Dakhleh Oasis Project: Monograph 14

THE OASIS PAPERS 3
Proceedings of the Third International Conference
of the Dakhleh Oasis Project

Dakhleh Oasis Project: Monograph 14

THE OASIS PAPERS 3
Proceedings of the Third International Conference of the Dakhleh Oasis Project

Edited by
Gillian E. Bowen and Colin A. Hope

assisted by
Bruce E. Parr

Contributing Authors:
A. C. Aufderheide, J. Biggerstaff, G. E. Bowen, L. Cartmell, C. S. Churcher, A. Cerroni,
T. L. Dupras, I. Gardner, R. F. Giegengack, S. Haddow, T. Herbich, C. A. Hope, O. E. Kaper,
M. R. Kleindienst, G. D. Madden, C. Maggiano, S. Marchand, C. Marchini,
M. M. A. McDonald, A. J. Mills, J. E. Molto, P. J. Reimer, A. Ross, P. Sheldrick,
T. N. Smekalova, J. R. Smith, B. Stern, J. D. Stewart, J. L. Thompson, M. W. Tocheri,
A. R. Warfe, H. V. Whitehouse, M. F. Wiseman, K. A. Worp and M. Zlonis

Oxbow Books

Published by
Oxbow Books, Park End Place, Oxford OX1 1HN
with the assistance of
The Monash University Publications Grants Committee

ISBN 1 84217 129 1

This book is available direct from
Oxbow Books, Park End Place, Oxford OX1 1HN
(Telephone: 01865-241249; Facsimille: 01865-794449)

and

The David Brown Book Company
Post Office Box 511, Oakville, CT 06779, U.S.A.
(Telephone: 860-945-9329; Facsimille: 860-945-9468)

and

from our website
www.oxbowbooks.com

Front Cover:
Tutu Stela from the Main Temple at Ismant el-Kharab

Frontispiece:
The Gladiator Jug from Area D/7 at Ismant el-Kharab

Printed in Great Britain at
Cambridge University Press

Editors' Preface

The Third International Conference of the Dakhleh Oasis Project was organized by the editors of this volume and held at the Bayview Conference Centre in Clayton, Victoria, Australia, on 10–12 August 2000. It was sponsored jointly by the Centre for Archaeology and Ancient History, Monash University and the Egyptology Society of Victoria. Participants came from Australia, Europe and North America, most members of the Dakhleh Oasis Project.

The papers presented at the conference, the programme of which follows, covered most of the major areas of investigation being undertaken by the Project, with the notable exception of geomorphology and Islamic studies. In general, the presentations reflected recent developments in research into Dakhleh and their significance for understanding human activity within north-eastern Africa. Discussions highlighted potential future directions the research might take. A welcome contribution came from Sylvie Marchand of L'Institut Français d'Archéologie Orientale in Cairo on one aspect of her work on the ceramics from the French concession within Dakhleh.

In preparing the papers for publication, authors were given the opportunity to extend the range of material that they covered and to incorporate material discovered subsequent to the conference. Several of the conference papers are not published in this volume; of these some represented work in progress, while others have been published elsewhere. In the latter case, the place of publication is indicated in the following conference programme. In addition, all members of the Project were invited to contribute further papers to this volume, so that it reflects on the one hand the content of the conference and on the other the research conducted on material from Dakhleh to 2002. The grouping of papers within this volume reflects the original conference format.

The editors' wish to acknowledge with gratitude the financial assistance received from the School of Historical Studies, through its Research Infrastructure Block Grant for 2003, and the Publications Grant Committee, both of Monash University, towards the preparation and publication costs of this volume. Without these the appearance of the volume would have been delayed considerably and it would not have been possible to include the colour illustrations. Without the skill and dedication of Bruce Parr this volume would not have taken its current form; his assistance is greatly appreciated.

Finally, the papers presented here have been subject to peer review. The editors and authors extend their thanks to all who have lent their expertise to this process.

July 2003

Gillian E. Bowen and Colin A. Hope
Centre for Archaeology and Ancient History
School of Historical Studies
Building 11, Clayton Campus
Monash University
Clayton, Victoria 3800
AUSTRALIA

Contents

Historical Archaeology II: Ptolemaic–Roman Period at Kellis

Conference Programme

THE THIRD INTERNATIONAL CONFERENCE
OF THE DAKHLEH OASIS PROJECT

Session 1   Prehistory

M. Kleindienst, University of Toronto/Royal Ontario Museum: First Characterization of the Earlier Middle
    Stone Age 'Teneida Unit'
M. Wiseman, University of Toronto at Scarborough/Royal Ontario Museum: The Chronology of the later
    Late Pleistocene: A 'Low-Tech' Approach (in absentia)
M. McDonald, University of Calgary: The Early Holocene Masara Cultural Unit: Puzzles and Prospects
U. Thanheiser, University of Vienna: Environment and Subsistence during the Epi-Palaeolithic Period*
J. Thompson and G. Madden, University of Nevada: Health and Disease of Neolithic Human Remains of
    the Sheikh Muftah Cultural Unit (in absentia)
C. S. Churcher, University of Toronto/Royal Ontario Museum: Hyaenas in Dakhleh Oasis (in absentia)

Session 2   Pharaonic Period: The Old Kingdom

A. J. Mills, Royal Ontario Museum: 'Ain el-Gazzareen: Developments in the Old Kingdom Settlement
J. Walter, University of Vienna: Flora of 'Ain el-Gazzareen*
T. Smekalova, Physical Institute of Saint Petersburg State University: Magnetometer Survey at 'Ain el-
    Gazzareen (in absentia)
O. Kaper, Humboldt University: Old Kingdom Watch Posts[1]

Session 3   Pharaonic Period: Middle–New Kingdoms

S. Marchand, L'Institut Français d'Archéologie Orientale: Late Middle Kingdom–Second Intermediate Period
    Ceramics from 'Ain Aseel (in absentia)
C. A. Hope, Monash University: Wine from *s3-wḥ3t*: An Overview of Contacts with the Nile Valley, the
    Ceramic Evidence[2]

Session 4   Kellis: Burial Practice and Physical Anthropology of the Ptolemaic–Roman Periods

A. Schweitzer, Institut d'Égyptologie de Strasbourg: Decorated Cartonnages from Kellis 1 (in absentia)[3]
A. Aufderheide, University of Minnesota: The Mummies from Kellis 1
E. Molto, Lakehead University: Palaeoepidemiological Research on Human Remains from Kellis*
A. Gravere: Mitachindrial DNA Variation in the Dakhleh Oasis: Past and Present*

Session 5   Kellis: The Settlement – Part 1

C. A. Hope, Monash University: The 2000 Season of Excavations
G. E. Bowen, Monash University: The Small East Church
C. McGregor, Monash University: Computer Simulation of Kellis Monuments[4]

Session 6   Kellis: The Settlement – Part 2

I. Gardner, University of Sydney: Progress in the Editing of the Coptic Texts
K. A. Worp, Universiteit van Amsterdam: Greek Ostraka: A Progress Report (in absentia)[5]
O. E. Kaper, Humboldt University: New Light on Tutu of Kellis
L. Blondaux, Le Creuso, and M. Berry, Museum of Victoria: Conservation of Wall Paintings[6]
M. Eccleston, Monash University: High Temperature Industries[7]
A. Stevens, Monash University: Terracotta Figurines[8]
A. Dunsmore, Melbourne: Imported Ceramics*
N. Hallam, Monash University: Wheat: Alive, Dead or Just Resting?*

---

* Paper not presented for publication.

[1] See O. E. Kaper and H. Willems, Policing the Desert: Old Kingdom Activity around the Dakhleh Oasis, in R. Friedman, ed., *Egypt and Nubia: Gifts of the Desert*, The British Museum Press, London, 2002, 79–94.

[2] See C. A. Hope, M. Eccleston, P. Rose and J. Bourriau, Oases Amphorae of the New Kingdom, in R. Friedman, ed., *Egypt and Nubia: Gifts of the Desert*, The British Museum Press, London, 2002, 95–131.

[3] See Annie Schweitzer, Les parures de cartonnage des momies d'une nécropole d'Ismant el-Kharab, in C. A. Hope and G. E. Bowen, eds, *Dakhleh Oasis Project: Preliminary Reports on the 1994–1995 to 1998–1999 Field Seasons*, Oxbow Books, Oxford, 2002, 269–76.

[4] See C. C. McGregor, Reconstructing the Temple of Tutu using Three-Dimensional Computer Modelling, in C. A. Hope and G. E. Bowen, eds, *Dakhleh Oasis Project: Preliminary Reports on the 1994–1995 to 1998–1999 Field Seasons*, Oxbow Books, Oxford, 2002, 225–38.

[5] See K. A. Worp, ed., *Greek Ostraka from Kellis*, Oxbow Books, Oxford, forthcoming.

[6] See L. Blondaux, Conservation of Archaeological Wall Paintings in the Temple of Tutu, in C. A. Hope and G. E. Bowen, eds, *Dakhleh Oasis Project: Preliminary Reports on the 1994–1995 to 1998–1999 Field Seasons*, Oxbow Books, Oxford, 2002, 61–3.

[7] See M. A. J. Eccleston, Metalworking at Kellis: A Preliminary Report, in C. A. Hope and G. E. Bowen, eds, *Dakhleh Oasis Project: Preliminary Reports on the 1994–1995 to 1998–1999 Field Seasons*, Oxbow Books, Oxford, 2002, 143–9.

[8] See A. Stevens, Terracottas from Ismant el-Kharab, in C. A. Hope and G. E. Bowen, eds, *Dakhleh Oasis Project: Preliminary Reports on the 1994–1995 to 1998–1999 Field Seasons*, Oxbow Books, Oxford, 2002, 277–95.

Strategies for Studying Pleistocene Archaeology based upon Surface Evidence: First Characterization of an Older Middle Stone Age Unit, Dakhleh Oasis, Western Desert, Egypt

Maxine R. Kleindienst

... if appreciable progress is ever to be made in the interpretation of the human past in this desert it seems probable that special methods involving comparative statistics concerning the surface density and distribution of the various types of artefacts will be necessary .... But, alas, human nature is such that the temptation to pick up and remove ancient artefacts seen lying on the ground is almost irresistible. Even now the original statistical pattern of artifact distribution must in some places have already spoilt (Bagnold 1981, vii).

Abstract

Larger-sized Middle Stone Age artefacts, mainly representing workshop activities, were recovered in 1987 from the surface of a P-II remnant below Balat Point near the Libyan Escarpment. Based upon morphology and condition, and comparisons with the cognate "Lower Levalloisian" unit at Kharga (Caton-Thompson 1952), these are estimated to be over 200,000 Uyrs old. Middle Stone Age artefacts, apparently representing occupation debris, were found in the north-eastern Teneida Palaeobasin in 1996, and discovered *in situ* within the basal Lake Teneida Formation deposits only in 1998. The geological setting indicates a comparable age, although the single chronometric determination only indicates that the Calcareous Silty Sediments deposits are older than *circa* 120,000 Aryrs. The provisionally-designated 'large-sized Middle Stone Age unit' at Dakhleh Oasis can now be characterized, and at Locality 187A this cultural stratigraphic unit is here designated as the Gifata Unit. The Teneida unit is not yet analysed in detail: it is as yet unclear whether it is a facies of the Gifata Unit, or one that is somewhat younger.

Introduction

In the Dakhleh Piedmont, three generations of complex, Pleistocene geomorphic surfaces have been recognized. The ancient surfaces are represented by the terraced remants of erosion surfaces/pediments that truncate bedrocks, and which are mantled by variable thicknesses of alluvial gravels overlain by soils. These have been designated, from oldest (highest elevation) to youngest (lowest elevation), P-I, P-II and P-III (Kleindienst *et al.* 1999, 20–3; Churcher *et al.* 1999, 303–4).

In 1987, a "large-sized Middle Stone Age unit" was discovered on the surface of a P-II terraced fan/*bajada* remnant below and west of Balat Point, at Locality 187A (Figure 1); (Kleindienst 1999, 92–4; Kleindienst *et al.* 1999, 23–4, Figure 1.25). In 1997, Hawkins, Ormerod and I found Middle Stone Age artefacts in the north-eastern Teneida Palaeolake basin north-west of el-Akoulah Pan (Locality 361). The placement of artefacts suggested derivation from the basal Lake Teneida Formation, Calcareous Silty Sediments facies (CSS), but limited test pitting could not prove this source. In 1998, Churcher and I discovered Middle Stone Age artefacts *in situ* in basal lake sediments at three localities (Localities 374, 391 and 392) to the south-west of Locality 361, together with scattered artefacts on the surface along the north-eastern and eastern edges of the large terraced remnant (Locality 211), lying in position to have eroded from the basal Calcareous Silty Sediments unit (Occurrences 211 NE, E and SE). The geological and geomorphological placements of these Middle Stone Age aggregates indicate that they either pertain to the time of the P-II surface found north of el-Akoulah Pan, or to the downcutting from that surface (Churcher *et al.* 1999, 306). The Middle Stone Age aggregates from the Piedmont at Locality 187A are here designated as the Gifata Unit, and those from the Lowland Teneida Palaeobasin are designated as the Teneida unit. Both are presently assigned to the older, generalized Middle Stone Age developmental stage of Egypt. Here, the aggregate from Locality 187A is used as the basis for describing the artefact inventory from a workshop area. Preliminary counts for the aggregates assigned to the Teneida unit indicate that these are characteristic of "occupation-type" areas rather than of workshops (Hawkins 2001, 218–20; Hawkins and Kleindienst 2002).

Maxine R. Kleindienst

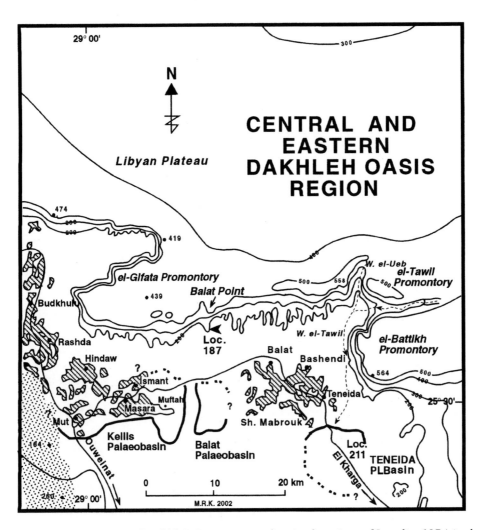

*Figure 1 Map of eastern and central Dakhleh Oasis region, showing locations of Locality 187A in the Piedmont
north-west of Balat, where Middle Stone Age artefacts are found in the desert pavement, and the Teneida Palaeobasin
south-east of Teneida where Middle Stone Age artefacts are related to outcrops of Lake Teneida Formation,
Calcareous Silty Sediments facies (CSS), laid-down in Palaeolake Teneida.*

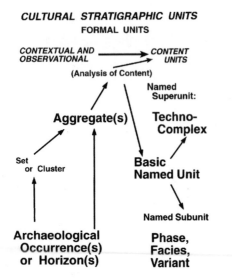

CULTURAL STRATIGRAPHIC UNITS
FORMAL UNITS

DESIGN THEORY/DECISION THEORY

1)   RECOGNIZE PROBLEM-->DEFINE PROBLEM-->

2)   CONSIDER POSSIBLE SOLUTIONS-->CHOOSE SOME-->

3)   IMPLEMENT SOLUTION(S)-->TRIAL AND ERROR-->

4)   <u>CHOOSE SOLUTION TO PROBLEM = 'Good Enough'</u>

5)   (± REFINE SOLUTION => MORE TRIAL AND ERROR.)

ANCIENT ARTISANS SOLVED PROBLEMS, FOR

REASONS;   ARCHAEOLOGISTS TRY TO IDENTIFY

PROBLEM(s) FROM THEIR SOLUTION(s).

*Figure 2 Classification of prehistoric Cultural
Stratigraphic Units, Dakhleh Oasis Project: formal
nomenclature.*

Figure 3 Steps in solving a design problem.

Nomenclature

At Dakhleh and Kharga, areas or points where prehistoric artefacts are found are designated Localities or Loci numbered in sequence of discovery (Kleindienst 1999), following Caton-Thompson and Gardner (Caton-Thompson 1952, 'Locus'). A Locality may include one or more Archaeological Occurrences with cultural materials. The first find is designated as Add 0 (Hawkins 2001, Appendix Eleven, 481–612). Finds in the same general area may then be designated as separate Adds numbered in sequence, if they come from different contexts and/or are collected at different times. Specific numbered localities may also be designated within a larger area that bears an earlier number. Localities are also designated by a Dakhleh Oasis Project grid number (Mills 1979, 167–8; Churcher and Mills 1999, 251).

The designations for cultural stratigraphic units discussed in Kleindienst (1999) are a modification from recommended Africanist nomenclature (Clark *et al.* 1966; Bishop and Clark 1967, 892–99) (Figure 2). The basic field or observational unit is an Archaeological Occurrence, defined as the minimal unit which comprises evidence of human behaviour and artefacts *in context*; these can be grouped into Occurrence Sets, or "Clusters" (Hawkins 2001, 166–7), according to context, by geographic location, or similar geomorphic or stratigraphic setting. If a Locality comprises more than one Occurrence, a number or name designates these arbitrarily. Artefacts recovered from Occurrences comprise aggregates or collections or, if single finds, isolates. An aggregate may include more than one component, based upon analyses of attributes of physical condition and typology.

The basic formal analytic entity is a named cultural stratigraphic unit which must be defined first; it comprises all aggregates that are considered sufficiently similar to be grouped together. Further work may show that a Unit can be subdivided into Phases, chronologically sequenced, or Facies, pene-contemporary and geographically distinctive, or simply into Variants, based upon more detailed analyses and more evidence. Possibly, some subdivisions may then be raised to Unit level; or Units can be placed within other Units as subdivisions at a lower analytic level. Units judged to be sufficiently similar are grouped into more inclusive, named Techno-complexes or Complexes. Units are named from local geographic features or places, or arbitrarily if no local names are available. Capital *U* designates formal usage and definition; lower case *u*, as in Teneida unit, designates informal usage, where the unit is recognized but not yet fully defined. The system is intended to provide maximum flexibility in the application of nomenclature.

The term 'Middle Stone Age' ('MSA') is retained strictly as a general, African developmental stage term. It is neither a chronostratigraphic term, nor a cultural stratigraphic unit term. Middle Stone Age here refers to flake-based lithic aggregates, which usually incorporate a form of specialized reduction method, often Levallois techniques (see Appendix). These have been designated as "mode 3" types of aggregates, seen as a stage of development in technological progress (Clark 1970, 72–4; Phillipson 1993, 60). The definition for the 'mode 3' is not always appropriate (McBrearty and Brooks 2000). Similarly, the term 'Earlier Stone Age' ('ESA') is regarded as an African developmental stage term.

Analytic units imply neither the ethnicity nor the social relationships of the artisans who originally made and/or used the artefacts. They do *not* imply the existence of prehistoric 'cultures', although further interpretation and testing may prove that some units do represent the garbage left by such self-recognized human groups in the past. Units refer only to the analysed content that has been interpreted to have human cultural origins.

Classification

An initial protocol for classification of Middle Stone Age aggregates at Dakhleh was developed in 1987. This scheme has been modified, as appropriate, to apply to materials recovered from localities and archaeological occurrences yielding Middle Stone Age since that time. The basic descriptive classification presented here (see Appendix) is a derivation of that developed for the Lupemban Techno-complex units at Kalambo Falls (Clark and Kleindienst 1974; 2001), with changes based upon observations of Middle Stone Age aggregates recovered from both the east and west banks of the Nile by the Yale Prehistoric Expedition to Nubia in 1963–64 (Kleindienst 1972), and upon continuing observations in Dakhleh. It should be noted that because Dakhleh artefacts are all analysed in the field, classification methods must be both appropriate for the material, and practical in terms of the restricted time and layout space available. Gross class ascriptions are recorded in the cataloguing of all recovered artefact aggregates, following the basic classification for the Middle Stone Age.[1] Technological and morphological attributes for all artefacts are recorded in detailed analyses of entire aggregates from archaeological occurrences, or for randomly sampled portions of large aggregates. Attribute analyses allow for refinement, and testing of the validity of the preliminary class ascriptions, as well as for other analytic approaches.

Note has been taken of other classifications for the Egyptian Middle Stone Age (Caton-Thompson 1952; Guichard 1965; Guichard and Guichard 1968; Schild and Wendorf 1977; Van Peer 1992; Close 1993) or the Middle Palaeolithic in the Levant (for example, Fish 1979; Marks 1983; Goren-Inbar 1990). A Bordesian typology (Bordes 1961) is not followed at Dakhleh, despite its use, more recently in a modified form, by the Combined Prehistoric

---

[1] Hawkins (2001, Appendix Eight, 465–6) has modified that for appropriate application to the Dakhleh Unit, as has Wiseman for the Sheikh Mabruk Unit (this volume).

IMPLICATIONS OF DESIGN AND DECISION THEORY: FEEDBACK DYNAMIC

SYSTEMS FOR ARTISANS

SELECTION (End product)-->USE (± modification)-->DROPPING

(S-->U-->D)

SELECTION-->PRODUCTION (End and Byproducts)-->SELECTION-

->(End product)-

->USE (± modification)-->DROPPING

(S-->P-->S-->U-->D)

SELECTION-->PRODUCTION(S) (End and Byproducts)-->SELECTION-

->(Blank)-

->PRODUCTION (End product)-->USE (± modification)-->DROPPING

(Multistage: S-->P(s)-->S-->P-->U-->D)

NB: ALL PRODUCTION STAGES PRODUCE BYPRODUCTS; RECYCLING CAN

OCCUR AT ANY STAGE, OR ANY LATER TIME. 'DROPPING' IS BY EITHER

ACCIDENTAL LOSS OR DELIBERATE DISCARD. RELATED 'TOOLS TO MAKE

TOOLS' ARE ALSO PRODUCED.

LITHIC ANALYISTS ARE INTERPRETING THE 'INTENTIONS' OF THE

KNAPPER FROM BROKEN BITS OF STONE: 1) THE STONES BROKEN; AND

2) THE STONES BROKEN-OFF FROM THOSE.

Figure 4 Lithic reduction or wasting sequences in the production of stone artefacts.

Expedition in the Western Desert (Wendorf *et al.* 1993). There are a number of problems with applying a typology developed for the French Mousterian (Bisson 2000; *contra* Moyer and Rolland 2001):

1) The boundaries of Bordes' type classes are ill-defined, so that consistent, reliable ascriptions by different analysts are unlikely.

2) Bordes' typology is a taxonomic and morphological descriptive classification, so that a number of Bordes' classes are lumped in the Dakhleh classification, which emphasizes attribute analysis: for example, morphological characteristics of 'scrapers' are recorded as attributes, and 'denticulation' is regarded as an attribute of edge retouch rather than as a separate category of "tool" (Clark and Kleindienst 1974; Isaac 1977, 154). We do use some descriptive classes in general use, which were also used by Bordes; see Kleindienst (1999, 100) on Bordes' retouched point classes.

Lithic analysts have come to accept that stone working is a production, or "reduction" (Baumler 1995) sequence beginning with the selection of the raw material to be broken, followed by one or more production stages to fashion an "end product" (Collins 1970). Hence, based upon knowledge or assumptions about how stone breaks, lithic analysis necessarily involves *interpretation* by the analyst of the actions, and thus the intentions, of the artisan that are represented by the attributes of *each* artefact. This is as true of attribute analysis, reflected in the choice of relevant attributes, as it is of descriptive typological classification. Refitting of broken material helps to test those interpretations (Van Peer 1992; Sellet 1995; Demidenko 1998); unfortunately, this is rarely possible with abraded and redistributed aggregates, although some refits are found.

Allowing for possible recycling stages, the process of production ends with the disposal or loss of artefacts into an archaeological context, a sequence most recently called *chaîne opératoire* by French prehistorians (Sellet 1993; Inizan *et al*. 1999, 14–16). Although implying dynamic processes, most descriptions of this 'operative chain'

Table 1 *Lithic raw material composition of Gifata Unit and Teneida unit aggregates, Locality 187A, central Piedmont zone, and localities in eastern Teneida Palaeobasin, Dakhleh Oasis. Key: TCH, Tarawan Chert; MCH, Mut Chert; OCH, Other cherts; CBS, Chert Ball Silicas; LST, limestone; QZT, quartzites; IST, ferruginous quartzites; SLS, siliceous sandstone; QTZ, quartz; PWD, petrified wood.*

LOCI		LITHIC RAW MATERIALS									
	N	TCH+	MCH	OCH	CBS	LST	QZT	IST	SLS	QTZ	PWD
Gifata Unit	405	402	-	1	2	-	-	-	-	-	-
%	100.0	99.3	0.0	0.2	0.5	0.0	0.0	0.0	0.0	0.0	0.0
Teneida unit (north to south)											
L. 361											
CORRIDOR†	1,243	1,087	-	7	97	-	29	19	-	1	3
RIDGE*	252	199	-	-	31	2	20		-	-	-
E RIDGE & PAN*	103	73	-	-	26	-	4		-	-	-
L. 392†	3	2	-	-	-	-	-	1	-	-	-
L. 374††	292	212	8	14	16	5	24	6	7	-	-
L. 211 NE/E†	146	94	-	-	10	11	6	23	2	-	-
L. 391†	33	28	-	-	1	-	2	2	-	-	-
L. 211 SE†	42	24	-	-	3	-	7	-	8	-	-
L. 211 S†	30	13	-	1	2	-	4	7	3	-	-
TOTAL NUMBER	2,144	1,732	8	22	186	18	154		20	1	3
%	99.9	80.8	0.4	1.0	8.7	0.8	7.2		0.9	0.01	0.1

+   Possible inclusion of unidentified Mut Chert (MCH) in Teneida unit Tarawan Chert (TCH).

†   Catalogue counts by Kleindienst.

*   Catalogue counts by Ormerod; QZT includes IST.

**   Catalogue counts by Ormerod; Lag cluster on east side of ridge, plus material redeposited from there into the pan below; QZT includes IST.

††   Basic analysis by Kleindienst, 1998; Sample includes lag from north-west, north-east and south-west grid quadrats, plus surface material from adjacent areas on Iron Balls talus, CSS talus and wadi floors.

concept lack a more general, explicit theoretical framework. Following principles of design theory (for example, Pye 1964; 1968) (Figures 3 and 4), all flaked stone is the product of a "wasting" or reduction sequence (Pye 1964, 47) involving the "workmanship of risk" (Pye 1968, 4–8), which begins with the *selection of particular pieces* of material (Pye 1964, 46). Large quantities of by-products are produced; but any of this debris may be used as blanks or tools, in addition to the produced end products. All production sequences involve multidimensional decision-making (Kleindienst 1979; Sheppard and Kleindienst 1996) and further stages of selection by the artisan(s).

For each flake removal, an individual artisan interacts with a piece of stone (with its own idiosyncratic properties) in a manner that combines muscular control, experience, and goals (Cross 1983, 89). Some methods of flake production are more "regulated" (Pye 1968, 17–20) in that deliberate core preparation more closely constrains the attributes of some flakes, and which may even produce a high degree of standardization in the replicability of the "preferential flakes" (Inizan *et al.* 1999, 65). Those flakes may be end products for use, or blanks for further reduction by trimming or retouch. The production of end products implies the achievement of acceptable solutions to design problems recognized by ancient artisans, that is, intentional problem solving. The problem need not be utilitarian usage. It could be practice, play or display. The basic descriptive classification for Middle Stone Age lithic artefacts explicitly incorporates those design principles (see Appendix).

Lithic Raw Materials

The Dakhleh Oasis region is unusual in having a variety of lithic raw materials available from different bedrock and secondary sources within a relatively small area, so that variable usage representing human selectivity can be assessed. Lithic raw material sources for knappable stone from the various geological formations are sought and mapped (Kleindienst 1999, 87–90; Kleindienst *et al.* 1999; Hawkins and Kleindienst 2002). The attributes of lithic raw materials used to make artefacts are recorded not only as to rock type, but also as to the incidence, original forms and sizes available (Hawkins 2001, 170–3; Hawkins and

Kleindienst 2001; Hawkins and Kleindienst 2002) (Table 1).[2]

The Gifata Unit artisans knapped Tarawan Group cherts (Tarawan Chert, TCH) in the workshops near the Libyan Escarpment below Balat Point; Teneida unit artisans imported Tarawan cherts into the Teneida Palaeobasin where such cherts are not available from either the capping limestones of el-Battikh Promontory or the Pleistocene gravels to the north of el-Akoulah Pan (Figure 1). The nearest known secondary sources of Tarawan Group cherts now existing are north-west of Teneida on the uplifted sandstone block north of Bashendi, *circa* 12 km distant, or in high P-II remnants north of Teneida in the Wadi el-Tawil, *circa* 14 km distant. These remnants suggest that P-II gravels bearing Tarawan Chert might once have existed south of Teneida that have been completely eroded away. Such gravels would have been >6 km distant. Their resistant components are now incorporated into the P-III gravels of that area. The scarcity of chert has resulted in significant selective holoporting of Middle Stone Age artefacts onto Masara Unit and younger Holocene localities where they were stockpiled in some cases, and used as raw material (McDonald, personal communication, 1998; personal observations). Consequently, most artefacts now found associated with Lake Teneida Formation deposits in Teneida Palaeobasin are likely to have been exposed only in the last 4,000 years. This age estimate is confirmed by the mint to fresh condition of most artefacts and the lack of desert varnish, indicating recent exposure to surface processes.

The localities within the Teneida Palaeobasin utilize a percentage of nodular chalcedony/chert, termed "Ball chalcedony" (Hawkins and Kleindienst 2002) or Chert Ball Silicas (CBS). I had speculated that these 'chert balls' might come from the Thebes Group formations (Kleindienst 1999, 89); but large nodules of varying banded composition and colour, white to pink to red to brown or yellow, were finally sourced by Churcher in 1994, north-east of Teneida in the upper Mut Formation Variegated Shales Member (Kleindienst *et al.* 1999, Figure 1.37, bottom). This outcrop (Locality 347) appears to have been exposed from below P-III gravels only in Holocene times. Similar nodules or geodes have been described from northern Kharga, where nodules also have a reticulated rind with

> ... a zonation from white cryptocrystalline quartz (chalcedony) in outer layers to clear, crystalline quartz toward the inside; interior cavities are lined with euhedral quartz crystals overgrown by celestite in a few places ... (Haynes 1980, 70).[3]

In Dakhleh, only some larger nodules are geodes with quartz crystals lining the interior cavity, while smaller ones are solid. As a knapping material, nodules are difficult to break, even with a heavy hammer. Once broken they provide some thickness of flakeable material in the outer portions, but a tough, durable material in the interior due to the intergrown crystal structure. Although the latter was used as a raw material for flaking, it was more favoured for hammer-stones. Entire nodules were often used as hammer-stones, and transported to areas well away from available sources: two have been found at Locality 187A, at least 10 km from a likely gravel source in the Lowland. The Chert Ball Silicas used for artefacts are usually identifiable in hand specimen due to the colourations, structure, or patination; and the development of desert varnish colours also differs from that of Tarawan Chert. Amorphous nodules of white chalcedony come from the Mut Formation in the area of the Balat Palaeobasin and southward, but none have yet been noted in the area of the Teneida Palaeobasin; this is the only similar Dakhleh lithic material yet found that might be confused with Chert Ball Silicas.

The Mut Formation chert ball nodules, some over 50 cm in diameter, are highly resistant, and are found in quantity redeposited in the lags and gravels north and north-east of Bashendi, and in the P-III gravels flanking the Wadi el-Tawil as far north as the western flank of Wadi el-Ueb. I have found relatively small chert balls only rarely in the P-II and P-III gravels north of el-Akoulah Pan, and even fewer small pieces of grey-brown chert. Small, complete chert balls were imported into the Locality 211 area, some used as hammer-stones. The rare pieces of chert derived from Mut Formation clay-stones and noted in the P-II gravels, Mut Chert (MCH), are too small to have been of much use in Middle Stone Age knapping except for small, unspecialized flakes or situational tools, although some Mut Chert was identified in the Teneida unit, Locality 374 Grid aggregate in 2002. Mut Chert tends to be more homogeneous in colour than Tarawan Chert. It can be identified by bearing a different cortex than Tarawan Chert if cortex is present.

The Mut Formation outcrops to the north of the Teneida Palaeobasin and el-Akoulah Pan are not yet surveyed for possible bedrock source(s) of chert balls or chert. Several transects in the southern portion of the Piedmont with Churcher indicate that the available geological mapping is incorrect in showing the entire area as Mut Formation (Egyptian Geological Survey and Mining Authority 1982; Klitzsch, List, and Pöhlmann 1987; Hermina 1990, 267, Figure 14.5). Masked by P-II gravels, the area is cut by

---

[2] It should be noted that classification of lithic resources for archaeological purposes is not necessarily identical to petrological or mineralogical classification. Our classification emphasizes bedrock sources, although rock or mineral composition might be highly variable within a given source.

[3] Haynes originally thought these to be of Quaternary age, but now assigns them to the uppermost Nubia Group (personal communication, 2000).

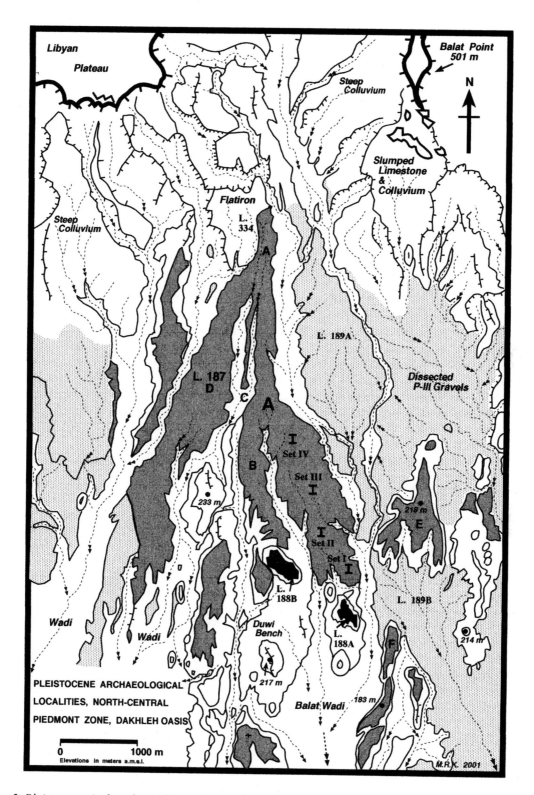

Figure 5 Pleistocene Archaeological Localities in the Piedmont Zone, south-west of Balat Point in north-central Dakhleh Oasis, showing the Locality 187 P-II remnant of terraced Pleistocene gravels, and the locations of Transect Sets I, II, III and IV on the Locality 187A lobe. Key: darkest infill, P-I gravels on terraced remnants; medium infill, P-II gravels on terraced remnants; lightest infill, P-III gravels on terraced remnants. Map based on air photographs and field observations.

faults, and includes outcrops of both Dakhla Formation shales and Duwi Formation phosphorites overlying the Mut Formation.

Quartzites (QZT) of varying colour, and grain size were also used in the chertless area of Teneida Palaeobasin, as was more friable siliceous sandstone (SLS). Both can be found in surface lags, and in the upper Nubia Group sandstone formations, the Taref Formation and Maghrabi Formation. Dark coloured, ferruginous quartzite, or 'ironstone' (IST) occurs in the upper Nubia Group sandstones, mainly as joint fillings or as concretions. Some grey to tan quartzites grading to siliceous sandstone are interbedded, but workshops have not been located. Ferruginous quartzites are also associated with Quaternary spring deposits, as at Iron Balls Spring, Locality 374, or at Locality 366. Rare use is made of quartz cobbles (QTZ) from the Nubia sandstone conglomerates, or of other Nubia Group rocks found to the south in older formations. Small pieces of petrified wood (PWD) may come either from the sandstones, or from the gravels to the north.

Context of Locality 187A

Locality 187, together with Localities 188 and 189, was selected for intensive investigation by I. A. Brooks and M. R. Kleindienst in 1987: air photographs indicated exposures of P-I, P-II and P-III veneered erosion surfaces on terraced remnants existed in close proximity below and west of Balat Point (Figure 1) (Kleindienst 1999, 90–2; Kleindienst *et al.* 1999, 22, Figure 1.25 top). Locality 187 is a four-lobed, *circa* 3 km-long remnant of P-II pedisediments (Locality 187A, B, C, D), one of the largest preserved (Figure 5). The P-II ramp is defined on the east by a steep face >10 m high, cut by the modern wadi which also dissects the lower elevation P-III terrace (Locality 189A). Modern wadi-cutting on the west also isolates the P-II. A small remnant of P-I (Locality 188A) stands above the south tip of the eastern Locality 187A lobe, cut off from the P-II by headward erosion of two small drainages. The head of the P-II terrace is separated from the steep colluvial slope of a flatiron, once the Escarpment face, by headward erosion of low drainages cutting into the Pediment II surface, which here stands *circa* 2 m above the dissected area.

At Locality 187A, the surface slopes north to south, with an elevation of *circa* 225 m above sea level at the head, and *circa* 215 m above sea level at the south tip. An erosion surface (pediment) cutting across the Duwi Formation is overlain by a variable thickness, to >2 m, of coarse boulder gravels, now highly cemented, which are overlain by ≥30 cm of silty soil under a desert varnished, chert-rich, stony veneer or desert pavement (Kleindienst

et al. 1999, 23, Figure 1.27). When exposed by erosion in lower areas where the soil cover has been removed by small drainages and sheet-wash, the limestone boulders of the gravels are planed-off and heavily fluted by sand-blasting, which continues today (Kleindienst *et al.* 1999, 22, Figure 1.25 bottom). The veneer/soil/gravels profile is retained on higher areas upslope, and over much of the downslope P-II surface. Erosional and depositional processes probably acted differentially during the several past palaeoclimatic episodes, and the chert-rich veneer might have resulted from erosion of the underlying gravels, as well as from distribution downslope from the colluvial face of the Escarpment. To test that question, detailed work was undertaken on the eastern lobe of the P-II, at Locality 187A. Despite evidence of erosion, sampling by Brooks and Kleindienst indicated that surface lowering of the gravels has not been more than *circa* one metre (Kleindienst *et al.* 1999, 23–4). This lowering process would, however, result in the lateral dispersal of any existing clusters of artefacts, as would surface wash.

Because the P-II surface has undergone multiple wet-dry-wet cycles during its existence, evidence of water action suggests that surface material may have been continuously distributed downslope from the foot of the Escarpment colluvium, adding to or redistributing any chert that might have been humanly deposited at various points on the surface. If water transport and 'desert creep'[4] have both acted over a long period of time, and if humans did most of their flaking nearer the raw material sources on the Escarpment or in the capping limestones, one can expect that the older materials would be found further south than younger material. Also, depending upon the relationship between size sorting and the incidence of chert nodules breaking-up naturally at the surface, one might expect that there would be more small pieces in chert-rich areas downslope than upslope. A series of Transect Set collections was made to test such hypotheses. as well as to obtain unselected samples of artefacts from a broad area of the terrace surface (Kleindienst 1999, 87). In the Sets, the artefact density falls off from 0.12/square m at Set IV in the middle of the 187A lobe to 0.02–0.05/square m in Sets I, II and III further south (Kleindienst 1999, Table 5.2), suggesting that material was redistributed down the P-II surface. Also, cores similar to those found in Sets I-II-III were found redeposited onto the Duwi Formation benches south of the P-II terrace.

The only available chronometric age on P-II gravels is a uranium series determination on a large block of tufa embedded in the south end of the Locality 187E remnant to the east, which proved to be beyond dating range: MRK 1988/DAK 1, >350,000 Uyrs[5] (Kleindienst *et al.* 1999, 17; forthcoming). The limited number of extant P-II

---

[4] 'Desert creep' is a term suggested by R. Schild for aeolian processes that move clasts (personal communication, 1998).

[5] Given the plethora of chronometric, relative dating methods for the Pleistocene, it has been suggested that a shorthand way of showing what method is quoted should be introduced (Smith 1999), especially when one is referring to numbers generated by different methods; for example: 14Cyrs or Cyrs (cal) or (uncal) for radioactive carbon; Uyrs for uranium-series methods; or Aryrs for argon isotope methods. The statistical measurements generated by different methods should not be regarded as necessarily equivalent, nor as being easily translated into calendric (solar) years.

Table 2 Artefact class composition of combined Gifata Unit aggregates from Locality 187A, Sets I-II-III+G and Set IV+G, by abrasion categories, Dakhleh Oasis.

LOCALITY 187A / ARTEFACT CLASS	SETS I-II-III+G N Abraded	%	Fresh	SET IV+G N Abraded	%	Fresh	ABRADED AGGREGATE N	%
CORES								
SPECIALIZED								
Levallois								
Struck	17	73.9	-	20	66.7	-	37	69.8
Unstruck	4	1.7	1r	6	20.0	-	10	18.9
Fragments	1	4.3	-	4	13.3	2	5	9.4
Earlier Stage	1	4.3	-	-		-	1	1.9
Total Levallois	*23*	*79.3*	*1*	*30*	*75.0*	*2*	*53*	*76.8*
Discoidal	3	10.3		4	10.0	-	7	10.1
Flake/Blade--1 platform				4		-	4	
--2 platform	1		-	1		-	2	
Blade--1 platform	1		-	-		-	1	
--2 platform	1		-	1		1	2	
Total Linear	*3*	*10.3*		*6*	*15.0*	*1*	*9*	*13.0*
Total Specialized	*29*	*80.6*	*1*	*40*	*78.4*	*3*	*69*	*79.3*
UNSPECIALIZED								
Flake--1 platform	4r		1r	2		-	6	33.3
--2 platform	-		-	2		-	2	11.1
Multidirectional	-		-	1		-	1	5.6
Earlier Stage	1		-	-		-	1	5.6
Initial Stage--1 platform	1		-	4		2	5	27.8
--2 platform	-		-	2		-	2	11.1
Fragments--Initial--1 platform	1		-	-		-	1	5.6
Total Unspecialized	*7*	*19.4*	*1*	*11*	*21.6*	*2*	*18*	*20.7*
Total Cores	*36*		*2*	*51*		*5*	*87*	*21.4*
ANGULAR DEBRIS*	(3 chips)			(1 chip)				
FLAKES								
SPECIALIZED								
Levallois								
Pointed	2		-	3		-	5	29.4
Broad	2		-	1		-	3	17.6
Other	2		-	5		1	7	41.1
Overpassed	1		-	1		-	2	11.8
Total	*7*	*21.7*		*10*	*28.6*	*1*	*17*	*29.3*
Linear								
Quadrilateral	4		-	8		-	12	63.2
Pointed	-		-	7		-	7	36.8
Total	*4*	*17.4*		*15*	*42.9*		*19*	*32.8*
Total Complete	*11*	*39.1*		*25*	*81.5*	*1*	*36*	*62.1*
Fragments--proximal	5		-	9		-	14	63.6
--distal	7		-	1		-	8	36.4
Total	*12*	*52.2*		*10*	*28.6*		*22*	*37.9*
Total Specialized Flakes	*23*	*16.2*		*35*	*23.2*	*1*	*58*	*19.9*
UNSPECIALIZED								
End Struck	75		3	65		11	140	83.8
Side Struck	9		-	18		1	27	16.2
Total Complete	*84*	*71.2*	*3*	*83*	*71.6*	*12*	*167*	*71.4*
Fragments--proximal	29		1	25		-	54	80.6
--distal	5		-	8		-	13	19.4
Total	*34*	*28.8*	*1*	*33*	*28.4*		*67*	*28.6*
Total Unspecialized Flakes	*118*	*83.7*	*4*	*116*	*76.8*	*12*	*234*	*80.1*
Total Flakes	*141*		*4*	*151*		*13*	*292*	
SHAPED TOOLS								
Points--Bifacial oval	-		-	1		-	1	4.8
Bifacial Points (Lanceolate)	2		-	-		-	2	9.6
Scrapers	3		-	3		-	6	28.6
Burins	-		1r	-		-		
Ventral Butt-Thinned Flakes	1		-	2		-	3	14.2
Core Axes	-			-		-		
Bifaces--Acheulian-type	2ff		-	-		-	2	9.6
--Balat-type	2		-	1		-	3	14.2
--Balat-type/MSA Coreaxes	2r		-	2		-	4	19.0
Total Shaped Tools	*12*	*100.0*	*1*	*9*	*64.3*		*21*	*80.8*
SITUATIONAL TOOLS	*0*		-	*1*	*7.1*	-	*1*	*3.8*
UTILISED TOOLS								
Edge-damaged	-		1	1		-	1	
Battered								
Hammerstones	-		-	3		-	3	
Total Utilized Tools	*0*		*1*	*4*	*28.6*		*4*	*15.4*
Total Tools	*12*		*2*	*14*			*26*	*6.4*
TOTAL AGGREGATE	189		8	216		18	405	
TOTAL BYPRODUCTS	36	19.0	2	51	23.6		87	21.5
TOTAL END/BYPRODUCTS	141	74.6	4	151	69.9		292	72.1
TOTAL END PRODUCTS	12	6.4	2	14	6.5		26	6.4
PSEUDO-ARTEFACTS (Natural)								
"Cores"	4		-	4		3	8	
"Flakes"	1		1	-		-	1	

r Recycled artefact
f Broken artefact

terraced surfaces, the depth of soil formation, and the black
to dark brown colours of the desert-varnished cherts on
terrace surfaces suggest that these remnants are likely to
be at least Middle Pleistocene in age of formation. Finds
of a dispersed Balat Unit biface cluster at Locality 187E
opposite isolated bifaces, some recycled, near the south-
eastern edge of Locality 187A, and rare, heavily-battered
Acheulian-type bifaces, support that estimate. Acheulian
sensu stricto is beyond uranium series dating range at
Kharga (Kleindienst *et al*. 1996; forthcoming) and in
southern Egypt (Schwarcz and Morawska 1993; Haynes
et al. 1997). The Balat Unit is now estimated to date
younger than *circa* 400,000 and older than *circa* 250,000
years ago. A uranium series determination for a tufa float
block found east of Sheikh Muftah on the Tawil anticline
by Giegengack and Nicoll in 1996 (McM #96007) is
210,000 ± 4,000 Uyrs. The tufa indicates surface water
availability that would sustain life at Dakhleh in the time
range of the water-laid tufas overlying older Middle Stone
Age "Lower Levalloisian" in Kharga, (Caton-Thompson
1952, 27–8; Kleindienst *et al*; forthcoming); artesian
springs could also have been erupting.

Dense clusters of Dakhleh Unit artefacts (Locality 334),
probably concentrated by water-action, lie in the dissected
area north-west and below the head of the P-II surface
with fewer redeposited further down-wadi or scattered on
the adjoining P-II terrace head (Kleindienst 1999, 101;
Hawkins 2001, 209–10). Those artefacts are much less
deeply varnished and abraded than the Balat Unit or Middle
Stone Age artefacts found further downslope, and are
probably less than 100,000 years in age. Their physical
condition indicates considerably greater antiquity for the
other Middle Stone Age artefacts on the P-II surface, based
upon the darker colouration and greater degree of abrasion.
Few pieces in fresh condition, which may belong with the
Dakhleh Unit, were found on the southern half of the terrace
(Table 2).

Nodules and fragments of chert occur in the colluvium
of the flatiron and in the P-II gravels. The modern Balat
Wadi to the east heads in two branches below the capping
Tarawan limestones of the Plateau. Both allow foot access
to the Plateau, although both branches head in chutes, and
the top ±10 m requires climbing the rock face. The east
branch limestone carries no chert, while the west branch
has abundant nodules in the limestone face and in huge
fallen blocks. These have been redistributed into the
colluvium and the Pleistocene to modern gravels. Some
are of large size, to *circa* 40 cm in length.

On the surface of the P-II, chert incidence in the colluvial
face and on lower surfaces decreases markedly to the west
and south along the 187D lobe. This suggests that the
Locality 187A area was attractive to Pleistocene humans
both because of the localized availability of chert, and
possibly because there was an access route via the
Escarpment face to the capping limestone, and the Plateau
above. Also, redeposited tufa boulders in Pleistocene
gravels indicate that springs, which would have supported
vegetation, erupted from the Escarpment face; and in 2002,

Churcher, Kleindienst and Walter found tufa terraces
incorporating vegetal casts preserved high on the face east
of Balat Point. Proximity to water, and other resources
may have been present in Gifata Unit times.

Evidence for later uses of the ramp are limited. A few
blade cores and blades in fresh to mint condition were
noted, with associated refitting debitage products lying
within an area of ≤2 m. These are of Masara Unit-type,
early Holocene or possibly older age; one, on the Set IV–
60E line, was collected but is not considered here. Only
one Holocene locality (Locality 219), and a few scattered
fresh to mint lithics typologically of Holocene age have
been found below and south of the P-II and P-III terraces.
Only two mule shoes and three abraded, shattered water
jugs indicate modern crossings of the terraced P-II surface,
although a trail goes up the ramp, and a cairned trail goes
up the east branch of Balat Wadi. Wild pigeons roost in
the holes of the capping limestones, and probably still are
hunted there.

At Locality 187A, artefact aggregates were collected
from six Transect Sets (Kleindienst 1999, 90–2 and 99–
100); these Occurrences are numbered Set I through Set
VI from south to north. Additional grab samples of
specialized cores and flakes or tools, General finds, were
selected from the areas between the Sets, or from the
adjacent surfaces (Figure 5). In 1987, detailed analyses
were done on aggregates from Sets I, II, and III, and basic
analysis on the Set IV aggregate. A few finds made in
later seasons were added to the General collection. These
collections from the southern half of the P-II terrace are
used here to characterize the features of the Gifata Unit in
the Piedmont zone near the Escarpment. The aggregates
appear to represent highly dispersed clusters resulting from
workshop activities, based upon the incidence of cortical
flakes (60.3% of complete primary flakes bearing >30%
of dorsal cortex). However, the find by P. Sheldrick of a
conjoining core and flake within ≤2 m distance (Set II)
may suggest less dispersion than might have been expected
on the long-exposed surface, or be just a unique find of
related pieces.

Analyses of Combined Aggregate from Locality 187A: Strategies for Assessing Surface Aggregates

Many archaeologists now regard the study of surface
aggregates as useless because they are mixed up. The
term 'mixed' is a misnomer. While every surface aggregate
potentially covers a time range from the formation of the
surface to the present day, as Bagnold noted (1981, vii),
the distributions of cultural materials may differ depending
upon how and when humans used a particular place. We
should recall that most of what is now found below the
surface of the ground was once on the surface, and subject
to all the vagaries of surface processes. The only essential
difference between surface and subsurface or 'sealed'
aggregates is in the potential time range represented:
subsurface material may or may not have been accumulated

*Table 3 Abrasion categories by artefact class for Sets I-II-III+G and Set IV+G, Locality 187A, Dakhleh Oasis.
Key: LA, lightly abraded; A, abraded; HA, heavily abraded.*

Loc. 187A	SETS I-II-III+G			SET IV+G			AGGREGATE			
	Abrasion Degree			Abrasion Degree			Abrasion Degree			
ARTEFACT CLASS	LA	A	HA	LA	A	HA	LA	A	HA	Total
CORES										
SPECIALIZED										
Levallois										
Struck	2	12	3	5	13	2	7	25	5	37
Unstruck	-	4	-	1	5	-	1	9	-	10
Fragments	-	-	1	1	3	-	1	3	1	5
Earlier Stage	1	-	-	-	-	-	1	-	-	1
Total Levallois	*3*	*16*	*4*	*7*	*21*	*2*	*10*	*37*	*6*	*53*
%	13.0	69.6	17.4	23.3	70.0	6.7	18.9	69.8	11.3	
Discoidal	*1r*	*1*	*1*	*0*	*0*	*0*	*1*	*5*	*1*	7
%	33.3	33.3	33.3	0.0	0.0	0.0	14.3	71.4	14.3	
Flake/Blade--1 platform	-	-	-	2	2	-	2	2	-	4
--2 platform	1	-	-	1	-	-	2	-	-	2
Blade--1 platform	1	-	-	-	-	-	1	-	-	1
--2 platform	-	1	-	1	-	-	-	1	-	2
Total Linear	*2*	*1*	*0*	*4*	*2*	*0*	*6*	*3*	*0*	*9*
%	66.7	33.3	0.0	66.7	33.3	0.0	66.7	33.3	.0.0	
Total Specialized	*6*	*18*	*5*	*11*	*27*	*2*	*17*	*45*	*7*	*69*
%	20.7	62.1	17.2	27.5	67.5	5.0	24.6	65.2	10.2	
UNSPECIALIZED										
Flake--1 platform	2r	2	-	1	1	-	3	3	-	6
--2 platform	-	-	-	-	2	-	-	2	-	2
Multidirectional	-	-	-	-	1	-	-	1	-	1
Earlier Stage	-	1	-	-	-	-	-	1	-	1
Initial Stage--1 platform	-	-	1	1	3	-	1	3	1	5
--2 platform	-	-	-	-	2	-	-	2	-	2
Fragments--Initial--1 platform	-	-	1	-	-	-	-	-	1	1
Total Unspecialized	*2*	*3*	*2*	*2*	*9*	*0*	*4*	*12*	*2*	*18*
%	28.6	42.9	28.6	18.2	81.8	0.0	22.2	66.7	11.1	
Total Cores	*8*	*21*	*7*	*13*	*36*	*2*	*21*	*57*	*9*	*87*
%	22.2	58.3	19.4	25.5	70.6	3.9	24.1	65.5	10.3	
FLAKES										
SPECIALIZED										
Levallois										
Total	*1*	*4*	*2*	*1*	*7*	*2*	*2*	*11*	*4*	*17*
%	14.3	57.1	28.6	10.0	70.0	20.0	11.8	64.7	23.5	
Linear										
Total	*1*	*2*	*1*	*3*	*11*	*1*	*4*	*13*	*2*	*19*
%	25.0	50.0	25.0	20.0	73.3	6.7	21.1	68.4	10.5	
Total Complete	*2*	*6*	*3*	*4*	*18*	*3*	*6*	*24*	*6*	*36*
%	18.2	54.5	27.3	16.0	72.0	12.0	16.7	66.7	16.7	
Fragments										
Total	*3*	*9*	*0*	*1*	*9*	*0*	*4*	*18*	*0*	*22*
%	25.0	75.0	0.0	10.0	90.0	0.0	18.2	72.8	0.0	
Total Specialized Flakes	*5*	*15*	*3*	*5*	*27*	*3*	*10*	*42*	*6*	*58*
%	21.7	65.2	13.0	14.3	77.1	8.6	17.2	72.4	10.3	
UNSPECIALIZED										
End Struck	13	39	23	13	46	6	26	85	29	140
Side Struck	3	5	1	1	13	4	4	18	5	27
Total Complete	*16*	*44*	*24*	*14*	*59*	*10*	*30*	*103*	*34*	*167*
%	19.0	52.4	28.6	16.9	71.1	12.0	17.9	61.7	61.7	
Fragments										
Total	*7*	*21*	*6*	*6*	*26*	*1*	*13*	*47*	*7*	*67*
%	20.6	61.8	17.6	18.2	78.8	3.0	19.4	70.1	10.4	
Total Unspecialized Flakes	*23*	*65*	*30*	*20*	*85*	*11*	*43*	*150*	*41*	*234*
%	19.5	55.1	25.4	17.2	73.3	9.5	18.4	64.1	17.5	
Total Flakes	*28*	*80*	*33*	*25*	*112*	*14*	*53*	*192*	*47*	*292*
%	19.9	56.7	23.4	16.6	74.1	9.3	18.1	65.8	16.1	
SHAPED TOOLS										
Points--Bifacial oval	-	-	-	-	-	1	-	-	1	1
Bifacial Points (Lanceolate)	-	1	1	-	-	-	-	1	1	2
Scrapers	-	3	-	2	1	-	2	4	-	6
Ventral Butt-Thinned Flakes	-	1	-	1	1	-	1	2	-	3
Bifaces--Acheulian-type	-	1	1	-	-	-	-	1	1	2
--Balat-type	-	2	-	1	-	-	1	2	-	3
--Balat-type/MSA Coreaxes	1r	1	-	-	1	1	1	2	1	4
Total Shaped Tools	*1*	*9*	*2*	*3*	*3*	*3*	*4*	*12*	*5*	*21*
%	8.3	75.0	16.7	33.3	33.3	33.3	19.1	57.1	23.8	
SITUATIONAL TOOLS	*0*	*0*	*0*	*0*	*1*	*0*	*0*	*1*	*0*	*1*
UTILIZED TOOLS										
Edge-damaged	-	-	-	1	-	-	1	-	-	1
Battered										
Hammerstones	-	-	-	-	2	1	-	2	1	3
Total Utilized Tools	*0*	*0*	*0*	*1*	*2*	*1*	*1*	*2*	*1*	*4*
%							25.0	50.0	25.0	
Total Tools	*1*	*9*	*2*	*4*	*6*	*4*	*5*	*15*	*6*	*26*
%	8.3	75.0	16.6	28.6	42.8	28.6	19.2	57.7	23.1	
TOTAL AGGREGATE	37	110	42	42	154	20	79	264	62	405
%	19.6	58.2	22.2	19.4	71.3	9.3	19.5	65.2	15.3	
TOTAL BYPRODUCTS	8	21	7	13	36	2	21	57	9	87
%	22.2	58.3	19.4	25.5	70.6	3.9	24.1	65.5	10.3	
TOTAL END/BYPRODUCTS	28	80	33	25	112	14	53	192	47	292
%	19.9	56.7	23.4	16.6	74.1	9.3	18.1	65.8	16.1	
TOTAL END PRODUCTS	1	9	2	4	6	4	5	15	6	26
%	8.3	75.0	16.6	28.6	42.8	28.6	19.2	57.7	23.1	
PSEUDO-ARTEFACTS (Natural)	2	2	1	1	2	1	3	4	2	9

r One recycled: disc core on disc core LA/A; flake core on Acheulian-type handaxe LA/HA; MSA biface on Balat biface LA/A.

Table 4 Desert varnish colours by artefact class for Sets I-II-III+G, Locality 187A, Dakhleh Oasis. Key: BNS, browns; DKBNS, dark browns; VDBNS, very dark browns; LGBRN, light grey browns; DKGRY, dark greys; RGRYS, reddish greys; YRED, yellowish reds.

ARTEFACT CLASS Loc. 187A	SETS I-II-III+G VARNISH ROCK COLOURS							N
	BNS	DKBNS	VDBNS	LGBRN	DKGRY	RGRYS	YRED	
CORES								
SPECIALIZED								
Levallois	2	16	3	-	-	2	-	23
Discoidal	1	-	1	-	-	1	-	3
Linear	1	1	1	-	-	-	-	3
Total Specialized	4	17	5	0	0	3	0	29
UNSPECIALIZED								
Flake--1 Platform	2	2	-	-	-	-	-	4
Initial/Earlier Stage	-	-	-	-	-	2	-	2
Fragments--Initial	-	-	-	-	-	-	1	1
Total Unspecialized	1	2	0	0	0	2	1	8
Total Cores	6	19	5	0	0	5	1	36
%	16.7	**52.8**	13.9	0.0	0.0	13.9	2.8	
FLAKES								
SPECIALIZED								
Levallois	2	4	1	-	-	-	-	7
Linear	-	3	1	-	-	-	-	4
Fragments	-	12	-	-	-	-	-	12
Total Specialized Flakes	2	19	2	0	0	0	0	23
%	8.7	**82.6**	8.7	0.0	0.0	0.0	0.0	
UNSPECIALIZED								
End Struck	14	39	18	1	1	1	1	75
Side Struck	1	3	4	-	-	1	-	9
Fragments*	4	27	-	-	1	1	-	33
Total Unspecial. Flakes	19	69	22	1	2	3	1	117
%	16.2	**58.9**	18.8	0.9	1.7	2.6	0.9	
Total Flakes	21	88	24	1	2	3	1	140
%	15.0	**62.9**	17.1	0.7	1.4	2.1	0.7	
SHAPED TOOLS								
Bifacial Points	-	2	-	-	-	-	-	2
Scrapers	-	3	-	-	-	-	-	3
Ventral Butt-Thinned	-	1	-	-	-	-	-	1
Bifaces- Acheulian-type	-	2	-	-	-	-	-	2
- Balat-type	-	2	-	-	-	-	-	2
- Balat/MSA-type	-	1	1	-	-	-	-	2
Total Shaped Tools	0	11	1	0	0	0	0	12
%	0.0	**91.6**	7.4	0.0	0.0	0.0	0.0	
TOTAL AGGREGATE	27	118	30	1	2	8	2	188
%	14.4	**62.8**	16.0	0.5	1.0	4.3	1.0	

* 1 not recorded

*Table 5 Desert varnish colours of artefacts by abrasion category, for Sets I-II-III+G, Locality 187A, Dakhleh Oasis.
Key: BNS, browns; DKBNS, dark browns; VDBNS, very dark browns; LGBRN, light grey browns;
DKGRY, dark greys; RGRYS, reddish greys; YRED, yellowish reds.*

ARTEFACT CLASS	SETS I-II-III+G		VARNISH ROCK COLOURS					
Loc. 187A	BNS	DKBNS	VDBNS	LGBRN	DKGRY	RGRYS	YRED	N
CORES								
SPECIALIZED								
Lightly Abraded	2	2	1	-	-	1	-	6
Abraded	2	12	3	-	-	1	-	18
Heavily Abraded	-	3	1	-	-	1	-	5
Total Specialized	*4*	*17*	*5*	*0*	*0*	*3*	*0*	*29*
UNSPECIALIZED								
Lightly Abraded	1	1	-	-	-	-	-	2
Abraded	1	1	-	-	-	1	-	3
Heavily Abraded	-	-	-	-	-	1	1	2
Total Unspecialized	*2*	*2*	*0*	*0*	*0*	*2*	*1*	*7*
Total Cores	*6*	*19*	*5*	*0*	*0*	*5*	*1*	*36*
TOTAL CORES			%					
Lightly Abraded	8.3	8.3	2.8	0.0	0.0	2.8	0.0	8
Abraded	8.3	36.1	8.3	0.0	0.0	5.6	0.0	21
Heavily Abraded	0.0	8.3	2.8	0.0	0.0	5.6	2.8	7
FLAKES								
SPECIALIZED								
Lightly Abraded	1	4	-	-	-	-	-	5
Abraded	1	13	1	-	-	-	-	15
Heavily Abraded	-	2	1	-	-	-	-	3
Total Specialized	*2*	*19*	*2*	*0*	*0*	*0*	*0*	*23*
UNSPECIALIZED								
Lightly Abraded	2	14	6	-	-	1	-	23
Abraded	10	42	8	1	1	1	1	64
Heavily Abraded	7	13	8	-	1	1	-	30
Total Unspecialized	*19*	*69*	*22*	*1*	*2*	*3*	*1*	*117*
Total Flakes	*21*	*88*	*24*	*1*	*2*	*3*	*1*	*140*
TOTAL FLAKES			%					
Lightly Abraded	2.1	12.9	4.3	0.0	0.0	0.7	0.0	28
Abraded	7.9	39.3	6.4	0.7	0.7	0.7	0.7	79
Heavily Abraded	5.0	10.7	6.4	0.0	0.7	0.7	0.0	33
SHAPED TOOLS								
Lightly Abraded	-	1	-	-	-	-	-	1
Abraded	-	8	1	-	-	-	-	9
Heavily Abraded	-	2	-	-	-	-	-	2
Total Shaped Tools	*0*	*11*	*1*	*0*	*0*	*0*	*0*	*12*
TOTAL SHAPED TOOLS			%					
Lightly Abraded	0.0	8.3	0.0	0.0	0.0	0.0	0.0	1
Abraded	0.0	66.7	8.3	0.0	0.0	0.0	0.0	9
Heavily Abraded	0.0	16.7	0.0	0.0	0.0	0.0	0.0	2
*TOTAL AGGREGATE**			%					
Lightly Abraded	3.2	11.7	3.7	0.0	0.0	1.1	0.0	37
Abraded	7.5	40.4	6.9	0.5	0.5	1.6	0.5	109
Heavily Abraded	3.7	10.6	5.3	0.0	0.5	1.6	0.5	42

* 1 not recorded

over much shorter periods of time. Dealing with the problems of surface aggregates is similar to dealing with the problems of sealed but potentially mixed, that is, multi-component, aggregates from geological contexts (Cole 1967; Sheppard and Kleindienst 1996). If we ignore the surface evidence in the desert, we ignore the bulk of the evidence for Pleistocene archaeology. Time-averaged aggregates covering greater time ranges may even be more useful for recognizing long-term trends than a combination of aggregates representing a series of short-period events.

Two main methods are used for assessing the integrity of surface aggregates:
1) observations of physical condition; and
2) both internal and external comparisons among artefact classes.

Complementary use of both lines of evidence is necessary, as has long been practiced in Pleistocene archaeology. These must be accompanied by quality control in assessing the various experiments in sampling and the effects of observer bias (Hawkins 2001, 115–33). Work on the surface occurrences at Dakhleh has been a learning process over the years.

In the early days of Egyptian Pleistocene archaeology, workers noted that they could discriminate between lighter-coloured 'gravel' patina, on artefacts found *in situ* or recently weathered-out, and darker-coloured 'desert' patinas (desert varnish) on artefacts which had rested on the surface for long periods of time (Caton-Thompson, 1952). C. T. Currelly and A. Sturge (Currelly 1909; 1967 (1956), 160–1) conducted one of the earliest, if not the earliest, systematic study of surface weathering rinds on chert as a tool for broadly discriminating between sets of artefacts of different relative ages, using a large surface collection from the Libyan Plateau and Escarpment at Thebes. They then tested their varnish stages against artefact typology. Geologists use similar observations on the colours of surface rinds in the desert to discriminate between the relative ages of different geomorphic surfaces (Dorn and Oberlander 1982; Dorn 1994), although attempts at chronometric dating of the desert varnish have proved less successful (Oberlander 1994, 113–4). Many possible factors influence the development of patina, in burial, and of weathering rinds and desert varnish on the surface, including the composition of the cherts or other rock types. However, the colour of desert varnish is a useful tool within the Dakhleh and Kharga regions for broadly discriminating between sets of artefacts of different relative ages when the cherts or chalcedonies or quartzites come from the same or similar sources, and for material in similar settings. In general, for similar rock material, the darker the colour the longer the piece has been exposed on the surface. If left in place, an exposed rock surface will progress from its original surface colour, usually first through a darkening of colour, and then to development of a light tan or brown rind, to progressively darker browns of varying tone, to black. Caton-Thompson termed the darker reddish browns 'mahogany' (1952, 111). If the piece has developed a weathering rind subsurface, the process begins altering that,

which is usually light coloured. Normally, the 'up' face of a rock is considerably darker than the 'down' face; if both have similar colours, or if both faces show variable colours, the piece has probably been repeatedly turned over, by sheet-wash, trampling, and/or wind action. One complication is that varnish can be removed and reformed. A "carbonate collar" is often observed (McFadden *et al.* 1998).

The Pleistocene artefacts in Dakhleh from surface contexts have been variably exposed to other weathering processes common to deserts, remembering also that the Western Desert was not always hyperarid, including pocking due to rapid changes in temperature combined with chemical weathering, surface erosion due to chemical weathering, and in particular, abrasion by sand blasting. Artefacts in areas exposed to wind-blown sand and silt exhibit 'nibbling' along edges, which makes identification of any fine retouch or use-damage problematic or impossible. Continued exposure results in abrasion of the pieces, first along the thinner edges and aretes, and then of the faces. The development of thick weathering rinds also affects the morphology of the pieces to some degree even without abrasion by sand blasting. Careful observations of physical condition, particularly of desert varnish colours and abrasion states, should allow assessment of the integrity of aggregates and in some cases, the separation of components from aggregates that may cover extended time periods of accumulation: 10,000s to 100,000s of years (Hawkins 2001, 142).

In analysis of the Locality 187A aggregates from Sets I-II-III+G on the southern end of the P-II terrace, and from Set IV+G in the centre of the terrace, abrasion was assessed by setting up a standard set of specimens representing five, intergrading, stages: mint (M, none found), fresh (F), lightly abraded (LA), abraded (A), and heavily abraded (HA). Mint indicates the condition as a piece was struck; fresh, that edge and arete sharpness is retained; lightly abraded, that edges and aretes are beginning to be rounded off; abraded, that both are clearly rounded; and heavily abraded, that abrasion has extended onto the faces of negative flake scars. Pieces that are barely recognizable as once having been artefacts may be noted as very heavily abraded, but none were found in this collection. Different abrasion states do not in themselves always indicate the relative ages of artefact disposal/loss, because of differential exposures in different micro-settings, or due to weathering out of the underlying sediments at different times. Rather, as with varnish colour, it is a question of whether there are marked differences in the distributions of abrasion states, or of whether the same range of stages is present among different artefact categories or types (Tables 3, 4 and 5).

A Munsell Rock Colour chart was used to describe the darkest colours of desert varnish on both artefact faces for Sets I-II-III+G, but it proved difficult to characterize colour in detail because of variable shades on the same face of many artefacts. Given that problem, the rock colour chart method proved to be too time consuming for practical use at Dakhleh, and general descriptive terms have proved to be more useful. Hence, more general terms are reported here for the darkest face, combining the yellow, red, and grey tones for browns as browns, dark browns, and very dark browns. Light grey brown, dark grey, reddish grey and yellowish-red are more distinctive but rare colours. Varnish colours were not recorded in the basic analysis for Set IV+G, but paralleled those recorded for the other sample.

Finally, in ascertaining the integrity of an aggregate, one can turn to comparisons of the artefact classes, both within the aggregate and externally. The data most comparable to Dakhleh in its contexts is that obtained at Kharga by Caton-Thompson and Gardner in the 1930s (Caton-Thompson 1952, 27–8): the "Lower Levalloisian Industry" (older Middle Stone Age) and "Upper Levalloisian Industry" (younger Middle Stone Age), distinguished on both geological and typological grounds (below). It is unlikely, given the extended time ranges involved, that any Dakhleh aggregate covers exactly the same time range as any at Kharga, nor need Dakhleh necessarily duplicate Kharga. However, we can expect a general level of similarity, given the distance involved (*circa* 125 km) and similarities in the geologic and geomorphologic settings of the two oasis depressions which are floored by Nubia Group sandstones and clay-stones, and bounded by piedmont terraces extending out from steep escarpments fronting the Libyan Plateau on the north or east.

Assessment of the Aggregate: Physical Condition, Locality 187A Artefacts

With respect to abrasion, the aggregates from Locality 187A span the range from fresh to heavily abraded (Tables 3 and 5). A few are fresh, with edges still sharp (8 from Sets I-II-III+G and 18 from Set IV+G). Although differential erosion from the soil is possible, the small number in itself suggests that some or all may not belong with the bulk of the abraded material. One piece was found weathering out at Set IV. As Currelly (1967 [1956], 161–2) noted long ago multiple patination/abrasion resulting from human recycling of older artefacts may be a useful device for establishing relative age. Four of the fresh artefacts are recycled: a burin worked on a lightly abraded specialized flake, which also shows different varnish colours (Set I-GE), two struck Levallois cores (Set IV), with fresh strikes attempted on cores already lightly abraded, and one flake core (Set II-60E). While these suggest that fresh material is probably Middle Stone Age, Dakhleh Unit or later, they also indicate that the fresh material is, indeed, likely to be younger in age. Consequently, the fresh material has been excluded from further consideration here.

Four other artefacts were recycled: a lightly abraded flake core made on a heavily abraded Upper Acheulian-type hand-axe (Set III/20-E); a lightly abraded biface worked on an abraded Balat-type biface (Set I/100E); and a lightly abraded scraper worked on a large abraded flake

(Set IV/20E). All of these recycled artefacts typologically belong with the Earlier Stone Age units. One lightly abraded discoidal core was worked on an abraded discoidal core (Set IIG, possibly Earlier Stone Age). Taken together with the fresh/lightly abraded recycles, they bracket the abraded material and indicate that it can be given consideration as a single Middle Stone Age aggregate, albeit one that probably covers an extended time range. Typologically, because coreaxes which closely resemble Balat Unit-type bifaces/coreaxes have been found elsewhere with Middle Stone Age units at Dakhleh, the less abraded Balat-type bifaces may be either Earlier Stone Age or Middle Stone Age. That the abraded aggregate is predominantly Middle Stone Age is confirmed by the overwhelming abundance of end-struck trimming flakes (non-specialized, 83.8%). In Africa, Earlier Stone Age units are characterized by a preponderance of side-struck flakes (Isaac and Keller 1968). The small component of abraded or heavily abraded Acheulian-type and Balat Unit-type bifaces can be excluded, but Earlier Stone Age flakes cannot be separated at present. The lightly abraded, recycled artefacts raise some question as to whether lightly abraded material as a group might actually be younger than more abraded material. It may still represent the older Middle Stone Age time range, however.

A consideration of the rock varnish colours indicates that the same range of colours is present for all artefact classes, although those with larger sample numbers have a broader range, as would be expected. Most are in the browns (BNS), dark browns (DBNS) or very dark browns (VDBNS): 93%: lightly abraded, 18.6%; abraded, 54.8%; heavily abraded, 19.6% (Tables 4 and 5). Of these, most are varnished in reddish-brown shades, while fewer are greyish or yellowish brown, variations that may relate to chert composition. Lightly abraded pieces have not yet developed the brown colourations; some of the surface varnish on some heavily abraded pieces probably has been removed, resulting in the grey to reddish grey shades. The bifaces that are typologically Earlier Stone Age do not segregate by varnish colour: all are dark browns.

Comparisons

Internal comparisons are facilitated because the Locality 187A knapped products are made entirely on Tarawan Chert. Only one unspecialized core fragment (Set III-0E) with yellowish-red varnish/patina is possibly a different chert, which may derive from the Plateau-top limestones rather than from the cliffs above. No obviously-imported chert was found on the terrace, although some nodules or artefacts of the more distinctive wood-grained variety were seen. Two hammer-stones are imported chert balls: both Set IVG and abraded (Table 2).

In internal comparison, similar ranges of variation occur for both abrasion and rock varnish colours for all artefact classes, although the small samples of tools and specialized flakes all fall within the browns and dark browns. Then, the abraded aggregate appears to be consistent as far as

Table 6 Dimensions of selected artefact classes by abrasion categories, Locality 187A, Sets I-II-III+G and Set IV+G, Dakhleh Oasis. Oriented maximum length is to long axis of piece, with flake talons on the base line (box/chart measurement); maximum width measured relative to orientation of long axis of the piece; maximum thickness of flakes usually at talon. Measurements not adjusted for abrasion. Key: n/c, samples numbering less than 5 not calculated.

ARTEFACT CLASS	Oriented Maximum Length mm				Oriented Maximum Width mm				Maximum Thickness mm			
	N	Mean	S.D.	Range	N	Mean	S.D.	Range	N	Mean	S.D.	Range
CORES												
Specialized Cores												
Levallois and Discoidal												
Lightly Abraded	8	91.5	13.3	70-110	8	80.4	15.3	51-100	8	34.6	9.0	25-50
Abraded	41	85.7	14.4	55-130	41	72.1	11.5	52-108	41	33.5	8.1	16-50
Heavily Abraded	6	92.3	15.3	74-112	6	80.3	11.4	66-96	6	34.0	5.3	27-40
Linear												
Lightly Abraded	7	94.0	42.8	63-185	5	66.4	17.4	48-95	5	37.8	4.2	32-43
Abraded	4	n/c	n/c	83-110	4	n/c	n/c	60-76	4	n/c	n/c	16-40

FLAKES	Oriented Maximum Length mm				Oriented Maximum Width mm				Maximum Thickness mm			
	N	Mean	S.D.	Range	N	Mean	S.D.	Range	N	Mean	S.D.	Range
Specialized Flakes*												
Lightly Abraded	6	88.5	21.2	58-124	6	52.0	17.0	33-82	6	14.3	3.3	10-20
Abraded	25	82.6	22.6	49-121	25	42.8	13.9	23-74	25	12.4	4.7	5-23
Heavily Abraded	7	93.0	16.4	67-114	7	53.9	11.4	34-65	6	12.8	2.6	10-17
Unspecialized Flakes*												
Lightly Abraded	25	74.0	19.1	50-124	25	54.6	16.3	34-84	25	13.8	5.0	6-26
Abraded	94	74.4	17.5	50-119	94	50.1	14.9	24-92	94	15.2	4.7	7-30
Heavily Abraded	30	72.8	14.9	50-105	30	46.6	17.0	20-107	30	14.4	5.0	7-30

* Unspecialized flakes under 50 mm in maximum piece dimension not included – not reliably collected. One specialized flake, 49 mm long, included.

exposure to conditions causing desert varnish as well as abrasion. The rarer colour variations could be excluded, but cross-correlation with abrasion does not support exclusion. In the larger samples, neither specialized cores nor unspecialized end-struck flakes show bimodality in abrasion.

One caution in dealing with measured attributes is that some collector bias may be operating: most lightly abraded material came from Set IV, where McDonald collected some Set lines and I did others. Different individuals tend to 'see' and to collect different objects, and different sizes of objects (Hawkins 2001, 128–9). Collector bias aside, experience shows that pieces under 50 mm in size are more difficult to see when walking transect lines, especially when the chert is darkly varnished. Also, the one square metre rock density squares collected at Sets I, II and III contained few small flakes, suggesting that smaller artefacts may be sorted-out on the southern portion of the P-II terrace. Therefore, flakes under 50 mm in length have been excluded from calculations in Table 6, in order to have better comparability between Sets I-II-III and Set IV.

Rough estimates of the amount of edge loss by abrasion can be made based upon conjoining cores and flakes from various oasis localities, by comparing the flakes with their negative flake scars. Using mint condition as no loss: fresh artefacts have lost *circa* 1 mm of edge; lightly abraded, *circa* 3 mm of edge; abraded, *circa* 5 mm of edge; and heavily abraded, 6+ mm of edge.

If abrasion states are compared (Table 6), not surprisingly lightly abraded, Levallois and discoidal specialized cores are longer than abraded cores, but given sample sizes do not differ greatly in mean oriented length: lightly abraded cores (n = 8), 91.5 ± 13.3 mm, are slightly larger than abraded (41), 85.7 ± 14.4 mm. Heavily abraded cores (6) are the largest, 92.3 ± 15.3 mm. All the cores, in mint condition, would have exceeded 90 mm in oriented length, congruent with adjusted lengths for specialized flakes. Roughly adjusted for abrasion: lightly abraded mean length of cores is *circa* 94.5 mm, and flakes, 91.5 mm; abraded cores, *circa* 90.7 mm and flakes, 87.6 mm; heavily abraded cores at least 98 mm, and flakes, 99 mm. In mean oriented flake chart length, lightly abraded unspecialized flakes are somewhat shorter than abraded or heavily abraded flakes: lightly abraded (n = 25), 74.0 ± 19.1 mm (+3 mm adjustment = 77 mm); abraded (94), 74.4 ± 17.5 mm (+5 mm adjustment = 79.4 mm); heavily abraded (30), 72.8 ± 14.0 mm (+6 mm = 78.8 mm). This could indicate that lightly abraded material differs from the more abraded material. However, given sample sizes, the adjusted lengths of cores and flakes and the similar ranges in lengths support treating all the abraded material as a single combined aggregate.

Turning to external comparisons with Kharga, after qualitative assessment of the 187A aggregates, I tentatively considered the 'large-sized Middle Stone Age' as cognate to the "Lower Levalloisian" (Caton-Thompson 1952, 27–

Table 7 Comparison of artefact classes found in Escarpment Loci, classed as "Lower Levalloisian" at Kharga Oasis, plus Lowland Locus K08A (Caton-Thompson 1952), with classes found in the Gifata Unit at Piedmont Locality 187A, Dakhleh Oasis. Key: X, present; Inferred, presence based on presence of struck cores or flakes; dash (–), not recorded at Kharga, or not found at Dakhleh.

ARTEFACT CLASS	KHARGA OASIS, "LOWER LEVALLOISIAN" LOCALITIES					CF. "L. LEVALLOISIAN" LOWLAND	DAKHLEH OASIS PIEDMONT
			ESCARPMENT				
	REFUF Locus IV	REFUF Locus VI	REFUF Locus VIII	ABU SIGHAWAL KO18	MATANA Site F	KO8A	P-II 187A
CORES	silt & gravel	gravel	gravel	silt, gravel, & scree	gravel	spring vent	veneer
SPECIALIZED							
Levallois	X	X	X	X	X	X	X
Triangular	X	X	X	X	X	X	X
Oval & Arch	X	X	-	X	-	X	X
Circular	-	-	-	-	X	X	X
Opposed platform	X	-	-	X	X	X	X
Earlier stages	X	-	X	X	-	-	X
Discoidal	X	-	-	-	-	X	X
Linear	-	-	-	Inferred	Inferred	Illustrated	X
UNSPECIALIZED & INITIAL	X	-	X	X	-	X	X
FLAKES							
SPECIALIZED							
Levallois	Inferred	X	X	X	X	X	X
Broad	Inferred	X	-	X	X	X	X
Pointed	Inferred	-	X	-	X	X	X
Other	Inferred	-	-	Inferred	-	X	X
Linear--Quad. & Pointed	-	-	-	X	-	X	X
UNSPECIALIZED							
Complete	X	X	X	X	X	X	X
Fragments	-	-	-	-	-	X	X
TOOLS							
SHAPED							
Bifacial points	-	-	-	-	-	-	X
Scrapers	-	-	-	X	-	X	X
Ventral butt-thinning	-	-	-	-	-	-	X
Bifaces/Core axes	-	-	-	-	-	-	X
Choppers	-	-	-	-	-	X	-
UTILIZED							
Edge damaged	X	-	X	X	-	X	X
Battered							
Anvil	-	X	-	X	-	-	Inferred
Hammerstone	-	-	-	-	-	X	X
[N]	[34]	[8]	[24]	[94]	[20]	[653]	[405]

8; Kleindienst 1999, 100). Although Caton-Thompson pioneered using quantitative methods for description of lithics, she unfortunately also used selected samples so that her data are of limited use, except for specialized flakes and cores where all were collected. "Wasters" were usually counted but not all collected, although talon faceting was usually recorded qualitatively. The discards can be found on the edges of the trenches at Kharga. She also only reported the composition of the aggregates from different occurrences found *in situ* within sediments.

Caton-Thompson characterized the older Middle Stone Age unit as being larger in size for both specialized cores and flakes, with less regulation of the knapping techniques than in the younger Middle Stone Age units. On specialized flakes, and therefore also on cores, there was less careful face or platform preparation. Flakes were reported to have wider talons than did younger Middle Stone Age flakes, but with lower talon/ventral face striking angles than in the Earlier Stone Age. Few pieces showed retouch into shaped tools, mainly scrapers. It is not surprising that she found a marked difference between the older and younger Middle Stone Age at Refuf: Schwarcz has provided U/Th determinations that indicate at least a 100,000-year time span separating "Lower" and "Upper Levalloisan" occurrences (Churcher, Kleindienst, and Schwarcz 1999, 305, Table 1; Kleindienst *et al.* forthcoming). The generalized Middle Stone Age of the Western Desert is similar in gross categories throughout that time span, the major differences being in greater regulation and refinement of knapping techniques,

Table 8 Comparison of artefact classes found in Escarpment Loci classed as "Upper Levalloisian" at Kharga Oasis (Caton-Thompson 1952) with classes found in the Gifata Unit at Piedmont Locality 187A, and in the Lowland Teneida unit occurrences, Dakhleh Oasis region. Key: X, present; Inferred, presence based on presence of struck cores or flakes; dash (–), not recorded at Kharga, or not found at Dakhleh.

	KHARGA OASIS "UPPER LEVALLOISIAN" LOCALITIES		DAKHLEH OASIS	
	ESCARPMENT LOCI		PIEDMONT	LOWLAND
ARTEFACT CLASS	REFUF	MATANA		Teneida unit
	Locus VII	Site G	187A	Localities
CORES	tufa terrace silts	tufa terrace silts	veneer	CSS or surface
SPECIALIZED				
Levallois	X	X	X	X
Triangular	-	X	X	Inferred
Oval & Arch	X	X	X	X
Circular	X	X	X	?
Opposed platform	X	X	X	Inferred
Earlier stages	X	X	X	X
Discoidal	X	X	X	X
Linear	Inferred	Inferred	X	Inferred
UNSPECIALIZED AND INITIAL	X	-	X	X
FLAKES				
SPECIALIZED				
Levallois	X	X	X	X
Broad	X	X	X	X
Pointed	X	X	X	X
Other	X	X	X	X
Linear	X	X	X	X
UNSPECIALIZED				
Complete	X	X	X	X
Fragments	Observed	-	X	X
TOOLS				
SHAPED				
Retouched points	-	X (small)	X (large)	X (varied)
Lanceolates	-	-	X	-
Scrapers	X	X	X	X
Denticulated edge	X	-	-	X
Ventral butt-thinning	-	-	X (large)	X (large)
Tabalbalat points	-	X (small)	-	-
Borers	X	X	-	X
Bifaces/Coreaxes	-	-	X	X
SITUATIONAL (varied)	X	-	X	X
UTILIZED				
Edge damaged	X	-	X	X
Battered				
Anvil	-	-	Inferred	X
Hammerstone	-	-	X	X
Depression	-	-	-	X
Spheroid	-	-	-	X
[N]	[106]	[153]	[405]	[2,154]
OTHER				
Potboiler	-	X	-	-
Burnt artefacts	X	X	-	-

Table 9 Combined aggregate assigned to Gifata Unit, Locality 187A, Sets I-II-III+G and Set IV+G, Piedmont zone, Dakhleh Oasis.

ARTEFACT CLASS: Loc. 187A	SETS I-II-III+G N	%	SET IV+G N	%	Total N	Percent
Cores--Specialized						
Levallois	22		26		48	
Discoidal	3		4		8	
Linear	3		6		9	
Fragments	1		4		5	
Total	*29*	*80.6*	*40*	*78.4*	*69*	*79.3*
Cores--Unspecialized	*7*	*19.4*	*11*	*21.6*	*18*	*20.7*
Total Cores	*36*	*19.5*	*51*	*23.7*	*87*	*21.8*
Angular Debris*						
Flakes--Specialized						
Levallois	7		10		17	
Linear	4		15		19	
Fragments	12		10		22	
Total	*23*	*16.2*	*35*	*23.2*	*58*	*19.9*
Flakes--Unspecialized						
End-struck	75		65		140	
Side-struck	9		18		27	
Fragments	34		33		67	
Total	*118*	*83.7*	*116*	*76.8*	*234*	*80.1*
Total Flakes	*141*	*76.2*	*151*	*70.2*	*292*	*73.0*
Shaped Tools						
Points--Bifacial oval			1		1	
Bifacial Points (Lanceolate)	2				2	
Scrapers	3		3		6	
Ventral Butt-Thinned Flakes	1		2		3	
Bifaces/Coreaxes--Balat type/MSA	2r		2		4	
Situational Tools			1		1	
Utilized Tools						
Edge-damaged Flakes			1		1	
Battered Hammerstones			3		3	
Total Tools	*8*	*4.3*	*13*	*6.0*	*26*	*5.3*
Total Aggregate	**185***		**215***		**400***	

*   **Earlier Stone Age-type artefacts and Angular Debris excluded from calculations for Gifata Unit artefacts.**

reduction in size, and more production of more shaped tool types (Tables 7 and 8). However, more shaped tools in occurrences may relate to factors other than chronological placement: aggregates from occurrences representing different sets of activities can be expected to differ in composition (Kleindienst 1999, 85–6; Hawkins and Kleindienst 2002). Fewer shaped tools might be dropped at workshop localities. Also, it should be noted that technique or size comparisons are valid only when the form, size or properties of available raw materials do not constrain production.

Allowing for differences in typology, a general comparison of Locality 187A with the Kharga Escarpment localities designated as "Lower Levalloisian" is shown in Table 7. Caton-Thompson (1952) considered *in situ* samples, only mentioning surface evidence, so that most aggregates are small. Only the sample from Abu Sighawal Locus KO18 is larger, with more artefact classes. She equivocates regarding Lowland spring vent KO8A, because it could not be placed into a geological sequence as could the localities on the Escarpment: she leaves it as undifferentiated "Levalloisian" in the text, but labels artefacts "probably Lower Levalloisian" on Plates 63 and 64. Based upon the flaking debris present, all aggregates represent workshops; no occupation-type, older Middle Stone Age occurrences are known at Kharga.

Comparison with the smaller-sized, and more regulated "Upper Levalloisian" (Table 8) shows only that the larger Locality 187A sample includes more classes than do the smaller samples from Kharga. The much larger sample from the occupation-type Teneida unit occurrences includes even more classes, so that sample size is likely to account for observed differences.

Despite problems, the classes present at both Kharga and Dakhleh are similar. Dakhleh does include three tool classes not noted at Kharga: bifacial lanceolate points, ventrally basally-thinned flakes and bifaces/coreaxes. Although not reported by Caton-Thompson, such points do occur at Kharga in surface contexts (Kleindienst 1999, 100). Caton-Thompson noted ventrally-thinned flakes only in her "Upper Levalloisian" at Kharga; smaller sample sizes could account for their lack in the older unit. The class cannot be excluded at Dakhleh either on the basis of abrasion or varnish, although this becomes a class requiring

Table 10 Striking face preparation on specialized cores and flakes, Locality 187A, Sets I-II-III+G, Dakhleh Oasis. Totals may be less than for the entire aggregate because some observations not recorded. Key: dash (–), not present.

SPECIALIZED CORE STRIKING FACE PATTERNS

ARTEFACT CLASS CORES	N	Radial	Convergent	Opposed	Nubia	Sub-Parallel/ Parallel	Parallel Opposed
Specialized Cores							
Levallois							
Struck	17	12	5	-	-	-	-
Unstruck	6	4	1	1	-	-	-
Total	23	16	6	1	0	0	0
%		69.6	26.1	4.3	0.0	0.0	0.0
Linear	4	-	1	-	-	1	2
Total	27	16	7	1	0	1	2
%		59.3	25.9	3.7	0.0	3.7	7.4

DORSAL FACE PATTERNS ON FLAKES

FLAKES	N	Cortex	Cortex + Scars	Radial	Convergent	Convergent-* Opposed	Sub-Parallel/ Parallel	Parallel Opposed	Parallel Transverse
Specialized Flakes									
Levallois	7	-	-	4	1	1	-	1	-
Levallois fragments	7	-	-	4	2	1	-	-	-
Total	14	0	0	8	3	2	0	1	0
%		0.0	0.0	57.1	21.4	14.3	0.0	7.1	0.0
Linear	4	-	-	-	-	-	3	-	1
Linear fragments	8	-	-	•	-	-	7	1	-
Total	12	0	0	0	0	0	10	1	1
%							83.3	8.3	8.3
Total Specialized	26	0	0	8	3	2	10	2	1
%		0.0	0.0	45.0	11.5	7.7	38.5	7.7	3.8
Unspecialized Flakes									
End struck	77	11	38	9	2	-	12	4	1
Side struck	8	-	-	1	6	-	-	1	-
Total Unspecialized	85	11	38	10	8	0	12	5	1
%		12.9	44.7	11.8	9.4	0.0	14.1	5.9	1.2
TOTAL FLAKES	111	11	38	18	11	2	22	7	2
%		9.9	34.2	16.2	9.9	1.8	19.8	6.3	1.8

* Nubia pattern (convergent opposed) difficult to distinguish from convergent on aeolised flakes.

future confirmation. Anvils were not found/recognized at Dakhleh Locality 187A, possibly because of the abrasion. Four cores from Sets I-II-III+G suggest the use of an anvil or rest technique of striking in the presence of battering on the base of the core, an attribute often observed on African Levallois or linear cores. The presence of anvils is, therefore, inferred.

In considering abrasion at Locality 187A, it can be noted that more specialized linear cores, blade or flake/blade, are lightly abraded than are abraded. Blade cores were assigned on the basis of the last strikes, but all linear cores could be considered as one class. This could suggest that some or all do not belong with the more abraded Middle Stone Age aggregate, although it is not surprising to find linear flake production in the African Middle Stone Age (McBrearty and Brooks 2000, 494–6). Caton-Thompson (1952, 111) notes that "narrow flakes occur at practically all Levalloisian sites in Kharga ...", but does not report finding linear cores. I would class one illustrated core from KO8A, (Caton-Thompson 1952, Plate 68-2), as flake/blade, although she regarded it as unspecialized. Some linear flakes do result from trimming Levallois cores; however, some illustrated Kharga linear flakes appear to have come from flake/blade cores (Caton-Thompson 1952, Plates 64-12 and 14, 66-5). The external comparison provides no reason to exclude the less abraded linear cores

Table 11 Attributes of specialized core platforms and specialized flake talons, Locality 187A, Sets I-II-III+G and Set IV+G, Dakhleh Oasis. Key: n/a, not applicable; n/r, not recorded; dash (–), not present.

SPECIALIZED CORE PLATFORMS

CORE CLASS	LOCATION*			PLAN SHAPES					PREPARATION				FACETTING DIRECTION	
	N	End	Side	N	Pointed	Convex	Strait	Concave	Cortex	Cortex+ Facet	Faceted		Direct	Trans-verse
LEVALLOIS CORES														
Struck	37	31	6	17	2	7	6	2	1	5	11		13	3
Unstruck	10	9	1	4	-	2	2	-	1	-	3		3	-
Total	47	40	7	21	2	9	8	2	2	5	14		16	3
%		85.1	14.9		9.5	42.9	38.1	9.5	9.5	23.8	66.7		84.2	15.8
LINEAR CORES														
Blade														
1 Platform	1	1	-	1	-	-	1	-	-	-	1		-	1
2 Platform	2	4	-	2	-	-	2	-	-	-	2		1	1
Flake/Blade														
1 Platform	4	3	1	n/r										
2 Platform	2	4	-	2	-	-	2	-	2	-	-		-	-
Total	9	12	1	5	-	-	5	-	2	-	3		1	2
TOTAL	56	52	8	26	2	9	13	2	4	5	17		17	5
%		92.9	7.1		7.7	34.6	50.0	7.7	15.4	19.2	65.4		77.3	22.7

SPECIALIZED FLAKE TALONS

FLAKE CLASS		PLAN SHAPES						PREPARATION				FACETTING DIRECTION	
	N	Irreg-ular	Dihed-ral	Chap-eau	Convex	Strait	Concave	Cortex	Cortex+ Facet	Faceted		Direct	Trans-verse
Levallois	8^	-	-	2	5	1	-	5	-	3		3	-
Linear	4	-	1	-	-	3	-	1	-	3		2	1
Fragments--Prox	7^	1	1	1	2	1	1	2	1	4		5	-
Total	19	1	2	3	7	5	1	8	1	10		10	1
%		5.3	10.6	15.9	36.8	26.3	5.3	42.1	5.3	52.6		90.9	9.1
Lev.--last strikes	17	n/a	-	-	-	-	-	3	-	14		13	3
Lin.--last strikes	4	n/a	-	-	-	-	-	2	-	2		1	2
Total	21	n/a	0	0	0	0	0	5	0	16		14	5
%			0.0	0.0	0.0	0.0	0.0	23.8	0.0	76.1		73.7	26.3

* Sets I-II-III+G & IV+G; otherwise only Sets I-II-III+G.
^ Including tools; not all fragments recorded.

Table 12 Dimensions of selected artefact classes, Locality 187A, Sets I-II-III+G and IV+G, Dakhleh Oasis. Oriented maximum length is to long axis of the piece; flake length measures point of impact to most distant distal edge; flake axis measured along striking axis; mid-width on flakes measured at mid-point of long axis of the piece. Measurements not adjusted for abrasion. Key: n/a, not applicable.

ARTEFACT CLASS	Oriented Maximum Length mm				Flake Length	mm			Maximum Width mm				Maximum Thickness mm			
	N	Mean	S.D.	Range	N	Mean	S.D.	Range	N	Mean	S.D.	Range	N	Mean	S.D.	Range
CORES																
Specialized Cores																
Levallois																
Struck	17	86.6	15.6	57-130	16	67.2	15.2	38-113	17	74.5	14.0	51-96	17	31.6	6.7	21-50
Unstruck	5	77.2	16.7	55-92	n/a				5	64.2	8.2	52-74	5	29.8	4.8	20-32
Total	22	84.5	16.0	55-130					22	72.2	13.5	51-96	22	30.3	6.7	20-50
Levallois*	48	87.5	14.5	55-130	36	67.6	15.2	38-113	48	74.0	13.0	55-108	48	32.6	7.7	16-50
Linear*	11	99.4	35.8	62-185	16	71.8	21.9	29-100	9	65.2	12.5	48-95	9	37.0	6.1	25-45
Discoidal*	7	85.4	14.7	69-106	8	52.5	10.8	37-69	7	75.7	7.2	57-65	7	41.1	4.7	35-47
Total Specialized*	67	89.0	19.7	55-185	63	66.0	17.5	29-113	65	72.8	12.7	48-96	65	34.1	7.6	16-50
Unspecialized Cores	5	79.0	14.5	65-98	5	59.4	16.2	37-77	5	65.0	11.0	51-79	5	29.2	5.8	23-38

FLAKES	Oriented Flake Length mm				Flaking Axis Length mm				Oriented Maximum Width mm				Mid-Thickness	mm		
	N	Mean	S.D.	Range	N	Mean	S.D.	Range	N	Mean	S.D.	Range	N	Mean	S.D.	Range
Specialized Flakes																
Levallois	7	91.0	24.3	89-120	7	88.9	22.2	59-108	7	51.3	11.6	32-65	6	10.3	4.7	5-17
Levallois scars	16	67.3	15.2	38-113	17	62.9	15.2	29-102	17	45.4	12.3	24-71	n/a			
Linear*	19	84.5	20.6	49-124	n/a				19	38.1	10.0	23-61	19	11.4	3.0	5-16
Unspecialized Flakes **	84	71.9	16.3	35-104	83	67.4	16.1	29-97	84	42.7	12.9	18-95	83	10.5	3.5	4-21

* Includes Set IV; otherwise Sets I-II-III
** Unspecialized flakes under 50 mm in maximum piece dimension not included – not reliably collected.

Table 13 Lengths and faceting of specialized core platforms and specialized flake talons, Locality 187A, Sets I-II-III+G and Set IV+G, Dakhleh Oasis. Key: n/a, not applicable; n/c, samples with n less than 5 not calculated.

ARTEFACT CLASS	CORE STRIKING PLATFORM ANGLE					
Levallois Cores	N	Mean	S.D.	Range	Mode	Median
Struck	37	70.5	12.6	40-105	80	68
Unstruck	5	73.4	11.6	64-92	n/c	n/c
Total	*42*	*70.9*	*12.4*	*40-105*	*80*	*68*
Linear Cores	14	73.6	13.3	49-100	70	68

	STRIKING PLATFORM ANGLE				BULBAR ANGLE				TALON WIDTH mm*			
	N	Mean	S.D	Range	N	Mean	S.D.	Range	N	Mean	S.D.	Range
Levallois flake scars	37	70.5	12.6	40-105	37	109.5	12.6	75-140	n/a			
Levallois Flakes	7	98.9	13.6	83-120	18	93.6	12.0	75-110	17	11.2	3.4	8.0-21
Levallois Fragments**	9	83.8	5.5	74-93	n/a				6	13.0	3.4	9.0-18
Total Levallois Flakes	*16*	*90.3*	*12.3*	*74-120*	*18*	*93.6*	*12.0*	*75-110*	*23*	*11.7*	*3.4*	*8.0-21*
Linear flake scars	14	73.6	13.3	49-100	14	106.4	13.3	80-131	n/a			
Linear Flakes	4	n/c	n/c	85-95	n/a				16	8.9	2.3	4.0-14
Linear Fragments	3	n/c	n/c	84-93	n/a				2	n/c	n/c	7.0,8.0
Total Linear Flakes	*7*	*88.6*	*4.2*	*84-95*	*5*	*92.8*	*15.6*	*74-108*	*18*	*8.6*	*2.4*	*4.0-14*

*   Includes Set IV+G; otherwise Sets I-II-III+G.
** Includes tools.

Table 14 Measured attributes of specialized core platforms and specialized flake talons, Locality 187A, Sets I-II-III+G, Dakhleh Oasis. Key: n/c, samples with n less than 5 not calculated.

ARTEFACT CLASS	PLATFORM LENGTH mm				PLATFORM FACETING*			FACETING/PLATFORM LENGTH*		
Levallois Cores	N	Mean	S.D.	Range	N	Mean	S.D.	Range	Mean	S.D.	Range
Struck	17	56.6	19.2	28-100	17	2.1	1.2	0-4	0.05	0.04	0-.12
Unstruck	5	46.0	12.6	30-60	5	2.6	2.1	0-5	0.05	0.04	0-.09
Total	*22*	*53.9*	*18.6*	*28-100*	*22*	*2.2*	*1.4*	*0-5*	*0.04*	*0.03*	*0-.09*
Linear Cores	5	33.6	6.9	25-44	5	0.8	0.8	0-2	0.02	0.03	0-.06

	TALON LENGTH mm				TALON FACETING*			FACETING/TALON LENGTH*		
	N	Mean	S.D.	Range	N	Mean	S.D.	Range	Mean	S.D.	Range
Levallois flake scars	17	27.6	8.3	14-42	17	1.4	1.2	0-4	0.04	0.02	0-.08
Levallois Flakes	7	43.3	21.1	20-55	7	1.6	2.9	0-8	0.04	0.06	0-.14
Levallois Fragments	5	41.0	11.0	32-60	5	1.8	2.1	0-4	0.05	0.06	0-.11
Total Levallois Flakes	*12*	*42.3*	*17.0*	*20-60*	*12*	*1.7*	*2.5*	*0-8*	*0.04*	*0.05*	*0-.14*
Linear flake scars	2	n/c	n/c	18,19	4	n/c	n/c	0-1	n/c	n/c	.05-.06
Linear Flakes	4	n/c	n/c	17-60	4	n/c	n/c	0-2	n/c	n/c	0-.12
Linear Fragments	2	n/c	n/c	22,37	2	n/c	n/c	1,3	n/c	n/c	.05,.12
Total Linear Flakes	*6*	*26.8*	*17.6*	*17-60*	*6*	*1.7*	*1.0*	*0-3*	*0.07*	*0.05*	*0-.12*

* Cortex counted as 0.

Table 15 Estimated percentage of cortex present on faces of specialized cores, Locality 187A, Sets I-II-III+G, Dakhleh Oasis. Key: dash (–), not present.

ARTEFACT CLASS	PERCENTAGE CORTEX ON BACK*						PERCENTAGE CORTEX ON STRIKING FACE**			
CORES	N	0	01-25	26-50	51-75	76-100	N	0	01-25	26-50
Specialized Cores										
Levallois										
Struck	17	2	5	4	2	4	16	12	4	-
Unstruck	4	-	-	-	1	3	6	5	1	-
Total	21	2	5	4	3	7	22	17	5	0
%		9.5	23.8	19.1	14.3	33.3		77.3	22.7	0.0
Linear	3	-	-	-	-	3	3	-	2	1
Discoidal	4	1	-	1	1	1	4	3	1	-
TOTAL SPECIALIZED CORES	28	3	5	5	4	11	29	20	8	1
%		10.7	17.9	17.9	14.3	**39.3**		**69.0**	27.6	3.4

*   Average percentage of platform face cortex on Levallois cores (N = 21): 52.9 ± 36.2; range 5-95% cortex where present.

** Average percentage of striking face cortex on Levallois cores (N = 22): 2.5 ± 6.1; range 1-20% cortex where present.

Table 16 Attributes of unspecialized core platforms and unspecialized flake talons, Locality 187A, Sets I-II-III+G, Dakhleh Oasis. Key: dash(–), not present.

UNSPECIALIZED CORE PLATFORMS

CORE CLASS		LOCATION		PLAN SHAPES				PREPARATION			FACETING DIRECTION	
	N	End	Side	Pointed	Convex	Strait	Concavo Convex	Cortex	Cortex +Facet	Faceted	Direct	Trans- verse
Flake--1 platform	4	2	2	-	1	1	2	-	1	2*	3*	-
Initial Stage--1 platform	2	2	-	-	1	-	1	1	-	1	1	-
Total	6	4	2	0	2	1	3	1	1	3	4	0
%		66.7	33.3	0.0	33.3	16.7	**50.0**	20.0	20.0	**60.0**	**100.0**	0.0

UNSPECIALIZED FLAKE TALONS

FLAKE CLASS		PLAN SHAPES						PREPARATION			FACETING DIRECTION	
	N	Irreg- ular	Dihed- ral	Chap- eau	Convex	Strait	Concave	Cortex	Cortex +Facet	Faceted	Direct	Trans- verse
End Struck												
Primary	39	5	1	-	13	18	2	29	1	7*	2*	4
Secondary	25	5	1	-	2	15	2	16	2	6*	8	-
Tertiary	11	-	2	-	3	4	2	3	-	6*	5*	1
Total	75	10	4	0	18	37	6	48	3	19	15	5
%		13.3	5.3	0.0	24.0	**49.3**	8.0	**68.6**	4.3	27.1	**75.0**	25.0
Side Struck												
Primary	7	-	2	-	3	2	-	4	1	2	3*	-
Secondary	2	-	1	-	-	-	1	1	-	1	-	1
Total	9	0	3	0	3	2	1	5	1	3	3	1
%		0.0	33.3	0.0	33.3	22.2	11.1	**55.6**	11.1	33.3	**75.0**	25.0
Fragments--Proximal	29	1	4	0	11	11	2	12	0	15*	9*	2
%		3.4	13.8	0.0	37.9	37.9	6.9	44.4	0.0	55.6	81.8	18.2
Total	113	11	11	0	32	50	9	65	4	37	27	8
%		9.7	9.7	0.0	28.3	**44.2**	8.0	**61.3**	3.8	35.9	**77.1**	22.9

* Some not recorded, absent (point talons on flakes) or indeterminate.

Table 17 Measured attributes of unspecialized core platforms and unspecialized flake talons, Locality 187A, Sets I-II-III+G, Dakhleh Oasis.

ARTEFACT CLASS

	CORE STRIKING PLATFORM ANGLE			
Unspecialized Cores	N	Mean	S.D.	Range
Flake/Initial-				
1 platform	5	80.0	12.5	68-101

	STRIKING PLATFORM ANGLE				**BULBAR ANGLE**				**TALON WIDTH mm**		
	Mean	S.D	Range	N	Mean	S.D.	Range	N	Mean	S.D.	Range
Unspecialized flakes											
End Struck	53	87.6	34.1	28-125	73	93.2	20.4	42-151	75	9.4	6.1	0-50
Side Struck	8	93.5	18.1	70-120	9	100.4	20.1	78-138	9	14.2	9.2	7-35
Total	*61*	*88.4*	*32.4*	*28-125*	*82*	*94.0*	*30.3*	*42-151*	*84*	*9.6*	*6.1*	*0-50*
Fragments-Proximal*	22	87.2	26.5	0-120	7	88.1	30.3	66-136	27	10.3	5.1	0-22

* Includes tools.

Table 18 Lengths and faceting of unspecialized core platforms and unspecialized flake talons, Locality 187A, Sets I-II-III+G, Dakhleh Oasis. Key: n/c, samples with n less than 5 not calculated.

ARTEFACT CLASS

	PLATFORM LENGTH mm				**PLATFORM FACETING***				**FACETING/PLATFORM LENGTH***		
Unspecialized Cores	N	Mean	S.D.	Range	N	Mean	S.D.	Range	N	Mean	S.D.	Range
Flake/Initial-												
1 platform	5	31.4	11.1	42-70	4	n/c	n/c	0-3	3	n/c	n/c	.02-.05

	TALON LENGTH mm				**TALON FACETING***				**FACETING/TALON LENGTH***		
	N.	Mean	S.D.	Range	N	Mean	S.D.	Range	N	Mean	S.D.	Range
Unspecialized flakes												
End Struck	75	24.6	16.2	0-72	75	0.63	1.16	0-5	75	0.03	0.05	0-.25
Side Struck	9	42.3	18.9	15-78	9	0.33	0.71	0-2	9	0	0	0-.05
Total	*84*	*26.5*	*17.4*	*0-78*	*84*	*0.6*	*1.12*	*0-5*	*84*	*0.03*	*0.05*	*0-.25*
Fragments-Proximal**	28	33.3	16.6	5-64	29	1.2	1.7	0-6	28	0.05	0.06	0-.16

*   Cortex counted as 0.
** Includes tools.

from the Locality 187A abraded aggregate, although, again, this becomes a class requiring confirmation in the future. Pending the acquisition of a larger sample of lightly-abraded versus more abraded material from the southern half of the P-II terrace, and statistical testing, the entire abraded aggregate will be considered here as one combined sample. Even if some oddly-coloured or less abraded pieces are younger than most of the more abraded artefacts, or some Earlier Stone Age flakes are included, their small numbers will probably not affect broader generalizations.

Characterization of the Combined Locality 187A Abraded Aggregate, Gifata Unit

The Gifata Unit is characterized by the use of both Levallois and linear methods of preferred flake production, with some use of discoidal methods as well (Table 9). Levallois flakes were produced mainly by radial, or 'centripetal', preparation of the core face (69.6 %) (Table 10), and less often prepared by convergent preparation (26.1 %). No Nubian cores were found, but two specialized flakes with a convergent-opposed dorsal scar pattern suggest that Nubian preparation may have been rarely used. Such flakes could also come from opposed platform linear cores, however. The attributes of specialized cores and resultant flakes are congruent (Table 11).

Specialized cores, and the resultant flakes, are relatively large in size (Table 12). Preferred flakes were often struck from cortical platforms, although more were faceted; preferred flake talons are relatively wide, with few facets (Tables 11, 13 and 14). Mean maximum talon width on Levallois flakes is 11.7 mm, and for linear flakes, 8.6 mm.

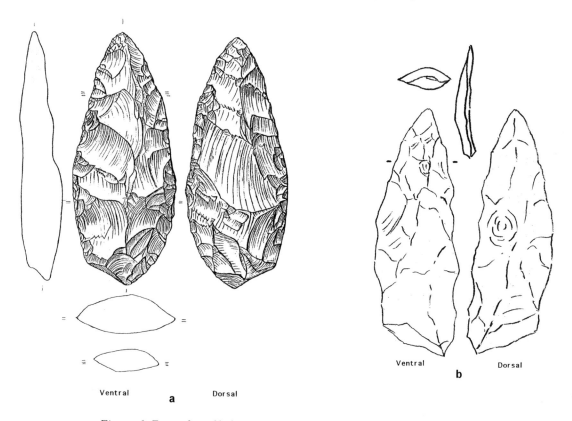

Figure 6 Examples of bifacially-worked 'Gifata points', Dakhleh Oasis.
a: Locality 310-1: Isolate found on surface of P-III gravel terrace west of Wadi el-Tawil, together with redeposited, isolated large specialized cores. Tarawan Chert, lightly abraded to abraded condition, dark grey brown varnish; point measures 135 x 57 x 25 mm (circa 139 x 61 x 25 mm adjusted for abrasion); bifacially worked with untrimmed cortex butt (end-struck flake talon); step-flaked secondary edge trimming. (Drawing by J. O'Carroll).
b: Locality 187A, Sets I/II-G-82: Veneer on P-II gravel terrace south-west of Balat point. Tarawan Chert, heavily abraded, dark brown varnish with pocking on both faces; point measures 133 x 50 x 20 mm (circa 139 x 56 x 22 mm adjusted for abrasion); bifacially work with untrimmed butt (end-struck flake talon); abrasion has obscured any secondary trimming. (Field sketch by M. R. Kleindienst).

The mean number of facets on both Levallois and linear flakes is 1.7; the facet number/talon length index is 0.04 for Levallois flakes, and 0.07 for linear flakes.

Discarded specialized cores often retain large areas of cortex on the platform face as well as on the platforms (Table 15), with less regulation in flake production than is noted in younger Middle Stone Age aggregates: 47.6% of Levallois cores bear over 50% of cortex, indicating that they were discarded after only marginal and platform trimming. The linear cores bear mostly cortex on the back face. Little cortex is retained on the striking face of either Levallois or linear cores; a few with some cortex give evidence of early discard or loss.

As is expected on workshop-type occurrences, large amounts of flaking debris are found (Table 9). The percentage of cortical flakes is high (primary and secondary flakes, Table 16). Few unspecialized cores were found, which together with the dorsal scar patterning of unspecialized flakes, suggests that most such flakes result from preparation of specialized cores (Tables 10, 16, 17 and 18). Attributes of flakes are consistent with those of the cores, and also with those of the preferred flakes produced. Only 35.9% of talons are faceted; and again the facet/talon length index is low, with means of 0.03 on complete flakes, and 0.05 on proximal fragments. Talon width averages 9.6 mm on complete flakes, and 10.3 mm on proximal fragments, which is consistent with averages for the small samples of specialized flakes.

Shaped tools left at the workshop locations are relatively infrequent, but include side scrapers, core axes, ventrally-thinned flakes, and a distinctive type of bifacial point. Some points, or bifacial foliates, are long, lanceolate or triangular in plan form, and retain a truncated cortex or talon butt that is often canted compared to the long axis. Except on the Locality 187A occurrences, these are found as isolates (Kleindienst 1999, 100), often redeposited onto younger geomorphic surfaces. They are here termed Gifata points (Figure 6).

Chert ball hammer-stones were imported for use on the P-II occurrences. Otherwise, lithic production was dependent upon the local sources of Tarawan Chert. Chert nodules were also used as hammer-stones. The use of anvils in striking specialized cores is inferred from damage to the distal edges of struck cores.

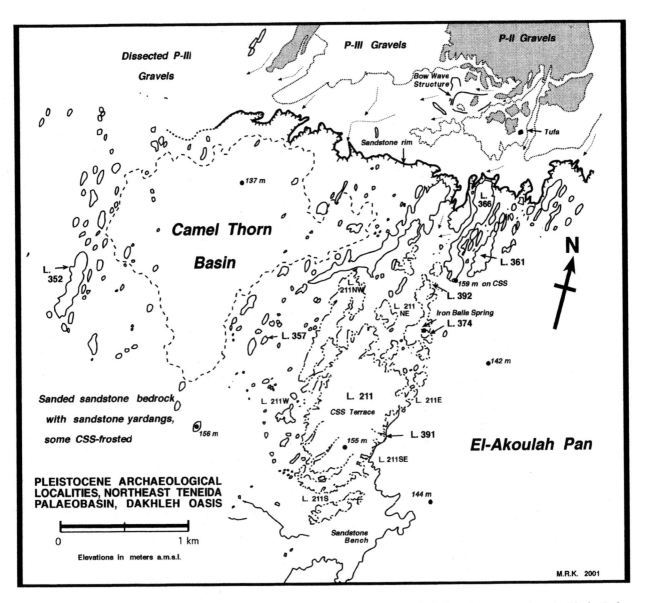

Figure 7 Pleistocene Archaeological Occurrences in the north-eastern Teneida Palaeobasin associated with the Lake Teneida Formation, Calcareous Silty Sediments facies, (CSS), and assigned to the Teneida unit, south-eastern Lowland, Dakhleh Oasis region. Map based on air photographs and field observations.

The presence of larger sized specialized flakes and cores, together with a relatively low degree of regulation in production, agrees with Caton-Thompson's characterization of older Middle Stone Age occurrences at Kharga (1952). That the Gifata Unit technologically and typologically can be assigned to a similar time range is also supported by the degrees of varnish and abrasion. Future finds of Gifata Unit aggregates retaining internal integrity can be expected only on P-II or older surfaces, although redeposited artefacts may occur on younger surfaces in proximity to remnants of older surfaces.

Context of the Teneida Palaeobasin Localities

None of the Middle Stone Age material from the Teneida Palaeobasin, here designated as the Teneida unit, has yet been analysed in detail. Cataloguing, however, indicates that the content contrasts with that of the Gifata Unit in raw material usage, and also in artefact classes, even though the geomorphic contexts indicate that the Teneida unit is probably within the older Middle Stone Age time range. Consequently, preliminary data is provided here. Counts may change somewhat after further analyses.

Table 19 gives the composition of the Locality 361 Corridor aggregate, and Table 20, compositions of the aggregates assigned to the Teneida unit. Table 21 shows physical condition of the aggregates, and Tables 22 and 23, the lithic raw materials used. For comparison with the Gifata Unit, Tables 24 and 25 compile data from a portion of the Locality 374 Grid aggregate. The grid sample includes much small debris, so that flakes ≥50 mm are calculated separately to allow equivalence with the Locality 187A Sets.

In the Teneida Palaeobasin, remnants of the Calcareous Silty Sediments facies, now assigned to the Lake Teneida Formation, are being eroded, exposing a yardanged surface of Taref sandstones (Figure 7). The deeply-incised surface testifies to a period of strong aeolian erosion prior to deposition of the lacustrine sediments. The largest outcrop is the Locality 211 terrace in the easternmost exposures of the formation, with numerous small outliers to the north below the rim of the modern el-Akoulah Pan, and to the south and west. Further small exposures frost some sandstone yardangs as far west as south of Sheikh Mabrouk (Figure 1). Calcareous Silty Sediments comprise several cycles of sandy-silts fining upward to silts and lacustrine marls, now reaching a thickness of >6m in places. No erosional breaks have been noted in the sequence. The original extent of the Teneida palaeolake basin may be much larger than originally estimated by Churcher *et al.* (1999, 302, Figure 1, 306); the area requires further survey. The eastern and southern confining margins for the palaeolake are unknown, but must have been over 160 m above sea level in elevation: the present eroding surface of the Locality 211 terrace stands at an elevation of ±155 m above sea level, but a higher remnant to the north-east is *circa* 159 m above sea level in elevation. Residual fragments of eroded Calcareous Silty Sediments lie on a sandstone ridge just below the north rim of el-Akoulah basin, at >160 m above sea level. Fossil bone and shell have been recovered from the surface and from *in situ* within the lake deposits, indicating an African-type fauna which inhabited the margins of a perennial freshwater lake, with surrounding forest-savanna and gallery forest (Churcher 1999; Churcher and Kleindienst 1999; Churcher, Kleindienst and Schwarcz 1999; Churcher *et al.* forthcoming).

Although McDonald noted occasional aeolised Middle Stone Age in her transect east from Camel Thorn Basin in 1983 (personal communication 1996), the first clustered aggregate of Middle Stone Age in the Teneida Palaeobasin was discovered only in 1997 (Locality 361), and Middle Stone Age artefacts eroding out of the basal Lake Teneida Formation units only in 1998. Middle Stone Age artefacts *in situ* in sediments were found at: Locality 391 on the eastern edge of the Locality 211 terrace; at Locality 374 at a remnant just to the north-east of the terrace; and at Locality 392 further to the north. Earlier surveys in 1987 and 1992 were confined to the southern edge of the Locality 211 terrace and to its surface.

At Locality 361, aeolised artefacts were concentrated on the sanded surface of a yardang corridor, or coulier, to the west of a low sandstone ridge, an eroded yardang, carrying Calcareous Silty Sediments in patches. Hawkins and Ormerod collected all visible lithic artefacts from the corridor lag in a series of nine 20 m wide strips, labelled '0–20 m' through '160–180 m' from south to north, which comprise the Corridor Occurrence (Tables 19 and 20). Denser accumulations in some strips probably relate to concentration by water action; even a small rainstorm might create rapid flow in quantity off the sandstones to the north

and west. The large number of small angular debris (26.2% of total sample) suggests an accumulation of sorted material. The corridors also channel wind and sand scour, allowing for possible desert creep processes. Based upon my cataloguing in 2000, the Corridor collection is a multi-component aggregate including some diagnostic, more abraded Sheikh Mabruk Unit lithic artefacts. These are probably derived from the high sandstone yardang to the west of the corridor on which a cluster is known to occur. None of the recorded Corridor chert artefacts are in mint condition (Table 21); most are lightly abraded. Sherdage was also found, probably trail garbage from historic use of the corridor. An Old Kingdom lookout is situated on the high sandstone yardang further west (Site 30/450-D4-2).

That the Corridor collection is a multi-component aggregate is indicated both by the condition and the sizes of specialized cores, as well as by their typology. Ten of 16 Sheikh Mabruk-type cores are abraded or heavily abraded, suggesting greater surface exposure and/or distance of transport than for the other specialized cores. Of these, only three of 10 are abraded or heavily abraded. Three of the nine unspecialized cores are abraded; these could belong with either component. Sheikh Mabruk-type cores range from 20–30 mm to 50–60 mm in length, with the mode at 40–50 mm. Other specialized cores overlap that distribution, but range from 40–50 mm to 89–90 mm long, Specialized flakes have a bimodal distribution, with modes at 40–50 mm length, and 70–80 mm length, suggesting that at least some of the smaller examples belong with the Sheikh Mabruk Unit rather than with the Teneida unit.

In 1997, Ormerod and I collected material from the surface of the adjoining sandstone ridge east of the coulier, with areas delimited by natural elevations in the sandstone or Calcareous Silty Sediments, together with some Middle Stone Age artefacts that had been displaced by water action off the sandstone onto the lower wadi and pan surface of el-Akoulah east of the ridge. Aggregates from the Ridge, the East Ridge Concentration and the Pan occurrences showed no obvious inclusion of later materials. Only one scraper of caramel chert was found; it could be of Holocene age based upon the form and type of retouch (Tables 20–22).

At Locality 392, Churcher discovered two Tarawan Chert flake fragments *in situ* in the reddish muds of the basal Lake Teneida Formation unit, which here includes derived red Mut Formation clay-stones from north on the sandstone rim of el-Akoulah. Only one specialized ironstone core fragment was found on the talus surface below the outcrop (Tables 20–22).

Locality 374, the Iron Balls Spring locality, is a surface exposure of lag artefacts resting in a small sandstone-floored depression, with a few pieces found *in situ* in the overlying sandy deposit. Upslope, pieces were found eroding from a thin dark sand layer overlying the sandstone. Surface and exposed *in situ* material was collected in 1998 using a one-square-metre grid; isolates were piece-plotted

Table 19 Composition of multi-component aggregate representing the Teneida unit and the Sheikh Mabruk Unit from Locality 361, Corridor Occurrence, in the Teneida Palaeobasin, Dakhleh Oasis region.

ARTEFACT CLASS	LOCALITY 361 CORRIDOR OCCURRENCE: STRIP COLLECTION (Meters south to north)									TOTAL NUMBER	
	0-20	20-40	40-60	60-80	80-100	100-120	120-140	140-160	160-180		
CORES											
Specialized	-	1	-	1	-	-	1	5	2	10	
'Sheikh Mabruk type'	-	2	3	3	-	1	-	3	4	16	
Unspecialized + Fgs.	1	2	-	1	-	-	-	2	3	9	*35*
%										*2.8*	*3.8*
ANGULAR DEBRIS≈	11	25	114	33	10	14	17	59	30	313	
%										*25.2*	*≈*
FLAKES											
Specialized + Fgs.	4	5	19	8	2	8	3	42	16	107	*107*
%										*8.6*	*11.5*
Unspecialized + Fgs.	45	58	163	62	14	16	45	275	59	737	*737*
%										*59.3*	*79.2*
TOOLS											
Shaped Tools											
Points	-	-	1	-	-	-	-	6	2	9	
Scrapers	-	-	1	3	-	1	-	4	3	12	
Knives	-	-	-	2	-	-	-	-	-	2	
Pointed/Borers	-	-	-	-	-	-	-	1	-	1	
Ventral Butt-Thinned	-	-	-	-	-	-	-	1	-	1	
Coraxes/Bifaces	-	-	-	1	-	-	1	-	1	3	
Broken	-	2	1	1	-	-	-	4	1	9	
Situational Tools	-	1	1	-	1	-	-	-	2	5	
Utilized Tools											
Edge damaged	-	-	-	-	-	-	-	-	1	1	
Battered	-	-	-	-	-	-	-	-	-		
Hammerstones	-	-	3	1	-	-	-	3	1	8	*51*
%										*4.1*	*5.5*
TOTAL NUMBER	61	96	306	116	27	40	67	405	125	1,243	930

≈ **Angular Debris excluded from percentage calculations in last column.**

Table 20 Composition of aggregates from Locality 361, multi-component Corridor Occurrence, and from single component Archaeological Occurrences assigned to the Teneida unit in the Teneida Palaeobasin, Dakhleh Oasis region. Key: Ridge Conc., lag concentration on eastern edge of sandstone ridge; Com., combined aggregate from several occurrences in area of Locality 374 Grid.

ARTEFACT CLASS	ARCHAEOLOGICAL OCCURRENCES													Total Number	%
	361 CORRI-DOR	361 Ridge*	361 Ridge Conc.*	361 PAN*	392**	374 Com.**	211 NE/E	391**	211 SE	211 S	357**	351	350 W		
CORES															
Specialized	26	2	1	1	1	11	11	-	1	1	1	-	-	56	3.3
Unspecialized + Fgs.	9	6	6	1	-	6	9	1	6	4	-	-	-	48	2.8
Total Cores	*35*	*8*	*7*	*2*	*1*	*17*	*20*	*1*	*6*	*5*	*1*			*104*	*6.1*
ANGULAR DEBRIS≈	313	52	16	8	-	27	5	1	6	3	1	-	-	432	≈
FLAKES															
Specialized + Fgs.	117	57	16	8	1	94	31	8	7	4	1	2	1	337	19.6
Unspecialized + Fgs.	737	115	26	15	1	117	66	15	20	16	2	-	-	1,130	65.6
Total Flakes	*854*	*172*	*42*	*23*	*2*	*211*	*97*	*23*	*27*	*20*	*3*	*2*	*1*	*1,467*	*85.2*
TOOLS															
Shaped Tools		19	3	1										23	
Points	9				-	1	1	1	-	-	-	-	-	12	
Scrapers	12				-	23	13	3	-	-	-	-	-	51	
Knives	2				-	3	-	-	-	-	-	-	-	5	
Pointed/Borers	1				-	5	3	1	1	-	-	-	-	11	
?Burins	-				-	2	-	-	-	-	-	-	-	2	
Ventral Butt-Thinned	1				-	-								1	
Coraxes/Bifaces	3				-	-	-	1	-	-	-	-	-	4	
Broken	9				-	2	-	-	-	-	-	-	-	11	
Situational Tools	3				-	1	1	2	1	1	-	-	-	11	
Utilized Tools															
Edge Damaged	1				-	-	-	-	-	-	-	-	-	1	
Hammerstones	8	1	1	-	-	3	3	-	-	-	-	-	-	16	
Anvils	-	-	-	-	-	1	-	-	-	-	-	-	-	1	
Depression	-	-	-	-	-	1	-	-	-	-	-	-	-	1	
Pecked spheroid	-	-	-	-	-	-	-	-	-	1	-	-	-	1	
Total Tools	*51*	*20*	*4*	*1*	*-*	*42*	*21*	*8*	*2*	*2*	*-*	*-*	*-*	*151*	*8.8*
TOTAL NUMBER	1,243	252	69	34	3	297	143	33	42	30	5	2	1	2,154	1,722 ≈

* Catalogued by Ormerod; other counts by Kleindienst.
** Some artefacts found *in situ* in CSS.
≈ Angular Debris excluded from percentage calculations.

Table 21 Physical condition of artefacts assigned to the Teneida unit from Archaeological Occurrences in the eastern Teneida Palaeobasin, Dakhleh Oasis. Key: dash (–), not present.

OCCURRENCES north to south	PHYSICAL CONDITION: ABRASION/WEATHERING					
	MINT	FRESH	L. ABR.	ABRADED	HEAVILY ABRADED	TOTAL
L. 361						
CORRIDOR*	-	100	244	114	11	469
%	0.0	21.3	52.0	24.3	2.4	100.0
L. 392	2	1	-	-	-	3
L. 374**	151	109	14	17	1	292
L. 211 NE/E	51	54	15	20	1	141
L. 391	32	1	-	-	-	33
Total	236	165	29	37	2	469
%	50.3	35.2	6.2	7.9	0.4	100.0
L. 211 SE	1	20	11	9	1	42
L. 211 S***	2	2	9	8	6	27
Total	3	22	20	17	7	69
%	4.3	31.9	29.0	24.6	10.2	100.0

*   Chert only; angular waste not included.
**   Combined aggregate from several occurrences at Locality 374; 5
        artefacts not recorded.
***   Three pieces not recorded.

Table 22 Lithic raw materials used for artefacts in aggregates from Archaeological Occurrences in the eastern Teneida Palaeobasin, Dakhleh Oasis region. Key: TCH, Tarawan Chert; MCH, Mut Chert; OCH, Other cherts; CBS, Chert Ball Silicas; LST, limestone; QZTS, quartzites, including ferruginous quartzites; SLS, siliceous sandstone; QTZ, quartz; PWD, petrified wood; dash (–), not present.

Occurrences North->South	Number and Percent of Raw Materials								
	TCH+ ?MCH	OCH	CBS	LST	QZTS	SLS	QTZ	PWD	N
L. 361 Lag	1,090	7	96	-	46	-	1	3	1,243
%	87.7	0.6	7.7	0.0	3.7	0.0	0.1	0.2	
L. 361 Ridge	198	1	31	2	20	-	-	-	252
%	78.6	0.4	12.3	0.8	7.9	0.0	0.0	0.0	
L. 361 E+Pan	73	-	26	-	4	-	-	-	103
%	70.9	0.0	25.2	0.0	3.9	0.0	0.0	0.0	
L. 392	2*	-	-	-	1	-	-	-	3
%	66.7	0.0	0.0	0.0	33.3	0.0	0.0	0.0	
L. 211NE+E	90	-	9	11	29	1	-	-	140
%	64.2	0.0	6.4	7.9	20.7	0.7	0.0	0.0	
L. 374 Occs.	224*	14	17	5	30	7	-	-	297
%	80.4	4.7	5.7	1.7	10.1	2.4	0.0	0.0	
L. 391	28*	-	1	-	4	-	-	-	33
%	84.8	0.0	3.0	0.0	12.1	0.0	0.0	0.0	
L. 211 SE	24	-	3	-	7	8	-	-	42
%	57.1	0.0	7.1	0.0	16.7	19.1	0.0	0.0	
L. 211S	13	1	2	-	11	3	-	-	30
%	43.3	3.3	6.7	0.0	36.7	10.0	0.0	0.0	

*   Some artefacts *in situ* in CSS, basal unit.

Table 23 Sample combined aggregate from locality 374 Occurrences, Teneida Palaeobasin, Dakhleh Oasis region. Key: TCH, Tarawan Chert; MCH, Mut Chert; OCH, Other cherts; CBS, Chert Ball Silicas; LST, limestone; QZT, quartzites; IST, ferruginous quartzites; SLS, siliceous sandstone; r, red-brown chert; b, black-patinated chert; dash (–), not present.

LOCALITY 374 ARTEFACT CLASS	LITHIC RAW MATERIALS								TOTAL NUMBER	%
	TCH+ ?MCH	MCH (NE Grid)	OCH	CBS	LST	QZT	IST	SLS		
CORES										
Specialized										
Struck Levallois	3	1	-	-	-	-	-	-	4	
Unstruck Levallois	2	2	-	-	-	-	-	-	4	
Linear	-	-	-	1	-	-	-	-	1	
Earlier stage	-	-	-	-	-	-	1	-	1	
Fragments	1	-	-	-	-	-	-	-	1	
Total	6	3	0	1	0	0	1	0	11	
%	54.5	27.3	0.0	9.1	0.0	0.0	9.1	0.0		3.7
Unspecialized	-	1	-	2	-	-	-	1	4	
Fragments	-	-	-	2	-	-	-	-	2	
Total	0	1	0	4	0	0	0	1	6	2.0
Total Cores	6	4	0	5	0	0	1	1	17	
%	35.3	23.5	0.0	29.4	0.0	0.0	5.9	5.9		5.7
ANGULAR DEBRIS*	16	2	5rrbb	1	-	3	-	-	27	
%	59.3	7.4	18.5	3.7	0.0	11.1	0.0	0.0		9.1
FLAKES										
Specialized + Frags.	79	-	-	4	-	6	2	3	94	31.6
Unspecialized + Frags.	85	2	4rrb	5	2	13	2	3	116	39.1
Other (rejuvination)	1	-	-	-	-	-	-	-	1	0.3
Total Flakes	165	2	4	9	2	19	4	6	211	
%	78.2	0.9	1.9	4.3	0.9	9.0	1.9	2.8		71.0
TOOLS										
Shaped Tools										
Points**	1	-	-	-	-	-	-	-	1	
Scrapers**	18	-	3rr	-	-	2	-	-	23	
Knives	2	-	1b	-	-	-	-	-	3	
Pointed tools/Borers	4	-	-	1	-	-	-	-	5	
Burins?	1	-	1	-	-	-	-	-	2	
Fragments	2	-	-	-	-	-	-	-	2	
Total	28	0	5	1	0	2	0	0	36	
%	77.8	0.0	13.9	2.8	0.0	5.6	0.0	0.0		12.1
Situational Tools	1	-	-	-	-	-	-	-	1	
%										0.3
Utilized Tools										
Hammerstones**	-	-	-	1	2	-	-	-	3	
Anvils	-	-	-	-	1	-	-	-	1	
?Depression on cobble	-	-	-	-	-	-	1	-	1	
Total	0	0	0	1	3	0	1	0	5	
%	0.0	0.0	0.0	20.0	60.0	0.0	20.0	0.0		1.7
Total Tools	29	0	5	2	3	2	1	0	42	
%	69.0	0.0	11.9	4.8	7.1	4.8	2.3	0.0		14.1
TOTAL NUMBER	216	8	14	17	5	24	6	7	297	
%	72.7	2.7	4.7	5.7	1.7	8.1	2.0	2.4		

*   In combined Loc. 374 sample, small angular debris, flakes and fragments likely to have been removed by water and wind action, and difficult to "see" on CSS talus. Raw materials not recorded for all collected artefacts. Grid material not screened, but lagged, resting directly on the sandstone in the Grid quadrats (SW, SE, NE = 236 pieces), with a few pieces still embedded in basal CSS.

** Three TCH scrapers and 1 point, 1 limestone hammerstone from Loc. 374 Grid, SE quadrat; other raw materials not yet recorded. (Field plot includes 6 additional scrapers in the 146 plotted piece SE sample; not all material under 3 cm long plotted.)

Table 24 Dimensions of selected measured attributes of specialized cores and flakes, assigned to the Teneida unit, from Locality 374 Grid, eastern Teneida Palaeobasin, Dakhleh Oasis region. No adjustment for abrasion – most artefacts in mint or fresh condition. Key: n/r, not recorded.

Loc. 374 Grid ARTEFACT CLASS	Oriented Length mm	Oriented Maximum Width mm	Oriented Maximum Thickness mm	Talon Length mm	Talon Facet Number	Facets/ Talon Length	Maximum Talon Width mm
CORES							
Specialized Cores*							
N	7	7	7	n/r	n/r	n/r	n/r
Mean	54.0	48.7	27.3				
S.D.	18.3	17.7	18.8				
Range	33-90	28-79	11-60				
FLAKES							
Specialized-- Levallois							
N	14	n/r	n/r	22	22	22	23
Mean	66.6			37.5	3.9	0.11	8.1
S.D.	11.2			14.8	1.8	0.04	2.8
Range	49-90			15-70	2-10	0.06-0.20	1-12
Specialized--Linear							
N	10	n/r	n/r	10	10	10	10
Mean	56.9			17.1	1.7	0.10	6.1
S.D.	11.4			2.3	1.1	0.05	3.5
Range	40-80			15-21	1-4	0.05-0.20	1-12
Specialized-- Total							
N	54**	n/r	n/r	32	32	32	33
Mean	61.6			31.1	3.2	0.11	7.5
S.D.	15.2			15.8	1.9	0.05	3.1
Range	20-92			15-70	1-10	0.05-0.20	1-12
Median	61			30.5	1	0.09	8
Mode	65			32	3	0.13	6
Specialized--Total ≥50 mm							
N	43**	n/r	n/r	31	31	31	32
Mean	66.2			31.0	3.2	0.10	7.5
S.D.	12.0			15.8	1.9	0.04	3.2
Range	50-92			15-70	1-10	0.05-0.20	1-12

*   NE quadrat only; no cores in NW or SW.
**   Includes Grid quadrats NW, SW, NE and lines 1-3 of SE; otherwise NW and SW only.

Table 25 Dimensions of selected measured attributes of unspecialized flakes, and total flakes, assigned to the Teneida unit, from Locality 374 Grid, eastern Teneida Palaeobasin, Dakhleh Oasis region. No adjustment for abrasion – most artefacts in mint or fresh condition.

Loc. 374 Grid ARTEFACT CLASS	Oriented Length mm	Talon Length mm	Talon Facet Number	Facets/ Talon Length	Maximum Talon Width mm
FLAKES					
Unspecialized					
N	16	13	21	13	13
Mean	60.4	20.9	1.4	0.10	6.3
S.D.	19.6	5.2	1.1	0.06	2.9
Range	34-98	12-33	0-4	0.05-0.25	3-14
Unspecialized ≥50 mm					
N	9	10	16	9	10
Mean	74.8	21.8	1.4	0.09	6.3
S.D.	12.1	6.1	1.0	0.06	3.3
Range	50-98	12-33	0-4	0.05-0.25	3-14
Total Flakes					
N	70*	45	53	45	46
Mean	61.3	28.2	2.5	0.10	7.2
S.D.	16.5	14.2	1.8	0.05	3.1
Range	29-98	12-70	0-10	0.05-0.25	1-14
Median	61	22	2	0.09	7
Mode	45	20	1	0.09	6
Total Flakes ≥ 50 mm					
N	53*	42	48	41	43
Mean	67.9	28.9	2.6	0.11	7.2
S.D.	12.5	14.4	1.8	0.05	3.2
Range	50-98	12-70	0-10	0.05-0.25	1-14

*   Includes Grid quadrats NW, SW, NE and lines 1-3 of SE; otherwise NW and SW only.

in the surrounding area from the talus slopes, and also collected from the small 'north' and 'south' wadis draining into el-Akoulah pan (Tables 20–25). The Middle Stone Age artefact concentration, mostly in mint to fresh condition (89%) is separated by north wadi from the ancient artesian Iron Balls spring vent. The vent was planed-off by erosion prior to the deposition of overlying Calcareous Silty Sediments. A few mint specimens were found on the slopes of the eroded vent, or on eye sediments, and also just to the east and below the basal lake sediment unit that here includes derived ferruginous pieces from the vent. Thus, it is possible that the Locality 374 artefacts were derived from the spring vent, or from the old sandstone surfaces, and that they predate Lake Teneida Formation deposition. The site awaits excavation.

Scattered surface finds of Middle Stone Age artefacts, many in mint to fresh condition and lacking desert varnish, were found southward from Locality 361 to the south-eastern corner of the Locality 211 terrace in 1998 and 2000, lying in positions to have been derived from the lake deposits (Localities 211NE, 211E, 211SE and 211S) (Tables 20–22). All artefacts seen were collected, noting point locations. A few Middle Stone Age artefacts were also found in earlier years, west and north-west along the Locality 211 terrace, but these areas have not yet been systematically collected.

The extent of recycling by Holocene peoples (above), as well as physical condition, indicate that most of the Middle Stone Age lithics have not been exposed for a long period of time. Many are less aeolised than are Holocene artefacts from the area of the South-east Basin. Patinas on Tarawan Chert artefacts, if present, vary from tan to light browns.

Locality 391 is a small wadi re-entrant cut into the eastern edge of the Locality 211 terrace, which discharges onto the sandstone bench standing above the surface of the el-Akoulah Pan. I found Middle Stone Age artefacts on the surface of the sanded wadi, on the slopes of the sandstone and capping Calcareous Silty Sediments north of the wadi, and two pieces *in situ* in the basal unit there. All artefacts seen were collected in 1998, and nothing further was found in 2000 (Tables 20–22).

Finds of artefacts that appear to relate to the Lake Teneida Formation rather than to the aeolised underlying sandstone surfaces have been rare at outcrops further west in the Teneida Palaeobasin (Table 20). Calcareous Silty Sediments-related (from east to west) are:
1) Locality 357, one Levallois core on the surface in position to have eroded from the basal sandy unit (Middle Stone Age); one specialized flake *in situ* at sandstone contact; two unspecialized flakes and one chip on the talus.
2) Locality 350, one large Levallois flake and one specialized flake fragment resting on a Calcareous Silty Sediments talus slope (Middle Stone Age).
3) Locality 350W, one Levallois flake on sandstone, in position to have derived from the basal lake sediments (Middle Stone Age).

Still further west and south of Sheikh Mabrouk, finds are:
1) Locality 355, one recycled biface on the surface of sandstone below a basal Lake Teneida Formation outcrop (found by C. S. and B. Churcher).
2) Locality 348, one small flake and one small core *in situ* in marls. At these localities, the affiliation of the artefacts is indeterminate Pleistocene Stone Age.

The incidence of finds drops off steeply moving south from Locality 374 along the Locality 211 margins, and finds are even rarer to the west of Locality 211, presumably because Calcareous Silty Sediments were deposited in the palaeolake further from shore (Table 20). That finds of Middle Stone Age artefacts in quantity in the Teneida Palaeobasin are limited to the easternmost area of exposures may suggest that the lakeshore was nearby. Except in the Locality 361 Corridor aggregate, artefacts also appear to become more abraded from north to south (Table 21). At localities where *in situ* specimens were found (Localities 392, 374 and 391), pieces are predominantly mint to fresh. If the Corridor aggregate abrasion is treated as a special case (above), the isolated pieces from the north-east and the eastern edge of the terrace show somewhat more abrasion; and more of the pieces found on the south-east and south are abraded, even heavily abraded. This could reflect water action rather than sand blasting, suggesting that artefacts were washed further into the palaeolake. Differences in surface wear may also reflect differences in raw materials (Table 22): siliceous sandstone becomes weathered and desilicified; quartzites probably abrade faster than cherts. Larger samples are needed to investigate variations in size and condition for each rock type.

No aeolised, diagnostic Middle Stone Age artefacts, such as Levallois cores or flakes, have been found in position to have come from the weathered and aeolised sandstone surfaces underlying the Lake Teneida Formation at the western localities or to the south of the Kharga road where small remnant Calcareous Silty Sediments yardangs are found (Locality 349). Only small, abraded, indeterminate Pleistocene Stone Age pieces occur. Again, excavations are required to test whether any Middle Stone Age artefacts were resting on the old sandstone surfaces.

The only chronometric determinations available for the Teneida Palaeobasin are Ar/Ar determinations on lagged Dakhleh Glass from the surface of Locality 211: the isochron age limiting the age of some pre-existing surface of the Lake Teneida Formation onto which the glass was deposited is 122,000 ± 40,000 years (Schwarcz *et al.* forthcoming), indicating that deposition cannot be younger than that broad age range. Although lacustrine deposits cannot be traced directly north to P-II gravel deposits north of the rim of el-Akoulah Pan, further west the Calcareous Silty Sediments stand at higher elevations than do P-III gravels, and must therefore be older than P-III. In el-Akoulah Pan, P-III gravels spill down the abrupt north rim, and are cut-off by *circa* 200 m from a low sandstone bench bearing similar gravels. Consequently, the Lake

Teneida Formation is thought to correlate with the deposition of the extensive, now dissected, P-II surface to the north, or to times of down-cutting from that surface (Churcher, Kleindienst and Schwarcz 1999).

Some additional archaeological evidence provides support for that estimate. A basal wadi gravel underlies the Calcareous Silty Sediments remnants north-east of Locality 374, in a channel cut into the sandstone that now forms a ridge extending north to the rim of el-Akoulah (Locality 366). I have found three bifaces of Earlier Stone Age-type whose condition and position indicate probable derivation from the gravel. A fourth Earlier Stone Age biface was found with gravel lag on the eroded surface of the Locality 366 sandstone ridge just to the north. Still further north, Thompson and I found an ancient spring seepage now marked by the formation of ironstone on the edge of the sandstone ridge overlooking the flanking modern wadi cut. Fragments of Earlier Stone Age bifaces and flakes were found on the talus below, and an Earlier Stone Age biface on the wadi floor. This locality may have been the source for the bifaces redeposited into the wadi gravel underlying Calcareous Silty Sediments to the south. These finds only indicate that their deposition is coeval with or, more likely, postdates the Earlier Stone Age. The small sample of bifaces may belong to either Balat Unit or the Upper Acheulian *sensu stricto*, both found on the P-II remnants at Locality 187 (above).

Preliminary Characterization of the Teneida Unit

As noted, a suite of raw materials was exploited at the eastern Teneida Palaeobasin localities, some probably locally available from beds in the Taref or Maghrabi formations: quartzites (QZT) including ironstone (IST), siliceous sandstone (SLS), quartz (QTZ) and possibly petrified wood (PWD), indicating their availability at the time of use from outcrops or surface lags. Some materials may come from gravels to the north: limestone cobbles (LST), chert balls (CBS), Mut Chert (MCH) and possibly petrified wood, again indicating availability (Hawkins and Kleindienst 2002).

Although Tarawan Group cherts had to be imported from a significant distance, Tarawan Chert (TCH) was preferred (Tables 22 and 23); most unspecialized flakes are tertiary, without cortex, indicating that blanks and partially-prepared cores were brought into the area, rather than unworked nodules. In the Locality 374 combined sample, only seven of 62 unspecialized flakes or fragments are primary or secondary corticals, and five retouched tools are made on secondary pieces: 17.9%. Cores of any material are few in number, and many are unspecialized or entirely exhausted nubbins. Mut Chert is difficult to differentiate in hand specimen; some homogeneous grey-brown pieces may be Mut Chert. In the Locality 374 NE Grid sample, seven of 152 chert artefacts were identified in 2002 as probably Mut Chert: 4.6%. Some rare types of chert appear to be imports. At Locality 374 Grid: six pieces of a reddish-

brown variety, two of them scrapers, are probably Other chert, but possibly Chert Ball Silicas; four pieces of a black-surfaced chert, which may indicate a different mineral composition, one a knife; and four pieces of a grey patinated chert, one a possible burin. These could all come from three cores. The sources for Other cherts are unknown. A few pieces of the black patinated type were found in the southern Lake Kellis Palaeobasin in 2002. One piece of caramel chert from Locality 211S is of Thebes Group type, which outcrops on the eastern Kharga Oasis Escarpment or far north of Dakhleh; this could be of Holocene age, but the one Levallois core from Locality 357, further west, is also of caramel chert. In the large lag sample from the Locality 361 corridor, four pieces are of caramel chert (three chips, two fresh and one lightly abraded, and one specialized flake proximal, lightly abraded). Two Levallois flakes are of chert with the unusual black patina. One hammer-stone is worked on a waterworn cobble of non-local, translucent chert, source unknown (Hawkins and Kleindienst 2002).

Only one larger nodule of poor quality, limey chert/siliceous limestone was found near the Locality 374 Grid, which may have come from the gravels to the north. It was used as an anvil. Limestone cobbles, as well as chert balls were used as hammer-stones, and chert balls were knapped. Although by-products indicate that knapping was done, the composition of the aggregates contrasts with those from Locality 187A, and suggests a different landscape usage (Tables 19 and 20). Whether the Teneida unit is directly related to the time of basal Lake Teneida Formation deposition, or predates that time, human uses of this Lowland area were related to the availability of water, either erupting as springs or forming a large lake, rather than to the easy availability of raw material as in the Piedmont. The presence of Other cherts indicates contacts with, or travel to, areas outside Dakhleh region.

Comparison with Kharga Oasis (Tables 7 and 8) shows that the much larger sample of Teneida unit artefacts compares more closely with the Kharga "Upper Levalloisian" than with the "Lower Levalloisian" in having more shaped tool types. However, as noted above, this may be a 'functional' rather than a chronostratigraphic indicator, because the Teneida aggregate compositions suggest occupation rather than mainly workshop activities. The sizes of some specialized flakes suggest an age older than *circa* 120,000–125,000 years (lengths to over 130 mm), but the average length is lower than at Locality 187A: at Locality 374 Grid (n = 54) 61.6 ± 15.2 mm; and 66.2 ± 12.0 mm if only flakes ≥50 mm are considered (n = 43) (Table 24). Nine unspecialized flakes ≥50 mm are somewhat larger: 74.8 ± 12.1 mm (Table 25), which is comparable to Locality 187A. The mean length of 25 specialized flakes ≥50 mm in the Locality 361 Corridor aggregate, including two tools, is somewhat longer than at Locality 374 Grid: 74.8 ± 16.1, range 50–130 mm. The larger specialized and unspecialized flakes have often been used as blanks for shaped tools; when used for scrapers,

Table 26 Cultural Stratigraphic Units recognized at Dakhleh and Kharga Oases, Western Desert, Egypt. Middle Stone Age units in Kharga Oasis originally defined by Caton-Thompson (1952).

| Chrono-Time | CULTURAL STRATIGRAPHIC UNITS | | | AFRICAN DEVELOPMENTAL STAGES |
| | BASIC UNITS | | TECHNO-COMPLEX | |
Estimated KUyrs ago	Dakhleh Oasis	Kharga Oasis		
20-30	Sheikh Mabruk Unit	"Khargan Industry"/Unit	KHARGAN	latest Middle Stone Age/MSA
40-50	[informal unit(s)]		Khargan?	
				latest Middle Stone Age/MSA
	Dakhleh Unit	"Kharga Aterian"	ATERIAN	
70-100				
	[informal unit(s)] "medium-sized"	"Upper Levalloisian" = Mata'na unit	REFUF	younger Middle Stone Age/MSA
150				
	Teneida unit		REFUF	older Middle Stone Age/MSA
		"Lower Levalloisian"		
	Gifata Unit	= Refuf unit	REFUF	
250-300				
	Balat Unit		BALAT	latest Earlier Stone Age/ESA
		Dharb el-Gaga unit	Balat?	
				ESA
		KO10 unit	Balat?	ESA
400				
	[informal unit(s)]	[informal unit(s)]	AFRICAN UPPER ACHEULIAN *sensu stricto*	Earlier Stone Age/ ESA

laterals are often much reduced, as are the tips and laterals on points.

Talon faceting and width also suggest that the Teneida unit is younger than the Gifata Unit (facet/talon length ratio, n = 22, 0.11 ± 0.04; talon width, n = 33, 7.5 ± 3.1 mm) (Tables 24 and 25). Although facets counted on fresher material may not be exactly comparable to those counted on the abraded material, narrower talons with more faceting indicate a more regulated flaking method than do the Levallois or unspecialized flakes at Locality 187A. However, specialized flakes at Locality 187A represent rejects for the most part, while many flakes in the Teneida Palaeobasin probably represent the flakes that were selectively chosen for transport away from their place of manufacture. Thus, they are a sample selected by the ancient inhabitants of Dakhleh, which may not be comparable to the workshop sample. Cores are few in number, making up only 2.8% of the total Locality 361 Corridor aggregate, and 0.8% specialized cores, if the Sheikh Mabruk-type cores are excluded, 3.7% of the Locality 374 Grid sample, and 4.8% of the total sample from all occurrences. Also, because local chert and chalcedony raw material is scarce, cores flaked in the area were worked down to minimum sizes. Although some or all of the small specialized flakes in the Locality 361 Corridor aggregate may belong to Sheikh Mabruk Unit,

small flakes are also found in the Locality 374 Grid sample. Production of extremely small, specialized flakes, ≤30 mm long, may relate to their use in tasks requiring greater precision, rather than only to conservation in the use of scarce lithic resources.

Most shaped tools are scrapers, including some with notched or denticulated edges. Both unifacial and bifacial points occur; some pieces classed as unifacial points may be early-stage scrapers, because triangular or pointed scrapers occur, including *dejeté* forms. Ventral butt thinning is found on both scrapers and points, as well as on otherwise unretouched flakes, executed with few blows. Knives are odd, backed flakes. Small, pointed tools or borers are common, but both burins are atypical forms. Small coreaxes and bifaces include one coreaxe found *in situ* in the basal Calcareous Silty Sediments at Locality 391, confirming the association with the Middle Stone Age aggregates.

External Comparisons: Egypt and Northern Africa

Van Peer (1998) has suggested that nearly all North African Middle Stone Age, including the Aterian Techno-complex, should be designated as the "Nubian Complex", more fully defined as including aggregates that are based upon Levallois methods of specialized flake production, specifically the Nubian I and II methods of striking face preparation. Additional features are

> ... bifacial foliates, various retouched point types including Mousterian and Nazlet Khater points, and truncated-facetted pieces. In addition, they all show the presence of significant proportions of side scrapers, denticulates and a good deal of Upper Palaeolithic types (Van Peer and Vermeersch 2000, 48–9).

Schild (1998) has disputed the validity of such a complex, noting the rarity of Nubian techniques in the Western Desert, both in his work at Dakhleh, and in southern Egypt. They are rare in both the Gifata and Teneida units, and elsewhere in the Dakhleh Middle Stone Age until the Aterian Dakhleh Unit, where there is a greater frequency of Nubian point cores (Hawkins 2001, 355). Otherwise, I have noted consistent use of Nubian methods only at one 'medium-sized Middle Stone Age' locality in the southern Balat Palaeobasin where relatively small and irregular nodules of Mut Chert were employed at artesian spring vent, Locality 153. In Kharga, so far as now known, Nubian cores are rare or lacking until the "Upper Levalloisian" and the Kharga Aterian. The typological features cited by Van Peer and Vermeersch (2000) might well fit many established and defined African complexes, especially the Lupemban Techno-complex. I see little merit in a vaguely-defined, generalized complex which denotes little more than 'North African Middle Stone Age' at its widest proposed extent (Van Peer 1998), or more locally, 'Egyptian Middle Stone Age outside the central Nile Valley' (Van Peer and Vermeersch 2000). I see no merit in subsuming the well-defined Aterian Techno-complex into any larger, less well-defined unit (Garcea 1998; 2001, 39; Kleindienst 2000). In addition, even in the Western Desert there are large swathes of territory for which evidence is lacking.

The level of comparability in content of cultural stratigraphic units within the Middle Stone Age developmental stage at Kharga and Dakhleh supports the designation of a named, regional techno-complex, hereafter designated as the Refuf Techno-complex (Table 26). The name is appropriate, because Caton-Thompson and Gardner regarded the Naqb el-Refuf, or "Refuf Pass" as the key area for their geoarchaeological sequence (Caton-Thompson 1952, xi). This Techno-complex includes all units previously formally or informally designated as Middle Stone Age, which pre-date the Aterian Techno-complex. Future detailed studies may allow for subdivision, but at present the included cultural stratigraphic units at Dakhleh comprise: Gifata Unit, Teneida unit, the 'medium-sized Middle Stone Age' unit(s), and the aggregates found associated with palaeolake deposits in the Kellis (Lake Kellis Formation) and Balat (Lake Balat Formation) Palaeobasins. At Kharga, the "Lower Levalloisian" unit, here designated as the Refuf unit, and the "Upper Levalloisian" unit, here designated

as the Mata'na unit, are included. Whether any greater regional extent is warranted for the Refuf Techno-complex must await detailed comparisons of the cultural contents of archaeological occurrences from elsewhere.

Appendix

Basic Descriptive Classification for Middle Stone Age Artefacts from Dakhleh and Kharga Oases, Western Desert, Egypt

> ... for the form of designed things is decided by choice or else by chance; but it is never actually entailed by anything whatever (Pye 1964, 9); original emphasis.

The implementation of solutions to design problems using lithic reduction processes begins with the selection of a 'suitable piece' of raw material (Pye 1964, 46). Primary lithic reduction processes were carried-out with the intent of producing either blanks selected for further treatment by secondary reduction, and/or end products selected to be used without further reduction. Secondary lithic reduction processes using either selected blanks, or selected pieces of raw material, were carried-out with the intent of producing end products for use(s), which may not have been utilitarian. In either case, one finds the selected rocks that were deliberately broken, and the pieces that were broken off those: see Isaac and Isaac (1997, 364), for "flaked pieces" versus "detached pieces". Natural breakage must be distinguished from human breakage, which may be difficult in some contexts.

Reduction, or wasting produces large amounts of lithic debris, any of which could have had use value. When lacking any evidence of secondary reduction, or of humanly-induced use-damage, this material has been termed "waste products" (Kleindienst 1962, 98), "waste" (Clark and Kleindienst 1974, 88; 2001, 49), or often recently in English and French, "debitage" (Clark and Kleindienst 2001, 49), although that word should apply to the knapping process (Balout 1967), and "debitage product" is suggested for the broken stones (Inizan *et al.* 1999, 138).

Potential *working surfaces* of artefacts can be characterized as:
1) edges where faces converge, designated as *lateral, distal* and *proximal*, given a standardized orientation of proximal being either the talon end of a flake, or arbitrarily defined;
2) points where edges and faces converge; or
3) faces confined by *edges*, or continuous.

On flakes, the standardized orientation is that the striking face of the core is *dorsal*, and the core release face is *ventral*; arbitrarily defined for other artefact classes.

Measurements of length, width and thickness depend upon the orientation of the artefact, and the measuring device used. Initial field measurements of maximum length, width and thickness, termed chart measurements, utilize measuring boxes; detailed analyses, in which the landmark for measurement may be specified, callipers.

Piece measurements are oriented to the longest axis of the artefact. Oriented measurements vary according to the class of artefact: for example, flakes are oriented to the talon for box/chart length, or to the striking point for calliper lengths, maximum or taken along the flaking axis. Measurements of angles employ a goniometer or a template.

I. By-products of lithic flaking reduction: Pieces resulting from lithic reduction which are discarded, or lost, during the production process, and which lack identifiable secondary trimming, retouch or use-damage. These are often termed waste or debitage.

A. Cores. The selected, larger pieces of lithic raw material from which flakes have been removed by directed force. Discarded when no longer wanted for producing flakes, or lost, but may be recycled. Earlier stages of working the core may be identifiable for any category.

    1. Specialized cores. Cores that result from the more regulated methods of flake production.

       a. Levallois cores: cores with varying preparation of the *striking face*, the "upper surface" of Van Peer (1992, 12–13) and *back*, the "under surface" of Van Peer (1992, 11–12), allowing some degree of regulation in the form and attributes of one or more "preferential flakes" (Inizan *et al.* 1999, 65)[6] removed after preparation. Yield Levallois flakes. May be subdivided according to striking face preparation as: radial or "centripetal" (Boëda 1993 and 1995); convergent; bi-directional; "Nubian Type 1; Nubian Type 2" (Guichard 1965; Guichard and Guichard 1965; 1968) and others. The radial pattern is not regarded as being any more "classical" (Van Peer 1992, 39) than the other patterns.

         i. Struck cores: cores from which one or more preferential flakes have been removed. The core was not retrimmed subsequent to the last removal.

         ii. Unstruck cores: cores with similar preparation to struck cores, or struck cores with evidence of re-preparation, without a final preferential flake removal.

         iii. Fragments of Levallois cores: broken struck or unstruck cores, including cores with overpassed core faces.

       b. Discoidal cores: cores which bear radial, alternatively centripetal, trimming on one or both faces, sometimes alternating, with a biconvex profile in side view, symmetrical or asymmetrical. May yield asymmetrical pointed flakes in series, sometimes from one face with platform preparation on the other face. Difficult to differentiate from unstruck cores in some cases. May represent a later stage of working down exhausted Levallois cores (Clark and Kleindienst 1974, 92).

Boëda (1993; 1995, 56, 65, Figure 4.34) has introduced the term "recurrent Levallois" for an asymmetrical core type, worked mainly on one face, based first upon the distribution of mass in the core, but then yielding more than one predetermined flake after striking face preparation. Any crafter knows that the major mass must be on the undersurface of any material if one face is the primary working surface. Boëda's usage seems to have introduced some confusion, in that *all* centripetally-worked asymmetrical cores may be termed 'Levallois' (Hawkins *et al.* 2001, 10). Lacking demonstrable evidence of multiple striking after repreparation of a multiply-struck face, I prefer to regard asymmetrically-profiled, radially-worked cores as a distinctive discoidal method. For instance, the simplest manner to achieve such reduction is to split a cobble or nodule, and to proceed to work around the split face without any further face preparation, and perhaps without any striking platform preparation either. I consider that specificity in the use of the term 'Levallois' should be retained to refer *only* to preferred flake removals, one or more, after striking face preparation, or repreparation (Van Peer 1995). A distinction between obtaining a single preferred flake rather than several from one stage of core preparation has implications for efficiency in raw material use. However, I doubt that ancient artisans were as stereotyped in their production methods as are modern analysts in their descriptive logic.

       c. Linear cores: cores prepared and struck in a manner to yield linear flakes.

         i. Flake/Blade cores: cores which yield a series of both long and short linear flakes with parallel to converging dorsal scars, which were struck from one or more platforms. May be subdivided according to the number and placement of the striking platforms, or according to morphology.

         ii. Blade cores: cores that yield a series of long linear flakes, that is, blades, struck from one or more platforms. May be subdivided according to the number and placement of the striking platforms, or according to morphology.

       d. Other Core fragments: Broken specialized cores. May be subdivided as to core types *b*, or *c*, if identifiable.

    2. Unspecialized cores. Cores which result from less regulated methods of flake production, or from initial stages of core preparation. Yield unspecialized flakes.

       a. Flake cores: cores which yield non-linear flakes with varying forms and dorsal scar patterns, struck in series off one or more platforms. May be subdivided according to the number and placement of the striking platforms.

---

[6] Also termed "predetermined blanks" (Boëda 1994; 1995, 46).

b. *Biconical cores:* more steeply worked cores, radially-trimmed on both faces, usually by alternating flaking, which produces a biconical profile in side view. These are more characteristic of the Earlier than of the Middle Stone Age aggregates.[7]

c. *Multidirectional cores:* cores on which flake removals have been achieved by repeatedly turning the core, often using pre-existing negative scars as striking platforms.[8]

d. *Nubbins:* 'exhausted cores' that have been worked-down to extremely small sizes.

e. *Earlier stage trimming cores:* cores that can be placed within a technological series of reduction stages. May be earlier stages in producing either specialized or unspecialized cores.

f. *Initial trim* or *Materials testing cores:* cores with minimal working, including "casual cores" (Isaac 1977) or "bashed chunks" (Kleindienst 1959, 72; 1962, 98), on which work was discontinued, which may indicate that the raw material was judged unsatisfactory.

g. *Core fragments:* broken cores, or large pieces off cores, which cannot be assigned to any more specific category.

B. *Angular flaking debris.* Debris resulting from stone working that does not exhibit the attributes of flakes. Cortical pieces may be segregated. Lithic analysts often ignore this material. Many rocks break naturally into sharp-edged fragments. Chert easily fragments, especially after transport, so that consistent identification of this category in many contexts is problematic; aeolised pieces are problematic in any raw material type.[9] Angular flaking debris is deliberately produced only by the bipolar method of reduction (Casey 1993; 2000, 83–97). Also called "chips and chunks" (Kleindienst 1962, 100).

A. *Chips:* relatively smaller, thinner pieces, which result from striking cores. Small pieces sometimes called 'shatter'.

B. *Chunks:* relatively larger, thicker pieces, which may be broken off cores.

C. *Microdebris* or *'dust':* identifiable only within sediments.

II. **End products and by-products of lithic flaking reduction:** Pieces resulting from the lithic reduction process which lack identifiable trimming, retouch or use-damage. Often termed waste or debitage. Based upon observed ancient selections for making or using end products, these could have been regarded as blanks, or as end products, or they may be the rejected by-products of reduction.

Flakes: The term has often been used for the distal form; (Inizan *et al.* 1999, 149–51) refer to the more general category as "plunging". Variously-shaped pieces struck off larger pieces of stone, which bear the characteristic attributes of removal through the application of directed force: a *talon*, 'butt', or 'striking platform'; a ventral release surface with evidence of conchoidal fracture, and a dorsal surface bearing evidence of the pre-existing core face. Attributes vary with different raw materials.

A. *Specialized Flakes.* Those flakes, either blanks for later working, or for use as such, or rejects, that can be identified as "preferential flakes" (Inizan *et al.* 1999, 65) produced by striking from specialized cores. These cores and flakes represent more regulated methods of lithic reduction, in that the attributes of the flakes are more closely defined by core preparation than is possible with other methods. Flakes more closely replicate each other in form and other attributes. Study of cores indicates that, while flakes can be confidently assigned to the general category, ascription to the specific types of cores is likely to be less reliable (Copeland 1983): similar flakes can come off the different specialized core types, and occasionally even off unspecialized cores. There is almost always more than one way to produce a similar-looking lithic product (Clark and Kleindienst 1974, 86).

1. *Levallois flakes.* Flakes whose attributes indicate removal from Struck Levallois cores:

a. *Pointed:* approach symmetrical triangular shape; may correspond to *"pointe levallois"* (Bordes 1961, 18–19, Figures 3-6, 4-1) and (Boëda 1994, 86), but here a less restrictive category for Levallois flakes with lateral edges converging to a point.

b. *Broad:* symmetrically shaped, with rounded or squared distal ends.

c. *Other:* irregularly-shaped, or flakes which hinged or broke-out; may be regarded as 'mistakes' in striking the preferential flake, but may be used as blanks or as tools.

d. *Overpassed:* flakes which take a section of the core edge in striking, subdivided as *distal, lateral,* or *core face.*[10] Intentional core rejuvenation or production, or 'mistakes' in striking, which may be used as blanks or as tools.

2. *Linear flakes.* End struck flakes whose attributes indicate that they were struck off flake/blade, or blade cores. These flakes exhibit parallel to convergent dorsal

---

[7] Original definition (Kleindienst 1959, 72; 1962, 98–9) following (Paterson and Fagg 1940; Paterson 1945).

[8] Originally termed "formless" (Kleindienst 1959, 72; 1962, 98) following (Paterson and Fagg 1940; Paterson 1945); also "changed orientation" cores (Schild and Wendorf 1977, 18).

[9] Note the problem of Isaac (1977, 234) of "Artifactual Rubble (Angular Waste)".

[10] The term has often been used for the distal form; (Inizan *et al.* 1999, 149–51) refer to the more general category as "plunging".

scars, and were removed in series after core striking-face preparation. Probably cannot be differentiated from some linear flakes that were produced during the trimming or striking of Levallois cores.

    a. *Quadrilateral:* defined as parallel-sided flakes with parallel dorsal scars; may be subdivided as *long* (length ≥ 2 x width), or *short* (length < 2 x width). Term introduced by Mason (1962, 92).

    b. *Pointed:* flakes whose laterals converge to a point, and on which the dorsal scars may be parallel to convergent; may be subdivided as *long* or *short*; termed "Triangular" in (Mason 1962, 92; Clark and Kleindienst 1974, 80).

    c. *Overpassed:* flakes that removed the edge, base or face of the core.

3. *Asymmetrical pointed flakes.* Flakes whose attributes indicate that they were struck off discoidal cores, possibly in series. Bordes (1961, 22–3, Figures 3-7 and 3-8) termed these "*pointes pseudo-Levallois*".

4. *Fragments.* Proximal, *medial* or *distal* fragments of broken specialized flakes. The specific type of flake may, or may not, be identifiable.

B. *Unspecialized Flakes.* Flakes produced from unspecialized cores, or in preparation of specialized cores, or in the shaping of tools from blanks or pieces of raw material. Subdivided as *end-struck* (length > width along the striking axis) versus *side-struck* (width ≤ length). Special types may be identifiable, although no attempt is made to differential the flakes struck off the different kinds of unspecialized cores because the margin of error in identification is considered to be too high (*contra* Schild and Wendorf 1977; Close 1993). Separated into:

    1. *Cortical or Primary:* flakes bear *circa* 30% to 100% of cortex, or original rock surface on the dorsal face, ± negative dorsal flake scars.

    2. *Secondary:* flakes bear less than *circa* 30% of cortex, or original rock surface on the dorsal face, plus negative dorsal flake scars.

    3. *Tertiary:* dorsal flake face bears no cortex, or original rock surface, often showing multiple negative dorsal flake scars.

    4. *Specific types:* flakes which originate from specific types of tertiary removals, such as *biface-trimming flakes* and *burin spalls*, or from specific types of core rejuvenation, such as *core tablets* or *core platform edges*.

    5. *Fragments:* proximal, *medial* or *distal* pieces of broken unspecialized flakes.

III. End products of reduction and/or selection:
Tools. Those blanks or selected pieces of raw material on which the form of the original piece has been humanly modified, either by secondary trimming and/or retouch, or through use in a manner which produces identifiable use-damage on edges or faces.

A. *Shaped Tools:* "Shaped tools" (Kleindienst 1959, 45; 1962, 85) are those modified pieces which exhibit a higher degree of consistent selection of the kind of the blank or original piece chosen for working, and consistent methods of alteration, resulting in a higher degree of replicability in morphology between similar objects. Sometimes called "formed" (for example, Casey 2000, 53) or "formal tools" (for example, Wadley 2001, 213, Table 1). Modification may occur sequentially during use for episodes, resulting in changes in attributes of scrapers, for example, or may be completed prior to use, which is often inferred and sometimes demonstrable for points.

1. *Points:* secondarily trimmed pieces with an acuate pointed tip, ranging from triangular to oval plan shapes, and with low-angled, sharp edges when retouched, which are biclinal if worked on both faces. Subdivided according to type and placement of retouch.

    a. *Unifacial points:* worked only on one face, dorsal or ventral.

    b. *Bifacial points:* Elongated, bifacially-trimmed lanceolate points with cortex or talon retained on the butt are associated with the Gifata Unit: *Gifata points* (Kleindienst 1999, 100). Completely worked points characterize the Dakhleh Unit. Completely-worked, and even partially-worked objects are sometimes called "bifacial foliate" (Guichard and Guichard 1965, 68); the artefacts from Nubia or the Western Desert which have been included in the category are highly variable.

2. *Ventral butt-thinned:* flakes with ventral bulb removal. Those found with the Kharga Aterian unit were termed "Tabalbalat" by Caton-Thompson (1952, 129–31); and with the Dakhleh Unit, "basal thinned" (Hawkins 2001, 328–30). Those found with the Gifata Unit and Teneida unit aggregates differ from Aterian in the type of ventral flaking.

3. *Scrapers:* secondarily trimmed pieces with low- to high-angled, planoclinal edge retouch. May be subdivided according to the placement of retouch relative to the long axis of the piece, for example, *end scrapers* versus *side scrapers*, or by plan shape, for example, *pointed scrapers*. Symmetrical pointed forms grade into unifacial points; an arbitrary edge-angle may be used to differentiate the classes.

4. *Core axes:* heavy duty tools, with emphasis upon trimming at the distal bit end and/or along one or both laterals; usually bifacial (Clark and Kleindienst 1974, 95–6). Characteristic of the Balat Unit, but also rarely occur in the Middle Stone Age, and later.

5. *Bifaces:* of variable plan shape, small-sized, and bifacially-trimmed over all or most of both faces, with sharp biclinal edges. These have often been termed 'handaxes', but are not of Acheulian type.

6. *Other categories as needed.*

B. *Situational Tools:* These may be made on any piece of lithic material or flaking product. They exhibit deliberate but minimal alteration, which does not result in any great degree of consistent replicable form in objects. May be subdivided according to: the placement of retouch, for example, *side, end*; type of edge, for example, *pointed, nosed*; and/or according to the blank type. Originally "modified tools" (Kleindienst, 1959, 71; 1962, 97; Clark and Kleindienst 1974, 84–5 and 93) or "miscellaneous trimmed pieces" (Isaac 1977, 234); sometimes called 'informal' or "expedient tools" (Parry and Kelly 1987). The term 'expedient' is considered to be inappropriate because it carries the negative connotation of something opportunistic, or less valued. Such tools represent foreknowledge of their usage, and deliberate selections of the pieces worked on the part of the makers. These tools comprise a consistent, and therefore important component of the Middle Stone Age toolkits. They may be curated.

C. *Utilized Tools:* any piece of rock, or flaking product that lacks secondary trimming or retouch, but on which any type of identifiable use-damage can be discerned. For worn or aeolised artefacts, this is limited to macro-use flaking, which may be difficult to differentiate from retouch; hence "utilized/modified" (Clark and Kleindienst 2001, 58). Except in sealed or sheltered locations, most surface artefacts in the Western Desert have fine 'nibbling' along all edges, probably resulting from the saltation of sand grains. Heavy-duty usage, resulting from battering or pounding, can be more easily determined. No micro-damage analyses have yet been attempted on the fresher materials.

  1. *Edge-damaged blanks:* can be subdivided according to the placement of damage and/or the kind of blank: for example, impact fractures on tips of points or pointed flakes.
  2. *Battered surfaces:* relatively large pieces with evidence of strong force applications on edges or faces, resulting in multiple step flaking, or Hertzian cones.
    a. *Hammer-stones:* pieces exhibiting heavy use-damage on one or more faces.
    b. *Anvils:* larger pieces of stone showing battering on edges and Hertzian cones on faces.
  3. *Ground surfaces:* pieces showing evidence of abrasion during use.

IV. Imports. Lithic pieces which must have been introduced to a locality by human agency, but showing no evidence of modification. Also called "unmodified" (Clark and Kleindienst 1974, 84), or "manuports" (Leakey 1971, 39).

Author's Affiliations:
Professor Emeritus, Department of Anthropolgy,
University of Toronto at Mississauga

Research Associate,
Department of Asian and Near Eastern Civilizations,
Royal Ontario Museum, Toronto

Research Associate, Department of Anthropology,
Field Museum of Natural History, Chicago

Author's Addresses:
Department of Anthropology
University of Toronto at Mississauga,
Mississauga, Ontario L5L 1C6,
Canada

and

1762 Angela Crescent,
Mississauga, Ontario L5J 1B9
Canada

REFERENCES

Bagnold, R. A., 1981 Foreword, The Results of the Field Studies Carried Out in the South Western Desert of Egypt in the Period between 25 September and 8 October, 1978, in B. Issawi, ed., *Annals of the Geological Survey of Egypt* XI, v–vii.

Balout, L., 1967 Procédés d'analyse et questions de terminologie dans l'étude des ensembles industriels du Paléolithique inférieur en Afrique du Nord, in W. W. Bishop and J. D. Clark, eds, *Background to Evolution in Africa*, University of Chicago Press, Chicago, 701–36

Baumler, M. F., 1995 Principles and Properties of Lithic Core Reduction: Implications for Levallois Technology, in H. L. Dibble and O. Bar-Yosef, eds, *The Definition and Interpretation of Levallois Technology*, Prehistory Press, Madison, 11–23.

Bishop, W. W. and J. D. Clark, eds, 1967 *Background to Evolution in Africa*, University of Chicago Press, Chicago.

Bisson, M. S., 2000 Nineteenth Century Tools for Twenty-First Century Archaeology? Why the Middle Paleolithic typology of François Bordes must be replaced, *Journal of Archaeological Method and Theory* 7, 1–48.

Boëda, E., 1993 Le débitage discoïde et le débitage Levallois récurrent centripéte, *Bulletin de la Société Préhistorique Française* 90, 392–404.

Boëda, E., 1994 *Le concept Levallois: variabilité des méthodes*, Centre de Recherches Archéologiques Monograph 9, Paris.

Boëda, E., 1995 Levallois: a volumetric construction, methods, a technique, in H. L. Dibble and O. Bar-Yosef, eds, *The Definition and Interpretation of Levallois Technology*, Prehistory Press, Madison, 41–68.

Bordes, F., 1961 *Typologie du Paléolithique ancien et moyen*, L'Institute de Préhistoire de l'Université de Bordeaux, Delmas, Bordeaux.

Casey, J., 2000 *The Kintampo Complex. The Late Holocene on the Gambaga Escarpment, Northern Ghana*, Archaeopress, Oxford.

Casey, J. L., 1993 *The Kintampo Complex in Northern Ghana: Late Holocene Human Ecology on the Gambaga Escarpment*, unpublished Ph.D. Dissertation, Department of Anthropology, University of Toronto.

Caton-Thompson, G., 1952 *Kharga Oasis in Prehistory*. Athlone Press, London.

Churcher, C. S., 1999 Our African Eden: Northeast Africa in the Mid-Pleistocene, in J. Lee-Thorp and H. Clift, eds, *Book of Abstracts, International Union for Quaternary Research, XV International Congress, 3–11 August, 1999, Durban, South Africa*, University of Cape Town, Rondebosch, 41.

Churcher, C. S. and M. R. Kleindienst, 1999 Mid-Pleistocene Fauna from Dakhleh Oasis, Western Desert of Egypt, *Journal of Vertebrate Paleontology* 19, *Abstracts of Papers, Fifty-Ninth Annual Meeting, Society of Vertebrate Paleontology, Denver, Colorado, October 20–23*, 38A.

Churcher, C. S., M. R. Kleindienst, and H. P. Schwarcz, 1999 Faunal Remains from a Middle Pleistocene Lacustrine Marl in Dakhleh Oasis, Egypt: Palaeoenvironmental Reconstructions, *Palaeogeography, Palaeoclimatology, Palaeoecology* 154, 301–12.

Churcher, C. S., M. R. Kleindienst, M. F. Wiseman, and M. M. A. McDonald, forthcoming, The Quaternary Faunas of Dakhleh Oasis, Western Desert of Egypt, in M. F. Wiseman, ed., *The Oasis Papers II: Proceedings of the Second Conference of the Dakhleh Oasis Project*, Oxbow Books, Oxford.

Churcher, C. S. and A. J. Mills, 1999 Appendix II. Index list of archaeological sites surveyed by the Dakhleh Oasis Project, in C. S. Churcher and A. J. Mills, eds, *Reports from the Survey of Dakhleh Oasis, Western Desert of Egypt, 1977–1987*, Oxbow Books, Oxford, 251–65.

Clark, J. D., G. H. Cole, G. L. Isaac and M. R. Kleindienst, 1966 Precision and Definition in African Archaeology, *South African Archaeological Bulletin* XXI, 114–21.

Clark, J. D. and M. R. Kleindienst, 1974 The Stone Age Cultural Sequence: Terminology, Typology and Raw Material, in J. D. Clark, ed., *Kalambo Falls Prehistoric Site, Volume II*, Cambridge University Press, Cambridge, 71–106.

Clark, J. D. and M. R. Kleindienst, 2001 The Stone Age Cultural Sequence: Terminology, Typology and Raw Material, in J. D. Clark, ed., *Kalambo Falls Prehistoric Site, Volume III*, Cambridge University Press, Cambridge, 34–65.

Close, A. E., 1993 The Analysis of Middle Paleolithic Artifacts, in F. Wendorf, R. Schild, A. E. Close and a. Associates, eds, *Egypt during the Last Interglacial. The Middle Paleolithic of Bir Tarfawi and Bir Sahara East*, Plenum Press, New York and London, 255–60.

Cole, G. H., 1967 The Later Acheulian and Sangoan of Southern Uganda, in W. W. Bishop and J. D. Clark, eds, *Background to Evolution in Africa*, University of Chicago Press, Chicago, 481–528.

Collins, D., 1970 Stone Artefact Analysis and the Recognition of Culture Traditions, *World Archaeology* 2, 17–27.

Copeland, L., 1983 Levallois/non-Levallois determinations in the early Levant Mousterian: problems and questions for 1983, *Paléorient* 9, 15–27.

Cross, J. R., 1983 Twigs, Branches, Trees, and Forests: Problems of Scale in Lithic Analysis, in J. A. Moore and A. S. Keene, eds, *Archaeological Hammers and Theories*, Academic Press, New York and London, 87–106.

Currelly, C. T., 1909 A Sequence of Egyptian Stone Implements. *Report of the 78th Meeting of the British Association for the Advancement of Science, Dublin, September, 1908*, John Murray, Dublin, 848–52.

Currelly, C. T., 1967 (1956) *I Brought the Ages Home*, The Ryerson Press, Toronto.

Demidenko, Y. E., 1998 Comment on Van Peer, 'The Nile Corridor and the Out-of-Africa Model', *Current Anthropology* 39, Supplement, S131.

Dorn, R. I., 1994 Surface Exposure Dating with Rock Varnish, in C. Beck, ed., *Dating in Exposed Surface Contexts*, University of New Mexico, Albuquerque, 77–113.

Dorn, R. I. and T. M. Oberlander, 1982 Rock Varnish, *Progress in Physical Geography* 6, 317–67.

Egyptian Geological Survey and Mining Authority, 1982 *Geological Map Sheet NG-35 Dakhla*, Cairo.

Fish, P. R., 1979 *The Interpretive Potential of Mousterian Debitage*, Arizona State University University, Tempe.

Garcea, E. A. A., 1998 Comment on Van Peer, 'The Nile Corridor and the Out-of-Africa Model', *Current Anthropology* 39, Supplement, S131–2.

Garcea, E. A. A., 2001 The Aterians of the Libyan Coast and the Sahara, *XIV Congress of the International Union of Prehistoric and Protohistoric Sciences, 2001, Liège*, (paper presented).

Goren-Inbar, N., 1990 *Quneitra: A Mousterian Site on the Golan Heights*, The Hebrew University of Jerusalem, Jerusalem.

Guichard, J., 1965 Contribution à l'étude du Paléolithique inférieur et moyen de la Nubie, Thésis de 3e cycle, Faculté des Lettres et Sciences Humaines, Université de Bordeaux, Bordeaux.

Guichard, J. and G. Guichard, 1965 Contributions to the Prehistory of Nubia, No. 3, The Early and Middle Paleolithic of Nubia: a preliminary report, in F. Wendorf, ed., *Contributions to the Prehistory of Nubia*, Fort Burgwin Research Center and Southern Methodist University, Dallas, 57–116.

Guichard, J. and G. Guichard, 1968 Contributions to the study of the Early and Middle Paleolithic of Nubia, in F. Wendorf, ed., *The Prehistory of Nubia, Volume 1*, Fort Burgwin Research Center and Southern Methodist University, Dallas, 148–93.

Hawkins, A. L., 2001 Getting a Handle on Tangs: The Aterian of the Western Desert of Egypt, unpublished Ph.D. Dissertation, Department of Anthropology, University of Toronto, Toronto.

Hawkins, A. L. and M. R. Kleindienst, 2001 Lithic Resources of the Dakhleh Oasis Region, Western Desert of Egypt. *Society for American Archaeology 2001, Abstracts of the 66th Annual Meeting, April 18–22, New Orleans*, Society for American Archaeology, Washington, D.C., 175.

Hawkins, A. L. and M. R. Kleindienst, 2002 Lithic Raw Material Usages During the Middle Stone Age at Dakhleh Oasis, Egypt, *Geoarchaeology: An International Journal* 17, 601–24.

Hawkins, A. L., J. R. Smith, R. Giegengack, M. M. A. McDonald, M. R. Kleindienst, H. P. Schwarcz, C. S. Churcher, M. F. Wiseman, and K. Nicoll, 2001 New Research on the Prehistory of the Escarpment in Kharga Oasis, Egypt, *Nyame Akuma* 55, 8–14.

Haynes, C. V., 1980 Geochronology of Wadi Tushka: Lost Tributary of the Nile, *Science* 210, 68–71.

Haynes, C. V., T. A. Maxwell, A. El Hawary, K. A. Nicoll, and S. Stokes, 1997 An Acheulian Site near Bir Kiseiba in the Darb el Arba'in Desert, Egypt, *Geoarchaeology: An International Journal* 12, 819–32.

Hermina, M., 1990 The Surroundings of Kharga, Dakhla and Farafra Oases, in R. Said, ed., *The Geology of Egypt*, Balkema, Rotterdam and Brookfield, 259–92.

Inizan, M.-L., M. Reduron-Ballinger, H. Roche, and J. Tixier, 1999 *Technology and Terminology of Knapped Stone. Volume 5*, Cercle de Recherches et d'Etudes Préhistoriques, Nanterre.

Isaac, G. L., 1977 *Olorgesailie*, University of Chicago Press, Chicago.

Isaac, G. L. and B. Isaac, eds, 1997 *Koobi Fora Research Project. Volume 5, Plio-Pleistocene Archaeology*, Clarendon Press, Oxford.

Isaac, G. L. and C. M. Keller, 1968 Note on the proportional frequency of side- and end-struck flakes, *South African Archaeological Bulletin* 23, 17–19.

Kleindienst, M. R., 1959 *Composition and Significance of a late Acheulian assemblage, based upon an analysis of East African occupation sites*, unpublished Ph.D. Dissertation, Department of Anthorpology, University of Chicago, Chicago.

Kleindienst, M. R., 1962 Components of the East African Acheulian assemblage: An analytic approach, in G. Mortelmans and J. Nenquin, eds, *Actes du IVe Congrès Panafricain de Préhistoire et de l'Étude du Quaternaire, Section III, Annales, sèrie in-8o, Sciences Humaines* 40, Musée Royale de l'Afrique Centrale, Tervuren, 81–111.

Kleindienst, M. R., 1972 Brief Observations on some Stone Age Sites Recorded by the Yale University Prehistoric Expedition to Nubia, 1964–1965, in H. J. Hugot, ed., *Congrès panafricain de Préhistoire, Dakar 1967. Actes de 6e Session*, Les Imprimeries Réunies de Chambéry, Chambéry, 111–2.

Kleindienst, M. R., 1979 Discussion: General Considerations. B. Design Theory, in B. Hayden, ed., *Lithic Use-Wear Analysis*, Academic Press, New York, 59–60.

Kleindienst, M. R., 1999 Pleistocene Archaeology and Geoarchaeology: A Status Report, in C. S. Churcher and A. J. Mills, eds, *Reports from the Survey of Dakhleh Oasis, Western Desert of Egypt, 1977–1987*, Oxbow Books, Oxford, 83–108.

Kleindienst, M. R., 2000 On the Nile Corridor and the Out-of-Africa model, *Current Anthropology* 41, 107–9.

Kleindienst, M. R., C. S. Churcher, M. M. A. McDonald, and H. P. Schwarcz, 1999 Geography, Geology, Geochronology and Geoarchaeology of the Dakhleh Oasis Region: An Interim Report, in C. S. Churcher and A. J. Mills, eds, *Reports from the Survey of Dakhleh Oasis, Western Desert of Egypt, 1977–1987*, Oxbow Books, Oxford, 1–54.

Kleindienst, M. R., H. P. Schwarcz, K. Nicoll, C. S. Churcher, J. Frizano, R. W. Giegengack and M. F. Wiseman, 1996 Pleistocene Geochronology and Palaeoclimates at Dakhleh and Kharga Oases, Western Desert, Egypt, based upon Uranium-Thorium determinations from spring-laid tufas, *Nyame Akuma* 46, 96 (Revised abstract).

Kleindienst, M. R., H. P. Schwarcz, K. Nicoll, C. S. Churcher, J. Frizano, R. W. Giegengack, and M. F. Wiseman, forthcoming, Water in the Desert: First Report on Uranium-Series Dating of Caton-Thompson's and Gardner's 'Classic' Pleistocene Sequence at Refuf Pass, Kharga Oasis, in M. F. Wiseman, ed., *The Oasis Papers II: Proceedings of the Second International Conference of the Dakhleh Oasis Project*, Oxbow Books, Oxford.

Klitzsch, E., F. K. List and G. Pöhlmann, 1987 *Geological Map of Egypt NG 35 SE Dakhla*, The Egyptian General Petroleum Corporation, Cairo.

Leakey, M. D., 1971 *Olduvai Gorge. Volume III: Excavations in Beds I and II, 1960–1963l*, Cambridge University Press, Cambridge.

Marks, A. E., ed., 1983 *The Avdat/Aqev Area, Part 3. Volume III. Prehistory and Paleoenvironments in the Central Negev, Israel*, Southern Methodist University Press, Dallas.

Mason, R., 1962 *Prehistory of the Transvaal*, Witwatersrand University Press, Johannesburg.

McBrearty, S. and A. S. Brooks, 2000 The Revolution that wasn't: a new interpretation of the origin of modern human behaviour, *Journal of Human Evolution* 39, 453–563.

McFadden, L. D., E. V. McDonald, S. G. Wells, K. Anderson, J. Quade, and S. L. Forman, 1998 The vesicular layer and carbonate collars of desert soils and pavements: formation, age and relation to climatic change, *Geomorphology* 24, 101–45.

Mills, A. J., 1979 Dakhleh Oasis Project. Report on the First Season of Survey, October–December, 1978, *Journal of the Society for the Study of Egyptian Antiquities* IX, 163–85.

Moyer, C. C. and N. Rolland, 2001 Understanding the Middle Palaeolithic Assemblage Typology, *Antiquity* 75, 39–43.

Oberlander, T. M., 1994 Rock Varnish in Deserts, in A. D. Abrahams and A. J. Parsons, eds, *Geomorphology of Desert Environments*, Chapman & Hall, London, 106–19.

Parry, W. J. and R. L. Kelly, 1987 Expedient Core Technology and Sedentism, in J. K. Johnson and C. A. Morrow, eds, *The Organization of Core Technology*, Westview Press, Boulder and London, 285–304.

Paterson, T. T., 1945 Core, culture and complex in the Old Stone Age, *Proceedings of the Prehistoric Society*, n.s. 11, 1–19.

Paterson, T. T. and B. E. B. Fagg, 1940 Studies on the Palaeolithic succession in England. No. 2. The Upper Brecklandian Acheul (Elueden), *Proceedings of the Prehistoric Society* 6, 1–29.

Pye, D., 1964 *The Nature of Design*, Studio Vista and Reinhold, London and New York.

Pye, D., 1968 *The Nature and Art of Workmanship*, Cambridge University Press, London.

Schild, R., 1998 Comment on Van Peer, 'The Nile Corridor and the Out-of-Africa model', *Current Anthropology* 39, Supplement, S134–5.

Schild, R. F. and F. Wendorf, 1977 *The Prehistory of the Dakhla Oasis and adjacent Desert*, Polish Academy of Sciences, Warsaw.

Schwarcz, H. and L. Morawska, 1993 Uranium-series dating of carbonates from Bir Tarfawi and Bir Sahara East, in F. Wendorf, R. Schild, A. E. Close and a. Associates, eds, *Egypt during the Last Interglacial. The Middle Paleolithic of Bir Tarfawi and Bir Sahara East*, Plenum Press, New York and London, 205–17.

Schwarcz, H. P., R. Szkudlarek, M. R. Kleindienst and N. Evenesen, forthcoming, Fire in the desert: the occurrence of a high-Ca silicate glass near the Dakhleh Oasis, Egypt, in M. F. Wiseman, ed., *The Oasis Papers II: Proceedings of the Second International Conference of the Dakhleh Oasis Project*, Oxbow Books, Oxford.

Sellet, F., 1993 Chaine operatoire: the concept and its applications, *Lithic Technology* 18, 108–12.

Sellet, F., 1995 Levallois or not Levallois, does it really matter? Learning from an African case, in H. L. Dibble and O. Bar-Yosef, eds, *The Definition and Interpretation of Levallois Technology*, Prehistory Press, Madison, 25–39.

Sheppard, P. J. and M. R. Kleindienst, 1996 Technological change in the Earlier and Middle Stone Age of Kalambo Falls, *The African Archaeological Review* 13, 171–96.

Smith, F. H., 1999 The real revolution: the impact of chronology on models of modern human origin, *Fryxell Symposium: Papers in Honor of Henry P. Schwarcz, 64th Annual Meeting, Society for American Archaeology, Chicago, March 25*, (paper presented).

Van Peer, P., 1992 *The Levallois Reduction Strategy*, Prehistory Press, Madison.

Van Peer, P., 1995 Current issues in the Levallois problem, in H. L. Dibble and O. Bar-Yosef, eds, *The Definition and Interpretation of Levallois Technology*, Prehistory Press, Madison, 1–9.

Van Peer, P., 1998 The Nile Corridor and the Out-of-Africa Model. An examination of the archaeological record, *Current Anthropology* 39, Supplement, S115–S140.

Van Peer, P. and P. M. Vermeersch, 2000 The Nubian complex and the dispersal of modern humans in North Africa, in L. Krzyzaniak, K. Kroeper and M. Kobusiewicz, eds, *Recent Research into the Stone Age of Northeastern Africa*, Poznan Archaeological Museum, Poznan, 47–65.

Wadley, L., 2001 What is cultural modernity? A general view and a South African perspective from Rose Cottage Cave, *Cambridge Archaeological Journal* 11, 201–21.

Wendorf, F., R. Schild, A. E. Close and a. Associates, eds, 1993 *Egypt during the Last Interglacial. The Middle Paleolithic of Bir Tarfawi and Bir Sahara East*, Plenum Press, New York and London.

Wiseman, M. F. W., this volume, The Chronology of the Later Late Pleistocene Occurrences at Dakhleh: A 'Low-Tech' Approach, 89–94.

The Early Holocene Masara A and Masara C Cultural Sub-Units of Dakhleh Oasis, within a Wider Cultural Setting

Mary M. A. McDonald

Introduction

Two major cultural stratigraphic units, Masara A and Masara C, are assigned to the Epipalaeolithic developmental stage of Dakhleh Oasis, Egypt. Masara A localities, campsites of mobile hunter-gatherers, resemble sites widely scattered across the eastern Sahara *circa* 9500–8000 bp uncalibrated radiocarbon years before present. Masara C sites, however, have seemed to be anomalous within the wider setting in both their timing and adaptation. Masara C, dated *circa* 8900–8500 bp, has been recorded only in the south-eastern corner of Dakhleh Oasis. Sites feature structures, stone hut circles, and a distinctive chipped stone assemblage including the 'Ounan-Harif point'. It appears that the best parallels elsewhere are either much older – the Harifian of the Negev and Sinai, at well before 10,000 bp (Scott 1977; Goring-Morris 1991), or much younger, the Al Jerar entity of Nabta Playa in southern Egypt, dated 7900-7300 bp (Wendorf *et al.* 2001). While the eastern Sahara in the Masara C era is considered by many to be hyperarid and largely deserted, Masara C palaeobotanical evidence suggests Sahelian conditions locally.

Now, as a result of two things, the opportunity for me, as part of the Kharga Oasis Prehistoric Project (KOPP) to do fieldwork on the escarpment in Kharga Oasis, and the full publication of the sequence from around Nabta Playa in southern Egypt by the Combined Prehistoric Expedition (CPE), Masara C no longer looks quite as isolated and anomalous as it did before. Sites sharing similar artefact assemblages have been recorded at several locations in the southern half of Egypt. Masara A, meanwhile, can be seen as part of a tradition traceable across much of the Sahara, and persisting in some areas into the mid-Holocene.

Masara A and Masara C defined

Masara A

Sites and Artefact Assemblages

Masara A localities are sparsely scattered throughout Dakhleh Oasis (Figure 1) and atop the plateau to the north.

Many are associated with muddy pans, while Locality 166 in Miramar Basin on the plateau lies within the 'playa sediments' of an 'intermittent lake' (Brookes 1993, 535; Kleindienst *et al.* 1999, 12). Masara A sites consist of scatters of chipped stone and sometimes a little grinding equipment associated, usually, with a hearth. They range in size from Locality 224, a sparse scatter about 5 m across on the desert floor in east central Dakhleh, to Locality 263, consisting of many separate scatters covering an area at least 800 x 200 m, around a large muddy pan in the vicinity of the Masara C sites in south-eastern Dakhleh. Typical perhaps is Locality 85, east of Ezbet Sheikh Muftah in central Dakhleh, where several small chipped stone scatters cover an area *circa* 150 x 95 m. Within that area as well are a few stone-capped hearths, a pair of grinding slab fragments, a possible handstone fragment, and sparse ostrich eggshell. Everything about these sites, including the organization of lithic technology, suggests that they are the temporary campsites of highly mobile groups of hunter-gatherers who routinely travelled into the desert beyond the oasis (McDonald 1991b). Similar scatters have been recorded for this era throughout the eastern and central Sahara (Gabriel 1987; Holl 1989).

In part because of the sparse and deflated nature of the sites, there are no large lithics collections from Masara A localities. Table 1 lists frequencies of tool types in controlled collections from two localities, 85 and 263, Grid A (263A). Masara A sites are characterized by blades knapped from good quality nodular chert and then notched, denticulated or continuously retouched (Figure 2). Backed bladelets are common, while geometric microliths are represented mostly by elongated scalene triangles. There are important differences between the sites as well, notably in the emphasis in the 263A collections on burins and perforators. Ounan points are listed here only for 263A, but one was noted on Locality 85 as well, lying off the grid.

The Masara B scatters located on the sandstone ridge south-west of Sheikh Muftah (McDonald 1991a; 1991b) may actually be a specialized component on the Masara A unit (*pace* McDonald 1991b, 106, which postulates a

Figure 1 Map of Egypt showing places mentioned in text.

relationship with Masara C). Masara B localities are special-purpose sites where Middle Stone Age (MSA) artefacts were systematically reworked into a limited range of tool types, mostly burins (Table 1). The few tools made on fresh nodular material include Masara A-like notched or retouched blades and various backed bladelets. Moreover, some Masara A sites such as Locality 263A also have high proportions of burins in the toolkit, and, at 263A, at least four of those burins are on MSA flakes. On the other hand, there are few parallels with the Masara C toolkit as defined below. Both Masara A and Masara B sites have yielded a few sherds with a distinctive shale-tempered fabric (Hope 2002, 40). Finally, on the Masara B ridge itself, there are also scatters of Masara A material.

Masara C

There have been questions in the literature as to whether Masara C should be considered a *bona fide* cultural entity (Close 1992, 167; Wendorf *et al.* 2001, 654). In fact, Masara C can be clearly delineated areally and chronologically; it has a distinctive chipped stone industry and well defined adaptive and settlement patterns.

Localities and site features

Virtually all recorded Masara C localities[1] are confined to a corner of south-eastern Dakhleh well beyond the extant oasis. Here, most are located within an area less than 2 km across (McDonald 1991b, 87 and Figure 2). Unlike the Masara A sites, and early Holocene sites elsewhere in the Western Desert, Masara C sites are not associated with playa deposits. Most are found on a low sandstone ridge where they occupy shallow hollows that may have acted to concentrate drainage. The ridge lies at the terminus of a major wadi system, the Wadi-el-Batikh that carries water from the plateau top.

On the Masara C ridge, some 20 localities have been recorded, 15 of them featuring apparent structures, the rest being surface scatters of lithics. Of those with structures, most are fairly small, ranging from two to about eight units, while four are larger, consisting of a dozen or more structures each. Masara C structures are rings of stone, oval, round or bilobed, and averaging 3 to 4 m in diameter. Surface remains usually consist of a single tier of vertical sandstone slabs, which can stand three to four slabs thick in places.

Work has been conducted on five of the Masara C localities so far: three of the large sites with structures, Localities 260, 264 and 265, and two others lacking structures, 300 and 308. Each locality was gridded, surface features and artifact scatters mapped, surface lithics collected in a controlled manner, and portions of the sites excavated. This work yielded much information on construction methods, lithic technology and toolkits and, from excavated organic remains, data on subsistence and the palaeoenvironment (McDonald 2002).

Two structures were excavated on each of the three large sites. The structures on Locality 264 (Figure 3) proved to be semi-subterranean. Hut 5 was a pit 40–50 cm deep, its walls lined with stone, with a probable hearth on its floor. The pit was encircled by a layer of stone at ground level. In Hut 1 at the other end of the same hut cluster (Figure 4), the floor had been scooped 30 cm down into the sandstone bedrock, and there was a sloped entryway to the east. Outside the hut, two successive occupation layers were detected, each with a hearth.

The structures tested on Locality 265, Huts 1 and 8, do not seem to have required as much work to build. The Hut 8 floor was only slightly concave, resting well above bedrock, with one main hearth and two other smaller patches of burning. These patches lay at different levels, sandwiching an eight cm thick layer of silt, suggesting a period of abandonment and reoccupation during the life of the structure.

In addition to the sites with structures, two apparent special-purpose sites were excavated. Locality 300, near 264, consists of five small hearths, a pit dug into bedrock, and a knapping floor. Here, typical Masara C tools were produced on good quality 'Tarawan' chert, which comes from the escarpment to the north of the oasis (M. R. Kleindienst, personal communication, January 2002).

Locality 308, also nearby, was of interest because of bone fragments on the surface, bone being rare of Masara sites. Locality 308 proved to be a shallow basin 4.5 x 2.0 x 0.3 m, scooped out of the soft sandstone bedrock, its floor red-stained and covered by an ashy layer 10–15 cm thick. Within and around this feature were seven smaller pits, averaging *circa* 40 cm across, also dug into bedrock, their fill rich in charcoal and animal bone.

The Lithic Assemblage

The published scepticism mentioned above concerning the integrity of the Masara C cultural unit, stems in part from the assumption that it is mostly surface material and arguably mixed (Close 1992, 167). In addition, some elements of the Masara C toolkit are found, within the CPE sequence (Wendorf *et al.* 2001), in separate cultural entities, for example double patinated end scrapers in the El Adam variant, 9500–8900 bp, and Ounan points in the Al Jerar variant, 7900–7300 bp.

Masara C material is largely from the surface, as are most early Holocene collections from the Eastern Sahara. Collections from all Masara C sites however, were made systematically (Table 2) and all include at least some excavated material. The collection from Locality 308 is almost all from excavated squares, and the few tools from

---

[1] One Masara C locality, 274, a small surface scatter of lithics, lies *circa* 10 km north of the other Masara C sites on the ridge north of the Southeast Basin (McDonald 1990).

Table 1 Absolute and percentage frequencies of retouched tool types at Masara A Localities 85 and 263A and Masara B Localities 194 and 200.

Locality	85[1] (n)	%	263A[2] (n)	%	194[3] (n)	%	200[4] (n)	%
4. Core-like end-scraper					16	*14.3*	1	*0.5*
5. Denticulated end-scraper			1	*1.6*				
12. Single perforator			1	*1.6*	2	*1.8*		
16. Double-backed perforator			3	*4.8*				
17. Dihedral burin			5	*7.9*	52	*46.5*	13	*41.9*
19. Burin on a break			4	*6.3*	10	*8.9*	2	*6.5*
20. Multiple dihedral burin			1	*1.6*	13	*11.6*	2	*6.5*
23. Burin on a concave truncation			2	*3.2*				
29. Dihedral burin on a backed blade			1	*1.6*				
31. Burin on a backed blade			1	*1.6*				
45. Pointed straight-backed bladelet	7	*14.3*					2	*6.5*
51. Pointed straight-backed bladelet, retouched base	1	*2.0*	1	*1.6*				
56. Curved-back bladelet	2	*4.1*						
63. Partially backed bladelet			2	*3.2*				
64. Shouldered bladelet							3	*9.7*
66. Fragment of backed bladelet	18	*36.7*	1	*1.6*			1	*3.2*
67. Obtuse-ended backed bladelet	1	*2.0*						
74. Notched flake			4	*6.3*	4	*3.6*	1	*3.2*
75. Denticulated flake			4	*6.3*	3	*2.7*	1	*3.2*
76. Notched blade or bladelet	3	*6.1*	5	*7.9*	4	*3.6*		
77. Denticulated blade or bladelet	1	*2.0*	8	*12.7*				
79. Notched or denticulated, continuous retouch			6	*9.5*	2	*1.8*		
80. Truncated piece	1	*2.0*	2	*3.2*				
82. Segment							3	*9.7*
90. Scalene triangle	1	*2.0*						
95. Elongated scalene triangle, v. short side	5	*10.2*						
97. Elongated scalene triangle, concave short truncation			1	*1.6*				
101. *Piquant-trièdre*					1	*0.9*		
102. Microburin	1	*2.0*			1	*0.9*	1	*3.2*
105. Piece with continuous retouch	7	*14.3*	4	*6.3*	4	*3.6*	1	*3.2*
106. Sidescraper			1	*1.6*				
107. Ounan point			5	*7.9*				
112. *Varia*	1	*2.0*						
Total	**49**	**99.7**	**63**	**99.9**	**112**	**100.1**	**31**	**100.0**

[1] Tools from 80 sq m surface collected and screened.

[2] From 72 sq m of shallow deposits excavated to sterile.

[3] From 150 sq m surface collected but not screened.

[4] From 64 sq m surface collected but not screened.

the surface elsewhere on the site are also good Masara C types. While tools on most Masara C sites are made on a variety of locally-available raw material including MSA artefacts (McDonald 1991b), Locality 300 is a knapping floor where all the standard Masara C tool types are produced on a good quality, distinctive 'Tarawan' chert that would have been imported (Kleindienst *et al.* 1999, 88; Kleindienst this volume). A lithic assemblage knapped on the spot from a distinctive, imported raw material is arguably nearly as secure as one excavated from an intact primary context.

All Masara C sites, including Locality 274 well to the north, share the same classes of tools: end scrapers, perforators, notched or denticulated items, geometrics in the form of equilateral triangles and trapezes, the Ounan point, and use of the microburin technique (Table 2).

Many of the Masara C tool types within these classes, moreover, are distinctive compared with those from Masara A and other early Holocene entities (Figure 5). Masara C end scrapers are broad, thick-sectioned tools. On most sites, MSA artefacts were chosen as blanks. On Locality 300, blanks of similar dimensions were fashioned from the fresh Tarawan chert. Double-backed perforators or drills, unlike the parallel-sided Masara A drills, tend to be backed for only part of their length, leaving a wider, unmodified proximal end, perhaps for easier handling or hafting (Figure 5e). Amongst the geometrics, most triangles and trapezes are concave-sided. Masara C notches and denticulates tend to be on thin-sectioned blanks and feature small but fully retouched notches, giving a roughly nibbled effect (Figure 5c). Masara A tools in contrast tend to be thicker-sectioned with steep retouch producing broad, deep notches or extensive denticulated edges (Figure 2g; McDonald 1991b, Figure 6, 2–4).

Lastly, while both Masara A and Masara C feature simple-stemmed points, often called Ounan points, an important distinction can be drawn between the two units on this basis. As early as 1980, Wendorf and Schild (1980, 110; 259) described a group of points from sites in the Nabta area which were less like the Ounan points of the Sahara, as defined by Tixier (1955, 98; 1963, 149), and closer to 'Harif' points from the Negev and Sinai (Marks 1973; Goring-Morris 1987, 354).[2] As illustrated in Figure 6, Ounan and Harif points are similar in some ways: the shank is a blade, or blade-like, with edge retouch at the tang or base, and sometimes also along the lateral or at the point. But Ounan points generally are longer and narrower,

usually have a definite tang, and only occasionally, some retouch toward the tip.[3] Harif points tend to be shorter and broader. They have a triangular base or a fairly short tang, and more retouch on at least one lateral toward the tip, in the form of backing or an oblique truncation. In Dakhleh, Masara A sites feature the Ounan point, and Masara C the Harif point (McDonald 19991b, Figure 6, 5–6, 23–27).

Finally, while all Masara C sites share the same tool classes and many of the same types, the collection from Locality 265 differs somewhat from the others (Figure 7). The only end-scraper is a denticulated one. MSA blanks tend to be worked instead into points or combination tools. Amongst the notches and denticulates are examples of the thin-sectioned tools with the 'nibbled' effect. On others, however, the notches are larger, and the patterning of retouch unique to this site, with notches often occurring as adjacent pairs (Figure 7k). Further, most of the arrowheads do not qualify as Harif (or Ounan) points (Figure 7a–e). Four of the six[4] are retouched bifacially either along the edge or more extensively. Bifacially-retouched points are in general typical of later, mid-Holocene collections in Dakhleh.

Other Artefact Categories

Masara C sites feature grinding equipment, both slabs and handstones. Grinding slabs are usually sub-rectangular or oval, and can measure up to 75 x 35 cm. The eight complete handstones on Locality 264 are well made, tend to be sub-rectangular or ovate, usually with a hint of corners, and in cross section, range from almost round, markedly biconvex, to flat and thin. Each of the large sites with structures, 260, 264 and 265, has, on its surface amongst the structures, a little cluster of three carefully worked handstones.

As for other artifact categories, no pottery has been found either on surface reconnaissance or in excavation of any Masara C site. One fragmentary bone tool, a point, was found on Locality 308. Ostrich eggshell beads occur commonly on Masara C sites. At Locality 264, beads were made on site, judging by the presence of fragments at various stages of manufacture. Finished beads are small, *circa* 9–10 mm in diameter. One fragment of decorated eggshell was noted on Locality 309, which is close to, and perhaps an extension of, Locality 260.

---

[2] The CPE were later (Wendorf *et al.* 184, 276) to call their points "Ounan-Harif points".

[3] Ounan points should also be distinguished from a type that Holmes (1991), studying a collection of 'post-Palaeolithic' projectile points from Umm el-Dabadib in northern Kharga Oasis, has labelled, somewhat confusingly, the 'Ounanian' point. An Ounanian point, like the Ounan point, is made on a blade, but with "a slightly constricted base tending towards a triangular shape ..." (Holmes 1991, 105) rather than a distinct tang, and often with *couvrante* or invasive retouch on its base (Holmes 1991, Figure 4f). Holmes' Ounanian points are found within a collection of otherwise Bashendi-like arrowheads, and based on observations in Dakhleh and Kharga, I suspect that the Ounanian is a post-Epipalaeolithic point.

[4] Two of the six were found just off the 265 grid. In Table 2, the three from the grid bearing bifacial retouch are listed as *Varia*.

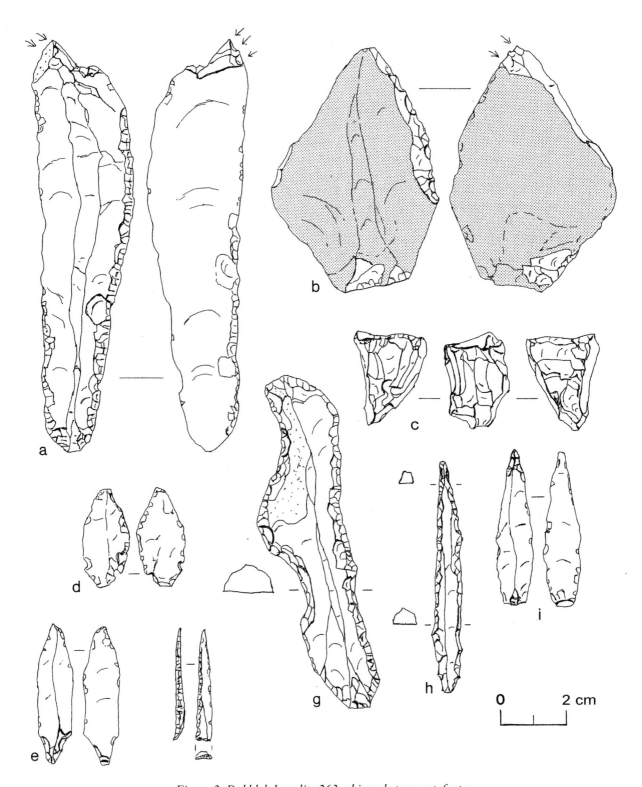

Figure 2 Dakhleh Locality 263, chipped stone artefacts:
a, burin on backed blade; b, burin (or bladelet core?) on Middle Stone Age flake (shaded area); c, small core;
d, rough point; e, Ounan point; f, elongated triangle; g, notched backed blade; h and i, drills.

Masara A and Masara C: Environment, Subsistence and Dating

Animal bone is relatively rare on Masara sites, but charred plant remains are abundant and can be used to elucidate environmental conditions and adaptations, and for dating purposes.

Faunal Evidence

For Masara A, fragmentary faunal remains[5] from Locality 263A appear to be Dorcas gazelle and something slightly larger. Dorcas gazelle was recovered also from Locality 166 on the plateau.

For Masara C, the fullest faunal collection is from Locality 308. Species ranging from hartebeest, gazelle and hare, to ostrich and smaller (wading?) birds, to tortoise, lizard and toad, suggest a broad spectrum, hunting-collecting adaptation. Some of these elements occur also at other sites: from Locality 265, gazelle and bird, of desert grouse size; from 264, hartebeest and bird; from 300, gazelle and hartebeest. In addition, Localities 264 and 300 each yielded what appears to be goat. Ostrich eggshell fragments occur on all sites; on Locality 265, they are so numerous that it appears the eggs were being eaten.[6]

Palaeobotanical Remains

The five excavated Masara C sites, and to a lesser extent the Masara A Locality 263A, had rich-looking ashy deposits, and a total of 39 samples were collected in the 1997 and 1998 field seasons. The analyst, U. Thanheiser, (personal communication, July 1998), reports that phytoliths were rare, but that both charcoal and plant macrofossils were found in virtually all samples. The picture emerging from her work is fairly consistent for all six sites, but seems at odds with evidence for aridity elsewhere in the desert at this time.

Twelve species of trees or shrubs were identified from the charcoal (U. Thanheiser, personal communication, October 2000). Amongst them were at least six that could be classed as southern or Sahelian elements: *Acacia nilotica, Balaites aegyptiaca, Calotropis procera, Capparis decidua, Leptadenia pyrotechnica* and *Salvadora persica*. Species were fairly evenly distributed amongst the sites: nine from each of Localities 263A, 260 and 308, seven from 264 and 265, and five from Locality 300. In comparison, of the other three areas in the Western Desert where early Holocene charcoal has

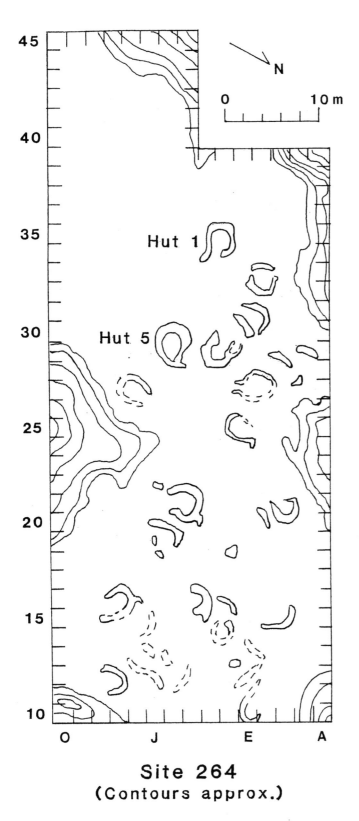

Site 264
(Contours approx.)

Figure 3 Plan of Dakhleh Locality 264 showing Huts 1 and 5.

[5] Faunal identifications are by C. S. Churcher.

[6] None of the fragments from the Hut 8 excavation showed the hole that would suggest they were being used as water bottles.

Table 2　Absolute and percentage frequencies of retouched tool types at five Masara C localities.

Locality	264[5]		300[6]		308[7]		260[8]		265[9]	
	(n)	%	(n)	%	(n)	%	(n)	%	(n)	%
1. End-scraper on flake	8	4.0	1	1.2			14	24.6		
3. Circular scraper							1	1.8		
4. Core-like end-scraper	1	0.5					2	3.5		
5. Denticulated end-scraper	7	3.5					1	1.8	1	2.3
6. Nosed end-scraper	2	1.0					8	14.0		
7. Notched end-scraper							1	1.8		
8. End-scraper on blade	4	2.0	7	8.1						
9. End-scraper on retouched blade					1	1.4				
11. Double end-scraper							2	3.5		
12. Single perforator	18	9.0	6	7.0			2	3.5	6	13.6
13. Perforator on backed bladelet	1	0.5								
16. Double-backed perforator	5	2.5	5	5.8	2	2.9	4	7.0	1	2.3
17. Dihedral burin	2	1.0			1	1.4				
20. Multiple dihedral burin					1	1.4				
45. Pointed straight-backed bladelet	1	0.5								
66. Fragment of backed bladelet	3	1.5								
72. Fragment, Ouchtata retouch	1	0.5								
74. Notched flake	18	9.0	1	1.2	6	8.6	3	5.3	5	11.4
75. Denticulated flake	12	6.0	1	1.2	2	2.9	5	8.8	5	11.4
76. Notched blade or bladelet	9	4.5	4	4.7	7	10.0	3	5.3	9	20.5
77. Denticulated blade or bladelet	6	3.0	8	9.3	15	21.4	4	7.0	2	4.5
78. Saw	2	1.0								
79. Notched or denticulated, continuous retouch	1	0.5	1	1.2						
80. Truncated piece	3	1.5	4	4.7						
82. Segment	1	0.5								
83. Isosceles trapeze	1	0.5	1	1.2						
85. Trapeze rectangle	1	0.5								
86. Trapeze, one side concave	5	2.5	1	1.2			1	1.8		
87. Trapeze, two sides concave	1	0.5	1	1.2					1	2.3
89. Isosceles or equilateral triangle	2	1.0	2	2.3						
90. Scalene triangle	1	0.5								
91. Triangle, one side concave	2	1.0	3	3.5						
92. Triangle, two sides concave	1	0.5	10	11.6	1	1.4				
101. Piquant-trièdre			1	1.2						
102. Microburin	14	7.0	12	14.0	6	8.6				
103. Krukowski microburin			1	1.2						
105. Piece with continuous retouch	32	16.0	4	4.7	9	12.9	3	5.3	10	22.7
107. Ounan point	23	11.6	12	14.0	19	27.1	3	5.3	1	2.3
108. Bou-Saâda point	1	0.5								
111. Tongued piece	1	0.5								
112. Varia	9	4.5							3	6.8
Total	**199**	**99.6**	**86**	**100.5**	**70**	**100.0**	**57**	**100.3**	**44**	**100.1**

[5] Tools from 68 sq m excavated to sterile soil, and from 40 sq m surface collected but not screened.

[6] All from surface to bedrock in 68 sq m.

[7] From surface of 320 sq m grid, and from excavated 24 sq m. All but 5 tools from excavated squares.

[8] From surface (not screened) of 2028 sq m grid, and from excavated 14 sq m.

[9] From surface (not screened) of 2100 sq m grid, and from excavated 24 sq m.

been recovered, site 83/39, 8200 bp, at Abu Ballas, south-west of Dakhleh Oasis, yielded five species, two of them southern, while ninth millennium bp sites in the Sand Sea yielded just two arboreal species (Neumann 1989). The other area with early Holocene charcoal, Nabta Playa, had 10 species (Wendorf *et al.* 2001, Table 21.26). However, this was not during the Masara C era, when there were at most three arboreal species (see below, Footnote 13), but later during the 'El Nabta/Al Jerar maximum humid interphase' starting 8050 bp (Wendorf *et al.* 2001, 650).

As for plant macro remains, some 49 types have been distinguished (U. Thanheiser, personal communication, October 2000). Aside from the grasses, all of the identified types require a moist environment (U. Thanheiser, personal communication, July 2002). The dominant type amongst the Masara C sites is *Portulaca oleracea*, an edible succulent herb found in open, wet habitats. Also prominent are *Scirpus maritimus* and *Cyperaceae*, a pair of sedges or marsh plants. Locality 263A, the Masara A site, lacks portulac, but has a relatively high proportion of grasses.

This palaeobotanical evidence for a fairly wet environment in south-eastern Dakhleh Oasis contrasts sharply with evidence for aridity elsewhere in the desert at the time. Hassan (1986; 1988, Figure 2; 1996; 2000) identifies a drier or erosional episode, dated *circa* 8800–8600 bp, in the sedimentological record for southern Egypt, and in a degradation of the Nile floodplain triggered by an oscillation in global climate. For the Nabta-Kiseiba area, Wendorf *et al.* (2001, 649) classify the period 8700–8600 bp as an arid phase. Within the Western Desert in general, there are relatively few radiocarbon dates for the first half of the ninth millennium, and particularly for the period *circa* 8700–8600 bp, suggesting a reduced human presence at the time (McDonald 1998a, Figure 3, 4).

Dating Evidence

For Masara A, considerable diversity is evident among the admittedly small, mostly surface collections in Table 1, and this may, in part, reflect a long span of time for the unit. The eight published dates for Masara A and B (Table 3) range from 9180 to 8170, or 9290 to 8060 at one standard deviation (McDonald 2001, 27). A new date of 7730 ± 110 (VRI-2054) for 263A may be too young (see below), but at face value indicates that this site is 1300 years younger than Locality 85.

The ten radiocarbon dates for Masara C, nine from the laboratory in Gliwice, and a new one from Vienna, are more clustered than the Masara A and B dates (Table 3). Except for one younger one, they fall between 9000 and 8500 bp, or 9070 to 8340 at one standard deviation, and average *circa* 8700 bp. The two dates from Locality 265

look somewhat younger than the others, although they do overlap with some of the older dates at one standard deviation. This conforms with the evidence from the toolkit, and particularly from the points, suggesting a somewhat later date for Locality 265.

The Evidence from Kharga Oasis

Wadi el-Midauwara

It now appears that the dichotomy between Masara A and Masara C, at least in terms of the lithic industry, is not confined to south-eastern Dakhleh. In 2000, KOPP geologists R. Giegengack and J. R. Smith drew my attention to sites in the Wadi el-Midauwara on the southern end of the Kharga Escarpment that show the same dichotomy. I did a little sampling of the area in 2000 and 2001 with Giegengack and Smith (Hawkins *et al.* 2001), and more detailed survey of part of the area in 2002 with C. S. Churcher and M. R. Kleindienst.

Several clusters and individual finds of Masara A-like material have been recorded. Locality MD-06 includes cobble-covered 'hearth mounds' and two or three probable slab structures on silts marking the west margin of a small basin. Scatters of Neolithic and later material also occur elsewhere in the basin. A grab sample of material was made in 2000, and the next year, a surface collection from 16 sq m around the hearth mounds. On MD-06 (Figure 8), all the points are fine Ounan points. There are drills, mostly parallel-sided, and a few short perforators on the ends of blades, including two on the distal ends of Ounan points (Figure 8i).[7] There are also notched and denticulated blades, and blades with backing. Ostrich eggshell fragments including a bead or two, and grinding stones, were recorded as well.

Small clusters of similar material, as well as isolated Ounan points, can be found in several of the aeolian depressions within the surveyed area. Masara A-like material constitutes one of the components on Locality MD-18, a large site with clusters of slab structures, which was occupied in the mid-Holocene as well (see below).

Only one Masara C-like locality has been recorded so far in this area. MD-05 consists of scatters of chipped stone and ostrich eggshell, several hearth mounds and a possible slab structure around playa silts on the margin of a basin. The lithic industry, mostly on local chert, is blade-oriented. Tools (Figure 9) include a dozen Harif points, denticulates with the nibbled notching, equilateral triangles and an elongated scalene triangle, various piercers and an end-scraper. A charcoal-rich soil sample was taken from one of the hearths, but no results are available yet. While one can find isolated examples of Ounan points throughout

---

[7] These two modified Ounan points are interesting in light of a long-standing debate as to whether 'Ounan points' might be *perçoirs* rather than arrowheads, the 'tang' in fact serving as the working end (for example Tixier 1955, 98; Clark 1976, 72). In this instance, we have apparently normal Ounan points with the *distal* end modified into a piercer.

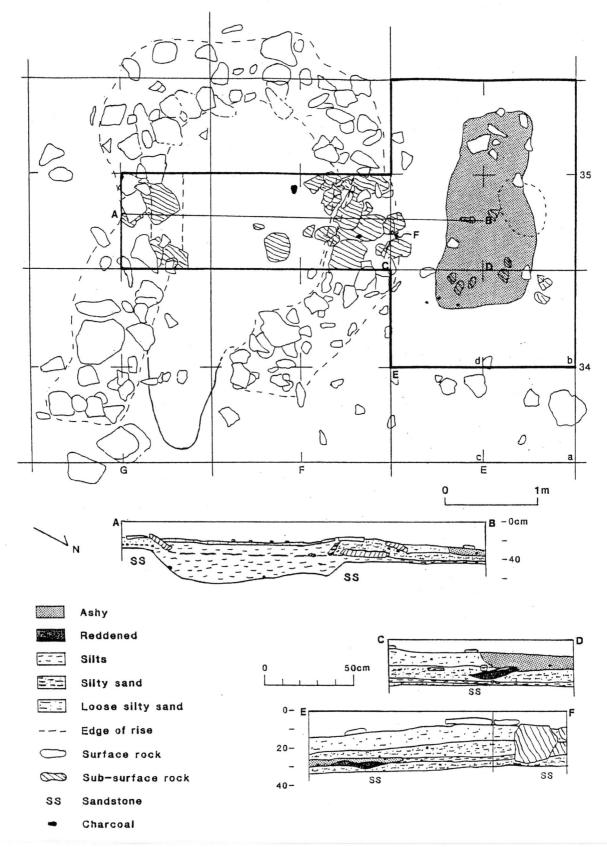

Figure 4 Dakhleh Locality 264, Hut 1: Plan, area excavated in 1998 (heavy line) and section across structure showing floor cut into bedrock (A–B). (To a different scale) sections of square E34d, W. balk (C–D) and E34d–E35c, S. balk (E–F) showing a surface hearth and a buried hearth respectively.
Solid line in G34a: outline of sloped entryway excavated in 2002.

this area, no Harif points were noted away from Locality MD-05.

The Epipalaeolithic elsewhere in Kharga Oasis

That there are Epipalaeolithic sites in Kharga Oasis is no surprise. Material, most of it Masara A-like, has been published by several earlier workers. The Epipalaeolithic is a component, together with mid-Holocene material, in Caton-Thompson's (1952) Bedouin Microlithic. Sites are recorded both on the oasis floor and atop the plateau to the east. She stresses (1952, 34) that these appear to be the temporary campsites of highly mobile desert dwellers, and indeed the Epipalaeolithic portion of the toolkit is predominantly Masara A-like, with deeply-notched blades, Ounan points, various backed bladelets, and elongated scalene triangles (Caton-Thompson 1952, Plates 94, 95, 97 and 98). On the other hand, the 'transverse arrowheads' (Caton-Thompson 1952, Plate 96) can be equated with the Masara C concave-sided trapezes and triangles.

Wendorf and Schild (1980, 188) recorded one 'Terminal Palaeolithic' site, E-76-6 on the oasis floor. The toolkit, with deeply notched blades, elongated scalene triangles and various backed bladelets, resembles Masara A. This was a small concentration near a spring vent representing one or more brief stops (Wendorf *et al.* 1984, 413). The CPE also noted another site at the edge of a basin on the Plateau well north of Kharga (Close 1992, 169; Wendorf *et al.* 2001, 655).

Simmons and Mandel (1986) report 'Terminal Palaeolithic' material on some of their survey transects on the northern part of the oasis and atop the Plateau. Most localities appear to be small campsites, but three on Transect 4 atop the Plateau are listed as 'villages' (Simmons and Mandel 1986, 118; 211), while a couple of the published artefacts, a possible Harif point, an end-scraper on an Aterian point (Simmons and Mandel 1986, Figures 27B and 28A) are reminiscent of Masara C.

In summary, Epipalaeolithic material has been recorded in spots on the floor of Kharga Oasis, and along stretches of the edge of the plateau top, where it is usually associated with silty pans. Most of this material resembles Masara A, but there is a little evidence to suggest a Masara C-like component as well.

The Nabta-Kiseiba Area of Southern Egypt

One other region where the dichotomy between Dakhleh's Masara A and Masara C can be detected is the Nabta-Kiseiba area of Southern Egypt. This area, with its rich early and mid-Holocene deposits, has been under investigation by the CPE since 1974. A good deal of fieldwork has been carried out, and the CPE has done an

admirable job of disseminating their results. Five monographs have been published to date (Wendorf and Schild 1980; Banks 1984; Wendorf *et al.*1984; Wendorf *et al.* 2001; and Nelson 2002), plus numerous articles and conference papers. Wendorf *et al.* (1984) published an archaeological sequence for 5000 years of the early and mid-Holocene. It consists of six successive taxonomic units distinguished on the basis of lithics, ceramics and dating evidence (Table 4). The 2001 volume presents a sequence revised to reflect new cultural, geomorphic and dating evidence suggesting a more complex history (Wendorf and Schild 2001, 648). One entity has been dropped from the sequence and new ones added, for a total of seven units, each terminated by an arid phase (Table 4).

Masara A and the CPE Sequence

The one date from Locality 263A suggests that it might be related to the Al Jerar phase of the CPE sequence dated 7900–7300 bp (Wendorf *et al.* 2001). In fact, while it shares with that entity the distinctive Ounan point, parallels on the whole are not close. Al Jerar lithic assemblages are less blady, with the ratio of blades to flakes rarely more than 10, while toolkits are dominated by pieces with continuous retouch, perforators, and sometimes scaled pieces. Locality 263A lacks the huts and other features of El Jerar, and of course, the pottery for which the phase was named (Wendorf *et al.* 2001, 325); at 263A, blades constitute 43% of blades and flakes in the debitage.

The radiocarbon chronology for Masara A and B as a whole suggests the unit may span two or more of the CPE early Holocene entities. As suggested in McDonald 1991b, however, the best parallels for Masara A in the CPE sequence, in terms both of artifact assemblages and site distribution, seem to be with the El Ghorab variant *circa* 8500–8200 bp (Wendorf *et al.* 2001, 654). On El Ghorab sites, good quality raw material was used to produce notched and denticulated blades and various bladelets. Other tools shared with Masara A include elongated scalene triangles, double-backed perforators, and a few Ounan points. El Ghorab sites are distributed widely across the eastern Sahara: besides the Nabta-Bir Kiseiba area, they occur in the Selima Sandsheet to the south, the Gilf el Kebir in south-western Egypt, the Dyke area between Nabta and Dakhleh, Farafra Oasis, and El Kab in the Nile Valley[8] (Close 1992, 168; Hassan *et al.* 2001, 38; Schuck 1993; Vermeersch 1978; Wendorf *et al.* 2001). Locality E-76-6 in Kharga Oasis, mentioned above, is an El Ghorab site.

Masara C and the CPE Sequence

For Masara C, the obvious parallel in the 2001 sequence initially might appear to be the Al Jerar unit, the only one

---

[8] Of these assemblages, the 263A collection most closely resembles that of the Dyke area site E-72-5 surface collection, in the percentages of various tool classes (Schild and Wendorf 1977, 129).

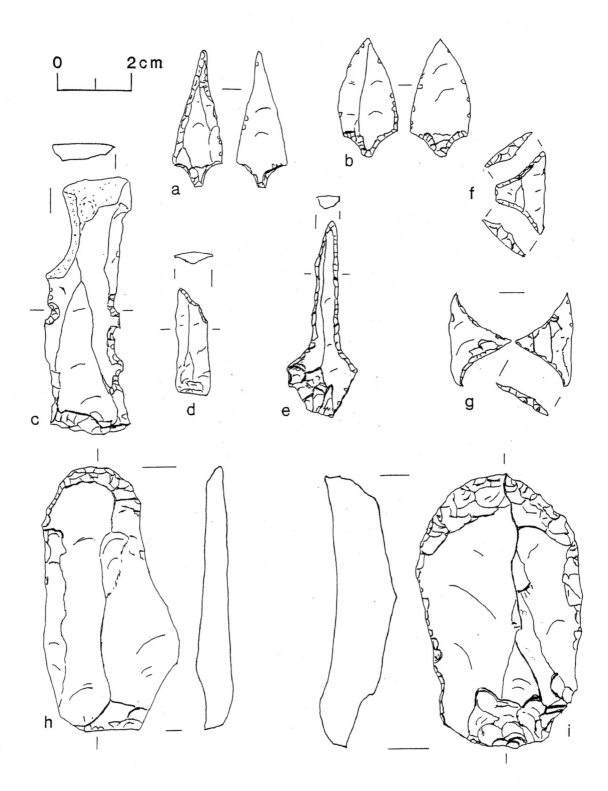

*Figure 5 Dakhleh Locality 300, chipped stone tools: **a** and **b**, Harif points; **c**, notch-denticulate; **d**, truncation; **e**, drill;*
***f**, trapeze with concave sides; **g**, triangle with concave sides; **h** and **i**, end scrapers.*

with the Ounan point, and one that also features hut structures and large pits. But Al Jerar is firmly dated *circa* 7900–7300 bp, many of its points arguably are different from the Harif points (see below), and the rest of the lithic toolkit, elongated scalene triangles, continuously retouched pieces, backed bladelets, etc., is not very similar to Masara C. Finally, pottery is abundant on Al Jerar sites, while not a sherd has been recorded on Masara C localities.

Another possible cognate is the El Adam, the earliest in the sequence (Wendorf *et al.*1984, 410). It does share with Masara C the double patinated end scrapers, a few trapezes, and such general traits as microburin technology, grindstones and abundant ostrich eggshell beads. Otherwise, though, it is not very close. The toolkit is dominated by backed bladelets, while geometrics are uncommon and consist mostly of elongated scalene triangles and the few trapezes. Denticulates are rare, there are no points, and there is pottery.

Much better parallels exist with the El Kortein entity (8800–8500 bp) that appears in the 1984 sequence but is left out of the 2001 version (Table 4). As defined in Wendorf *et al.*1984, the half-dozen El Kortein sites are small, widely scattered and poorly dated. In the 2001 version, these sites have been absorbed into the El Adam or El Ghorab units or the newly-defined Al Jerar entity, and the period 8700–8600 bp is reclassified as an arid phase (Wendorf *et al.* 2001, 319, 648–9). However, I would argue, partly of the basis of parallels with Dakhleh's Masara C, that the El Kortein is a legitimate unit as originally defined.

The principal El Kortein sites are E-75-6 (lower level) at Nabta Playa, E-77-3 at El Kortein Playa to the north, E-80-1 Area A and E-80-2 at El Adam Playa, E-79-1, Trench 1, lying northeast of Bir Kiseiba, and E-85-1, E-85-3 and E-85-5 at Bir Safsaf, 70 km west of Bir Kiseiba (Banks 1984, 67; Wendorf and Schild 1980, 108; Wendorf *et al.* 1984, passim; Wendorf *et al.* 1987, 58). All of them appear to be short-lived campsites associated with playas. Some have a few features: E-77-3, clusters of fire-cracked rock, a pair of 'hearth basins' with charcoal, and a slab-lined feature (Wendorf and Schild 1980, 108; Figure 3.34); E-75-6, a few firepits; E-80-1, possibly a deflated hearth. Most are quite small concentrations of artefacts: those at Bir Safsaf, no more than 4 to 6 m across (Wendorf *et al.* 1987, 58). All of these sites occupy the centre of their respective playas, and are thought to be dry-season occupations. Site E-80-2 on the other hand, a tight concentration *circa* 3 m across, is located near the southern margin of El Adam Playa and is thought to be a small wet season camp (Wendorf *et al.* 1984, 305). Faunal remains from El Kortein sites include two types of gazelle, hare, and from E-75-6 and E-77-3, cattle (Wendorf and Schild 1980, Table A4.3; Wendorf *et al.* 1984, 306). There are four radiocarbon dates from El Kortein sites (Wendorf *et*

al. 1984, 411). Two, from E-75-6 and E-79-1 are on ostrich eggshell, and when adjusted for isotopic fractionation, date to 8580 ± 80 and 8560 ± 70. Charcoal from the hearth basins on E-77-3 dates to 8840 ± 90. Another date on charcoal from E-75-6, 9320 ± 70, was not firmly associated with the assemblage and was rejected as too old.

El Kortein sites vary somewhat among themselves in their lithic assemblages (Wendorf *et al.* 1984, 296), and they differ from Masara C, notably in their emphasis on various backed bladelets. However, they share with Masara C many of that unit's distinctive traits. All El Kortein sites have Harif-like points (Wendorf and Schild 1980, Figure 3.39; Banks 1984, Figure IV:7; Wendorf *et al.* 1984, Figures 12.11, 13.3, 5.6, 5.8; Wendorf *et al.* 1987, Figure 13). Indeed, it was on the basis of tools from these sites that the CPE defined the 'Ounan-Harif' point (Wendorf and Schild 1980, 110, 259; Wendorf *et al.* 1984, 276, 304, 411). Moreover, I would argue that the El Kortein points as a whole are distinguishable from the points of the Al Jerar unit. Some of the Al Jerar points would fit easily in the El Kortein collections (e.g. Wendorf *et al.* 2001, Figures 7.18n; 8.28f, o; 8.43k). Others though are much closer to Ounan points (Wendorf *et al.* 2001, Figures 8.43g–j; 8.59e; 9.14f; 9.18e), while yet others may be evolving into something else (Wendorf *et al.* 2001, Figures 8.29i; 8.48c; 8.53h, i; 8.61j, k). Like Ounan points in general, Al Jerar points are longer and narrower than the El Kortein version,[9] and indeed, the CPE authors (Wendorf *et al.* 2001) refer to the Al Jerar tools as 'Ounan points' rather than 'Ounan-Harif points'.

Other Masara C tool types shared by El Kortein sites include thin-sectioned notches and denticulates with the small 'nibbled' notching (Wendorf and Schild 1980F Figures 3.38; Banks 1984, Figure IV:6; Wendorf *et al.* 1984, Figures 12.11; 13.3). With one or two exceptions (Wendorf *et al.* 2001, Figure 4.6o, for the El Adam unit), tools with that kind of notching do not occur in other CPE units. El Kortein sites have equilateral triangles and trapezes, often with concave sides (Wendorf and Schild 1980, Figures 3.39; 3.40; Banks 1984, Figure IV:7; Wendorf *et al.* 1984, Figures 12.10; 13.3; 5.8e). There are some examples of the drills with one end unmodified (Wendorf and Schild 1980, Figure 3.38g, h; Banks 1984 IV, 7r). End scrapers, while not numerous, are present, and some are fashioned on MSA flakes (Banks 1984, Figure IV:6m).

As for other artefact categories, grinding stones are rarely very distinctive. A pair of illustrated El Kortein handstones however, one from E-79-1 (a surface find), rectangular in outline with an oval cross section (Wendorf *et al.* 1984, Figure 5.10), and a flatter one from a pit on E-77-3 (Wendorf and Schild 1980, Figure 3.40 l) closely resemble Masara C tools from Locality 264. Close

---

[9] The 62 Ounan-Harif points from E-80-1 have a mean length:width ratio of 2.22 (Wendorf *et al.* 1984, 277), while the illustrated Al Jerar points (Wendorf *et al.* 2001) have a ratio of 2.82.

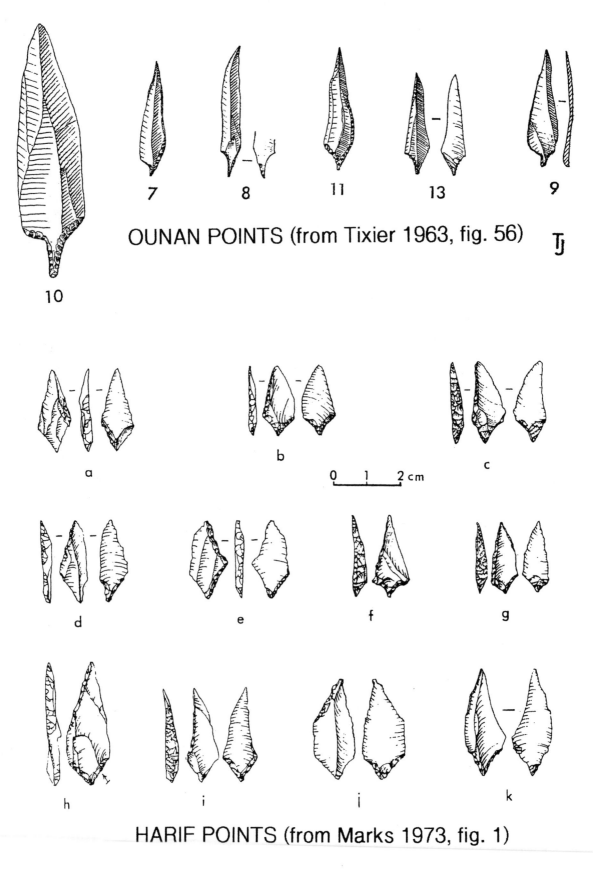

OUNAN POINTS (from Tixier 1963, fig. 56)

HARIF POINTS (from Marks 1973, fig. 1)

Figure 6 Ounan and Harif points.

(Wendorf *et al.* 1984, 278) reports a little cluster of handstones on E-80-1, Area A, that might be analogous to the clusters of three found on each of the large Masara C localities. Ostrich eggshell beads, usually < 10 mm in diameter, occur on El Kortein sites, as they do on many other Epipalaeolithic sites. On some sites, they were being manufactured (Banks 1984, Figure IV:8; Wendorf *et al.* 1984, 91). A few bone tools were found on E-75-6 (Banks 1984, Figure IV:8). Finally, although pottery occurs in the earlier El Adam unit, and in all later units in the Nabta-Kiseiba area, El Kortein sites, like Masara C sites, appear to be aceramic.

In summary, the half-dozen El Kortein sites share a number of traits, a distinctive point type, several other lithic tool types, even a lack of pottery, that mark them as different from sites in any of the other cultural units in the Nabta-Kiseiba area. These traits are, however, shared with the Masara C sites in Dakhleh Oasis. There are two pieces of excavated evidence that might help to confirm El Kortein's position as a separate entity within the CPE sequence. In the 2001 publication, site E-77-3, which had been the El Kortein type site, is said to consist instead of two components, an earlier El Adam occupation marked by backed bladelets and the dated hearth basin, and a later one with Ounan points and storage pits, assumed to belong to Al Jerar, but not yet studied (Wendorf *et al.* 2001, 319, 648). In fact, some of the contents of the dated hearth basin have been published and seem typical of El Kortein (Wendorf and Schild 1980, Figure 3.40). Aside from the backed bladelets they include an Harif point, a trapeze with one concave side, a denticulate and a notch, both with the small 'nibbled' notching, a truncation, a microburin and the flattish, sub-rectangular handstone mentioned above – all good Masara C (and El Kortein) material. The date on the basin, as mentioned above, is 8840 bp.

The other bit of excavated evidence to support a separate El Kortein entity comes from site E-80-1, Trench 2. Here some Ounan-Harif points were excavated in deposits that were stratified over material like that of site E-79-8 (an El Adam site dated *circa* 9000 bp) and under the El Nabta type of occupation of E-80-1, Area C, dated *circa* 8100 bp (Wendorf *et al.* 1984, 256, 305).

To conclude, there is considerable evidence to suggest that the El Kortein should be restored as a separate entity within the early Holocene sequence for the Nabta-Kiseiba area. Some of that evidence, as mentioned, comes from excavations. The bulk of it rests on comparisons with Masara C localities in Dakhleh Oasis. El Kortein and Masara C are quite dissimilar in terms of site location and site structure. The similarity lies rather in their artifact assemblages, and particularly their lithic toolkits. The radiocarbon dates seem to correspond fairly closely as well. The members of the CPE who contributed to the 2001 publication are not to be faulted for deciding to eliminate the El Kortein unit. As mentioned, it is largely when it is compared with the Masara C corpus that the distinctiveness

of the El Kortein within the CPE sequence becomes apparent. Little of the information on Masara C was available when the 2001 volume was being prepared, as Masara C has, to date, been but sketchily published. Only when all of us working in the area follow the CPE example and fully publish our material will the late prehistory of the eastern Sahara be put on a truly sound footing.

There is one other cultural unit defined by the CPE that might be related to Masara C. In the Nile Valley, Shamarkian sites on the west of the Nile at the Egyptian-Sudanese border have a chipped stone industry reminiscent of the Epipalaeolithic of the desert, including what could be Harif points (Wendorf 1968, Figure 45, 2–4 for site DIW 3; Figures 42, 30, 31 for DIW 53). There are triangles and trapezes as well, some with concave sides, and the notches, though made on Nile pebbles, are small and 'nibbled-looking' (Wendorf 1968, Figure 41, 14–18). However, such types as Bou Saadi points, backed bladelets and segments are more common here than on Masara C sites. The early Shamarkian sites are small compact camps on recessional beaches of the Nile (Wendorf 1968, 1052). There is a date of 7910 ± 120 for site DIW-53, and 8810 ± 90 for DIW-51 (Wendorf *et al.* 1979).

Finally, sites with remarkably similar artifact assemblages have now been documented in three widely separated regions within the Egyptian Western Desert: Dakhleh Oasis, Kharga Oasis, and the Nabta-Kiseiba-Safsaf area. There may be a similar presence in the Nile Valley. I propose that these three or four groupings of similar sites be termed the *Masara Complex*. The Masara Complex would include the Masara C sites from Dakhleh Oasis, MD-05 from Kharga Oasis, the El Kortein sites from the Nabta-Safsaf area and possibly the Shamarkian sites in the Nile Valley.

Masara A and Masara C within a Wider Cultural Setting

Masara A and the 'Ounanian'

The Ounanian in the Central Sahara

As noted above, Masara A localities in Dakhleh are best characterized as the temporary campsites of highly mobile hunter-gatherers. The closest cognate within the CPE sequence, in terms both of site distribution and artifact assemblages, is the El Ghorab unit. Sites of this type have been recorded across Southern Egypt including the Nile Valley. Further, Wendorf *et al.* (1984; also Schild and Wendorf 1977, 144) point to close similarities between El Ghorab assemblages, and those from certain Upper Capsian sites in the eastern Maghreb such as Dakhlat es-Saâdame (Tixier 1955). They cite the shared high indices of retouched, notched and denticulated blades, and of elongated scalene triangles.

It was the collection from Dakhlat es-Saâdame that Tixier used for his definitions of the Ounan point and the

Mary M. A. McDonald

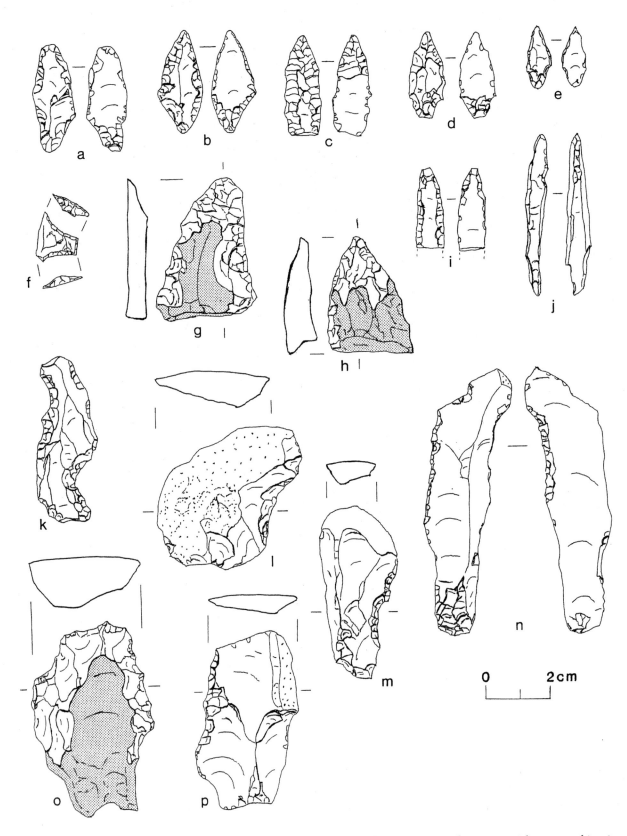

*Figure 7 Dakhleh Locality 265, chipped stone tools: **a–e**, arrowheads; **f**, trapeze with concave sides; **g**, combination tool, double patinated; **h**, point, double patinated; **i** and **j**, drills; **k–m**, notches/denticulates; **o**, denticulated end scraper, double patinated; **n** and **p**, retouched pieces.*

Bou Saada point[10] (Tixier 1955; 1963, 149–52 and Figures 56, 57). The name Ounan, however, comes from the site of Bir Ounan, far to the west in Mali, where the type was first recognized, in 1930, by H. Breuil. Breuil's term for his industry, 'Ounanian', has since been adopted by various authors (Alimen 1957; Camps 1974; Clark 1976; MacDonald 1998). There is as yet no consensus, however, as to what the term entails. Camps and Clark seem to agree that it is an early Holocene phenomenon, widespread across the Sahara from Mauritania to the Nile, and that it consists of small scattered sites left by highly mobile hunter-gatherers. It is characterized by the Ounan point, and sometimes the Bou Saada point, and otherwise by notched blades, by variously retouched, backed or truncated blades and bladelets, by piercers, and sometimes by burins. There is disagreement, however, about dating, about whether or not it has pottery, even about whether the Ounan point must be present.[11]

Clark (1980, 564) suggests that the Ounanian originated in the eastern Maghreb or Cyrenaica, and that its spread reflects the post-Pleistocene repopulation of the Sahara from this direction. Unfortunately, little firm dating evidence is available. Dakhlat es-Saâdame and related Maghrebi sites with Ounan points are assigned to the early Upper Capsian (Tixier 1963) which Lubell *et al.* (1984, 153) date to before 8000 bp. A. B. Smith (1993) argues, based on the sequence of lacustrine deposits near the Aïr mountains of Niger, where he and Clark found early to mid-Holocene material, that their Ounanian sites probably date to before 9500 bp.

As to pottery, Tixier (1963) reports Ounan points associated with pottery at Adrar Bous III (near Aïr) *circa* 5100 bp, while Roset (1987) describes an assemblage consisting of Ounan points and blade tools plus geometric microliths and pottery, from sealed deposits at Adrar Bous 10. This material is dated by conventional radiocarbon methods, as well as by thermoluminesence dating of the pottery, to between 9000 and 10500 bp (Roset 1996). Smith (1993) however argues that both Tixier's and Roset's are mixed industries. Tixier's collection is a surface sample where the Ounan points are mixed with later Ténérian Neolithic artifacts (Clark *et al.* 1973, 274). But Roset's excavated material likewise may have been mixed, through processes of deposition and deflation in the early Holocene (Smith 1993). Smith asserts, on the basis of the (mostly surface) material described in Clark *et al.* (1973; and Clark 1976), that there are three discrete post glacial industries in the Aïr – Adrar Bous area. The earliest is an Epipalaeolithic macroblade industry with the Ounan points. The second is the *Kiffian*, with geometric microliths, pottery, bone harpoons, and an aquatic fauna, which post-dates 7300 bp. The last is the *Ténérian*, with pottery, bifacial disc knives, adzes, polished axes etc., and food production.

Moving westward within the Ounanian distribution area, Breuil's industry from Bir Ounan in northern Mali, and another from nearby Araouan, were surface collections and are undated (Camps 1974). M. Raimbault (1990), based on a survey conducted 100 km south of Bir Ounan at Foum el Alba, uses the term Ounanian for one of his 'Neolithic' facies of the Malian Sahara. At a series of surface sites along the shore of a palaeolake dated *circa* 7000 bp, he found a blade industry made, as was that of Bir Ounan itself, on red quartzite. Tools include end scrapers, notches, piercers and other backed items, and a few Ounan points, associated with many grinding stones and two kinds of pottery. This is the earliest material he found in the area, which he had called 'Epipalaeolithic' in an earlier report (Raimbault 1983), although he suggests that there may be older sites buried under the lake deposits (Raimbault 1990, 70).

The Ounanian in the Eastern Sahara

In the eastern Sahara, as noted above, Ounanian sites can be traced right across to the Nile Valley, indeed to the coast of the Red Sea at Sodmein Cave (Vermeersch *et al.* 1996). It is interesting to note as well where the Ounanian, as defined at least by the presence of the Ounan point, is *not* found. None has been recorded in the Tadrat Accacus region of south-western Libya, which has been intensively studied for decades by teams from Italy (Close in Barich 1987; Cremaschi and Di Lernia 1999). These points however, are found nearby in the Fezzan, in the Wadi esh Shati (Petit-Maire 1982; Close 1992, 167), and possibly in the Wadi Lagaba (Alimen 1957, 158). No Ounan points are reported for the Besiedlungsgeschichte der Ost-Sahara (B.O.S.) sites along the western edge of Egypt and the Sudan (Kuper 1989). None has been found in the northern oases of Baharia (Hassan 1979), the Fayum (Caton-Thompson and Gardner 1934; Wendorf and Schild 1977; Wenke *et al.* 1988), or Siwa and the Qattara Depression (Hassan and Gross 1987). 'Shanked points' said to be comparable to the Ounan points of Kharga Oasis, were reported in the collections made by Willett-Cunnington in 1918 on the plateau above Siwa (McBurney and Hey 1955, 254). The illustrations (McBurney and Hey 1955, Figure 35, 6–9), however, are of 'Ounanian points' (see above, Footnote 3) which are probably later in time.

In the Western Desert of Egypt, the Ounanian initially appears to survive into the mid-Holocene, and pottery is associated with it throughout its span. If it is defined strictly by the presence of the Ounan point, within the CPE sequence it spans 1200 years to 7300 bp, from El Ghorab through the Al Jerar phases. In Farafra Oasis, Hassan *et al.* (2001, 39) report 'Ounan-Arif' points, described as laminar points with unifacial retouch, in an assemblage

---

[10] A pointed blade with basal concave retouch.

[11] Clark (1980, 563) for instance includes the Dyke site on his list, although no points were found there.

Table 3 Radiocarbon dates from Masara A, Masara B and Masara C localities in Dakhleh Oasis. Dates uncalibrated. Ostrich eggshell (OES) dates adjusted for isotopic fractionation; charcoal (CH).

Lab. No.	Material	Age bp	Adjusted Age bp	Locality Number
Masara A				
B 23684	OES	8720±100	9070±100	85
B 23694	OES	8650±150	9000±150	75
Gd-4563	OES	8650±170	9050±170	166
B 17022	OES	8270±160	8620±169	166
TO 2360	CH	8170±110		166
VRI-2054	CH	7730±110		263
Masara B				
B 23693	OES	8830±110	9180±110	194
B 23687	OES	8110±110	8460±110	200
Masara A or B				
B 23696	OES	8630±130	8980±130	197
Masara C				
Gd-6320	CH	8950±120		264
Gd-6318	CH	8660±90		264
Gd-5720	OES	8340±70	8730±70	264
Gd-7964	CH	8840±100		300
Gd-11323	CH	8220±140		300
Gd-7962	CH	8810±70		308
Gd-7965	CH	8710±80		308
VRI-2053	CH	8660±80		308
Gd-7966	CH	8590±100		265
Gd-11324	OES	8130±140	8480±140	265

Table 4 CPE archaeological sequence for the early and mid-Holocene for the Nabta-Kiseiba Area, following Wendorf et al. 1984 and Wendorf et al. 2001.

Wendorf *et al.* 1984	Wendorf *et al.* 2001
El Adam: 95–8900 bp	El Adam: 95–8900 bp
El Kortein: 88–8500 bp	Arid Phase: 87–8600 bp
El Ghorab: 85–8200 bp	El Ghorab: 85–8200 bp
El Nabta: 81–7900 bp	El Nabta: 81–7900 bp
	Al Jerar: 79–7300 bp
Middle Neolithic: 77–6200 bp	El Ghanam: 71–6600 bp
	El Baqar 65–5800 bp
Late Neolithic: 60–4600 bp	El Ansam 57–4500 bp

dated 5380 ± 110 bp. If however, the characteristic Ounanian adaptation of mobile hunter-gathering is the defining criterion, the Ounanian really ends in the CPE sequence at the close of the El Ghorab unit *circa* 8200 bp,[12] as the subsequent El Nabta and Al Jerar phases represent new, more settled ways of life, termed the 'intensive collector stage' in Wendorf *et al.* 2001, 658. Likewise in Farafra, the Ounan-Arif points are associated with Bashendi B-like ceramics and lithics, and so probably with a pastoralist adaptation (McDonald 1998b).

In Dakhleh Oasis, the 'Ounanian' or Masara A seems to have started earlier than around Nabta (Table 3), ends by 7700 bp at the latest, and is clearly distinguishable from the later Bashendi cultural unit. Very little pottery has been found on Masara sites, but in all cases, the finds are on Masara A and B localities. Sherds are profusely tempered with shale, fired to a wide range of colours and have uncoated compacted surfaces. Vessels are coil-built with apparently open forms (Hope 2002, 9).

The Bedouin Microlithic of Kharga Oasis

If in Dakhleh Oasis the Masara unit can be defined as strictly of early Holocene age, in Kharga Oasis, the case is not so clear. Caton-Thompson's Bedouin Microlithic includes artefacts that would in Dakhleh be classed as both Masara and Bashendi material, and the assumption is that her collections are mixed (Clark 1980, 563). Now, the new work in the Wadi el-Midauwara (see above) suggests that, in this part of Kharga at least, the two cultural units can indeed be distinguished. In Wadi el-Midauwara there are pure Masara-like sites such as MD-05 and MD-06, and pure Bashendi-like sites such as MD-24, which has bifacial arrowheads, knives and side-blow flakes. It also yielded a few sherds of rocker-stamped pottery, perhaps imported from the south (A. Warfe personal communication, January 2003).

MD-18, on the other hand, is the sort of site that Caton-Thompson would have used in defining the Bedouin Microlithic. The surface scatter includes such good Epipalaeolithic artefacts as Ounan points, double-backed perforators and notched blades, and Bashendi-like items such as bifacial arrowheads, knives and side blow flakes. Even here, though, the two units can be separated. MD-18 is a large site with three distinct clusters of stone circles, probable structures, for a total of about 85 units. The site was gridded and mapped, and controlled samples taken within two of the clusters. One of these, in fact the cluster where the structures are most deteriorated, yielded Epipalaeolithic artefacts: Ounan points, double-backed perforators, and so on. On the other, Cluster 2, the 10 sq

m sampled area yielded later material including seven Bashendi-like arrowheads and three knife fragments. Judging from its surface scatter, the third cluster (Cluster 3) likewise is of Bashendi age.

On the evidence from MD-18 and other Midauwara sites, then, it seems likely that in Kharga, as in Dakhleh, the Ounanian is strictly an early Holocene phenomenon.

Masara C and the Masara Complex within a Wider Setting

The Masara Complex: Accounting for the Unity

Sites with Harif points have a much more limited distribution in space and time than those with Ounan points. None are known from the Sahara beyond Egypt. Within Egypt, apart from the Sinai peninsula, recorded sites are confined to a few localities in the southern third of the country, most of them in the desert: in Dakhleh and Kharga Oases, Nabta Playa, Bir Kiseiba and Safsaf. The Nile Valley at Wadi Halfa with its Shamarkian sites may be included as well.

The homogeneity in the toolkits among the sites of the Masara Complex can not be explained in terms of similar adaptations to similar environments. Indeed, the environment of south-eastern Dakhleh Oasis in Masara C times, and that of the Nabta-Safsaf area, appear to be strikingly different. For the Masara C area, the palaeobotanical evidence, and particularly that from the plant macrofossils, suggests a verdant, even marshy environment (see above). There is some supporting evidence for this picture in the rich faunal remains from Locality 308, particularly from the possible wading birds. These apparent wetlands seem to have attracted people to settle to a degree unprecedented up to that time in the post-Pleistocene Eastern Sahara.

Environmental conditions in the Nabta-Kiseiba-Safsaf area seem to have been very different. In the 2001 publication, Wendorf and Schild classify the period 8700–8600 bp as an arid phase, although stating that the evidence, increased aeolian deposition under one of the El Ghorab sites, is not strong. It is clear, as stated above, that for the period 8800–8500 bp, there are very few sites in this part of Egypt, they are scattered over a wide area, and that each represents a small, short-lived campsite. There would have been some water about, as all El Kortein sites are associated with playa silts. Still, the little palaeobotanical evidence available, two charcoal samples that bracket the period, contained only tamarisk and acacia,[13] suggesting an impoverished arboreal vegetation compared with

---

[12] In a sense, even the El Ghorab would not qualify as a strictly hunter-gatherer adaptation. El Ghorab groups in the Nabta-Kiseiba area are listed as 'cattle-keepers', although the evidence consists of a single 'large bovid' bone from one site (Wendorf *et al.* 1984, Table 4.1).

[13] The samples were from site E-77-7, dated 8963 bp, with *Tamarix sp.*, and from E-91-1, Area B, dated 8500–8200 bp, with *Tamarix sp.*, *Acacia raddiana* type and *A. ehrenbergiana* (Barakat 1996, 64).

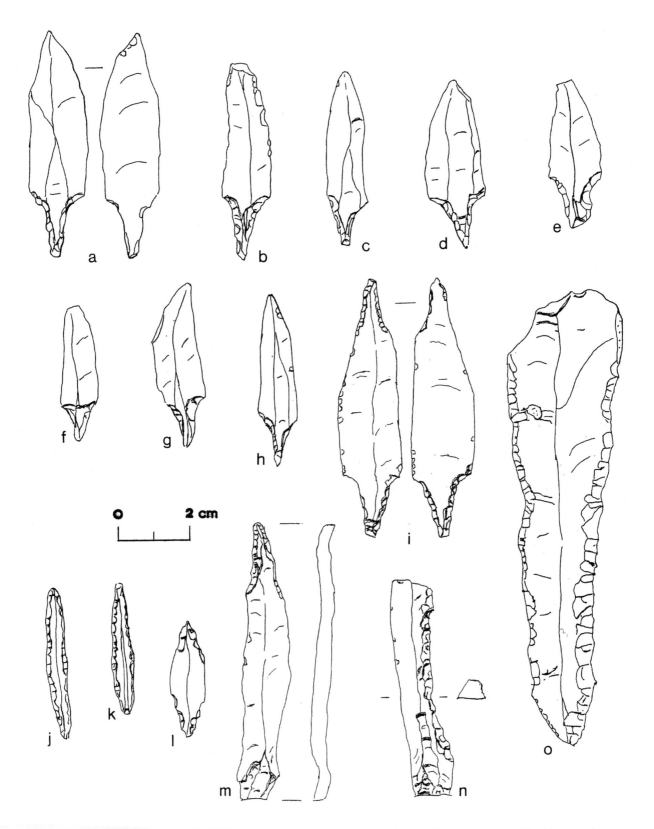

Figure 8 Kharga Locality MD-06, chipped stone tools: **a–h**, *Ounan points;* **i**, *Ounan point modified into perforator;* **m**, *perforator on end of blade;* **j–l**, *drills;* **n**, *steeply retouched blade;* **o**, *retouched blade.*

contemporary Dakhleh (see above), or with Nabta Playa itself by 8000 bp (Wendorf *et al.* 2001, 584 and Table 21.26). The short faunal list for the El Kortein sites supports the picture of an arid environment.

The third locale with a Masara C-like site, the small basin of Locality MD-05, just under the lip of the Plateau high above Kharga Oasis, is dramatically different from the other two. The soil sample from a hearth on Locality MD-05 will, it is hoped, shed light on conditions there at the time. The Wadi el-Midauwara must have been an attractive location generally in early to mid-Holocene times, judging by the number of sites recorded there, some, such as MD-18, with numerous structures.

The Nile Valley at the Egyptian border may also have been occupied by these groups. It appears to have been a somewhat impoverished environment at this time, to judge by the size of the Shamarkian sites.

Given the diverse environments occupied by these localities of the Masara Complex, plus the obvious differences in the sites themselves, in length of occupation, site features, in access to raw materials and so on, it appears that the shared toolkits are not explicable primarily in functional terms, as similar adaptations to similar environments. As difficult as it may be for a North American-trained archaeologist of a certain age to admit (Binford and Sabloff 1982), and despite the limited potential for lithics to carry stylistic information, in this case perhaps the most parsimonious explanation for the traits shared by these far-flung sites of the Masara Complex, is that they were all occupied by members of a single social (ethnic?) group (Bar-Yosef 1991; Henry in Goring-Morris *et al.* 1996).

This putative social entity seems in some ways to be intrusive to the Western Desert. It does not appear to have evolved from groups already in the area, such as Masara A or the El Adam entity in southern Egypt. In a region that already had a pottery-making tradition of several hundred years standing, the Masara Complex appears to be aceramic. It seems to be a relatively short-lived entity, with no obvious ties to the subsequent El Ghorab, for instance. Nevertheless, its characteristic point form, the Harif, seems to reappear several hundred years later in the El Jerar entity. In short, it remains in some ways ill defined.

The Masara Complex and the Harifian

If the Masara Complex is in fact a new group arriving in the Western Desert *circa* 8800 bp, an obvious question concerns its origins. New information on the subject may emerge when the Eastern Desert is more thoroughly explored. At present though, the only credible antecedent seems to be the Harifian itself, although it is a much older entity. In addition to the Harif point, it does share a number of traits with the Masara Complex.

Some 22 Harifian sites are recorded in the Negev and Northern Sinai (Goring-Morris 1987; 1991). Two major zones were occupied, probably on a seasonal basis. In the Negev highlands, sites are large and possess architecture, while in the lowland dune fields of the northern Sinai and western Negev, there are small, ephemeral campsites. On the highland sites, the largest of the structures are roughly circular, up to 3.5 m in diameter, semi-subterranean (up to 1.5 m deep), with walls built of local slabs and stones. There are hearths, work surfaces with cup-marks, stationary mortars and trash pits, but no storage facilities.

As for subsistence, the pounding and grinding equipment, and limited palaeobotanical evidence, suggest the exploitation of nuts and wild cereals (Goring-Morris 1987, 367). Faunal collections from the highland sites (Butler *et al.* 1977) include 12 species, ranging in size from rodent to onager, but they are dominated by gazelle and caprovines (ibex/wild sheep). Both these species would have been locally available, and there seems to be no question of incipient domestication (Butler *et al.* 1977, 342). Still, there are some oddities in the caprovine statistics. There is a far greater emphasis on goat at these sites than at most Natufian sites. The presence of heads shows that goat carcasses were carried intact to the site, and quite a high proportion of caprovines were under 2.5 years, although about half were over 3.5 years at death.

For their lithics industry, Harifians chose mostly local raw material, and their approach to knapping is characterized as 'opportunistic' and 'expedient' in terms of the manufacture, use and abandonment of artifacts (Goring Morris 1987, 386; 1991, 168).

Goring-Morris (1987, 354) lists several variants of the Harif point including the Proto-Harif and the Shunera, both thought to be forerunners of the Harif point, and perhaps some of the earliest arrowheads anywhere, and the Ounan point, which he describes as having a base like the Harif point, but with no retouch distally.[14] As for the Harif point, while generally similar to the Masara C point, the Harifian version is normally retouched on only one lateral, often using the microburin technique. Masara C points are more varied, ranging from little or no retouch on either lateral, through to full retouch on both.

Other Harifian tools include end scrapers on flakes or blades, described as shorter, squatter and thicker than those of other Epipalaeolithic industries in the area (Goring-Morris 1987, 349). Many bear a fine but somewhat irregular denticulation (Scott 1977, Figure 11.8). The denticulates *per se* include massive tools, but there are also thin-sectioned denticulates and notches with fine, somewhat irregular, almost 'nibbled' notching (Scott 1977, Figure 11.9). Geometrics are dominated by the somewhat elongated 'lunate/triangle' (Goring-Morris 1987, 350), although a few equilateral triangles are present as well (Goring-Morris 1987, Figure IX–7, 43–46). Other items

---

[14] Some of his illustrations look like classic north African Ounan points, others less so. Compare for example Goring-Morris 1991 figure 17, numbers 13 and 15.

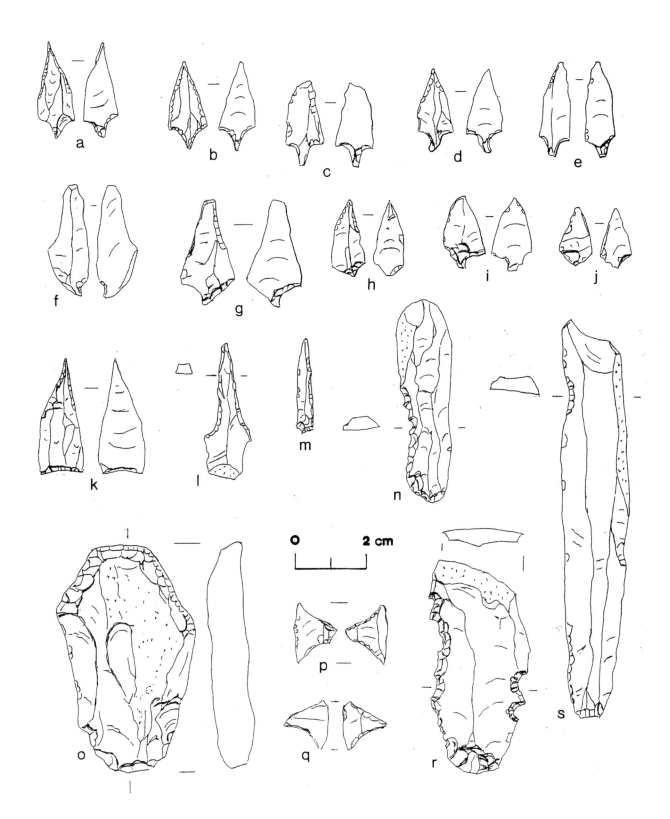

*Figure 9 Kharga Locality MD-05, chipped stone tools: **a–e**, **g–j**, Harif points; **k**, Bou Saada point; **f**, distal microburin; **l**, perforator or drill; **m**, elongated triangle; **n** and **r**, denticulates; **o**, end scraper; **p**, equilateral triangle; **q**, triangle, one side concave; **s**, retouched blade.*

in the toolkit include double-backed perforators and various retouched, truncated and backed items. The microburin technique was in use.

Other categories of artifact include various handstones, shaft straighteners, bone tools, and beads made of ostrich eggshell and stone, including turquoise and malachite. The Harifian, like all Levantine cultures of the early Holocene, is aceramic. Numerous marine shells attest to ties with the Mediterranean and the Red Sea, particularly the latter.

Concerning settlement patterns, highland sites are thought to be semi-sedentary residential base camps occupied from spring through autumn by perhaps two to three families engaged in hunting and harvesting wild plant foods. In the winter, people dispersed to small camps in the lowlands. Goring-Morris (1991, 209) estimates a total population of 200–500 individuals, given the size of the Harifian range (*circa* 20–30,000 sq km). He emphasizes the apparent stability and homogeneity of the Harifian entity over time.

The Harifian is dated *circa* 10750 to 10000 bp. It has been interpreted as an ultimately unsuccessful attempt by a Late Natufian population to adapt to the harsh dry conditions of the Younger Dryas (Bar-Yosef 1998; Goring-Morris 1987, 442). The Harifians are said to have disappeared without a trace (Goring-Morris 1987, 442), and their homeland would then be deserted for 1000 years (Goring Morris 1987, Figure XI-8; Bar-Yosef 1998).

Some time in the ninth millennium (there are two dates of 8640 and 8220 bp), the southern Sinai was reoccupied by groups associated with the Pre-Pottery Neolithic B (PPNB) of the Levant, but in this area, subsisting as hunter-gatherers and living in winter base camps somewhat reminiscent of the Harifian hamlets (Bar Yosef 1984). Helping to bridge the time gap between the Harifian and this PPNB entity is the site of Abu Maadi I, a Pre-Pottery Neolithic A (PPNA) site in the southern Sinai, with dates ranging from 10100 to 9800 bp. The lithic industry is said to resemble the Harifian, but the Harif point is replaced by a somewhat similar tool called the Abu Maadi point (Gopher 1994, 31).

As for ties with Egypt, there is some evidence for contact earlier in the Levantine Epipalaeolithic. The period 14500–11500 bp was a relatively wet one in the southern Levant (Bar-Yosef 1998), and there seems to have been traffic across the Sinai at this time. Tchernov (1976) reports African faunal elements in the Sinai and Negev, and the Mushabian and Ramonian industries of the Sinai and Negev (*circa* 14000–12500 bp) are thought to have originated in Africa (Goring-Morris 1987, 443). Indeed, Schmidt (1996), who has examined old surface collections from the site of Helwan near Cairo, the type site for Helwan retouch, the Helwan lunate and the Helwan point, reports Mushabian and Ramonian material at this site. He also suggests that the 'Helwan point' actually is part of the Sinai PPNB, and that its presence at Helwan shows that that culture had spread into the Nile Valley. As for the interval between the Mushabian and the PPNB, there is not much evidence of contact across the Sinai. However,

Schmidt (1996, 127) does report, without elaborating "… Harifian (without Harif points) type inventories …" in the collections from Helwan.

To sum up, there are some intriguing parallels between the Harifian and the Masara Complex. Aside from the Harif point, the two entities share a number of tool classes (many of them, of course, widespread in the Epipalaeolithic), and a few specific tool types, for instance among the scrapers, denticulates and geometrics. Comparing the Harifian highland sites and the Dakhleh Masara C sites, both take a largely expedient approach to their chipped stone industries. Both seem semi-sedentary, and they build their structures to roughly the same pattern. Both the Harifian and the Masara Complex also use small ephemeral campsites. If the faunal evidence for caprovines from a pair of Masara C sites is not simply intrusive, both units show an unusual focus on goats. Finally, both entities seem to display a marked cohesion and homogeneity, at least for the Masara Complex, in certain artefact classes, amongst far-flung sites. Of course there is the problem of the large chronological and spatial gap between the two entities. Indeed there is very little information for the critical tenth millennium bp from the lower Nile Valley or anywhere in Egypt. A few tentative links have been suggested, such as the PPNA and PPNB material from the southern Sinai, and the collections from Helwan. If there are ties between the Harifian and the Masara Complex however, they might not have flowed through the PPNA and PPNB, as the crucial Harif point, shared by the Harifian and the Masara C sites, disappears in those later industries.

Discussion

In summary, the two major Epipalaeolithic cultural units in Dakhleh Oasis, Masara A and Masara C, represent two dramatically different traditions. Masara A spans a long period, and the collections from individual sites are somewhat diverse. On the whole, though, it fits comfortably within a tradition known locally as El Ghorab, and more widely across the Sahara as the Ounanian. Sites in this grouping share a distinctive blade and bladelet dominated toolkit and usually, the Ounan point. Clark suggests that the Ounanian may have originated in the Maghreb at the end of the Pleistocene, although, as noted, a tool resembling the Ounan point occurs in the Harifian of the Negev and Sinai at roughly the same time.

Ounanian sites are characterized as the small temporary camps of highly mobile hunter-gatherers. The description is generally applicable to the El Ghorab sites as well, although these seem somewhat more varied in size and features than sites to the west. Some localities such as the Dyke site and Locality 263 in Dakhleh are extensive, and seem to represent repeated occupations of, or tethering to, favoured locales (McDonald 1991b, 104). There is also some evidence for structures on a few sites, usually the larger ones. At the Dyke site there are stone slabs and blocks that may be the dispersed foundations of huts (Wendorf *et al.* 2001, 655). In Dakhleh, somewhat enigmatic alignments of slabs were noted on Locality 263, and on Masara B Locality 194 (McDonald 1991b, 90). In Kharga Oasis, there are two or three probable slab structures on Locality MD-06, while on MD-18, the Masara A-like component is almost certainly associated with the remains of over a dozen structures. In the Nabta-Kiseiba area, there is some evidence for seasonality in site location, with plateau-top and basin centre sites possibly occupied in the rainy season and dry season respectively (Wendorf *et al.* 2001, 655).

The Masara Complex is much more restricted in time and space than the Ounanian. Masara Complex localities share a toolkit, but they otherwise vary dramatically, from the large semi-sedentary sites of the well-watered Masara C ridge in Dakhleh, to the small surface scatters in basin bottoms elsewhere in the Western Desert. Various questions remain respecting the nature of the unit, how the various sites are related, and concerning the origins and ultimate fate of the entity.

Given the relatively short time frame for the Masara Complex, the assumption that a single social group may be involved, and the somewhat restricted area geographically, it is possible that the various sites are components of a single seasonal round. On the whole though, this seems unlikely, given the still-substantial distances involved, *circa* 300 km from south-eastern Dakhleh to the Nabta-Safsaf area, for instance, and the fact that Masara C groups may have been tethered to their ridge for a substantial part of the year. In addition, there is a little evidence from the location of sites in the Nabta-Kiseiba-Safsaf area to suggest that that region itself may have been occupied during both the wet and the dry seasons (see above). If the Shamarkian sites are part of the Masara Complex, one might postulate a 'Southern Branch' of the Complex occupying the desert basins during and after the rainy season, but retreating to the Nile Valley for the latter part of the dry season, or during particularly arid years. The 'Northern Branch' then, in Dakhleh Oasis, or Kharga-Dakhleh, enjoyed a generally better watered environment where somewhat larger groups could gather, and a greater degree of sedentism was possible. Alternatively, the various localities in the southern third of the Western Desert might have been occupied sequentially over the course of the few centuries of the life of the Complex.

The question of the origins of the Masara Complex has been discussed above. As to its ultimate fate, there seem to be at least two possibilities. The Masara Complex might, as was suggested of the earlier Harifian, have been an ultimately unsuccessful attempt to adapt to the generally very arid conditions on the Western Desert in the first half of the ninth millennium bp. Alternatively, the Masara Complex may have survived to evolve or be absorbed into some later cultural entity. There are, for example, some intriguing parallels with the Al Jerar entity, in the survival there of Harif-like points, and in some site features, such as huts with hollowed out floors and tongue-like sloped entryways oriented to the east, similar to Locality 264,

Hut 1 in Dakhleh (Figure 4) and E-91-1, Area 9, Ft 1 in Nabta Playa (Wendorf *et al.* 2001, Figure 8.47).

There are still a number of avenues to pursue in investigating these issues. To date, the Masara Complex has been defined largely on the basis of lithic toolkits. Analysis of the debitage should reveal the extent to which these sites shared a similar approach to core preparation and reduction. Of course, more radiocarbon dates are needed. It would be particularly interesting to learn how dates from Kharga Locality MD-05 compare with the Masara C dates from Dakhleh. In addition, further fieldwork is needed in several areas. There is much yet to do on the rich Masara C ridge, particularly in testing the variety of sites and features there, and to pursue the questions surrounding the discovery of goat and ass bones on some of these sites. As yet, there has been little survey done on the south-western margins of Dakhleh Oasis, where one might expect Epipalaeolithic finds analogous to those in the south-east. Finally, the few days spent surveying the Wadi el-Midauwara in 2002, plus the material published by others for areas within that oasis, shows that there is still a great deal to learn about the Epipalaeolithic in Kharga Oasis.

Acknowledgements

Support for this research came from the Social Sciences and Humanites Research Council of Canada, the National Geographic Society, the Dakhleh Trust and the Department of Archaeology, University of Calgary. My thanks to F. A. Hassan, M. R. Kleindienst, U. Thanheiser and F. Wendorf who read and commented on an earlier version of this paper. Any errors of fact or interpretation are my own.

Author's Address:
Department of Archaeology
University of Calgary
Calgary,
Alberta,
Canada

REFERENCES

Alimen, H., 1957 *The Prehistory of Africa*, Hutchinson Scientific and Technical, London.

Banks, K. M., 1984 *Climates, Cultures and Cattle: the Holocene Archaeology of the Eastern Sahara*, Southern Methodist University Press, Dallas.

Barakat, H., 1996 Anthracological Studies in the Northeastern Sahara: methodology and preliminary results from the Nabta Playa, in L. Krzyzaniak, K. Kroeper and M. Kobusiewicz, eds, *Interregional Contacts in the Later Prehistory of Northeastern Africa*, Poznan Archaeological Museum, Poznan, 61–9.

Barich, B. E., 1987 *Archaeology and Environment in the Libyan Sahara: the Excavations in the Tadrat Acacus, 1978–1983*, BAR, Oxford.

Bar-Yosef, O., 1984 Seasonality among Neolithic Hunter-Gatherers in Southern Sinai, in J. Clutton-Brock and C. Grigson, eds, *Animals and Archaeology:3. Early Herders and their Flocks*, British Archaeological Reports, International Series 202, Oxford, 145–60.

Bar-Yosef, O., 1991 Stone Tools and Social Context in Levantine Prehistory, in G. A. Clark, ed., *Perspectives on the Past: Theoretical Biases in Mediterranean Hunter-Gatherer Research*, University of Pennsylvania Press, Philadelphia, 371–95.

Bar-Yosef, O., 1998 The Natufian Culture in the Levant, threshold to the origins of agriculture, *Evolutionary Anthropology* 6 (5), 159–77.

Binford, L. R. and J. A. Sabloff, 1982 Paradigms, Systematics, and Archaeology, *Journal of Anthropological Research* 38, 137–53.

Brooks, I. A., 1993 Geomorphology and Quaternary Geology of the Dakhla Oasis Region, Egypt, *Quaternary Science Reviews* 12, 529–52.

Butler, B. H., E. Tchernov, H. Hietala and S. Davis, 1977 Faunal Exploitation during the Late Epipalaeolithic in the Har Harif, in A. E. Marks, ed., *Prehistory and Paleoenvironments in the Central Negev, Israel, Vol. II, The Avdat/Aqev Area, Part 2, the Har Harif*, Southern Methodist University Press, Dallas, 327–45.

Camps, G., 1974 *Les Civilisations préhistoriques de l'Afrique du Nord et du Sahara*, Doin, Paris.

Caton-Thompson, G., 1952 *Kharga Oasis in Prehistory*, Athlone Press, London.

Caton-Thompson, G. and E. W. Gardner, 1934 *The Desert Fayum*, Royal Anthropological Institute, London.

Clark, J. D., 1976 Epi-palaeolithic aggregates from Greboun Wadi, Aïr, and Adrar Bous, North-western Tenere, Republic of Niger, in B. Abebe, ed., *Proceedings of the Panafrican Congress of Prehistory and Quaternary Studies, VIIth Session – 1971*, Addis Abada, 67–78.

Clark, J. D., 1980 Human Populations and Cultural Adaptations in the Sahara and the Nile during Prehistoric Times, in M. A. J. Williams and H. Faure, eds, *The Sahara and the Nile: Quaternary Environments and Prehistoric Occupation in Northern Africa*, Balkema, Rotterdam, 527–82.

Clark, J. D., M. A. J. Williams and A. B. Smith, 1973 The Geomorphology and Archaeology of Adrar Bous, Central Sahara: a preliminary report, *Quaternaria* XVII, 245–97.

Close, A. E., 1992 Holocene Occupation of the Eastern Sahara, in F. Klees and R. Kuper, eds, *New Light on the Northeast African Past*, Heinrich Barth Institut, Koln, 155–83.

Cremaschi, M. and S. DiLernia, 1999 Holocene Climate Changes and Cultural Dynamics in the Libyan Sahara, *African Archaeological Review* 16, 211–38.

Gabriel, B., 1987 Palaeoecological Evidence from Neolithic Fireplaces in the Sahara, *African Archaeological Review* 5, 93–103.

Gopher, A., 1994 *Arrowheads of the Neolithic Levant: a Seriation Analysis*, Eisenbrauns, Winona Lake.

Goring-Morris, A. N., 1987 *At the Edge: Terminal Pleistocene Hunter-Gatherers in the Negev and Sinai*, BAR, Oxford.

Goring-Morris, N., 1991 The Harifian of the Southern Levant in O. Bar-Yosef and F. R. Villa, eds, *The Natufian Culture in the Levant*, Ann Arbor, 173–216.

Goring-Morris, N., D. O. Henry, J. L. Phillips, G. A. Clark, C. M. Barton and M. P. Neeley, 1996 Pattern in the Epipalaeolithic of the Levant: debate after Neeley and Barton, *Antiquity* 70, 130–47.

Hassan, F. A., 1979 Archaeological Explorations at Baharia Oasis and the West Delta, Egypt, *Current Anthropology* 20, 806.

Hassan, F. A., 1986 Desert Environment and Origins of Agriculture in Egypt, *Norwegian Archaeological Review* 19, 63–76.

Hassan, F. A., 1988 The Predynastic of Egypt, *Journal of World Prehistory* 2, 135–85.

Hassan, F. A., 1996 Abrupt Holocene Climatic Events in Africa, in G. Pwiti and R. Soper, eds, *Aspects of Archaeology: Papers from the 10th Congress of the Pan-African Association for Prehistory and Related Subjects*, University of Zimbabwe Publications, Harare, 83–9.

Hassan, F. A., 2000 Holocene Environmental Change and the Origins of Food Production in the Middle East, *Adumatu* 1, 7–28.

Hassan, F. A., B. Barich, M. Mahmoud and M. A. Hemdan, 2001 Holocene playa deposits of Farafra Oasis, Egypt, and their palaeoclimatic and geoarchaeological significance, *Geoarchaeology* 16, 29–45.

Hassan, F. A. and G. T. Gross, 1987 Resources and Subsistence during the early Holocene at Siwa Oasis, Northern Egypt, in A. E. Close, ed., *Prehistory of Arid North Africa: Essays in Honor of Fred Wendorf*, Southern Methodist University Press, Dallas, 85–103.

Hawkins, A. L., J. R. Smith, R. Giegengack, M. M. A. McDonald, M. R. Kleindienst, H. P. Schwartz, C. S. Churcher, M. F. Wiseman and K. Nicoll, 2001 New Research on the Prehistory of the Escarpment in Kharga Oasis, Egypt, *Nyame Akuma* 55, 8–14.

Holl, A., 1989 Social Issues in Saharan Prehistory, *Journal of Anthropological Archaeology* 8, 313–54.

Holmes, D. L., 1991 Analysis and Comparison of some Prehistoric Projectile Points from Egypt, *Institute of Archaeology Bulletin* 28, 99–132.

Hope, C. A., 2002 Early and Mid-Holocene Pottery from the Dakhleh Oasis: traditions and influences, in R. Friedman, ed., *Egypt and Nubia; Gifts of the Desert*, British Museum Press, London, 39–61.

Kleindienst, M. R., this volume, Strategies for Studying Pleistocene Archaeology based upon Surface Evidence: First Characterization of an Older Middle Stone Age Unit, Dakhleh Oasis, Western Desert, Egypt, 1–42.

Kleindienst, M. R., C. S. Churcher, M. M. A. McDonald and H. P. Schwarcz, 1999 Geography, Geology, Geochronology, and Geoarchaeology of the Dakhleh Oasis Region: an interim report, in C. S. Churcher and A. J. Mills, eds, *Reports from the Survey of Dakhleh Oasis, Western Desert of Egypt, 1977–1987*, Oxbow Books, Oxford, 1–54.

Kuper, R., 1989 The Eastern Sahara from North to South: data and dates from the B.O.S. Project, in L. Krzyzaniak and M. Kobsiewicz, eds, *Late Prehistory of the Nile Basin and the Sahara*, Polish Academy of Sciences, Poznan, 213–23.

Lubell, D., P. Sheppard and M. Jackes, 1984 Continuity in the Epipalaeolithic of Northern Africa with Emphasis on the Maghreb, *Advances in World Archaeology* 3, 143–91.

MacDonald, K., 1998 Archaeology, Language and the Peopling of West Africa: a consideration of the evidence, in R. Blench and M. Spriggs, eds, *Archaeology and Language II: Archaeological data and Linguistic Hypotheses*, Routledge, London, 33–66.

Marks, A. E., 1973 The Harif point: a new tool type from the Terminal Epi-paleolithic of the central Negev, Israel, *Paléorient* 1, 97–9.

McBurney, C. B. M. and R. W. Hey, 1955 *Prehistory and Pleistocene Geology in Cyrenaican Libya*, Cambridge University Press, Cambridge.

McDonald, M. M. A., 1990 The Dakhleh Oasis Project: Holocene Prehistory: interim report on the 1991 season, *Journal of the Society for the Study of Egyptian Antiquities* XX, 65–76.

McDonald, M. M. A., 1991a Systematic Reworking of Lithics from Earlier Cultures in the Early Holocene of Dakhleh Oasis. *Journal of Field Archaeology* 18, 269–73.

McDonald, M. M. A., 1991b Technological Organization and Sedentism in the Epipalaeolithic of Dakhleh Oasis, Egypt, *African Archaeological Review* 9, 81–109.

McDonald, M. M. A., 1998a Adaptive Variability in the Eastern Sahara during the Early Holocene, in S. di Lernia and G. Manzi, eds, *Before Food Production in North Africa*, A.B.A.C.O., Forlì, 127–36.

McDonald, M. M. A., 1998b Early African Pastoralism: view from Dakhleh Oasis (South Central Egypt), *Journal of Anthropological Archaeology* 17, 124–42.

McDonald, M. M. A., 2001 The Late Prehistoric Radiocarbon Chronology for Dakhleh Oasis within the Wider Environmental Setting of the Egyptian Western Desert, in C. A. Marlow and A. J. Mills, eds, *The Oasis Papers 1: The Proceedings of the First Conference of the Dakhleh Oasis Project*, Oxbow Books, Oxford, 26–42.

McDonald, M. M. A., 2002 Holocene Prehistory: Interim Report on the 1997 and 1998 Seasons: the Masara Sites, in C. A. Hope and G. E. Bowen, eds, *Dakhleh Oasis Project: Preliminary Reports on the 1994–1995 to 1998–1999 Field Seasons*, Oxbow Books, Oxford, 7–14.

Nelson, K., 2002 *Holocene Settlement of the Egyptian Sahara. Volume 2: The Pottery of Nabta Playa*, Kluwer Academic/ Plenum Publishers, New York.

Neumann, K., 1989 Zur Vegatationsgeschichte der Ostsahara im Holozan. Holzkohlen aus prahistorischen Fundstellen, in R. Kuper, ed., *Forschungen zur Umweltgeschichto der Ostsahara*, Heinrich-Barth-Institut, Köln, 13–181.

Petit-Maire, N., 1982 *Le Shati. Lac pléistocène du Fezzan (Libye)*, Editions du Centre National de la Recherche Scientifique, Paris.

Raimbault, M., 1983 Industrie Lithique, in N. Petit-Maire and J. Riser, eds, *Sahara ou Sahel? Quaternaire récent du Basin de Taoudenni (Mali)*, Editions du Centre National de la Recherche Scientifique, Paris.

Raimbault, M., 1990 Pour une approche du Néolithique du Sahara ien, *Travaux du LAPMO*, 67–81.

Roset, J.-P., 1987 Paleoclimatic and Cultural Conditions of Neolithic Development in the Early Holocene of Northern Niger (Aïr and Ténéré), in A. Close, ed., *Prehistory of Arid North Africa: Essays in Honor of Fred Wendorf*, Southern Methodist University Press, Dallas, 211–34.

Roset, J.-P., 1996 La ceramique des debuts de l'Holocene au Niger Nord-oriental. Nouvelles datations, bilan des recherches, *The Prehistory of Africa, Volume 15, The Colloquia of the XIII International Congress of Prehistoric and Protohistoric Sciences*, A.B.A.C.O., Forlì, 175–82.

Schild, R. and F. Wendorf, 1977 *The Prehistory of Dakhla Oasis and Adjacent Desert*, Ossolineum, Wroclaw.

Schmidt, K., 1996 Helwan in Egypt – a PPN site?, in S. K. Kozlowski and H. G. K. Gebel, eds, *Neolithic Chipped Stone Industries of the Fertile Crescent, and their Contemporaries in Adjacent Regions*, Ex Oriente, Berlin, 127–35.

Schuck, W., 1993 An Archaeological Survey of the Selima Sandsheet, Sudan, in L. Krzyzaniak, M. Kobusiewicz and J. Alexander, eds, *Environmental Change and Human Culture in the Nile Basin and Northern Africa until the Second Millennium B.C.*, Poznan Archaeological Museum, Poznan, 215–22.

Scott, T. R., 1977 The Harifian of the Central Negev, A. E. Marks, ed., in *Prehistory and Paleoenvironments in the Central Negev, Israel, Vol. II, The Avdat/Aqev Area, Part 2, the Har Harif*, Southern Methodist University Press, Dallas, 271–322.

Simmons, A. H. and Mandel, R. D., 1986 *Prehistoric Occupation of a Marginal Environment: An Archaeological Survey near Kharga Oasis in the Western Desert of Egypt*, BAR, Oxford.

Smith, A. B., 1993 Terminal Palaeolithic Industries of the Sahara: a discussion of new data, in L. Krzyzaniak, M. Kobusiewicz and J. Alexander, eds, *Environmental Change and Human Culture in the Nile Basin and Northern Africa until the Second Millennium B.C.*, Poznan Archaeological Museum, Poznan, 69–75.

Tchernov, E., 1976 Some Late Quaternary Faunal Remains from the Avdat/Aqev Area, in A. E. Marks, ed., *Prehistory and Paleoenvironments in the Central Negev, Israel, Volume I, The Avdat/Aqev Area, Part 1*, Southern Methodist University Press, Dallas, 69–73.

Tixier, J., 1955 Les abris sous roche de Dakhlat es-Saâdane (Commune mixte de Bou-Saâda): I. – Les industries en place de l'Abri B, *Libyca* 3 (1), 81–128.

Tixier, J., 1963 Typologie de l'Epipaléolithique du Maghreb. *Mémoires du Centre de Recherches Anthropologiques, Préhistoriques et Ethnographiques, No. 2*, Artes et Métiers Graphiques, Paris.

Vermeersch, P. M., 1978 *Elkab II. L'Elkabien, Epipaléolithique de la Vallée du Nil Egyptien*, Fondation Egyptologique Reine Elisabeth, Leuven.

Vermeersch, P. M., P. Van Peer, J. Moeyersons and W. Van Neer, 1996 Neolithic Occupation of the Sodmein Area, Red Sea Mountains, Egypt, in G. Pwiti and R. Soper, eds, *Aspects of Archaeology: Papers from the 10th Congress of the Pan-African Association for Prehistory and Related Subjects*, University of Zimbabwe Publications, Harare, 411–19.

Wendorf, F., 1968 *The Prehistory of Nubia*, Volume II, Southern Methodist University Press, Dallas.

Wendorf, F., A. E. Close and R. Schild, 1987 A Survey of the Egyptian Radar Channels: an example of applied archaeology, *Journal of Field Archaeology* 14, 43–63.

Wendorf, F. and R. Schild, 1976 *Prehistory of the Nile Valley*, Academic Press, New York.

Wendorf, F. and R. Schild, 1980 *Prehistory of the Eastern Sahara*, Academic Press, New York.

Wendorf, F., R. Schild and Associates, 2001 *Holocene Settlement of the Egyptian Sahara. Volume 1: The Archaeology of Nabta Playa*, Kluwer Academic / Plenum Publishers, New York.

Wendorf, F., R. Schild (assemblers) and A. E. Close (editor), 1984 *Cattle-Keepers of the Eastern Sahara: the Neolithic of Bir Kiseiba*, Department of Anthropology, Institute for the Study of Earth and Man, Southern Methodist University, Dallas.

Wendorf, F., R. Schild and H. Haas, 1979 A New Radiocarbon Chronology for Prehistoric Sites in Nubia, *Journal of Field Archaeology* 6, 219–23.

Wenke, R. J., J. E. Long and P. E. Buck, 1988 Epipalaeolithic and Neolithic Subsistence and Settlement in the Fayyum Oasis of Egypt, *Journal of Field Archaeology* 15, 29–51.

Health and Disease of Neolithic Remains from Sheikh Muftah, Dakhleh Oasis

Jennifer L. Thompson and Gwyn D. Madden

Introduction

The dental and skeletal remains of six individuals, from the mid-Holocene (late Neolithic to Old Kingdom) of Dakhleh Oasis, Egypt, were excavated between 1997 and 2000. Preliminary reports on the dentition (Thompson forthcoming) and the skeletons (Thompson 2002) are presented elsewhere. The purpose of this paper is to report on the pathologies associated with these individuals that give insight into the lifeways, behaviour, and health of the mid-Holocene peoples of Dakhleh Oasis.

Artefacts attributed to the Sheikh Muftah Unit are loosely associated with the burials, found on a deflated surface near and/or above each individual. McDonald *et al.* (2001) provide details of these artefacts, which include pottery, ground stone, copper fragments, and chipped stone. These authors state that this cultural unit probably dates to *circa* 5200–4000 bp (see also McDonald 2001, 35).

McDonald *et al.* (2001), report that the Sheikh Muftah sites are located near the centre of the oasis, possibly near the remaining water sources. Faunal fragments from various Sheikh Muftah Localities were examined by Churcher (1983, 183; see also Churcher 1999). These remains were highly fragmented, which may indicate that these people were attempting to maximize any resources available to them (McDonald 1999, 124). This is an interesting find, as during this time the environs of Dakhleh Oasis were becoming increasingly more arid. McDonald (1993; 1996; 1998; 1999; 2001) reports that by 5000 bp, the desert surrounding the Dakhleh Oasis would have provided little in the way of dietary resources to the local peoples. The question at hand, then, is to assess the skeletal remains of these peoples to determine if they reveal any evidence reflecting their biological and/or cultural response to an increasingly arid environment. We appreciate that such a small sample of individuals cannot be representative of an entire population. Together with the available archaeological material, however, the results of this analysis are pertinent to the overall picture of the mid-Holocene of Dakhleh Oasis and provide comparative biological data against which to assess future discoveries.

Skeletal Remains

The skeletal material that is the subject of this paper comes from two regions in Dakhleh Oasis. As reported by Thompson (2002), five individuals were discovered south and west of the cultivation near the village of Sheikh Muftah, and one individual was discovered west of the cultivation near Balat (McDonald *et al.* 2001 for a map of Sheikh Muftah Localities and village locations; Thompson 2002 for GPS readings). Three individuals were recovered from Locality 365 near Sheikh Muftah and are numbered 365-1, 365-2 and 365-3 in order of their discovery. 365-1 was a male of about 17–20 years of age, 365-2 was a male of about 40–45 years of age, while 365-3 was a female about 20–25 years of age (Thompson 2002). This Locality is particularly interesting because it was once capped by sandstone fragments that were likely imported from several hundred meters away. Most of the skeletal material was recovered from the north-western side of the mound, although bone was scattered over the whole surface. Two of the skeletons were found north of the mound and are mostly intact, while the third individual was on the west slope of the mound. This latter individual, 365-1, had probably been buried, but wind action had exposed the bones for a number of years before it was discovered by M. Kleindienst in 1997 and so now it is mainly in fragments. These surface remains were recovered in 1997 by J. L. Thompson. The two articulated skeletons, 365-2 and 365-3, both had their heads at the west end of their graves. They were located in situ and excavated in 1998 and 1999 by J. L. Thompson.

Locality 375 is several hundred meters from Locality 365. Here, two burials were exposed to the surface and most of the remains were fragmentary, 375-1, a male about 25–35 years old; and 375-2, unknown sex, about 30–35 years old. Both specimens were flexed burials with their heads at the south end. They were excavated in 1997 by J. L. Thompson. The surface around Localities 365 and 375 includes one or several deflated spring mounds and it is covered with archaeological material attributed to the Sheikh Muftah Unit.

Table 1 Sheikh Muftah Dental Pathologies.

Pathology	100-1	365-1	365-2	365-3	375-1	375-2
Abscess		X				X
Dental Caries			X	X	X	X
Enamel Hypoplasia	X?	X	—	X	X	X
Enamel Hypocalcification	—	X	—	X	X	X
Periodontal Disease		X	X			

Locality 100, near Balat, was discovered by M. McDonald and a colleague in 1982. Remains of a burial were found and the more intact pieces of skeleton removed at that time. The authors of this paper recently, in 2000, re-excavated the site and located several teeth and many bone fragments from this individual (100-1) who was an adult male. A second individual was buried close by and will be excavated in future. Sheikh Muftah cultural remains are also abundant on the surface of this locality.

Links between Regions and Sites

The one associated artefact, found with the male individual, 365-2, consisted of a copper pin. While this copper pin could be interpreted as a status symbol, "the lack of noticeable burial monuments or of elaborate grave goods … reinforces the picture of small, egalitarian groups" (McDonald *et al.* 2001, 9) during Sheikh Muftah times. Of interest is the fact that copper pins were also recovered from burials of several males in a Predynastic cemetery at Hierakonpolis, dating to *circa* 3600–3400 BC. One pin from that site was found in a leather pouch tied at the man's waist and hanging from the hip (Friedman 1998, 5). The discovery of a copper pin under the hip of the male individual 365-2 suggests a common behavioural practice. The fact that McDonald (personal communication) estimates that the Sheikh Muftah cultural unit extended from 3800 to 2200 BC certainly indicates a temporal overlap between the two sites. This does not mean a direct connection between Hierakonpolis and Dakhleh Oasis (see Hope 2002, 58) although this has been suggested by Friedman (cited 2002, 58 in Hope). It simply provides additional evidence for a connection between the Nile Valley and Dakhleh.

Ceramics imported from the Nile Valley have been recovered from several Sheikh Muftah Localities (Hope 2002, 51), including Locality 100, as well as at older localities associated with the Bashendi Cultural Unit. According to Hope (2002, 52) "Ceramics indicate that the Dakhleh occupants maintained contacts with regions far to the west, to the south and south-east during the Bashendi B and early Sheikh Muftah Cultural Units, while imports from the Predynastic cultures of Egypt occur from the early phase of the Sheikh Muftah Cultural Unit onward in small numbers". Thus there is convincing cultural evidence of links between Dakhleh and other places within Egypt prior to, and during, Sheikh Muftah times.

As there is only one artefact directly associated with the burials in Dakhleh, and no radiocarbon dates are available for them, it is more difficult to decide whether the individuals from the three localities were contemporaries. Ceramics from Locality 100 are from the Late Sheikh Muftah Cultural Unit (Hope 2002, 51). Ceramics from the other two localities, 365 and 375, while attributed to the Sheikh Muftah Cultural Unit, have not yet been analysed in detail. Several of the more complete individuals were buried in a flexed position indicating that a similar mortuary pattern was practised (365-2, 365-3, 375-1 and 375-2). This pattern was likely practised throughout Sheikh Muftah times, however, and so does not indicate synchronous habitation of the region by these individuals. Thus the archaeological evidence does not currently help to address this issue.

The biological evidence does not resolve this issue either. Three of individuals, two from near the village of Sheikh Muftah (365-1 and 365-2) and one from Locality 100, share the biological characteristic of expansion of the protocone, resulting in a large increased bucco-lingual breadth of one or more maxillary molars. This shared feature requires further investigation to determine its significance.

It is not improbable that individuals buried at each locality were in some way related to each other. The likelihood that two or three individuals were buried in such close proximity to each other, at each of these separate localities, simply by coincidence is difficult to credit. Thus, some relationship, genetic or cultural, between individuals buried adjacent to each other at Locality 365, for example, is feasible. Convincing evidence of any connections between the three localities however, must await further research.

Pathologies

Each individual was examined for the presence of dental and skeletal pathologies. These pathologies are listed in Tables 1 and 2 and will be discussed further below.

Several individuals experienced both enamel hypoplasia and enamel hypocalcification in several of their teeth (Table 1). The location, number of episodes per tooth, and teeth affected will be published elsewhere as this degree of detail is beyond the scope of the present paper. Presence of hypoplastic lines are suggestive of stress events during the developmental period, including periods of poor nutrition,

Table 2 Sheikh Muftah Skeletal Pathologies.

Pathology	100-1	365-1	365-2	365-3	375-1	375-2
Porotic Hyperostosis		X				X
Compression Fracture			X			
Arthritis			X			
Sclerotic Bone					X	
Enthesopathic Lesion			X			

infectious disease, high parasite load, and weaning practices (Goodman and Rose 1991, 1992; Buikstra and Ubelaker 1994, 56; Malville 1997, 351; Wright 1997, 233). While some enamel defects may have occurred at weaning, others appear to occur throughout the teeth and indicate long-term stress throughout the formation of the dentition. For example, 375-1 and 365-3 both exhibit several hypoplastic pits on at least one of their third molars, which probably occurred at about the age of 10 years. Whereas in rare instances hypoplastic events can also be caused by hereditary anomalies and localized trauma (Goodman and Rose 1991; Malville 1997), the added presence of enamel opacities suggests that systematic stress from disease or poor nutrition may have been the cause of these events. Additionally, it has been demonstrated that individuals suffering from enamel defects experience a reduced life expectancy (Duray 1996).

Another of the dental pathologies noted in several individuals is root caries (Table 1). This type of carious lesion begins at the neck of the tooth and works its way up to the crown; once the lesion reaches this state it can lead to tooth loss or infection of the alveolar bone possibly creating an abscess. Once an abscess is formed, this can lead to blood poisoning and, without treatment, can cause death (Aufderheide and Rodriguez-Martin 1998, 403). In fact, two of the individuals in this study each suffered from an abscess (365-1 and 375-2), possibly the condition that led to their death.

Root caries are the product of periodontal disease (Aufderheide and Rodriguez-Martin 1998, 404), which in turn is most commonly caused by severe attrition in archaeological populations. When the tooth crown is worn down below the point of interproximal contact, a sulcus can result between the gingiva and tooth cervix, creating a food trap. Plaque calcifies to form calculus, widening the sulcus and can lead to a vertical defect in the bone next to the root, ultimately leading to tooth loss (Aufderheide and Rodriguez-Martin 1998, 401–4). This type of periodontal disease is known as vertical bone loss, affecting one or two teeth at a time (as opposed to horizontal bone loss affecting the bone under several teeth along the tooth row) (Hillson 1996, 263–6). The food trap also allows bacteria to multiply near the neck of the tooth, contributing to the formation of root caries. Periodontal disease was present in two individuals, 365-1 (*circa* 17–25 years of age) and 365-2 (40+ years old) with erosion of the alveolar bone around one or more teeth.

Turning to the skeletal evidence (Table 2), porotic hyperostosis affected two of the individuals in the study, 365-1 and 375-2. Small perforations were seen on both the frontals and the parietals, but can be described overall as minimal. Due to the age of the individuals, and what appears to be bone thickened from the healing process, the perforations appear to be remnants of a past event (Buikstra and Ubelaker 1994, 151). The etiological agent or process causing porotic hyperostosis has not yet been identified; however, it is known that individuals suffering from the condition are anaemic, indicating physical stress (Fairgrieve and Molto 2000). Researchers are debating whether diet (malnutrition), infectious agents, or malaria are responsible for the anaemic condition (Angel 1967; Stuart-Macadam 1992; Fairgrieve and Molto 2000).

Periostitis, or sclerotic bone (Buikstra and Ubelaker 1994, 136), was noted on the femoral shaft of individual 375-1 during analysis. This condition is recognizable during the healing phase as new bone is formed. Periostitis can be caused by trauma, infection, or disease and is therefore a non-specific indicator of diminished health. It also correlates with other biological indicators of stress, like porotic hyperostosis (Aufderheide and Rodriguez-Martin 1998, 129; Ortner 2003, 208–9).

Individual 365-2, the 40+-year-old male, presented with a compression fracture (stage 2–3, following Rah and Errico 1998) of one of the cervical vertebrae, probably C3 or C4 but the bone is still covered in matrix. This stage of severity indicates that the fracture was stable and would not have caused the death of this individual. It likely required little, if any, medical treatment. Compression fractures of this type can be related to repetitive micro-trauma, trauma, and loss of bone mass (Rah and Errico 1998). According to Lovell (1994), cervical compression fractures are more common among individuals who carry objects on their heads.

Arthritis or Degenerative Joint Disease is influenced by age, sex, genetics, and mechanical stress (Larson 1997). Individual 365-2, shows signs of Degenerative Joint Disease in the presence of bony spicules or osteophytes on the bodies of the vertebrae. This individual also showed signs of Degenerative Joint Disease at the shoulder and elbow. Arthritic changes in these joints frequently point to repetitive occupational activities (Aufderheide and Rodriguez-Martin 1998, 93–6).

This 40+-year-old male, 365-2, (Thompson 2002) was powerfully built, as indicated by the muscle attachment areas. In addition, this individual presented with several enthesophytes on the heel. Enthesophytes are musculoskeletal markers of strenuous activities and appear as bony spicules at ligament and tendon attachments (Larson 1997, 188; Cox and Mays 2000, 387–8). These are thought to be the result of mechanical stresses related to high levels of walking and running (Larson 1997, 189), suggesting that this individual was very physically active.

Discussion

Climatic information indicates that the Sheikh Muftah period was a decreasingly hospitable time, with an increase in aridity in the surrounding region (McDonald *et al.* 2001). Shallow, open water or swamp is suggested by the presence of oysters, at least west of the Balat cultivation (McDonald 1982) and this is an indication that the water in the region may have been drying up, and may have contributed to the restriction of the inhabitants to the more central part of the oasis. The stress evidenced in the dental and skeletal pathologies of this group may be due to worsening conditions imposed by the changing environment and give some insight into the economy, behaviour, and health of these people.

No archaeological materials are directly associated with the burials to suggest their economic strategy but, assuming they lived during Sheikh Muftah times, the presence of domestic fauna imply pastoralism, while the presence of wild fauna indicate limited hunting (McDonald *et al.* 2001). The occurrence of root caries and heavy dental wear however, suggests an increased dependence on starch-rich plant foods.

Patterns of dental caries and types of subsistence patterns have been linked. Hillson (1996, 283) states that the rate of dental caries is low in hunter-gatherer diets that contain meat and plant foods low in carbohydrates. In contrast, carious lesions at the root are most common in adults among people practising cereal agriculture. This is not only due to the change in diet, which includes more dietary starch, but to the ingestion of food items that continuously abrade the occlusal surface of the teeth, which may reduce the incidence of pit or fissure caries on those surfaces, the initial carious lesion being abraded away before it can affect the remaining tooth. In populations whose diet includes refined food, high in sugars, pit, fissure, and inter-proximal caries are more common (Hillson 1996, 283–4). Thus the incidence of root caries in this sample suggests that some degree of agriculture was being practised.

The degree of dental wear in the Dakhleh dental sample supports this finding. According to Aufderheide and Rodriguez-Martin (1998, 404), "The addition of abrasives to the food by grinding grains with stone mills or manes and metates (grinding stones) can accelerate attrition enormously, leading to loss of proximal contact, periodontitis, and root caries". McDonald *et al.* (2001) report the presence of ground stone in the Sheikh Muftah Cultural Unit indicating that some grinding of food took place. They also hypothesize that archaeological changes

seen over the course of the Holocene may reflect increasing sedentism or an increased reliance on cultivars during the Sheikh Muftah period. This hypothesis may be substantiated, in the future, by the analysis of dental calculus found on the teeth of the individual 100-1 (Dobney and Brothwell 1986; Fox *et al.* 1996). Thus these findings need further corroboration, but suggest that these people were practising some form of agriculture, or else were incorporating more cereals or wild plant food into their diet.

Inferences of past behaviour can be made from biological information in combination with archaeological data. For example, individual 365-2 lived to about 40+ years and thus survived long enough to develop several incidents of what appear to be age-related arthritis throughout his body. Evidence of arthritis linked to repetitive activities and the presence of a mechanically-induced enthesopathic lesion on his heel however, suggests a highly active lifestyle for this person. The association of a copper pin with this active individual, an artefact also found associated with men buried in the Nile Valley, supports the idea (McDonald *et al.* 2001) that there was some contact between the Nile Valley occupants and peoples of the outlying oases, a fact confirmed by the ceramic evidence (Hope, 2002).

In terms of health, many of these individuals are dying young compared to life expectancy rates today. Although age estimates are slightly confounded by the amount of wear on the occlusal surface of the dentition (Thompson 2002), it can be estimated that the average life expectancy for these people was approximately 30 years of age. It can be seen from both the dental and skeletal pathological evidence that these individuals were subjected to consistent periods of health stress. As seen in Tables 1 and 2, diminished health is indicated by enamel hypoplasia and/or hypocalcification in all but one individual (365-2). Root caries and/or periodontal disease is seen in all but individual 100-1, whose molar teeth are coated in calculus. The two individuals with a dental abscess both present porotic hyperostosis (365-1, 375-2), which is related to anaemia, while one with enamel defects and root caries also presented periostitis (375-1). Thus there are multiple signs of impaired health in this small sample. The causes of these health stress-producing events are unknown, but possibilities may include diet (including food preparation techniques), malarial infection, or parasitic infestation.

Conclusions

As reported above, McDonald (1993; 1996; 1998; 1999; 2001) states that by 5000 bp, the desert surrounding the Dakhleh Oasis would have provided little in the way of dietary resources. Thus any skeletal and dental finds from the mid-Holocene are important, not simply because this time period was previously undocumented in terms of physical remains, but because they may provide information about how people adapted to, or were impacted by, the changes in their environment. The analysis presented in this paper and elsewhere (Thompson 2002), while based only on a small sample of six individuals, provides biological data that can be interpreted in conjunction with the more plentiful archaeological evidence. The dental evidence points to an increase in plants as part of the diet, a result that is in accord with the archaeological data. Together, these findings may indicate a shift in food availability, as well as a shift in economic strategy as the result of environmental deterioration in this area. The discovery of a copper pin, like ones found with burials in the Nile Valley, is consistent with evidence indicating that people travelled between the Nile Valley and the outlying oases of the western desert. Finally, the pathological evidence indicates that nutritional stress, and perhaps disease, affected the health of these people, lending support to the hypothesis that the mid-Holocene was a period of economic stress for the Sheikh Muftah people.

Acknowledgements

In 1997 and 1998, this project was supported by travel grants from Social Sciences and Humanities Research Council and from the Division of Social Sciences, University of Toronto at Scarborough. Funding for the 1999 season was provided from the Department of Anthropology and Ethnic Studies, University of Nevada, Las Vegas. We would like to thank the Egyptian authorities for permission to work in the Dakhleh Oasis. The authors would also like to acknowledge the continued support of the Department of Anthropology and Ethnic Studies, University of Nevada, Las Vegas.

Authors' Address:

Department of Anthropology
University of Nevada,
4505 Maryland Parkway,
Box 455012,
Las Vegas,
Nevada 89154-5012,
U. S. A.

REFERENCES

Angel, J. L., 1967 Porotic hyperostosis or Osteoporosis symmetrica, in D. Brothwell and A. T. Sandison, eds, *Diseases in Antiquity: A Survey of the Diseases, Injuries & Surgery of Early Populations*, Charles C. Thomas, Springfield, 378–89.

Aufderheide, A. C. and C. Rodriguez-Martin, 1998 *The Cambridge Encyclopedia of Human Paleopathology*, Cambridge University Press, Cambridge.

Buikstra, J. E. and D. H. Ubelaker, eds, 1994 Standards for Data Collection from Human Skeletal Remains, *Arkansas Archaeological Survey Research Series* 44.

Churcher, C. S., 1983 Dakhleh Oasis Project – Palaeontology: Interim Report on the 1982 field season, *Journal Society for the Study of Egyptian Antiquities XIII*, 178–87.

Churcher, C. S., 1999 Holocene faunas of the Dakhleh Oasis, in C. S. Churcher and A. J. Mills, eds, *Reports from the Survey of the Dakhleh Oasis, Western Desert of Egypt, 1977–1987*, Oxbow Books, Oxford.

Cox, M. and S. Mays, 2000 *Human Osteology in Archaeology and Forensic Science*, Greenwich Medical Media, London.

Dobney, K. and D. Brothwell, 1986 Dental Calculus: its relevance to ancient diet and oral ecology, in E. Cruwys and R. A. Foley, eds, *Teeth and Anthropology*, BAR, Oxford, 55–81.

Duray, S. M., 1996 Dental indicators of stress and reduced age at death in prehistoric Native Americans, *American Journal of Physical Anthropology* 99, 275–86.

Fairgrieve, S. I. and J. E. Molto, 2000 Cribra orbitalia in two temporally disjunct population samples from the Dakhleh Oasis, Egypt, *American Journal of Physical Anthropology* 111, 319–31.

Fox, C. L., J. U. Juan and R. Albert, 1996 Phytolith analysis on dental calculus, enamel surface, and burial soil: information about diet and paleoenvironment, *American Journal of Physical Anthropology* 101, 101–14.

Friedman, R., 1998 More Mummies: The 1998 Season at HK 43, *Nekhen News* 10, 4–6.

Goodman, A. H. and J. C. Rose, 1991 Dental enamel hypoplasias as indicators of nutritional stress, in M. A. Kelley and C. S. Larsen, eds, *Advances in Dental Anthropology*, Wiley Liss, New York, 279–94.

Hillson, S., 1996 *Dental Anthropology*. Cambridge University Press, Cambridge.

Hope, C. A., 2002 Early and Mid-Holocene Ceramics from the Dakhleh Oasis: Traditions and Influences, in R. Friedman, ed, *Egypt and Nubia Gifts of the Desert*, The British Museum Press, London, 39–61.

Larson, C. S., 1997 *Bioarchaeology: Interpreting Behavior from the Human Skeleton*, Cambridge University Press, Cambridge.

Lovell, N. C., 1994 Spinal arthritis and physical stress at Bronze Age Harappa, *American Journal of Physical Anthropology* 93, 149–64.

Malville, N. J., 1997 Enamel hypoplasia in ancestral Puebloan populations from southwestern Colorado: I. Permanent Dentition, *American Journal of Physical Anthropology* 102, 351–67.

McDonald, M. M. A., 1982 Unpublished Field Notes.

McDonald, M. M. A., 1993 Cultural Adaptations in Dakhleh Oasis, Egypt, in the Early to Mid-Holocene, in L. Krzyzaniak, M. Kobusiewicz and J Alexander, eds, *Environmental Change and Human Culture in the Nile Basin and Northern Africa until the Second Millennium B.C.*, Poznan Archaeological Museum, Poznan.

McDonald, M. M. A., 1996 Relations between Dakhleh Oasis and the Nile Valley in the Mid-Holocene: a discussion, in L. Krzyzaniak, K. Kroeper and M. Kobusiewicz, eds, *Interregional Contacts in the Later Prehistory of Northeastern Africa*, Poznan Archaeological Museum, Poznan, 93–9.

McDonald, M. M. A., 1998 Early African Pastoralism: View from Dakhleh Oasis (South Central Egypt), *Journal of Anthropological Archaeology* 17, 124–42.

McDonald, M. M. A., 1999 Neolithic Cultural Units and Adaptations in the Dakhleh Oasis, in C. S. Churcher and A. J. Mills, eds, *Reports from the Survey of the Dakhleh Oasis, Western Desert of Egypt, 1977–1987*, Oxbow Books, Oxford, 117–32.

McDonald, M. M. A., 2001 The Late Prehistoric radiocarbon chronology for Dakhleh Oasis within the wider environmental and cultural setting of the Egyptian Western Desert, in C. A. Marlow and A. J. Mills, eds, *Proceedings of the First Conference of the Dakhleh Oasis Project*, Oxbow Books, Oxford, 26–42.

McDonald, M. M. A., C. S. Churcher, U. Thanheiser, J. L. Thompson, I. Teubner and A. R. Warfe, 2001 The mid-Holocene Sheikh Muftah Cultural Unit of Dakhleh Oasis, South Central Egypt: a preliminary report on recent fieldwork, *Nyame Akuma* 56, 4–10.

Ortner, D. J., 2003 *Identification of pathological conditions in human skeletal remains*, Elsevier Science, New York.

Rah, A. D. and T. J. Errico, 1998 Classification of lower cervical fractures and dislocations, in C. Clark, ed., *The Cervical Spine*, Lippincott-Raven, Philadelphia, 449–56.

Stuart-Macadam, P., 1992 Anemia in past human populations, in P. Stuart-Macadam and S. Kent, eds, *Diet, Demography, and Disease: Changing Perspectives on Anemia*, Aldine De Gruyter, New York, 151–70.

Thompson, J. L., 2002 Neolithic Burials at Sheikh Muftah, A Preliminary Report, in C. A. Hope and G. E. Bowen, eds, *Dakhleh Oasis Project: Preliminary Reports on the 1994–1995 to 1998–1999 Field Seasons*, Oxbow Books, Oxford, 43–5.

Thompson, J. L., forthcoming Neolithic Dental Remains from Sheikh Muftah, Dakhleh Oasis: A Preliminary Report, in M. F. Wiseman, ed., *The Oasis Papers II: Proceedings of the Second International Conference of the Dakhleh Oasis Project*, Oxbow Books, Oxford.

Wright, L. E., 1997 Intertooth patterns of hypoplasia expression: implications for childhood health in the Classic Maya Collapse, *American Journal of Physical Anthropology* 102, 233–47.

Interregional Contacts with the Sudan: Ceramic Evidence from the Mid-Holocene Period

Ashten R. Warfe

Introduction

For several decades, evidence accumulated across northern Africa has shown that interregional contact during the mid-Holocene was extensive in range and frequency. One of the most accepted arguments for this rests on the widespread distribution of pottery with impressed designs, in particular the 'dotted wavy-line' motif, or variations thereof, first defined by Arkell (1949, 84–7). Examples have been recovered across the Sahara from early and mid-Holocene sites in central and northern Niger (Roset 1987, 218–22), south-western Libya (Barich 1987, 105) through to the south of Egypt (Banks 1980, 307). The dotted wavy-line pottery is, of course, found also in the Middle Nile Valley region (Mohammed-Ali 1982; Caneva 1988) where it was thought to have originated (Arkell 1949; 1953). While this point of origin is now disputed, it is still unclear where, exactly, the beginnings of this tradition lie (Mohammed-Ali 1982, 160; 1987, 132; Caneva 1987, 250–1; 1993, 409–10). In any case, the spread of impressed pottery and several other Neolithic traits is generally believed to have occurred along an east-west transect, to and from the Middle Nile Valley. It is within this expanse that Camps' (1974, 219) Saharo-Sudanese Neolithic is placed. For some time the boundaries of this cultural horizon were not considered to extend into Egypt much beyond the Nabta-Kiseiba region. The oases of the central Western Desert of Egypt,[1] for instance, are still often seen as peripheral to the wider spread of cultural flow in north-

eastern Africa during prehistoric times (Barich and Hassan 1984–7, 184; cited in McDonald 1992, 57–8). Yet recent studies are beginning to suggest otherwise.

During the early 1990s pottery reminiscent of the Saharo-Sudanese Neolithic was found at Dakhleh along with other items that compare with the Neolithic assemblages of central Sudan. These unexpected finds inspired McDonald (1992) to investigate possible links between the mid-Holocene oasis groups and those at home in the Middle Nile Valley region. In her paper McDonald (1992, 63–6) concluded, primarily on account of lithic and ground-stone evidence, that Dakhleh was included within the wider circulation of traits associated with the Saharo-Sudanese Neolithic. Moreover, McDonald suggested that Dakhleh may have played a central role in the innovation and spread of cultural traits at this time.

The current paper looks to the ceramic record to see if it supports McDonald's (1992) argument. Preliminary studies on the early Dakhleh pottery (Hope 2002) found that a few examples compare with the material produced to the south of the oasis, well beyond the central Western Desert. The intent of this paper is to determine whether these examples can be used to demonstrate ties with the Neolithic of the Sudan. In addition, this paper looks at whether the exchange of pottery between Dakhleh and central-northern Sudan was a two-way affair, or whether the oasis was simply on the receiving end of the cultural flow.[2] Some comments on the causal mechanisms behind the spread of pottery are also offered.

---

[1] For convenience, the term 'central Western Desert' is used here in reference to the region of Egypt in which Dakhleh, Farafra, Kharga, Lobo, Abu Mingar, Abu Gerara and Abu Ballas are located (Figure 1). Although this term is not intended to carry any further meaning, it should be noted that these areas appear to belong to one regional tradition. Thus the term assumes cultural as well as geographical boundaries. In contrast, areas south of Abu Ballas (but still within Egypt) including the Nabta Playa, Bir Kiseiba and the Gilf el-Kebir, are referred to here collectively as the southern Western Desert of Egypt.

[2] In a recent overview of the Neolithic pottery from Dakhleh, Hope (2002, 41–5) argued that several of these examples may be compared with Sudanese pottery traditions. Hope (2002, 41–5) also points out that pottery from the oasis resembles material found in regions further west. While this is something that certainly requires further attention it is beyond the scope of the current paper, which is intended primarily as a study in drawing ceramic associations with the south.

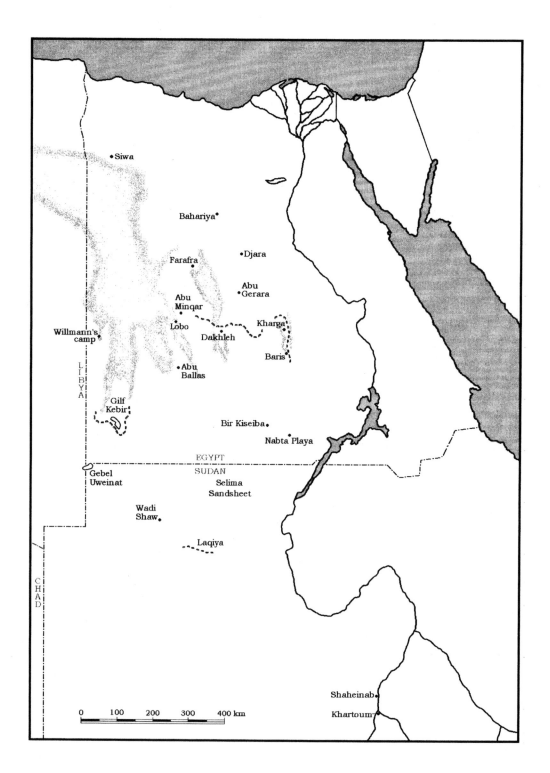

Figure 1 Map of Egypt and Sudan with sites mentioned in the text.

The Mid-Holocene Bashendi Cultural Unit: Settlements and Subsistence

The mid-Holocene cultural units that are of interest here are the Bashendi A, dated 7600–6800 bp, and the Bashendi B, dated 6500–5200 bp. Besides being temporally separate, the units differ in subsistence strategies, patterns of adaptation and in site location. The following is a brief overview of each cultural unit (for more detailed reports see McDonald 1998; 2001, 33–5).

Bashendi A sites are found atop the northern plateau and throughout Dakhleh. Most sites are located, however, in the south-eastern portion of the oasis, in and around the Southeast Basin. On the basin floor, as elsewhere, Bashendi A sites are sometimes associated with playas, often still eroding out of playa silts. Exceptions to this include Locality 387 and the sites surrounding and including Locality 270 that are found on a sandstone embankment. Locality 270 and its neighbours, Localities 269, 306 and 307, are notable also for their stone slab structures, which suggest a move towards sedentism at this time. McDonald (1998, 134) has suggested that the raised position of these sites might indicate a wet season occupation, whereas those positioned on the playas were occupied during the dry season. Thus it is possible that Bashendi A groups occupied the oasis year round, oscillating from one set of sites to another depending on seasonality (McDonald 1998, 134). Extensive artefact scatters are present on most of these sites alongside a relatively rich faunal assemblage that includes gazelle, hartebeest, fox, hare and ostrich. As yet there is no definite evidence for either domesticated plant or animal species (M. McDonald personal communication, 2001). The Bashendi A is divided into 'early A' and 'late A' based on two clusters in the radiocarbon suite around 7300 bp and 6900 bp. Only the late A sites have yielded pottery.

Bashendi B sites are also found within a concentrated area in the Southeast Basin, though they tend to be situated on the edges of the playa rather than on the basin floor. Elsewhere, sites are found atop the escarpment and there appears to be a shift in site location during the sixth millennium bp towards the central lowlands of the oasis. This relocation probably reflects an oasis shrinking in response to the increasing aridity occurring in north-eastern Africa at this time (McDonald 2001, 33). Evidence for sedentary adaptations is scarce with only one site, Locality 385, yielding a total of six hut circles. As with the previous sub-unit, the Bashendi B sites may be identified by groupings of hearth mounds and artefact scatters. Again, the faunal remains consist of gazelle and perhaps hartebeest, and for the first time clear evidence of cattle and goat has been documented, both of which are believed to be domesticated (McDonald 1998, 134). Although the Bashendi B groups are considered to be predominantly pastoral in nature, the remains of wild fauna suggests there was a partial reliance on hunting. Little botanical data has been recovered from Bashendi B sites, and it is not yet known whether plants were domesticated at this time (M. McDonald personal communication, 2001).

Bashendi Pottery

In reviewing the Bashendi pottery there are a few things that should be noted from the outset. To begin with, the collection comprises a small number of sherds, several of which are badly eroded, and most of which come from one area within the oasis, the South-east Basin. In the past this area has attracted considerable attention for its concentration of material culture, and most of our knowledge of the Bashendi groups, and their pottery, comes from here. It is perhaps to be expected that future studies conducted beyond the South-east Basin could yield material that calls for a revision of some conclusions reached in this paper.

Second, as the study of Bashendi pottery is still in its early stages, only macroscopic methods of analysis are used here to distinguish imported pottery, or for that matter, locally-made pottery that exhibits non-local traits. Ideally, laboratory-assisted analysis, particularly chemical composition and thin-section studies, would be used in combination with macroscopic methods of analysis to make this distinction. As yet, a comprehensive study based on laboratory-assisted analyses has not been carried out and it might be expected that when this does occur, some of the findings presented here could require further consideration.

Bashendi A

Of the 15 known late A sites, 10 have yielded pottery. In total, 89 sherds have been examined by this writer, probably representing no less than 15 complete vessels, and no more than 17. The most common fabric, attested by 36 sherds, is usually open-bodied and medium-textured, and comprises fine sand and shale inclusions that are often profuse in distribution. They are found in quantities that constitute 40% or more of the fabric body. This fabric is provisionally classified as Fabric IV (Fine Quartz and Shale).[3] An additional nine sherds found on late A sites are considered to represent a finer version of the Fabric IV (Hope 2002, 41). A sherd of this finer fabric retrieved from a sealed deposit at Locality 270 is, so far, the only pottery excavated on a late A site.

Almost all Fabric IV sherds are compacted on both the interior and exterior surfaces, and a few display a lustre that has resulted from burnishing. While most examples are uncoated and undecorated, one sherd from Locality 174 preserves a red-slip, and a few display short oblique

---

[3] Until the current pottery analysis is finalized the descriptions used here will be in keeping with the published literature (Eccleston 2002; Hope 2002).

Plate 1 Decorated sherds from Locality 275 (Bashendi A).

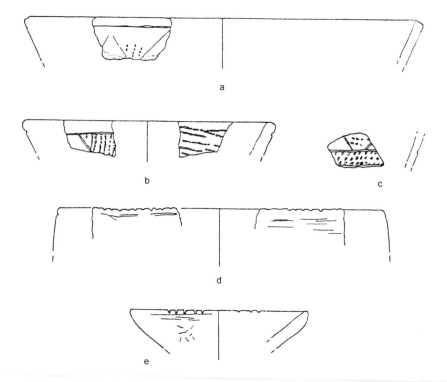

Figure 2 Decorated sherds from Locality 74 (Bashendi B); Scale 1:2.

lines, fingernail incisions, below the rim. The complete vessels were mostly unrestricted semi-ellipsoidal or hemispherical bowls with a wall thickness ranging between 3–7.5 mm, and made by coil construction. It is more than likely that the Fabric IV pottery is a local product given its high frequency in this and later collections, and for the fact that shale is naturally occurring throughout the oasis (Kleindienst *et al.* 1999). Indeed, the absence of shale inclusions is often taken as a first sign in identifying imports from this period.

As a second sign, it is also necessary to look for fabric inclusions that are uncommon in the pottery found at Dakhleh, though care must be taken with this approach. For instance, three sherds found on Locality 103, that are most likely from the same vessel, stand out for their straw-rich fabric. Although the use of organic temper is uncommon in Dakhleh, the fabric also contains sand and shale in similar quantities to the standard Fabric IV. As such, the vessel in question are considered a product of the local industry, and the presence of straw temper may be explained in terms of Bashendi potters experimenting with their more common fabric. The Locality 103 sherds have reddish-brown exterior surfaces (10R 5/6) with pale red-beige interior surfaces (2.5YR 6/4). The wall thickness ranges between 5.8 and 6.4 mm and none of the sherds bears decoration.

The only imports identified among the late A collection come from two sites. This includes two sherds from Locality 103 and 38 sherds from Locality 275. In both cases, the fabrics were found to contain profuse, coarse sand inclusions; the Locality 275 sherds also contain red, black and white pebbles. This fabric, classified as Fabric III, is rare among the Dakhleh pottery collections of all periods. That neither contains shale suggests these are most probably non-local in manufacture (Hope 2002, 41), which seems to be confirmed by the decoration found on several Locality 275 sherds. The Locality 103 examples are compacted and undecorated with reddish-brown exterior surfaces (10R 5/6), brown-grey interior surfaces (10YR 5/3) and grey-black cores. They probably came from the one vessel which had a medium wall thickness of between 5.9–7.6 mm and was coil-built.

The sherds from Locality 275, which are also likely to have come from one vessel, are compacted and have coarse brown (5YR 6/2) surfaces with a dark brown core. The sherds range in thickness from 6.3–8.7 mm, and 10 of these preserve impressed or punctated decoration (Plate 1). Six sherds are entirely covered with rows of punctates, another three display rows of closely spaced punctates which initially appear to form incised lines, and one sherd has undulating rows of punctates. The decoration was most likely applied with a square-toothed comb, probably using the rocker-stamp technique; the sherds are too small and eroded to determine precisely. In any case, the decoration is reminiscent of that belonging to the Saharo-

Sudanese Neolithic and may be considered a product of this widespread tradition (Hope 2002, 41).

Bashendi B

Seventeen phase B sites have yielded close to 300 sherds. A single sherd was also retrieved some 200 m west of Locality 200. There are probably no more than 62 vessels represented in this collection, 40–45 of which may be identified as the Fabric IV. Of these, three vessels belong to what Hope (2002, 41) describes as a finer version of the Fine Quartz and Shale Fabric IV.

The descriptions of the Fabric IV pottery noted in the previous section apply here also. There are, however, some additional points relevant to the Bashendi B collection that may be mentioned briefly. These include the more frequent use of coatings, that is, self-slips and red-slips, an increase in the deliberate blackening of the upper exterior of vessels, and an increase in the variety of vessel shapes and sizes including whole-mouthed jars and restricted forms (Hope 2002, 41–3). In several instances the vessel walls are very thin (2.6–2.9 mm) and some examples appear to have been fired in especially low temperatures; the sherds are quite friable and soft. Although decoration has become more frequent and elaborate, it is still an uncommon attribute. While the short oblique dashes noted on a few phase A sherds are again present, longer oblique grooves and finger channelling on the exterior surface are now notable. Whether the latter are decorative motifs or applied for functional purposes remains unknown. A small collection of sherds found on Locality 74 preserve incised triangular motifs and impressed dots (Figure 2a–c), and other examples from this site display rim notching/incising (Figure 2d–e). The sherds with triangular designs are uncoated and preserve the most elaborate decoration recorded so far amongst the mid-Holocene collection.

Two sherds recovered from Localities 104 and 200W, contain calcareous inclusions, including gypsum, and a sherd from Locality 258 preserves voids in the section and on the surface that are indicative of burnt-out straw temper. Although both tempers are uncommon in the oasis, the presence of sand and shale in the same quantity as the Fabric IV suggests a local manufacture. Calcareous inclusions and voids left by burnt-out straw can be found in several other sherds retrieved from Bashendi B sites.

These examples do not comprise shale inclusions and might, therefore, be considered imports. Twenty-four examples of a calcareous-tempered fabric come from three separate sites, and a small collection of sherds with straw temper were recovered from Localities 74, 212 and 257. The collection of straw-tempered sherds from Locality 74 were reconstructed to form a short-necked jar. Hope (2002, 44–5) has compared this with shape 5a in the Lower Egyptian Ma'adi corpus (Rizkana and Seeher 1987, 23–6, Figure 6).[4] A further three sherds with straw temper

---

[4] As Hope (2002, 44–5) points out, if this vessel is from the Ma'adi complex it should be treated as intrusive to Locality 74, as this complex postdates the Bashendi B (Hassan 1985, 98).

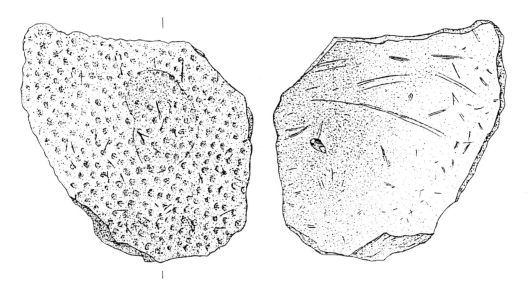

Figure 3 Imitation basketry sherds from Locality 212 (Bashendi B).

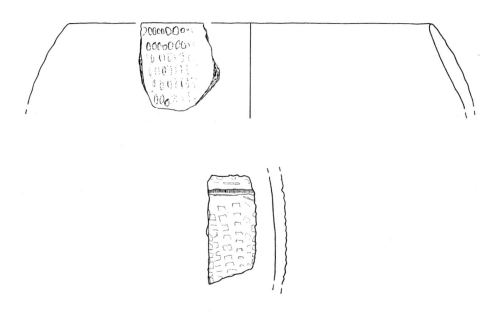

Figure 4 Decorated sherds from Kharga site MD-24; Scale 1:2.

recovered from Locality 212 are decorated with an imitation basketry design (Figure 3), as defined by Hope (2002, 45). Also recovered from Locality 212, as well as Locality 257, are examples of the sand-rich fabrics comparable to that found on Bashendi A sites. Unlike the Locality 275 examples, those from Bashendi B sites are undecorated.

Ceramic Evidence for Interregional Contact: The View from Dakhleh

There are two things to consider when searching for evidence for interregional contacts; pottery that was manufactured elsewhere and brought into the oasis, and, locally-made pottery that exhibits non-local traits. Identifying examples of the latter is particularly difficult as we must recognise anomalies amongst attribute states that are less likely to be the product of local innovation, as they are of non-local sources. Identifying imports, is somewhat easier. The sherds on Locality 275, for instance, are most certainly imports judging by their wall thickness, fabric and decoration, all of which stand out within the Bashendi pottery collection. The sherds in question bear the impressed designs reminiscent of the Saharo-Sudanese Neolithic.

Until recently, pottery belonging to the Saharo-Sudanese tradition had not been encountered in the Egyptian Western Desert north of the Nabta-Kiseiba region, where it is found in 'Early' and 'Middle Neolithic' contexts (Banks 1980; 1984; Wendorf and Schild 1998, 100–5). With the finds at Dakhleh and a few other Western Desert sites this picture is beginning to change. Pottery identified as 'Khartoum-related' has been retrieved from site 85/56 at Abu Ballas (Kuper 1993, Figure 4.2-3.5), and sherds with impressed decoration, similar to the Locality 275 examples, were found recently in Kharga on site MD-24 (Figure 4, personal observation, February 2002). At 'Ain Raml, in the Farafra Oasis, some poorly preserved pottery was recovered that might bear the dotted wavy-line pattern (Barich and Hassan 1990, 60). Although these examples are few, they demonstrate that features of the Saharo-Sudanese Neolithic were reaching the central Western Desert, and probably on several occasions.[5]

The other late A pottery to be mentioned here are the two sand-rich sherds from Locality 103. Although these are apparently non-local in manufacture, a point of origin cannot be offered. The sand-rich paste could have been manufactured anywhere in the surrounding desert regions or beyond, and these examples cannot be given an exact provenance. This said, it might be noted that fabrics with profuse, coarse sand inclusions are reported from roughly contemporaneous sites in the more southerly areas of the

Egyptian Western Desert (McHugh 1975, 53; Banks 1980; 1984, 159) and in the north of the Sudan (Schuck 1993, 245).

The Bashendi B collection offers several more examples of what appear to be imports, in addition to a few examples of locally-made pottery that exhibit non-local traits. This point is well illustrated by a collection of Fabric IV sherds from Locality 74. The sherds in question preserve dotted lines and triangular designs (Figure 2a–c). Hope (2002, 42) has compared these with material from Nabta Playa, Gebel Uweinat, Wadi Bakht and Wadi el-Akhdar, stating nonetheless, that no exact parallels can be determined.

Comparisons may be drawn also with material from the Middle Nile Valley region. Sherds bearing triangular patterns have been recovered from Khartoum and the Shaheinab Neolithic site of el-Geili (Arkell 1949, Plate 89.2–2a; Caneva 1988, Figure 15). While the examples from Khartoum do not bear a close resemblance to the Locality 74 examples, a marked similarity may be observed with the examples from el-Geili, classified as 'Simple impression: stipple lines' (compare Figure 2b–c with Caneva 1988, 100–1). Despite these similarities, Dakhleh and el-Geili are separated by a considerable distance (Figure 1), and this is something to consider in drawing direct links between Shaheinab Neolithic groups and the Bashendi B. If an actual connection exists here, keeping in mind that McDonald (1992) associates the groups on the grounds of shared adornment items, it might be assumed that the Bashendi potters borrowed the decoration. So far, we have nothing in Dakhleh that signals the development of such elaborate designs, whereas the 'Simple impression' is considered derivative of earlier traditions in the Middle Nile Valley region (Caneva 1988, 101).

Rim-top decoration is another feature of the Bashendi pottery that is of relevance here. Four examples have been recovered from Locality 74. Three of these have incised rims and the fabrics are undoubtedly local in manufacture. The fourth example has a notched rim, and does not resemble the local pottery in fabric; the fabric is sand-rich and does not contain shale. Hope (2002, 45) is tempted to see this latter example originating in Lower Nubia, in the context of either the Khartoum Variant or Abkan traditions. It is important to note that examples have been found also in the southern Western Desert (Banks 1984, Figure 4a, c–e and g; Kobusiewicz 1984, Figure 5.1) and the rim-top decoration is a feature of the pottery tradition emerging in the central Western Desert during the eighth millennium bp (Kuper 1995, 129).

Whether this import served as a prototype for the three locally-made examples bearing rim-top decoration is impossible to tell with certainty. On the one hand, rim-top decoration is hardly an elaborate or unusual design and its

---

[5] The sherds from Farafra come from early Holocene contexts (Barich and Hassan 1990, 60), whereas those from Dakhleh, Abu Ballas and Kharga come from mid-Holocene contexts. Site 85/86 has a cluster of dates around 7500 bp (Kuper 1993, 215) which only slightly predates Locality 275, with its range of dates from (Gd-5981) 7450 ± 60 to (Gd-5990) 6850 ± 50 bp (McDonald 2001, Table 3.1). So far no absolute date has been determined for the Kharga site MD-24, though associated material compares with the Bashendi B which suggests a mid-seventh or sixth millennium bp date (M. McDonald personal communication, 2002).

appearance among locally-made material need not demonstrate outside influences. In addition there is a notable difference between the non-local notched rim and the local incised rim (compare Figures 2d and 2e). On the other hand, it is noteworthy that all four examples are found on the one site. Further, Locality 74 has yielded several other sherds that bear decoration that could be of a non-local origin (see above).

A similar problem exists with the straw-tempered fabrics. There appears to be both local and non-local examples of straw-tempered fabrics; two sherds from the late A Locality 103 and one sherd from Bashendi B Locality 258 are considered local in origin, whereas the reconstructed jar from Locality 74, three sherds from Locality 212, and one sherd from 257 are identified as imports. As the Locality 103 sherds are from a Bashendi A context, this tells us that local potters were using straw temper before the imported examples were brought into the oasis. As such, it may be assumed that the use of straw temper by Bashendi B potters was also a local development.

The imported examples of straw-tempered pottery probably came into Dakhleh from different directions. If the jar from Locality 74 belongs to the Ma'adi complex (see above) then its origins are to be found in the north-east. The examples from Locality 257 may have come from anywhere within the immediate vicinity of the oasis. Straw-tempered pottery has been recorded north of Dakhleh at Abu Gerara (Riemer in press), to the west of the oasis at sites 81/55–2 and 81/55–3 in Abu Minqar (Klees 1989, 229), and further south at 'Late Neolithic' sites in the Nabta-Kiseiba region (Wendorf and Schild 1998, 108).

The three straw-tempered sherds found on Locality 212 also preserve what Hope (2002, 45) describes as imitation basketry designs (Figure 3). Pottery with similar fabric and decoration is recorded at various mid-Holocene sites across the southern region of the Western Desert (listed in Hope 2002, 45) and in the Middle Nile Valley region (Arkell 1949, 87–8; Nordström 1972, Plates 60 and 122 cited in Hope 2002, 45). It is from this general direction that the Locality 212 examples probably came, though it is difficult to say whether they originated in the Western Desert or somewhere further south.

To sum up, only a few imports have been identified amongst the Bashendi pottery collection and there are even fewer examples of locally-made pottery exhibiting non-local traits. The small number of examples listed here is not surprising as pottery was extremely scarce in the Egyptian Western Desert during the eighth and seventh millennia bp (Close 1995). While most of the imports seem to originate from somewhere to the south of the oasis, a more precise point of origin cannot be offered, at least until more detailed, laboratory-assisted, provenance studies are undertaken. It might be assumed, however, that the impressed sherds from Locality 275 originated in the Sudan as a product of the Saharo-Sudanese Neolithic. The elaborately-decorated sherds from Locality 74 also deserve

mention here as they may demonstrate links with the Shaheinab Neolithic of the Middle Nile Valley.

It is important to note that, for the most part, the presence of imported pottery did not impact on the local tradition in any significant manner. Only the elaborately-decorated sherds from Locality 74 seem to reflect an influence as such. Even then, decoration was never fully incorporated into the pottery tradition at Dakhleh during the mid-Holocene.

A Tradition of Undecorated Pottery

This apparent disinterest in decoration distinguishes the Bashendi material from the 'extensively decorated' pottery that prevailed in north-eastern Africa until *circa* 6000 bp (Close 1995, 26; Hope 2002). The Bashendi potters are not alone here as a similar pottery was appearing elsewhere in the Egyptian Western Desert during the mid-Holocene. These appearances seem to represent a new tradition of sorts and one to compare with the more well-known decorated tradition of the Saharo-Sudanese Neolithic (Friedman 1994, 894; Kuper 1995). Although this new pottery is characteristically plain, rim-top designs feature occasionally (Kuper 1995, 129) and the burnishing of vessel exteriors is also occasional. There is also a notable thinning of vessel walls and increasing variety in vessel shape. In tracing the spread of this tradition it is clear that contact between the central Western Desert and the Sudan did result in two-way flow of cultural traits. It is less clear whether Dakhleh Oasis played an active role in this process.

The origins of the undecorated pottery tradition are not yet known. It appears to have originated in the Egyptian Western Desert some time during the first half of the eighth millennium bp and seems to have spread quickly within the confines of the Western Desert; its first appearance in both the central and southern desert regions gives the impression of almost simultaneous development. The earliest dated examples come from the south-western corner of Egypt where, at Wadi el Akhdar (Gilf Kebir), numerous sherds of an 'undecorated ceramic type' were recovered from a layer dated 7700 bp (Schön 1989, 216). By the mid- to late-eighth millennium bp undecorated pottery was present at Dakhleh, Abu Ballas and Lobo (Kuper 1993, 219; 1995 Figure 2; Figure 1). Examples have been found also at Kharga, on sites that yield Bashendi-like material (personal observation, 2002), and further to the north-west at Abu Gerara (Riemer in press). It is difficult to tell how far north this tradition extended as pottery is not yet reported from eighth–seventh millennium bp sites at Siwa or Bahariya (Hassan 1978; 1979). A few undecorated sherds were, however, found at Djara alongside material that compares with the Bashendi A and B (Kuper 1996, 89). As for Farafra, there is little evidence of pottery, which is somewhat surprising given that the lithic assemblage compares well with the Bashendi B (Barich and Hassan 2002, 19). Still, it is important to keep in mind that impressed pottery has been recovered here, which suggests participation in the spread of cultural traits.

South of Abu Ballas, and not counting the Gilf Kebir, the first signs of the new pottery tradition come from 'Late Neolithic' sites in the Nabta-Kiseiba region, *circa* 7500 bp (Wendorf and Schild 1998, 108). Over the following millennia the tradition appears to spread further south, into northern Sudan (for overview see Kuper 1995, 135–6). By 6000 bp the tradition is thought to have reached Wadi Shaw (Kuper 1995, 135), though the extent of distribution beyond this point is unclear. It is suggested that pottery found in the Laqiya region with decoration restricted to the rim might be a related occurrence (Kuper 1995, 130). In summarizing these points, a tradition of undecorated pottery can be seen to emerge somewhere in the Egyptian Western Desert during the eighth millennium bp, spreading rapidly within the immediate vicinity. During the following two millennia this tradition gradually spreads south into the Sudan though the full extent of this process is unknown. From where the tradition began to spread south is also unknown. On the one hand, it might be assumed this occurred somewhere near the modern political border, perhaps in the Gilf Kebir or Nabta-Kiseiba regions. As far as one can tell from dated examples, undecorated pottery appears along this latitude around the same time, or even slightly earlier, than elsewhere in the Western Desert. On the other hand, several Sudanese traits were making their way into the central Western Desert around this time. This would suggest that Dakhleh, and several other neighbouring sites, were part of an extensive network of interregional contacts, and as such, may have had some influence over the spread of cultural traits.

The Dakhleh Oasis is singled out here for several reasons. The north-south spread of cultural traits in the Western Desert was most likely facilitated by a scatter of sites forming a corridor in the desert regions west of the Nile Valley. It is likely that Dakhleh served as one of the principal way stations along this corridor. In addition to holding a central position within the Western Desert, the oasis had a relatively abundant water-supply and sufficiently rich environment to sustain habitation through mid-Holocene times (McDonald 1991, 50; 1992, 64). Naturally, these features would attract mobile desert groups moving throughout the area, particularly during times of increased aridity (see below). Dakhleh's importance in the region can also be argued on account of the numerous 'exotic' material items recovered from the oasis. To date, no other location in the central Western Desert has yielded exotic items in comparative numbers to those recovered from Dakhleh.

While there is good evidence to suggest that Dakhleh served an important role in the region, it cannot be shown that the oasis was a point from which undecorated pottery spread south. Until regional variations are recognized within the pottery tradition of the central Western Desert, it is difficult to tell the role that individual locations played in the spread of this tradition.

A Brief Comment on the Spread of Pottery

The following discussion looks briefly at the spread of pottery and whether this occurred by way of widespread human migration or as part of exchange/trade networks. While it is likely that both scenarios are correct, and interrelated, a strong case can only be made for migration. Knowledge of the exchange/trade networks of the mid-Holocene desert groups is still nascent and with this in mind, the conclusions offered herein should be treated as tentative.

The mid-eighth millennium bp presents a suitable starting point for discussion. At this time undecorated pottery was spreading across the central Western Desert and shortly afterwards impressed, Khartoum-related, pottery was being brought into the region. The causes for this apparent increase in activity might be due to fluctuating palaeoenvironmental conditions. It is more than likely that climate shifts, and particularly those of increasing aridity, forced desert groups to become more mobile, and this in turn accelerated the spread of cultural traits. The increasing homogeneity of the material record around the late seventh to early sixth millennia bp probably reflects a similar chain of events (Barich 1993).

Kuper's (1995, Figure 2) 'proposed archaeological sequence' considers the events in question. The Middle Ceramic phase (*circa* 7800–6000 bp) of Kuper's model sees the northward movement of the Khartoum tradition following a wetting front into the central Western Desert. There is good archaeobotanical evidence to show that a Sahelian environment was moving north into Egypt during the first half of the eighth millennium bp and continued in this direction, reaching the central Western Desert by the second half of the millennium (Neumann 1993, 164; McDonald 1998, 127). From here the Khartoum tradition is thought to have developed in one of three separate ways:
a) meeting and being influenced by a non-decorating tradition,
b) developing into its own tradition in which decoration is no longer applied, or,
c) encouraging non-ceramic-bearing groups to take up the craft, who after doing so, decided not to decorate their pottery.

Although Kuper (1995, 135) does not seem to favour any one explanation, the first point agrees in part with that argued above. In summing up the model, Kuper (1995, 135) suggests that groups bearing undecorated pottery migrated south following the retreat of the Sudanic environment sometime around 6000 bp. At this point we see the beginnings of the so-called 'Late Ceramic' phase.

Within the wider setting of environmental change and human response, Kuper's model demonstrates that full-scale migration was a causal factor in the spread of pottery. The full impact of this migration on the central Western Desert is not yet clear. While the population count at a few sites increases during the first half of the seventh millennium bp (McDonald 2001, Figure 3.3) this is not uniform across the region.

As Kuper's model covers a wide geographic scope over a considerable period of time, it is not overly sensitive to the spread of pottery on a small scale. It does, however, provide a framework in which this can be investigated. Within the temporal/spatial boundaries of Kuper's model various material traits were being developed and circulated. Significantly, the distribution of several of these traits, and certain domesticated species also, does not follow the direction or timing of the migratory movements outlined by Kuper (1995). An example of this can be seen with the elaborately decorated sherds from Locality 74 and with the exotic items listed by McDonald (1992, 59). That the same traits are appearing, at roughly the same time, in both the central Western Desert and Middle Nile Valley is indicative of interregional trade/exchange networks more so than full-scale migrations.

It might be assumed that these trade/exchange networks were operated by nomadic or semi-nomadic desert groups, and as such, the process occurring here can be treated as a migration of sorts, but one to distinguish from the full-scale migration type noted by Kuper (1995). Even though the patterns of movement on a seasonal/episodic basis are still not fully known, small-scale migrations seem to have occurred with relative frequency and ease during the mid-Holocene. Gabriel's (1987) study of desert fireplaces is seen as sufficient evidence for this (McDonald 1992, 63) and so too is the evidence accumulating at several major Western Desert sites. The Bashendi B groups from Dakhleh, for instance, appear to have been predominantly mobile in nature (see above). The numerous exotic traits found on Bashendi B sites tends to confirm extensive interregional relations.

One explanation for the extensive range of these networks links in with Kuper's (1995) model. Once the initial, large-scale, migration saw contacts established between the Middle Nile Valley and the central Western Desert, new channels were opened up for cultural exchange. Whatever the motivation was for exploring these channels, gift-giving exercises and/or trade practices seem to have become fully integrated. It might even be that after a while the channels were maintained for these reasons, more so than for migratory purposes. Evidence supporting this may be found in the items themselves.

A few material traits that McDonald (1992, 62–3) focuses on are those that may be defined as 'prestige' items (Hayden 1998). These are worked items made of barite, marine shell and amazonite, or green feldspar. It is noteworthy that two of the three items, amazonite and marine shell, cannot be found in their raw material form in the central Western Desert (for anecdotal evidence on the sourcing of amazonite see Lucas and Harris 1962, 393–4; McDonald 1992, 63; Aston *et al.* 2000, 46). The marine shell is obviously non-local to the Middle Nile Valley region as well. The importance of these items might be inferred from the fact that they were traded, or at least transported, over considerable distances, and because they are apparently non-utilitarian in function. The amazonite had been worked into beads, the marine shell into pendants

or armlets, and the barite into what are probably labrets or ear studs. In all cases, the items were almost certainly used for personal adornment.

It is possible that pottery too falls into the category of prestige items though relatively few studies have looked at this in relation to the early desert material. Of those that have, the general feeling is that the rarity of pottery is the best indicator of its importance in the 'symbolic sphere' (Close 1995, 26; McDonald 2001). There are a few other signs that support this. The very thin-walled and low-fired sherds from Dakhleh, for example, are not what one would expect from pottery that was intended for everyday purposes. The general absence of use-wear indicators, carbon deposits and attrition marks, also points to this conclusion.

In assuming that there were certain items valued above others, it follows that groups or even individuals would actively seek to procure such items. It is on these grounds that arguments for trade and gift-giving exercises may be postulated. Although such arguments require more scrutiny before statements can be made with certainty, there is evidence to suggest that interregional networks were maintained for purposes of migration and for the upkeep of exchange.

Concluding Remarks

The intent of this paper was to build on McDonald's (1992) argument and this has met with some success. As with the lithic assemblage and items of adornment, the pottery collection also indicates that Dakhleh was included in the wider circulation of cultural traits during mid-Holocene times. On the basis of decorative motifs and fabric comparisons it is argued that at least some of these traits came from the Sudan. Although there are only a few examples that demonstrate this, it must be kept in mind that pottery was scarce during Bashendi times both in Dakhleh and elsewhere in the Western Desert.

In terms of the spread of pottery, the role that Dakhleh played in this process remains inconclusive and in this sense the argument presented here differs to McDonald's (1992). Where McDonald (1992) would see a direct involvement in this process, in so far as the lithic and adornment items are concerned, the same cannot be argued for the ceramic evidence. Until the pottery of the undecorated tradition is differentiated on the basis of regional variations, there is no way of telling whether pottery spread south from Dakhleh.

As a final comment, one thing to emerge from this study is that despite the presence of non-local pottery, groups in the central Western Desert maintained their own distinct pottery tradition. This suggests that the Bashendi potters, and those from neighbouring regions, resisted adopting non-local traits. While it remains unclear whether this was actually the case, it would be interesting to pursue this line of inquiry in future studies that look at interregional relations across north-east Africa during the mid-Holocene.

Acknowledgments

I am grateful to Colin Hope for commenting on this paper and for inviting me to submit it to the Conference Proceedings. Thanks also go to Mary McDonald for commenting on an earlier version of this paper and for providing information that was not at my disposal. I would also like to thank Heiko Riemer for allowing me to use unpublished material. Figure 4 was drawn by Damon Kowarsky whose participation in the 2002–3 field season in Dakhleh was funded by the Ian Potter Foundation. Bruce Parr kindly assisted with the illustrations, all of which are the property of the Dakhleh Oasis Project. Naturally, any errors herein are the responsibility of the author.

Author's Address:
Centre for Archaeology and Ancient History
School of Historical Studies
Building 11, Clayton Campus,
Monash University,
Victoria 3800,
Australia

REFERENCES

Arkell, A. J., 1949 *Early Khartoum*, Oxford University Press, London.

Arkell, A. J., 1953 *Esh Shaheinab*, Oxford University Press, London.

Aston, B. G., J. A. Harrell and I. Shaw, 2000 Stone (Inorganic materials), in P. Nicholson and I. Shaw, eds, *Ancient Egyptian Materials and Technology*, Cambridge University Press, Cambridge, 5–78.

Banks, K. M., 1980 Ceramics of the Western Desert, in F. Wendorf and R. Schild, eds, *Prehistory of the Eastern Sahara*, Academic Press, New York, 300–15.

Banks, K. M., 1984 Early ceramic-bearing occupations in the Egyptian Western Desert, in L. Krzyzaniak and M. Kobusiewicz, eds, *Origin and early development of food-producing cultures in North-Eastern Africa*, Poznan Archaeological Museum, Poznan, 149–61.

Barich, B. E., 1987 The Wadi Ti-n-Torha facies, in Barbara E. Barich, ed., Archaeology and environment in the Libyan Sahara. The excavations in the Tadrart Acacus, 1978–1983, *BAR*, Oxford, 97–114.

Barich, B. E., 1993 Culture and environment between the Sahara and Nile in the early and mid-Holocene, in L. Krzyzaniak, M. Kobusiewicz and J. Alexander, eds, *Environmental change and human culture in the Nile Basin and Northern Africa until the second millennium B.C.*, Polish Academy of Sciences, Poznan, 171–83.

Barich, B. E. and F. A. Hassan, 1984–87 The Farâfra Oasis archaeological project (Western Desert, Egypt), *Origini* 13, 117–91.

Barich, B. E. and F. A. Hassan, 1990 Il Sahara e le oasi: Farafra nel Deserto Occidentale Egiziano, *Sahara* 3, 53–62.

Barich, B. E. and F. A. Hassan, 2000 A stratified sequence from Wadi el-Obeiyd, Farafra: new data on subsistence and chronology of the Egyptian Western Desert, in L. Krzyzaniak, K. Kroeper, and M. Kobusiewicz, eds, *Recent research into the Stone Age of Northeastern Africa*, Poznań Archaeological Museum, Poznan, 11–20.

Camps, G., 1974 *Les civilisations préhistoriques de l'Afrique du Nord et du Sahara*, Doin, Paris.

Caneva, I., 1987 Pottery decoration in prehistoric Sahara and Upper Nile: a new perspective, in B. E. Barich, ed., *Archaeology and environment in the Libyan Sahara. The excavations in the Tadrart Acacus, 1978–1983*, BAR, Oxford, 231–54.

Caneva, I., 1988 The cultural equipment of the Early Neolithic occupants of Geili, in I. Caneva, ed., *El Geili: The history of the Middle Nile environment 7000 B.C.–A.D. 1500*, BAR, Oxford, 65–150.

Caneva, I., 1993 Pre-pastoral Middle Nile: local developments and Saharan contacts, in L. Krzyzaniak, M. Kobusiewicz and J. Alexander, eds, *Environmental change and human culture in the Nile Basin and Northern Africa until the second millennium B.C.*, Polish Academy of Sciences, Poznan, 405–11.

Close, A. E., 1995 Few and far between: Early ceramics in North Africa, in W. K. Barnett and J. W. Hoopes, eds, *The emergence of pottery: Technology and innovation in ancient societies*, Smithsonian Institute Press, Washington, 23–37.

Eccleston, M. A. J., 2002 Early and mid-Holocene ceramic from the Dakhleh Oasis: Macroscopic, petrographic and technological descriptions, in R. F. Friedman, ed., *Egypt and Nubia, Gifts of the Desert*, London, 62–73.

Friedman, R. F., 1994 Predynastic settlement ceramics of Upper Egypt: A comparative study of the ceramics of Hemamieh, Nagada, and Hierakonpolis, unpublished Ph.D thesis, Berkeley.

Gabriel, B., 1987 Palaeoecological evidence from Neolithic fireplaces in the Sahara, *African Archaeological Review* 5, 93–103.

Hassan, F. A., 1978 Archaeological explorations of the Siwa Oasis region, Egypt, *Current Anthropology* 19 (1), 146–8.

Hassan, F. A., 1979 Archaeological explorations at Baharia Oasis and the West Delta, Egypt, *Current Anthropology* 20 (4), 806.

Hassan, F. A., 1985 Radiocarbon chronology of Neolithic and Predynastic sites in Upper Egypt and the Delta, *African Archaeological Review* 3, 95–116.

Hayden, B., 1998 Practical and prestige technologies: The evolution of material systems, *Journal of Archaeological Method and Theory* 5 (1), 1–55.

Hope, C. A., 2002 Early and mid-Holocene ceramics from the Dakhleh Oasis: Traditions and influences, in R. F. Friedman, ed., *Egypt and Nubia, Gifts of the Desert*, London, 39–61.

Klees, F., 1989 Lobo: A contribution to the prehistory of the eastern Sand Sea and the Egyptian Oases, in L. Krzyzaniak and M. Kobusiewicz, eds, *Late Prehistory of the Nile Basin and the Sahara*, Polish Academy of Sciences, Poznan, 223–31.

Kleindienst, M. R., C. S. Churcher, M. M. A. McDonald and H. P. Schwarz, 1999 Geography, Geology, Geochronology and Geoarchaeology of the Dakhleh Oasis region: an interim report, in C. S. Churcher and A. J. Mills, eds, *Reports from the Survey of Dakhleh Oasis, Western Desert of Egypt, 1977–1987*, Oxbow Books, Oxford, 1–54.

Kobusiewicz, M., 1984 The multicultural early Holocene site E-79-4 at El Ghorab Playa, Western Desert of Egypt, in L. Krzyzaniak and M. Kobusiewicz, eds, *Origin and early development of food-producing cultures in North-Eastern Africa*, Poznañ Archaeological Museum, Poznan, 171–84.

Kuper, R., 1989 The Eastern Sahara from north to south: data and dates from the B.O.S. Project, in L. Krzyzaniak and M. Kobusiewicz, eds, *Late Prehistory of the Nile Basin and the Sahara*, Polish Academy of Sciences, Poznan, 213–23.

Kuper, R., 1993 Sahel in Egypt: Environmental change and cultural development in the Abu Ballas area, Libyan Desert, in L. Krzyzaniak, M. Kobusiewicz and J. Alexander, eds, *Environmental change and human culture in the Nile Basin and Northern Africa until the second millennium B.C.*, Polish Academy of Sciences, Poznan, 213–23.

Kuper, R., 1995 Prehistoric research in the South Libyan desert: A brief account and some conclusions of the B.O.S. project, *Cahier de recherches de l'Institut de Papyrologie et d'Égyptologie de Lille* 17, 123–40.

Kuper, R., 1996 Between the Oases and the Nile: Rohlfs' Cave in the Western Desert, in L. Krzyzaniak, K. Kroeper, and M. Kobusiewicz, eds, *Interregional contacts in the later prehistory of Northeastern Africa*, Poznan Archaeological Museum, Poznan, 81–92.

Lucas, A. and J. R. Harris, 1962 *Ancient Egyptian Materials and Industries*, Edward Arnold, London.

McDonald, M. M. A., 1991 Origins of the Neolithic in the Nile Valley as seen from Dakhleh Oasis in the Egyptian Western Desert, *Sahara* 4, 41–52.

McDonald, M. M. A., 1992 Neolithic of Sudanese tradition or Saharo-Sudanese Neolithic? The view from Dakhla Oasis, South Central Egypt, in J. Sterner and N. David, eds, *An African commitment: Papers in honour of Peter Lewis Shinnie*, University of Calgary Press, Calgary, 51–70.

McDonald, M. M. A., 1998 Early African pastoralism: View from Dakhleh Oasis (South Central Egypt), *Journal of Anthropological Archaeology* 17, 124–42.

McDonald, M. M. A., 2001 The Late Prehistoric radiocarbon chronology for Dakhleh Oasis within the wider environmental and cultural setting of the Egyptian Western Desert, in C. A. Marlow and A. J. Mills, eds, *The Oasis Papers 1: The Proceedings of the First Conference of the Dakhleh Oasis Project*, Oxbow Books, Oxford, 26–42.

McHugh, W. P., 1975 Some archaeological results of the Bagnold-Mond expedition to the Gilf Kebir and Gebel 'Uweinat, southern Libyan Desert, *Journal of Near Eastern Studies* 34, 31–62.

Mohammed-Ali, A. S., 1982 *The Neolithic Period in the Sudan 6000–2500 B.C.*, BAR, Oxford.

Mohammed-Ali, A. S., 1987 The Neolithic of Central Sudan: a reconsideration, in A. E. Close, ed., *Prehistory of arid North Africa: essays in honor of Fred Wendorf*, Southern Methodist University, Dallas, 123–36.

Neumann, K., 1993 Environmental change and human culture in the Nile Basin and Northern Africa until the second millennium B.C., in L. Krzyzaniak, M. Kobusiewicz and J. Alexander, eds, *Environmental change and human culture in the Nile Basin and Northern Africa until the second millennium B.C.*, Polish Academy of Sciences, Poznan, 153–68.

Riemer, H., in press, Abu Gerara: mid-Holocene sites between Djara and Dakhla Oasis, in L. Krzyzaniak, K. Kroeper, and M. Kobusiewicz, eds, *Cultural markers in the later prehistory of Northeastern Africa*, International Symposium, Poznan.

Rizkana, I. and J. Seeher, 1987 *Maadi I: The pottery of the Predynastic settlement*, Philipp von Zabern, Mainz am Rhein.

Roset, J., 1987 Palaeoclimate and cultural conditions of Neolithic development in the early Holocene of Northern Niger (Aïr and Ténéré), in A. E. Close, ed., *Prehistory of arid North Africa: essays in honor of Fred Wendorf*, Southern Methodist University, Dallas, 211–34.

Schön, W., 1989 New results from two playa-sites in the Gilf Kebir (Egypt), in L. Krzyzaniak and M. Kobusiewicz, eds, *Late Prehistory of the Nile Basin and the Sahara*, Polish Academy of Sciences, Poznan, 215–22.

Schuck, W., 1993 An archaeological survey of the Selima Sandsheet, Sudan, in L. Krzyzaniak, M. Kobusiewicz and J. Alexander, eds, *Environmental change and human culture in the Nile Basin and Northern Africa until the second millennium B.C.*, Polish Academy of Sciences, Poznan, 237–48.

Wendorf, F. and R. Schild, 1998 Nabta Playa and its role in Northeastern African Prehistory, *Journal of Anthropological Archaeology*. 17, 97–123.

The Chronology of the Later Late Pleistocene Occurrences at Dakhleh: A 'Low-Tech' Approach

Marcia F. Wiseman

Abstract

Reconnaissance since 1993 on the fringes of Dakhleh Oasis has led to the conclusion that, though sparse, there appears to have been a human presence in the region during the very arid, later Late Pleistocene. Cultural material presumed to belong to this time-period has been recovered and attributed to the Sheikh Mabruk Unit (= Khargan Complex). Lithic artefacts from another occurrence, Locality 318, appear late on stylistic grounds, but differ from both the Sheikh Mabruk and the Dakhleh Unit (= Aterian Complex) cultural material. In the absence of both stratigraphic control and datable material, however, we are forced to determine the relative chronology of these occurrences by resorting to techniques employed in archaeology's earlier, pre-chronometric days, and to rely almost exclusively on physical condition and techno-typological considerations of the lithics themselves. These criteria, plus two limiting dates on underlying deposits at Dakhleh and Dungul Oases respectively, point to a relatively late, that is, a post-Aterian, date for the Sheikh Mabruk Unit, and a chronological position intermediate between the Dakhleh Unit and Sheikh Mabruk for the artefacts from Locality 318. If these 'guesstimates' are sustained, the relative chronology of similar material found elsewhere in the Western Desert, such as Kharga, Dungul and Kurkur Oases, will require re-assessment.

Introduction

"The first, and in some ways the most important, step in much archaeological research involves ordering things into sequences" (Renfrew and Bahn 2000, 118). This task has been revolutionized during the past half century by a variety of sophisticated techniques, for example, those based on the disintegration of radioactive isotopes, as well as those which employ trapped electrons. For reasons which will become apparent below, however, the nature of the later Late Pleistocene data in the Dakhleh Oasis requires us to turn our backs, however reluctantly, on this brave new archaeological world, and revert to a 'low-tech', or more accurately, a 'retro-tech', approach to the sequencing and chronology of this poorly documented period of prehistory in the Western Desert.

For purposes of discussion, the later Late Pleistocene is arbitrarily defined as roughly that period of time between 40 and 12 thousand years ago. Essentially, we are speaking of the latter part of Oxygen Isotope Stage 3, dated to between 59 and 24 thousand years ago, and all of Oxygen Isotope Stage 2, dated approximately 24 to 13 thousand years ago (Renfrew and Bahn 2000, 126). By all accounts this was a period of increasing climatic stress which manifested itself in progressive aridity in the Western Desert. Prevailing sentiment among many scholars holds that this increasing desiccation provoked a total withdrawal of human habitation from the Western Desert during this prolonged period of time (Close and Wendorf 1992, 63).

On the contrary, the term 'everlasting oasis' was coined by Kleindienst to emphasize her contention that Dakhleh had been occupied continuously since humans first arrived there over four hundred thousand years ago (Thurston 1987); moreover, an increasing body of evidence has been put forward that convincingly supports the notion of a human presence in other, nearby desert environments. For example, renewed excavations at the site of Jerf Ajla have confirmed that there was a lengthy and relatively unbroken occupation in the Palmyra Basin of the Syrian Desert throughout much of this time-span (Julig et al. 1999). Phillips' (1988) work on the Abu Noshra sites in Sinai demonstrates habitation there dating to circa 30 through 36 thousand years ago. More recently, several sites of similar age have been reported from the Eastern Desert, for example, in the Suez Rift (Gawarecki and Perry 1992) and in the Red Sea Mountains (Vermeersch et al. 1994). In light of these finds, it appears increasingly improbable that Dakhleh, which sits on top of the Nubian Aquifer System, estimated by Thorweihe (1986, 95) to have a ground-water mass of 50,000 cubic km within Egypt alone, should have been completely devoid of human occupation during the prehistory of the later Late Pleistocene.

Lithic Prototypes

In 1993, therefore, it was decided to put this 'hiatus hypothesis' to the test (Wiseman 1993; 1999; 2001). The first problem was one of finding suitable lithic prototypes that might lend support to a human presence in the oasis during that period of time, equivalent elsewhere to the Upper Palaeolithic. The experience of several previous seasons' reconnaissance at Dakhleh, however, suggested that looking for Upper Palaeolithic-type blade and bladelet industries which are so characteristic of much of North Africa and the Levant during this time, and increasingly characteristic of the Nile Valley as well (see Van Peer and Vermeersch 1990), would result in yet another declaration of an empty desert. While prismatic blades and both unidirectional and bidirectional prismatic blade-cores are known at Dakhleh in presumed later Late Pleistocene context, they appear to be comparatively rare, and always numerically subordinate to a very strong, and apparently late-lingering, Levallois presence.

Since 1993, two lithic candidates for this later Late Pleistocene time-slot have presented themselves. The first is a lithic assemblage from one occurrence only, Locality 318, found on a high, P-I gravel-terrace quite close to the escarpment in the piedmont north of Bashendi. This locality was found by Kleindienst in 1992, grid-collected by Kleindienst and Wiseman in 1996, and analyzed by Wiseman during the 1998 field-season. Briefly, Locality 318 is represented by a blady, less-than-classic Levallois industry, for lack of a better descriptive term; however, 22% of the total core inventory (n = 134) are composed of non-Levallois cores, inclusive of two bidirectional prismatic blade-cores, four bladelet cores, and a total of 18 flake/blade and flake/bladelet cores.

The second candidate has been designated the 'Sheikh Mabruk Unit' at Dakhleh. To date approximately 15 relatively small, discrete occurrences have been found, primarily on the southern margins of the oasis, and typically situated on moderately elevated, usually deflated areas, on or between sandstone yardangs. Briefly, these occurrences are characterized by small, very flat-backed Levallois cores, first noted in mixed context in Dakhleh by McDonald (1981, 227–30; 1982, 118–21), who referred to them as a 'Southern Middle Palaeolithic' or a 'southern variant of the Middle Stone Age.'

The diminutive Levallois cores found since 1993 are often worked on 'recycled' older flakes, and are found in frequent association with thick, stubby Levallois flakes, many either truncated, or intentionally snapped and abruptly retouched along the fracture plane, sometimes into enigmatically amorphous or quasi-geometric forms. At Kharga Caton-Thompson (1946, 112–3) refers to strikingly similar artefacts as 'mutilated flakes'. On the whole, the retouch on these Sheikh Mabruk artefacts varies from the half-hearted, slap-dash variety, to that which is executed with sufficient finesse to merit being called 'backing' if lateral, or 'truncation' if proximal or distal. The resemblance of this material to Caton-Thompson's (1952,

Plates 76–80) Khargan Industry at Kharga is striking; however, first-hand examination in 1995 of the Khargan material curated at the British Museum and in Cambridge confirmed that there was sufficient variability between the Sheikh Mabruk and the Khargan to justify a distinct, regional name for the Dakhleh material.

Chronological Conundrums

With these proposed lithic prototypes in hand, the issue becomes one of verifying their suggested chronological position in the near absence of both relative and chronometric indicators. Since both the Sheikh Mabruk and Locality 318 materials from Dakhleh are found in surface context, relative stratigraphic dating is not an option; moreover, material suitable for any type of chronometric dating is rare to nonexistent. Thanks to the efforts of H. P. Schwarcz at McMaster University, there is one isochron U/Th date of 40,000 ± 10,000 uranium years bp (McM 91080/McM 91079/McM 90056) on calcareous sediments similar to those which underlie a Sheikh Mabruk occurrence at Locality 332, thereby suggesting a *terminus post quem* for the Sheikh Mabruk Unit as a whole. It must be emphasized, however, that the above is an averaged uranium-series date of three samples, two of which required correction for detrital contamination (Kleindienst *et al.* 1999, 33).

Other limiting dates are suggested on the basis of the evidence from both Wadi Kubbaniyeh and Dungul Oasis. Hill *et al.* (1989, 374) report that at Wadi Kubbaniyeh a Sebilian occurrence stratigraphically overlies the Kubbaniyan, and therefore ". . . the Sebilian artifacts at the site cannot be older than about 19,000 BP, and are probably much younger". In view of Caton-Thompson's (1952, 30) observations concerning the analogous relationship between the Sebilian and the Khargan Industry at Kharga, which in turn bears a striking resemblance to the Sheikh Mabruk Unit at Dakhleh, this date may provide something of a *terminus post quem* for the Sheikh Mabruk as well. An additional limiting date of 22,900 ± 600 bp (WSU-256) has been obtained at Dungul Oasis by ^{14}C on a tufa that underlies lithic material very similar to the Sheikh Mabruk. The lithics from Dungul have been attributed to the Khargan Industry (Hester and Hobler 1969, 14, 49); yet, in spite of the relatively late date obtained on the underlying tufa, Hester and Hobler (1969, 124) have chosen to follow the sequential order tentatively (see below) adopted by Caton-Thompson (1952), and to declare the Khargan at Dungul 'pre-Aterian'.

According to this view, if the recently reported OSL dates on the Aterian from the Libyan Sahara are accepted (Cremaschi *et al.* 1998, 272), the Khargan would have to predate a *minimal* age of 61 ± 10 thousand years ago (UTI c–g). This scenario is possible in light of a U/Th date of 68 ± 2 thousand years ago (E95-10) on a wadi travertine from Kurkur Oasis (Crombie *et al.* 1997, 348–9) which could be regarded as an additional limiting date for the surface material attributed to the Khargan Industry (Hester and Hobler 1969). It should be emphasized, however, that the Khargan material at Kurkur is not directly associated with the dated travertine; moreover, this early date for the Khargan seems less likely given the evidence from Kubbaniyeh, Dungul and Dakhleh itself.

At this point, Caton-Thompson's (1952: 29, 133) own ambivalence concerning the relative chronological relationship between the Aterian and Khargan at Kharga bears noting. Referring specifically to the Khargan Industry, she notes that, "Its chronological relationship to the Aterian remains uncertain" (Caton-Thompson 1952, 29); moreover, she repeats unequivocally that, "The time and industrial relationship between Khargan and Aterian . . . pose unanswered questions [which] [s]tratified evidence alone can resolve . . ." (Caton-Thompson 1952, 133). Unfortunately, this happy coincidence has yet to be found. With two possible, and as-yet-unexplored, exceptions, Locality 393, a spring-mound in the initial stages of excavation situated in the Sheikh Muftah Valley (Wiseman in Kleindienst 2001, 5–6), and Locality 414, a potential workshop eroding out of pan/sand-sheet sediments south of the oasis rim south of Mut (C. S. Churcher and M. R. Kleindienst personal communication 2002), all known Sheikh Mabruk occurrences are in surface context. A recent re-examination of Caton-Thompson's sections at Bulaq A by Smith and Hawkins (Hawkins *et al.* 2001, 11), moreover, indicates that in the singular situation at Kharga where stratification of Aterian over 'Levalloiso-Khargan', from which the Khargan claims 'descent and affiliation', according to Caton-Thompson (1952, 29), the pebbly sand underlying the Aterian appears to have been redeposited. This situation has led to doubts concerning the usefulness of the location for establishing chronological relationships, and furthermore has raised concerns that the battered appearance of the artefacts within this deposit may have contributed to their misattribution as 'Levalloiso-Khargan' (A. Hawkins personal communication 2002; Hawkins and Wiseman 2002; Kleindienst 1999, 102).

A 'Retro-Tech' Approach

It would seem, therefore, that in the absence of both stratigraphic evidence and conclusive chronometric dating we are obliged to employ technological criteria in an attempt to establish 'guesstimates' of relative age and sequential order. Two criteria which may prove time-sensitive in the context of the material being discussed are suggested here:
1. relative mean length of Levallois core; and,
2. differential retouch.

Core size alone in archaeological context is problematic, in that metric attributes may be as much a reflection of the quality and availability of raw material as it is a technological indicator. Nevertheless, at Dakhleh the trend through time, from the first appearance of Levallois technique in the older Middle Stone Age to what may be its dying gasp in the Sheikh Mabruk Unit, has been in the direction of a progressive reduction in core size. If we

Table 1

MEAN LENGTH OF LEVALLOIS CORES FROM ATERIAN AND SHEIKH MABRUK LOCS					
LOCALITY	REF.	SITE TYPE	N	MnL	SD
Dak 216tp	ALH	At-Workshop	181	71	15
Bulaq Site A	GCT	At	19	71	
Bulaq Pan C	GCT	At	2	70	
Kharga K06E	GCT	At	171	68	
Bulaq Pan B	GCT	At	32	68	
Dak 299	ALH	At-Occupation	13	66	14
Dak 80	ALH	At-Sp Use	30	65	14
Dak 342	ALH	At-Workshop	121	65	13
Dak 318	MRK/MFW	Workshop	98	59	15
*Dak 294	ALH	At-Occupation	57	59	11
**Dak 130	ALH	At-Occupation	23	55	11
**Dak 325	ALH	At-Occupation	51	53	14
Dak 324	MFW	ShM-Sp use	19	49	8
Dak 328	MFW	ShM-Sp use	24	43	7
Dak 332	MFW	ShM-Sp use	12	41	12

At = Aterian
ShM = Sheikh Mabruk   Dak = Dakhleh
N = Number   Locs = Localities
MnL = Mean length
SD = Standard deviation
Sp Use = Special use

*Heavily abraded **Far from raw material sources

look at core dimensions, particularly length, we see a reduction in size between the Aterian cores, both those published by Caton-Thompson (1952, 88, 119, 129, 130) and the numerous samples from Dakhleh analyzed by Hawkins (2001), and those from the three Sheikh Mabruk occurrences noted here (Table 1). Similarly, if we are correct in positing a directional reduction in size through time, this differential in mean core length suggests that the Sheikh Mabruk Unit does indeed post-date the Aterian, as the limiting dates cited above would indicate.

In contrast to this relatively marked differential in core length between the Sheikh Mabruk and the Aterian, there would appear to be continuity between the mean core length in the Dakhleh Unit occurrences (= Aterian Complex) analyzed by Hawkins and that shown in Locality 318, a workshop site to judge by the total number of cores present (n = 134, or 8% of the total number of artefacts), and also on the basis of the core-to-tool ratio (0.75). In fact, there is a certain amount of overlap between the mean core length for Locality 318 and three of the Dakhleh Unit localities. At the lower end of the range displayed by the Dakhleh Unit occurrences, Locality 294 equals Locality 318 in mean core length, and two occurrences, Localities 130 and 325, are marginally smaller (Hawkins 2001, 238). The artefacts from Locality 294, however, are reported to be heavily abraded, and mean length was not corrected to reflect this condition; whereas the latter occurrences, Localities 130 and 325, both abraded, are situated far from the terrace gravels near the southern oasis margins, and therefore are likely to show more intense utilization of raw material

Table 2

FREQUENCY OF LOCALITY 318 ARTEFACTS (N=1700)		
ARTEFACT TYPE	NUMBER	PERCENT
FLAKES	553	33
Specialized flakes	(78)	(5)
Unspecialized flakes	(475)	(28)
FLAKE FRAGMENTS	552	32
Specialized flake fragments	(74)	(4)
Unspecialized flake fragments	(478)	(28)
CORES	134	8
Levallois, struck	(69)	(4.1)
Levallois, unstruck	(29)	(1.7)
Initial trim	(7)	(0.4)
Flake	(5)	(0.3)
Blade	(2)	(0.1)
Bladelet	(4)	(0.2)
Flake/blade	(3)	(0.2)
Flake/bladelet	(15)	(0.9)
CORE FRAGMENTS	111	7
TOOLS	178	10
VARIA	19	1
CHIPS/CHUNKS	153	9
	1700	100

Table 3

FREQUENCY OF LOCALITY 318 TOOL TYPES (N=178)		
TOOL TYPE	NUMBER	PERCENT
SCRAPERS	63	35
End	(9)	(5)
Side	(4)	(2)
Side and end	(3)	(2)
Convergent	(3)	(2)
Steep	(31)	(17)
Core	(9)	(5)
Heavy-duty	(4)	(2)
NOTCHES	29	16
BURINS	13	7
AWLS	5	3
PERFORATORS	5	3
MULTIPLE TOOLS	11	6
"MUTILATED" FLAKES	7	4
RETOUCHED FLAKES	17	10
RETOUCHED FRAGMENTS	26	15
CORE-AXES	1	0.5
HAMMERSTONES	1	0.5
	178	100.0

resources (A. Hawkins personal communication 2000; Hawkins 2001, 286; Hawkins and Kleindienst 2002). All three Dakhleh Unit examples, therefore, exhibit reduced values associated with specific circumstances. In contrast, the physical condition of the Locality 318 artefacts displays only a light varnish and relatively fresh edges; moreover, the proximity of Locality 318 to the escarpment, and to Pleistocene gravels which include chert, suggests easy access to raw material. Consequently, if the proposed directional model regarding size holds true, and the three 'exceptional' Dakhleh Unit cases are excluded, the values for mean core length would suggest a chronological position for Locality 318 that follows much more closely on the heels of the Dakhleh Unit than does the Sheikh Mabruk Unit.

Additional support for this relative chronological position for Locality 318 may be found in such 'late' typological indicators as the presence of true bidirectional blade-cores and prismatic blades, and a relatively high percentage of flake/bladelet cores (Table 2). Although typological considerations tend to be allied to function, it may be of some chronological significance that tool types which are deemed characteristic of later inventories are present in the Locality 318 repertoire (Table 3). For example, the ratio of end- to side-scrapers is approximately 2:1. Included in the tool inventory of Locality 318, moreover, are several abruptly retouched, quasi-geometric pieces, for example, Caton-Thompson's 'mutilated flakes', which would foreshadow their more pronounced appearance in the Sheikh Mabruk Unit. To date, none has been reported from Aterian assemblages.

In terms of retouch, one of the hallmarks of the Dakhleh Aterian is the basal thinning of flakes, characteristically by fine, sometimes parallel, retouch on the ventral surface (Hawkins 2001, 327–8). In contrast to this frequently elegant treatment of the base, the people who trimmed the proximal ends of the Sheikh Mabruk flakes attempted to achieve the same thing by the removal of large irregular flakes, or alternatively, by the complete removal of the thick proximal end through deliberate fracture. Neither technique shows any trace of the finesse demonstrated in the Aterian. Although on occasion these intentionally snapped surfaces are retouched into what, with charity, might be called a truncation, the general impression of this treatment of the base is one that appears more indicative of a technique in a state of 'devolution', than one in the process of realizing the refinement of Aterian craftsmanship.

Conclusions

In conclusion, although difficult to establish in the absence of both chronometric and relative dates, on the basis of the technological and typological attributes discussed, and contrary to the opinions expressed, albeit tentatively, by Caton-Thompson (1952, 132–3) and by Hester and Hobler (1969, 124), the Khargan Industry, and consequently the Sheikh Mabruk Unit at Dakhleh, appear to post-date the

Aterian. Moreover, on the basis of at least one of these attributes, that is, mean core length, supported by physical condition and typological considerations, it is suggested here that Locality 318 occupies a chronological position younger than the Dakhleh Unit, but one which anticipates, at least in the presence of abruptly retouched, quasi-geometric 'mutilated flakes', the subsequent Sheikh Mabruk Unit.

Perhaps the true legacy of this hyperarid period was, as Smith (1982, 374) has suggested, a high degree of regional differentiation as a result of decreased interaction between the inhabitants concentrated in the better-watered oases, such as Dungul, Kurkur, Kharga and Dakhleh, and those in the Nile Valley. Although, for reasons still obscure, the cores and tools of both the oases and the Nile Valley were becoming smaller, at least some of the groups in the Nile Valley were producing these objects by means of blade and bladelet techniques, whereas those in the oases seemed to maintain their commitment to a Levallois-based technology.

Acknowledgments

Much of the research on which this paper is based was carried out with the generous support of the National Geographic Society. I should like to extend my sincere thanks to the society for Grants Nos 5341-94, 5827-96, and 6724-00 awarded to the Dakhleh Oasis Project Prehistory Group. I am very grateful to Maxine Kleindienst, who read this paper for me in Melbourne in August 2000, and who has since added many valuable comments; to Rufus Churcher for both desert transport and enlightenment, frequently at one and the same time, and for his unfailing support and advice; to colleagues Mary McDonald and Alicia Hawkins, my 'chronological book-ends' in the field; and last, but always first, to Tony Mills for his incomparable logistical and moral support.

Author's Affiliations and Addresses:

Department of Anthropology
University of Toronto at Scarborough
1265 Military Trail,
Toronto,
Ontario M1C 1A4,
Canada

and

Research Associate
Department of Near Eastern and Asian Civilizations
Royal Ontario Museum,
100 Queen's Park,
Toronto,
Ontario M5S 2C6,
Canada

REFERENCES

Caton Thompson, G., 1946 The Levalloisian Industries of Egypt, *Proceedings of the Prehistoric Society* 12 (4), 57–120.

Caton-Thompson, G., 1952 *Kharga Oasis in Prehistory*, Athlone Press, London.

Close, A. E. and F. Wendorf, 1992 The beginning of food production in the Eastern Sahara, in A. B. Gebauer and T. D. Price, eds, *Transitions to Agriculture in Prehistory*, Prehistory Press, Wisconsin, 63–72.

Cremaschi, M., S. Di Lernia and E. A. A. Garcea, 1998 Some insights on the Aterian in the Libyan Sahara: chronology, environment and archaeology, *African Archaeological Review* 15 (4), 261–86.

Crombie, M. K., R. E. Arvidson, N. C. Sturchio, Z. El Alfy and K. Abu Zeid, 1997 Age and Isotopic Constraints on Pleistocene Pluvial Episodes in the Western Desert, Egypt, *Palaeogeography, Palaeoclimatology, Palaeoecology* 130, 337–55.

Gawarecki, S. L. and S. K. Perry, 1992 Late Pleistocene Human Occupation of the Suez Rift, Egypt: a key to landform development and climatic regime, in R. Friedman and B. Adams, eds, *The Followers of Horus: Studies dedicated to Michael Allen Hoffman, 1944–1990*, Oxbow Books, Oxford, 139–46.

Hawkins, A. L., 2001 Getting a Handle on Tangs: Defining the Dakhleh Unit of the Aterian Technocomplex – a Study in Surface Archaeology from Dakhleh Oasis, Western Desert, Egypt, unpublished Ph.D. dissertation, University of Toronto, Toronto.

Hawkins, A. L. and M. R. Kleindienst, 2002 Lithic Raw Material Usages during the Middle Stone Age at Dakhleh Oasis, Egypt, *Geoarchaeology* 17 (6), 601–24.

Hawkins, A. L., J. Smith, R. Giegengack, M. M. A. McDonald, M. R. Kleindienst, H.P. Schwarcz, C. S. Churcher, M. F. Wiseman and K. Nicoll, 2001 New Research on the Prehistory of the Escarpment in Kharga Oasis, Egypt, *Nyame Akuma* 55, 8–13.

Hawkins, A. L. and M. F. Wiseman, 2002 Contrasting Behavioural Adaptations in the Aterian and Khargan of the Western Desert, Egypt, *Abstracts of the Society for American Archaeology 67th Annual Meeting, Denver, Colorado, March 20–24, 2002*, Society for American Archaeology, 134.

Hester, J. J. and P. M. Hobler, 1969 *Prehistoric Settlement Patterns in the Libyan Desert*, University of Utah, Salt Lake City.

Hill, C. L., F. Wendorf and R. Schild, 1989 Report on Site E-84-1: a multicomponent Paleolithic site at Wadi Kubbaniya, in F. Wendorf, R. Schild (assembly) and A. E. Close, ed., *The Prehistory of Wadi Kubbaniya*, Volume 3, Southern Methodist University Press, Dallas, 365–74.

Julig, P., D. G. F. Long, H. B. Schroeder, W. J. Rink, D. Richter and H. P. Schwarcz, 1999 Geoarchaeology and New Research at Jerf al-Ajla Cave, Syria, *Geoarchaeology* 14 (8), 821–48.

Kleindienst, M. R., 1999 Pleistocene Archaeology and Geoarchaeology of the Dakhleh Oasis: A Status Report, in C. S. Churcher and A. J. Mills, eds, *Reports from the Survey of the Dakhleh Oasis, Western Desert of Egypt, 1977–1987*, Oxbow Books, Oxford, 83–108.

Kleindienst, M. R., 2001 National Geographic Society Grant 6724-00: Interim Report, January/February 2001 Field Season, Prehistory Group, Dakhleh Oasis Project, Unpublished Report.

Kleindienst, M. R., C. S. Churcher, M. M. A. McDonald and H. P. Schwarcz, 1999 Geography, Geology, Geochronology and Geoarchaeology of the Dakhleh Oasis Region: An Interim Report, in C. S. Churcher and A. J. Mills, eds, *Reports from the Survey of the Dakhleh Oasis, Western Desert of Egypt, 1977–1987*, Oxbow Books, Oxford, 1–54.

McDonald, M. M. A., 1981 Dakhleh Oasis Project: Second Preliminary Report on the Lithic Industries in the Dakhleh Oasis, *Journal of the Society for the Study of Egyptian Antiquities* 11 (4), 225–31.

McDonald, M. M. A., 1982 The Dakhleh Oasis Project: Report on the Fourth Season of Survey, October 1981–January 1982, *Journal of the Society for the Study of Egyptian Antiquities* 12 (3), 93–101.

Phillips, J. L., 1988 The Upper Palaeolithic of the Wadi Feiran, Southern Sinai, *Paléorient* 14 (2), 183–200.

Renfrew, C. and P. Bahn, 2000 *Archaeology: Theories, Methods and Practice,* 3rd edition, Thames and Hudson, New York.

Smith, P. E. L., 1982 The Late Palaeolithic and Epi-Palaeolithic of Northern Africa, in J. D. Clark, ed., *The Cambridge History of Africa,* Volume 1, *From the Earliest Times to c. 500 BC,* Cambridge University Press, Cambridge, 342–409.

Thorweihe, U., 1986 Isotopic Identification and Mass Balance of the Nubian Aquifer System in Egypt, *Berliner Geowissenschaftliche Abhandlungen* 72 (A), 87–97.

Thurston, H., 1987 Everlasting Oasis, *Equinox* Sept./Oct., 30–43.

Van Peer, P. and P. M. Vermeersch, 1990 Middle to Upper Palaeolithic Transition: the Evidence from the Nile Valley, in P. Mellars, ed., *The Emergence of Modern Humans*, Edinburgh University Press, Edinburgh, 139–59.

Vermeersch, P. M., P. Van Peer, J. Moeyersons and W. Van Neer, 1994 Sodmein Cave Site, Red Sea Mountains (Egypt), *Sahara* 6, 31–40.

Wiseman, M. F., 1993 The Dakhleh Oasis during the Terminal Pleistocene: Is Anyone Home?, in R. W. Jamieson, S. Abonyi and N. Mirau, eds, *Culture and Environment: A Fragile Coexistence. Proceedings of the Twenty-Fourth Annual Conference of the Archaeological Association of the University of Calgary*, Calgary, 283–5.

Wiseman, M. F., 1999 Late Pleistocene Prehistory in Dakhleh Oasis, in C. S. Churcher and A. J. Mills, eds, *Reports from the Survey of the Dakhleh Oasis, Western Desert of Egypt, 1977–1987*, Oxbow Books, Oxford, 109–15.

Wiseman, M. F., 2001 Problems in the prehistory of the Late Upper Pleistocene of the Dakhleh Oasis, in C. A. Marlow and A. J. Mills, eds, *The Oasis Papers 1: The Proceedings of the First Conference of the Dakhleh Oasis Project*, Oxbow Books, Oxford, 15–25.

Hyaenas in the Dakhleh Oasis II [1]

Charles S. Churcher

Abstract

Hyaenas are recorded to have been recently present or to be still extant according to local lore in Dakhleh Oasis. Evidence for their presence in the Holocene (Neolithic and Historic Recent) and Middle Pleistocene is now available in the forms of bones, teeth, shattered bones of prey mammals and coprolites. A complex of low tunnels beneath a hard calcareous marl cap in a small hill south-west of Balat has yielded mammal bones broken in the manner typical of hyaenas. Fragmentary skeletal elements of hyaena have been recovered from excavated deposits of Middle Holocene/Neolithic and Middle Pleistocene/ Older Middle Stone Ages. Bone fragments broken as by hyaenas have been recovered from Neolithic occupation sites. The evidence indicates that hyaenas, probably the striped hyaena, *Hyaena hyaena*, found in Egypt today, was present in Dakhleh Oasis throughout the Holocene. The Middle Pleistocene hyaena may have been either the extant striped hyaena, *H. hyaena*, or the spotted hyaena, *Crocuta crocuta*, now extant only south of the Sahara.

Introduction

The hyaena resident in the New Valley is the striped hyaena, *Hyaena hyaena*, subspecies *dubbah* (Dorst and Dandelot 1970, 134; Haltenorth and Diller 1980, 218). Osborn and Helmy (1980, 428 and Figure 130) note a sighting in Dakhleh Oasis at Bir Karawein, near the main oasis town of Mut by Hoogstraal (1964, 221), but this reference mentions no such sighting. A dubious sighting on the shore of Lake Mut by Harry and Cathy Thurston, Anthony Mills and Alan Hollett in 1987, was first believed to be of an Egyptian jackal, *Canis aureus lupaster*, and is recorded as 'An individual was seen on 15 February, 1987, on the south shore of Lake Mut' (Hollett and Churcher 1999, 167). H. Thurston (personal communication, 2000) said he considered it was possibly a hyaena as it was 'skulking

around the water's edge', definitely a 'very stealthy looking animal [quotation from Thurston's field notes]', with a 'posture which was ... low in the hind end, again, a characteristic that better suits a hyaena'. Thurston's field notes state 'Jackal running along lake edge – sandy [coloured] with black spots' which suggest hyaena by colouring but not identification. Thurston admits that it might have been either as he had not seen a jackal or hyaena before or since! A specimen was shot in neighbouring Kharga Oasis, for which a £E50 bounty was paid, and was reported to D. J. Osborn by I. Helmy (Osborn personal communication, 1988).

I have observed no evidence of recent hyaena activities on the Libyan Escarpment or its Piedmont in the field seasons since 1985 when I quartered that broken country and investigated its various caves, crevices and rock shelters. I was particularly interested in finding remains of extinct local fauna and evidence of carnivore occupation of such shelters but, apart from jackal-, feral dog- or fox-transported skeletal elements of domestic stock or Dorcas gazelle, found none. It thus appeared that any hyaenas extant in the oasis during the past few hundred years must have kept to the peripheries of the inhabited areas, subsisted mainly on dead domestic animals and scavenged garbage, and did not hide out far from human habitation.

Indirect evidence of hyaena activity is shown by split long bone shafts in all three horizons: Middle Pleistocene, Neolithic and Historic. These breaks are green longitudinal splits of dense long bone shafts that proliferate from discrete pressure points. Such fragments are present in the lake marls' (Calcareous Silty Sediments [CSS] of Palaeolake Teneida, Churcher *et al.* 1999, 304–5; Kleindienst *et al.* 1999, 31–2; Churcher 2000, 3) Iron Balls Fauna (Localities 348 and 357), in Neolithic occupation sites (Localities 308, 385 and 387) and in the recent den at Hyaena Hill (Plates 1 and 2) and two other dens in the hill field south-west of Balat. Some Neolithic fragments

---

[1] The text was revised and expanded during 2000 and 2001.

Plate 1 View of Hyaena Hill from north-east. The flat-topped hill is composed of an erosional remnant of lake bottom and marsh deposits, and is capped by a consolidated marl, circa 1.5–2.0 m thick, from the floor of Palaeolake Teneida. The marl forms the roof of both the east and north dens' passages which are excavated in the contact lacustrine deposits and underlying Mut Formation shales beneath. The aeolian eroded plain is armoured with a lag gravel mainly composed of sandstone fragments from the underlying Taref Formation. In the right middle distance is a mound formed from a defunct spring mound. Beyond in the far distance is the Libyan Escarpment. Aeolian sand mantles the lee slopes of the mound and the small rise to its right foreground. Blocks of marl lie on the sloping sides of Hyaena Hill. The shaded lip of the marl layer (centre) shows the larger northern and smaller southern entrances. The northern entrance lies below the large block lying on the crest of the marl stratum and at the head of the mound of rock and spoil leading towards the block. The southern entrance is to the left of the leftmost block and at the head of the sand-filled gully. The far small block indicates the position of the roof entrance. The large block is the large one to the left and the small block is the far one in Plate 2. Debris below the entrances are spoil removed from the entrances by tomb robbers and marl blocks on the roof are presumably moved there by human agency. Fallen blocks tilted in the lip or lying on the glacis slope are probably the results of weathering. Land Rover to right for scale: crest of mound circa 52.5 m in length.

Plate 2 Main den entrance with geological hammer in centre, on shadow edge, for scale. Note: Entrance filled with secondary wind-blown sand; rough marl crust (Palaeolake Teneida marl) with separated blocks above, probably moved by humans; and bone fragment on marl edge to right of photo (arrow). A roof entrance is located by blocks on horizon beyond near left-hand block.

Table 1 Comparative measurements of Neolithic hyaena and modern striped (H. hyaena) *and spotted* (C. crocuta) *mandibular dimensions.*

Dimension	Locality 387 D 14b Dakhleh Oasis	C. crocuta Zimbabwe (No Data)	H. hyaena Ol Donyo Sambuk, ?Nr. Arusha, Tanzania M. 73305[1,2]	H. brunnea or C. crocuta Kalkpan ? S. Africa ? M. 91482[1,3]
Depth in diastema to symphysial flange	30.5	35.5	31.4	29.9
Height of mental foramen above ventral margin	18.4	19.0	14.1	13.8
Depth of ramus between P_2 and P_3	31.4	34.9	29.7	27.8
Width of ramus between P_2 and P_3	16.3	19.1	16.6	16.9
Mesiodistal diameters of roots on buccal faces P_2	14.1	13.2	11.9	12.3
P_3	18.0	21.1	13.5	17.1
P_4	19.5+	22.3	17.8	17.1
Mesiodistal length over roots of P_2 and P_3	53+	57.6	48.2	47.2

[1] Specimens M. 73305 and M. 91482 are held in the Collection of Mammals, Department of Mammalogy, Royal Ontario Museum.

[2] M. 73305 is male and has single large and 2 small accessory mental foramina. Locality given as 'Ol Donyo Sambuk', possibly west of Arusha, Tanzania.

[3] Skull M. 91482 has pencilled on it 'Georg[e] Backhouse', '1908', a locality that may read 'Kalk[p]an', and identification to hyaena. The skull has the large transverse M's and robust heels to M,s, characteristic of the genus *Hyaena*. This specimen may be *Hyaena brunnea* or *Crocuta crocuta*, if a South African location is correct and if the identification to 'hyaena' is general and not generic. *H. hyaena*, the striped hyaena, is not endemic in southern Africa.

can be reassembled (Plate 4A, B), and the green spiral manner of breakage (Plate 4F) supports a probable hyaena causation for the damage.

Specimens will be referred to by Field Numbers (FNo. or FNos) in the text. Field Numbers include the year and order of collection, for example, FNo. 20-57 indicates the year 2000 CE and the 57th specimen collected. Sites yielding hyaena materials or associated items are identified as 'Localities' with Grid Square (for example D3) and Quadrant (for example D3a), and Level. See below for further examples.

Evidence

Bone fragments that appear broken by hyaenas occur in the Mid-Pleistocene marls of Palaeolake Teneida (Localities 348, 350, 357) and include coprolites (FNo. 20-57, Locality 357). A few fragments appear to have been etched by stomach acid (Locality 348). Split bones and skeletal fragments have been recovered from Holocene Neolithic occupation sites (Localities 308, 385 and 387) or coeval pan deposits (Locality 358) (Churcher 1999, 49).

Specimens include part of a hyaena dentary, in two fragments, with damaged teeth (FNo. 20-30, Locality 387, Plate 3A, B), a proximal phalanx (Locality 358), damaged and partial metapodials (FNo. 20-32, Locality 387, Plate 3C, D; Localities 357 and 358) and a coprolite (FNo. 20-37, Locality 308, Level D3a, Plate 4D). These may represent scavenging hyaenas that visited these sites either during or between human occupations. Bones broken by hyaenas are present in Neolithic occupation sites (bone flakes, FNo. 20-36; Localities 308 and 387) and mainly represent hartebeest (*Alcelaphus buselaphus*, FNo. 20-31, Locality 387, Plate 4A, B). The presence of hyaenas around a Neolithic encampment is expected and recovery of an identifiable jaw confirms this expectation and assists identification to species.

The hyaena jaw fragments (FNo. 20-30, Plate 3A, B) from Locality 387 are badly weathered, lack the crowns of the teeth, and are too fragmentary for simple comparison of dental features or standard dimensions to be possible. It retains roots of the canine and premolars, partial symphysial surface, diastema and some ventral margin. Comparisons of the available dimensions with those from

Plate 3 Weathered right lower jaw fragment and metapodials of hyaena.
A and B: Lingual and buccal aspects of dentary fragments (FNo. 20-30, Locality 387, Level D14b), with roots of lower
canine, third and fourth premolars and molar (C₁, P₃₋₄ and M₁). C: Weathered left metacarpal III (FNo. 20-32, Locality
387, surface) in lateral aspect, and D: in medial aspect, showing plaster restoration. Scales: 30 mm.

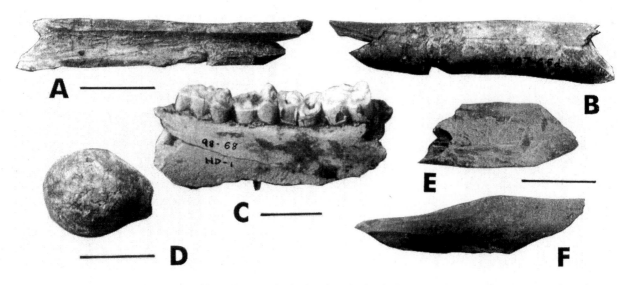

Plate 4 Tibial shaft fragment of hartebeest (Alcelaphus buselaphus) *(FNo. 20-31, Locality 387, Level G5d),*
reassembled from fragments. A: internal and B: external aspects. C: Ass (Equus asinus) *lower jaw fragment (FNo.*
98-68, Hyaena Den). D: Hyaena coprolite (FNo. 20-37, Locality 308, Level D4c). E and F: Bone flakes (FNo. 20-36,
Locality 308, Level D3a). Scales: 30 mm.

C. crocuta, *Hyaena hyaena* and *H. brunnea* (Table 1) show it better resembles *Hyaena* in the dimensions of the ramus (three out of four dimensions) and *Crocuta* in dental dimensions (3/4). As the crowns of the fragment's teeth are absent, no information as to the size and morphology of the premolars is available to help in identifying the genus. This specimen is possibly either *C. crocuta* or *Hyaena striata*.

The left metatarsal III from Locality 387 (FNo. 20-32, Plate 3C, D) is gracile and suggestive of *Hyaena*. Both proximal and distal epiphyses are fused to the diaphysis, and thus the individual was an adult. It measures 90 mm long, with mid-shaft antero-posterior and transverse diameters 7.0 and 7.7 mm respectively; some plaster restoration is present. The salient points on both ends are worn and unreliable for measurements.

The coprolite from Neolithic Locality 308 (FNo. 20-37, Plate 4D) is ovate or pear-shaped, with a smooth rounded face, rough narrow end, and creased broad end. Its obverse face is smoothly undulating and small lengths of vegetable matter are present. There is some weathering. It measures 31 mm long by 22 mm in greater diameter. The coprolite from Mid-Pleistocene Locality 357 (FNo. 20-57) is a subrectangular 'pillow' with one smooth undulating face and a rough obverse through which show surfaces of an enclosed black bone fragment. The dropping appears to be modelled over a bone fragment by a layer of phosphate rich faeces. It measures 25 mm long by 20 mm wide by 15 mm thick.

At this juncture it is impossible to state which hyaena is present in any of the levels or cultures from which evidence has been obtained, although it is presumed that closer to the present it is more likely that it is the striped hyaena, *Hyaena h. dubbah*.

The hyaenas identified in the Neolithic occupation sites span some 3,000 years. Locality 308 is a Masara C cultural unit occupation with two radiocarbon ages of $8,710 \pm 80$ and $8,810 \pm 70$ years bp, Locality 387 is probably late Bashendi A, and dates to about 7,000 bp (McDonald 2002), and Locality 385 is Bashendi B and is dated from three dates on nearby Locality 271 that range from 6,360 to 5,810 bp (McDonald 1991, 69–71). All radiocarbon dates are based on ostrich egg shell analysis and are uncalibrated; calibrated dates would be older.

Description of Hyaena Dens

Abandoned hyaena dens have been discovered south-west of Balat with associated bone fragments from ass, goat, cow, camel and hartebeest. These fragments are typical of those found in hyaena lairs (A. J. Sutcliffe personal communication, 1998). The first den found, but unrecognized at the time as a den, is an irregular excavation roofed by CSS marl noted in 1998 some 500 m north-east of Locality 368 at Latitude 25° 30.799' N, Longitude 29° 10.785' E, and well to the north-west of the lairs described below. It is within the northern nose of a small marl-capped hill and has three entrances on the north, east and west sides. The main chamber has been cleared of its fill, is tall enough to enter stooped, and could have contained coffins, but appeared unplanned and irregular, and contains pottery and human skeletal debris. Two smaller low passages lead from the main burial chamber to the north and west entrances. At the time of discovery M. R. Kleindienst and I assumed it to have been a robbed grave of lowly design but it now appears to have been an enlarged hyaena den with its floor lowered and used for burials, but later desecrated and robbed. A hyaena coprolite was recovered from the west passage on 1 February, 2001.

Another den was located in marl-topped conical hill of Mut Formation shale on 1 February, 2001. It faces south, is 'Y' shaped in plan with the entrance at the foot of the 'Y', and large enough in section for a small person to crawl into. Fragments of camel, cow and ass are scattered down slope from the entrance, as described by Sutcliffe and Collings (1972, 497–8). These two dens are excavated below the marl cap into the Mut Formation shale, as described next.

The low flat-topped hill, dubbed 'Hyaena Hill', in which the main hyaena dens are present, lies south-west of Balat in a field of flat-topped yardanged hills capped by the CSS marls of Palaeolake Balat (Figure 1). Its GPS co-ordinates are Latitude 25° 28.06' N: Longitude 29°11.65' E. These marls are compact, 1.5–2.0 m thick, and form a unit of sufficient integrity that chambers or tunnels may be excavated beneath it. In some hills this stratum was used as a roof for Roman-Byzantine era tombs. Two hyaena dens are present in the crest of the hill, a larger one on the east margin (Plate 1) and a smaller one on the south end (Figure 1). It is assumed that the extant Egyptian striped hyaena, *H. h. dubbah*, occupied both these dens. There are therefore four hyaena dens located to date in the hill field south-west of Balat.

The large hyaena den was signalled by the fragments of bone on a debris slope visible from the general level of the plain supporting the hills (Plate 1). A quick examination of these bones, including jaw fragments with teeth, suggested damage by hyaena crushing. These bones were from ass, goat and smaller mammals such as hare, Dorcas gazelle and fox or jackal. The condition of the bones was clean, unweathered, with spiral green breaks with unworn sharp edges and points, indicating no lengthy exposure to weathering or abrasion (Plate 4A–C, E, F).

The east den is a branching 'V', as far as it can be traced, with two entries on the east face of the hill and another through the roof about six metres from the edge, suggestive of a central chamber or an extensive tunnel system. Excavation at the main entrance, *circa* 1.75 m across, where the margin of the roof marl has collapsed as a number of large blocks (Plates 1 and 2), quickly led into a tunnel about 60 cm high by 90–100 cm wide. The tunnel was too narrow for me to enter but sufficient for a striped hyaena, which is smaller than both the spotted hyaena or the brown hyaena (*H. brunnea*) of southern Africa.

The entrance was filled with wind-blown sand, marl blocks, some large ones as they lay after coming loose

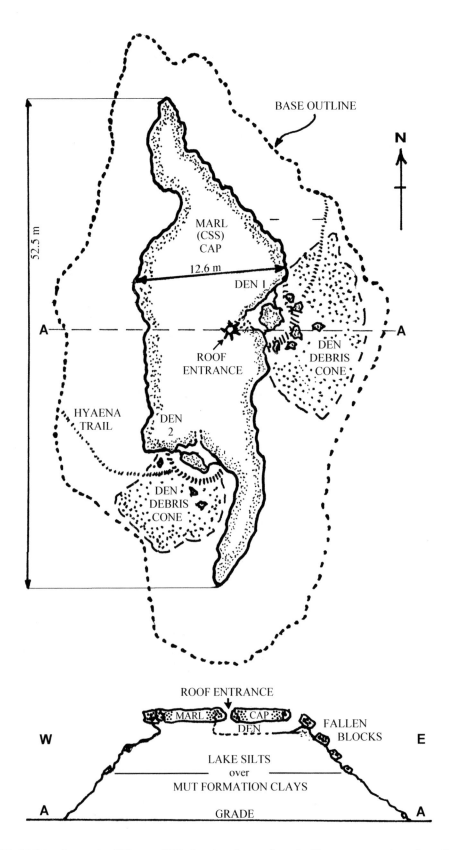

Figure 1 Sketch map of summit of Hyaena Hill showing den and vertically exaggerated section of hill. Dens are shown as though the roofs to tunnels and chambers have been removed. Areas in front of entrances are approximately level and form an entrance terrace or step above a debris cone. Marl cap margin lightly stippled. Debris cones with bone fragments from dens heavily stippled. Not to scale.

from the roof, fragments of bone, date pits, charcoal and a few lengths of palm cordage. At the back of the entrance, where the tunnel became too confined for excavation except by lying prone and working a trowel with one arm extended into the tunnel, the fill was in two units. An outer and upper yellow sand was loose and unconsolidated, with bone fragments in the sand among the marl blocks. The inner and lower sand was darker, finer, browner and more consolidated; within the tunnel there were few rock fragments and some bone riven by hyaena action. The tunnel was clear of obstructions and most debris and in many aspects corresponds to those in Wadi el-Sitbu (Becker and Reed 1973, 158–9), particularly in the fine flooring silt comprising much of the older unit and the narrowness of the tunnel entrance. Large blocks of marl are perched on the capping roofing marl (Plates 1 and 2), probably having been moved there by human agency.

This situation is interpreted as an accumulated original hyaena-occupation floor deposit with some scattered hyaena carried bone debris and a later aeolian infilling after excavation by local grave robbers who did not recognize the tunnels as the work of hyaenas. The robbers had cleared the entrance of all but the largest rocks and ceased work when it became apparent that the cavity was neither a grave nor a tomb. The easily-reached outer deposits with any contained bone fragments had thus been thrown down the side of the hill. They had also tested around the hill with a hoe just below the capping marl for tomb entrances, but found none. Thus the hyaena-deposited bone fragments on the side of the hill had only recently been freed from the matrix and were still pristine when examined by M. R. Kleindienst and myself. Hyaenas usually keep their lairs clear of refuse debris, and thus little is found within the occupation chambers of the animals. Bones may lie around the entrance as much as anything as 'toys for the children'. Scats or pellets are always outside the chambers and usually removed from the habitation area if not deposited in latrines around their territory. This is true also of both spotted and brown hyaenas (Skinner and Smithers 1990, 378–91).

The bones of smaller mammals, fox, jackal or hare, are interpreted as remnants of animals that occupied the den after the hyaenas had been extirpated, or who entered it when the hyaenas were absent, as their small bones would have been destroyed or removed by the hyaenas. Foxes or jackals would not remove such debris.

A sample of the spirally-cracked bones was collected in 1998 and examined by Anthony J. Sutcliffe of the Natural History Museum, South Kensington, a recognized authority on hyaena dens and bone debris, for confirmation on their hyaena modification (Sutcliffe 1970). His confirmation of their hyaena association encouraged me to carry out a small field excavation in the major entrance at my next opportunity, which came in 2000. The aim of this investigation was to confirm, or deny evidence, that hyaenas were relatively-recently resident in Dakhleh Oasis, that the remains of their prey or scavenging would show them to have coexisted with humans in the area if domesticates were present, or to give evidence of animals now extirpated from the oasis such as hartebeest. Fortunately all three aims were accomplished.

Towards the back of the entrance or at the beginning of the narrow passage, fragments of hartebeest long bone were recovered from the darker and more consolidated sand, two of which fitted together across a green spiral break (Plate 4A, B). This find supports the presence of hartebeest in the area in Historic time (Osborn and Helmy 1980, 484–6) and demonstrates its continuity with the reports of occurrence in Romano-Byzantine Kellis (Ismant el-Kharab), Old Kingdom 'Ain el-Gazzareen, Bashendi and Sheikh Muftah Neolithic occupation sites, and possibly as far back as the Middle Pleistocene Older Middle Stone Age Iron Balls fauna present in the marls of palaeolakes Teneida and Balat, and possibly Kellis (Churcher *et al.* 1999, 308).

Discussion and Conclusions

Epipalaeolithic hyaenas are known from Kom Ombo whence Churcher (1972, 44) reported *H. hyaena* and Gaillard (1934, 13–17) a partial right dentary of the spotted hyaena '*Hyaena crocuta = Crocuta crocuta*, race *spelaea*'. Gautier (1984, 43) reported spotted hyaena from the Palaeolithic of Helwan. Thus both striped and spotted hyaena appear to have been present in Egypt between 17,000 and 12,500 bp (that is 15,000 and 10,500 BCE) as well as during modern times. A series of dens of the striped hyaena, *H. hyaena dubbah*, in Taref Formation sandstone in Wadi el-Sitbu, some 70 km south of Aswan in Egyptian Nubia, was found by C. A. Reed and a party including M. R. Kleindienst, from the University of Chicago, Department of Anthropology, in 1962. These dens had abundant deposits of discarded bones, typical of *H. hyaena* (Skinner and Smithers 1990, 390); one of these provided a grab sample of bone debris which was reported on by Becker and Reed (1973, 158).

During the past few seasons sufficient evidence has been recovered to demonstrate that hyaenas, presumably the extant striped hyaena, *Hyaena hyaena*, and possibly the spotted hyaena, *Crocuta crocuta*, during the Pleistocene, inhabited the Dakhleh Oasis. They appear to have favoured dens near human habitation during times when villages and towns were present, and may have visited the occupation sites of Neolithic peoples in the greater Dakhleh Oasis region. When the region was well watered, as during the Middle and Late Pleistocene and the first half of the Holocene, they may have been able to range more widely because of the ease of available water. Thus, bones of and broken by hyaenas are to be expected in all sites within Dakhleh Oasis, but infrequently. They would have constituted the major scavenger of animal matter in all settlements and probably skulked down the alleys of the Old Kingdom town of 'Ain el-Gazzareen and Romano-Byzantine Kellis (Ismant el-Kharab) or Trimithis (Amheida) after dark when the human habitants had retreated into their houses, although no skeletal materials of hyaenas have been identified in refuse recovered from any historic site (Churcher 1999, 51; 2002).

Acknowledgements

I thank Harry Thurston for helping me in a particularly dusty excavation of the hyaena den and for allowing me to cite his field notes of an apparent live hyaena observation in Dakhleh Oasis, Anthony Mills for his support arrangements for use of a Land Rover and the base support in Bashendi, Mary McDonald for collecting the evidence of hyaena presence and activity in the Neolithic occupation sites, and particularly for the unarguable evidence of the hyaena jaw fragment, my wife Bee for photographing the specimens, and Maxine Kleindienst for willingly reading my paper in Melbourne *in absentia*, and most particularly for being the great field companion when the hyaena dens were first noted and over many years.

Author's Affiliations and Addresses:
Professor Emeritus
Department of Zoology
University of Toronto,
Toronto, Ontario M5S 32G5,
Canada

Research Associate Emeritus
Department of Palaeobiology
Royal Ontario Museum,
100 Queen's Park,
Toronto, Ontario M5S 2C6,
Canada

2230 Windecker Drive,
Gabriola Island, British Columbia V0R 1X7,
Canada

REFERENCES

Becker, B. and C. A. Reed, 1973 Studies of bone detritus of the striped hyena (Hyaena hyaena) at a site in Egyptian Nubia, and the interpretation of the bone breakage by striped hyenas, in A. Clason, S. Payne and H.-P. Uerpman, eds, *Skeletons in her Cupboard: Festschrift for Juliet Clutton-Brock*, Oxbow Books, Oxford, 157–82.

Churcher, C. S., 1972 Late Pleistocene Vertebrates from Archaeological Sites in the Plain of Kom Ombo, Upper Egypt, *Royal Ontario Museum, Life Sciences Contribution* 80, 1–172.

Churcher, C. S., 1999 The Neolithic fauna from archaeological contexts in Dakhleh Oasis, Egypt, *Archaeozoologia* 10, 47–54.

Churcher, C. S., 2000 Dakhleh Oasis Project Report for the 2000 Field Season, in A. J. Mills, ed., *Report to the Supreme Council of Antiquities on the 1999–2000 Field Season of The Dakhleh Oasis Project*, 2–3.

Churcher, C. S., 2002 Faunal Remains from Kellis, in C. A. Hope and G. E. Bowen, eds, *Dakhleh Oasis Project: Preliminary Reports on the 1994–1995 to 1998–1999 Field Seasons*, 105–13.

Churcher, C. S., M. R. Kleindienst and H. P. Schwarcz, 1999 Faunal Remains from a Middle Pleistocene lacustrine marl in Dakhleh Oasis, Egypt: palaeoenvironmental reconstructions. *Palaeogeography, Palaeoclimatology, Palaeoecology* 154, 301–12.

Churcher, C. S., M. R. Kleindienst, M. F. Wiseman and M. M. A. McDonald, in press The Quaternary Faunas of Dakhleh Oasis, Western Desert of Egypt, in M. F. Wiseman, ed., *The Oasis Papers II: Proceedings of the Second International Conference of the Dakhleh Oasis Project*, Oxbow Books, Oxford.

Dorst, J. and P. Dandelot, 1970 *A Field Guide to the Larger Mammals of Africa*, William Collins Sons and Co. Ltd., London.

Gaillard, C., 1934 Contribution à l'étude de la Faune Préhistorique de l'Egypte, *Archives du Museum d'Histoire Naturelle de Lyon*, Memoire 3, 1–126.

Gautier, A., 1984 Quaternary Mammals and Archaeozoology of Egypt and the Sudan: a survey, in L. Krzyzaniak and M.

Kobusiewicz, eds, *Origin and Development of Food Producing Cultures in North Eastern Africa*, Polish Academy of Sciences/Poznan Archaeological Museum, Poznan, 43–56.

Haltenorth, T. and H. Diller, 1980 *A Field Guide to the Mammals of Africa including Madagascar*, William Collins Sons and Co. Ltd., London.

Hollett, A. F. and C. S. Churcher, 1999 Notes on the Recent Fauna of Dakhleh Oasis, in C. S. Churcher and A. J. Mills, eds, *Reports from the Survey of the Dakhleh Oasis, Western Desert of Egypt*, Oxbow Books, Oxford, 153–70.

Hoogstraal, H., 1964 A brief review of the contemporary land mammals of Egypt (including Sinai), 3: Carnivora, Hyracoidea, Perissodactyla and Artiodactyla, *Journal of the Egyptian Public Health Association* 39 (4), 205–39.

Kleindienst, M. R., C. S. Churcher, M. M. A. McDonald and H. P. Schwarcz, 1999 Geography, geology, geochronology and geoarchaeology of the Dakhleh Oasis Region: An interim report, in C. S. Churcher and A. J. Mills, eds, *Reports from the Survey of Dakhleh Oasis, Western Desert of Egypt, 1977–1987*, Oxbow Books, Oxford, 1–54.

McDonald, M. M. A., 1991 Dakhleh Oasis Project: Holocene Prehistory: Interim Report on the 1991 Season, *Journal of the Society for the Study of Egyptian Antiquities* 20, 65–76.

McDonald, M. M. A., 2002 Holocene Prehistory: Interim Report on the 1997 and 1998 Seasons – the Masara Sites, in C. A. Hope and G. E. Bowen, eds, *Dakhleh Oasis Project: Preliminary Reports on the 1994–1995 to 1998–1999 Field Seasons*, Oxbow Books, Oxford, 7–14.

Osborn, D. J. and I. Helmy, 1980 The Contemporary Land Mammals of Egypt (including Sinai), *Fieldiana (Zoology)* N.S., No. 5, 1–579.

Skinner, J. D. and R. H. N. Smithers, 1990 *The Mammals of the Southern African Subregion* (New Edition), University of Pretoria, Pretoria.

Sutcliffe, A. J., 1970 Spotted hyaena: crusher, gnawer, digester and collector of bones, *Nature* 227 (5263), 1110–13.

Sutcliffe, A. J. and H. D. Collings, 1972 Gnawed bones from the Crag and Forest Bed deposits of East Anglia, *Suffolk Natural History* 15 (6), 497–8.

Spatial and Temporal Distribution of Fossil-Spring Tufa Deposits, Western Desert, Egypt: Implications for Palaeoclimatic Interpretations

Jennifer R. Smith and Robert F. Giegengack

Introduction

The terrain of the Western Desert of Egypt is underlain by a sequence of conformable sedimentary rocks ranging in age from lower Paleozoic, exposed where sediments directly overlie the basement complex at the Aswan Cataract and at Gebel Uweinat, to the Miocene sediments of the Mediterranean coast. These sediments are typically slightly deformed, with a dip to the north of one degree or less, though more intensive deformation does occur in a few locations, for example the Wadi Midauwara region. Superimposed on this northward dip is a system of broad flexures and faults of slight displacement; many of those faults, and the axes of the subtle folds, are oriented north-east to south-west (Hermina 1990).

The lower part of the sedimentary section in the Western Desert lies exposed in the cliffs of the Sinn el-Kiddab (Libyan Escarpment), a 300-metre-high escarpment that extends across the Western Desert from cliffs bordering the Nile to the edge of the Sand Sea (Figure 1). Carbonate rocks of either the Tarawan group or the Thebes Group form a 20- to 30-metre vertical cliff at the crest of the escarpment in Dakhleh and Kharga. These cliff-forming carbonate rocks allow passage of camel caravans, and in recent years, motor vehicles, only at those localities where the carbonate rocks are slightly offset, or rendered more erodible, by displacement along faults. The terrain above the Sinn el-Kiddab, the 'limestone plateau', is characterized by carbonate yardangs ('kharafish'), solution weathering, and lag accumulations of resistant chert; the terrain below Sinn el-Kiddab, that of the floors of the oasis depressions, is underlain primarily by shales of the Quseir Group and sandstones of the Taref Formation in Dakhleh and shales of the Quseir Group and Dakhla Formation in Kharga (Hermina 1990, 266–7).

Deposits of spring tufa, predominantly from springs now dry, are preserved at many localities along the Sinn el-Kiddab and in the oasis depressions excavated below the surface of the limestone plateau. Major deposits of tufa have been described from the limestone cliffs along the Nile Valley (Hamdan 2000), from Kurkur and Dungul Oases west of Aswan (Butzer and Hansen 1968, 355–80; Issawi 1969; Crombie et al. 1997), from several locations along the northward-trending escarpment east and south-east of Kharga (Caton-Thompson 1952; el-Hinnawi et al. 1978; Sultan et al. 1997; Nicoll et al. 1999); from the north-eastern edge of the Gebel Abu Tartur plateau (Caton-Thompson 1952, 11), from a number of localities in Dakhleh Oasis (Kleindienst 2002, 3–4), and, most recently, from Farafra and Bahariya Oases. These deposits are superimposed on the major features of the present topography, but clearly have experienced some erosion since they were deposited. At many localities, clear stratigraphic evidence of repeated episodes of deposition of spring tufa has been described. In Dakhleh, carbonate-rich spring waters are likely to have issued from either the base of the Tarawan Group, or at the base of limestone beds within the Dakhla Shale. In Kharga, tufa-depositing springs were located at the Thebes Group/Esna Shale contact, or at the base of limestone beds within the Esna Shale.

In this paper, we describe the fossil-spring tufas we have studied from Kharga and Dakhleh Oases, and undertake to explain the distribution of those deposits in time and space. These tufas (Figure 1) have proven to be a valuable, directly-datable record of climate change in the now hyperarid Western Desert of Egypt (Sultan et al. 1997; Nicoll et al. 1999; Smith 2001; Kleindienst et al. forthcoming). A simple and direct interpretation of the climate record contained in the tufas, however, is confounded by the observation that variability in the processes whereby tufas are deposited may result from factors that are not climatically controlled. Many chemical and physical characteristics of tufas that can be used as palaeoclimatic indicators in other carbonate deposits are difficult to interpret in tufas. For example, the stable-isotope composition of tufas is subject to a multitude of non-climatic influences, such as stream gradient (Chafetz and Lawrence 1994; see Smith 2001 for review). Simply establishing the timing of spring discharge based on the ages of tufas can be difficult, as the degree of diagenetic recrystallization of tufa carbonate may vary with tufa facies,

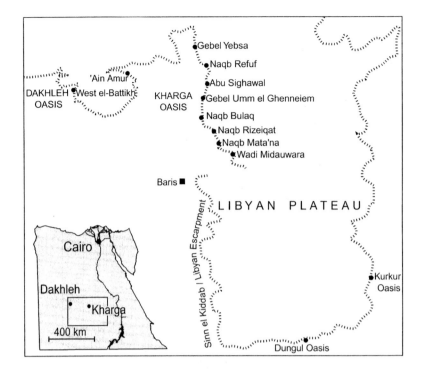

Figure 1 Tufa deposits in the Western Desert, after Smith 2001; Caton-Thompson 1952; Crombie et al. *1997;*
Sultan et al. *1997.*

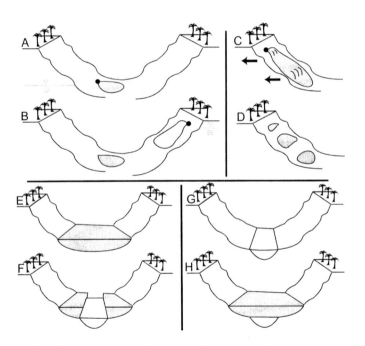

Figure 2 Differing formational mechanisms can result in variable topographic relationships of sequential generations
of tufa. In each diagram, a black circle represents an active spring and the dark grey and light grey areas indicate
older and younger tufas, respectively. A: A spring issues from a relatively low orifice, with tufa deposition occurring
downslope of the spring. B: A raised water table feeds a spring at a higher elevation, while the old orifice is blocked.
Younger tufa is thus deposited above older tufa. C: Tufa is deposited in steps along a slope, with curved beds marking
cascade locations. Following deposition, the slope retreats, with cascade locations particularly vulnerable to erosion.
D: Cascade deposits are completely removed, leaving same-age tufa deposits at distinctly different elevations. E and
F: Customary clastic-style terrace deposition. E: Tufas are deposited by rivers flowing parallel to the valley.
F: Subsequent incision causes younger tufas to be deposited below the level of the older terrace.
G and H: Simple aggradational model where younger tufa is deposited on top of older without significant incision
between depositional episodes.

leading to differences in the suitability of tufa samples for direct dating (Nicoll *et al.* 1999, 858). Even establishing the number of humid events recorded by spring carbonates in Egypt's Western Desert is not without difficulty, as the number of tufa depositional events preserved as discrete stratigraphic units may vary between localities only tens of kilometres apart (Smith *et al.* 2000). While the sources and magnitudes of geochemical and petrologic variability in tufas can be identified and estimated through studies of modern tufa-depositing systems in different climatic settings (Giegengack *et al.* 1979; Chafetz and Lawrence 1994; Nicoll 1996), it is the larger scale stratigraphic variation that has proven particularly difficult to constrain. The stratigraphy of the Western Desert tufas represents periodic rainfall during hundreds of thousands of years of predominantly arid to hyperarid conditions. Thus, modern tufa-depositing systems, most of which occur in temperate regions, can not provide all the uniformitarian keys necessary to reconstruct the environmental conditions under which the fossil tufas accumulated.

In order to assign climatic significance to the deposition, or non-deposition, of spring carbonates, it is necessary to understand the fundamental controls on spring-carbonate formation. Furthermore, in order to distinguish between a climate record unique to an individual locality and one with regional applicability, we must understand the physical and chemical factors that control where tufa will be precipitated within a region, and those factors that control the geomorphic relationship of each tufa body to other tufa bodies deposited before or since.

Controls on Tufa Deposition

Spring tufa is deposited by direct chemical precipitation of $CaCO_3$ on the beds and banks of streams, and on obstacles to flow that lie or hang in the water; spring tufa also accumulates as particles of $CaCO_3$, precipitated on crystallization nuclei suspended in the water column, which settle to the floor of streams as calcareous ooze.

The C in spring $CaCO_3$ comes from several sources (for example, Turi 1986, 210–11):

A. Reaction of rain water with atmospheric CO_2:
(1) $H_2O + CO_2 <\text{-}> H_2CO_3$
(2) $H_2CO_3 <\text{-}> H^+ + HCO_3^-$

B. A similar reaction occurs as water that infiltrates below the ground surface reacts with CO_2 included in soil air. That soil air may contain 3% or more CO_2, hundreds of times the CO_2 concentration in the atmosphere (Brady and Weil 1996, 20).

C. H^+ ions released from dissociation of H_2CO_3 (Eq. 2) may react with limestone bedrock in the subsurface:

(3) $H^+ + CaCO_3 <\text{-}> Ca^{++} + HCO_3^-$

If H^+ ions are provided only from dissolution of CO_2, the number of limestone-derived HCO_3^- ions will not exceed the number of HCO_3^- ions derived from dissolution of gaseous CO_2; if H^+ ions are provided from another source or sources, then limestone-derived HCO_3^- can exceed CO_2-derived HCO_3^- (Frumkin *et al.* 2000, 865).

Thus, ground water circulating underground may contain C, in the form of HCO_3^- ion, from three sources, the atmosphere, the soil atmosphere, and limestone bedrock. When that water emerges from the ground as spring flow, it will begin to equilibrate with the atmosphere; if the spring water is supercharged with HCO_3^-, a consequence of reaching equilibrium with soil air enriched in CO_2, CO_2 will escape from the flowing water, and equations 1, 2 and 3 will run to the left, leading to precipitation of $CaCO_3$. Escape, or evasion, of CO_2 is facilitated by agitation; thus, $CaCO_3$ will be precipitated preferentially at sites of turbulence in the stream (Merz-Preiss and Riding 1999, 113; Zhang *et al.* 2001, 205). In addition, aquatic vegetation may extract CO_2 directly from the water, leading to precipitation of $CaCO_3$ at any site where photosynthesis takes place (Ford and Pedley 1997, 107; Pentecost and Spiro 1990, 18).

To produce a tufa body of 0.2 cubic km, the approximate volume of tufa now present at each of several localities in the Western Desert, 100 cubic km of spring water, carrying ~500 ppm HCO_3^-, an average composition for modern tufa-depositing water, (from data in Giegengack *et al.* 1979, 723; Usdowski *et al.* 1979, 269; Dandurand *et al.* 1982, 301; Herman and Lorah 1988, 2348; Chafetz *et al.* 1991, 1020; Lu *et al.* 2000, 39),[1] would have to be stripped of its entire content of HCO_3^-. This is a conservative estimate, as tufa volumes prior to erosion would have been considerably greater at some localities. Though this amount of water is equivalent to only slightly more than a year's discharge of a major river such as the modern Nile, it would represent ~2000 years of constant spring flow at rates similar to those of Havasu Springs in the Grand Canyon, a tufa-depositing spring in a semi-arid climate (Giegengack and Pardi 1982, 35). Modern precipitation over the Western Desert averages <1 cm/yr; that value must have been much greater at times in the past when bodies of spring tufa accumulated. The absence of tufa deposits of a certain age, however, cannot be taken as an unequivocal indication of arid climate during that time period; there are a number of factors that may halt tufa deposition despite available water, or may remove it after deposition. The response of tufa-depositing systems to climatic change can be complex; as stated by Goudie *et al.* (1993, 183):

---

[1] A number of assumptions are necessary for this estimate. An average thickness of 5 metres for the Wadi Midauwara tufas was used to calculate tufa volume. 2.2 g/cm^3 is taken as tufa density, and tufa is presumed to be 100% $CaCO_3$. It is also assumed that calcium availability is never a limiting factor in tufa precipitation, and that all bicarbonate is consumed during tufa precipitation.

Fluvial landscapes vary enormously in their sensitivity to disturbance, and the presence of thresholds within a landscape can mean that a very localized, small-scale event can result in a basin-wide change in regime. Conversely, under some circumstances a large-scale change in climate may not be reflected by a sudden, dramatic change in tufa deposition.

Atmospheric CO_2

The late Holocene tufa 'decline' in Great Britain and continental Europe has been attributed to a number of causes, among them changes in atmospheric pCO_2 (Goudie *et al.* 1993; Griffiths and Pedley 1995). Griffiths and Pedley (1995) suggest that a biogenic response to increasing atmospheric CO_2 levels at the end of the last glacial period may have led to enhanced uptake of CO_2 from spring waters, causing extensive tufa precipitation. Though the correlation between timing of atmospheric CO_2 changes and the onset and cessation of tufa formation in Great Britain is intriguing, it is difficult to assess the importance of atmospheric CO_2 as a controlling factor in tufa formation. It is possible that the same climatic processes driving atmospheric CO_2 levels are also driving tufa precipitation but via a different mechanism, for example, via changes in rainfall amounts or seasonal distribution, temperature changes, associated floral change; thus, the temporal correlation between CO_2 changes and tufa formation is not evidence of causation. Carbonate formation in the Sahara, as in Great Britain, however, did occur during glacial-interglacial transitions, especially during transitions between oxygen-isotope stages 6–5 and 8–7 transitions (Petit-Maire 1989, 638; Szabo *et al.* 1989 and 1995). Though certainly a precipitation increase and not merely a change in atmospheric chemistry is needed to allow for tufa formation in the Sahara, it is possible that tufa precipitation may have halted despite available water due to unfavourable atmospheric conditions, or may have been removed by erosion.

Precipitation

Tufa deposits are relatively rare in areas with high rainfall; only a few reports have been made on tufas in 'tropical' settings (for example, Smith 1998; Das and Mohanti 1999). In these settings, spring or river water is too dilute to allow for carbonate precipitation. The various processes responsible for removing CO_2 from the water (for example, photosynthesis and degassing) cannot proceed at rates fast enough to result in supersaturation of $CaCO_3$. In some climatic settings, tufas are precipitated only during the dry season, and may be physically and chemically eroded by the relatively dilute waters of the rainy seasons. This pattern of tufa deposition can be observed in the semi-arid 'monsoonal' climate of the Grand Canyon region. During times of no rainfall, the entire flow of the Little Colorado River consists of the discharge from Blue Spring, a limestone spring supersaturated with HCO_3^-, with respect

to the atmosphere. The Little Colorado precipitates $CaCO_3$ throughout 18 miles of flow below Blue Spring; but, in the frequent, often annual, episodes of overland flow, which occur in mid to late summer, all the tufa precipitated in preceding months is swept away. When the flood subsides, and the murky run-off is replaced by the clear water of Blue Spring, tufa precipitation begins again.

While it is unlikely that the Sahara received >>600 mm of precipitation per year during pluvial events (Hoelzmann *et al.* 2001, 214), a highly seasonal distribution of that rainfall could thus result in a very low preservation potential for the tufas. Tufa preservation would reflect a balance between dry season deposition and rainy season erosion, and thus would be dependent not on the amount of precipitation during a given year, but the distribution of that precipitation throughout the year. High-amplitude variability in river discharge also tends to inhibit tufa precipitation because it prohibits growth of mosses and algae, which provide nucleation sites for tufa precipitation as well as contribute to photosynthetic uptake of CO_2 from the water (Goudie *et al.* 1993, 183). Discharge on a tufa-depositing tributary of the Nakatsugawa River, Japan, however, can vary from 40 to 3000 L/min over the course of one year with no apparent cessation of precipitation or erosion of tufas (Matsuoka *et al.* 2001, 33).

Temperature Changes

A decrease in temperature may also cause tufa precipitation to cease; colder temperatures enhance the solubility of CO_2, and reduce both evaporative potential and photosynthetic activity. Some effects of changing seasonal temperatures on modern tufa precipitation have been observed (Chafetz *et al.* 1991, 1023), though those effects may have as much to do with biochemical mediation of tufa deposition as with temperature-driven changes in solubility. Though tufa formation in the Western Desert is largely correlative with warm interglacial periods, as warming of the north tropical Atlantic causes a northward migration of the Atlantic monsoon, bringing rainfall to North Africa, (Kutzbach and Liu 1997, 441; Sultan *et al.* 1997, 34), a cooling climate may have been able to halt tufa precipitation if tufa-depositing waters were already near the solubility threshold prior to cooling. Temperatures in North Africa during glacial maxima are reconstructed as ~2–6° lower than average interglacial temperatures (Bonnefille *et al.* 1990, 347).

Tufa Distribution in the Western Desert

The uneven distribution of tufa deposits throughout Kharga Oasis was commented upon by Elinor Gardner, based on two seasons of field work. She noted that tufa was "strangely absent from the high scarps of the north and north-west, and also from the eastern scarp south of latitude 25° 6'" (Gardner 1932, 388), and mentioned optimistically that "... it is hoped to discover the significance of these facts next season ..." (Gardner 1932, 389). Additional reconnaissance by Gardner herself, and by other workers in the decades since Caton-Thompson and Gardner's expeditions, has shown that tufa deposits are somewhat more extensive throughout Kharga and Dakhleh than earlier workers had described (Nicoll *et al.* 1999; Smith 2001; Kleindienst 2002, 3–4). Tufas extend south along the Libyan escarpment at least to 24° 54' (Wadi Midauwara; el-Hinnawi 1978), but have not yet been documented along the stretch of the escarpment between Midauwara and Dungul Oasis (Figure 1). Tufas have been found in place along the escarpment in Dakhleh in only three locations, though tufa blocks in gravel terraces in Dakhleh have been noted in several other locations (M. R. Kleindienst personal communication, 2003).

The lack of detailed reconnaissance of the Libyan Escarpment between Dakhleh and Kharga may be a factor in the dearth of tufa deposits recorded from that region. It seems unlikely, however, that tufas as extensive as those in Kharga could have escaped notice in Dakhleh for the last 70 years, and thus there is likely also either a preservational or depositional reason for the relative paucity of tufas in Dakhleh. If the lack of tufas in Dakhleh is depositional rather than simply preservational, that is, tufas were never deposited in Dakhleh, the water resources represented by escarpment springs may not have been the same in the two oases. As a disparity in the distribution of water resources across the landscapes of Dakhleh and Kharga Oases would be expected to be reflected in different patterns of prehistoric exploitation of the landscape, it is important to try to distinguish between tufa absence due to lack of preservation and absence due to lack of deposition.

If it is differential preservation that accounts for the pattern of tufa distribution in Dakhleh and Kharga, there would have to be either faster erosion rates in Dakhleh or higher resistance to erosion in the Khargan tufas. Kleindienst and Churcher (personal communication, 2001) have noted that the predominantly east-west trend of the Libyan Escarpment in Dakhleh may make it more susceptible to eolian erosion by prevailing north-south winds than the north-south trending escarpment segment which bounds Kharga Oasis. If the escarpment in Dakhleh were subjected to more erosion via ground-water sapping than the Khargan escarpment, ground-water sapping being the predominant mode of escarpment erosion in the Western Desert (Luo *et al.* 1997), one would expect more rather than fewer tufas as the result of the greater ground-water activity that one might expect during periods of relatively rapid scarp retreat. It is also unlikely that there was a significant difference in the amount of precipitation that fell on Dakhleh and Kharga Oases during pluvial events; thus there is no reason to suspect that increased activity of dilute surface waters in Dakhleh may have contributed to heightened erosion rates there. The tufas in Dakhleh, in place and in gravels, appear to be similar in texture and morphology to those in Kharga. Dense networks of plant casts observed in tufa-terrace remnants in Dakhleh resemble the plant-cast facies common to tufas at all localities studied in Kharga. It is highly unlikely that

Dakhleh tufas would have been in some way intrinsically less resistant to erosion than Khargan tufas. As resistance to erosion does differ by facies in tufas, it is possible that a higher proportion of less-resistant facies was deposited in Dakhleh. As the most common easily erodible tufa facies is a silty lacustrine tufa, however, which requires a basin in which to accumulate, it is doubtful that the absence of tufa along the escarpment slope in Dakhleh can be explained this way.

Most probably it is more than a simple preservational bias that accounts for the relative lack of tufa deposits in Dakhleh compared to Kharga. It is certainly possible that, despite the high likelihood that both oases received similar amounts of precipitation during pluvial events, there may have been a discrepancy in the volume of tufa deposition between the two oases. Studies of modern ground-water chemistry show that carbonate concentrations are significantly higher in Kharga Oasis ground-water which averages 122 ppm HCO_3^-, than in Dakhleh waters, which average 52 ppm HCO_3^- (Swanberg *et al.* 1984, 135–6). This may be the result of a more extensive Cretaceous carbonate section in Kharga (Hermina 1990, 276). If Khargan spring water during pluvial events was also higher in carbonate concentration than Dakhleh water, it may be that the processes which act on spring water to cause the carbonate supersaturation necessary for tufa formation were only effective enough to reach the threshold for tufa deposition in the Khargan springs. In that case, spring flow along the Dakhleh escarpment may have been just as great as that in Kharga; we are simply left with less evidence of it in the form of spring carbonates. Rather, in Dakhleh, carbonate-rich surface waters are recorded by extensive lacustrine deposits in the lowlands (Churcher *et al.* 1999, 304).

Alternatively, there may have been differences in the magnitude of spring flow between the oases. The enhanced permeability of rock along faults that cut the section exposed in the Sinn el-Kiddab can channel ground water to spring orifices that accommodate the outflow of subsurface watersheds. The bedrock faults mapped at a number of tufa localities: Wadi Midauwara, 'Ain Amur, Wadi Battikh, Gebel Umm el Gheneiem (Hermina 1990, 266–7) would certainly have concentrated ground-water flow in those areas. The detailed geometry of the relationship between faults and tufa deposits remains unknown to us, as we have not yet been able to observe these faults in the field. Based on geologic maps of Dakhleh and Kharga (Hermina 1990, 266–7), the bedrock section along the escarpment east of Kharga is more fault-dissected than the escarpment north of Dakhleh; thus, there may have been more opportunities for the concentration of ground-water flow in Kharga than in Dakhleh. It is possible, however, that additional faults exist in Dakhleh that have simply not been mapped.

Even if unmapped faults exist in Dakhleh, the potential for substantial spring flow at these faults is fairly low due to another structural control on the location of active springs in the Dakhleh-Kharga region. As the bedrock section along the escarpment in the Dakhleh-Kharga region

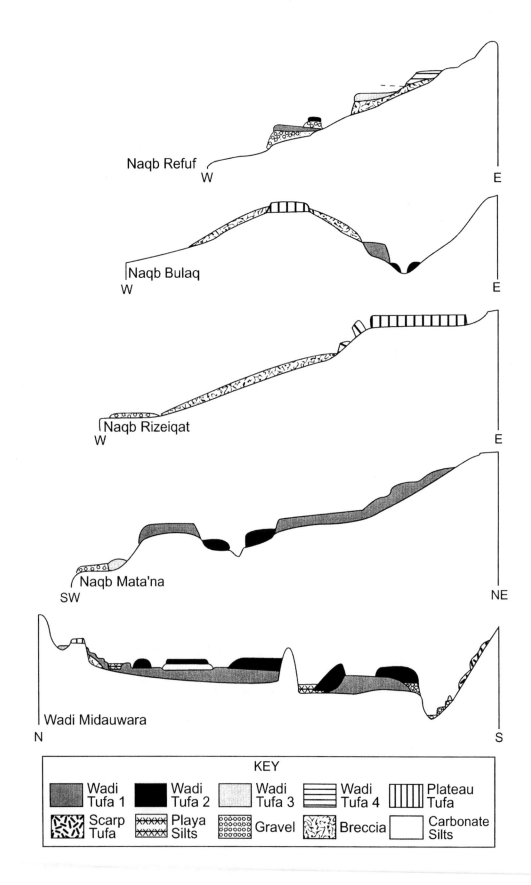

Figure 3 Schematic cross sections of tufa stratigraphy at Naqb Refuf, Naqb Bulaq, Naqb Rizeiqat, Naqb Mata'na and Wadi Midauwara (Naqb Refuf drawn from Caton-Thompson 1952; all others, this study. See Figure 1 for locations).

generally dips to the north (Caton-Thompson 1952, 11), the principal direction of ground-water movement would also be towards the north. The major tufa accumulations along the north–south-trending escarpment along the eastern border of Kharga all occur where major east–west-trending faults probably capture subsurface flow, and deliver relatively large amounts of water to spring outlets. Even 'Ain Amur, a major tufa centre along the east–west-trending scarp, has access to the entire catchment area of the Gebel Abu Tartur plateau to the south. Thus, along the east–west-trending scarp in Dakhleh, structural folding with the appropriate geometric relationship to faults would be required to generate a ground-water catchment area large enough to produce substantial spring deposits.

Stratigraphic Variability among Individual Tufa Localities

Even when tufa is deposited and preserved, there is significant variation in the number of stratigraphic units at each locus of deposition, and in the geomorphic relationship of successive stratigraphic units, despite the geographic proximity of the individual loci. Extracting regionally-important patterns of tufa deposition and non-deposition from this local variability requires an understanding of the nature and causes of tufa stratigraphic variability. The variation in number of tufa strata represented is the result of presumably non-systematic variation in the location of active springs over the course of successive pluvial events. There may be a fault-controlled component to that variation, in that tufa-depositing localities may have become active more frequently if they were located along bedrock faults that yielded more ground-water. However, without more direct dating to support the stratigraphies developed at a number of localities, it is difficult to determine whether or not such a pattern can be observed.

The range of possible geomorphic relationships between tufas of the same or different ages is summarized in Smith (2001, 31–3), and is recapitulated here (Figure 2). All of these possibilities are represented in the Kharga Oasis tufas; it is possible, after survey and mapping of four different tufa localities and brief reconnaissance of two additional localities (Hawkins *et al.* 2001, 9; Smith 2001, 26–60), to make some generalized statements on the determining factors of the particular depositional styles at each locality. One fundamental control on the geomorphic relationship of successive tufa strata may be the pre-existing geometry of the escarpment or wadi down which tufa-depositing water flowed. Where tufa-depositing waters flowed down a gentle gradient through major wadi systems with broad floors, aggradation was the principal mode of tufa accumulation: for example at Wadi Midauwara, Naqb Refuf (Figure 3). Conversely, where tufa-depositing waters flowed down the escarpment slope, progressively more deeply-incised inclined sheets was the predominant style of tufa deposition: for example at Naqb Mata'na, Naqb Bulaq (Figure 3).

Another basic control on tufa depositional style, which may be specific to systems in which periods of tufa deposition are separated by arid climatic phases, is the extent to which a tufa unit becomes topographically inverted during non-depositional phases. Should a tufa stratum remain as a topographic low throughout the arid phase subsequent to the deposition of the tufa, the tufa-depositing water of the following pluvial event will be concentrated in the same areas, resulting either in aggradation or in an incised tufa terrace (Figure 4a). If, however, the process of topographic inversion is begun during an arid phase, previously deposited tufa would represent a raised topographic feature at the onset of the subsequent pluvial event. Spring waters would flow parallel to previous deposits, and result in the formation of a tufa terrace parallel to the older deposits, but topographically lower (Figure 4b). Multiple humid phases separated by arid phases would result in the formation of a stepped landscape, 'steps' parallel to the topographic gradient, with elevation of a tufa terrace generally correlating with age for adjacent terraces. This particular sequence of events in tufa formation would not tend to create symmetrical, paired terraces, as can be common in clastic fluvial systems. As rates of erosion would be higher along the slopes of the escarpment than in broad wadis at the escarpment's base, the process of topographic inversion would progress faster along the escarpment slope. That is where the development of the stepped landscape resulting from topographic inversion would be expected to occur. Indeed, that landscape is present on the escarpment flanks at Naqb Bulaq, at Wadi Midauwara, and, to a lesser extent, at Naqb Mata'na.

Summary and Conclusions

The causes of variation in the distribution of tufa deposits in space and in time throughout the Western Desert of Egypt are many. Though certainly greater precipitation than occurs today was required to cause the onset of tufa deposition, cessation of spring-carbonate precipitation does not necessarily indicate that spring flow has also ceased. Age determinations on spring carbonates, then, reflect times of increased water availability relative to today; however, a lack of age determinations from a particular time does not necessarily indicate a lack of water. Spring flow without carbonate precipitation was probably not a frequent occurrence; rather, it may have occurred during the height of pluvial-phase rainfall when spring water was diluted by carbonate-poor surface waters, or at the end of a pluvial phase spanning a glacial-interglacial transition, as atmospheric CO_2 levels rose, though the magnitude of change in atmospheric CO_2 is not likely to have been able to halt carbonate precipitation unless spring-water chemistry were already near the precipitation threshold.

Spatial controls on tufa distribution are somewhat more complex. The primary control is the systematic northward dip and lithology of the section of sedimentary rock that underlies terrain near the escarpment: simply put, potential spring orifices along east–west-trending sections of the escarpment drain tiny watersheds. Concentration of tufas in Kharga Oasis relative to Dakhleh Oasis may be a result of greater amounts of carbonate in Kharga ground-water

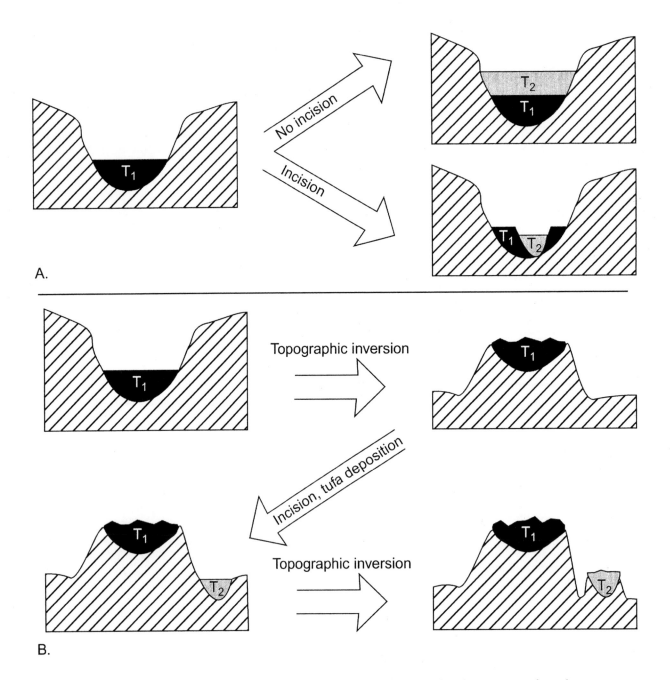

Figure 4 A: Tufa formed during an initial humid event (T1) may be either overlain by younger tufa, or have a younger tufa stratum incised into it, depending on whether or not there has been a lowering of base level. B: If a tufa, deposited along a valley floor, is subject to topographic inversion, subsequent tufa units will most probably be deposited in a valley running parallel to the older tufa. Aggradation is in this case highly improbable.

due to differences in aquifer units and ground-water-flow paths in Kharga and Dakhleh. Alternatively, the Libyan Escarpment appears to be more heavily dissected by faults in Kharga than in Dakhleh; as a number of tufa localities in Kharga are located along faults, it may be that fault conduits for ground-water were necessary for the development of significant spring carbonate deposits. The stratigraphic and geomorphic variability between different tufa localities can be in part explained by the pre-existing morphology of the escarpment, where broad, flat open valleys tend towards aggradation of tufa units and steep slopes towards incision of younger units into older.

Thus, while fossil-spring deposits in hyperarid regions provide an important record of changing climate, interpretation of that record is anything but simple. Tufas, like many terrestrial palaeoclimate proxies, provide discontinuous records of times when climatic conditions allowed for their deposition, with subsequent erosion causing additional complications. Though the multiple sources of variability in tufa deposition and preservation limit the certainty with which palaeoclimatic reconstructions based on studies of fossil tufas can be made, the spring carbonates of the Western Desert of Egypt still remain one of the best archives of humid conditions in the Eastern Sahara during Pleistocene time.

Acknowledgments

Field research was carried out under the auspices of the Dakhleh Oasis Project and the Kharga Oasis Prehistory Project, with concessions granted by the Supreme Council of Antiquities to A. J. Mills and M. R. Kleindienst, respectively. Funding was provided by the Leakey Foundation, the University of Pennsylvania (through the University Research Fund, the Center for the Study of Catastrophes and Human Culture, and the Geobiology Fund), the Geological Society of America (Student Research Grants and the Archaeological Geology Division's Albritton Fund) and Emilie deHillebranth. Thanks are due to the Dakhleh Oasis Project, as always, for logistical and scientific support. M. R. Kleindienst and C. S. Churcher provided thoughtful commentary and valuable suggestions on this paper.

Authors' Addresses:

Jennifer R. Smith
Department of Earth and Planetary Sciences
Washington University,
Campus Box 1169, 1 Brookings Drive,
St. Louis, Missouri 63160,
U. S. A.

Robert F. Giegengack
Department of Earth and Environmental Science
University of Pennsylvania,
240 South 33rd Street,
Philadelphia, Pennsylvania 19104-6316,
U. S. A.

REFERENCES

Bonnefille, R., J. C. Roeland and J. Guiot, 1990 Temperature and rainfall estimates for the past 40,000 years in equatorial Africa, *Nature* 346, 347–9.

Brady, N. C. and R. R. Weil, 1996 *The Nature and Properties of Soils*, Prentice Hall, New Jersey.

Butzer, K. and C. Hansen, 1968 *Desert and River in Nubia*, University of Wisconsin Press, Madison.

Caton-Thompson, G., 1952 *Kharga Oasis in Prehistory*, Athlone Press, London.

Chafetz, H. S. and J. R. Lawrence, 1994 Stable isotopic variability within modern travertines, *Géographie physique et Quaternaire* 48, 257–73.

Chafetz, H. S., N. M. Utich and S. P. Fitzmaurice, 1991 Differences in the $\delta^{18}O$ and $\delta^{13}C$ signatures of seasonal laminae comprising travertine stromatolites, *Journal of Sedimentary Petrology* 61, 1015–28.

Churcher, C. S., M. R. Kleidienst and H. P. Schwarcz, 1999 Faunal remains from a Middle Pleistocene lacustrine marl in Dakhleh Oasis, Egypt: palaeoenvironmental reconstructions, *Palaeogeography, Palaeoclimatology, Palaeoecology* 154, 301–12.

Crombie, M. K., R. E. Arvidson, N. C. Sturchio, Z. E. Alfy and K. A. Zeid, 1997 Age and isotopic constraints on Pleistocene pluvial episodes in the Western Desert, Egypt, *Palaeogeography, Palaeoclimatology, Palaeoecology* 130, 337–55.

Dandurand, J. L., R. Gout, J. Hoefs, G. Menschel, J. Schott and E. Usdowski, 1982 Kinetically controlled variations of major components and carbon and oxygen isotopes in a calcite-precipitating spring, *Chemical Geology* 36, 299–315.

Das, S. and M. Mohanti, 1999 Tufa deposition in tropical setting, Orissa State, India; Insights from carbonate petrography, water chemistry and stable isotopes, *Journal of Conference Abstracts, 11th Bathurst Meeting* 4.

el-Hinnawa, M. A., A. Abdallah and B. Issawi, 1978 Geology of Abu Bayan, Bolaq stretch, Western Desert, Egypt, *Annals of the Geological Survey of Egypt* 8, 19–50.

Ford, D. T. and H. M. Pedley, 1997 Tufa and travertine deposits of the Grand Canyon, *Cave and Karst Science* 24, 109–16.

Frumkin, A., D. Ford and H. Schwarcz, 2000 Paleoclimate and vegetation of the glacial cycles in Jerusalem from a speleothem record, *Global Biogeochemical Cycles* 14, 863–70.

Gardner, E. W., 1932 Some problems of the Pleistocene Hydrography of Kharga Oasis, Egypt, *Geological Magazine* 69, 386–409.

Giegengack, R. and R. R. Pardi, 1982 Field measurement of CO_2-exchange rate between the atmosphere and the water of Havasu Creek, Arizona, in *11th International Radiocarbon Conference*, American Journal of Science, New Haven, 35.

Giegengack, R., E. K. Ralph and A. M. Gaines, 1979 Havasu Canyon – A natural geochemical laboratory, in R. M. Linn, ed., *First Conference on Scientific Research in the National Parks*, Volume II, U. S. Department of the Interior, 719–26.

Goudie, A. S., H. A. Viles and A. Pentecost, 1993 The late-Holocene tufa decline in Europe, *The Holocene* 3, 181–6.

Griffiths, H. I. and H. M. Pedley, 1995 Did changes in late Last Glacial and early Holocene atmospheric CO_2 concentrations control rates of tufa precipitation?, *The Holocene* 5, 238–42.

Hamdan, M. A., 2000 Quaternary travertines of Wadi Abu Haddib area Eastern Desert, Egypt: Paleoenvironment through field, sedimentology, age and isotopic study, *Sedimentology of Egypt* 8, 49–62.

Hawkins, A. L., J. R. Smith, R. Giegengack, M. M. A. McDonald, M. R. Kleindienst, H. P. Schwarcz, C. S. Churcher, M. F. Wiseman and K. Nicoll, 2001 New research on the prehistory of the escarpment in Kharga Oasis, Egypt, *Nyame Akuma* 55, 8–14.

Herman, J. S. and M. M. Lorah, 1988 Calcite precipitation rates in the field: Measurement and prediction for a travertine-depositing stream, *Geochimica et Cosmochimica Acta* 52, 2347–55.

Hermina, M., 1990 The surroundings of Kharga, Dakhla and Farafara oases, in R. Said, ed., *The Geology of Egypt*, A. A. Balkema, Rotterdam, 259–92.

Hoelzmann, P., B. Keding, H. Berke, S. Kropelin, and H.-J. Kruse, 2001 Environmental change and archaeology: lake evolution and human occupation in the Eastern Sahara during the Holocene, *Palaeogeography, Palaeoclimatology, Palaeoecology* 169, 193–217.

Issawi, B., 1969 *The Geology of Kurkur-Dungul Area*, Organization for Government Printing Office, Cairo.

Kleindienst, M. R., 2002 Pleistocene Archaeology and Geoarchaeology, *Brief Report to the Supreme Council of Antiquities*, 1–6.

Kleindienst, M. R., H. P. Schwarcz, K., Nicoll, C. S. Churcher, J. Frizano, R. Giegengack and M. F. Wiseman, forthcoming, Water in the Desert: First report on Uranium-series dating of Caton-Thompson's and Gardner's "classic" Pleistocene sequence at Refuf Pass, Kharga Oasis, in M. Wiseman, ed., *The Oasis Papers II: Proceedings of the Second International Conference of the Dakhleh Oasis Project*, Oxbow Books, Oxford.

Kutzbach, J. and Z. Liu, 1997 Response of the African monsoon to orbital forcing and ocean feedbacks in the Middle Holocene, *Science* 278, 440–3.

Lu, G., C. Zheng, R. J. Donahoe and W. B. Lyons, 2000 Controlling processes in a $CaCO_3$ precipitating stream in Huanglong Natural Scenic District, Sichuan, China, *Journal of Hydrology*, 230, 34–54.

Luo, W., R. E. Arvidson, M. Sultan, R. Becker, M. K. Crombie, N. Sturchio and Z. E. Alfy, 1997 Ground-water sapping processes, western Desert, Egypt, *Geological Society of America Bulletin*, 109, 43–62.

Matsuoka, J., A. Kano, T. Oba, T. Watanabe, S. Sakai, and K. Seto, 2001 Seasonal variations in stable isotopic compositions recorded in a laminated tufa, SW Japan, *Earth and Planetary Science Letters* 192, 31–44.

Merz-Preiss, M. and R. Riding, 1999 Cyanobacterial tufa calcification in two freshwater streams: ambient environment, chemical thresholds and biological processes, *Sedimentary Geology* 126, 103–24.

Nicoll, K., 1996 Deposition and diagenesis of freshwater spring-deposited travertines from Oklahoma, Arizona and Egypt, unpublished MA Thesis, Bryn Mawr College.

Nicoll, K., R. Giegengack and M. Kleindienst, 1999 Petrogenesis of Artifact-bearing fossil-spring tufa deposits from Kharga Oasis, Egypt, *Geoarchaeology: An International Journal* 14, 849–63.

Pentecost, A. and B. Spiro, 1990 Stable carbon and oxygen isotape composition of calcites associated with modern freshwater cyanobacteria and algae, *Geomocrobiology Journal* 8, 17–26.

Petit-Maire, N., 1989 Interglacial environments in presently hyperarid Sahara: Palaeoclimatic implications, in M. Leinen and M. Sarnthein, eds, *Paleoclimatology and Paleometeorology: Modern and Past Patterns of Global Atmospheric Transport*, Kluwer Academic Publishers, 637–61.

Smith, J. R., 2001 Geoarchaeology, Stable Isotope Geochemistry and Geochronolgy of Fossil Spring Tufas, Western Desert, Egypt, in *Earth and Environmental Science*, University of Pennsylvania, Philadelphia, 180.

Smith, J. R. and R. Giegengack, 1998 Carbonate hydrogeochemistry of a tropical, tufa-depositing river, Belize, *Geological Society of America Abstracts with Program* 30, 374.

Smith, J. R., R. Giegengack, H. Schwarcz and M. Kleindienst, 2000 Variability in tufa stratigraphy along the Sinn el-Kiddab, Kharga Oasis, Egypt: Implications for the formation and preservation of the Pleistocene archaeological record, *Geological Society of America Abstracts with Program*, 30, 276.

Sultan, M., N. Sturchio, F. A. Hassan, M. A. R. Hamdan, A. M. Mahmood, Z. E. Alfy and T. Stein, 1997 Precipitation source inferred from stable isotopic composition of Pleistocene groundwater and carbonate deposits in the Western Desert of Egypt, *Quaternary Research*, 48, 29–37.

Swanberg, C. A., P. Morgan and F. K. Boulos, 1984 Geochemistry of the groundwaters of Egypt, *Annals of the Geological Survey of Egypt* 14, 127–50.

Szabo, B. J., C. V. J. Haynes and T. A. Maxwell, 1995 Ages of Quaternary pluvial episodes determined by uranium-series and radiocarbon dating of lacustrine deposits of Eastern Sahara, *Palaeogeography, Palaeoclimatology, Palaeoecology* 113, 227–42.

Szabo, B. J., W. P. McHugh, G. G. Schaber, C. V. Haynes Jr. and C. S. Breed, 1989 Uranium-series dated authigenic carbonates and Acheulian sites in Southern Egypt, *Science*, 243, 1053–6.

Turi, B., 1986 Stable isotope geochemistry of travertines, in P. Fritz and J. C. Fontes, eds, *Handbook of Environmental Isotope Geochemistry*, Elsevier, 207–38.

Usdowski, E., J. Hoefs and G. Menschel, 1979 Relationship between ^{13}C and ^{18}O fractionation and changes in major element composition in a recent calcite-depositing spring – a model of chemical variations with inorganic $CaCO_3$ precipitation, *Earth and Planetary Science Letters* 42, 267–76.

Zhang, D. D., Y. Zhang, A. Zhu and X. Cheng, 2001 Physical mechanisms of river waterfall tufa (travertine) formation, *Journal of Sedimentary Research* 71, 205–16.

La Céramique Datée de la Fin de la XIIIe Dynastie (Deuxième Période Intermédiaire) Découverte en Contexte Artisanal à 'Ain Aseel (Oasis de Dakhleh)

Sylvie Marchand

Les céramiques dont il sera question dans cet exposé sont issues de la fouille du niveau de la Seconde Période Intermédiaire de la ville de 'Ain Aseel, réalisée entre 1995 et 1999. Les divers sondages pratiqués dans toute la partie méridionale du site, en particulier dans la zone du palais des gouverneurs de l'Ancien Empire (Soukiassian *et al.* 1990a, 353–4; Soukiassian *et al.* 2002), ont révélé des structures d'habitat, de production alimentaire et de stockage, silos à grains et magasins à jarres (Baud 1997).

Les céramiques et le mobilier exhumés, dont de nombreuses figurines animales et humaines de terre cuite, offrent une grande cohérence typologique. Le problème de la chronologie, en l'absence de tout document épigraphique, reste bien évidemment crucial. Cependant, il est raisonnable de penser que la céramique exhumée lors de la fouille recouvre globalement la fin de la XIIIe dynastie.[1]

Les céramiques datées de la Deuxième Période intermédiaire sont déjà bien connues ailleurs dans l'oasis de Dakhleh. On peut citer la nécropole de Qila al-Dab'a toute proche (fouilles IFAO), Aufrère et Ballet (1990) qui a fourni un abondant matériel contemporain du site urbain de 'Ain Aseel. Il existe d'autres secteurs dans l'oasis de Dakhleh qui ont livré des ensembles importants de céramiques datés de cette période grâce aux fouilles et aux prospections réalisées par le Dakhleh Oasis Project (Edwards *et al.* 1987). Mais dans presque tous les cas, à l'exception d'un site, les céramiques sont associées à des tombes.

Face à ces grands ensembles funéraires, le matériel urbain de 'Ayn-Asîl est d'une nature différente. Cependant, l'étude *stricto sensu* des céramiques qui va être faite ici n'est pas le seul axe de réflexion proposé. C'est le contexte archéologique de leur découverte dans un secteur à vocation artisanale et domestique qui sera l'autre regard porté sur ces récipients lors de cette brève présentation.

Nous développerons successivement les trois points suivants:

Tout d'abord nous décrirons les critères de reconnaissance les plus évidents des pâtes et des techniques de façonnage des productions céramique datées de la XIIIe dynastie trouvées à 'Ain Aseel.

Dans un second temps, nous donnerons un catalogue des céramiques. Parallèlement, la question de la fonction des céramiques et de leurs utilisations sera évoquée. Bien entendu, seules les formes les plus courantes ou les plus évocatrices seront présentées.

Enfin, nous mettrons en parallèle les céramiques trouvées en site urbain et celles issues des tombes.

Il conviendra, en guise de conclusion, de préciser les limites d'une telle démarche.

---

[1] La fouille du secteur a été conduite par M. Baud. Rappelons que le secteur situé au sud du palais des gouverneurs a fait l'objet d'une prospection réalisée par Michel Baud et Sylvie Marchand. Le matériel collecté en surface post Ancien Empire/Première Période intermédiaire, essentiellement représenté par la céramique, couvre toute la Deuxième Période intermédiaire, le Nouvel Empire et la Basse Époque (XXVIe et XXVIIe dynastie). Quatre sondages ont été menés en 1998 et 1999 sous la direction de Pierre Tallet. Le résultat des fouilles, avec la publication des céramiques datées du Nouvel Empire, est publié par S. Marchand et P. Tallet 1999.

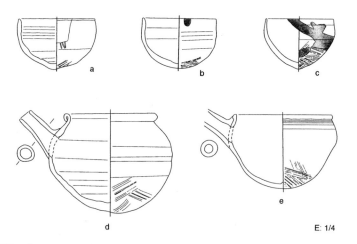

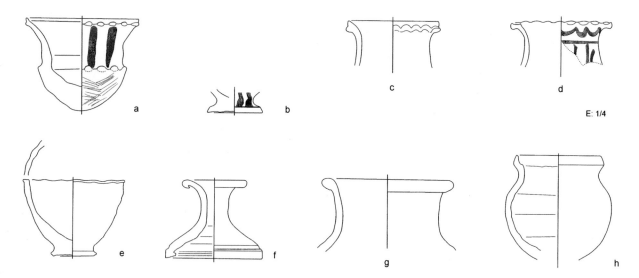

Figure 1 La céramique XIIIe dynastie. Bols hémisphériques F1A (a–c); aiguière F1A (d) et bol à bec verseur F1E (e).

Figure 2 La céramique XIIIe dynastie. La production locale en pâte F1E.

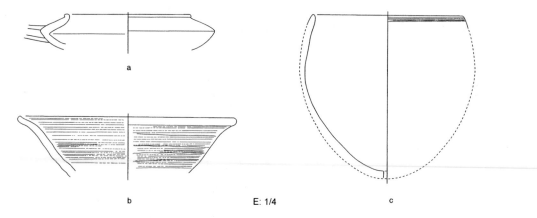

Figure 3 La céramique XIIIe dynastie. Bol à bec verseur F1B (a); assiette F1F (b) et pot sans col F1E (c).

1. Classification des Pâtes et des Techniques de Façonnage Pour le Matériel Daté de la XIIIe Dynastie[2]

1.1 L'argile locale des Oasis et la production locale

L'argile utilisée dans presque tous les cas est locale. Les caractéristiques des argiles rouges des Oasis, sur la base du matériel daté de l'Ancien Empire et de la Première Période intermédiaire, ont déjà fait l'objet d'une publication par P. Ballet et M. Picon dans le cadre des fouilles du secteur des ateliers de potiers de 'Ain Aseel (Soukiassian *et al.* 1990b, 75–85). Nous n'y reviendrons donc pas. Rappelons toutefois que pour les périodes plus récentes, l'étude des argiles oasiennes a bénéficié des études réalisées par l'auteur lors des sondages dans des niveaux datés du Nouvel Empire à Balat, (Marchand and Tallet 1999, Figures 8–75) et de celles de C. Hope dans le cadre du Dakhleh Oasis Project (Hope 1999, 215–43; Hope *et al.* 2002, 95–131). Il faut également signaler l'existence de nombreux autres programmes sur les céramiques des Oasis trouvées sur des sites situés dans la Vallée du Nil hors des Oasis.[3]

On remarque, d'une manière générale, que la céramique fine pour les productions oasiennes datées de la XIIIe dynastie n'existe pas. Du moins pas telle qu'on peut la concevoir pour la céramique trouvée dans la Vallée du Nil pour les mêmes périodes. Ce constat a déjà été fait par de nombreux auteurs travaillant sur le matériel plus ancien daté de l'Ancien Empire (P. Ballet et M. Picon in: Soukiassian *et al.* 1990b, 85).

De fait, c'est la taille et la fréquence des inclusions minérales et-ou végétales (souvent élevées), le soin donné au façonnage et au traitement de surface, le tour de main, mais également la qualité de la cuisson, qui déterminent une céramique dite 'fine' par rapport à une autre qui peut être qualifiée de moyennement fine à grossière.

Il a été choisi de privilégier les argiles locales les plus courantes. Quatre groupes seront examinés: F1E, F1A, F1B et F1F. Une description détaillée des pâtes plus rares dont celles des céramiques d'importation ne sera pas donnée. Seules les pâtes alluviales utilisées dans le façonnage des céramiques nubiennes seront décrites.

1.2 La pâte locale F1-E

Formes céramiques: bol à bec verseur (Figures 1e, 8b et 10a), bol à carène (Figures 2a et 9b), coupe à pied (Figure 2b), jarre à lèvre pincée (Figure 2c–d), encensoir (Figure 2e), petit support 'en trompette' (Figure 2f), jarre à col à lèvre retournée (Figure 2g), jarre à lèvre à ressaut interne marqué (Figure 2h), pot sans col (Figure 3c).

Il s'agit du type de pâte qui caractérise le mieux la production céramique de cette période.

La texture est de qualité très moyenne. Elle recèle un grand nombre de petites inclusions minérales: nodules blancs, micas, sable. La texture poreuse laisse apparaître un dégraissant végétal très abondant qui est particulièrement visible en négatif à la surface des récipients. Ce traitement de l'argile est une véritable 'marque de fabrique' qui se prolongera au-delà de la XIIIe dynastie, tout au long de la Deuxième Période Intermédiaire et jusqu'au Nouvel Empire.

L'engobe est peu épais et mat. C'est ce qui le différencie rapidement à l'œil nu du matériel daté de l'Ancien Empire qui possède des engobes de couleur rouge couvrants et parfois polis.

On note également l'existence d'un engobe blanc qui est parfois associé à certaines catégories de jarres (Figure 2g). Lorsque la surface n'est pas engobée, l'aspect est 'chamois', avec un simple lissage.

La cuisson est de qualité inégale, cela tient vraisemblablement en partie à une porosité nettement épaisses. On constate une telle fréquence des cas de surcuisson qu'ils en deviennent presque une "marque de fabrique".

Le décor peint de couleur rouge est courant (Figure 2 a–b et d). Le répertoire décoratif est répétitif et stéréotypé. Il consiste pour l'essentiel en bandes ou coulures verticales. Plus rarement, pour les jarres (Figure 2d), le motif est composé de lignes ondulées, et dans un cas, on observe des lignes horizontales. On trouve sur un individu une croix simple disposée sur la base du bec verseur des bols (forme identique Figure 1e).

Le cas le plus fréquent reste le rehaut de couleur rouge déposé sur la lèvre (Figure 8b).

L'autre catégorie de décors est le décor pincé des lèvres des jarres (Figure 2c–d) ou des bords et des carènes de

---

[2] Toutes les argiles locales et importées du matériel céramique daté de la Deuxième Période Intermédiaire ont fait l'objet d'un examen sous la loupe binoculaire. Les échantillons de pâte ont tous été examinés sur des cassures fraîches. Des prises de vue ont été réalisées avec une binoculaire Zeis Stemi 2000 et à l'aide d'une caméra vidéo numérique Sony. Le choix des grossissements s'est réduit à deux, l'un faible (X8) pour obtenir une vue d'ensemble de la cassure afin de mieux évaluer la densité et la taille des inclusions les unes par rapport aux autres, et l'autre plus élevé (X15) afin d'affiner l'identification de certaines inclusions. Une échelle est figurée sur chaque cliché. Ces photos seront présentées en annexe de la publication définitive de la fouille qui est en cours.

[3] Il s'agit principalement des travaux menés sur les amphores datées du Nouvel Empire trouvées sur des sites de la Vallée du Nil. Citons les publications de David Aston sur les formes et les fabriques oasiennes, dont D. Aston, *Die Keramik des Grabungsplatzes Q1. Teil 1. Corpus of Fabrics, Wares and Shapes*, Mayence, 1998, 73 Fabric Group V: clays from Dakhleh Oasis?. Enfin, signalons l'étude en cours à l'Institut Français d'Archéologie Orientale sur les étiquettes de jarres à vin trouvées à Deir el Medineh par Laurent Bavay, Janine Bourriau, Sylvie Marchand et Pierre Tallet. Dans ce large ensemble de documents, un petit groupe d'étiquettes provient des Oasis: L. Bavay, S. Marchand et P. Tallet, 'Les jarres inscrites du Nouvel Empire provenant de Deir al-Médina', *Cahiers de la Céramique Égyptienne* 6, 77–86; plus particulièrement la figure 6.

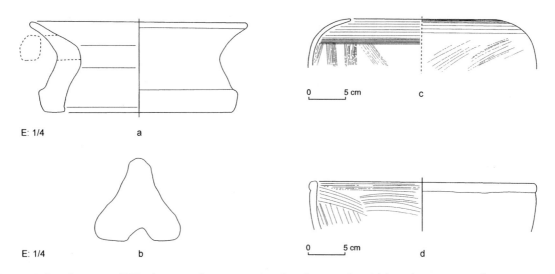

E: 1/4   a

0   5 cm   c

E: 1/4   b

0   5 cm   d

Figure 4 La céramique XIIIe dynastie. Support en pâte locale grossière (a) bouchon conique de terre crue (b); pot de stockage et jatte en pâte locale montée à la main (c–d).

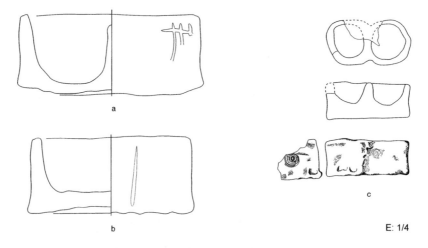

a

b

c

E: 1/4

Figure 5 La céramique XIIIe dynastie. Moules à pain 'double corps' (a et c) et terrines rondes (b).

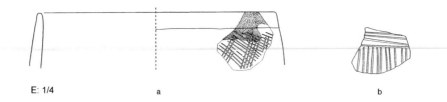

E: 1/4   a   b

Figure 6 La céramique XIIIe dynastie. Céramiques nubiennes en pâte alluviale. Kerma Moyen.

certains bols (Figure 2a et e). Ce décor se retrouve fréquemment associé aux motifs peints en rouge décrit plus haut (Figure 2a, c et d).

1.3 La pâte locale F1-A

Formes céramiques: petit bol hémisphérique (Figure 1a–c), aiguière (Figure 1d).

La céramique dite 'fine' recèle de nombreuses inclusions minérales, mais de petite taille. Nous retrouvons les nodules blancs, les micas et le sable. La texture est qualifiée de fine dans le sens où la porosité est réduite. Un engobe rouge parfois épais la recouvre, il est peu couvrant. Même pour cette catégorie, on identifie la présence d'un dégraissant végétal. L'engobe rouge est souvent partiel, disposé en taches (Figure 1c). On remarque de fréquents rehauts de couleur rouge sur les bords des récipients (forme identique présentée Figure 1d).

1.4 La pâte locale F1-B

Formes céramiques: bol très caréné à bec verseur (Figure 3a), assiette (Figure 8a).

La céramique moyennement fine présente un nombre important d'inclusions minérales visibles à l'œil nu. Un engobe rouge parfois épais, dans de rares cas polis la recouvre (Figures 3a et 8a).

1.5 La pâte locale F1-F

Formes céramiques: assiette (Figure 3b).

Il s'agit d'une pâte identique à la précédente, mais généralement non engobée, d'aspect 'chamois' brun clair. Le dégraissant végétal est cependant moins dense que pour la pâte F1-E.

1.6 Les céramiques de tradition nubienne

Formes céramiques: large bol de cuisson (Figure 6a–b).

Dans presque tous les cas, il s'agit d'une pâte alluviale à fort dégraissant végétal, sableuse et fortement micacée. Le cœur est le plus souvent totalement noir en cassure. La couleur de la surface externe est brun clair, souvent douce, parfois à bord noir mat (Figure 6a). L'intérieur des pots présente dans certains cas une surface de couleur noire

uniforme et polie. Le décor consiste en incisions fines (Figure 6a) ou débordantes et rugueuses (Figure 6b).

L'existence d'une céramique en pâte alluviale fine rouge à bord noir n'a été révélée qu'à deux reprises et dans des contextes perturbés, hors de la fouille du secteur sud.

2. Les Principales Formes dans la Production des Céramiques Datées de la XIIIe Dynastie du Secteur Artisanal de 'Ain Aseel

Le répertoire qui va suivre ne se prétend pas exhaustif. Il n'a d'autre but que de présenter les formes les plus courantes.[4] Ou encore celles qui, même rares, peuvent fournir des indices pour la datation de cet ensemble.

La fonction et l'utilisation de certains récipients seront données au fur et à mesure, lorsque le contexte de leur découverte le permet.

2.1 Les bols hémisphériques (Figure 1a–c)

Cette catégorie de récipients représente 9,2 % de la documentation recueillie. On les retrouve communément dans tous les secteurs de la fouille, il s'agit selon toute vraisemblance d'un bol à boire ou à verser des liquides en petite quantité.

Cette série de bols, en fait, nous pose problème. Elle devrait logiquement constituer notre 'fossile directeur' le plus sûr, et permettre des comparaisons précises avec le matériel issu des fouilles de la Vallée du Nil. La classification des bols hémisphériques, réalisée par Dorothea Arnold (1988, 140), comprend les bols de la XIIe dynastie à la fin de la XIIIe dynastie.[5] Cependant, le système de calcul des indices qui est établi par l'auteur à partir des bols hémisphériques trouvés à Lisht engendre pour notre matériel une certaine confusion.[6] Les exemplaires provenant de la fouille de 'Ain Aseel possèdent un diamètre très faible et un fond moyennement conique. Le résultat du calcul des indices donne des indications très inégales voir incohérentes pour la datation de cette série. Cependant, la forme générale des bols avec des parois très droites et une lèvre amincie, reste le critère le plus significatif. En l'adoptant, ces bols hémisphériques s'inscrivent sans problème majeur dans les séries datées par Do. Arnold de la XIIIe dynastie (Arnold 1988, 61, Figure 17 n° 9–13).

---

[4] Les pourcentages qui vont être donnés dans le cours de l'exposé concernent les secteurs G20, G25 et les niveaux de surface/ou perturbés du palais des gouverneurs (saisons 1995–1997). Ils sont liés à la présentation archéologique du secteur publié par Michel Baud (1997, 19–34).

[5] Pour suivre l'évolution de ce calcul des indices sur les bols hémisphériques jusqu'à la fin de la Deuxième Période Intermédiaire: M. Bietak, Egypt and Canaan during the Middle Bronze Age, *Bulletin of the American Schools of Oriental Research* 281, 50 figure 14. On consultera également les résultats des fouilles d'Eléphantine, C. Von Pilgrim, *Elephantine XVIII*, Mayence, 1996, Figure 4b bols hémisphériques de la fin de la XIIe dynastie, Figure 147–148 datés de la XIIIe dynastie, Figure 145–146 datés de la XVIIe dynastie.

[6] Précisons que ce calcul des indices n'est valable que si l'individu est archéologiquement complet. Nos séries qui permettent le calcul sont peut-être insuffisantes par le nombre d'exemplaires recueillis.

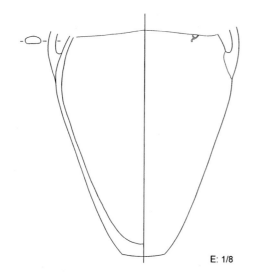

Figure 7 La céramique XIIIe dynastie. Jarre cananéenne.

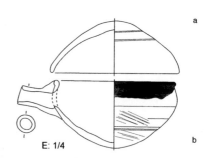

Figure 8 La céramique XIIIe dynastie. Bol à bec verseur FlE (b) muni de son couvercle FlB (a).

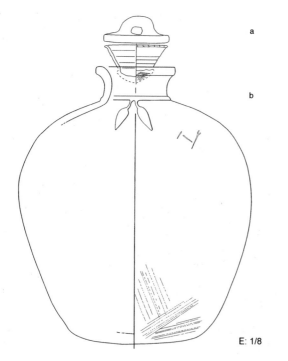

Figure 9 La céramique XIIIe dynastie. Jarre de stockage de grande taille FlE à engobe rouge, munie de ses deux couvercles.

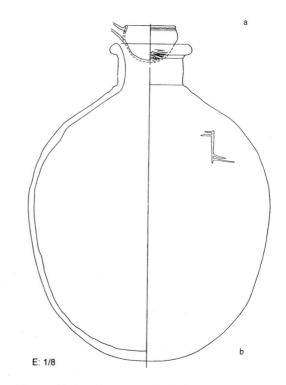

Figure 10 La céramique XIIIe dynastie. Jarre de stockage de grande taille FlE à engobe rouge, munie de son couvercle.

2.2 Les aiguières (Figure 1d)

Cette catégorie de céramiques ne représente que 0,70 % de la céramique exhumée. Il s'agit donc d'une forme rare, vraisemblablement un vase à verser les liquides. On a également retrouvé ce récipient réutilisé mais en contexte cultuel. En effet, trois de ces aiguières ont été découvertes déposées à intervalle régulier, *in situ*, dans le sable de fondation d'un mur délimitant la cour enclose d'un grand bâtiment. On est indubitablement en présence d'un rituel de fondation, fait inhabituel pour un habitat (Baud 1997, 21 et Figure 4).

2.3 Les bols à bec verseur (Figures 1e, 8, 10a)

Ce type de céramique est le plus fréquemment retrouvé dans les fouilles, puisqu'il représente à lui seul presque 33 % des individus comptabilisés. Tous les secteurs de la fouille sont concernés. Ce bol sert vraisemblablement à verser, à puiser ou à la conservation des liquides. L'un d'eux a été découvert en contexte sur un sol muni de son couvercle (Figure 8).

2.4 Les bols évasé à lèvre et carène pincées avec ou sans décor peint (Figures 2a et 9b)

Cette forme ne représente que 1,5 % de la documentation et concerne l'habitat. Il s'agit d'un bol de présentation pour éléments solides. Comme réutilisation possible, il a été retrouvé en place comme premier couvercle pour une jarre de stockage découverte *in situ* (Figure 9).

2.5 Les jarres à haut col à lèvre pincée (Figure 2c–d)

Cette catégorie est à rattacher directement à la précédente, avec la même fabrique, la même lèvre pincée et le même décor peint que ce qui a été décrit précédemment. Ces jarres de petite taille ne représentent que 1,7% de la documentation, aucun individu intact n'a été découvert. On la retrouve associée à l'habitat.

2.6 L'encensoir (Figure 2e)

Cet objet qui est façonné à la main est le seul exemplaire de ce type découvert à 'Ain Aseel. La lèvre est pincée de façon régulière sur son pourtour. La présence de traces de feu à l'intérieur et sur les bords, ainsi que la taille de la pièce, fait penser à un encensoir.

2.7 Les jarres à col à lèvre retournée (Figure 2g)

Il s'agit du type de jarre le plus massivement représenté (15 % de la documentation). On la retrouve invariablement dans tous les secteurs de la fouille. Cette jarre ne porte

jamais de décor, le façonnage est peu soigné. Ces récipients de taille moyenne sont vraisemblablement utilisés pour le transport et la conservation des denrées diverses. Il est possible que certains des bouchons de terre crue de forme conique qui ont été découverts en grand nombre y soient associés (Figure 4b). Précisons qu'aucun de ces bouchons n'a été découvert en place sur une jarre.

2.8 Les larges assiettes évasées (Figure 3b)

Ces récipients sont représentés à 3%. Présentation ou couvercles, ces assiettes peuvent servir à de multiples usages.

2.9 Le pot sans col (Figure 3c)

Il s'agit de l'unique exemplaire découvert. Il a été recueilli *in situ* dans une grande cour qui était consacrée à des activités de production alimentaire (Baud 1997, 21–2).

2.10 Les supports de jarre de grande taille (Figure 4a)

Ils représentent moins de 1 % de la documentation. Ils sont tous de grande taille courts et tronconiques.

2.11 Les jarres sans col montées à la main à bord rentrant (Figure 4c)

Ces larges pots représentent 1% de la documentation. Il s'agit de pots de stockage de denrée alimentaire.

2.12 Les jattes (Figure 4d)

Elles concernent plus de 11% de la documentation recueillie. Elles sont façonnées à la main et de grande taille. Aucune ne présente de trace de feu, l'intérieur est toujours lisse et sans aspérité. Il s'agit vraisemblablement d'un récipient utilisé pour les préparations alimentaires.

2.13 Les moules à pain 'double corps' et les terrines rondes (Figure 5)

Pour tous les secteurs étudiés, ils constituent la majorité écrasante du matériel céramique représenté. Les comptages ont été systématiquement réalisés dans les sondages stratigraphiques, mais pas dans les fosses/dépotoirs qui contenaient du matériel chronologiquement mélangé. Cependant, un test a été réalisé pour l'une d'entre elle afin d'évaluer cette masse. Prenons l'exemple d'une couche de type dépotoir[7] qui livre: 2688 moules à pain (87,9 %), 58 terrines (1,8 %) contre 310 individus céramiques autres (10 %).

---

[7] Secteur G20. US d1118.

Les moules à pain 'double corps' (Figure 5a) illustrent un particularisme oasien au sens large. En effet, cette forme n'est attestée, dans l'état actuel de nos connaissances, que dans le matériel céramique de l'oasis de Dakhleh et de Kharga, mais également dans celui de Baharyia.[8]

Signalons qu'au moins un individu complet a été répertorié dans le matériel conservé en magasin à la suite des fouilles du Service des antiquités de la nécropole de 'Ain-Askar à Kharga. Il s'agit d'un ensemble de tombes datées de la XIIIe dynastie à la fin de la Deuxième Période intermédiaire/début Nouvel Empire.[9]

Il est important de signaler que les moules à pain 'double corps' ont été également identifiés hors des oasis, en Nubie à Toshka (Simpson 1963, 44 et Plate XXII). Ils étaient associés à du matériel *'Pan-graves'*.

Il existe également un petit lot de moules à pain double corps miniaturisés (Figure 5c).

Les moules de taille normale (Figure 5a) ou miniaturisés (Figure 5c) portent fréquemment des marques incisées, de même pour les terrines rondes (Figure 5b) que l'on rencontre en nombre conséquent. Ces incisions sont des signes schématiques.[10]

Les moules à pain de forme identique à ceux attestés pour la même période dans la vallée du Nil existent, mais ne concernent qu'un très petit nombre d'individus.

2.14 Les céramiques nubiennes (Figure 6a–b)

La presque totalité des céramiques nubiennes découvertes sont des pots ou grands bols de cuisson façonnés dans une argile de type alluviale grossière à fort dégraissant végétal. Il s'agit donc d'une vaisselle à usage domestique. La céramique fine rouge à bord noir n'est représentée que par deux individus apparentés à des bols de taille moyenne trouvés hors du contexte de la fouille. Précisons que si le nombre des céramiques nubiennes reste faible, on ne doit plus les considérer comme anecdotiques. En effet, on recense pour l'ensemble de la fouille: 30 individus apparentés au *Kerma moyen* (Figure 6a–b) et 10 avec impressions de natte ('nids d'abeilles') apparentés au *Kerma Classique*.[11] Ces premières attributions sont susceptibles d'évoluer encore. En effet, il est parfois difficile de trancher sur l'appartenance d'une céramique à un groupe plutôt qu'à un autre. Le problème se pose pour les céramiques fines rouge à bord noir, ou pour d'autres tessons qui 'flottent' entre le *groupe C* ou la culture *Pan Grave*.

La méconnaissance des cultures nubiennes il y a encore peu, fait que la culture Kerma (*Kerma Moyen*) n'apparaît jamais dans les fouilles anciennes qui présentent des céramiques nubiennes trouvées en Égypte. L'attribution trop systématique de ces tessons à la culture *'Pan Graves'* ne doit pas faire oublier la culture du *Groupe C* ou celle du *Kerma Moyen* qui lui sont contemporaines. L'attribution des tessons trouvés en contexte daté de la fin de la XIIIe dynastie à 'Ain-Aseel, à la culture du *Kerma Moyen* est une hypothèse de travail qu'il faut maintenant considérer. Je remercie Brigitte Gratien d'avoir attiré mon attention sur ce problème et d'avoir expertisé quelques tessons d'après photographies.[12]

2.15 Les jarres cananéennes (Figure 7)

Seuls deux individus ont été découverts pour l'ensemble des secteurs fouillés.[13] Il s'agit donc d'une forme rare.

---

[8] Les fouilles récentes et la prospection d'une partie de l'oasis de Baharyia ont permis de localiser des nécropoles du Moyen Empire-Deuxième Période Intermédiaire et de la XVIIIe dynastie. Ces moules à pain 'double corps' ont été identifiés sur deux nécropoles. La première est située à Qaret et-Tub; F. Colin, D. Laisney, S. Marchand, 'Qaret el-Tub: un fort romain et une nécropole pharaonique. Prospection archéologique dans l'oasis de Baharyia 1999', *Bulletin de L'Institut Français d'Archéologie Orientale* 100, 2000, 145–92, figure 9 moule à pain 'double corps' associé à du matériel céramique daté de la XIIIe dynastie à la XVIIIe dynastie (figures 1–29). La deuxième nécropole est celle de Khataba qui a été prospectée en 2000. Des moules à pain 'double corps' complets ont été ramassés en surface, ils étaient associés à des céramiques qui s'échelonnent de la XIIIe dynastie à la XVIIIe dynastie. Signalons que des moules à pain 'double-corps' ont été identifies à Dakhla par le Dakhleh Oasis Project dans ce qui pourrait être des niveaux dates de la VIe dynastie (je remercie Colin Hope pour cette information.

[9] Les fouilles ont été conduites en 1997 sous la responsabilité de Ahmed Bahgat (Responsable de l'inspectorat de Kharga). Qu'il me soit permis de le remercier pour m'avoir autoriser à dessiner et à étudier l'ensemble de la documentation conservée à l'Inspectorat de Kharga.

[10] Le répertoire de ces marques incisées avant cuisson sur les moules à pain et les terrines sont à l'étude. Les jarres (figures 9 et 10) sont également porteuses de ce type de marque.

[11] Les tessons de céramique nubienne apparentés au *Kerma Classique* sont principalement collectés en surface des sondages ou dans certaines zones perturbées du palais des gouverneurs. Ils sont souvent associés à des céramiques datées de la fin de la Deuxième Période intermédiaire au début du Nouvel Empire.

[12] On se référera à l'article de B. Gratien qui fait le point sur la documentation publiée à ce sujet. B. Gratien, 'Les pots de cuisson nubiens et les bols décorés de la première moitié du IIe millénaire avant J.-C. Problèmes d'identification', *Cahiers de la Céramique Egyptienne* 6, 2000, 113–48. On consultera également P. Lacovara, 'Egypt and Nubia during the Second Intermediate Period', in E. Oren, éd., *The Hyksos: New Historical Archaeological Perspectives*, Philadelpie, 1997, 69–83; et J. Bourriau 'Relations between Egypt and Kerma during the Middle Kingdom and the New Kingdom', in W. Davies, éd., *Egypt and Africa*, Londres, 1991, 129–43.

[13] Pour comparaison (forme, pâte et chronologie identiques), on consultera: D. Arnold, F. Arnolds et S. Allen, 'Canaanite Imports at Lisht, The Middle Kingdom Capital of Egypt', *Egypt and the Levant* V, 1995, 13–32, figure 6 Canaanite Pottery n° 21–3.

En général le nombre des importations est extrêmement réduit sur le site.

Cette rareté concerne aussi les céramiques issues de la vallée du Nil. Seuls trois individus ont été exhumés.

2.16 Les jarres de stockage de grande taille (Figures 9 et 10)

La jarre (Figure 9) munie de ses deux couvercles est un exemplaire unique avec son décor floral d'argile appliquée. Les jarres apparentées au type présenté (Figure 10) représentent 5% de la documentation examinée. Une jarre de ce type, muni de son couvercle, a été découverte *in situ* dans une grande cour qui était consacrée à des activités de production alimentaire (Baud 1997, 25). Ces jarres de grande taille constituent le grand module de celles qui sont présentées sur la Figure 2g.

3. La Détermination des Groupes de Céramiques Selon Leur Contexte

La céramique recueillie lors des fouilles des boulangeries et de l'habitat nous invite à pousser plus loin leur étude en relation avec la nature artisanale et domestique des bâtiments fouillés. En fonction des données qui ont été publiées pour les tombes datées de la XIIIe dynastie (Deuxième Période Intermédiaire) découvertes dans l'oasis de Dakhleh, il est en effet souhaitable de comparer le matériel céramique d'une même période l'une en contexte urbain, 'Ain Aseel, et l'autre en contexte funéraire, Qil'a al-Dab'a et les tombes publiées par le Dakhleh Oasis Project. On se contentera d'explorer quelques pistes très générales qui demanderont à êtres étudiés de façon plus systématique.

Tous ces indices ne sont valables que si le matériel que l'on compare est exactement contemporain.

3.1 Les groupes de céramiques communs (contextes urbain et funéraire)

Cela concerne les groupes les plus nombreux. On constate qu'il s'agit des formes les plus usuelles retrouvées en grand nombre en contexte urbain. On se reportera aux pourcentages indiqués plus haut.

Les formes qui se retrouvent indifféremment dans le matériel céramique provenant des tombes ou de la ville sont principalement les suivantes:
- Les bols hémisphériques (Figure 1a–c)
- Les bols à bec verseur à puiser et-ou à verser (Figure 1e)
- Les encensoirs (Figure 2e)

- Les supports hauts à col en 'trompette' de petite taille (Figure 2f)
- Les jarres à col de dimension moyenne de toutes catégories (Figure 2g–h)
- Les coupes à carène (Figure 3a)
- Les assiettes évasées (Figure 3b).

3.2 Les groupes de céramiques ou les décors spécifiques en contexte urbain

- Les jarres à décor peint en rouge et de lèvre pincé (Figure 2c–d)
- Les supports tronconiques de grande taille (Figure 4a)
- Les jarres de stockage (Figure 4c)
- Les jattes de préparation alimentaire (Figure 4d)
- Les moules à pain 'double corps' (Figure 5 a)
- Les céramiques de tradition nubienne: *Kerma Moyen* en majorité[14] (Figure 6)
- Les jarres/amphores d'origine cananéenne (Figure 7)
- Les jarres de stockage de grande taille (Figures 9 et 10)

3.3 L'adaptation des modèles

À l'examen du matériel, on constate un phénomène d'adaptation d'un modèle à usage domestique pour son usage funéraire. Cela concerne principalement deux catégories. Celle des bols à bec verseur (Figure 1e). Dans le premier cas, la forme générale est identique pour le matériel provenant de la ville ou des tombes. Cependant, on les distingue par la présence d'une base systématiquement aplatie pour les modèles qui proviennent des tombes (Aufrère et Ballet 1990, 24 n° 17; Edwards *et al.* 1987, 42, Plate XX n° 11 et 85, Figure 2 k–l; Hope, 1999, 277, n° 16–17). Le constat est le même pour les bols à carène (Figure 2a) dont les fonds deviennent systématiquement plats, mais ils conservent leur décor peint (Edwards *et al.* 1987, 42 n° 14, sans lèvre pincée).[15]

Conclusion

En guise de conclusion, il convient de préciser les limites du schéma proposé. Si ce cadre théorique, dans l'état actuel de nos connaissances, fonctionne correctement dans les limites géographiques de l'oasis de Dakhleh, il ne s'applique pas systématiquement pour le matériel découvert dans l'oasis voisine de Kharga ou pour celui de Baharyia. Les céramiques datées de la XIIIe dynastie provenant des fouilles du Service des Antiquités dans la nécropole de 'Ain Askar le montrent clairement. On remarque par exemple que le phénomène d'adaptation évoqué ci-dessus

---

[14] Edwards *et al.*, 1987, 29 et plate XXVIIIa 'Pangrave sherds'. Ces deux tessons ont été collectés sur le site 32/390-I5-1 très endommagé.

[15] Il convient de noter la présence de matériel identique dans la Vallée du Nil pour la même période (bols à carène à base plate, avec ou sans décor de bandes verticales peintes). On consultera: A. L. Kelley, *The Pottery of Ancient Egypt*, Royal Ontario Museum, 1976; plate 45.3–4 (site d'Armant); plate 44.2 (site de Khargeh); plate 43.1 (sites de Qau et de Badari); plate 48.1 (site d'Abydos).

n'existe pas à 'Ain Askar. En effet, les bols à bec verseur trouvés dans ces tombes sont identiques à ceux qui sont découverts en contexte urbain à 'Ain Aseel. On constate également que les moules à pain 'double corps' qui sont absents en contexte strictement funéraire à Dakhleh se retrouvent dans les tombes de 'Ain Askar[16] à Kharga, et en surface de deux nécropoles de l'oasis de Baharyia.

Il convient donc pour le moment de se contenter de ces quelques éléments de réflexion générale, et de se limiter au cadre géographique de l'Oasis de Dakhleh.

On remarque que les formes spécifiques à vocation exclusivement domestique ou spécifiquement funéraire sont finalement peu nombreuses. Ces dernières concernent le plus souvent les formes les plus courantes trouvées en contexte urbain. Quant à la fonction des objets en contexte urbain elle reste le plus souvent bien vague. Ce qui est le schéma le plus courant pour les époques pharaoniques.[17] Bien souvent le bon sens demeure le seul indicateur. Le manque de rationalisation et de spécificité des vaisselles culinaires pharaoniques est assez évident, à la différence des vaisselles culinaires grecques et romaines très spécialisées et très diversifiées dans le choix de la pâte et dans ses formes.[18]

On remarque pour l'Égypte dynastique, à l'exception des pots utilisés pour le pain et la bière[19] ou encore du cas très spécifique de quelques vaisselles cultuelles, Du Mesnil du Buisson 1935, que les pots en terre cuite à usage domestique n'ont pas clairement de nom, si ce n'est très générique sans rapport clair avec les formes (Du Mesnil du Buisson 1935, 10–11, 142–7; Vandier, 1964, 144–70). La fonction des objets découverts est souvent aventureuse. Il n'existe pas de glossaires de la céramique domestique égyptienne pour l'Égypte pharaonique qui soit comparable à ceux qui existent pour le monde grec et romain.

Author's Address:
L'Institut Français d'Archéologie Orientale
37 Shariya Sheikh Aly Youssef,
Mounira, Cairo,
Arab Republic of Egypt

REFERENCES

Arnold, D. and Do. Arnold, 1988 *The pyramid of Senwosret I*, Metropolitan Museum of Art, New York.

Aufrère, S. and P. Ballet,1990 La nécropole sud de Qila 'Al-Dabba, *Bulletin de L'Institut Français d'Archéologie Orientale* 90, 1–28.

Baud, M., 1997 Balat/'Ayn-Asîl, oasis de Dakhla. La ville de la Deuxième Période intermédiaire, *Bulletin de L'Institut Français d'Archéologie Orientale* 97, 19–34.

Du Mesnil du Buisson, R., 1935 *Les noms et signes égyptiens désignant des vases ou objets similaires*, Librairie Paul Geuthner, Paris.

Edwards, W. I., C. A. Hope and E. R. Segnit, 1987 *Ceramics from the Dakhleh Oasis, Preliminary Studies*, Victoria College Press, Burwood, Australia.

Hope, C. A., 1999 Pottery Manufacture in the Dakhleh Oasis, in C. S. Churcher and A. J. Mills, eds, *Reports from the Survey of the Dakhleh Oasis Western Desert of Egypt 1977–1987*, Oxbow Books, Oxford, 215–43.

Hope, C. A., M. Eccleston, P. Rose and J. Bourriau, 2002 Oases Amphorae of the New Kingdom, in R. Friedman, ed., *Egypt and Nubia: Gifts of the Desert*, The British Museum Press, London, 95–131.

Marchand, S. and P. Tallet, 1999 'Ayn-Asîl et l'oasis de Dakhla au Nouvel Empire, *Bulletin de L'Institut Français d'Archéologie Orientale* 99, 307–52.

Simpson, W. K., 1963 *Heka-Nefer*, Yale University-University of Pennsylvania, New-Haven, Philadelphie.

Soukiassian, G., L. Pantalacci and M. Wuttmann, 2002 *Le palais des gouverneurs du règne de Pepy II: les sanctuaires de Ka et leurs dépendances*, Balat VI, Institut Français d'Archéologie Orientale, Cairo.

Soukiassian, G., M. Wuttmann and D. Schaad, 1990a La ville d'Ayn-Asîl à Dakhla. Etat des recherches, *Bulletin de L'Institut Français d'Archéologie Orientale* 90, 347–58.

Soukiassian, G., M. Wuttmann, L. Pantalacci, P. Ballet and M. Picon, 1990b *Balat III, Les ateliers de potiers d'Ayn-Asîl*, Institut Français d'Archéologie Orientale, Cairo.

Vandier, J., 1964 *Manuel d'Archéologie égyptienne* IV, Éditions Picard, Paris, 144–70.

---

[16] Le seul exemplaire conservé dans le magasin du service est complet, nous ignorons l'existence de fragments appartenant à d'autres individus qui auraient été laissés sur le site.

[17] Pour des remarques d'ordre général sur la fonction des céramiques de la vie de tous les jours aux époques pharaoniques: P. Paice, 'The pottery of daily life in Ancient Egypt', *Journal of the Society for the Study of Egyptian Antiquities* XIX, 1989, 50–88. Pour les quelques recettes et modes de préparations pour l'époque pharaonique à notre disposition, on consultera Hérodote, *L'enquête*, Livre I à IV, H. Barguet, éd., Paris, 1985, 199, chapitre 77 Moeurs des Égyptiens: le crû, le séché, le salé, le rôti et le bouilli pour poissons et oiseaux, 205, chapitre 92 Lotus et papyrus: cuisson à l'étouffée à four chaud des tiges de papyrus. On consultera un article qui fait le point sur ces processus alimentaires, S. Ikram, 'Meat Processing', in P. T. Nicholson et I. Shaw, éd., *Ancient Egyptian Material and Technology*, Cambridge University Press, 2000, 656–71.

[18] Pour les époques plus tardives (époques ptolémaïque et romaine) le schéma est totalement différent : les céramiques ont un nom et une fonction précise, notamment la vaisselle culinaire (préparation, cuisson et présentation des denrées alimentaires), si difficile à étudier pour les périodes plus anciennes en Egypte. Le meilleur ouvrage qui fait le point sur ce sujet pour tout le monde antique et qui s'adapte également à l'Egypte reste M. Bats, *Vaisselle et alimentation à Olbia de Provence (v. 350-v. 50 av. JC.), Modèles culturels et catégories céramiques*, Centre Nationale de Recherches Scientifiques, Paris, 1988.

[19] D. Faltings, *Die Keramik der Lebensmittelproduktion im Alten Reich*, Heildelberg, 1988, pour les céramiques datées de l'Ancien Empire.

'Ain el-Gazzareen:
Developments in the Old Kingdom Settlement

Anthony J. Mills and Olaf E. Kaper

Abstract

'Ain el-Gazzareen, in Western Dakhleh Oasis, has been under excavation for the past four seasons. Initial prospecting at the site showed great promise, which subsequent geophysical surveying enhanced. Excavation confirmed the geophysical results and the 1999–2000 season has revealed a large building with considerable symmetry which may be an indicator of the importance of the site. It has also revealed our first real architectural stratigraphy. Next season should prove particularly important for our appreciation of the Old Kingdom settlement in the oasis.

Previous Work

In October 1979, Rosa Frey investigated some of the area between Amheida and Mushiya as a part of the walking survey of the Dakhleh Oasis. This was during the initial phase of the Dakhleh Oasis Project's field programme to ascertain the number and variety of ancient remains in the oasis and each site, as it was found, was given a surface inspection to determine its apparent extent and dated from the artefacts that were collected from the surface. At the same time, a small test excavation was made to assess the depth of fill each the site, the occurrence of any stratigraphy, the sub-surface condition of the site, and the quality of preservation at the site. Frey's initial assessment of 'Ain el-Gazzareen was that it was an Old Kingdom town-site covering an area of over 500 x 150 m with an extensive surface scatter of Old Kingdom pottery, flints, sandstone grindstones, and ostrich eggshell. Several mud-brick buildings were located, particularly at the west side of the site. It was given the index number 32/390-K2-2 (Mills 1980, 257–8) in the system utilized by the Dakhleh Oasis Project. Two separate tests were excavated by Frey, close to one another with a resulting description of

architecture and artefactual finds. The survey then moved on and the Project's interest in the site remained dormant for a couple of decades.

In 1997 it was realized that while the Project had 200 prehistoric sites and approximately 220 sites ascribed to the late Pharaonic to the Roman Period, other than ceramics (Hope 1999, 221–9) there had been little to provide information of a substantial nature, except at the cemetery at 'Ain Tirghi, about the intervening millennia between the Neolithic and the Roman Periods. To excavate in a settlement site with not such an obviously official capacity but of a date similar to that of the Old Kingdom capital of the oasis at 'Ain Aseel, it seemed especially useful to make a search amongst the 50 or so Old Kingdom sites indexed by the survey. Eventually, 'Ain el-Gazzareen was chosen as seemingly the most appropriate site to complement the work of the Institut Français d'Archéologie Orientale team and to present a picture of life in the oasis during the third millennium at the beginning of pharaonic settlement.

As has been explained (Mills 1995, 61–5; Mills 2002a and b), the quantity and quality of surface material on the site, the type of site, its probable connexion with the official capital at 'Ain Aseel, and the potential of the site to explain so much about the activity of the period in the area, were among the reasons for its investigation. The first two seasons, 1996–7 and 1997–8, were occupied in excavating a bakery structure in a square of 10 x 15 m, and in the recovery and assessment of floral and faunal materials, as well as artefacts, which well demonstrated the nature of the buildings and of the industry in them. Dating the site is mainly based on the ceramics and is at least Dynasty V and VI.[1] There is also a series of seal impressions which help to fortify this dating (see Kaper below and Figures 2 and 3). Surface assessments have now placed the site's extent at nearly 5 hectares in total, with a maximum width from east to west of about 125 m.

---

[1] The study of this material under the supervision of Colin Hope commenced in the 2001/2 season and continued in the 2002/3 season. The results will be reported at a later date.

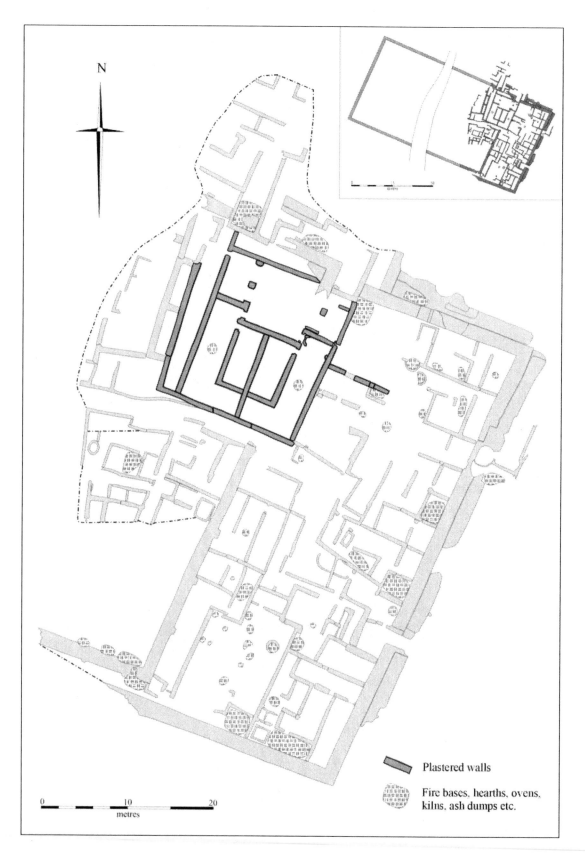

N

Plastered walls

Fire bases, hearths, ovens,
kilns, ash dumps etc.

0   10   20
         metres

Figure 1 'Ain el-Gazzareen (32/390-K2-2); plan of excavated area.

Plate 1 The heavy eastern wall of the enclosure with the series of interior rooms abutting it.

Recent Excavations

Work has now been conducted at the site, with the assistance of Richard Mortimer and Natasha Dodwell, in two subsequent seasons, in 1999–2000 and 2000–2001, with interesting results. It was suggested to the writer by Tomasz Herbich, the then secretary of the Polish Centre for Mediterranean Studies, that 'Ain el-Gazzareen would be a good subject for a geophysical survey. It was agreed and he began surveying early in January 2000, together with his colleague Tatyana Smekalova, using a Geoscan fluxgate gradiometer and Overhauser gradiometer GSM-19WG magnetometers (Herbich and Smekalova 2001, 259–62). The results were most satisfying. The survey, in the general vicinity of the previous season's excavations, revealed the presence of a large enclosure, some 55 m from north to south and 125 m from east to west. There appeared to be, under the architecturally-featureless surface, a rectangular structure which contained small architecture as well as traces of burning in many places: perhaps the remains of industrial activity, or simple cooking fires. One other large feature was an internal wall, apparently as heavy as the enclosure wall, running parallel to the outer east wall and some 25 m to its west, and apparently dividing the 'enclosure' into two unequal parts (Figure 1).

These results had then to be tested by excavation, which proved the accuracy of the geophysic's results. In the season following the geophysical survey we excavated along the eastern wall of the enclosure and exposed a heavy mud-brick wall, with a width of some 3.50 m, together with a series of rooms built against the interior, west, face of the wall (Plate 1). This wall turned westwards at each end and the three walls together formed the eastern end of the great enclosure. These walls were traced to their ends, at a distance of some 25 metres. The western ends of the eastern enclosure walls approach but do not connect with the north and south walls of the larger, western enclosure.

The eastern enclosure would seem to have been a subsequent addition to the larger enclosure as the western wall of the smaller utilizes the east wall of the larger enclosure but does not join it. The ends of the north and south walls are not attached to the western enclosure and do not in fact form an enclosed space but leave openings at both of the western ends. Excavation has largely been with brush and scraping. This serves to disclose wall tops and the upper 30 cm of each space, without disturbing floor deposits. One test of about one metre square was excavated in the corner of the south-easternmost room and disclosed a complete wall height for the enclosure wall corner of 0.75 m. The floor of the room is, of course, above the wall bottom.

The interior is divided by mud-brick walls, generally one brick thick, into nearly fifty 'spaces'. There are 13 of these 'rooms' built against the inside of the eastern enclosure wall (Plate 1), and the remainder across the enclosure. The architecture of this eastern enclosure will not, of course, be completely understood until it has been fully excavated, but it appears to have been constructed in a planned, but rather haphazard fashion. The row of 13

Plate 2 Deposit of ceramics, flints and bone artefacts at a high floor level in Room 51.

Plate 3 Building 'C', showing the southern symmetrical rooms; view from the north.

rooms across the inner face of the eastern enclosure wall have more or less straight walls and right angled corners, but to the west of these lies a much more irregular set of spaces. A few of the spaces are too large to have been roofed and must have been courtyards or open spaces for industrial process or gathering areas. As the plan now stands, access to most of the rooms is uncertain, but may become obvious when excavations are deeper. There are no obvious corridors or access to many of the spaces. There is a large, built entrance gap in the eastern wall, but access is only into a very few rooms. Possibly, there was other access into this eastern enclosure from the west, at either end or via the passage leading eastwards between buildings at the side of the bakery.

There are several features within the eastern enclosure. These include areas of ash deposits as indicated on the plan. The deposit in the rectangular room against the southern wall was particularly dense and thick, rather like that in the bakery area (Mills 1980, 61–5) excavated previously. Other ash deposits are less dense and probably represent cooking or other more domestic fires. Samples have been taken from most of these deposits for botanical analysis by Johannes Walter and virtually all the fuel found in these deposits is tamarisk and acacia. There are also a number of areas where water seems to have affected the soil and deposits. This may have been contemporaneous but could as easily represent activity, human or even natural, after the site had been abandoned. Finally, there are a number of round or rounded pits, up to a metre deep, which also may be post-abandonment. In one of these, a large limestone column element was found, although it seemingly was not *in situ*.

Potsherds of various late Old Kingdom wares have been found in the upper fill of these spaces and, exceptionally, entire vessels (Plate 2). The heavy bread moulds are not common, unlike in the area of the bakery. Chipped stone materials occur, although these are more concentrated in surface deposits, which are the amalgamation of up to two metres of deflation. Objects are rare; the seal impressions that were common in the bakery (Mills 2002b, 28–9) are absent. In a scattered deposit in one room there was a variety of beads in stone and faience, a few bone and copper awls, three complete pottery vessels, one drop-shaped jar and two bowls, seven long bones of a ?goat perhaps collected for preparation into awls, and some chipped stone artefacts (Plate 2). This was an unusually rich deposit. The fill of the area of the eastern enclosure was largely sand, mixed with some ash and soil.

The eastern enclosure abuts the western or main enclosure. The walls of this larger enclosure are some one metre thick and have rectangular buttresses at intervals of up to 3.50 m on the outer face. These buttresses are seen on the eastern, southern and northern segments. The buttresses are small and may serve a decorative function, rather than a structural one. No deliberately-made doorway or entryway has yet been discerned. The eastern wall of this main enclosure has been interrupted. At a distance of 18.2 metres from the south corner, a lane cuts across the wall and immediately north of the lane is a large building, 'Building C' (Plate 3), which has been built at a level above the top of this wall. At a distance of about 12 metres northwards from the break in the wall, it is resumed, just before a corner at which it turns at a right angle to the west. The geophysical survey results do not indicate any break in this wall and it is expected to be able to trace it at a lower level.

It is the large building which lies atop the eastern wall of the main enclosure and is partly within the area of the eastern enclosure, but mostly within the main enclosure, that is now our main focus. This building is quite different from the rest of the structures seen to date. The building has straight walls with good rectangular corners. The walls are well built and are 1½ bricks wide. The southern part of the structure has four rooms or spaces. There is a symmetry in the internal arrangement of the rooms, with two opposed L-shaped rooms at the outside and two rectangular rooms on the inside. Doorways into each of the two outer rooms are from behind a 'partition' wall on the north, and then the entrance into each of the inner, rectangular room is from the outer L-shaped room adjacent to it. There is no communicating door between these two 'pairings'. To add to the symmetry, there is a round pit, 80 cm in diameter, at the centre of each of the L-shaped rooms. These two pits were identical in size, position, shape, and both contained an ashy fill, although the sides do not display any particular evidence of burning. On all of the walls in this part of the building, there is a heavy, grey mud plaster, up to 5 cm thick. On the western wall of the western room there are traces of a rather thin wash of yellow pigment, and in the entrance at the north into this same room is a thick red coating of paint. A number of large fragments of packed mud with the impression of palm-leaf stems on one side betray the existence of flat roofs on this part of the building. As the mud layer is thick, there may have been a second storey above.

A surface examination of the remainder of the building to the north of these four rooms indicates an open court with two rows of square pillars and buttresses. This gives the structure an even, more formal aspect, with hidden rooms at the southern end and more open spaces towards the north. It is interesting that while the fill of many of the rooms in the eastern enclosure contained potsherds and other debris that might be attributed to a living space, none of the rooms in this Building C contained much artefactual debris at all. In the inner, western room, was a mound of sherds of red polished ware vessels which appeared to have been collected together at the north-eastern corner to tidy up other spaces. There were several column drums, each approximately 20 cm in diameter and about 25 cm high. They are of limestone and each has two opposed flat surfaces, on one of which are traces of red paint, apparently from the painted (?wooden) column that rested on each of them. None of these bases was found *in situ* and none of the four rooms is wide enough to warrant a ceiling support.

It would be premature to offer an interpretation of this structure, until the northern part has been fully examined. However, it is difficult to avoid comparison with the remainder of the architecture on the site. This structure is well and regularly built with comparatively heavy walls of 1½ brick thickness, whereas the other building in the eastern enclosure is less regular and has generally thin walls of a single brick. Within these rooms almost no living debris was found and the rooms' contents were few; some sherds and a few circular limestone column bases of about 25 cm diameter and some 25 cm thick. None of these were *in situ*. In the eastern enclosure there are signs of activity everywhere. The walls are thickly and carefully plastered and there is evidence for decorated wall surfaces, none of which is visible in the remainder of the site. A similar structure has been reported from 'Ain Aseel as a large, symmetrical apartment (Soukiassian 1997, 16). However, that structure is less complex than the one at 'Ain el-Gazzareen.

It is also appropriate to report here that Michal Kobuseiwicz of the Polish Academy of Sciences in Poznan, has begun an analysis of the chipped stone industry found at 'Ain el-Gazzareen. Intensive pick-up has been accomplished in a 100-metre square on the site as well as collection of large groups, probably representing knapping areas, that have been seen at various places on the site. These collections, as well as excavated materials in the future, will be analysed in order to come to an understanding of the industry at the site. This will be compared with the industry on the contemporaneous Sheikh Muftah sites, and that from other Old Kingdom sites from other parts of Egypt. This is intended to give us a broad and detailed insight into the chipped stone industry of late Old Kingdom Egypt and to provide an example of collection, recording and analysis of the industry throughout dynastic Egypt. With chert and flint so widely available, ancient Egyptians must have utilized the material in an easily-understood industry throughout their history.

The work at 'Ain el-Gazzareen will continue to provide considerable information about the life of the Dakhleh Oasis community, its internal composition and interactions, as well as its relationships with the Nile Valley and with Saharan and other oasis communities of a similar date. So far, it has greatly rewarded the Dakhleh Oasis Project.

(AJM)

Preliminary Remarks on the Seal Impressions from 'Ain el-Gazzareen

A total of 45 seal impressions and a few inscribed sealings are currently known from the excavations at 'Ain el-Gazzareen. These impressions provide evidence for Egyptian administrative practice in this part of the oasis, and their interpretation will be largely dependent upon a comparison with the hundreds of impressions found at the oasis' capital at 'Ain Aseel (Pantalacci 1996). Recently, a collection of 164 seal impressions and related material from the *ka*-chapels of the governors at 'Ain Aseel were

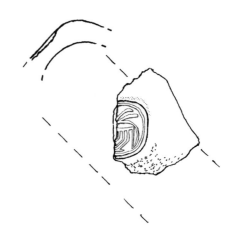

Figure 2 The seal impression with a bee used for sealing a bolt (drawing by B. Parr). Scale 1:1.

published by Pantalacci (Soukiassian *et al.* 2002, 365–74, 385–445). Smaller collections of seal impressions have already been published from the cemetery at Qal'a ed-Dabba and the pottery workshops at 'Ain Aseel, but the recent publication provides the first evidence from the urban area. This comparative material has prompted the following preliminary remarks on the finds from 'Ain el-Gazzareen.

One actual stamp seal was found at 'Ain el-Gazzareen, made of ceramic, and six examples made of this material may be cited from the *ka*-chapels complex at 'Ain Aseel (Soukiassian *et al.* 2002, 385–91). As Pantalacci has noted, this material is unknown for contemporary seals from the Egyptian Nile Valley and there are only a few parallels from Nubia (Soukiassian *et al.* 2002, 385, citing Wiese 1996, 99). The shape of the stamp seal from 'Ain el-Gazzareen is different to those found at 'Ain Aseel, and its study is continuing.

The majority of the seals employed at 'Ain el-Gazzareen were button seals, and a smaller number of seal impressions was stamped with a cylinder seal. This division, the range of devices and the shapes of the seals generally conform with the finds at 'Ain Aseel.

One broken sealing found in 2001 in Building C carries the impression of a door bolt on its back. Two other sealings are known from other locations at 'Ain el-Gazzareen with clear impressions of bolts. This particular door in Building C had been sealed with a button seal with a bee as its device (Figure 2). The bee is a frequent theme among the seal impressions at 'Ain Aseel. Pantalacci has explained it as a symbol of royal power, and she has compared it to the frequent depictions of falcons and crouching lions upon the seals (Soukiassian *et al.* 2002, 395).

There are 17 stamped bread moulds from 'Ain el-Gazzareen. All of these were found in the excavation squares H13 and I13, which was identified as a bakery. The seals are stamped in the outer face of the moulds, a practice that should evidently be related to the more frequent incised marks found in the bread moulds at 'Ain

Figure 3 The drawing of the device on seven bread moulds, composed on the basis of different impressions. Scale 1:1.

el-Gazzareen and also Balat (Soukiassian *et al.* 2002, 446–56). This is confirmed by one of the fragmentary bread mould that has both an incised mark and a seal impression side by side. Unfortunately, most of the devices are indistinct, and two even appear completely blank, which demonstrates the unsuitability of the fabric of these vessels for rendering the delicate designs of the seals. All impressions in the moulds were made with button seals, as at Balat (Soukiassian *et al.* 2002, 392). Most devices are round in shape, two are oval, and one is square. One mould carries two stamps of the same device, an oval stamp with a lizard, which is a well-known theme among the seal devices in the Old Kingdom.

The stamped bread moulds make up a large proportion of the seal impressions at 'Ain el-Gazzareen. Similarly, at Balat, 10% of all recorded stamps occur on bread moulds (Soukiassian *et al.* 2002, 392), but their number is marginal when compared to the number of incised marks in moulds, of which the excavations at 'Ain el-Gazzareen and Balat have yielded several hundred examples each.

It is remarkable that there are seven bread moulds from 'Ain el-Gazzareen carrying the same device. This is the impression of a large stamp seal, 2.8 cm in diameter, which shows a heraldic device with two birds flanking the hieroglyph for 'life' (*ankh*) and a fallen captive at the bottom (Figure 3). The royal symbolism of this device is clear. In Balat and elsewhere, similar large devices were found, in which a crouching lion takes the place of the fallen captive (Soukiassian *et al.* 2002, number 6307). Pantalacci has noted that the larger seal impressions, which measure more than 2 cm in diameter and which are of good quality manufacture, are specifically associated with the governor's palace at 'Ain Aseel (Soukiassian *et al.* 2002, 394, note 104). It is not clear how this observation should affect our interpretation of the occupants of 'Ain el-Gazzareen, but some high official presence at the site is not to be excluded.

It is important to conclude that the seal impressions prove to be extremely similar at both Balat and 'Ain el-Gazzareen, and it is evident that the same system of administration was practiced in both. No identical impressions have yet been found that would link the two settlements more directly, but it is clear that close connections existed between the different parts of the oasis and such a conclusion would not be inconceivable.   (OEK)

Authors' Addresses:

Anthony J. Mills
The Barn, Above Town,
Egloshayle, Wadebridge,
Cornwall PL27 6HW,
England

Olaf E. Kaper
Honorary Reseach Associate
Centre for Archaeology and Ancient History
School of Historical Studies
Building 11, Clayton Campus,
Monash University, Victoria 3800,
Australia

and

Netherlands-Flemish Institute in Cairo
1 Dr Mahmoud Azmi Street,
Post Office Box 50,
11211 Zamalek, Cairo,
Egypt

REFERENCES

Herbich, T. and T. N. Smekalova, 2001 Dakhleh Oasis Magnetic Survey 1999–2000, *Polish Archaeology in the Mediterranean*, Warsaw, 259–62.

Hope, C. A., 1999 The Pottery Manufacture in the Dakhleh Oasis, in C. S. Churcher and A. J. Mills, eds, *Reports from the Survey of the Dakhleh Oasis 1977–1987*, Oxbow Books, Oxford, 215–43.

Mills, A. J., 1980 Dakhleh Oasis Project. Report on the Second Season of Survey, September–December 1979, *Journal of the Society for the Study of Egyptian Antiquities* X, 251–82.

Mills, A. J., 1995 A Note on a New Old Kingdom Site in the Dakhleh Oasis, *Journal of the Society for the Study of Egyptian Antiquities* XXV, 61–5.

Mills, A. J., 2002a Another Old Kingdom Site in the Dakhleh Oasis, *Egypt and Nubia: Gifts of the Desert*, The British Museum Press, London, 74–8.

Mills, A. J., 2002b Deir el-Hagar, 'Ain Birbiyeh, 'Ain el-Gazzareen and El Muzawwaqa, in C. A. Hope and G. E. Bowen, eds, *Dakhleh Oasis Project: Preliminary Reports on the 1994–1995 to 1998–1999 Field Seasons*, Oxbow Books, Oxford, 25–30.

Pantalacci, L., 1996 Fonctionnaires et analphabètes: sur quelques pratiques administratives observées à Balat, *Bulletin de l'Institut Français d'archéologie orientale* 98, 359–67.

Soukiassian, G., 1997 A Governors' Palace at 'Ayn Asil, Dakhla Oasis', *Egyptian Archaeology* 11, 15–17.

Soukiassian, G., M. Wuttmann and L. Pantalacci, 2002 *Le palais des gouverneurs de l'époque de Pépy II. Les sanctuaires de ka et leurs dépendances*, Institut Français d'Archéologie Orientale, Cairo.

Wiese, A. B., 1996 *Die Anfänge der ägyptischen Stempelsiegelamulette. Eine typologische und religionsgeschichtliche Untersuchung zu den "Knopfsiegeln" und verwandten Objekten der 6. bis frühen 12. Dynastie*, Rupprecht, Freiburg.

Magnetic Survey at 'Ain el-Gazzareen

Tatyana N. Smekalova, Anthony J. Mills and Tomasz Herbich

A magnetic survey on the Old Kingdom site 'Ain el-Gazzareen (32/390-K2-2) was carried out during January 1999 and January–February 2000 over an area of 3.86 hectares by Tomasz Herbich and Tatyana Smekalova. A test square of 10 x 15 m excavated in 1997 under the direction of Anthony Mills (Mills 1995 and 2002, 28) recorded architectural remains, filled with ground rich in ceramics, ash, faunal remains and stone artefacts. There were traces of burning in several places. The depth of the cultural remains is up to one metre. For a discussion of recent work at the site, see the report by Mills in this volume.

Magnetic Properties of Archaeological Objects

It was suggested that a magnetic survey could be useful for the investigation of the site because there is a significant contrast in magnetic properties between mud-brick walls and the fill of the rooms (Table 1), and also as these structures are situated just below the surface. The magnetic test in Dakhleh Oasis in 1988 at Ismant el-Kharab (Smekalova 2002) showed that magnetic prospecting is an efficient method for identifying the location of ancient industrial activity such as pottery kilns and blacksmith furnaces, and also for mud-brick architectural remains. Samples of the elements of the cultural layer were collected on the site 'Ain el-Gazzareen and their magnetic properties measured at the Geological Faculty of Saint Petersburg State University with help of a 'Kappabridge' (Brno, Czech Republic).

Magnetic Anomalies and Archaeological Objects

Considering the figures in Table 1 one could conclude that the difference between the magnetic susceptibility of mud-brick and surrounding ground is quite significant and sufficient for the observation of negative magnetic anomalies (10÷20nT) with smaller positive anomalies from the northern side from mud-brick walls. Because the inclination of the earth's magnetic field on the latitude of

Table 1 Magnetic susceptibility of archaeological objects from 'Ain el-Gazzareen.

Archaeological material	Magnetic susceptibility, $\mathit{æ}, 10 \cdot ^{-5}$ ISO
Mudbrick	*130*
Ground of the cultural layer	*230*
Ceramics	*600÷3200*
Sandstone	*10-15*

Dakhleh Oasis (*circa* 25°30' N parallel) is about 30°, one can see that there is quite a strong displacement of the position of the minimum of the negative anomaly towards the south of centre of a mud-brick wall (Vacquier *et al.* 1951). Therefore, the centre of the wall is situated somewhere between the minimum and maximum of the anomaly.

Rooms filled with burnt earth and ash will be reflected on the magnetic maps as positive anomalies with an intensity of 20–30 nT. There should be a considerable displacement of the anomaly towards the south of the centre of the object (Vacquier *et al.* 1951, 91). Another peculiarity of the anomalies of magnetized objects, such as the magnetic filling of the rooms, pits, ovens and kilns, is that the negative parts are almost equal to the positive ones. Ovens and kilns will create quite strong positive magnetic anomalies (40÷160 nT) with negative anomalies immediately to the north of the main positive signals. Such features, constructed of mud bricks, which were fired during their functioning, process their own thermoremanent magnetization, the direction of which corresponds to the direction of the earth's ancient magnetic field during cooling after the last heating. Heaps of spoiled vessels, ceramic slags and ash will be reflected in the magnetic field as intensive positive anomalies (80–130 nT) with smaller negative addition to the north of the maximum of anomalies.

Other archaeological features like pits filled with fragments of ceramics, ash, burnt earth and so on, could

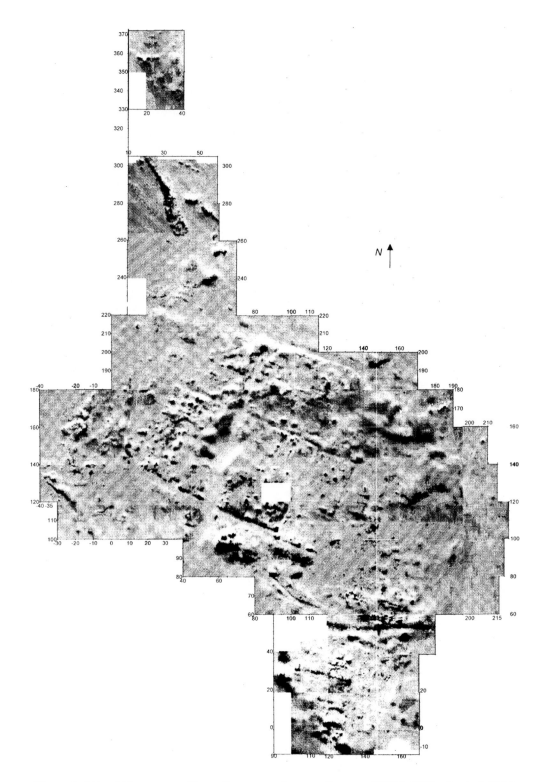

Figure 1 'Ain el-Gazzareen. Magnetic grey-scale map. Survey of 1999–2000. Scale 1:2000.

create rather strong positive anomalies (up to 50–60 nT) with negative parts to the north of the positive ones.

Method and Equipment

There were two main instruments used for the magnetic survey on the site. Tomarsz Herbich used a fluxgate gradiometer FM-36 of Geoscan Research (England) and Tatyana Smekalova used an Overhauser gradiometer GSM-19WG of Gem Systems (Canada, Ontario). Both instruments were operated in the so-called walking mode, which means that the measurements were carried out along the parallel lines spaced 0.5 m one apart. The frequency of measurements along the profiles was not more than 0.3–0.4 m. The height of survey was 0.25 m above the surface.

One sensor of the Overhauser gradiometer served as a base point. It was placed in the more or less normal magnetic field and was connected by a 50-metre cable to the measuring unit. The signals of the working sensor and a base station were subtracted to remove temporal daily variations of the earth's magnetic field. The data from the magnetic survey was stored in the memory of the gradiometers and later was transferred to portable computers. The programmes used for the data presentation were *Geoscan* and *Surfer* (Golden Software, Colorado).

Results of the Magnetic Survey

The results of the magnetic survey by Overhauser gradiometer are presented as a grey-scale magnetic map (Figure 1) drawn at the scale of 1:2000 for the amplitudes ±30 nT around the 'zero' level with the contour interval of different colours equal to 5 nT. The negative anomalies are marked in white and positive anomalies in black. The anomalies stronger than +30 nT are marked in black and anomalies lower than -30 nT are marked in white. An eastern part of the site was surveyed also with the help of the Geosan fluxgate gradiometer and the results are shown in Figure 2.

Studying the grey-scale maps (Figures 1 and 2) it is possible to identify the following structures:

1. Main Enclosure

There is a large rectangular mud-brick structure approximately 54 x 112 m in the centre part of the site. It is distinguished by long negative anomalies (light grey) that form a rectangle. The direction of the short axis is about 25° from north to east. One could suppose that this rectangular structure is surrounded by a mud-brick wall of about 1–1.5 m thick. This wall surrounds living and working quarters, which are visible on the magnetic map as mutually perpendicular negative anomalies of oblong-shaped houses and positive local anomalies such as ovens, kilns, places with traces of burning and ash.

This main rectangular structure probably consists of three parts: an eastern, a central and a western one. It seems that the eastern part, 54 x 20 m, is about one metre to the south of the others. It is possible that this eastern part has been constructed at a different time, later, than the other parts. The eastern part of the main enclosure was cleaned by brushing the surface and the plan of the structure is presented elsewhere in this volume. There is a very good correspondence between the map (Mills and Kaper, this volume, Figure 1) and the grey-scale map. The magnetic map reveals mud-brick walls that are not visible on the surface even after brushing and that are covered by later structures (Figure 1).

There is an interruption in the central part of the long walls resulting from a deep modern irrigation trench that crosses the site.

2. Inner Parts of the Main Structure

There are several parts within this main rectangular structure, which have, probably, different functions.

Many positive local anomalies are concentrated in some parts of this inner area that could be related to the food or other production. The working quarters with ovens (bakeries ?) are reflected in the magnetic field as many intensive positive anomalies. Most quiet magnetic fields could correspond to the living quarters.

Many smaller negative anomalies parallel and perpendicular to the main walls are probably caused by the inner mud-brick walls of the structures. Some of these without positive anomalies inside could be dwellings and others with intensive positive anomalies inside could be working rooms such as bakeries, cooking places, smelting areas and so on.

3. Areas Outside the Main Structure

There are three areas with groups of very strong positive magnetic anomalies outside the main structure. One could suggest that they are probably industrial areas such as pottery workshops with kilns for the firing of ceramic vessels. These industrial quarters might have been placed outside the main construction because of the danger of fire and to avoid the smoke from the kilns.

There is a curved structure surrounding the eastern part of the site, which caused positive and negative anomalies. This structure could be a fence and ditch, making the boundary of the site, because outside it there are almost no magnetic anomalies. It is interesting that this possible ditch is reflected in the magnetic field as a rather strong magnetic anomaly in an area close to the possible pottery kilns, which implies that the 'ditch' is filled with magnetic material (ash, burned clay, etc.).

There is a rectangular pattern of the long negative anomalies from possible mud-brick walls to the south of the main enclosure, which consists of two parts, different in magnetic field. There are many positive anomalies on the western part of the area, which may indicate the presence of fire places, ovens, ash, etc. The eastern part of the area is characterized by weaker anomalies and could be a habitation area.

An interesting anomaly is situated in the most northern part of the area surveyed. It is a 25-metre-long positive and negative anomaly. This could be a ditch filled with

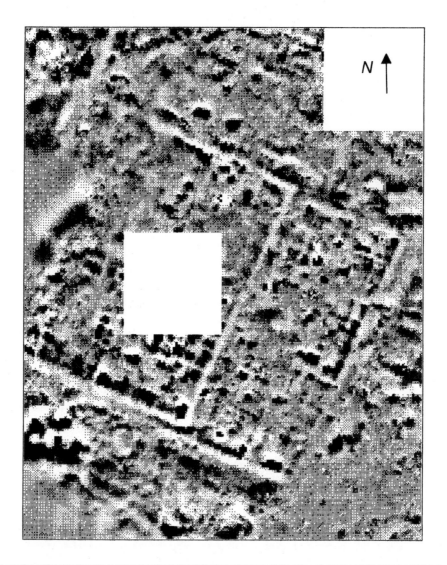

Site : dah99	Gradiometer Survey		Scale	1:738
Comp. : dah99				
Shade Plot (Clip)		Size x 0.5	Block	Off
Minimum -2	Grey Levels 17			
Maximum 2	Palette Positive			
Contrast 2			Black	Positive
Units Std.Dev.			White	Negative

Figure 2 'Ain el-Gazzareen. Magnetic map. Geoscan fluxgate gradiometer. Survey of 1999.

vitrified clay, ceramics, ash and so on. There are several other rather strong positive anomalies in the vicinity of this long structure that might be caused by ovens or kilns.

Conclusions

The magnetic prospection on the Old Kingdom site of 'Ain el-Gazzareen demonstrated the high effectiveness of the magnetic survey for the investigation of mud-brick architecture. It is necessary to note that the magnetic field measured there is much more clear than the one measured on the Roman Period sites of ancient Kellis (Ismant el-Kharab) and Trimithus (Amheida). The important result of the magnetic survey in 1999 was the identification of the main enclosure, which seems to be the central part of the site. The magnetic map of 1999–2000 shows the locations of industrial activities and other parts of the settlement outside the main enclosure. Magnetic surveying allows archaeologists to choose the places for trial excavations, giving at the same time a general idea about the site as a whole.

REFERENCES

Andreasen, G. E. and I. Zietz, 1969 Magnetic Fields for a 4x6 Prismatic Model, *Geological Survey Professional Paper* 666, Washington.

Mills, A. J., 1995 A Note on a New Old Kingdom Site in the Dakhleh Oasis, *Journal of the Society for the Study of Egyptian Antiquities* XXV, 61–5.

Mills, A. J., 2002 Deir el-Hagar, 'Ain Birbiyeh, 'Ain el-Gazzareen and El-Muzawwaqa, in C. A. Hope and G. E. Bowen, eds, Dakhleh Oasis Project: *Preliminary Reports on the 1994–1995 to 1998–1999 Field Seasons*, Oxbow Books, Oxford.

Mills, A. J. and O. E. Kaper, this volume 'Ain el-Gazzareen: Developments in the Old Kingdom Settlement, 123–30.

Smekalova, T. N., 2002 Magnetic Testing using Overhauser Gradiometer GSM-19WG and Cesium Magnetometer MM-60, in C. A. Hope and G. E. Bowen, eds, Dakhleh Oasis Project: *Preliminary Reports on the 1994–1995 to 1998–1999 Field Seasons*, Oxbow Books, Oxford.

Vacquier, V., N. C. Steenland, R. G. Henderson and I. Zeitz, 1951 Interpretation of Aeromagnetic Maps, *Geological Society of American Memoirs* 47, Baltimore, Maryland.

Authors' Addresses:

Tatyana N. Smekalova
Physical Institute of Saint Petersburg State University
198904 Saint Petersburg,
Russia

smek@niif.spb.su

Anthony J. Mills
The Barn, Above Town,
Egloshayle, Wadebridge,
Cornwall PL27 6HW,
England

Tomasz Herbich
Institute of Archaeology and Ethnology
Polish Academy of Sciences
Al. Solidarności 105,
00-140 Warszawa,
Poland

Bio-anthropological Features of Human Mummies from the Kellis 1 Cemetery: The Database for Mummification Methods

Arthur C. Aufderheide, Larry Cartmell and Michael Zlonis

Abstract

Forty-nine mummies have been excavated in the Kellis 1 cemetery in the Dakhleh Oasis and examined. A large number of these had become mummified naturally as a result of environmental conditions. The remainder were anthropogenically mummified as a result of human efforts to enhance soft tissue preservation: evisceration and resin application internally and externally. Extensive looting in antiquity has resulted in body fragmentation. Later efforts to repair, reconstruct and rewrap these bodies included the use of wood splinting of body parts and internal resin application, often via atypical resin ports. Several body reconstructions utilized body parts from more than one mummy.

Introduction

During the 1993 and the 1998 excavation seasons the authors of this article examined a total of 49 partial or complete mummified human bodies excavated in a series of Late Ptolemaic to Roman Period tombs in the Kellis 1 (31/420-C5-1) cemetery at Ismant el-Kharab. In this initial publication we focus on the mummification methods that resulted in soft tissue preservation of some of the bodies excavated from this burial site.

The Cemetery

At Kellis, the dead were interred principally in two primary cemeteries. The Kellis 2 cemetery, 31/420-C5-2, was used by Christians whose dead were buried without coffins in an extended position in graves (Birrell 1999, 38–41; Bowen this volume). These bodies had almost invariably decayed into skeletons. About one kilometre to the west of Kellis 2 is another cemetery, Kellis 1, 31/420-C5-1, (Birrell 1999, 29–38). Many of the bodies buried there were intentionally mummified and had retained much of their soft tissue. These are the focus of this article. The burial chambers are cut into the face of the sandstone terrace; the dimensions are on average 3 x 2 metres and about one metre in height

(Plate 1). Several vertical stones flank the entrance that was closed by a larger stone. On excavation, it was found that some of these had not sealed the entrance with sufficient effectiveness to prevent drifting sand from filling much of the tomb space. The tombs are linearly located along the terrace's vertical face, and are serially numbered. Twenty-one of these tombs have been excavated. Bodies had not been placed in coffins or other containers in these tombs, but several had painted cartonnage coverings (Birrell 1999, 35–8; Schweitzer 2002).

Selection of Mummies for Study

Fifteen of the many bodies in Tombs 1 to 12 were selected for examination in 1993 and 34 more from Tombs 16 to 21 in 1998. Removal of the sand from these tombs generally exposed a chaotic distribution of bodies. Some were merely scattered, disarticulated skeletons while others were completely wrapped in linen. However, evidence of looting in these tombs during antiquity was obvious everywhere. The wrappings on few of these were intact (Plate 2). Most had been at least partially torn open, most frequently exposing the head. The head of many mummies had not only been exposed but actually disarticulated, most commonly by twisting it while pulling on it, as judged by the appearance of the soft tissues at the separated edges. Some heads dangled by only a narrow band of soft tissues. Heads totally separated from their bodies were common and distributed in a pattern that commonly defied identification of the body from which the head had been torn.

In others a large fraction of the body had been exposed. In these it was common to find that hands and feet or even entire extremities had been disarticulated, all probably in efforts to retrieve jewellery or other artefacts. As is detailed below, some of the apparent intact mummy 'bundles' proved to be rewrapped, looted, partially disarticulated mummies or composite mummies composed of body parts from multiple mummies.

Our criteria for selection of those we examined focused principally on those bundles whose external appearance

Plate 1 Kellis 1 cemetery, exterior of Tomb 12.

Plate 2 Interior of Tomb 16 reveals two unwrapped intact bodies, several isolated body parts including several heads and a jumble of commingled bones. Photo by Peter Sheldrick.

Table 1 Autopsy features of viscera in each of dissected mummies.

Age was estimated on the basis of dental eruption, long bone length and epiphyseal fusion in sub-adults. In adults alterations in pubic symphysis, cranial suture closure and dental attrition were employed. Sex was estimated by external genitalia, breast preservation and pelvic skeletal features (Ubelaker 1999).

Legend: **Age**: in years (in adults = ± 5 yrs). **Sex**: M = Male, F = Female, I = Indeterminate. **SM/AM** = Spontaneous mummification/Anthropogenic mummification, I = Indeterminate. **Evisc. Site** = Evisceration site: A = Abdominal, P = Perineal, I = Indeterminate, N = None, B = Back. **Remaining Viscera**: A = Absent, P = Present.
Autopsy Numbers: 116–121 = Isolated heads only.

Autopsy #	Age	Sex	SM/AM	Evisc. Site	Hair	Eyes	Breast	Ext. Gen.	Heart	Lung	Esoph.	Liver	Spleen	Stomach	Ileum	Colon	Kidney	Aorta	Trachea	Brain	Diaphragm	Coprolites
1	15	M	S	N	P	P	A	P	P	P	A	P	A	A	P	P	A	P	P	A	P	P
2	2	I	S	I	P	A	A	A	A	A	A	A	A	A	A	A	A	A	A	A	A	A
3	25	M	A	A,P	P	A	P	P	A	P	A	A	A	A	A	A	A	A	A	A	A	A
4	21	F	S	N	P	P	P	P	P	P	A	P	A	A	A	A	A	A	A	A	P	A
5	48	M	I	N	A	A	A	P	P	P	A	P	A	A	A	A	A	A	P	A	P	A
6	25	F	S	N	P	P	P	I	A	P	A	A	A	A	A	A	A	A	A	A	A	A
7	23	F	A	N	P	P	A	A	A	A	A	A	A	A	P	A	A	A	A	A	A	A
8	10	I	S	N	P	P	A	A	A	A	A	P	A	A	P	A	P	A	A	A	A	P
9	5	M	S	I	P	P	A	P	A	A	A	P	A	A	P	P	A	A	P	A	P	A
10	45	F	S	N	P	P	A	P	A	A	A	A	A	A	P	A	A	A	A	A	P	A
11	28	F	A	I	A	A	A	A	A	A	A	A	A	A	A	A	A	A	A	A	A	A
12	58	M	S	N	P	P	A	A	A	A	A	A	A	A	A	A	A	A	A	A	A	A
13	55	M	S	N	P	A	A	P	P	P	A	P	A	A	A	P	A	A	P	A	P	P
14	58	M	S	I	P	A	A	A	A	A	A	A	A	A	A	A	A	A	A	A	A	A
15	48	F	S	N	P	P	A	A	A	A	A	A	A	A	A	A	A	A	A	A	A	A
101	25	M	S	N	A	P	A	P	A	P	A	P	A	A	P	P	A	A	A	A	P	P
102	11	M	S	N	A	P	A	P	P	P	A	P	A	A	P	P	A	A	P	P	P	P
103	Adult	M	I	N	A	A	A	P	A	A	A	A	A	A	A	A	A	A	A	A	A	P
104	55	F	A	I	A	A	A	A	A	A	A	A	A	A	A	A	A	A	A	A	A	A
105	22	M	I	I	P	P	A	A	A	P	A	A	A	A	A	A	P	A	A	A	A	P
106	15	F	S	N	P	P	P	P	A	A	A	P	A	A	P	P	A	A	A	A	A	P
107	8	M	A	N	A	A	A	P	A	A	A	P	A	A	P	A	A	A	A	A	P	A
108	23	M	S	N	P	P	A	P	P	P	P	P	A	P	P	P	A	P	P	A	P	A
109	10	I	I	I	P	P	A	A	A	A	A	A	A	A	A	A	A	A	A	A	P	A
110	35	M	A	B	A	A	A	P	A	P	A	A	A	A	P	A	A	P	A	P	A	A
111	23	M	S	N	P	P	A	P	A	P	A	P	A	A	P	P	A	A	A	A	P	A
112	7	I	S	N	A	A	A	A	A	A	A	A	A	A	P	A	A	A	A	A	A	A
113	Fetus	I	S	I	A	A	A	A	A	A	A	A	A	A	A	A	A	A	A	A	A	A
114	7	M	A	A	A	A	A	P	A	A	A	A	A	A	A	A	A	A	A	A	A	A
115	30	F	A	A	P	A	P	A	A	A	A	A	A	A	A	A	A	A	A	A	A	A
116	Adult	M	S	I	P	P	A	A	A	A	A	A	A	A	A	A	A	A	A	A	A	A
117	Adult	M	I	I	P	P	P	A	A	A	A	A	A	A	A	A	A	A	P	A	A	A
118	7	I	S	I	P	P	A	A	A	A	A	A	A	A	A	A	A	A	A	A	A	A
119	45	M	I	I	P	A	A	A	A	A	A	A	A	A	A	A	A	A	A	A	A	A
120	10	I	I	I	P	P	A	A	A	A	A	A	A	A	A	A	A	A	A	A	A	A
121	7	I	S	I	P	P	A	A	A	A	A	A	A	A	A	A	A	A	A	A	A	A
122	37	M	I	P	P	P	A	P	A	A	A	P	A	A	A	A	P	A	A	A	P	A
123	50	M	A	A	P	P	A	P	A	A	A	A	A	A	A	A	A	A	A	A	A	A
124	50	M	A	P	I	I	A	P	A	A	A	A	A	A	A	A	A	A	A	A	A	A
125	40	F	A	A	P	P	P	P	A	A	A	A	A	A	A	A	A	A	A	A	P	A
126	35	M	A	N	A	A	A	P	A	P	A	P	A	A	P	A	A	P	P	A	P	A
127	Adult	M	I	I	A	A	A	A	A	A	A	A	A	A	A	A	A	A	A	A	A	A
128	7	F	A	A	A	A	A	A	A	A	A	A	A	A	A	A	A	A	A	A	A	A
129	6	M	A	N	P	P	A	P	A	A	A	P	A	A	P	P	A	A	A	A	A	A
130	7	M	A	A	P	A	A	P	A	A	A	A	A	A	A	A	A	A	A	A	A	A
131	8	M	I	N	P	P	A	P	A	A	A	A	A	A	A	A	A	A	A	A	A	A
132	4	I	A	I	P	A	A	A	A	A	A	A	A	A	A	A	A	A	A	A	A	A
133	2.5	I	A	P	A	A	A	A	A	A	A	A	A	A	A	A	A	A	A	A	A	A
134	50	F	A	A	A	A	P	P	A	A	A	A	A	A	A	A	A	A	A	A	A	A

Table 2 Miscellaneous autopsy features of individual dissected mummies.

In Mummy 4, some viscera had been removed prior to our examination. A ceramic item was present within the abdomen of Mummy 104. In Mummies 108 and 129 resin gained access to cranial cavity from the abdominal cavity via the spinal canal. Mummies 116–121 are isolated heads only. A surplus humerus was lying loose in thoracic cavity of Mummy 132.

Legend: **Age**: in years (in adults = ± 5 yrs). **Sex**: M = Male, F = Female, I = Indeterminate. **SM/AM** = Spontaneous mummification/Anthropogenic mummification. In this table in all other columns A = Absent, P = Present, I = Indeterminate. **Wrap** = Linen wrappings around body. **Abdomen** = Abdominal cavity. **Chest** = Thoracic cavity. **Skull** = Cranial cavity. V = Resin deposited on cranial cavity walls as delicate, web-like structure suggestive of condensed vaporized resin. **Portal** = Portal of resin entry into body cavity. A = Abdomen, P = Perineum, C = Cranium, N = None, I = Indeterminate, B = Back muscles (retroperitoneum). **TNC** = Transnasal craniotomy. **Side**: L = Left, R = Right, B = Both, I = Indeterminate, N = None. **Resin**: N = No, Y = Yes, I = Indeterminate. **Tampon**: As in Resin column. **Splint** = Wood stick in cranium, spinal canal or abdomen. **STP** = Soft Tissue Preservation Score. **BP** = Bone Preservation Score. **STI** = Soft Tissue Index. **Stature**: in cm. I = Indeterminate. **Nose**: Nasal tampon: P = Present in situ; D = Nares dilated but tampon absent, I = Indeterminate. **OPS** = Organ Preservation Score. **Circum** = Circumcision.

Autopsy #	Age	Sex	SM/AM	Wrap	Skin	Eyes	Hair	Perineum	Abdomen	Chest	Skull	Portal	Side	Resin	Tampon	Splint	STP	BP	STI	Head	Stature	Nose	OPS	Circumc.
1	15	M	S	A	P	A	A	A	A	A	A	N	L	N	N	A	96	96	100	P	157	D	70	P
2	2	I	S	A	A	A	A	A	A	A	A	N	I	I	I	A	0	100	0	P	I	I	10	I
3	25	M	A	P	P	A	A	P	P	P	A	A,P	B	N	N	A	96	99	97	P	171	I	30	P
4	21	F	S	I	P	A	P	A	A	A	A	N	L	N	N	A	56	100	56	P	156	D	60	A
5	48	M	I	I	P	P	A	A	P	P	P	P	B	Y	N	A	96	96	100	P	164	P	40	P
6	25	F	S	I	A	A	A	A	A	A	A	N	B	N	N	A	72	90	80	P	158	D	30	A
7	23	F	A	I	P	A	A	I	P	P	A	C	B	N	N	P	47	59	80	P	155	P	20	I
8	10	I	S	I	P	A	A	A	A	A	A	N	B	N	N	A	32	60	51	P	I	D	30	I
9	5	M	S	I	P	P	A	I	P	P	P	I	L	Y	Y	A	100	100	100	P	I	D	40	I
10	45	F	S	I	P	A	A	A	A	A	A	N	B	N	N	A	99	100	99	P	149	D	30	A
11	28	F	A	P	P	I	I	I	P	P	I	I	I	I	I	P	4	20	20	A	159	I	0	A
12	58	M	S	I	P	A	A	A	A	A	A	N	B	N	N	A	12	56	21	P	166	D	10	I
13	55	M	S	I	P	A	A	A	A	A	A	N	B	N	N	A	99	100	99	P	167	D	50	A
14	58	M	S	I	P	I	I	I	I	I	I	N	I	I	I	A	4	12	33	A	166	I	10	I
15	48	F	S	P	A	A	A	I	A	A	A	I	L	N	N	P	90	90	100	P	152	D	10	I
101	25	M	S	P	P	A	A	A	A	A	A	N	B	N	N	A	96	100	96	P	185	D	30	P
102	11	M	S	P	P	A	P	A	A	A	A	N	B	N	N	A	72	99	73	P	103	D	40	A
103	Adult	M	I	P	P	A	A	A	A	A	I	N	I	I	I	A	20	20	100	A	I	I	10	A
104	55	F	A	P	P	I	I	I	P	P	I	I	I	I	I	P	12	44	27	A	170	I	0	A
105	22	M	I	I	P	A	P	I	I	I	I	I	L	N	N	A	48	60	80	P	188	I	0	I
106	15	F	S	I	P	A	P	A	A	A	A	N	B	N	N	A	90	96	94	P	I	D	50	A
107	8	M	A	A	P	A	A	A	A	P	A	C	I	I	I	A	70	70	100	A	I	I	30	A
108	23	M	S	I	P	A	P	A	A	A	A	N	B	N	N	A	90	90	100	P	167	D	60	A
109	10	I	I	P	P	A	P	I	I	I	P	I	L	N	N	P	20	20	100	P	I	D	10	I
110	35	M	A	P	P	I	I	A	P	P	I	B	I	I	I	A	54	70	77	A	167	I	30	P
111	23	M	S	P	P	A	P	A	A	A	A	N	B	N	N	A	100	100	100	P	183	D	50	P
112	7	I	S	I	P	I	I	I	A	I	I	N	I	I	I	A	4	20	20	A	I	I	0	I
113	Fetus	I	S	P	A	A	A	A	A	A	A	N	I	I	I	A	0	8	0	A	I	I	0	I
114	7	M	A	P	P	I	I	A	P	P	I	A	I	I	I	A	10	20	50	A	I	I	10	A
115	30	F	A	P	P	A	I	A	P	P	A	A	B	N	N	A	44	76	58	P	161	D	10	A
116	Adult	M	S	I	P	A	P	I	I	I	I	I	B	I	I	A	20	20	100	P	I	D	0	I
117	Adult	M	I	P	P	A	I	I	I	I	A	I	N	N	N	A	8	12	67	P	I	I	10	I
118	7	I	S	I	P	A	A	I	I	I	A	I	B	N	N	A	9	20	45	P	I	I	0	I
119	45	M	I	P	P	I	P	I	I	I	P	I	B	Y	N	A	12	20	60	P	I	P	10	I
120	10	I	I	I	P	A	I	I	I	I	A	I	L	N	N	A	16	20	80	P	I	P	10	I
121	7	I	S	I	P	A	A	I	I	I	A	I	B	N	N	A	16	20	80	P	I	D	10	I
122	37	M	I	P	P	A	P	P	P	P	P	P	B	I	I	A	36	100	36	P	168	P	40	P
123	50	M	A	I	P	A	I	A	P	P	P	A	B	Y	N	A	100	100	100	P	174	P	10	P
124	50	M	A	I	P	P	I	I	I	P	P	I	L	Y	N	A	30	36	83	P	185	D	10	I
125	40	F	A	P	P	P	I	A	P	P	V	B	B	N	N	A	100	100	100	P	155	D	30	A
126	35	M	A	P	P	I	I	I	P	P	I	B	I	I	I	A	52	66	79	A	168	I	40	P
127	Adult	M	I	P	P	I	I	I	I	I	I	I	I	I	I	A	20	20	100	A	165	I	0	I
128	7	F	A	P	P	I	I	I	P	P	I	A	I	I	I	A	80	80	100	A	I	I	0	A
129	6	M	A	P	P	A	A	I	P	P	V	B	R	N	N	A	100	100	100	P	I	D	30	A
130	7	M	A	P	P	I	I	A	P	P	I	A	I	I	I	A	80	80	100	A	I	I	20	I
131	8	M	I	P	P	A	P	A	A	A	A	N	B	N	N	A	100	100	100	P	I	D	20	I
132	4	I	A	P	P	A	A	I	P	P	A	I	N	N	N	P	32	52	61	P	I	I	10	I
133	2.5	I	A	P	P	I	I	P	P	P	I	P	I	I	I	A	28	40	70	A	I	I	0	I
134	50	F	A	P	P	I	I	A	P	P	I	A	I	I	I	A	44	68	65	A	157	I	10	A

offered the strongest suggestion that the body's chest and abdomen remained intact. As became evident during later dissection, the outer aspect of a mummy bundle was unreliably predictive of its content. Eventually we examined 49 mummified bodies or body parts. These probably represented less than one-fourth of such bodies found in these tombs.

Examination Procedure

Wrappings

Initially the body was photographed as received. Photographs were also prepared at many subsequent stages of the examination. Following the initial photos the wrappings, in spite of their extensive destruction, were removed in a manner permitting reconstruction of the wrapping process. This effort was commonly hampered by hardened resin that had been applied to the wrapping liberally in antiquity.

External Examination

After removal of the wrappings and photography of the exposed body, the external aspect of the body was inspected closely, and all aspects of interest photographed. In some bodies resin had been applied to the skin in a layer several centimetres thick. Samples of hair, toenails, skin and leg muscle were retained for later study. Detailed examination was carried out to identify evisceration, abdominal, perineal, thoracic or other wounds. Breast and external genitalia were examined to help identify the body's sex. All body orifices were inspected closely for the presence of tampons, resin ports or foreign bodies. Special attention was paid to the application of resin to the skin and scalp surfaces. In addition an effort was made to detect the possible use of body orifices as resin entry ports.

Internal Examination

Since bio-anthropological information was the primary focus of our study, procurement of tissue samples from the individual visceral organs was of great interest. This was achieved in many cases by removing the ventral wall of the thorax and the abdomen, though in quite a few cases decay defects in this area provided direct access to the thoracic and abdominal cavities. The skull's calvarium was also removed to gain access to possible preserved brain tissue, to determine cranial cavity content and to evaluate the creation of transnasal craniotomy. Appropriate photographs were prepared at each stage of these procedures. The Femur was examined for length to estimate living stature (Table 2) and to obtain compact cortical bone for study. A vertebra sample was also acquired for trabecular bone study. Dentition was examined in detail. The body and body parts were then placed in labelled large bags and returned to the tomb from which the body had been removed.

A method described in Aufderheide (2003, 335) was employed to provide an expression of soft tissue and skeletal preservation that is more informative than the usual 'well-preserved' or similar adjectives as estimated in the field. For Bone preservation (BP), five numerical units ('points') are assigned to each of five major body parts, cranium, thorax, abdomen, both arms and both legs. Their sum is multiplied by four and expressed as a percentage. the presence of soft tissue covering each of these skeletal units is similarly estimated (STP). The soft tissue index (STI) is obtained by the fraction STP/BP and reflects the fraction of preserved skeletal tissue that is covered by preserved soft tissue. The retained samples were submitted to the appropriate Egyptian agency. After receiving their approval for further study they were forwarded to the author's laboratories for analysis.

Mummification Methods

Mummy Wrappings

Most of the mummies showed evidence of having been wrapped at the time of burial. When excavated, however, most of them also demonstrated obvious evidence of having been damaged by looting. In many, the wrappings about the face had been torn to expose the head. In others, much of the body had been exposed and in still others, all wrappings had been completely stripped from the body. In a moderate number the looted body had been rewrapped and sometimes looted again.

The wrappings were entirely linen. The shape of the wrappings varied. In some, broad sheets up to the total body length formed part of the wrappings, while in other areas such sheets had been torn into band-like strips from four to eight centimetres wide. Those near or next to the body often were more coarsely wound than the more superficial layers. The broad sheets were sometimes intact woven products but more often had been constructed by sewing smaller fragments together. In one instance an intact child's tunic had been employed. Many of the larger pieces had apparently been used for utilitarian purposes earlier as evidenced by the presence of numerous patches.

Although intact mummy bundles were rare among the examined bodies, the succession of applied wrappings could be reconstructed from observations on multiple bundles. Variation in wrapping, especially over the head, was not unusual. Nevertheless the following steps could be identified as a general model.

The process was initiated by the application of a thin layer of resin to the skin. The firm adherence of the first wrapping layer to this resin provides evidence that the resin was applied at the time of wrapping, suggesting also that the purpose of this thin resin layer probably may not have been soft tissue preservation, but rather an aid to the wrapping process. The adhesive nature of partially cooled resin could have held the first, broad sheet in position until the circular linen bands could be applied. These sheets were applied to the trunk and, separately, to the arms. In most cases the sheets enveloped both legs as a single unit. One or several layers of the narrow linen bands were then applied horizontally in a circular manner to hold the broad sheets in position. Broad sheets were then again applied, followed by more circular bands. This pattern was continued until about eight to ten cloth layers had been applied separately to the trunk, each arm and the combined legs. The arms were then brought, extended, against the trunk with the hands on the lateral aspect of the thighs. Thereafter the arms were included in the trunk wrappings. This process was continued until a total of 20–30 wrapping layers, even more in a few mummies, had been achieved. Several bodies had an outer covering comprising red shrouds (Birrell 1999, 35).

Various methods were employed to cover the head. The most common was to attach several long sheets about 10–15 cm wide to the back of the trunk. These when laid out flat, extended beyond the top of the head about 50 cm. This extended portion was then folded forward across the hair at the top of the head and downward, covering the face and anterior neck, reaching to the upper sternum. With several layers of these in position, narrow linen strips were then wound circularly beginning in the lowest part of the neck. Here they were drawn tightly with sufficient tension to fix and hold the head immovably into position. The circular bands were sometimes continued across the already-covered face.

Neither the broad sheets nor the narrow bands were of uniform size. In some the narrow bands had first been torn from a larger sheet; the lateral edges were then folded over about one centimetre or less and sewn to produce a hem. In others the edges were unaltered, revealing their torn or roughly cut edges. Periodically during the wrapping process resin was applied to the wrapping, obviously to act as an adhesive material. Often these were mere daubs of about five centimetres in diameter. On occasion, however, a much larger amount was applied, sufficient to soak through several layers. Frequent applications of this type frustrated efforts to unwrap the bundle in an orderly manner. In a few, the superficial wrappings were covered broadly with a resin layer as much as two or three centimetres thick. Although the linen was examined for evidence of inscriptions, none were found, nor were any artefacts found to have been included between the layers. Though some artefacts may have been removed from the wrappings by looters, one would not have expected them all to have been detected, unless such postulated artefacts had only been placed between wrappings in the facial area. No effort had been made to make the superficial layers assume a geometric or other wrapping pattern.

General Features of Human Mummification

Many of the interred bodies had no preserved soft tissues, presenting as simple, disarticulated skeletons. These, of course, were not selected for study. In several cases, however, mummy bundles selected for study proved to contain only disarticulated bones within the wrappings.

The remainder of the examined mummy bundles can be grouped into two distinctly different types: spontaneous that is, natural mummification (SM) and anthropogenic or artificial mummification (AM).

Spontaneous Mummification. This term is employed to describe a body in which the soft or non-skeletal tissue became preserved without the exercise of any human effort to achieve such preservation. While several different natural mechanisms are known to produce this result, in the Dakhleh mummies it occurred exclusively by desiccation: removal of tissue water of sufficient degree to paralyse the action of decay enzymes. In Dakhleh, this undoubtedly was due to the arid climate, enhanced principally by hot summer temperatures. The arid climate enhanced dehydration, hot summer temperatures assisted the evaporation process and the wicking action of wrappings acted to conduct water away from the body, thus maintaining a high gradient of water concentration at the skin surface. (Aturaliya and Lukasewycz 1999). It is clear, however, that the effectiveness of multiple processes were necessary to achieve desiccation of the corpse before it decayed, since the many skeletonized bodies testified to the failure of such preservation mechanisms in those cases. These skeletons may, for example, have been bodies of individuals who died during winter temperatures, or were interred in tombs that prevented sand infiltration. Alternatively, the interval between death and burial may have been prolonged for various possible reasons.

The viscera in such spontaneous desiccation processes undergo characteristic changes as they become dehydrated. The air in lungs passes through the lungs' filmy membranes and they collapse into a flat, plaque-like structure moulded to the posterior wall of the thoracic cavity's inner lining, measuring only 2–3 mm in thickness. The blood-filled heart dries so slowly that its muscular wall often decays but the fibrous valves and aorta commonly remain intact. The epithelial cells of the liver usually decay rapidly reducing this organ to only one-fifth of its normal size when dehydrated. The kidneys frequently decay to a similar degree, while the spleen is often not identifiable. Parts of the intestine, however, are often evident. While these various desiccated organs in spontaneously mummified bodies have an appearance that is profoundly different from their configuration in living persons, those researchers with dissection experience of such mummies become very familiar with these changes.

Anthropogenic Mummification. This term is applied to *post-mortem* retention of soft tissue as a result of some deliberate human act whose effect is designed to enhance soft tissue preservation after death. In the Dakhleh mummies, as is traditional throughout Egypt, that human act is principally the removal of the intestine with its bacterial content, the lungs, liver, heart and kidneys. Resin was applied as a very hot liquid that hardens when it cools. It was applied to the skin surface only in some Dakhleh mummies, and to the lining of the thoracic and abdominal cavities in the eviscerated bodies. The liquid resin was hot enough to have some thermal bactericidal effect. Majno

Plate 3 Type 1 bodies. Environmental conditions did not prevent complete soft tissue decay in these 18 bodies from Tomb 13. No human effort had been made at time of burial to preserve soft tissues in these corpses.

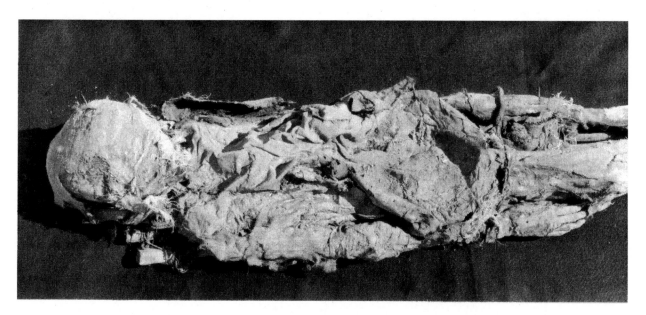

Plate 4 Type 2 body: Mummy 15 Tomb 2. This partially unwrapped, looted bundle presents the external appearance suggestive of an intact mummy (but see Plates 5 and 6).

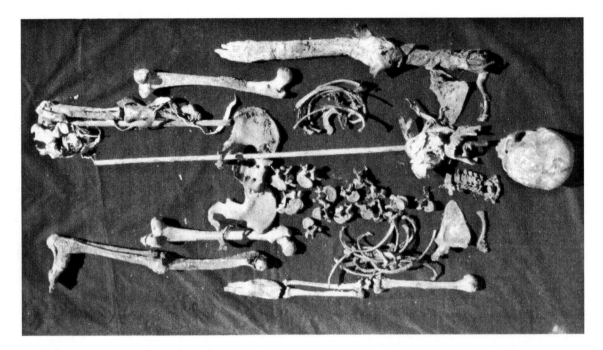

Plate 5 Type 2 body: Mummy 15 from Tomb 2. Complete unwrapping of the body displayed in Plate 4 reveals a mass of principally-skeletal tissue that had been lashed to a wooden rack. Note the mummified left leg of a 6-year-old child, bones of the right leg of a 3-year-old child, the head of a young adult female and the pelvis and spine of a 40–45-year-old female. This is a reconstructed composite mummy.

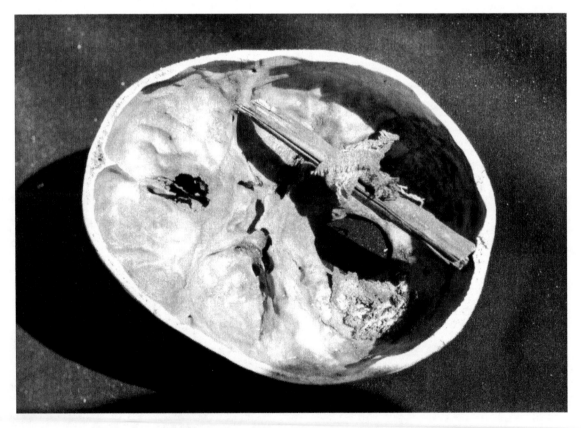

Plate 6 Cranial cavity of Type 2 body: Mummy 15 from Tomb 2. Note the transnasal craniotomy. The segment of a palm rib was inserted into the cranial cavity via the foramen magnum. The linen strap tied to it extended through the foramen magnum and was used to lash the cranium in anatomic position to the wood rack. A small amount of desiccated, residual brain tissue can be seen in the posterior fossa.

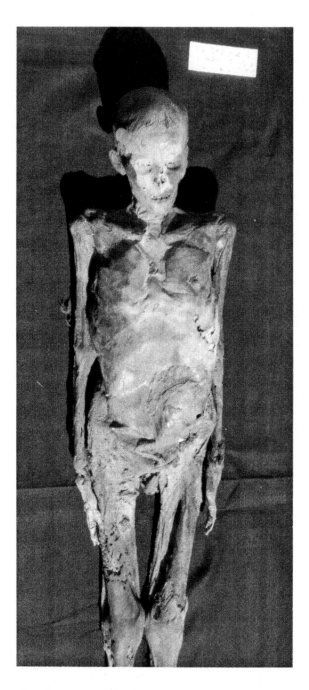

Plate 7 Type 3 mummification: Mummy 6 from Tomb 8. Spontaneous mummification without evisceration or resin application; well-preserved, desiccated lungs were present in the thorax.

Plate 8 Type 4 mummification: Mummy 1 from Tomb 3. Similar to Mummy 6 in Plate 7 but with resin application to the skin; spontaneous mummification with well-preserved desiccated heart, lungs, liver, aorta and bowel. See also Plate 9.

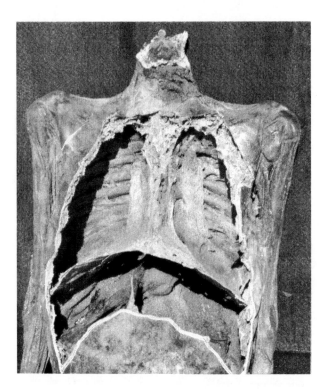

Plate 9 Type 4 mummification: Mummy 1 from Tomb 3. The spontaneously-mummified body of a 15-year-old male. The anterior wall of the thorax has been removed revealing the pericardial sac in the midline, the flattened, collapsed lung in the medial aspect of each thoracic cavity, the intact diaphragm and the liver in the abdomen's right upper quadrant. See also Plate 8.

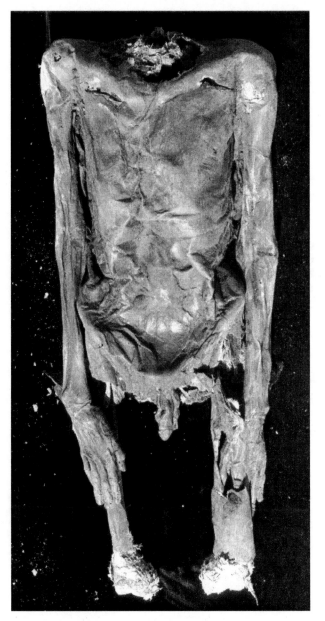

Plate 10 Type 5 mummification: Mummy 110 from Tomb 17. This partial body demonstrates no evidence of evisceration. See also Plates 11, 12 and 13.

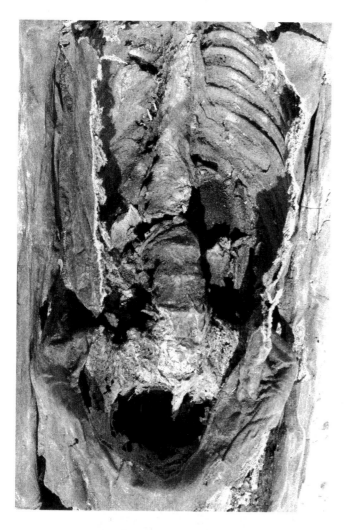

Plate 11 Type 5 mummification: Mummy 110 from Tomb 17. The anterior wall of the thorax and abdomen have been removed. Spontaneously desiccated, collapsed right lung is evident. The back fragments in the right lumbar areas represent the inner aspect of the back defect seen in Plate 12.

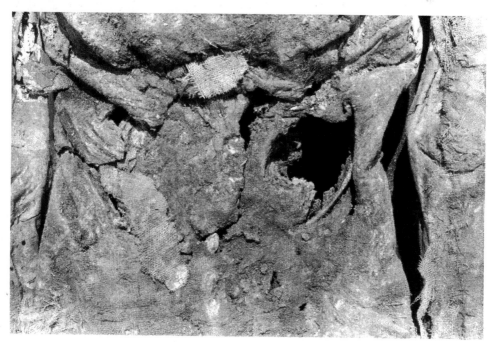

Plate 12 Type 5 mummification. The posterior aspect of Mummy 110 from Tomb 17 (see also Plates 10 and 11) is shown. The posterior abdominal portion of the back had been fractured during looting and reconstructed using resin and linen as adhesive patches. The demonstrated defect was used with the body in a prone position as a resin entry port (then obstructed by a resin-soaked linen, removed for photography).

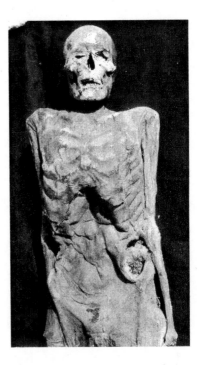

Plate 13 Type 5 mummification: Mummy 110 from Tomb 17. The photo demonstrates that the resin introduced into the body cavities pooled on the inner aspect of the sternum, as expected if resin was introduced via the back defect with the body in a prone position. See also Plates 10, 11 and 12.

Plate 14 Type 6 anthropogenic mummification: Mummy 3 from Tomb 3. A resin layer more than two centimetres thick over the skin has been removed; note evisceration wound in the left upper abdominal quadrant. See also Plate 15.

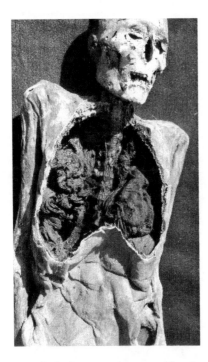

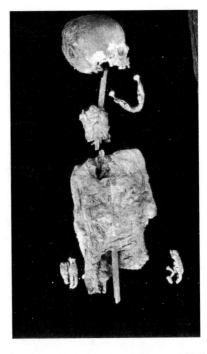

Plate 15 Type 6, Anthropogenic mummification: Mummy 3 from Tomb 3. The anterior thoracic wall has been removed, demonstrating the absence of thoracic viscera; these have been replaced by multiple resin-soaked linen rolls.

Plate 16 Type 7 mummification: Mummy 132 from Tomb 21. This looted, fragmented body was originally prepared with a Type 6, anthropogenic mummification process (see Plates 14 and 15) but subsequent looting fragmented the body; reconstruction (and rewrapping) required splinting of the body parts using a palm rib to support the trunk fragments.

(1975, 217) has provided laboratory evidence for an additional antibacterial effect of some resins. Resin was also used as a permanent adhesive to hold wrappings in position. Its principal value, however, may have simply been its moisture-repellent effect that prevented rehydration of already desiccated tissue. During the Middle and especially New Kingdoms (Ikram and Dodson 1998, 112–20) desiccation of soft tissue was achieved by packing a salty ore, natron, around the body after evisceration. However, the use of natron declined during the Late and particularly the Roman Periods as a result of increasing dependence upon liberal resin application. Conceivably at Dakhleh, deliberate exposure to a hot summer sun may have contributed some desiccating effect.

The abdominal evisceration wound was generally also used as an entry port for resin introduction by Nile-Valley embalmers (Smith and Dawson 1924, 81, 97, 125, 126) and also by those at Dakhleh. Alternatively, perineal evisceration could be achieved by an incision surrounding the anus through which a hand could be inserted to extract the viscera. This method was employed on several Dakhleh mummies. In addition, as described below, some Dakhleh bodies display the use of novel resin entry ports.

Finally, since the brain could not be reached via an abdominal incision, Nile-Valley embalmers traditionally created a defect in the base of the skull by forcing a metal rod through the nose and thin ethmoid bone into the cranial cavity. In some bodies they poured hot resin into the cranial cavity and even stuffed linen into it via the created channel. As noted below, Dakhleh embalmers created this defect, that we call transnasal craniotomy, in all but two mummies, including some which were otherwise allowed to undergo spontaneous mummification.

Mummification Methods Employed at Dakhleh

The mummies extracted from the Kellis 1 cemetery and subsequently examined, present an initially bewildering array of appearances. Some ideas about the nature of these were presented after examination of 15 mummies in 1993 (Aufderheide *et al.* 1999). It was not, however, until we had examined an additional 34 bodies in 1998, that it was possible to understand more fully the processes employed at this site. The bodies can be grouped into two major types: those in which no effort was made to enhance soft tissue preservation at time of burial (Types 1 to 5) and those in which major efforts to prevent soft tissue decay were employed in a manner not dissimilar from that of contemporary Nile-Valley embalmers (Types 6 and 7). Efforts to deal with looted bodies appear to be responsible for the variations noted within these two major groups. The individual types are described below, and examples illustrated in the plates. A listing of our findings in these bodies is presented in Table 1.

Type 1 (Plate 3). This type presented simply as disarticulated bones without any soft tissue preservation. These bodies were buried without any effort to enhance soft tissue preservation. The naturally-occurring environmental conditions were too ineffective to cause rapid desiccation. Mummy 113 is an example of a few bare foetal bones wrapped to present the external appearance of a bundle containing the mummy of a child.

Type 2 (Plates 4, 5 and 6). Disarticulated bones like those of Type 1, free of soft tissue, had been lashed to a wooden rack and then wrapped to provide the external appearance of a mummified adult body. Mummy 15 is an example. Most of the body consists of disarticulated adult bones from two different adult bodies plus the bones of a three-year-old child's right leg while the mummified left leg is that of a six-year-old child.

Type 3 (Plate 7). Soft tissue retention of variable degree is present without evidence of resin application either externally or internally. Some visceral organs are preserved. No effort was made in this type to prevent soft tissue decay at time of burial. Soft tissue preservation including some visceral organs was entirely the effect of environmental conditions. Of the Dakhleh bodies we have only one example: Mummy 6.

Type 4 (Plates 8 and 9). These are identical to Type 3 with one exception: a thin layer of resin had been painted on the skin surface. We cannot be certain whether the resin was applied at the time of burial or later, but we can be sure that preservation of the soft tissue is the result of environmental conditions. The layer of resin on the skin is so thin that in some it is only evident on close examination. It is too thin to have provided any significant preservative effect on viscera. It is conceivable that it was applied for some other reason, such as adhesive to hold the first layer of wrappings in position though this is speculative. The visceral preservation pattern is that of spontaneous mummification and no resin is present on the viscera or other internal sites. We conclude this is simply spontaneous mummification in a body that had been painted with a layer of resin too thin to have contributed to soft tissue preservation. Examples are numerous and include Mummies 1, 8, 10, 12, 13, 101, 102, 106, 108, 111 and 131.

Type 5 (Plates 10, 11, 12, 13). These are mummies without evisceration but with both external and internal resin application, yet they demonstrate a pattern of spontaneous visceral organ mummification. This produces apparent conflicting evidence of burial without human effort to prevent decay: no evisceration; visceral organs are present and show a pattern of spontaneous mummification. They also have evidence, however, of anthropogenic effort to preserve soft tissue in the form of extensive resin application both externally and internally. This apparent conflict is resolved by the identification of resin introduction into the body cavities via atypical resin entry ports. In several it was introduced through a defect in the back with the body in a prone position, while the position of the lungs indicates the body viscera dried while the body position was supine. These findings define a scenario in which the body was buried without effort to preserve soft tissue, achieved spontaneous mummification in the usual supine position and then, at a later time, probably following body damage by looting, the tomb was entered and the resin instilled via an atypical entry port. In addition to defects in the back, other atypical entry ports include one body in which the liquid, hot resin, was poured into the mouth, entered the bronchi, penetrated the lung pleura, burrowed through the diaphragm and drained into the abdomen. In still another case the entry point was via a defect in the anterior chest wall just above the left clavicle. It is conceivable these atypical resin entry ports were used when the tomb was entered some interval after these bodies had been interred, and the mummies found to have been looted. Examples include the Mummies 5, 9, 107, 110, 126 and 219.

Types 6 and 7 (Plates 14, 15, 16). These bodies had been eviscerated at the time of burial and elaborate applications of resin carried out both externally and internally in an effort to preserve soft tissue. This is precisely the method employed by contemporary Nile-Valley embalmers. In Type 6 (Plates 14 and 15) the bodies remained undisturbed except for some violation of the wrappings. In Type 7 the mummies had been prepared at the time of death and burial precisely as in Type 6, but had subsequently been looted. When this was discovered later, attempts had obviously been made to reconstruct these fragmented, looted bodies by rejoining their various disarticulated heads and extremities with their original bodies and splinting them with wood sticks into position before rewrapping them meticulously (Plate 16). In some of these reconstructed bodies the heads seem inappropriate for the body so that these probably constitute composite mummies. Type 6 mummification includes Mummies 3, 114, 115, 123, 125, 128, 130, 133 and 134, while examples of Type 7 include Mummies 7, 11, 104, 109, 122, 124 and 132.

Resin Analysis. Gas chromatography/mass spectrometry analysis of resin samples from Mummies 3, 5, 7 and 9 were carried out under the direction of Dr Arie Nissenbaum at the Weitzman Institute of Science in Rehovot, Israel. Results indicated that all samples were mixtures of materials in which the dominant elements were plant resins, principally of coniferous trees (cedar or pine) but mixed with small amounts of beeswax and fossil hydrocarbons (bitumen, asphalt). The asphalt from Mummies 3 and 9 had chromatographic signatures identical with reference samples of Palestine's Dead Sea asphalt (Maurer *et al.* 2002).

Summary of Mummification at Dakhleh

About half of the examined bodies had been buried with no apparent effort to prevent their decay. Some of these progressed to complete skeletonization. Most of the bodies became desiccated spontaneously with variable degrees of preservation of their visceral organs. Transnasal craniotomy had been performed and their skin surface had been painted with a very thin layer of resin. Almost all of these bodies had been the target of looting in antiquity, resulting in variable degrees of fragmentation of both the bodies and their wrappings. Apparently amateur efforts at

reconstruction of these damaged bodies resulted in rewrapped bundles containing bones and body parts that were held in position by splints and palm-frond rib racks. In a few, abundant resin was applied both internally and externally as part of the reconstruction effort.

The remainder of the bodies were prepared soon after death and before burial with a high level of professional skill. This involved evisceration, usually via an abdominal incision, with very extensive resin application both internally and externally. Resin-soaked linen towels were rolled up and placed inside the emptied body cavities. No visceral tissue was found inside these rolls. The evisceration wound was left unsutured but obstructed by a linen roll. Such preparation was identical with that employed by contemporary professional embalmers in the Nile Valley. Some of such prepared bodies in the Nile Valley had been damaged by looting and reconstruction efforts of these also occasionally involved extensive splinting of reassembled body parts, sometimes employing parts of several different bodies (Smith and Wood Jones 1910).

Authors' Addresses:

Arthur C. Aufderheide
Paleobiology Labratory
Department of Pathology and Laboratory Medicine
University of Minnesota, Duluth School of Medicine,
10 University Drive,
Duluth, Minnesota 55812-2487,
U. S. A.

Larry Cartmell
Department of Pathology
Valley View Regional Hospital,
Ada, Oklahoma
and
Research Affiliate of Paleobiology Laboratory at
University of Minnesota, Duluth School of Medicine

Michael Zlonis
Department of Pathology
St. Luke's Hospital, Duluth
and
Research Affiliate of Paleobiology Laboratory at
University of Minnesota, Duluth School of Medicine

REFERENCES

Aturaliya, S. and A. Lukasewycz, 1999 Experimental forensic and bioanthropological aspects of soft tissue taphonomy. I. Factors affecting soft tissue desiccation rate, *Journal of Forensic Sciences* 44 (5), 893–6.

Aufderheide, A. C., M. Zlonis, L. Cartmell, M. R. Zimmerman, P. Sheldrick, M. Cook and J. E. Molto, 1999 Human mummification practices at Ismant el-Kharab, *Journal of Egyptian Archaeology* 85, 193–210.

Birrell, M., 1999, Excavations in the Cemeteries of Ismant el-Kharab, in C. A. Hope and A. J. Mills, eds, *Dakhleh Oasis Project: Preliminary Reports on the 1992–1993 and 1993–1994 Field Seasons*, Oxbow Books, Oxford, 29–41.

Bowen, G. E., this volume Some Observations on Christian Burial Practices at Kellis, 167–81.

Ikram, S. and A. Dodson 1998, *The Mummy in Ancient Egypt*, Thames and Hudson, London.

Majno, G., 1975 *The Healing Hand*, Harvard University Press, Cambridge.

Maurer, J., T. Möhring, J. Rullkötter and A. Nissenbaum, 2002 Plant lipid and fossil hydrocarbons in embalming material of Roman Period mummies from the Dakhleh Oasis, Western Desert, Egypt, *Journal of Archaeological Science* 29, 751–62.

Schweitzer, A., 2002 Les parures de cartonnage des momies d'une nécropole d'Ismant el-Kharab, in C. A. Hope and G. E. Bowen, eds, *Dakhleh Oasis Project: Preliminary Reports on the 1994–1995 to 1998–1999 Field Seasons*, Oxbow Books, Oxford, 269–76.

Smith, G. E. and W. R. Dawson, 1924 *Egyptian Mummies*, Keegan Paul International, London.

Smith, G. E. and F. Wood Jones, 1910 Report of the Human Remains. Mode of Burial and Treatment of the Body, in G. Reisner, *The Archaeological Survey of Nubia*, Volume II: Report for 1907–1908, Printing Department, Cairo, 181–220.

Ubelaker, D. J., 1999 *Human Skeletal Remains*, Taraxacum, Washington D.C., Third Edition.

The Small East Church at Ismant el-Kharab

Gillian E. Bowen

Introduction[1]

The East Church complex is located upon a terrace overlooking the south-eastern wadi (Hope this volume, Figure 1). The architectural survey of this region revealed an extensive complex comprising numerous rooms, courts and corridors, much of which has been imprecisely mapped, due to the degree of preservation and the extensive alterations that had been carried out (Knudstad and Frey 1999, 205; Bowen 2002, 65; Figure 1). Knudstad and Frey (1999, 205) report that the enclosure wall surrounding the complex is 47 m wide north-south; however, its east-west length can only be traced for 60 m. The Small East Church is located within the south-eastern sector of the enclosure and is built against the eastern wall, 10 m north of the south-eastern corner (Bowen 2002, Figure 1). The Large East Church, located north-east of the small church, is set against the outer side of the enclosure wall and clearly post-dates the construction of the latter (Figure 1) (Knudstad and Frey 1999, 205; Hope and Bowen 1997, 49–51; Bowen 2002, 65–7). The access rooms to the large church (Rooms 5a and 5b) are on the west and are located within the enclosure. These rooms are separated from the north room of the small church by a narrow corridor, 1.2 m wide (Figure 1). This east-west corridor terminates in a doorway in the enclosure wall. The doorway opens onto a north-south corridor that separates the north room of the small church from the south rooms of the large church.

Minimal clearance was undertaken in the Small East Church during the 1981–82 field season (Mills 1982, 99–100). This entailed the excavation of the apse and the partial clearance of its two side chambers (Knudstad and Frey 1999, 205). In the 2000 field season it was decided to excavate the church in order to gain an understanding of its architecture, its antiquity, function, and to determine its relationship, if any, to the Large East Church.

Room 2

The Small East Church is a two-roomed, mud-brick structure: the church in the south, Room 1, and an adjoining room on its north, Room 2 (Figure 1). The overall dimensions are 10.5 m north-south x 9.5 m east-west. To the immediate north of the structure is the narrow corridor referred to above. The corridor has not been excavated. Work commenced in the expectation that both rooms would be excavated. The density of collapse in Room 2, however, made it impossible to clear the entire room in the time at our disposal. *Circa* 2 metres of wind-blown sand was removed and the floor was reached in a small section of the south-west corner. Sand-clearance revealed that it was a barrel-vaulted room, the internal measurements of which are 9.0 x 4.5 m with a height of just over 4 m. The room had been gypsum plastered throughout. The springing for the vaulting is built into the north and south walls at a point 2.8 m above the floor; it extends 23 cm from the wall. A window is set high into the west wall to the north of its centre (Plate 1). This window is 45 cm wide, 60 cm deep and is preserved to a height of 73 cm. An arched doorway, 1.25 m wide, was exposed in the north wall, 4.65 m from the west wall and 4.20 m from the east wall. This doorway had once opened off the corridor but had been blocked from the corridor side in antiquity with two courses of mud bricks (Plate 2). The doorway is set directly opposite another arched doorway which once opened off the corridor into the southern access room of the Large East Church, Room 5b (Plate 3). This doorway had also been blocked with mud bricks, covered with gypsum plaster and a niche set into it (Bowen 2002, 65). No attempt had been made to plaster over the bricking in the door in the north wall of Room 2. The blocking of the two doorways suggests that, at least in the latter stages of use, the two churches functioned independently. Three other doorways were exposed. One is in the southernmost

---

[1] A shorter version of this paper was published in the *Bulletin of the Australian Centre for Egyptology*, 11 (2000), 29–34.

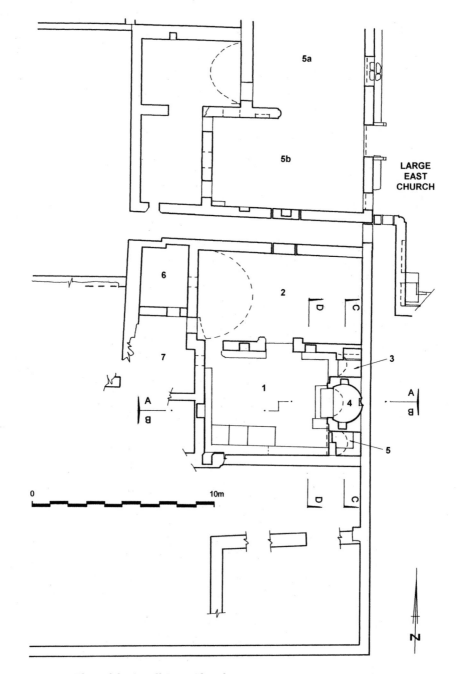

Figure 1 Plan of the Small East Church (drawing by J. Dobrowolski and B. Rowney).

Plate 1 Small East Church, Room 2, west wall showing barrel vault and the window.

Plate 2 Small East Church, Room 1 looking north into Room 2. The blocked doorway that opens into the corridor is visible in the north wall of Room 2.

Plate 3 Large East Church, access Room 5b, showing the blocked doorway and niche in the south wall.

Plate 4 Small East Church, Room 1 looking west before final clearance of the floor.

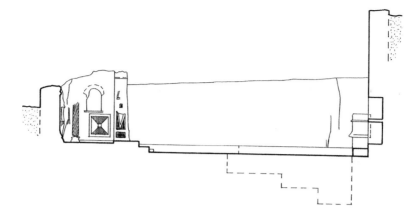

Figure 2 Small East Church, east-west section (B-B) through the centre of the church looking south; the dotted line indicates the test trench (drawing by B. Rowney). Scale: 1:100.

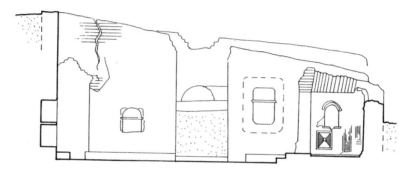

Figure 3 Small East Church, east-west section (A-A) through the centre of the church looking north through to Room 2 (drawing by B. Rowney). Scale 1:100.

Plate 5 Small East Church, Room 1 looking east into the sanctuary.

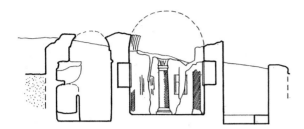

Figure 4 Small East Church, north-south section (D-D)
through the centre of the sanctuary
(drawing by B. Rowney). Scale 1:100.

Figure 5 Small East Church, north-south section (C-C)
through the east end
(drawing by B. Rowney). Scale 1:100.

part of the west wall and communicates with a small room
to the west, Room 7; this doorway provided the only access
to the church in the final stage of its use. The doorway is
1.75 m high, 1.10 m wide and 63 cm deep. The removal
of surface sand to the north of Room 7 revealed another
small room, Room 6, which opens off the former (Figure
1). Two further doorways were constructed in the southern
wall; these are described below with the discussion of
Room 1.

Room 1

Room 1 was fully excavated. It is well preserved with the
west wall standing 3.95 m; the east wall has been subject
to erosion and at the south-eastern corner the wall is 1.45
m high. The room was filled with windblown sand to
within 20 cm of the floor. The floor itself was strewn with
ceramic vessels and potsherds; there were fragments of
glass vessels, a cylindrical sandstone object and a single
palm log lying amongst the debris (Plate 4).

The room had undergone a series of modifications in
order to convert it into a church and a description of the
room prior to its conversion is given first. Originally, the
room appears to have been a simple rectangular, flat-roofed
structure, 8.5 x 5.5 m, with gypsum-coated walls throughout
and a window set high in the west wall, immediately to the
south of the north wall.[2] A gypsum-coated bench lined
the west wall (Figure 2). It continued along the south wall
for a distance of 2.94 m at which point there was a gap of
2.4 m before it resumed and continued along the remainder
of the south wall, turning and continuing along the east
wall only for a distance of 2.85 m (Figures 1 and 2). A
bench was also situated against the north wall (Figures 1
and 3), with an appropriate break to accommodate the
doorway; at its eastern end, the bench abuts a wall bin that
was built into the north-eastern corner of the room (see
below). A wide central door was set into the north wall
directly opposite the arched door that led from the north
room into the corridor beyond. This door and its

counterpart in what was later to become the access room
of the large church were also aligned with the gap between
the benches on the south wall. A cupboard was built into
each of the south, west and north walls; the latter also had
a niche (below) (Figures 1, 2 and 3; Plates 4 and 5). The
entire room was gypsum coated. The architecture of this
early room suggests that it may have functioned as a
meeting hall that had a focal point in the centre of the
south wall.[3] From surface observations, the other structures
within the enclosure wherein the small church and the
access rooms to the large church are situated do not appear
to be of a domestic nature and one is tempted to suggest
that the area fulfilled a civic function.

The Modification for the Church

With the modification of Room 1 to form the church, the
window in the west wall was blocked and a new section
was added to that same wall. A door was cut into the
westernmost end of the north wall and a short section of
the bench along the west wall immediately to the south of
the doorway was removed for ease of access (Figure 3,
Plate 2). The central doorway in the north wall was
narrowed at its eastern jamb by 37 cm. The gap between
the benches on the south wall was filled and an apse was
constructed against the east wall creating a tripartite
sanctuary: a central apse with north and south side
chambers (Figure 4, Plate 5). The sanctuary was set higher
than the nave and hence it was possible for the builders to
leave the bench against the east wall and simply cover it
with the floor of the apse and south side-chamber (Plate
5). The apse was covered with a cupola and the side
chambers were vaulted. The sanctuary in its entirety was
framed by three arches with pilasters on either side of the
apse (Figure 5; Plate 5).

The Apse

The curve of the apse was cut into the existing wall (Figure
1). The lack of bonding between the apse and exterior

---

[2] The excavation has shown that Knudstad and Frey's (1999, Figure 13.29) plan of the internal features of both churches is
inaccurate. There were no columns in the small church.

[3] This observation was made by C. A. Hope.

Plate 6 Small East Church, detail of the southern section of the apse showing the painted column (centre), the south niche and the geometric square.

Plate 7 Small East Church, apse, decoration on the northern face of the south pilaster.

wall, together with insubstantial foundation for the apse, have resulted in a slumping of the latter, exposing the undecorated gypsum plaster on the exterior wall. The maximum dimensions of the apse, Room 4, are 1.87 m north-south x 1.32 m east-west; the entrance is 1.48 m wide (Plate 5); the height from the floor to the commencement of the cupola is 1.72 m. The apse is approached by a single step paved with sandstone, 1.58 m long, 26 cm deep and 12 cm high, which gives access to the apse threshold, which is raised 9 cm above the step. The threshold is 63 cm deep and extends 20 cm into the nave. A groove, flush with the exterior of the pilasters, suggests that the apse could have been screened off. The apse floor was removed in antiquity but the presence of a few sandstone blocks amongst the rubble suggests that it was flagged.

The apse in its entirety was first coated in white gypsum and elaborately decorated both inside[4] and on the pilasters that frame it. An engaged half-column was set upon the back wall, slightly north of the centre (Figures 4 and 5; Plate 5). This column is preserved from the base of its

pedestal to the lower section of its capital; the latter comprises three-pointed leaves rising and spreading from a horizontal moulding. The shaft is 1.15 m high and the estimated height of the capital is 37 cm. From the traces of paint that remain it can be determined that the pedestal was deep yellow, the lower horizontal moulding, shaft and upper horizontal mouldings were dark red, with the leaves of the capital deep yellow on a dark-red ground. Two painted columns were placed either side of the engaged half-column (Plate 6). The column shafts are painted dark red and set upon a deep-yellow plinth; the capitals have eroded away. Between the engaged half-column and each of the painted columns are two painted frames containing representations of panelled, double-leaf doors. These panels each comprise a series of eight rectangles decorated with stylised palm fronds. Much of the colour has faded but Knudstad and Frey (1999, 207) note that most of the detail is rendered in dark red and deep yellow with some red; the frames are on a light-red or pink field and the doors on white with a dark-red filling. The panels clearly imitated cupboards. Two niches are on the western side

---

[4] For a description of the decoration as revealed in 1981–2 see Knudstad and Frey 1999, 205–7.

Plate 8 Small East Church, looking down into the north apse side chamber. The wall bin is on the right; the apse wall is on the extreme left.

Plate 9 Small East Church, looking down into the south apse side chamber. The bench is exposed along the south and east walls.

of each of the painted columns (Figures 2, 3 and 4; Plate 6); the top of each is framed by a sunken arch, painted in deep yellow and outlined in dark red, as are the ledges below the niches. A narrow, vertical dark-red border completes the decoration (Plate 6). The niches are 83 cm above the floor. They are 58 cm high, 41 cm wide at the opening, and 37 cm deep. A wooden sill was presumably inserted into the base and wooden doors added. Below the niches are painted squares with an alternating deep-yellow and dark-red border. The inner square is divided into four alternating, dark-red and deep-yellow triangles (Plate 6). In the centre is a rectangle within which is a *crux ansata*, outlined in dark red on a pale-yellow base. The *cruces ansatae* are 7 cm in length and 5 cm wide at the cross bar. The circular top is painted upon the vertical shaft and is slightly raised above the cross bar. Plaster fragments from another *crux ansata* were found amongst the debris on the *bema* of the Large East Church. This early Egyptian form of the Christian cross presumably adorned the apse or its vicinity (Bowen 2002, 71). The entire apse has a narrow light-red dado; this colour is continued along the inner edge of the outer pilaster and presumably framed the cupola.

Both faces of the pilasters are decorated with geometric designs painted dark and light red, deep and pale yellow. The decoration on the north face of the south pilaster is far better preserved than its counterparts. The surviving decoration on the inner-facing pilaster faces consists of two panels: the lower contains a light-red rectangle within a pale-yellow border all within a frame of vertical and horizontal zigzag red lines; the upper panel has a dark-red ground, framed with deep yellow, with double vertical lines radiating from the base (Figure 2; Plate 7). The decoration on the west-orientated faces of the pilasters is poorly preserved; the lower panel comprises a deep yellow square into which a pale-yellow diamond with dark-red points was set. A dark-red disc was painted in the centre of the diamond.

The narrow sections of wall flanking the apse pilasters were decorated to represent stone columns to give the effect of supporting the vaults of each room. The shaft was rendered in a pale yellow with the lower moulding, outline of the shaft and vertical, wavy lines picked out in a deep red; the shaft was set upon a deep-yellow painted plinth above a dark-red base line. Two further columns painted on the north and south walls of the nave immediately outside of the side chambers fulfilled the same decorative function. Traces only remain of the painting on the south wall that has been partly obscured by the addition of a wall to the side room.

The Apse Side Chambers

In the final stage of use as a church, both apse side chambers functioned as storage rooms. Room 3, on the north, measures 1.20 x 1.18 m and contains a large shelf and a substantial wall bin set well back into the north wall leaving a space of only 80 cm between the bin and the wall that divides the room from the apse (Plates 5 and 8).

The step into the room was raised 20 cm above the floor of the nave from which it was closed off by a narrow wooden door. Room 5, the south chamber, is slightly larger than its northern counterpart, 1.20 x 1.50 m, but is devoid of features. During the alterations to the room, the bench in this corner was retained but the floor level was filled in and raised to bench height (Plate 9). A wall was constructed to block it off from the nave. Access to the room was through a small doorway placed 35 cm above the floor of the nave. The door is only 63 cm high and 45 cm wide, which indicates that the room could only have functioned as a cupboard (Plate 5). The fact that the painted column on the south wall is obscured by the insertion of the blocking suggests that the blocking may post-date the conversion of the room into a church. Both chambers, including the bin and shelf in the north room, were gypsum coated and vaulted.

The Nave

The nave occupies the remainder of the room (Figure 1). The floor was originally gypsum coated. The only features are the benches, three cupboards and a niche in the north, south and west walls (Plates 2, 4 and 5), and to the south of the step to the apse, immediately to the west of the south apse pilaster, is a narrow water-hardened platform, 40 x 62 x 5 cm (Plate 5). The cupboard in the western corner of the south wall at a point 30 cm above the bench, is 60 cm high, 51 cm wide and 35 cm deep; the wooden shelf that had once divided it into two equal parts is missing. A second cupboard is cut midway along the west wall 15 cm above the bench (Plate 4). It is 1.21 m high, 70 cm wide and 45 cm deep. The wooden shelf is still *in situ*. The niche, which had a rounded top, is in the western section of the north wall (Plate 2). It is located 53 cm above the bench and is 69 cm high, 50 cm wide and 36 cm deep. It also had a wooden shelf placed 37 cm above the base. A third cupboard is located on the eastern section of the north wall, 75 cm above the bench. The dimensions are 97 cm high, 61 cm wide and 32 cm deep (Plate 2). It had a wooden shelf placed 60 cm from the base. All cupboards were closed with wooden doors and were gypsum-coated on the inside as was the niche.

Doorways

Room 1 could only be accessed from Room 2 through two doorways: a narrow doorway in the extreme west of the north wall and a large doorway in its centre (Plate 2). The doorway in the west of the north wall of the church was cut during the modification of the south room (see above). The dimensions are 1.82 m high and 85 cm wide. The pivot emplacement is preserved in the north-western side of the opening, indicating that the door opened into the north room. The central doorway connecting the two rooms is 1.51 m wide. The dividing wall was thickened on either side to form the jambs (Figure 1). The east jamb was added after the construction of the cupboard; the plaster that surrounds the cupboard and continued into the original doorway is observable behind the addition (Plate 2). As with the door on the west, the central door opened into Room 2.

Sub-Floor Excavations

North Apse Side Chamber

The floor of the north apse side chamber was removed in an effort to determine the relative chronology of the architecture (Plate 8). The fill comprised compacted earth with potsherds; three coins were retrieved from this context. A layer of compacted mud was laid at a depth of 1.84 m beneath the floor. This appears to have served as a foundation; a similar compacted-mud foundation was encountered in test trenches in the large church (Hope this volume). This foundation was cut through in order to erect the enclosure wall a section of which forms the east wall of the church. The bin abuts the east wall; it was set upon rubble some 12.5 cm above the compacted foundation. The front of the wall bin is gypsum plastered to the depth of the floor level of the nave; thereafter the unclad mud brick extends for a further 94 cm. This indicates that the bin was part of the original room; the fact that the bin extends into the room for the same width as the bench in the church, which abuts the bin, confirms this. The apse was the last to be constructed; its north wall abuts the east wall and extends only one course of bricks beneath the floor level, hence the slump.

The Nave

A test trench was excavated east-west along the bench on the south wall for a distance of 3.6 m commencing at the bench on the west wall, and extending one metre into the nave (Figure 2). This area was chosen because the section that had been added to the bench along the south wall suggested that it was a later addition. Excavation revealed that the bench along the entire south wall had been built directly onto the floor of the church. At a depth of 1.45 m below the floor a thick layer of mud was encountered yet again; this may have formed a foundation platform for the south wall but, as excavation was not undertaken beneath this bench, this cannot be confirmed. The fill comprised rubble, with bones and sherds; no ash was present. The ceramic assemblage was fourth-century. No earlier structure was detected.

Artefacts

The artefactual remains found in the church were few; they comprised ceramics, glass, three ostraka, coins, a single bead and a cylindrical piece of worked sandstone with a shallow depression in the top and a groove (Plate 10). The block, which has a diameter of between 42 cm and 46 cm, and a height of 21 cm was not found *in situ* (Plate 2), and its function cannot be determined. The glass has been identified by C. Marchini (personal communication, January 2000) as originating from lamps. One of the ostraka, registration number 31/420-D-6-1/A/8/21, preserves the noun Irene (Worp forthcoming; O. Kellis 272); whether a personal name or simply 'peace' cannot be determined as the ostrakon is broken. The coins and ceramics are crucial for the date of the foundation and period of use of the church. Four of the 15 coins are third-century *tetradrachms*. Three were found in the wall bin in the north apse side chamber and the fourth was from the cupboard on the south wall.[5] They may well have been contemporary with the earlier use of the room as *tetradrachms* were rendered obsolete with Diocletian's currency reforms of 296 and were removed from circulation soon after (West and Johnson 1967, 111; W. Metclaf personal communication, 1997).[6] A coin retrieved from beneath the lower course of bricks on which the apse wall was built dates to the reign of Maxentius: 31/420-D6-1-A/8/29. This indicates that the modification of the room cannot pre-date his reign, which spanned the years 306–12. The ceramics evidence complements that of the coins; all vessels can all be placed within a third-fourth century context (see below).

Discussion

Although minimal excavation was undertaken in Room 2 it became clear that it was an integral part of a larger church complex. Following the blocking of the door that opened into the north corridor, the sole access to the church was through a doorway in the extreme south of its west wall that communicated with a room to the west (see above). One can only speculate upon the function of this north room, but the retention of the large central doorway suggests a ceremonial use. It may have served as a room for the catechumens who could hear, but not view the mass and where they might receive instruction; it could also have functioned as a place for the congregation to partake of the communal meal. It seems unlikely that it was a baptistery or that it was associated directly with the large church.

The structure is a good example of a *domus ecclesiae*, 'house of the church', a community house owned by the congregation and converted according to its needs (Krautheimer 1981, 27). As such, the small church predates the construction of the purpose-built Large East Church. The earliest known *domus ecclesiae* is that at Dura-Europos in Syria, which was destroyed in the conflict of 256/57

---

[5] The registration numbers of the coins are 31/420-D6-1-A/8/11, 12 and 14 for those coins in the wall bin and A/8/10 for that in the cupboard.

[6] I am most grateful to Dr Metcalf for providing me with details of his study of the *tetradrachms*.

Plate 10 Small East Church, the sandstone object found on the floor of the nave.

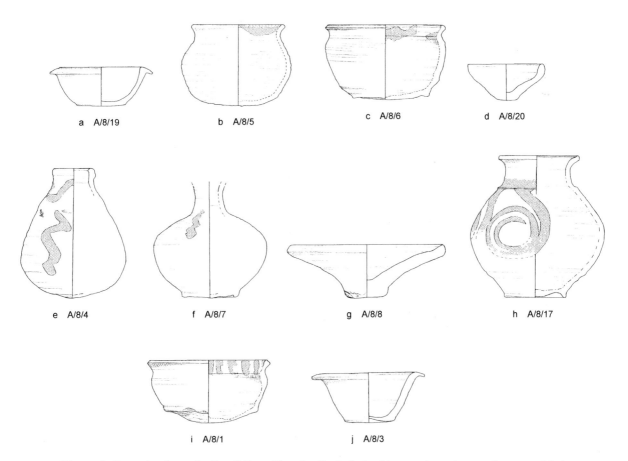

Figure 6 Ceramics from the Small East Church. Scale 1:4; object registration numbers provided.

(MacDonald 1986, 45–68). The basilica form in church architecture is said to have been introduced by Constantine I following the *Edict of Milan* in 313 (Krautheimer 1981, 43). It did not replace the *domus-ecclesiae* form, however, and structures were modified for ecclesiastical use throughout the fourth century, especially in the provinces (White 1990, 23).

The *domus ecclesiae* at Kellis has all the hallmarks of later Christian architectural conventions: that is, it is aligned on an east-west axis with the sanctuary on the east. The sanctuary is raised and the apse is closed off from the congregation. It cannot be shown whether the *domus ecclesiae* went out of service with the erection of the large basilica; indeed the two could well have functioned side by side, as did the numerous churches at Medinet Madi (Bresciaini 1987, 1–3; Grossmann 1987, 7–16). There is no evidence of post-abandonment activity within the church itself except for Coptic graffiti incised into the plaster on the apse wall. Olaf Kaper has distinguished three separate texts; however, they are mostly illegible.

The pottery vessels found at floor level in the nave may well have been associated with the functioning of the church, for cleaning of the floor revealed several impressions where pots once stood. Eight complete ceramic vessels were found on the floor in the nave (Figure 6a–h). One (Figure 6a), is an Oasis Red Ware bowl, a family of wares that has been dated to the fourth–fifth centuries (Hope 1985, 123; see Hope 1999, 236); Figures 6b, 6c and 6d have parallels in the fourth-century houses at Kellis (Hope 1986, Figure 6c 1/60; Patten 1999, 84–5). Figure 6e, however, has parallels in the well area of the Main Temple and in Tomb 13 of the cemetery known as Kellis 2, which dates to the third-early fourth centuries, if not earlier (Dunsmore 2002, 131 and Figure 1b), whilst Figures 6f, 6g and 6h also have parallels from third or early fourth-century contexts (Hope 1986, Figure 7f 3/3; Dunsmore 1999, Figure 1a); all such vessels are absent from the fourth-century houses. A vessel that was retrieved from the floor of the north apse side chamber, Figure 6i, also has parallels from the houses whilst a further Oasis Red Ware bowl was in the rubble of the south side chamber, Figure 6j.[7] Numismatic evidence for the period of use of the church is inconclusive as seven of the 15 are either broken or too corroded to identify. The remaining coins are a *Sol Invictus,* struck by Constantine I before 318, A/8/23, one issued by Crispus, A/8/32, sometime before his death in 326, and a third that appears to be of a similar date, A/8/31.[8] This indicates that the church functioned within the first half of the fourth century.

Onomastic evidence from dated texts attests a Christian presence at Kellis by the 280s, if not earlier (Bowen 1998, 158–61). It is not known where these early Christians met for purposes of worship, nor can their numbers be determined. Coins retrieved from the Large East Church at Kellis indicate that it was built during the reign of Constantine I (Bowen 2002, 81–3), which suggests that the residents of Kellis quickly outgrew their *domus ecclesiae* and opted for the new basilica form. The need to build a church of such proportions in the first half of the fourth century is not only testimony to the growing number of Christian converts in the village but also the rapid pace of that conversion.

Acknowledgements

The work in the Small East Church was funded by a grant from Monash University; for this I am most grateful. I also with to thank Colin A. Hope for permitting me to excavate and publish the churches at Ismant el-Kharab.

Author's Address:

Centre for Archaeology and Ancient History
School of Historical Studies
Building 11, Clayton Campus,
Monash University,
Victoria 3800,
Australia

---

[7] I am most grateful to C. A. Hope for the identification of the ceramics and providing me with information on the dates and parallels.

[8] Both the portrait and the flan size suggest a that the coin was struck before the mid-fourth century. This specimen was found together with the Crispus issue on the floor of the north apse side chamber.

REFERENCES

Bowen, G. E., 1998 The Spread of Christianity in Egypt in Light of Recent Discoveries from Ancient Kellis, unpublished Ph.D. dissertation, Monash University.

Bowen, G. E., 2002 The Fourth-Century Churches at Ismant el-Kharab, in C. A. Hope and G. E. Bowen, eds, *The Dakhleh Oasis Project: Preliminary Reports on the 1994–5 to 1998–9 Field Seasons*, Oxbow Books, Oxford, 65–85.

Bresciani, E., 1987 L'Attivita" Archeologica del" Universita di Pisa in Egitto (1987): Medinet Madi nel Fayum, in E. Bresciani, ed., *Egitto e Vicino Oriente* X, 1, 1–3.

Grossmann, P., 1987 Madinat Madi – die Kirche (1987) Beschreibunng Der Bearbeiten Kirchen, in E. Bresciani, ed., *Egitto e Vicino Oriente* X, 1, 7–16.

Hope, C. A., 1985 Dakhleh Oasis Project: Report on the 1986 Excavations at Ismant el-Gharab, *Journal of the Society for the Study of Egyptian Antiquities*, XV, 4, 114–25.

Hope, C. A., 1986 Dakhleh Oasis Project: Report on the 1987 Excavations at Ismant el-Gharab, *Journal of the Society for the Study of Egyptian Antiquities*, XVI, 3/4, 74–91.

Hope, C. A., 1999 Pottery Manufacture in the Dakhleh Oasis, in C. S. Churcher and A. J. Mills, eds, *Reports from the Survey of the Dakhleh Oasis 1977–1987*, Oxbow Books, Oxford.

Hope, C. A. and G. E. Bowen, 1997 The Excavations at Ismant el-Kharab in 1995/6 and 1996/7: A Brief Report, in *Bulletin of the Australian Centre for Egyptology* 8, 49–64.

Knudstad, J. E., and R. A. Frey, 1999 Kellis: the Architectural Survey of the Romano-Byzantine Town at Ismant el-Kharab, in C. S. Churcher and A. J. Mills, eds, *Reports from the Survey of the Dakhleh Oasis 1977–87*, Oxbow Books, Oxford, 189–214.

Krauthheimer, R., 1981 *Early Christian and Byzantine Architecture*, Penguin Books, Harmondsworth.

MacDonald, D., 1986 Dating the Fall of Dura-Europos, *Historia* 35, 45–68.

Mills, A. J., 1982 Dakhleh Oasis Project. Report on the Fourth Season of Survey. October 1981 – January 1982, in *Journal of the Society for the Study of Egyptian Antiquities* XII, 3, 93–101.

Patten, S. F., 1999 Reports on the Study of the Ceramics: 1993–1994 Seasons, C. A. Hope and G. E. Bowen, eds, *Dakhleh Oasis Project: Preliminary Reports on the 1992–1993 and 1993–1994 Field Seasons*, Oxbow Books, Oxford, 83–8.

West, L. C. and A. C. Johnson, 1967 *Currency in Roman and Byzantine Egypt*, Adolf M. Hakkert, Amsterdam.

White, L. M., 1990 *Building God's House in the Roman World*, The Johns Hopkins University Press, Baltimore and London.

Worp, K. A., Forthcoming *Greek Ostraka from Kellis*, Oxbow Books, Oxford.

Some Observations on Christian Burial Practices at Kellis

Gillian E. Bowen

Introduction

In 1997 I was invited by Anthony Mills to publish the archaeology of the Kellis 2 cemetery as an adjunct to my work on early Christianity in Egypt. Since that time further Christian burials have been discovered at Kellis other than in this cemetery. The primary aim of this paper is to publish preliminary observations on the burial practices adopted by the Christian community at Kellis in light of what is known of such practices in Egypt. The graves in Kellis 2 are being excavated by archaeologists under the direction of Eldon Molto, who co-ordinates the work of the physical anthropologists. Molto and his team are conducting a range of analyses on the skeletal remains that have added a new dimension to our knowledge of the community. Molto's analyses include radiocarbon tests of twelve samples in an effort to determine the date of the interments. The interpretation of the results of those analyses presents a broad time-frame that is seemingly at variance with the data from the settlement. This paper, therefore, presents an ideal opportunity to consider this dichotomy and how it might be addressed by archaeologists and physical anthropologists alike.

Kellis 2 Cemetery

The Kellis 2 cemetery (31/420-C5-2) is located to the north-east of the settlement (Birrell 1999, 38–41). Systematic excavations of the burials commenced in 1992 (Birrell 1999, 38) and to date 450 graves have been excavated (Stewart *et al.* this volume). Molto (2002, 241) has estimated the number of graves in the cemetery to be between 3,000 and 4,000, if the density of the burials in

the cemetery as a whole is reflected by the area excavated so far (Molto 2002, Figures 2 and 4). All graves are aligned on an east-west axis with minor deviations that may reflect winter or summer burials.[1] The graves are simple rectangular pits cut into the bedrock to an average depth of 1.3 m; the other dimensions are variable but for adults the average graves are *circa* 1.9 m long by 65 cm wide.[2] Four distinct types of grave are recorded. In the most elaborate the upper part of the pit, 35 cm above the floor, was widened and lined with mud bricks that terminated in a subsurface vault; the grave was then covered with a mud-brick mastaba superstructure. The second type is a rectangular pit with sloping sides, narrowing towards the bottom. The rubble fill, thrown directly onto the body, was covered with a false mud-brick floor and finished with a mastaba. A variation on this type omits the false floor and the fill extends into the superstructure. Many of the mastabas have traces of gypsum plaster coating. All of the superstructures have suffered the effects of erosion and it is not possible to determine their original height. The fourth type is the simple pit with the fill above the body covered by a low earth mound that was gypsum coated.

A number of mud-brick tomb enclosures have been identified; two, Enclosures 1 and 2 located two metres apart, have been excavated (Birrell 1999, 38–40, Figure 3). The enclosures are badly eroded and little survives of their superstructures. The external dimensions of Enclosure 1 are 3.4 metres square, the walls are preserved to a height of three courses; the exterior and interior walls and the floor were gypsum coated. The doorway was not located. The enclosure contained four burials: three adults and one young child. The most southerly of the graves (1D) is of

---

[1] This interpretation was suggested by M. Birrell (personal communication 1994). Jeffreys and Strouhal (1980, 34) observed the same phenomenon in the Christian cemetery at the site of the Sacred Animal Necropolis in North Saqqara. Based upon the east-west azimuthal orientation of the graves, they estimated that 50.9% of the interments took place in winter, 23.6% in each of spring and autumn and 1.5% in summer.

[2] The following information is taken from various field notebooks and personal observation.

the first type; the mastaba was preserved to a height of 60 cm above the floor and retained some of its gypsum coating. No surviving superstructure is recorded for the remaining adult graves. Enclosure 2 is *circa* 4 metres square and was more elaborate in design with two columns on its north-western corner and a third on the north wall towards the north-eastern corner. The door opened to the east. The walls are badly eroded and preserve only two courses of mud bricks. Although no remains of gypsum plaster were detected, it may be assumed that it too was coated in white. It cannot be determined whether or not this or the neighbouring structure was roofed. Enclosure 2 contained six graves but only three were excavated. Graves 3 and 5 were intrusive shallow pits dug for infants and had no superstructures. Grave 8 was badly eroded with the mastaba preserved to a height of 16 cm; it is of the same type as grave 1D. The grave was undisturbed and contained the body of a young woman; there were no accompanying grave goods. The plan indicates that the three remaining unexcavated graves had mastaba superstructures. These enclosures may well have been family tombs.

Burial practice throughout the cemetery, as illustrated by the excavated graves, was uniform. The bodies were placed directly onto the floor of the pit with the head on the west and with one exception they were single interments.[3] The corpse was wrapped in a linen shroud that was secured with woven linen ties wound in a criss-cross or lateral fashion and placed directly into the pit in a supine position; the hands were to the sides or over the pelvic region (Birrell 1999, 41). In some instances, large broken pots had been placed above the body (Birrell 1999, 41, Plate 10). The ceramic vessels included reused pigeon pots, presumably collected from a *columbarium* located near the cemetery, and large decorated vessels of the type found in the fourth-century houses in Area A, and elsewhere in the settlement (Birrell 1999, 40–1, Plate 10; Patten 1999, 88, Figure 1:10; Hope this volume) other sherds found in the fill include those from decorated vessels that are typical of the fourth-century ceramics from the settlement (Patten 1999, Figure 1:2). Although many of the graves have been disturbed, it can be determined from those still intact that burial goods were minimal: one string of beads, a reused glass vessel (Birrell 1999, 41; Marchini 1999, 81–2), the occasional ceramic bowl with red painted ticks on the rim (Patten 1999, 83, Figure 1:2) and sprays of rosemary and myrtle (U. Thanheiser personal communication, 1998). Infant burials were dispersed amongst those of the adult population; they were placed in shallow pits again cut on an east-west orientation, heads on the west. Such burial practices equate with the Christian tradition and, consequently, those interred have been identified as belonging to the Christian community at Kellis.

Twelve samples taken by Molto from eleven of the bodies exhumed have been subjected to radiocarbon dating and initial results, based upon the 2-sigma calibration, although inconclusive, indicate that the cemetery could have been in use from the end of the Ptolemaic Period until around 600 CE (Stewart *et al.* this volume). The early date is impossible if those interred were Christian. Molto and his team acknowledge that such a broad time span is unlikely and propose that the solution may be to narrow the margins by taking the latest end of the early date and the early end of the latest date, which gives a date range of between 220–380 CE. This, however, they regard as methodologically unsound and equally improbable and suggest that the date range for the use of the cemetery lies somewhere between those extremes (Stewart *et al.* this volume). Archaeological evidence from the settlement indicates that Kellis had a sizeable Christian community by the first half of the fourth century; this is attested by three churches at the site, two of which date to that time (Bowen 2002, 84; this volume). The earliest documentary attestation of a Christian from the village, however, is dated 319 (*PUG* 20 and *P. Med.* inv. 68.82; Wagner 1987 327–8). Papyrological, numismatic and ceramic evidence indicate that Kellis was abandoned towards the close of the fourth century (Hope 1999, 54–7). If the cemetery is indeed Christian, and if Kellis was abandoned at the end of the fourth century, the interpretation of the radiocarbon dates and archaeological data are at variance. If, however, the narrow range, considered to be improbable by the physical anthropologists, can be accepted, it would render the two sets of data more compatible, although a date of 220 for the first burials in the cemetery is problematic in light of what is known of the nature of Christianity at that period. With this in mind, an investigation of what is understood of early Christian burial practices in Egypt and Kellis and a discussion of the abandonment of the village is warranted before proceeding with further evidence for Christian interment at Kellis.

Early Christian Burial Practices in Egypt

The Problem of Identity

First, it should be established, as far as possible, that the cemetery belonged to and was used by Christians. This necessitates a brief statement of the nature of early Christianity together with evidence for comparable, contemporary burial practices. Christians, identifying as such, are undetectable in the archaeological record until at least the mid-third century. As there was no prohibition on Christians and pagans being buried within the same tombs or cemeteries (Johnson 1999, 42), the practice was continued by some Christians beyond the fourth century (Hauser 1932, 44–50; Thomas 2000, 34; Venit 2002, 181–

---

[3] The exception is Grave 92 that contained the bodies of two infants (Bodies 95 and 96).

6). Many who adopted the new religion held an amalgam of beliefs and practices. In Egypt, the iconography of the old religion was adapted by the new. For example, Isis and Horus became the Mother and Child, whilst the *ankh*, the pharaonic symbol for life, was modified and became the Christian *crux ansata*.

Regardless of whether or not the church imposed a dogma, some Christians continued to venerate the old gods along with the new, and to continue the age-old practice of mummification and pagan burial rites. Evidence for the continued practice of mummification and the employment of Christians as necropolis workers during the late third century is contained in a letter found amongst those in the dossier of the necrotaphs from Kysis, modern Dush in Kharga Oasis. It concerns the transportation of the mummified remains of a Christian woman, Politike whose body was entrusted to the care of Christian necrotaphs, on the instructions of Psenosiris to his fellow presbyter Apollon (Deissmann 1902, 10–12). Further evidence for the continuation of the practice by some Christians comes in the form of a mummy labels; one undated example bears the name Psentheos, son of Apollonius, son of Patses; the patronym is followed by the Christian *chi-rho* monogram (Scott-Moncrieff 1913, 102–3). The mummified bodies of three women, covered with painted shrouds, were found by Gayet at Antinoopolis; the shrouds are now dated to the early fourth century (Aubert 2000, 147–8; Walker 2000, 36).[4] Each woman is shown in her finery holding a *crux ansata* to her breast with her left hand and her right hand raised in what might be termed a gesture of prayer (Doxiadis 1995, 118, 120, 161). The *crux ansata* is well attested within a Christian funerary context and is the most prominent symbol depicted on the wall paintings in the necropolis at Bagawat (Fakhry 1951). The use of the symbol on the Antinoopolis shrouds indicates that the women presented as Christian in death (Scott-Moncrieff 1913, 107–9; Dunand 1998, 164), although some authorities remain reluctant to accept this identification (Aubert 2000, 147–8).

As no separate Christian cemetery has been found at Dush and the archive suggests that the necrotaphs served the pagan community, it could be assumed that Politike was buried in a tomb alongside members of the pagan population. The records from Gayet's excavations at Antinoopolis indicate that the bodies of the three women were interred in simple pits in Necropolis E (Doxiadis 1995, 151) that included pagan and Christian burial.[5]

Separate Cemeteries; Separate Customs

At some undetermined point in time Christians made a conscious effort to adopt a distinctive mode of burial from that of their pagan contemporaries. The earliest public Christian cemetery is St Callixtus' Catacomb in Rome, commissioned by Pope Zephyrinus in the early third century (Toynbee 1971, 236).[6] Tertullian (*ad scapulam* 3) implies a separate cemetery for Christians at the important see of Carthage by 203; the text, however, is ambiguous and should be treated with caution. In Alexandria, an exclusively Christian hypogeum in the Hadra necropolis was excavated by Breccia in 1908 (Venit 2002, 181). Frog lamps found there could date it as early as the third century; however as these lamps were manufactured in Egypt during the third and fourth centuries and may have continued into the fifth century (Bailey 1988, 217), they do not confirm an early date for the cemetery. Separate cemeteries for Christians, therefore, should not be expected prior to the third century.

The *Didascalia Apostolorum*, composed in Greek during the third century in Syria and translated into Syriac and Latin (Cross and Livingston 1974, 401), provides information on what Davies (1999, 199)[7] terms 'ordinary' early Christian burial practices: the body was washed, anointed and sometimes embalmed; it was then carried to the grave where it was buried with a Eucharist. The grave was aligned on an east-west axis and the body placed directly onto the floor of the pit, face upward, with the feet to the east in order to rise facing the Son of Man on the day of resurrection (Davies 1999, 199). Such practices were not confined to Syria but spread throughout the Christian world. Whilst some regarded modest graves as exemplary, they were not mandatory and wealthy Christians were also buried in expensive mausolea. These are attested in Egypt from the fourth century and are best exemplified by the tombs at Bagawat in Kharga Oasis and at Oxyrhynchus (below). Even within these expensive tombs, however, the bodies were simply shrouded and placed in the traditional east-west position with few, if any grave goods (Lythgoe 1908, 205–6; Petrie 1925, 16–9).

In the early fourth century it was usual for Christians to follow the traditional custom found throughout the ancient world of locating cemeteries outside of the town or city. Unlike pagans, Christians regarded the body as 'sleeping' or lying in the grave to await the day of resurrection and, as such, the person interred was considered to be a part of the world of the living. As a consequence of this doctrine,

---

[4] The shrouds were previously dated by B. Borg, (Problems in the Dating of Mummy Portraits, in E. Doxiadis, *The Mysterious Fayum Portraits*, Thames and Hudson, London, 1995, 232–3) to the first half of the third century. Borg has now accepted the later date (S. Walker personal communication, 2000).

[5] Gayet's publications are not available in Australia.

[6] Toynbee (1971, 236) notes that the information is recorded in an early third-century Greek text, the *Elenchos*.

[7] The *Didascalia Apostolorum* is not readily available and consequently the comments are based upon those provided by Davies.

towards the end of the fourth century in Rome, burial grounds were established within the city walls, often in association with martyria and churches (Davies 1999, 193). The practice was followed in other regions within the Empire (Brown 1981). Whilst many graves outside churches continued the east-west alignment, by the sixth century this attention to orientation was often abandoned.[8]

Christian Cemeteries in Dakhleh, Kharga and the Nile Valley

The funerary practices adopted by the Christian community in Kellis 2 and other places of interment associated with the village (below) conform to what Davies terms 'ordinary' burials. Parallels are attested elsewhere in Dakhleh, in Kharga Oasis and in the Nile Valley. This paper does not allow for an exhaustive catalogue of such; a single example from each of the above areas will suffice. In the west of Dakhleh, a cemetery (33/390-I7-2) of around 40–45 pit graves, aligned on an east-west axis with deviations, lies adjacent to a small settlement (33/390-I7-1); the bodies found within the excavated graves were buried in the standard Christian position and contained no burial goods (Mills 1979, 182). Two small rock-cut dwellings (33/390-I6-1), presumably used by Christian ascetics, are located in the sandstone hills to the north-west within sight of the village and cemetery (Mills 1979, 182) and may have been associated with it. The settlement has been dated tentatively to the fourth–fifth centuries CE on ceramic evidence (Hope 1980, 299–300).

The elaborate mausolea in the necropolis of Bagawat, Kharga Oasis, are predominantly Christian. Those tombs that were excavated fully contained both single and multiple burials, the bodies were not mummified but wrapped and placed on the floor with the head on the west (Lythgoe 1908, 205–6; Hauser 1932, 50). There is a single exception: a tomb that contained 13 bodies, including four babies. The five earlier burials were in pit graves beneath the floor; above these were three reused wooden coffins containing four bodies. The remaining bodies were placed on the floor, one beneath a coffin and the other three laid on top of two of the coffins (Hauser 1932). All bodies, including those in coffins, were placed with their heads to the west and the earlier interments were buried in a typically Christian fashion. Grave goods were minimal and included none of the traditional pharaonic items; the inclusion of infants is atypical of pagan practices and it is not unreasonable to assume that many, if not all of the occupants were Christian. Hauser (1932, 49–50) identifies the bodies as pagan because of the reuse of pharaonic-style coffins, the presence of a Greek figurine and a gilded

bronze coin of Nero that had been incorporated into a pendant. Hauser (1932, 50) argues that no Christian would be buried with pharaonic iconography or wear a coin depicting the archenemy of Christianity. The reuse by Christians of sections from pagan coffins, however, is attested in the cemetery at Saqqara (below) (Martin 1974, 21); moreover, Christians had no compunction about being buried in pagan tombs painted with traditional funerary motifs (see below), so why not in reused coffins? Hellenistic iconography is not out of place within a Christian context; a bronze Greek-style figurine and a ring with an engraving of a *menaid* were found in the Large East Church at Kellis (Bowen 2002, 75, Plates 6 and 7). The coin incorporated into the pendant was struck at least 225 years earlier and one wonders whether the emperor depicted was of relevance to the wearer. There is every possibility that the pendant was an heirloom. Coins of Diocletian, an even greater enemy of Christians than Nero, were found in both the Large and Small East Churches at Kellis (Bowen 2002, 81–2; this volume).

In 1908 about one hundred simple pit graves that form part of a larger pit-grave cemetery located on the slopes of the Bagawat necropolis, were excavated (Lythgoe 1908, 203–8). The graves are aligned on an east-west axis and had low mud-brick superstructures,[9] a headstone and foot-stone; the former was engraved with the name of the interred (Lythgoe 1908, 207; Wagner 1991, 327–8). Lythgoe (1908, 207) describes the superstructures as being either a mud-brick mastaba above a fill of rubble and gravel, and an oval mound of rubble and gravel with a mud-plaster coating. They resemble, therefore, two of the superstructure types in Kellis 2. From the photograph published in 1908, these pit graves also show some deviation in alignment (Lythgoe 1908, 208, Figure 7). The bodies were wrapped in burial shrouds secured variously with bands. Most were devoid of grave goods although some bodies had hairpins and small items of personal adornment. They were laid with the head on the west, hands to the sides or over the pelvic region. Several of the graves can be dated to the fourth century on the evidence of coins of Constantine I and Constantius II found with the bodies (Hauser 1932, 40). As the cemetery has only been published in preliminary reports, little more is known of the graves, the contents or the skeletal remains.

The final example is the cemetery located within the Sacred Animal Necropolis at Saqqara. It is dated by its original excavator to the late fourth and early fifth centuries (Martin 1974, 19); the subsequent excavators declined to give a date, due to lack of internal evidence, but note that occupation in the village to which the cemetery is attached 'cannot be dated more closely than sometime between the

---

[8] See, for example, the cemetery outside the small church at Dime (Badawy 1978, 100, Figure 2.66). Monks buried outside monastery walls do not always conform to the east-west tradition (Prominska 1986; Bács 2000, 35).

[9] Lythgoe (1908, 207) describes the superstructures as being either a mud-brick mastaba above a fill of rubble and gravel, and an oval mound of rubble and gravel with a mud-plaster coating. They resemble, therefore two of the superstructure types in Kellis 2 (Birrell 1999, 40).

beginning of the fifth and the middle of the sixth century' (Jeffreys and Strouhal 1980, 33). A total of 160 graves were excavated, this represents between 60 per cent and possibly as much as 80 per cent of the entire cemetery (Jeffreys and Strouhal 1980, 28). The graves are simple pits aligned on an east-west axis with deviations (see Footnote 2) (Jeffreys and Strouhal 1980, 34). Some had mud-brick superstructures and inscribed grave stelae, whilst certain of those without a superstructure were covered with large potsherds, a practice reminiscent of that in the Kellis 2 cemetery; the excavator reports that the potsherds included pieces of large red-ware storage vessels with roughly-inscribed Coptic texts (Martin 1974, 20). The bodies were wrapped in coarse linen shrouds, bound in either a criss-cross or lateral manner, and placed in the grave with the head to the west and feet to the east and the arms to the sides (Martin 1974, 21). The bodies were devoid of grave goods with a single exception (Martin 1974, 21).[10] Unlike the burials in Kellis 2 cemetery, the majority of the bodies at Saqqara were laid on and bound to planks of wood that had been reused from coffins of the Saite and Ptolemaic periods, others were placed in reed or basketry carriers (Martin 1974, 21). Martin (1974, 21) notes in particular that one of the reused planks depicts the goddess Nut, together with a hieroglyphic inscription. The use of pagan funerary iconography was clearly not an anathema within this community.

This brief survey has shown that the Christian residents of Kellis adopted similar burial practices to those of their co-religionists in other parts of Egypt.[11] An overview of pagan burial practices in the Roman Period is useful for comparative purposes and to test the likelihood of pagans being amongst those interred in Kellis 2. The survey is restricted to sites within the oases because of the abundance of material throughout Egypt.

Pagan Burial Practices in the Oases during the Roman Period

Generalizations

Although there was a diversity of burial practices in the Roman Period, pagans conformed to the millennia-old tradition of equipping the deceased for the next life. The following are characteristic of such practices: mummification of the body; multiple interments in rock-cut chamber tombs or mausolea where bodies could be buried in pits, placed in coffins or on a bier, laid directly onto the floor with or without decorated cartonnage coverings. The deceased was accompanied by an array of grave goods.

Pagan Burial Practices at Bahariya Oasis

The bodies from the tombs at Bahariya Oasis, currently being excavated by Zahi Hawass (2000), are typical of Roman-Period examples found in the Nile Valley. Those interred represent an affluent section of the community. Their bodies were mummified and were fitted with guilded anthropomorphic head coverings, cartonnage, some depicting scenes from the traditional funerary repertoire, and footstalls; they were equipped with standard grave goods amongst which were jewellery, amulets, figurines of deities, glass and ceramic vessels (Hawass 2000, 42, 46–7, 71–3). The subterranean tombs are rock-cut multi-chambered structures, large enough to accommodate a substantial number of burials. The spaces within had been maximized with bodies placed shoulder-to-shoulder on ledges prepared for that purpose; Tomb 54 was 'so full that mummies had also been placed upon the floor' (Hawass 2000, 34). Some of the interments can be dated by the presence of coins, found mostly in the hands (Hawass 2000, 78). Hawass (2000, 78) notes that the coins range in date from Kleopatra VII (51–30 BCE) to Constantine I; all of those illustrated in his publication were struck prior to 318 CE (Hawass 2000, 78).

Pagan Burial Practices at Dush, Kharga Oasis

Seventy-two tombs have been excavated and recorded at the necropolis at Dush; the tentative date range is from the first century BCE to the fourth century CE (Dunand *et al.* 1992, 263–4). The tombs vary in size but all are multi-chambered, subterranean structures that contain multiple burials; they differ in plan and design to those at Bahariya. The bodies display a similar range of mummification techniques to those employed in the Kellis 1 cemetery, including the use of palm-frond rib frames to support the body (Dunand *et al.* 1992, 199–206, Plate 61; Aufderheide this volume). Some of the bodies were covered with cartonnage, including masks and footstalls decorated with traditional funerary iconography (Dunand *et al.* 1992, Plates 54–7). The variation in the quality of treatment of the bodies and their coverings reflects the economic status of the interred (Dunand *et al.* 1992, 99). Some tombs were clearly for the less affluent amongst the community but even these contained some grave goods (Dunand *et al.* 1992, 99, 158–9). The funerary assemblage was representative of the standard pharaonic repertoire: biers, *ba* birds, statues of deities, items of personal adornment, clothing, lamps, baskets, ceramic and glass vessels, fruit, grain myrtle and garlands of flowers (Dunand *et al.* 1992, 237–45 and Plates 58–93). The tombs were used over a considerable period of time; bodies were placed on the

---

[10] The exception is the body of a female; she was buried clothed and wearing jewellery (Martin 1974, 21).

[11] The practice was not restricted to Egypt. A Christian cemetery with around 4,500 simple pit graves, cut on an east-west axis with bodies placed with heads to the west, has been discovered at Poundbury, Dorset, England (Davis 1999, 195 citing Painter 1989, 2049).

floor in no particular alignment and in some instances, bones were simply moved to one side when space was at a premium (Dunand *et al.* 1992, 159). Although a Christian community is attested at Dush (Deissmann 1902; Wagner 1987, 355–6), no pit-burial cemeteries have been found.[12]

Pagan Burial Practices at Kellis

Pit-grave cemeteries have been identified throughout Dakhleh Oasis; these are cut either into spring mounds or into the desert floor. The graves have a single interment, some within coffins, some without; they are distinguished from Christian burials in that there is no conformity of alignment (Mills 1979; 1980; 1981; 1982; 1983).

The pagan community at Kellis was buried either in single-chamber rock-cut tombs in a cemetery to the north-west of the village, designated Kellis 1 (31/420-C5-1), or in the numerous mud-brick mausolea that are located on the outskirts of the village to the north and south: the North Tomb Group and the South Tomb Group (Knudstad and Frey 1999, 208–13; Hope this volume). The chamber tombs of Kellis 1 each contain multiple burials with the bodies placed directly onto the floor but in no particular alignment (Birrell 1999, 29–38). No coffins have been found. Seven patterns of body treatment have been identified ranging from full mummification, which entailed the removal of the viscera, to natural desiccation of the body without human interference (Aufderheide *et al.* this volume); some had palm ribs inserted alongside the spinal column or were strapped to palm-rib frames (Birrell 1999, 35).[13] A few of the bodies had head and/or full cartonnage coverings and footstalls adorned with traditional funerary iconography (Schweitzer 2002, 269–76); grave goods are similarly representative of the standard Egyptian funerary assemblage, such as *ba* birds and offering tables (Birrell 1999, 38). The quality of the mummification and the coverings, together with the provision of funerary goods, is no doubt wealth related. It is of particular interest to note that both elaborate and simple burials were placed within the same tomb and that bodies were piled one on top of the other; earlier burials were simply pushed to one side to make room for later interments (Birrell 1999, 33–5).[14] Study of the cartonnage indicates that the same tombs were used over a considerable period of time with interments throughout the cemetery as a whole ranging in date from the late Ptolemaic Period to the third century CE (Schweitzer 2002, 269–76); ceramics confirm the date (Patten 1999, 88). There is, therefore, some overlap in the dates of the interments in Kellis 1 and Kellis 2.

Two of the North and one of the South Tombs have been excavated (Hope this volume). These are large, mud-brick mausolea that were erected for the affluent amongst the pagan community of Kellis. North Tomb 1 is decorated in a combination of pharaonic and classical design (Hope this volume; Kaper this volume). The only bodies found in situ in this tomb were those of Christians (below), although a surplus of bones for the number of graves (Dupras and Tocheri this volume) and the discovery of traditional grave goods amongst the rubble may well have belonged to the original burials (Hope this volume).

Tomb 2 was badly looted and the skeletal material is commingled. The commingled remains indicate a minimum number of 14 adults and six juveniles, plus two wrapped bodies: a female and an infant (Dupras and Tocheri this volume). The skeletal remains in Room 2 were disturbed but the bodies appear to have been placed directly onto the floor in an east-west direction with the heads on the east (Hope this volume). Decorated wooden fragments from what might have been a funerary bed, together with pieces of cartonnage, were found in Room 3 and elements from a funerary bed were retrieved from the fill of Room 4. Three intrusive pit graves had been cut against the northern, southern and western walls of the transverse hall, Room 4; the bodies had been placed in ceramic coffins. The mummified body of a young woman was found *in situ* within its coffin; it was elaborately wrapped and accompanied by a mummy label. A mummified head and torso of a male, found in the same vicinity, may once have occupied one of the other damaged ceramic coffins (Hope this volume). The burials have been dated tentatively prior to the early third century (Hope this volume). The modes of interment within the tomb reflect the variety of possibilities within the pagan tradition. The inclusion of six children is of interest; these far outnumber the ratio of adults/child burials found in Kellis 1 but reflect that of West Tomb 1 (below). The youngest individual represented by the skeletal remains was aged around 3 years at death; the others range from 8.75 to 15.5 years (Dupras and Tocheri this volume, 191, Table 9).

South Tomb 4 had been looted but the remains of six adults and two juveniles were identified (Dupras and Tocheri this volume). Items from the traditional funerary repertoire were found amongst the debris; no grave pits were found (Hope this volume).

The investigation so far indicates that whilst early Christians had no compunction about burial alongside pagans, the reverse was not so. Pagans in Bahariya and

---

[12] Dunand and Lichtenberg (1998, 161–3) identify the occupants of a single tomb located about 800 metres from the main necropolis as Christian. The identification rests upon the method of mummification and wrapping that parallel those used for the bodies of the monks from St Mark's Monastery, Thebes, but is not otherwise attested at Dush. No indication of the orientation of the burials is given. Coins found in the tomb date to 375–8 (Dunand and Lichtenberg 1998, 163).

[13] The use of resin (old carbon) in the mummification process contaminates samples and consequently no radiocarbon dates derived from these bodies can be relied upon.

[14] Birrell (1999, 33) notes that the average tomb size is 370 x 220 cm; they contained as many as 42 bodies.

Dush continued the traditional burial practices into the fourth century and therefore it is unlikely that those at Kellis would have chosen a simple pit grave within a Christian cemetery when interment within a rock-cut tomb or mausoleum was available. On this evidence it can probably be agreed that Kellis 2 was for the exclusive use of Christians and therefore a first–second century CE date for its foundation is untenable.

The Suggested Period of Use of the Kellis 2 Cemetery

If one accepts that the human remains from Kellis 2 analysed by Molto's team belonged to Christians, the radiocarbon results (Stewart *et al.* this volume) indicate that the people of Kellis had not only converted to Christianity, but in sufficient numbers to argue for and to warrant the foundation of a separate cemetery by the beginning of the third century at the latest. This argument, however, is not sustainable on current evidence from the site, nor in light of the absence of contemporary data from Egypt as a whole. As stated earlier, Christians identifying as such are invisible in the archaeological record until the mid-third century. This is due to several factors amongst which are the probable slow rate of conversion, the fear of persecution, and the lack of need or desire in some instances for an independent identity. Change in burial practices in the *chora* can only be expected with the adoption of doctrinal developments promoted by the authorities in Alexandria during the Little Peace of the Church from the third quarter of the third century (Eusebius *Ecclesiastical History* vii. 13).

The Earliest Evidence of Christians at Kellis: An Onomastic Approach

The earliest documented evidence for a Christian presence at Kellis is 319 (*PUG* 20 and *P. Med.* inv. 68.82), although it is likely that the religion had been introduced to the village much earlier. A method is required, therefore, that allows us to trace the introduction of the religion back in time. One possible avenue, although tenuous, is to adopt an onomastic approach based upon that of Roger S. Bagnall (1982) who suggested that the study of onomastic evidence could be useful in determining the pace of conversion to Christianity in Egypt. The basic premise for this model is that Christians are apt to give their offspring Christian names and therefore if one has a body of such names, together with Christian patronyms, in dated papyri it can be assumed that the child with the Christian name was given such by his or her parent a generation earlier. The first task is to determine which names are likely to be Christian. Bagnall (1982, 110–11) identified the following: biblical names, names compounded with the Coptic *noute*, names based upon abstract nouns and adjectives of theological content, and names of saints and martyrs. The second requirement is to determine the average years for a

generation. Bagnall and Frier (1994, 118–46) in their demographic study of Roman Egypt based upon census data suggest a generation gap of between 33–35 years. With these criteria in mind, one can cautiously adopt the model and consider the relevant data from Kellis.

The vast majority of dated documents from Ismant el-Kharab that attest Christians in the village derive from House 3, with some from House 2, in Area A. These contiguous houses were occupied from the end of the third century (Hope 2001, 54–5). It must be acknowledged that the sample is too small to function as anything other than an indicator of a possible Christian presence. Furthermore, as no ages are given for the men documented in the papyri, an element of conjecture is required. As it is not known at what age a man could be a party to a contract or to subscribe to a document, I have applied an arbitrary age of 25 years for men listed in official documents and have taken the upper figure of 35 years for a generation; the figure for both could well be higher as it cannot be determined whether or not the son was the eldest child. The most popular Christian name attested in the papyri from Kellis is Timotheos followed by variants upon Papnouthios (Worp 1995). The use of these names by Christians in the village is verified in personal letters. What is also notable from the Kellis papyri is that many Christian parents gave their offspring pagan names. Tithoes, the name of the principal god of Kellis, is the most common name to be found and was used by pagan and Christian alike (Worp 1995). Because of this practice, it is assumed that the son of a man with a Christian name is himself Christian. The rapid spread of Christianity in the village as shown by the demise of temple worship, the erection in the first part of the fourth century of a basilica church, and the lack of fourth-century burials in the Kellis 1 cemetery, lends credence to this assumption.

The study commences with firmly dated documents containing Christian patronyms. The first, P.Kell. I Gr. 24, dated 352 (Worp 1995, 72–6), lists at least 33 male residents of Kellis who have subscribed; four have Christian names, two have both Christian names and patronyms: Aurelius Timotheos, son of Timotheos (1.16) and Psenouphis, son of Psenouphis, alias Besas (1.17). Assuming Timotheos and Psenouphis were both 25 years old when the document was drawn up and their fathers aged 35 years at the time of their birth, the fathers were likely to have been born into a Christian family *circa* 292 at the latest. The second document, P.Kell. I Gr. 23, dated 353 (Worp 1995, 68–72), is a petition to the *praeses* of the Thebaid. The person implicated is Timotheos, described as 'the boy' (line 15); others include Psekes, son of Psennouphis (line 18), Psenouthes, Theotimes and Pachoumis (line 18). Using the same formula, Psennouphis' birth date was *circa* 293. The third text, P.Kell. I Gr. 8, dated 362 (Worp 1995, 29–31), records the sale of a slave. Whilst none of those involved in the sale are identified overtly as Christian, the purchaser, Aurelius Tithoes, son of Petesis, is known from other documents to have followed the faith.[15] The witness to the sale, Aurelius Horion, son of Timotheos (1ine 19) is of relevance to this study. Horion's father, Timotheos, was presumably born to Christian parents around 302.

The following are documents that the editor has dated by association, palaeography, formulaic evidence, commodity prices, or a combination of the above. The first, P.Kell. I Gr. 60, is a wooden board with a list of names, which Worp (1995, 161–2) dates to the late third to early fourth centuries. Worp (1995, 161–2) states:

> ... most names are pagan Egyptian, Greek and Latin names and they seem to point to an earlier period; only the fathers' names Timotheos and Elias (ll. 8, 11), may be related to the spreading of Christianity ... Given the fact that none of the persons mentioned seem to occur elsewhere in the Greek papyri from Kellis one may be tempted to think that perhaps the board belongs to another, slightly earlier period. ... there is no palaeographical obstacle against dating the text to ca. 300–310 rather than ca. 290–300.

The names of interest in this text are Psais, son of Timotheos, and Tithoes, son of Elias. Taking the document midway between the suggested date given by Worp, 300, Timotheos and Elias would have been born to Christian parents *circa* 275. P.Kell. I Gr. 61 is dated *circa* 360, or slightly later, by commodity prices (Worp 1995, 162–4). Names in this document include: Jacob the potter (line 1), Rachel (l. 5), Thermouthis, daughter (?) of Papnouthis (line 6), Mar(i)a or Marsha or Mar(s)a, daughter of Apollon (line 11), Isidora, daughter of John (line 12), Isid (), son of Papnouthis (line 13). If a date of 360 is taken for the document, one could expect both Papnouthis and John to have been born to Christian parents *circa* 300. P.Kell. I Gr. 74 is dated mid-fourth century (Worp 1995, 193–5) without further qualification. This private letter is from Psais the potter (lines 1–2) to his father Aron who is addressed variously as 'my father Aron' (line 1), 'brother Aron' (line 32) and 'my lord father brother in Kellis' (lines 34–5); one assumes a spiritual brotherhood. The text is further complicated by reference to two mothers Agape/Tagape, one of who appears to be with Psais (lines 4–6) and one with Aron (lines 6–7). Should the date and parentage be correct, Aron and Agape/Tagape must have been born in the closing years of the third century. Returning to *PUG* 20 and *P. Med.* inv. 68.8, and applying the same criteria, Timotheos would have been born to a Christian father some time before 295.

If the onomastic hypothesis is valid within this context, and assuming Worp's palaeographic dating to be correct, the birth dates cluster between 292 and 305, with the earliest being *circa* 275. Keeping in mind that most of these dates represent the birth of children to fathers who were given those names by Christian fathers, the grandfathers must themselves have been born at least 35

years earlier. Whether or not these grandfathers were born to Christian fathers or whether they were converts to the religion cannot be determined. An argument against the model is that the men changed their names upon conversion; the naming pattern at Kellis, however, indicates that this was unlikely. Pagan names continued to be used within Christian families until the end of occupation at Kellis, as attested by the latest documents from House 3: P.Kell. I Gr. 44 and 45 (Worp 1995, 130–6). A further difficulty faced by such an approach is that it does not take into account the possibility of immigration to Kellis by these men. With all of these variables taken into consideration, one can suggest, albeit tentatively, a Christian presence in the village from the 250s. It can be stated with confidence that by the first half of the fourth century, the Christian community was large enough to warrant and to fund the building and pay for the upkeep of a sizeable basilica alongside a smaller church that was operational from the early years of the fourth century (Bowen 2002, 65–85; this volume).

Evidence of squatter activity in the Temple of Tutu indicates that it was no longer functioning in a formal capacity by the mid-fourth century. From the names recorded on the numerous ostraka found in the temple precinct, especially Shrine III, many of those using the facility following its abandonment were Christian (Worp, forthcoming). The last recorded priest of Tutu was Stonios who in 335 acted as *hypographeus* for Aurelius Pekysis, in a contract of division of property (P.Kell. I Gr. 13, line 14; Worp 1995, 38–42). It is of interest to note that one of the parties to the division bears a probable Christian name: Pachoumis. The document cannot be used as evidence that the temple was still functioning in a formal capacity. Stonios is first attested as a priest in documents found in the Temple of Tutu that are dated 298–300, 299 and 311 (Worp 2002, 333–9). By 335 he was likely to have been around 60 years of age. Whilst age would not preclude him from performing his duties as a priest, it is equally possible that he retained the title after the temple cult had ceased to function. Although there is no way of confirming such a hypothesis, fourth-century papyri from the Nile Valley show that priests may be listed as private individuals who retain their titles as a means of identification rather than in relation to their religious duties (Bagnall 1992, 291). It is also of interest to note that in 337, a priest of the catholic church, Aurelius Harpokrates, was witness to a contract in the village (P.Kell. I Gr. 58, l. 8; Worp 1995, 158–9). It should be noted that in the early years of the fourth century the priests anticipated that the cult of Tutu would continue. This is attested by a document regarding circumcised priests that was sent to a government official in the Mothite Nome; it includes infants, not yet circumcised, but who were required to be before holding priestly office (Worp 2002, 346 number 10).

---

[15] The documents that establish Aurelius Tithoes as a Christian are P.Kell. I Gr. 10, 11, 12, 19 and P.Kell. V Copt. 12.

Archaeological Evidence for the Abandonment of Kellis

Returning to the radiocarbon data, the suggested latest interments in Kellis 2 cemetery are somewhere within the date-range 380–600, although Stewart *et al.* (this volume) acknowledge that the 600 date is unlikely. Archaeological evidence indicates that Kellis was abandoned towards the end of the fourth century. The latest dated documents from House 3 are 382 and 386 (P.Kell. I Gr. 44 and 45; Worp 1995 130–6); the latest dated document from Kellis is 392 (Worp, cited in Hope and Bowen 1997, 61; Hope 2002, 204). Amongst the 600 plus coins found at the site, only two examples of the massive *SALVS REPVBLICAE* issue that was struck between 388–95 have been identified (Bowen 1998, 236–7). Evidence from hoards deposited in Egypt indicate that this issue accounts for the greatest percentage of coins in circulation in the early fifth century: 55% of the De May Hoard, containing 289 coins, closed shortly after 402; 41% of the Hawara Hoard (H6) containing 2,248 identifiable coins, closed sometime after 410; 32% of the Kom Aushim Hoard A, comprising 582 identifiable coins, closed *circa* 410; 34% of the Kom Aushim Hoard B, comprising 604 identifiable coins, closed *circa* 423 and 32% of the Hawara Hoard B, containing 1,929 identifiable coins, closed *circa* 426; (Bowen 1998, 216–27). The issue is well represented at Dush in Kharga Oasis[16] and so it cannot be argued that there was a time-lag in the currency circulating in the Western Desert. Both the Large East Church and the West Church appear to have been abandoned in the late fourth century (Bowen 2002, 81–3). The latest coin from the large church is an issue struck by Theodosius between 378–383; the majority of coins from the church date between 348–378 (Bowen 2002, 81). The latest coin from the West Church is one of the two *SALVS REPVBLICAE* issues with the remainder dating from the mid-fourth century (Bowen 2002, 83). In the 15 years of excavation at the site, no diagnostic ceramics of the fifth-century have been found amongst the ubiquitous sherds and vessels at the site (C. A. Hope personal communication, 2002); one would expect such from the houses and from the churches if the latter were operative in the fifth century. It is likely that the residents were forced to abandon the village because of the effects of salinity and the activity of sand dunes that threatened to cover the village (Hope 2001, 56–7). The residents of House 3 had responded to this threat by raising the front door and building a retaining wall around it in order to curtail the sand's encroachment (Hope 2001, 57).

Possible Post-Abandonment Use of the Kellis 2 Cemetery

It could be argued that insufficient excavation has been undertaken at Ismant el-Kharab to confirm that Kellis was abandoned in its entirety at the end of the fourth century.[17] Surface surveys and test excavations have provided no evidence to indicate that there was any habitation, other than squatter activity in Area B during the fourth century and Area C seems to have been abandoned by the end of the third century. It appears that by the fourth-century the residential area had moved into Area A (Hope 2001, 57). There is evidence for post-abandonment activity in various areas of the site, for instance, the Coptic graffiti in the apse of the Small East Church and some late activity within the North Pastophorium in the Large East Church (Bowen 2002, 75; this volume), and Coptic graffiti on the walls of the *mamissi*, some of which was written by the goose-herders George and Kyris who were using the shrine, presumably as a shelter (Kaper this volume). It should be kept in mind, however, that any occupation must have been minimal for one would expect the churches to remain open to serve the congregation.

Other Christian Burials at Kellis

The Christian Cemetery in Enclosure 4

The remainder of the paper focuses upon Christian burials in other parts of Kellis: cemetery D/6 and D/7 in Enclosure 4 and the interments in North Tomb 1. A small Christian cemetery (D/7) lies within the walls of Enclosure 4, on the extreme north-west of the village (Hope 2000, 58; this volume, Figure 11). The cemetery is associated with two classical-style monumental tombs (below), possibly of first-century CE date (Hope in Bowen *et al.* 1993, 21–3; Hope and McKenzie 1999, 54–68; Hope 2000, 57–8) and a two-roomed church, with a sizeable annex, to its west (Hope 1993, 23–5; Bowen 2002, 75–81). All are pit graves, oriented east-west with the bodies placed with their heads to the west. No grave goods were found with the burials, none of which had been disturbed. Graves 1 and 2 were built against the exterior east wall of the church, behind the north apse side chamber; these graves each had a mud-brick superstructure (Hope 1995, 57–8) and contained the skeletonized remains of two females (Bodies 1 and 2, Molto *et al.* this volume). Their location indicates that they post-date the erection of the church (Hope 1995, 58; this volume). The seven remaining graves are to the west of the classical-style tombs: three beside West Tomb 1 (Graves 3–5) and the remaining four grouped in the south-eastern corner of the enclosure (Graves 6–9). The graves had no surviving superstructure but were sealed with mud bricks; Grave 9 had a small bowl set into the ground at the head end and the impression for another was found in Grave 7 (Hope this volume). The bowl contained pieces of charcoal and a second, smaller bowl had been placed

---

[16] I am indebted to Michel Amandry, Directeur du département des Monnaies, Médailles et Antiquites, Bibliothéque nationale de France, for providing me with copies of his inventories for the coinage of Dush and giving me permission to use his material for comparative purposes.

[17] The domestic structures in Area D (D/8) show activity in the fourth century but not the fifth (Hope 2002, 202–4).

inside the first; the latter retained the burnt remains of some substance that may have been part of the Eucharist offered at the grave side. The graves contained the remains of three females (bodies 3, 5 and 7), two males (bodies 8 and 9), one infant aged about 18 months (body 6) and a foetus or perinate (body 4) (Molto *et al.* this volume). The sex representation in the cemetery is of interest: five females, two males and two infants of undetermined sex. The two males were buried next to one another in the extreme-south eastern corner of the enclosure; the ceramic vessels were associated with one of the male burials (body 9), the missing bowl with a female burial (body 7). The foetus/perinate was buried beside a woman aged 60 ± 5 years (Molto *et al.* this volume).

Two east-west burials were found beneath the floor in the nave of the West Church, D/6 (Graves 10 and 11) (Hope 2000, 58; this volume, Figure 11): a male (body 1) and an infant aged about six months (body 2) (Molto *et al.* this volume). Their location in front of the apse, with the male to the north and the infant on the south side of the *bema*, suggest that the burials post-date the building of the church. No other burials were found in the floor of the nave although further excavation in the room to its west where laid mud bricks have been exposed beneath the floor, could reveal more.

West Tomb 1

The location of the cemetery within Enclosure 4 and the burials in the West Church require discussion. The focus of Graves 3–5 was West Tomb 1; they were located in the most prominent position, that is, to either side of the sandstone steps that formed the approach to the tomb (Hope 2000, 57–9; this volume). The tomb itself, which was excavated in 1992–1993, contained 12 bodies, probably secondary interments: five adults and seven juveniles, the latter aged between 5–8 years at death (Hope and McKenzie 1999, 55–6). The bodies were shrouded and some attempt at mummification had been carried out (Hope and McKenzie 1999, 56–60). The treatment of the bodies differed to that found within the Kellis 1 cemetery and in North Tomb 2, in that the chests and abdomens of several of the bodies were filled with dark brown, hardened sand (Hope and McKenzie 1999, 56); the remains were skeletal. Two of the bodies had finger rings but no other items of personal adornment. The funerary assemblage included pots, a basket, glass vessels, a spatula, a pair of small lead sandals, a small funerary bed and 39 funerary bouquets of rosemary and myrtle (Hope and McKenzie 1999, 56–61; Thanheiser 1999, 89); the bouquets are similar to those found in the graves in Kellis 2. Notable was the lack of traditional funerary items such as *ba* birds, altars or iconography that characterize the burials in the rock-cut tombs and the North Tombs. Although the bodies had

been disturbed, they were oriented roughly east-west with the heads placed both to the east and the west; two lay on top of two sandstone blocks that had been placed upon the floor (Hope and McKenzie 1999, 55–6). The burials in West Tomb 1 have been dated tentatively to the late third to early fourth century (Hope and McKenzie 1999, 61). It cannot be determined whether the bodies were those of pagans or Christians; the absence of any remnants of traditional funerary items argues against the former whilst the orientation of the heads, if that was the original position, might, though not necessarily, preclude the latter. Birrell (1999, 33–4) notes that the latest interments in Group 2 tombs in Kellis 1 were skeletal remains, simply wrapped, often placed on sandstone blocks or large potsherds and almost invariably laid on the floor with the head on the west. The similarity of burial practice could indicate that the two are contemporary and may reflect early, or an alternative form of Christian burial, although, there is no way of proving this. The development of the D/7 cemetery against the tomb wall and the proximity of the church might favour the identification of the interments as Christians, or at least regarded as such, by the community. If this was the case, the tomb could have functioned as a martyrium, for such held the bodies of martyrs or saintly Christians. This could explain the erection and location of the church for cemetery churches were built within close proximity to the martyria (Grossmann 1989, 434; 1991, 208).

The West Church

The West Church probably functioned as a cemetery church. It was in such buildings that the relatives congregated to offer prayers for the dead both at the time of the funeral and on anniversaries. Church burials are well attested; wealthy patrons could afford such a privilege (Grossmann 1991, 208). The West Church sanctuary differs to those of the other two churches at Kellis in that it has a two-stepped platform built directly in front of the apse and the benches are built against all four walls with a break only for the doorway, the platform of the apse, and the area in front of the pilasters that flank the apse (Bowen 2002, 75–8). The apse side chambers parallel those of the Small East Church in that the north chamber is fitted with storage bins whilst the south chamber is empty; neither communicates directly with the apse (Bowen this volume, Figures 1, 4 and 5, Plates 5, 8 and 9). There is no evidence for cupboards in the nave, which are characteristic of the East Churches,[18] and no remains of gypsum wall plaster were found. The nave communicates with the west room and the doorway between the two was narrowed on either side by two metres (Bowen 2002, Figure 8, Plate 8). The west room has benches along three of its walls but none in the south-eastern corner. Three ceramic vessels were found on one of the benches next to the door that opens into

---

[18] The north wall is too eroded to determine whether or not it was fitted with cupboards; the other walls are preserved sufficiently to indicate the lack of such.

Room 8. Preservation is too poor to determine whether there were any cupboards. As neither of the outer rooms of the East Churches has been excavated, no comparisons can be drawn.

The West Church is similar to some of the so-called apse tombs at Oxyrhynchus (Petrie 1925, 16–17, Plates XLI and XLV). In Tombs 23 and 42 at Oxyrhynchus, the bodies were placed in shallow pit graves beneath the floor directly in front of the sanctuary (Petrie 1925, 16). Neither tomb is published in any detail but from the plan Tomb 23 appears to have two randomly placed graves. The plan of the much larger Tomb 42 does not indicate the location of the pit graves; Petrie (1925, 16), however, states that they were in front of the sanctuary. Grossmann (2002, 337) suggests that Tomb 42 functioned as an independent church.

The West Church at Kellis has a contiguous seven-roomed structure to its south, through which the church is accessed; its function has not been explained adequately but it can now be assumed to have been associated with burials and/or funerary rituals (Bowen 2002, 78). The south-western room, Room 1, gives access to the complex as a whole. This is equipped with benches and impressions found on the floor indicate that many large jars had been used in the room; the room was also furnished with a hearth, presumably for the preparation of food. A flight of stairs leading to an upper storey above the church itself was built against the west wall, directly opposite the entrance door; the corridor that leads to the west room of the church runs parallel to the staircase opening from the easternmost end of the north wall of Room 1. Room 3, opening off Room 1, was probably an open courtyard. It has storage bins and a covered shelter; several pots were found in the room. There were a number of imprints of donkey hooves on the floor and chicken feathers and eggshells attest the presence of these animals. The suite of four rooms opening off Room 3 has no features other than a wall niche; the architecture and artefacts found within give no indication of their function. The majority of coins derived from just inside the entrance to Rooms 6 and 7. Several mud sealing were also retrieved from the complex. The numerous ostraka, found in Room 3 and in Room 8, a small room adjacent to the staircase but opening into the west room of the church, are mostly receipts for commodities such as chickens, eggs, oil, pigs, wheat, wine, donkeys, probably for purpose of transportation, and payment of amounts in talents and various commodities (Worp forthcoming).

Enclosure 4

The building of the church and a substantial enclosure wall, preserved to at least three metres in height in the north-eastern corner, and the incorporation of the West Tombs within that enclosure, was not a random development but a conscious act by the Christian community of Kellis to define and isolate a sacred space. The complex is itself isolated from Enclosure 3 to its south and Enclosure 2 to its east. The only means of access is from the west, somewhere to the south of the church annex. The enclosure, therefore, remained separate from the village. The incorporation of the West Tomb identifies the structure as a Christian monument at that period of its use and as integral to the nature and function of the enclosed space. Sufficient land was made available for burials and it would appear that those buried in the south-western corner and those abutting the church wall were interred after the building of the enclosure wall (Hope this volume, Figure 11). The small two-roomed structure erected close to the north wall of the enclosure is associated with the cemetery and was presumably erected along with the church. As there was no evidence for the presence of graves, it is unlikely to have been a family tomb. The paucity of burials in the D/7 cemetery is perplexing. It could be suggested that the cemetery was reserved for a specific sect; a Manichaean community was resident at Kellis (Gardner 1996; Gardner *et al.* 1999). This, however, is purely speculative and has no corroborative evidence. An alternative suggestion is that it was the domain of a particular family, perhaps descendants of those buried in West Tomb 1. The rare genetic trait identified by Molto (this volume) and his team in bodies 3, 5 and 10: the male buried in the church and the two females buried next to the tomb, and the evidence of spina bifida in all three males, could be offered as supporting evidence.

In Dakhleh, the practice of burials around a church was not restricted to Kellis. In 1980, Colin Hope excavated four pit graves dug along the north wall of the church of Deir Abu Metta (32/405-A7-1) in the west of the oasis; the bodies were in the traditional Christian east-west burial position, heads on the west, shrouded and without burial goods Two coins found in the vicinity, although not necessarily associated with the burials, were issues of Constantine I.[19] As the purpose of the excavation was a trial test and the area exposed only 7.9 m north-south by 5.6 m east-west, the extent of the cemetery is not known, nor was it possible to determine whether there were burials within the church itself. Only one other church has been identified in Dakhleh: Deir el-Molouk (31/405-M6-1); the plan has been determined but only a small area in the south half of the sanctuary was tested (Mills 1981, 185, Plate XI).

Christian Burials in North Tomb 1

North Tomb 1 is the largest of the mud-brick mausolea at Kellis; it is located to the north of Area A and the west of Area B (Hope this volume, Figures 1 and 12). It was built for members of the pagan community (above), but the latest interments are those of Christians. There are 24 pit graves cut on an east-west axis; the heads of those bodies that

---

[19] I am indebted to Colin Hope for providing me with a copy of his field notes from which the information is taken.

remained *in situ* were placed to the west. There were no funerary goods, although Grave 3, an undisturbed burial in Room 2, yielded a fragment of gypsum sealing that preserved the impression of the Christian *crux ansata* (Hope this volume). The bodies were confined to the western Rooms 2, 3 and 4, the outer corridors 6 and 14 and a small room to the east of the north entrance to the tomb, Room 8 (Hope this volume, Figures 12 and 16). Those bodies buried within Rooms 2–4 were badly disturbed and it was uncertain in some instances which of the skeletal remains belonged to individual graves (Dupras and Tocheri this volume, 185). It would appear, however, that those interred in graves in Room 2 were mostly juveniles, those in Room 3 all adult, whilst Room 4 contained the remains of three adults and a perinate. The burials in Room 6 were of a juvenile and an infant, that in Room 8 was an infant and the six graves in Room 14, which are located beneath the outer west wall of Rooms 2 and 3, contained the remains of seven individuals, the oldest being an infant aged about eight to nine months, three were newborn and the remainder were foetuses in various stages of development (Dupras and Tocheri this volume). It is possible that North Tomb 1 was a family mausoleum and that the later interments were descendants of the original owner who continued to use it following conversion to Christianity. Such practice is attested in Roman tombs in Italy where no member could be denied burial in a private family tomb on the basis of belief unless the head of the family so decreed (Johnson 1999, 40–1). Molto (this volume) and his team have identified an unusual disease in two skeletons found in Room 3 that could well indicate a family group; no mention is made of whether or not this is genetic, however, and as remains of earlier burials are probably co-mingled with later ones the hypothesis cannot be tested.

A tomb at Amheida in the west of the oasis is probably a further example of Christian burials within a pagan mausoleum. This multi-chambered monumental tomb is built of sandstone and mud brick (Mills 1980, 269–71). In a test excavation carried out during the 1979 field season three east-west orientated pits were found beneath a stone-lined floor of the western half of the central chamber (Mills 1980, 270, Plate XIV). Mills (1980, 270) identifies them as probably Christian but as there is no indication that the graves were excavated a positive identification cannot be made.

Burials in North Tomb 2 and South Tomb 4

There is no evidence for Christian reuse of North Tomb 2 or South Tomb 4. The intrusive child burial in Room 2 of North Tomb 2 is anomalous. Although the interment of infants is typical of Christian tradition, the north-south alignment of the grave renders such an identification inconclusive.[20] The absence of Christian graves within these mausolea might suggest that the usurpation of monumental tombs was not common practice.

Foetal Burials

The burial of foetuses is of considerable interest for our understanding of early Christian concepts of the nature and status of unborn children, and of the entrance of the soul into the body. As such they warrant further study. The foetuses were individually wrapped with the same attention was paid to the orientation within the grave, implying, therefore, the expectation of resurrection. Foetuses have also been found amongst the burials in Kellis 2 cemetery (Marlow 1999, 107; Tocheri *et al.* in press) indicating that it was common practice amongst Christians. Marlow (1999, 107–8, Figure 10.Ib) identified six foetal remains amongst her sample group of 56, with a further nine falling within the range of 38–43 weeks after conception; one of the foetuses (Burial 28) was of about 18 weeks gestation. Of particular note is the discovery of a foetus of approximately 14 weeks gestation amongst the debris of an upper room in House 4 in Area A; it is the youngest example of such from Kellis (Dupras *et al.* forthcoming). The body had been carefully wrapped in linen in the same manner as those of a later stage of development. Whilst the context in which it was found does not identify it as originating in House 4, it is not unreasonable to suggest that the foetus was conceived and prepared for burial by Christians, for both Manichaean and what might be loosely termed 'catholic' documents have been retrieved from the house. How the body came to be in the debris is not known, nor can it be certain whether or not it was intended for interment in the cemetery.

No foetal burials are attested in Kellis 1 cemetery (Marlow 1999, 106; T. Dupras personal communication, 2001); in fact, few infant or children's bodies have been retrieved from that necropolis (Marlow 1999, 108),[21] a phenomenon that is also noted at Dush (Dunand *et al.* 1992, 216–8). It would appear, therefore, that it was not customary for the pagan community to bury foetuses or infants in communal of family tombs. The body of a child aged around two years was found buried within the north wall of a room C/2/3 (Hope 1999, 62); this could suggest that such were placed within the home, a practice known from pharaonic times.

Conclusions

The number of Christian burials at Kellis and the lack of identified pagan burials from the end of the third century attest the rapid conversion of the community. There is no

---

[20] The skeletal remains of the child have not yet been analyzed and so an age at death cannot be determined.

[21] By contrast, Marlow (1999, 107) in her provisional report of 1994, noted that of 137 bodies exhumed in the Kellis 2 cemetery, 30% were infants and of those 37% were neonates.

archaeological or documentary evidence, however, to suggest that Christians identifying as such had arrived before the mid-third century. This conforms to the paucity of evidence for Christianity for that period throughout Egypt and indeed the Empire. This presents difficulties in accepting the suite of early dates yielded by radiocarbon analyses.

Evidence for the abandonment of the village at the end of the fourth century is strong. Dated documents may well be the result of serendipity but Worp has found no palaeographic evidence amongst the numerous undated texts to assign them to the fifth century or later. No fifth-century issues are found amongst the coins that have been retrieved from excavated structures and from the surface of the site; those struck after 375 are at a premium. A thorough surface survey, and eighteen years of excavation at the site, has yielded none of the diagnostic fifth-century ceramic evidence that is present at other oasis sites such as Mut, Amheida, the small Christian settlement in the west to name a few. The earlier forms of North African Red Slip and the imitation oasis ware, that one expects within a mid-late fourth-century context, are present but these are concentrated in the region of fourth-century occupation, Area A, and have not been found elsewhere (C. A. Hope personal communication, 2003). The archaeological data is again at odds with the dates assigned at the upper end of the radiocarbon range. A feasible explanation for any use of Kellis 2 in the fifth century has been proposed by Hope (personal communication, 2002), that is, that having abandoned the village through necessity, the people returned in order to bury their dead.

Whilst it can be argued that the abandonment was protracted, it is not known where the population relocated or whether it was scattered. It is difficult, therefore, to maintain that the successive generations of families continued to bury their dead at Kellis for upwards of one hundred years after abandonment. Molto (personal communication 2002) has acknowledged the need to analyze significantly more samples than has been possible so far; these are anxiously awaited by all.

The decision made by the Kellis community to reject traditional burial practices and commence a new cemetery along what must have been the preferred Christian lines, indicates an awareness of such practices and willingness to conform to Church doctrine. Little social differentiation is obvious in death and there was no display of wealth. Grave goods, where found, are minimal and of little commercial value, yet the texts, the architecture and artefacts from the site do not suggest an impoverished Christian community. Even those burials within the church, the D/7 cemetery, North Tomb 1 and Enclosures 1 and 2 in Kellis 2, which might represent an affluent section of the community, are devoid of burial goods.

As implied by the title, this paper is very much a summary of work in progress. Much more study and analyses of Christian burial practices at Kellis remains to be undertaken. Further work is required to consider the likely continuing use of the family mausolea following the conversion of the descendants to Christianity. For this study to progress it is necessary to excavate other mausolea in the North and South Tomb groups in the expectation that the remains of pagan, as well as later Christian interments, have survived and that DNA analysis can be applied. The implication of the foetal burials for Christian doctrine relating to unborn children is yet another area that demands attention and will be considered further in subsequent publications. For now, one can do no more than stress the importance of the site of Ismant el-Kharab for our understanding of the formative years of Christianity in Egypt.

Acknowledgements

The excavations in D/6, D/7 and North Tomb 1 were funded by Monash University, which also provided funding to assist with the publication of the Christian burials. I am greatly indebted to Colin A. Hope for his generosity in providing me with unpublished data from his personal research to incorporate into this paper, for his extensive comments on the latter and for his guidance in details of archaeological interpretation. I thank Anthony Mills for inviting me to publish the archaeology of the Kellis 2 cemetery (work in progress), Eldon Molto for discussing the pathology, radiocarbon dating and other details of the bodies from the Kellis 2 cemetery and Tosha Dupras for reading and commenting upon this paper and providing me with information on infant and foetal burials.

Author's Address:

Centre for Archaeology and Ancient History
School of Historical Studies
Building 11, Clayton Campus,
Monash University,
Victoria 3800,
Australia

REFERENCES

Ancient Sources

Eusebius, *Ecclesiastical History*, J. E. L. Oulton, editor and translator, Loeb Classical Library, William Heinemann Ltd., London, Harvard University Press, Cambridge Massachusetts, 1932.

Tertullian, *Ad Scapulam*, in *The Writings of Tertullian*, Volume XI, A. Roberts and J. Donaldson, editors and translators, T. T. Clark, Edinburgh.

Modern Sources

Aubert, M-F, 2000 Catalogue Entry 99, in S. Walker, ed., *Ancient Faces Mummy Portraits from Roman Egypt*, British Museum Press, London, 147–8.

Aufderheide, A. C., L. Cartmell and M. Zlonis, this volume Bio-anthropological Features of Human Mummies from the Kellis 1 Cemetery: The Database for Mummification Methods, 137–51.

Bács, T. A., 2000 The so-called 'Monastery of Cyriacus' at Thebes, *Egyptian Archaeology*, 17, 34–6.

Badawy, A., 1978 *Coptic Art and Archaeology*, The MIT Press, Cambridge, Massachusetts.

Bagnall, R. S., 1982 Religious Conversion and Onomastic Change in Early Byzantine Egypt, *Bulletin of the American Society of Papyrologists* 19, 105–24.

Bagnall, R. S., 1992 Combat au vide: christianisme et paganisme dans l'Égypte romaine tardive, *Ktema*, 13, 285–96.

Bagnall, R. S., 1993 *Egypt in Late Antiquity*, Princeton University Press, New Jersey.

Bailey, D. M., 1988 *A Catalogue of the Lamps in the British Museum III Roman Provincial Lamps*, British Museum Publications, London.

Birrell, M., 1999 Excavations in the Cemeteries of Ismant el-Kharab, in C. A. Hope and A. J. Mills, eds, *Dakhleh Oasis Project: Preliminary Reports on the 1992–1993 and 1993–1994 Field Seasons*, Oxbow Books, Oxford, 29–41.

Bowen, G. E., 1998 The Spread of Christianity in Egypt in Light of Recent Discoveries from Ancient Kellis, unpublished Ph.D. Dissertation, presented at Monash University, Melbourne.

Bowen, G. E., 2002 The Fourth-Century Churches at Ismant el-Kharab, in C. A. Hope and G. E. Bowen, eds, *Dakhleh Oasis Project: Preliminary Reports on the 1994–1995 to 1998–1999 Field Seasons*, Oxbow Books, Oxford, 65–85.

Bowen, G. E., this volume The Small East Church at Ismant el-Kharab, 153–65.

Bowen, G. E., C. A. Hope and O. E. Kaper, 1993 A Brief Report on the Excavations at Ismant el-Kharab in 1992–93, *Bulletin of the Australian Centre for Egyptology* 4, 17–28.

Brown, P., 1981 The cult of the Saints: its rise and function in Latin Christianity, University of Chicago Press, Chicago.

Cross, F. L. and E. A. Livingstone, eds, 1974 *The Oxford Dictionary of the Christian Church*, Oxford University Press, London, New York and Toronto.

Davies, J., 1999 *Death, Burial and Rebirth in the Religions of Antiquity*, Routledge, London and New York.

Deissmann, A., 1902 *The Epistle of Psenosiris an original document from the Diocletian Persecution (Papyrus 713 Brit.Mus)*, Adam and Charles Black, London.

Doxiadis, E., 1995 *The Mysterious Fayum Portraits: Faces from Ancient Egypt*, Thames and Hudson, London and New York.

Dunand, F. and R. Lichtenbery, 1998 *Les Momies et la Mort en Égypte*, Éditions Errance, Paris.

Dunand, F., J-L Heim, N. Henein and R. Lichtenberg, 1992 *La Nécropole de Douch (Oasis de Kharga)*, Institut Francais d'Archéologie Orientale du Caire, Cairo.

Dupras, T. L. and M. W. Tocheri, this volume Preliminary Analysis of the Human Skeletal Remains from North Tombs 1 and 2, 183–96.

Dupras, T. L., M. W. Tocheri, C. A. Hope, D. Frankfurter, P. Sheldrick and E. Molto, forthcoming A Fetus from Kellis: A Bioarchaeological Approach, *International Journal of Osteoarchaeology*.

Fakhry, A., 1951 *The Necropolis of el-Bagawat in Kharg Oasis*, Government Press, Cairo.

Frankfurter, D., 1998 *Religion in Roman Egypt*, Princeton University Press, Princeton.

Gardner, I., ed., 1996 *Kellis Literary Texts Volume 1*, Oxbow Books, Oxford.

Gardner, I., A. Alcock and W-P Funk, 1999, *Coptic Documentary Texts from Kellis Volume 1*, Oxbow Books, Oxford.

Grossmann, P., 1985 Some Observations on the late Roman necropolis of al-Bagawat, in *Al-sahraa al-masriya, Gabaana al-Bagawat fi al-waaha al-khaariga (The Egyptian Deserts: the necropolis of el-Bagawat in Kharga Oasis)*, Egyptian Antiquities Organisation, Cairo, 414–38.

Grossmann, P., 1991 Architectural Elements of Churches, in A. S. Atiya, ed., *The Coptic Encyclopedia*, Volume 1, Macmillan Publishing Company, New York, 194–225.

Grossmann, P., 2002 *Christliche Architektur in Ägypten*, Brill Leiden, Boston Köln.

Hauser, W., 1932 The Christian Necropolis in Khargeh Oasis, *Bulletin of the Metropolitan Museum of Art*, 38–50.

Hawass, Z., 2000 *Valley of the Golden Mummies*, Virgin Publishing Ltd, London.

Hope, C. A., 1980 Dakhleh Oasis Project – Report on the Study of the Pottery and Kilns, *Journal of the Society for the Study of Egyptian Antiquities* X, 4, 283–313.

Hope, C. A., 1995 The Excavations at Ismant el-Kharab in 1995: A Brief Report, *Bulletin of the Australian Centre for Egyptology* 6, 51–8.

Hope, C. A., 1997 The Find Context of the Kellis Agricultural Account Book, in R. S. Bagnall, ed., *The Kellis Agricultural Account Book*, Oxbow Books, Oxford, 5–14.

Hope, C. A., 1999 The Excavations at Ismant el-Kharab in 1998/9: a Brief Report, *Bulletin of the Australian Centre for Egyptology* 10, 59–66.

Hope, C. A., 2000 Excavations at Ismant el-Kharab, *Bulletin of the Australian Centre for Egyptology* 11, 49–66.

Hope, C. A., 2001 Observations on the Dating of the Occupation at Ismant el-Kharab, in C. A. Marlow and A. J. Mills, eds, *The Oasis Papers 1: The Proceedings of the First Conference of the Dakhleh Oasis Project*, Oxbow Books, Oxford, 43–59.

Hope, C. A., this volume The Excavations at Ismant el-Kharab from 2000 to 2002, 207–89.

Hope, C. A. and G. E. Bowen, 1997 The Excavations at Ismant el-Kharab 1995/6 and 1996/7: A Brief Report, *Bulletin of the Australian Centre for Egyptology* 8, 49–64.

Hope, C. A. and J. McKenzie, 1999 Interim Report on the West Tombs, in C. A. Hope and A. J. Mills, eds, *Dakhleh Oasis Project: Preliminary Reports on the 1992–1993 and 1993–1994 Field Seasons*, Oxbow Books, Oxford, 53–68.

Jeffreys, D. G. and E. Strouhal, 1980 North Saqqara 1978–9: The Coptic Cemetery Site at the Sacred Animal Necropolis Preliminary Report, *Journal of Egyptian Archaeology* 66, 28–35.

Johnson, M. J., 1999 Pagan-Christian Burial Practices of the Fourth Century: Shared Tombs? *Christianity and Society The Social World of Early Christianity*, Garland Publishing, Inc. New York and London, 37–59.

Kaper, O. E., this volume The Decoration of North Tomb 1, 323–30.

Knudstad, J. E and R. A. Frey, 1999 Kellis, the Archaeological Survey of the Romano-Byzantine Town at Ismant el-Kharab, in C. S. Churcher and A. J. Mills, eds, *Reports from the Survey of the Dakhleh Oasis 1977–1987*, Oxbow Books, Oxford, 189–214.

Lythgoe, A. M., 1908 The Oasis of Kharga, *Bulletin of the Metropolitan Museum of Art* 3: 11, 203–8.

Marchini, C., 1999 Glass from the 1993 Excavations at Ismant el-Kharab, in C. A. Hope and A. J. Mills, eds, *Dakhleh Oasis Project: Preliminary Reports on the 1992–1993 and 1993–1994 Field Seasons*, Oxbow Books, Oxford, 75–82.

Marlow, C. A., 2001 Miscarriages and Infant Burials in the Dakhleh Oasis Cemeteries: An Archaeological Examination of Status, in C. A. Marlow and A. J. Mills, eds, *The Oasis Papers 1: Proceedings of the First International Symposium of the Dakhleh Oasis Project*, Oxbow Books, Oxford, 105–10.

Martin, G. T., 1974 Excavations in the Sacred Animal Necropolis at North Saqqara, 1972–3: Preliminary Report, *Journal of Egyptian Archaeology* 60, 15–29.

Mills, A. J., 1979 Dakhleh Oasis Project Reports on the First Season of Survey October – December 1978, *Journal of the Society for the Study of Egyptian Antiquities* IX, 4, 163–85.

Mills, A. J., 1980 Dakhleh Oasis Project Reports on the Second Season of Survey September – December 1979, *Journal of the Society for the Study of Egyptian Antiquities* X, 4, 251–82.

Mills, A. J., 1981 The Dakhleh Oasis Project Report on the Third Season of Survey September – December, 1980, *Journal of the Society for the Study of Egyptian Antiquities* XI, 4, 175–92.

Mills, A. J., 1982 The Dakhleh Oasis Project. Report on the Fourth Season of Survey. October 1981 – January 1982, *Journal of the Society for the Study of Egyptian Antiquities* XII, 3, 93–101.

Mills, A. J., 1983 The Dakhleh Oasis Project Report on the Fifth Season of Survey October 1982 – January, 1983, *Journal of the Society for the Study of Egyptian Antiquities* XIII, 3, 121–41.

Molto, J. E., 2002 Bio-archaeological Research of Kellis 2: An Overview, in C. A. Hope and G. E. Bowen, eds, *Dakhleh Oasis Project: Preliminary Reports on the 1994–1995 to 1998–1999 Field Seasons*, Oxbow Books, Oxford, 239–55.

Molto, J. E., P. Sheldrick, A. Cerroni and S. Haddow, this volume The Late Roman Period Skeletal Remains from D/6 and D/7 and North Tomb 1 at Kellis, 345–63.

Parr, R. L., 2002 Mitochondrial DNA Sequence Analysis of Skeletal Remains from the Kellis 2 Cemetery, in C. A. Hope and G. E. Bowen, eds, *Dakhleh Oasis Project: Preliminary Reports on the 1994–1995 to 1998–1999 Field Seasons*, Oxbow Books, Oxford, 257–61.

Patten, S. F., 1999 A Brief Report on the Study of the Ceramics, in C. A. Hope and A. J. Mills, eds, *Dakhleh Oasis Project: Preliminary Reports on the 1992–1993 and 1993–1994 Field Seasons*, Oxbow Books, Oxford, 83–8.

Petrie, F., 1925 *Tombs of the Courtiers and Oxyrhynkhos*, British School of Archaeology in Egypt, London.

Prominska, E., 1986 Ancient Egyptian Traditions of Artificial Mummification in the Christian Period in Egypt, in A. R. David, ed., *Science in Egyptology*, Manchester University Press, Manchester, 113–21.

Rowell, G., 1977 *The Liturgy of Christian Burial*, SPCK Publishing, London.

Schweitzer, A., 2002 Les parures de cartonnage des momies d'une nécropole d'Ismant el-Kharab, in C. A. Hope and G. E. Bowen, eds, *Dakhleh Oasis Project: Preliminary Reports on the 1994–1995 to 1998–1999 Field Seasons*, Oxbow Books, Oxford, 269–76.

Scott-Moncrieff, P. D., 1913 *Paganism and Christianity in Egypt*, Cambridge University Press, Cambridge.

Stewart, J. D., J. E. Molto and P. J. Reimer, this volume The Chronology of Kellis 2: The Interpretative Significance of Radiocarbon Dating of Human Remains, 373–8.

Thanheiser, U., 1999 Plant Remains from Ismant el-Kharab: First Results, in C. A. Hope and A. J. Mills, eds, *Dakhleh Oasis Project: Preliminary Reports on the 1992–1993 and 1993–1994 Field Seasons*, Oxbow Books, Oxford, 89–93.

Thomas, T. K., 2000 *Late Antique Egyptian Funerary Sculpture*, Princeton University Press, Princeton.

Tocheri, M. W., T. L. Dupras, P. Sheldrick and E. Molto, in press Roman Period Fetal Skeletons from Kellis, Egypt, *International Journal of Osteoarchaeology*.

Toynbee, J. M. C., 1971 *Death and Burial in the Roman World*, Thames and Hudson, London.

Venit, M. S., 2002 *Monumental Tombs of Ancient Alexandria*, Cambridge University Press, New York.

Wagner, G., 1987 *Les Oasis d'Égypte*, Institut Français d'Archéologie Orientale, Cairo.

Wagner, G., 1991 Bagawat, Al-, Greek Inscriptions, in *The Coptic Encyclopedia*, Volume 2, Macmillan Publishing Company, New York, 326–8.

Walker, S., 2000 Mummy Portraits and Roman Portraiture, in S. Walker, ed., *Ancient Faces Mummy Portraits from Roman Egypt*, British Museum Press, London, 23–5.

Worp, K. A., 1995 *Greek Papyri from Kellis*, Oxbow Books, Oxford.

Worp, K. A., 2002 Short Texts from the Main Temple, in C. A. Hope and G. E. Bowen, eds, *Dakhleh Oasis Project: Preliminary Reports on the 1994–1995 to 1998–1999 Field Seasons*, Oxbow Books, Oxford, 333–9.

Worp, K. A., forthcoming *Greek Ostraka from Kellis*, Oxbow Books, Oxford.

Preliminary Analysis of the Human Skeletal Remains from North Tombs 1 and 2

Tosha L. Dupras and Matthew W. Tocheri

Introduction

On the north-western side of Kellis there are two rows of mausolea known as the North Tombs. They run in a line from south-south-west to north-north-east (Hope this volume, Figure 1). During the 1999–2000 field season two of the largest tombs, North Tomb 1 and North Tomb 2 were excavated (Hope this volume).

North Tomb 1 is the largest tomb structure at Kellis (Figure 1). It was first documented by Moritz in 1900, and later photographed and published in 1908 and 1936 respectively by H. E. Winlock. The large interior central chamber was stone-lined with adhering-gypsum plaster, originally with funerary scenes painted on the walls (Kaper this volume). Knudstad and Frey (1999, 209) documented the architecture of North Tomb 1 during the 1981–1982 field seasons.

North Tomb 1 comprises an antechamber, a rear stone-lined central chamber and two flanking chambers and an elaborate portico. There is also evidence (Hope this volume) of a wall that, in conjunction with the portico, is thought to have completely enclosed the tomb. This enclosure is important in our analysis of the human remains as several burials were located in between the wall and the tomb structure, space 14 (Hope this volume).

North Tomb 1 shows evidence of at least two phases of modification to the architecture. Excavations revealed no *in situ* evidence of the original burials. Only burials from the latest phase of use were found in the pitted floors of the three rooms located in the western part of the tomb (Hope this volume). All of these burials were mostly disturbed, but they were buried in an east-west orientation, with heads toward the west, indicative of the Christian burial tradition.

North Tomb 2 lies to the north of North Tomb 1 and both are architecturally similar (Figure 2). It has the same internal structure as North Tomb 1, but its decoration is much simpler as is the portico. North Tomb 2 has a stone floor in the transverse hall that is broken in several places by intrusive burial pits. In addition to the adult remains, an intrusive burial of a complete infant wrapped in linen was found oriented in a north-south position. Unlike North Tomb 1, excavation of this tomb revealed the inclusion of a range of burial goods associated with the adults in the central chamber and others elsewhere (Hope this volume).

In the past, the northern chamber of North Tomb 2, Room 3, was burnt in a high temperature fire. The fire melted glass and burnt much of the wooden funerary furniture. Human remains in this chamber are also charred, and in some cases have adhered melted glass on the bone surface. The fire was restricted to this chamber, leaving the other chambers and the transverse hall untouched. Several complete burials with tissue and linen wrappings were found in the transverse hall. Based on a provisional study of the burial goods found within North Tomb 2, the tomb was most likely built and first used during the first or second centuries CE as was North Tomb 1 (Hope this volume).

Preliminary Analysis of the Human Remains

The skeletal remains recovered from the North Tombs at Kellis were typically badly disturbed. Although a few intact burials were found, the majority of the recovered remains were commingled, consisting of incomplete bone fragments likely representing several individuals. The distribution of remains in both tombs is similar to what occurs in ossuary style burials. In many cases an ossuary is a secondary burial where bones from several individuals, mostly skeletonized, are deposited, resulting in a commingled mass of bones. Although both tombs analyzed in this study have the appearance of an ossuary, this was not the original burial practice as witnessed in other cultures. Instead, the ossuary nature of the North Tombs may be the result of tomb reuse where later populations made room for their dead by removing previous interments. Alternatively, commingling and fragmentation may have also occurred during grave pillaging.

Within North Tomb 1 and North Tomb 2, the preservation of bone and tissue is highly variable, ranging from completely desiccated body parts to severely burnt

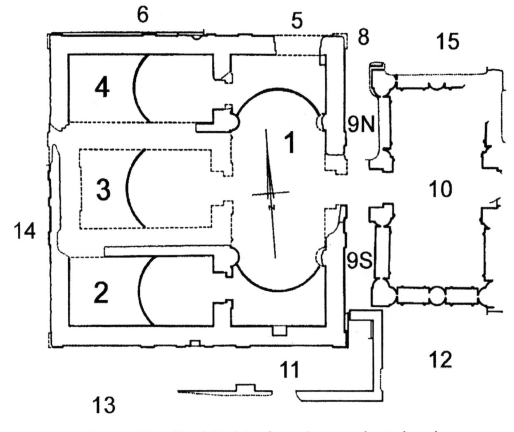

Figure 1 Plan of North Tomb 1 with room/space numbers indicated (adapted from Knudstad and Frey 1999).

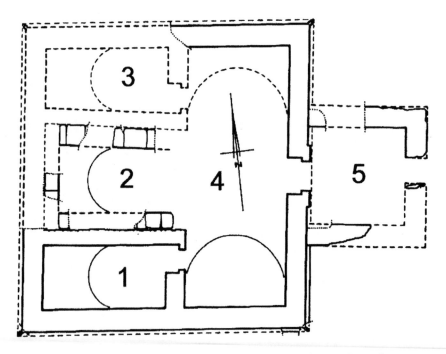

Figure 2 Plan of North Tomb 2 with room numbers indicated (adapted from Knudstad and Frey 1999).

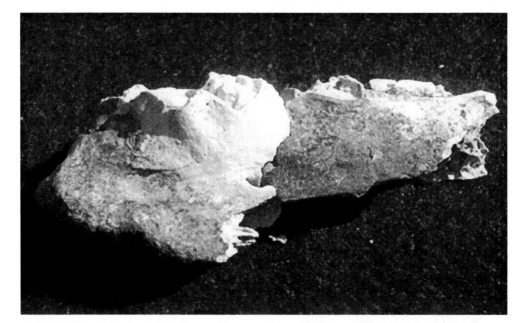

Plate 1   Mandible fragment from North Tomb 2, broken post-mortem then exposed to fire.

bone fragments. The burnt bones show characteristic signs that they were completely dry when exposed to fire. In other words, burning took place long after death and the processes of decomposition. Several bone fragments were found that fit together, with each fragment showing a different burning pattern (Plate 1), indicating that the bones were broken after death and separated spatially before being exposed to fire. Some bones were covered with a black vitreous substance resembling melted glass.

Initial examination of the skeletal material revealed that the majority of bone was fragmentary and a great deal of commingling of individuals had occurred. Therefore, the analysis of the material was approached as one would study ossuary material. Room by room, all bone fragments were identified, aged, and sided where possible. Then, the minimum number of individuals (MNI) represented by the skeletal remains was estimated as the number of anatomically identical skeletal elements found in each room. Many skeletal pathologies were noted and are discussed separately (Molto *et al.* this volume).

North Tomb 1

In North Tomb 1, 11 rooms/spaces yielded skeletal remains (Hope this volume, Figure 12). Room 1 had remains that were bagged from three contexts, 7, 8, and 45. Three distal tibia fragments suggest at least two individuals, one adult and one juvenile, are represented in Context 7. Several non-human bone fragments were also recovered. Four complete humeri, one of which is juvenile, suggest Context 8 contained remains from at least three individuals.

At least three individuals appear to be represented in Context 45, as three left calcanei were identified. Matching right and left hipbones were also recovered from this context and the morphology suggests this individual was female. In total, Room 1 has a MNI of eight individuals, seven of which are adults and one is juvenile.

Room 2 contained three burials[1] and further skeletal material from one other archaeological context. Context 2 contained at least one individual. Burial 1 consisted of a fairly complete juvenile skeleton. The proximal humeral epiphyses and the proximal and distal epiphyses of the femora and tibiae are all unfused suggesting that this individual died in his/her mid- to late-teens. Burial 2 consisted of several fragments belonging to a juvenile. Burial 3 consisted of a complete juvenile skeleton. Over 200 complete bones and bone fragments were recovered from the remainder of this room. The majority of this material was juvenile with foetal and infant bones also present whereas less than 10 fragments could be adequately identified as adult. The total number of individuals is difficult to determine based on the fragmentary condition of many skeletal elements, but at least three juveniles are represented.

Room 3 contained seven individual burials found in six graves (4a, 4b, 5a, 5b=6, 10, 12 and 16; Hope this volume, Figure 16). Burial 4 consisted of two commingled adult skeletons, renumbered 4a and 4b during analysis. Burial 5a consisted of a relatively complete skeleton of a female with an age at death estimation of 22 ± 3 years; a male, 23.4 ± 3.6 years, is represented by Burial 5b found with 5a. Burial 6 consisted of several skeletal elements

---

[1] In this paper 'burial' refers to complete or semi-complete skeletons, not an archaeological feature, though many were found in dug graves.

Table 1 Summary of the Minimum Number of Individuals (MNI) in North Tomb 1 based on individual burials and the presence of multiple skeletal elements.

Room	Number of Adults	Number of Juveniles	MNI
1	7	1	8
2	1	3	4
3	7		7
4	5	1	6
6		2	2
8		1	1
14		7	7
TOTAL	20	15	35

including both fibulae and feet that belong to the male of Burial 5b. An incomplete female skeleton, approximately 45 ± 5 years of age at death, is represented by Burial 10 (Contexts 85 and 86). Burial 12 is an adult male, likely 28 ± 3 years when he died. Burial 16 consisted of an adult male skeleton approximately 30 ± 5 years of age. In total, Room 3 has a MNI of seven individuals.

Room 4 likely contained three individual burials. Graves 8 and 9 are two separate adjacent features, but the remains attest only one complete individual, classified as Burial 8 for purposes of this analysis. Burial 7 represents a mid- to late-adult female. Burial 8 represents a young adult male, 23 ± 3 years, and Burial 11, a mid-adult male. Burial 13 consisted of an almost complete perinatal skeleton, missing only a pubis and ischium, that is, hip-bones. The burnt remains from Contexts 27, 58, 62 and 66 from this room have a MNI of two individuals. There are two right humeri, an axis, a sacrum and a manubrium. Because all the complete burials have an axis, sacrum and a manubrium, these are thought to represent other individuals. The number of fragmentary elements clearly do not represent two complete individuals and it is unknown if these remains are from individuals in other rooms in North Tomb 1. With this in mind, Room 4 has at least six individuals represented.

Room 5 yielded two bone fragments, the proximal end of a radius, and another proximal radius with one third of the shaft and the proximal end. Both fragments were burnt.

Room 6 contained two burials, 14 and 17. Burial 14 represents a fairly complete juvenile skeleton. Burial 17 represents a complete infant individual with charred soft tissue and cloth still remaining.

Room 8 contained one burial of an infant, Burial 18. The skull was skeletonized, with only a few teeth missing. The body was wrapped in linen, with the hands bound with red string and placed over the abdomen, and the feet were crossed left over right.

Room 10 contained two bone fragments; a lower right second premolar and an adult rib fragment, both likely from individuals represented in other rooms.

Space 14 contained the remains of six foetal/infant burials: 19, 20, 21, 22, 23 and 24. These burials were located outside the western wall of the main building of North Tomb 1. Burial 19 represents the almost complete

remains of an eight to nine month old infant. Burials 20 and 21 represent the almost complete remains of two newborns, *circa* 40 weeks gestation. Burial 22 represents the complete remains of an early third trimester foetus, 30 weeks gestation. Burial 23 represents the remains of a late third trimester foetus, 36 weeks gestation. Burial 24 contains the remains of two individuals; one appendicular skeleton of a newborn, relabelled as 24a for the analysis, and one complete skeleton of a foetus that appears to be late third trimester, or perinate numbered 24b. In total, Space 14 contains at least seven individuals.

Space 15 contained two right femoral fragments, both from Context 68. Space 16 does not appear to contain a complete individual, rather only fragments that likely come from other rooms. Bones represented include fragments of the femur, temporal, maxilla, radius, ribs, vertebra, scapula and a calcaneus. All fragments are burnt.

A summary of the MNI from each room and as a total for North Tomb 1 is presented in Table 1. While calculating the estimate for MNI in each room, care was taken to avoid counting an individual more than once in the case where the burial was not complete. However, because we are calculating MNI for each room within the tomb and the likelihood of commingling between rooms is high, it is likely that the MNI is over estimated.

Alternatively, all the skeletal elements from the entire tomb are also used to calculate a total tomb MNI (see below). Therefore, when considering distinguishable burials and multiple skeletal elements from each room, North Tomb 1 has a MNI of 35 individuals, with 20 adults and 15 juveniles represented.

North Tomb 2

Room 1 of North Tomb 2 contained a partial adult skeleton. Several bone elements and fragments were also found in Contexts 10 and 44. Duplication of these elements suggests that at least two adults are represented as well as one juvenile as two complete immature clavicles were recovered.

Bone was recovered from five contexts (2, 12, 13, 15 and 40) in Room 2. The majority of the bone is burnt with some being completely charred while others are vitrified, and range in colour from grey/white to blue/grey with some orange tint as well. Context 13 appears to contain four fairly complete adult individuals, all exposed to fire, which the excavator labelled Burials 1 to 4 (Hope this volume, Plate 59), and one unburnt wrapped infant. This infant is completely wrapped in linen and has not yet been analysed. One of the adults, Burial 2, was recovered with several perinatal remains. In addition to these remains, over 250 additional bones and bone fragments were collected from Room 2. Several fragments, mainly rib and vertebral, are not burnt, and likely have come from the individuals in other rooms where no burning is evident. This may indicate that commingling had taken place before and after the fire occurred. When all remains are examined, including the four fairly complete adults, the duplication of long bone fragments suggest at least four adult and three subadults (including the wrapped infant) are represented in Room 2. The presence of a pubic bone exhibiting dorsal pitting and a very thin pubic symphysis indicates that one of the females from Context 13 was a female. Another pubic bone (although sex is not determinant) indicates one of the other adults from Context 13 was of middle age or older. The subadult skeletal elements represent a foetus, another possible foetus/perinate and an infant (age yet to be determined).

The majority of bone from Room 3 was badly fragmented and burnt. Contexts 3, 9, 11, 16, 17 and 41 contained bone. Context 3 only contained two parietal fragments. Context 9 contained many burnt and charred fragments, mostly representing adults, with two juvenile fragments. Based on multiple bones, these contexts in Room 3 have a MNI of three adults based on the presence of three left tali and three right patellae, and possibly one juvenile also. The condition of the remains in Context 11 made it difficult to estimate a MNI greater than one, as no elements were recognizably duplicated and most were burnt and fragmented. Most of the skeletal remains from Room 3 were excavated from Context 16. Once again most remains were fragmentary and burnt. While most represent adult remains, there is evidence of at least four juveniles based on the presence of four right ischial bones. The MNI for adults is five based on the presence of five right calcanei and five left patellae. A small number of burnt fragments with no recognizable duplication of elements came from Context 17. Several small burnt fragments were recovered from Context 41, again with no duplication of elements. The MNI for Room 3 is seven adults, based on seven right calcanei, and four juveniles, based on four right ischial bones.

Bone was recovered from eight contexts in Room 4: Contexts 6, 7, 8, 23, 26, 27, 30 and 37. The skeletal material ranged from fragmentary and burnt to complete bones with some soft tissue still remaining. Context 6 did not contain any distinguishable burials and the fragmentary condition of the remains complicates an estimation of the MNI. Both adult and juvenile remains are present, however, suggesting at least two individuals are represented. Context 7 did not reveal any obvious burials, and the presence of juvenile remains and two right tali

indicate a MNI of two adults and one juvenile. Neither burnt bones nor any observable burials were contained in Context 8. Multiple occurrences of bones indicate a MNI of three adults, based on three right tali and three left calcanei, and two juveniles, based on two left femora. All bone recovered from Context 23 is burnt with the exception of five rib fragments and one second metacarpal. No obvious burials are present in this context, and two left adult tali and one complete juvenile humerus indicate a total MNI of three. Contexts 26 and 27 represent the fill of a grave against the northern wall (Hope this volume, Figure 19), which originally contained a ceramic coffin found completely fragmented. Context 26 revealed mostly fragmentary, burnt bone. Skeletal elements present indicate a MNI of one adult and one juvenile. The fragmentary and burnt condition of remains from Context 27 again complicates an estimation of the MNI; however, both juvenile and adult bones are present representing at least two individuals. The fifteen bone fragments excavated from Context 30 were not burnt, but their very fragmentary condition renders estimating a MNI impossible. Context 37 is the fill from a pit against the southern wall (Hope thos volume, Figure 19) that contained the remains of another ceramic coffin and had mostly unburnt bone fragments, with both juvenile and adult bone present. The presence of two right and two left clavicles indicate the presence of at least two adults, and the presence of immature bones indicates at least one juvenile. A completely mummified adult female was recovered from a third grave in front of the door to Room 1, bearing a mummy label revealing her name as Senpsais (Hope this volume, Figure 24 and Plates 68–70). In addition, the wrapped torso of an adult male was recovered from Room 4. In total, Room 4 of North Tomb 2 contained at least nine adults, based on the presence of seven left tali and one complete individual, a partial adult mummified torso, and two juveniles, based on the presence of two right clavicles and two left femora.

Although not assigned a room number, there were remains recovered from North Tomb 2 that were only assigned to Context 1, that represents a general surface deposit. Within this context the majority of the bones were fragmentary and burnt and grey-white in colour. The presence of two complete left adult calcanei indicates a MNI of two.

In addition to all the bones recovered in North Tomb 1 and North Tomb 2, there are several scattered bones with no provenience. All the bones are charred or burnt and are most likely from North Tomb 2, Room 2 (Context 13) or Room 3 (Context 16). Most of the remains are fragmentary and represent both juvenile and adult individuals. No distinguishable duplication is observed. All bones are included in the total estimate of MNI for North Tomb 2.

A summary of the MNI from each room and as a total for North Tomb 2 is presented in Table 2. When burials were not complete, care was taken to consider the missing elements so that an individual would not be counted more than once in the MNI. The possibility of commingling

Table 2 Summary of the Minimum Number of Individuals (MNI) in North Tomb 2 based on individual burials and the presence of multiple skeletal elements.

Room	Number of Adults	Number of Juveniles	MNI
1	2	1	3
2	4	3	7
3	7	4	11
4	9	2	11
TOTAL	**22**	**10**	**32**

Table 3 Summary of complete burials excavated from North Tomb 1.

Room	Burial	Sex	Age
2	1		Juvenile
2	2		Juvenile
2	3		Juvenile
3	4a		Adult
3	4b		Adult
3	5a	Female	Adult
3	5b	Male	Young adult
4	7	Female	Mid-late adult
4	8	Male	Young adult
3	10		Adult
4	11	Male	Mid-adult
3	12	Male	Adult
4	13		Perinate
6	14		Juvenile
4	16	Male	Adult
6	17		Infant
8	18		Infant
14	19		Infant (8–9 months)
14	20		Perinate
14	21		Perinate
14	22		Foetus (third trimester)
14	23		Infant
14	24a		Perinate
14	24b		Foetus (third trimester)

Table 4 Measurements (mm) of long bone diaphyses from foetal/perinate remains from North Tomb 1.

Room	Burial Number	Clavicle	Humerus	Radius	Ulna	Femur	Tibia
14	23	42.12	59.87	48.67	55.70	67.35	58.04
4	13	42.69	64.63	52.85	60.10	73.20	65.40
14	24b	44.74	63.14	49.65	57.36	70.71	60.07
14	22	32.66	48.35	38.78	44.74	52.85	45.18
14	21					63.57	54.99
14	20	51.53	71.23	59.88	67.43	80.96	71.81
14	19	30.77	45.42	37.93	43.64	50.59	

between rooms in this tomb is high and as such the MNI based on room-by-room calculations is most likely overestimated. As with North Tomb 1, all the skeletal elements from the entire tomb are considered in the calculation of a total tomb MNI (see below). Therefore, considering distinguishable burials and multiple skeletal elements from each room, North Tomb 2 has a MNI of 32 individuals, with 22 adults and 10 juveniles represented.

Minimum Number of Individuals in Each Tomb

While examining all the bones from each individual room in North Tomb 1 and North Tomb 2, the presence of multiple, unique skeletal elements was used to calculate the MNI in each room. Given the ossuary-like nature of the tomb, with very disturbed and fragmentary remains, we recognize the possibility that bones were commingled within and between rooms. Further evidence of commingling between rooms comes from the fact that badly charred and burnt remains are found throughout most of the rooms; however excavations in North Tomb 2 indicate that a high temperature fire had only occurred and was contained in the northern chamber, Room 3 (Hope this volume). The same assumption of commingling between rooms is also made for North Tomb 1. Given this, when examining the total array of bones from the entire tomb, we calculated the MNI in the entire tomb based on the multiple occurrences of skeletal elements.

North Tomb 1 contained many distinguishable burials, with a total of 24 individuals from 22 graves, including 10 adults and 14 foetal/juvenile remains (Table 3). Not all of these burials were complete individuals, so the likelihood that elements from these burials are commingled throughout the tomb is high. When all skeletal elements not assigned to individual burials are examined there is a MNI of six adults, based on six complete sacra, and two juveniles, based on two left humeri. It is recognized that some of the bones from the burials are commingled, but those used to calculate the MNI of commingled remains are present in the burials, so there is little, if any, overlap. In summation, there appears to be a total MNI of 16 adults and 15 juveniles for a total of 31 individuals in North Tomb 1. This estimate equates to four less individuals than the estimate calculated when each room was considered separately (see Table 1). This suggests that commingling in and between the rooms has likely occurred.

North Tomb 2 also contained many complete single burials; however, much of the skeletal remains was highly fragmentary and burnt. The burials that are assigned individual numbers (1, 2, 3 and 4) all appear to contain multiple individuals, and therefore are not representative of burials as seen in North Tomb 1. In North Tomb 2, Rooms 1, 2, 3 and 4 contained bone, and based on the MNI calculated for each room (see Table 2) there appears to be a total of 22 adults and 10 juveniles for a total of 30 individuals. Again, based on the strong likelihood of commingling, this number is likely overestimated. When MNI is calculated from all the commingled skeletal

elements in the entire tomb there are 14 adults represented by 14 left tali, and six juveniles represented by five right clavicles and one foetal calcaneus. In addition there are two completely wrapped bodies in the tomb, one adult and one juvenile for a total of 23 individuals in North Tomb 2. This estimate equates to eight less individuals than the estimate calculated on a room-by-room basis (Table 2), again suggesting that commingling of the remains has occurred.

The Demographic Profile

The determination of age at death and sex of skeletonized individuals can provide information about many facets of life. In this study we are specifically dealing with two mausolea, and this may mean that the individuals buried there may have been related in some way or may have had a similar level of status. The later interments in the tombs are oriented east-west, an indication of a Christian-style burial, which means their use was likely contemporary with the use of the Kellis 2 cemetery (Dupras 1999; Molto 2000; Tocheri *et al.* in press). If this is the case, then a certain portion of the population was being buried in the tomb structures and in areas in Kellis, such as D/6 and D/7, while others were being buried in the larger Kellis 2 cemetery. The reason for the dichotomy in burial location is currently unclear.

Due to the fragmentary and burnt nature of the remains, particularly within North Tomb 2, constructing a demographic profile is difficult. We are able to estimate the age at death and sex of the most complete adult individuals, with the exception of those that still remain wrapped, although in many cases, age is difficult to determine beyond categories of juvenile versus adult. In addition, determining the sex of juveniles is also very challenging as most sex differences in skeletal structure do not become apparent until after the advent of puberty. Hence, only the estimated ages are provided for the skeletal remains of juveniles.

The age estimations for foetuses/perinates are calculated from long bone diaphysis measurements using standard formulae (Scheuer *et al.* 1980; Scheuer and Black 2000; Sherwood *et al.* 2000). Table 4 presents the osteometrical data from the foetal/perinatal remains from North Tomb 1; none were identified in North Tomb 2. Bones that were too fragmentary or not available for measurement are left blank. Table 5 presents age estimates in foetal weeks for foetal/perinate remains from North Tomb 1 using the methods described in Scheuer *et al.* (1980) and Scheuer and Black (2000). Table 6 presents age estimates for the same foetuses/perinates from North Tomb 1 in foetal weeks based on formulae from Sherwood *et al.* (2000). Table 7 presents the average and median age estimates in foetal weeks based on all age estimates.

The diaphyseal measurements from individuals in North Tomb 1 suggest that approximately six individuals are of foetal or perinatal age. These ages range from approximately 29.4 to 42.6 foetal gestational weeks. With

Tosha L. Dupras and Matthew W. Tocheri

Table 5 Gestational age estimates in foetal weeks for foetal/perinates from North Tomb 1 based on Scheuer et al. *(1980) and Scheuer and Black (2000).*

	Method Number[1]				
ID	1.01	1.02	1.04	4.01	4.03
19			30.3	28.7	27.9
22	30.0	30.2	31.0	29.6	29.5
21		34.6	34.6	33.8	
23	36.1	36.0	35.8	35.2	35.9
24b	37.4	37.1	36.9	36.6	37.7
13	38.9	38.9	37.7	37.5	38.5
20	42.2	41.9	40.3	40.6	42.1

[1] Based on data provided in Scheuer *et al.* (1980); Scheuer and Black (2000).
Method 1.01 = (0.1724(FEM) + 0.1538(TIB) + 0.0674(HUM) - 0.0718(RAD) + 0.1397(ULN) + 7.2624) ± 1.88
Method 1.02 = (0.1984(FEM) + 0.2291(TIB) + 9.3575) ± 1.87
Method 1.04 = (0.3303(FEM) + 13.5583) ± 2.08
Method 4.01 = (0.3922(FEM) + 8.83) ± 1.49
Method 4.03 = (0.5524(HUM) + 2.7825) ± 1.24

Table 6 Gestational age estimates in foetal weeks for foetal/perinates from North Tomb 1 based on Sherwood et al. *(2000).*

	Method Name[1]					
ID	Femur	Tibia	Ulna	Humerus	Radius	Fibula
19	30.1	.	30.0	29.3	29.5	.
22	31.0	30.0	30.6	30.7	30.0	30.5
21	35.1	35.0	.	.	.	.
23	36.5	36.6	37.0	36.6	36.4	.
24b	37.8	37.7	38.0	38.3	37.0	39.1
13	38.7	40.8	39.8	39.2	39.3	41.0
20	41.7	44.8	44.8	43.0	44.6	.

[1] Based on data provided in Sherwood *et al.* (2000).
Method FEM = (10.91 + 0.38(FEM)) ± 2.05
Method TIB = (15.13 + 0.19(TIB) + (0.0031)(TIB^2)) ± 2.06
Method ULN = (14.28 + 0.19(ULN) + (0.0039)(ULN^2)) ± 2.08
Method HUM = (12.98 + 0.25(HUM) + (0.0024)(HUM^2)) ± 2.12
Method RAD = (13.53 + 0.25(RAD) + (0.0045)(RAD^2)) ± 2.14
Method FIB = (14.72 + 0.21(FIB) + (0.0036)(FIB^2)) ± 2.19

Table 7 Average and median gestational age estimates for individuals from North Tomb 1 based on Scheuer et al. *(1980), Scheuer and Black (2000) and Sherwood* et al. *(2000).*

ID	Average[1]	Median[1]
19	29.4	29.5
22	30.3	30.2
21	34.6	34.6
23	36.2	36.2
24b	37.6	37.7
13	39.1	38.9
20	42.6	42.2

[1] Data sorted by average gestational age estimate (in weeks).

Table 8 Age estimations (years) based on long bone (diaphysis) measurements for juvenile individuals. All individuals in this table are from North Tomb 1.

Room	Burial	Clavicle	Humerus	Radius	Ulna	Femur	Tibia	Fibula	Average Age
2	1	6	3	2.5	2.5	2.5	2.5	2.5	2.5
2	3	>18	13	12.5	13.5	13	13	12	13
3	4a	>18		18	16		15.5	14	16
3	5a	>18	13	13.5	13.5			11	13
3	6							14.5	14.5
4	7	>18	13				13	12	12.5
4	8	>18	14.5	>18	16.5		13.5		15
6	14	6		3.5	4	3.5	3.5		3.5

Table 9 Age estimates (years) of commingled long bones of juveniles from contexts within North Tomb 1 and North Tomb 2.

Tomb	Room	Context	Clavicle	Humerus	Radius	Ulna	Femur	Tibia	Fibula	Average Age	Median Age
1	1	8		13						13	13
1	1	8		13						13	13
1	1	8	15							15	15
1	1	8	10	7						8.5	8.5
1	1	8			7	7.5				7.25	7.25
1	1	45			13	13.5		13	11.5	12.75	13
1	1	45						12.5		12.5	12.5
1	1	45							11.5	11.5	11.5
1	1	45				13.5				13.5	13.5
1	1	45			13					13	13
1	1	45			14					14	14
1	2	1			7					7	7
1	2	3					6.5			6.5	6.5
1	2	3		7						7	7
1	2	3	1							1	1
1	2	24				0.5				0.5	0.5
1	2	24							0.5	0.5	0.5
1	3	32		15						15	15
1	3	32				16				16	16
1	3	32			13					13	13
1	3	32		14.5						14.5	14.5
1	3	test trench 1	>18		13					13	13
1	4	58		13			14	13.5		13.5	13.5
2	1	44	11	9	8	9	7		8.5	8.75	8.75
2	4	8		15.5						15.5	15.5
2	4	8		14						14	14
2	4	8						16	15	15.5	15.5
2	4	8						13.5		13.5	13.5
2	4	8							12	12	12
2	4	8					3			3	3

Table 10 Estimation of sex and age at death for complete or partial adult burials from North Tomb 1 and North Tomb 2.

Tomb	Room	Burial	Sex	Age
1	3	4b		
1	3	5a	female	22 ± 3
1	3	10	female	45 ± 5
1	3	12	male	28 ± 3
1	3	16	male	30 ± 5
1	4	7	female	> 50
1	4	8	male	20 ± 2
1	4	11	male	
1	6	17		
2	2	3		37 ± 10
2			female	

Table 11 Estimation of age for commingled pelvic bones from North Tomb 1 and North Tomb 2.

Tomb	Room	Context	Bone	Side	Age
1	4	58	Pubic Symphysis		51 ± 14
2	4	8	Pubic Symphysis	R	37 ± 10
2	4	8	Pubic Symphysis	R	37 ± 10
2	None	1	Pubic Symphysis	R	37 ± 10
2	None	1	Pubic Symphysis	R	37 ± 10
2	3	16	Pubic Symphysis	R	19 ± 2
2	3	16	Pubic Symphysis	R	19 ± 2

the exception of Burial 20, all of these individuals are estimated to be in the third trimester of development. Most likely, several of these individuals were born prematurely and would not have had sufficient lung development for postnatal survival. Burial 20 is probably a newborn. All the foetal/perinatal remains, with the exception of Burial 13 from Room 3 were found buried in Space 14, which is the area outside the western wall of the main tomb building (Figure 1). This may indicate burial segregation of the very young within the tomb structure. The inclusion of foetal remains within the context of an area reserved for adult burial is different from what has so far been observed in earlier burial practices at Kellis (Birrell 1999, 33–41; Molto 2000; Tocheri *et al.* in press), where no individuals under the age of five have yet been found buried with adults, as in the Kellis 1 cemetery.

Age estimates for juvenile individuals are calculated using long bone diaphysis measurements. Measurements are compared to standards presented by Scheuer and Black (2000), Maresh (1970), Gindhart (1973) and Anderson *et al.* (1964). Age estimates for individuals recovered in distinct burials are reported in Table 8. All obvious burials of juveniles were recovered from North Tomb 1. Eight individuals are represented in the juvenile category, and they range in estimated age from three to 16 years of age. Interestingly, all clavicular measurements provided inflated age estimates in comparison to associated diaphyseal measurements by approximately three years. Because of the discrepancy, the age estimates derived from

measurements of the clavicle are not used in the calculation of the average age of each individual.

Age estimates of commingled bones from contexts within each tomb are reported in Table 9. Because of the commingled nature of these remains each line entry does not necessarily represent an individual and it is very likely that several entries could be from one individual. The estimated age range of the juvenile remains spans from six months to 16 years of age.

Determination of sex for the adult remains was accomplished by analyzing pelvic morphology (Phenice 1969) and features of the skull (Bass 1995). Age estimates for adults are based on pubic symphyseal morphology (Katz and Suchey 1986; Brooks and Suchey 1990). Vital statistic profiles for individual burials are shown in Table 10, while Table 11 contains the adult data for age from commingled pubic symphyses from both Tombs. Tables 12, 13, 14 and 15 contain the osteometrical data from all commingled juvenile and adult long bones from both tombs.

Summary

The human remains recovered from North Tombs 1 and 2 at Kellis have been briefly described herein. We have reported on the age and sex of the individuals, where possible, to give a demographic overview as to whom was buried in these tombs. Although the fragmentary and burnt condition of many of the remains complicated the analysis,

Table 12 Raw osteometrical data for clavicles and humeri for juveniles and adults.

Tomb	Room	Burial	Context	Rcml[1]	Lcml[2]	Rhml[3]	Lhml[4]	Rmhh[5]	Lmhh[6]	Rmhm[7]	Lmhm[8]
1	1		8			292		38		19	
1	1		8				289		38		18
1	1		8			289		40		18	
1	1		8	133							
1	1		8	102		207					
1	2		3				203				
1	2		3	57							
1	2	3		145	143	297	291				
1	2	1		77	78	145	143				
1	3		32				326		48		22
1	3		32			329	324	49	49	21	20
1	3		32				326		47		22
1	3		Test Trench1		157						
1	3	4a		160							
1	3	4b		160	148						
1	3	5a		139	143	291	291	39	39	19	18
1	3	5b		156	158	329	324	49	48	21	20
1	4		58				293		39		20
1	4	7	60		144						
1	4	11	62	161							
1	4	7			144		293		42		20
1	4	8		159	157	323	319	45	45	20	19
1	4	11		160							
1	6	14	102		84						
1	6	17			55.24						
2	1		44	105	104		220				
2	2		13								
2	4		8			338		51		22	
2	4		8				319		43		18

[1] Rcml: right maximum clavicular length.
[2] Lcml: left maximum clavicular length.
[3] Rhml: right maximum humeral length.
[4] Lhml: left maximum humeral length.

[5] Rmhh: right maximum humeral head diameter.
[6] Lmhh: left maximum humeral head diameter.
[7] Rmhm: right maximum humeral midshaft diameter.
[8] Lmhm: right maximum humeral midshaft diameter.

there is still much useful information that can come from this type of study. In this situation, our data suggest that the best estimate of the MNI in a tomb is to consider all remains, and not to calculate room by room, as it appears very likely that remains were commingled throughout the tomb.

Analysis of all the remains from each tomb allowed us to calculate a MNI in each tomb. North Tomb 1 has a MNI of 31 individuals, 16 adults and 15 juveniles, while North Tomb 2 has a MNI of 23, 16 adults and 7 juveniles. Male and female adult remains appear to be represented fairly equally in each tomb. Age at death estimates span from early third trimester foetus to greater than 50 years of age. The earliest use of the tombs likely dates back to the early Roman Period (Hope this volume). Although it is presently unknown if the tombs were reserved for familial burials or for individuals of high status, it is likely that the tombs were re-used at the same time as the Kellis 2 cemetery. Similar trends, such as orientation and the inclusion of foetal burials, are found in both locations, suggesting that the tombs may have been used during the late third and fourth centuries CE.

Table 13 Raw osteometrical data for radii and ulnae for juveniles and adults.

Tomb	Room	Burial	Context	Rrml[1]	Lrml[2]	Ruml[3]	Luml[4]
1	1		8		157		171
1	1		45	230		246	
1	1		45			246	
1	1		45		223		
1	1		45	230			
1	2		1	159			
1	2		24				79
1	2	3		219	218	246	245
1	2	1		107	107	118	117
1	3		32			273	
1	3		32	226			
1	3		32		251		
1	3		Test Trench 1		223		
1	3	4a					271
1	3	4b		252	251	273	272
1	3	10		265	261	278	279
1	3	5a		226	225	244	242
1	3	5b			251	275	271
1	4	11	62	271			
1	4	8		258	258	276	
1	4	11		270			
1	6	14	102	119	118	134	133
2	1		44	170	169	189	187

[1] Rrml: right maximum radial length.
[2] Lrml: left maximum radial length.
[3] Ruml: right maximum ulnar length.
[4] Luml: left maximum ulnar length.

Table 14 Raw osteometrical data for femora for juveniles and adults.

Tomb	Room	Burial	Context	Rfml[1]	Lfml[2]	Rfmhd[3]	Lfmhd[4]	Rmfm[5]	Lmfm[6]
1	1		8			39			
1	2		3	298					
1	2	3			422				
1	2	1		193	193				
1	3	10	86	478	476	49	49	34	31
1	3	10		478	476	49	48	34	31
1	4		58		432		42		26
1	4	7			432		42		27
1	4	8					45		
1	6	14	102	218	219				
2	1		44	308	308				
2	2		13		473		53		
2	4		8		205				
2	4		8			38			
2	4		8			43			
2	4		8			38			

[1] Rfml: right maximum femoral length.
[2] Lfml: left maximum femoral length.
[3] Rfmhd: right maximum femoral head diameter.
[4] Lfmhd: left maximum femoral head diameter.
[5] Rmfm: right maximum femoral midshaft diameter.
[6] Lmfm: left maximum femoral midshaft diameter.

Table 15 Raw osteometrical data for tibiae and fibulae for juveniles and adults.

Tomb	Room	Burial	Context	Rtml[1]	Ltml[2]	Rtmn[3]	Ltmn[4]	Rttd[5]	Lttd[6]	Rfbml[7]	Lfbml[8]
1	1		45	350	349	27	28	19	19	332	332
1	1		45	350		27		19			
1	1		45		349		27		20		
1	1		45								330
1	1		45							331	
1	1		45								346
1	2		24							90	
1	2	3		356						350	341
1	2	1		158	157					155	154
1	3	10	86	416	418	38	37	24	25		
1	3	4a		394	397	34	34	21	21	381	384
1	3	6								387	385
1	3	4b		394	398	34	34	21	21	381	384
1	3	10		413	415	38	37	24	24	403	
1	3	5a									326
1	3	5b				32	34	24	23	387	385
1	4		58	363		29		21			
1	4	7	60		355		30		20		340
1	4	11	62							407	
1	4	7			355		30		20		340
1	4	8		363		28		21			
1	4	11									407
1	6	14	102		181						
1	6	17		94						91.41	
2	1		44								256
2	4	8		401		34		23		395	
2	4	8			363		29		21		
2	4	8									345

[1] Rtml: right maximum tibial length.
[2] Ltml: left maximum tibial length.
[3] Rtmn: right maximum tibial diameter at nutrient foramen.
[4] Ltmn: left maximum tibial diameter at nutrient foramen.

[5] Rttd: right minimum tibial diameter at nutrient foramen.
[6] Lttd: right minimum tibial diameter at nutrient foramen.
[7] Rfbml: right maximum fibular length.
[8] Lfbml: left maximum fibular length.

Acknowledgements

We thank the Egyptian Supreme Council of Antiquities and members of the Dakhleh Oasis Project. In particular we thank A. J. and L. Mills, for their continuous support and taking care of the many logistics that go into running a project of this magnitude. We also thank Drs C. A. Hope and G. E. Bowen for their assistance in understanding tomb architecture and use patterns. Thanks also to Drs E. Molto and P. Sheldrick. We also thank C. Maggiano for his work on data entry. Various aspects of this research were supported by the Wenner-Gren Foundation for Anthropological Research, a SSHRC regular grant and a SSHRC doctoral fellowship (MWT) and the University of Central Florida.

Authors' Addresses:

Tosha L. Dupras
Department of Sociology and Anthropology
University of Central Florida
Orlando, Florida 32816
U. S. A.
tdupras@pegasus.cc.ucf.edu

Matthew W. Tocheri
Department of Anthropology
Arizona State University
Tempe, Arizona 85287-2402
U. S. A.
matt.tocheri@asu.edu

REFERENCES

Anderson, M., M. B. Messner and W. T. Green, 1964 Distribution of lengths of the normal femur and tibia from one to eighteen years of age, *Journal of Bone and Joint Surgery*, 46A, 1197–202.

Bass, W. M., 1995 *Human Osteology: A Laboratory and Field Manual*, 4th Edition, Missouri Archaeological Society, Columbia.

Birrell, M., 1999 Excavations in the Cemeteries of Ismant el-Kharab, in C. A. Hope and A. J. Mills, eds, *Dakhleh Oasis Project: Preliminary Reports of the 1992–1993 and 1993–1994 Field Seasons*, Oxbow Books, Oxford, 29–42.

Bowen, G. E., 1998 *The Spread of Christianity in Egypt in Light of Recent Discoveries from Ancient Kellis*, unpublished Ph.D. Dissertation, Monash University, Australia.

Brooks, S. T. and J. M. Suchey, 1990 Skeletal age determination based on the os pubis: A comparison of the Acsadi-Nemeskeri and Suchey-Brooks Methods, *Human Evolution* 5, 227–38.

Dupras, T. L., 1999 *Dining in the Dakhleh Oasis, Egypt: Determination of Diet from Documents and Stable Isotope Analysis*, unpublished Ph.D. Dissertation, McMaster University, Canada.

Hope, C. A., this volume The Excavations at Ismant el-Kharab from 2000 to 2002, 207–89.

Kaper, O. E., this volume The Decoration of North Tomb 1, 323–30.

Katz, D. and J. M. Suchey, 1986 Age determination of the male os pubis, *American Journal of Physical Anthropology* 69, 427–35.

Knudstad, J. E. and R. A. Frey, 1999 Kellis: The Architectural Survey of the Romano Byzantine Town at Ismant el-Kharab, in C. S. Churcher and A. J. Mills, eds, *Reports from the Survey of the Dakhleh Oasis 1977–1987*, Oxbow Books, Oxford, 189–214.

Maresh, M. M., 1970 Measurements from Roentgenograms, in R. W. McCammon, ed., *Human Growth and Development*, C. C. Thomas, Springfield, 157–200.

Molto, J. E., 2000 The comparative skeletal biology and palaeoepidemiology of the People from Ein Tirghi and Kellis, Dakhleh Oasis, Egypt, in C. A. Marlow and A. J. Mills, eds, *The Oasis Papers 1: The Proceedings of the First Conference of the Dakhleh Oasis Project*, Oxbow Books, Oxford, 81–100.

Molto, J. E., P. Sheldrick, A. Cerroni and S. Haddow, this volume Late Roman Period Human Skeletal Remains from Areas D/6 and D/7 and North Tomb 1 at Kellis, 345–63.

Scheuer, L. and S. Black, 2000 *Developmental Juvenile Osteology*, Academic Press, London.

Scheuer, J. L., J. H. Musgrave and S. P. Evans, 1980 The estimation of late fetal and perinatal age from limb bone length linear and logarithmic regression, *Annals of Human Biology* 7, 257–65.

Sherwood, R. J., R. S. Meindl, H. B. Robinson and R. L. May, 2000 Fetal age: Methods of estimation and effects of pathology, *American Journal of Physical Anthropology* 113, 305–15.

Tocheri, M. W., T. L. Dupras, P. Sheldrick and J. E. Molto, in press The Roman Period Fetal Skeletons of Kellis, Egypt, *International Journal of Osteoarchaeology*.

Preliminary Analysis of Human Skeletal Remains from South Tomb 4

Tosha L. Dupras and Matthew W. Tocheri

Introduction

A series of mud-brick tombs that appear to be arranged in two distinct clusters are located on the southern perimeter of Kellis. The South Tomb Group has approximately 15 tombs in total, however the second cluster of tombs is poorly preserved and there may have been more tombs that have been destroyed by wind erosion and water (Knudstad and Frey 1999, 212). The first cluster, consisting of Tombs 1 through 5, are the best preserved. Of these five tombs, South Tomb 4 is the largest and most well preserved.

First described by Knudstad and Frey (1999, 211–13), South Tomb 4 was excavated during the 2000–2001 field season (Hope this volume). It comprises a T-shaped porch, Room 4, which provides access to a transverse room that was divided into two areas of unequal size, Rooms 1 and 2; another transverse room, Room 3, lies to their south (Figure 1). Unlike the tombs excavated in the North Tomb series, there is no major use of stone in South Tomb 4 and only minimal evidence of plaster survives. Artefacts discovered in South Tomb 4 included items that could be dated between the second and third centuries CE (Hope this volume).

Room 3 was found to have been heavily burnt at some point in the past, similar to what was observed in North Tombs 1 and 2. Throughout the tomb human remains were found to be very disturbed, fragmentary and in varying states of preservation including burnt fragments. Due to the disturbed nature of the human remains, description of burial treatment and orientation is not possible.

Skeletal Analysis

Throughout South Tomb 4, human remains were found to be badly disturbed and fragmentary, resulting in significant commingling of individual remains. None of the individuals were recovered as distinct burials during excavation. Due to the commingled nature of the tomb, skeletal analysis was undertaken as one would when dealing with an ossuary type burial in which skeletal remains are secondarily deposited into a mass burial and significant commingling occurs. As witnessed during the excavations of North Tombs 1 and 2, the ossuary nature of South Tomb 4 was not due to customary burial practices; rather tomb reuse by later populations and/or grave robbing is the likely cause. Analysis included an examination of all fragments from each room, identifying bone, side, age and sex when possible. Although pathological conditions were noted, they are not discussed in this paper. Because the remains were highly fragmented and/or burnt, it was only possible to reconstruct a minimum number of individuals (MNI) for each room, and a total for the entire tomb.

Room 1 revealed three contexts, 2, 6 and 7, that contained human remains. The condition of the remains ranges from highly fragmentary and burnt to complete bones with some desiccated tissue. All remains recovered from the north-western corner in Context 6 were burnt. Based on duplication of skeletal elements and maturity, there appears to be a MNI of four in Room 1. There are two atlases present, that is, the first cervical vertebra, both are completely fused, indicating a minimum of two adults. Also within the room are various bones from a juvenile and an infant.

Human remains were recovered from Context 2 in Room 2. Two crania represent the only duplication of skeletal material in this room. The crania give us an indication of the possible sex and age of the individuals in the room. The first cranium represents an adult male, based on the presence of square eye orbits and a protruding brow ridge. The other skull represents an older juvenile, approximately 15 years of age based on the eruption of the second molars, the absence of the third molars, and little to no wear on the second molars. This skull is gracile in build, has round eye orbits and sharp supraorbital ridges, suggesting a female, but given that

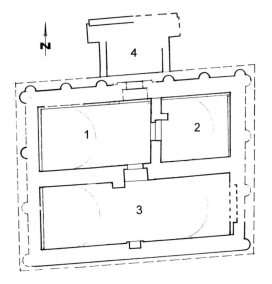

Figure 1 Architectural plan of South Tomb 4 with new room numbers illustrated (adpted from Knudstad and Frey 1999; Hope personal communication).

this individual is still a juvenile an estimation of sex is problematic.

The preservation of the human remains from Room 3 ranges from desiccated to fragmentary skeletal elements. No burnt remains were found in this room. Remains were excavated from Context 2 and from the north-eastern corner of the room. Skeletal elements represent a MNI of seven. There are four complete left adult humeri, two complete right juvenile clavicles, and several skeletal elements from an infant. In addition there are two adult crania, one male, with soft tissue features present, and one female, based on the presence of round eye orbits, a vertical forehead, parietal bossing, and the absence of brow ridges.

When each room is examined independently, there is a MNI of 11, seven adults and four juveniles. Because of the disturbed nature of the tomb, however, it is imperative that all skeletal elements are considered as a unit as commingling in and between rooms is likely to have occurred. When examining all the remains from the entire tomb the MNI is less than if each room is considered separately. Recurrence of skeletal elements indicates a MNI of six adults based on the presence of six left adult humeri. Two right clavicles indicate the presence of two juvenile individuals, and multiple skeletal elements represent one infant. Of these individuals, the cranial elements indicate that two of the adults are males and one is female and one of the juveniles is approximately 15 years. Unfortunately it is impossible to reconstruct the age of most individuals, as the most diagnostic skeletal elements are damaged or unavailable for analysis. In total, there is a MNI of nine represented in South Tomb 4.

The highly fragmentary nature of the remains made it possible to only obtain one long bone measurement from an intact femur (266 mm). The femoral length suggests that it most likely belongs to a juvenile individual between 5 and 6 years old (Anderson *et al.* 1964, 1199; Maresh 1970, 57–65; Scheuer and Black 2000, 394–5).

Summary

Excavation of South Tomb 4 uncovered highly fragmentary and commingled remains throughout the tomb. As witnessed in other tombs in Kellis (Dupras and Tocheri, this volume), the likelihood that skeletal remains were scattered throughout the tomb is high, and therefore complicates the skeletal analysis. In conditions such as these it is very difficult to reconstruct individuals and most often only information regarding the MNI can be obtained. All remains were examined in an attempt to identify the element and side of each fragment, as well as estimating the sex and age of the individual to which it belonged in order to provide a demographic profile of who was buried in South Tomb 4.

The occurrence of multiple skeletal elements within South Tomb 4 revealed a MNI of nine, six adults, two juveniles and one infant. Skeletal evidence indicates that two of the adults are male and one is female. Although there are no diagnostic skeletal elements present to provide a good estimate of age at death, all three of the adult crania appear to represent middle-aged adults, based on dental wear and suture closure. Due to the unavailability of appropriate skeletal elements for the determination of age, only two of the juveniles were assigned an age. One of the juveniles is approximately 15 and the other is between 5 and 6 years of age. Although fetal skeletal remains have been identified in North Tomb 1 and the Kellis 2 cemetery (Tocheri and Molto 2002; Tocheri *et al.* in press; Dupras and Tocheri, this volume), the youngest individual in South Tomb 4 is an infant likely to have been under one year at the time of death.

Acknowledgements

We thank the Egyptian Supreme Council of Antiquities and members of the Dakhleh Oasis Project for making this research possible. In particular we thank A. J. and L. Mills, for their continuous support and taking care of the many logistics that go into running a project of this magnitude. We also thank Drs C. A. Hope and G. E. Bowen for their assistance in understanding tomb architecture and use patterns. Thanks also to Drs E. Molto and P. Sheldrick. We also thank C. Maggiano for his work on data entry. This research was supported by the Wenner-Gren Foundation for Anthropological Research, aSSHRC regular grant and a SSHRC doctoral fellowship (MWT) and the University of Central Florida.

Authors' Addresses:

Tosha L. Dupras
Department of Sociology and Anthropology
University of Central Florida
Orlando,
Florida 32816,
U. S. A.

tdupras@pegasus.cc.ucf.edu

Matthew W. Tocheri
Department of Anthropology
Arizona State University
Tempe,
Arizona 85287-2402,
U. S. A.

matt.tocheri@asu.edu

REFERENCES

Anderson, M., M. B. Messner and W. T. Green, 1964 Distribution of lengths of the normal femur and tibia from one to eighteen years of age, *Journal of bone and Joint Surgery*, 46A, 1197–202.

Dupras, T. L. and M. W. Tocheri, this volume Preliminary Analysis of the Human Skeletal Remains from North Tombs 1 and 2, 183–96.

Hope, C. A., this volume The Excavations at Ismant el-Kharab from 2000 to 2002, 207–89.

Knudstad, J. E. and R. A. Frey, 1999 Kellis: The Architectural Survey of the Romano Byzantine Town at Ismant el-Kharab, in C. S. Churcher and A. J. Mills, eds, *Reports from the Survey of the Dakhleh Oasis 1977–1987*, Oxbow Books, Oxford, 189–214.

Maresh, M. M., 1970 Measurements from Roentgenograms, in R. W. McCammon, ed., *Human Growth and Development*, C. C. Thomas, Springfield.

Scheuer, L. and S. Black, 2000 *Developmental Juvenile Osteology*, Academic Press, London.

Tocheri, M. W. and J. E. Molto, 2002 Ageing Fetal and Juvenile Skeletons from Roman Period Egypt using Basiocciput Osteometrics, *International Journal of Osteoarchaeology* 12, 356–63.

Tocheri, M. W., T. L. Dupras, P. Sheldrick and J. E. Molto, in press The Roman Period Fetal Skeletons of Kellis, Egypt, *International Journal of Osteoarchaeology*.

Report on the editing of both the Coptic and the Manichaean Texts from Ismant el-Kharab

Iain Gardner

I have entitled this the 'Report on the editing of both the Coptic and the Manichaean texts'; this is because the linguistic and the religious delineations of my charge on behalf of the Dakhleh Oasis Project are by no means the same. As regards the definition 'from Ismant el-Kharab', this is by necessity as there has been little of substance in the way of Coptic texts, and certainly no Manichaean, yet found by our Project elsewhere in the Oasis. It remains to be seen if future work will expand this focus; I certainly hope so, as we are in real need of comparative data by which to judge what we have at present. In any case, in this report I will briefly summarize the progress with editing and publication, and then turn to discussion of the trajectories of this research as they point towards the future.

1. Progress with Editing and Publication

It would be reasonable to state that we are at a half-way stage with the publishing of both the Coptic and the Manichaean texts, and are substantially ahead of this as regards the foundational editorial work. I can only refer, of course, to what has already been uncovered by the archaeological work. Two 'series' of text volumes have been envisaged by myself and have been initiated, that is *Kellis Literary Texts* and *Coptic Documentary Texts from Kellis*. The first volume in the literary series was published in 1996 (= P.Kell. II, Gardner 1996) and the first in the documentary series late in 1999 (= P.Kell. V, Gardner *et al.* 1999). For an overall view of the papyrological work, it is probably helpful to think of Klaas Worp's *Greek Papyri from Kellis* as a third 'series', and the first volume there appeared in 1995 (= P.Kell. I, Worp 1995). I leave out of discussion here the publication of major codices in

individual volumes, namely the Kellis Isocrates Codex and the Kellis Agricultural Account Book, which appeared as P.Kell. III (Worp and Rijksbaron 1997) and IV (Bagnall 1997). Thus, in these three series one is Coptic documentary, one is Greek documentary, and one is multilingual literary, the primary purpose here being to keep the Manichaean scriptures and other religious writings together.

My own charge is with the Coptic and the literary series. The next volume that I will complete and put forward for publication will be *Kellis Literary Texts II*. I expect to have this finalized by the end of 2002, though realistically one should not expect publication until 2003 at least. The major pieces that it will contain are: the reconstructed leaves from two codices identified as containing Mani's *Epistles*, in Coptic, jointly edited by Wolf-Peter Funk and myself; an amulet in the form of a miniature papyrus codex, edited by myself; the Manichaean 'Prayer of the Emanations'[1] and the 'Leaves from a Manichaean Codex',[2] in Greek, jointly edited by Klaas Worp and myself. There are also a number of small text fragments that can be identified as literary and which will be included; one of these is in Syriac. Publication of the volume will complete work on this series until such a time as new textual material of this type may be uncovered.

As regards the Coptic documentary series, much of the basic research for a second volume has already been completed. Fifty further discrete texts from House 3 have been selected as worthy of publication at this time, and a full listing of all Coptic fragments from House 3 (A/5) will be included. Thus, it should be expected that the second volume will be of a similar substance to the first, which contained 45 texts from A/1–5, that is everything

---

[1] An edition of this text has previously been published by R. G. Jenkins, The Prayer of the Emanations in Greek from Kellis (T. Kellis 22), *Le Muséon* 108 (1995), 243–63.

[2] An edition of this text has previously been published by Gardner and Worp, Leaves from a Manichaean Codex, *Zeitschrift für Papyrologie und Epigraphik* 117 (1997), 139–55, with discussion of the archaeological context by C. A. Hope following, 156–61.

from A/1–4 and a first selection from the major archive of A/5. Publication must be expected after 2004.

There still remains to account for the other Coptic material recovered from Ismant el-Kharab, mostly from House 4 (A/6), but also some small but important amount from the Main Temple area. Then, there are fragments recovered from elsewhere in the oasis by the Project during the initial survey period. These disparate pieces will perhaps be collected in a third volume of the series, together with whatever future excavations may uncover, but they could be included in the second.

2. Some Trajectories of Research

I will now turn to a discussion, perhaps of more broad interest, about some of the implications of this editorial work. I have become increasingly concerned to utilize the basic data, as provided by the textual discoveries, in order to push the boundaries of our understanding in the relevant fields of knowledge. I must emphasize that the textual discoveries from Ismant el-Kharab are exceptional; they are outstanding and they provide an opportunity to re-examine and perhaps even revolutionize a number of the most important ideas in Coptology, papyrology, codicology, Manichaeology etc. I cannot summarize this all here, but I will discuss three recent papers that I have written, two jointly with colleagues, in order to give evidence of some of the trajectories of my current and future research.

i). The 'Old Coptic' Ostrakon

One of the principal issues in Coptic studies is that of the origin of the Coptic language and script itself. If I may simplify a series of complex issues: we can be certain that the indigenous language of Egypt continued as spoken, but evolving as all languages do, throughout the Roman and Byzantine periods. However, the native scripts became increasingly unwieldy and restricted in usage, so that through, say, the second and the third centuries of the common era there was essentially an hiatus, between the demise of Demotic and the birth of Coptic, wherein the Egyptians had no proper means by which to write their own language. Coptic thus marks a re-birth of the writing of the language whereby an adapted Greek alphabet was utilized, supplemented by native letters derived from Demotic. Coptic is not just a script, however, it equally refers to the latter stages of the spoken indigenous language, marked in particular by changes to the lexicon, notably a massive influx of Greek loan words, and syntax.

Obviously, the reasons for these developments are a foundational issue for the study of Coptic. To simplify, again, the general thesis is that the development of Coptic was driven by an urban, and perhaps monastic, elite; and

was inextricably linked to the Christianisation of Egypt, as Coptic provided an ideal vehicle for the promotion of the scriptures and the faith to the speakers of the indigenous language. In particular, Christians may be supposed to have wanted to avoid the pagan associations of the native scripts.

To turn now to the data provided by the excavations at Ismant el-Kharab: in the first place, it was something of a surprise to discover, particularly from House 3, such a vibrant and varied, and, indeed, often secular, use of Coptic evidenced *circa* 360–380 CE in this provincial village. Various reasons might be posited for this, for example, the Manichaean or trading context might have been an especial encouragement to native literacy, but the general lack of securely-dated comparative sites makes such arguments somewhat speculative. In any case, I am more concerned at this moment with the diachronic issue, that is to trace the rise, spread, type, etc, of Coptic usage through its formative period. As regards this, Coptologists count a particular category of texts as 'Old Coptic' (given the sigla OC or O), by which they may be understood to mean a phase between the simple transcription of Egyptian words, commonly proper names, into Greek letters and mature Coptic with its mostly standardized alphabet, orthography and lexicon, leaving aside the question of dialectical variation here. This transitional phase, 'Old Coptic', is marked in particular by variation in the number and form of the letters adapted from Demotic, and these generally remain closer to their Demotic prototypes than the standardized script of mature Coptic. We may say, then, that Old Coptic represents a number of competing systems for writing the language that were trialled during the formative period before standardization was achieved.

Ever since the start of my work for the Dakhleh Oasis Project I had been 'on watch' for any discoveries that might help to illuminate that curious transition or void between Demotic, which is also present at Ismant el-Kharab, and the fluid Coptic that had been found in some abundance. In January 1997 Colin Hope, excavating in the north-western corner of the Inner Temenos of the Main Temple, recovered an ostrakon from a barrel-vault that could reasonably be dated, from contextual and material evidence, to the later third century. The text is very short and can not be completely read; whilst the content, a brief personal message of greeting, is of no particular importance in itself. However, it is apparent that it is written in an Old Coptic script, I emphasize that the designation OC in fact refers to a variety of unsuccessful and presumably competing writing systems, and that the lexicon must be understood to pre-date that of mature Coptic.[3] Most obviously, the number of the letters derived from Demotic differs from that of the standardized alphabet, and in their forms they are noticeably closer to their origins.

---

[3] Most important is the use of the word ϭⲣⲱⲧ which can now be identified as a part of the OC lexicon that was rendered obsolete in the face of ϣⲏⲣⲉ throughout the southern dialect regions.

One further point needs to be emphasized: until this time all known Old Coptic texts were of pagan magical or astrological content. I now quote from the conclusion to the article I have recently published on this ostrakon (Gardner 1999), in order to highlight what I take to be the extraordinary importance of this piece.

OC was not simply a rather restricted attempt to write out a number of pagan religious (magical and astrological) texts; but rather refers to a number of competing systems for writing the emerging Coptic language. These could be used for purely secular purposes, and (as indeed the substantial finds of fourth-century Coptic documentary texts from Ismant el-Kharab also evidence) the dominant role generally assumed for temple and church in the collapse of Demotic and rise of Coptic may need to be reassessed. Whether the triumph of a standardized Coptic orthography, and the demise of its rivals, was exactly linked to the process of Christianisation (and what exactly Christianisation might mean in view of the evident promotion of Coptic by Manichaean missions) remains to be confirmed. If that were so, then the piece published here would be a most rare remnant of pagan Coptic from prior to the (complete) evangelisation of the oasis.

ii). The Coptic Palaeography Project

From the above discussion it can be seen that I hope to utilize the data recovered from the Ismant el-Kharab excavations in order to develop substantially our understanding of the development of Coptic, and to challenge some of the common assumptions or arguments about fundamental matters. My second example continues this theme, and refers to a project I have initiated in collaboration with Malcolm Choat. A first discussion paper concerning this project was read to the International Association of Coptic Studies conference in Leiden (2000), and will be published in the proceedings volume (Gardner and Choat, in press).

Palaeography is the science of studying the development of writing systems, and has been much advanced and utilized by Greek papyrologists as one of their major dating mechanisms. However, the science has hardly been developed as regards Coptic studies, and this is a crucial lack for Coptic papyrology. A principal problem has been the limited material available that could be securely dated to the early period of the language's development. The palaeography project, then, has as its ultimate aim the goal of establishing a scientific palaeography for Coptic. Such an holistic study, however, would be a massive undertaking; and at this early stage we prefer to focus on the more modest ambition of working with documentary hands prior to 400 CE. Of course, I am in an ideal situation for this, because the majority of securely-dated material of this type and date in fact derives from Ismant el-Kharab, material which I am in the process of editing. Thus, the basic aim is to make a systematic study of Coptic documentary

palaeography prior to 400 CE, essentially almost all in fact from the fourth century; but I should emphasize that this basic aim is foundational to a more far-reaching re-evaluation of the development of Coptic as a language, and has major social implications as regards issues such as literacy, dialect and religious affiliation in Romano-Byzantine Egypt.

In order to explain this, I will now summarize in brief three of the essential building blocks of the argument that Malcolm Choat and I put forward in our paper to the Leiden conference. I will not here evidence the actual details of the data upon which these are based.

a) Our provisional study, aided by access to the Ismant material, suggests that what had previously been identified as the distinctive fourth century Coptic hand is, in fact, only one of a much wider variety of styles that were employed contemporaneously. Thus, with the availability now of a greater range of material, a proper typology of fourth century Coptic documentary palaeography can be established, and this has the potential for redating extant material of unknown provenance.

b) Previous study of Coptic palaeography had emphasized the divergence in orthography between Greek and Coptic, and thus rendered Greek palaeography of dubious value for any understanding of Coptic. Our study will show that there were more cursive types of Coptic hands, and that some scribes would switch between the two languages without altering their script. This has the potential to reintegrate the study of Greek and Coptic palaeography, the latter having been cast unnecessarily adrift by earlier assumptions.

c) At Ismant el-Kharab we find important correlations between dialect and script, with the previously-dominant fourth century paradigm now able to be identified as the orthography of emerging standardized Sahidic, and which in the Ismant corpus is rivalled by the widespread use of a Lycopolitan *koine*. Furthermore, these correlations in the corpus can be extended to issues of religious affiliation, text type, lexicon and find site. This has massive implications for our understanding of the development of rival Coptics, their social usage contexts, and consequently for an understanding of the social and cultural change in fourth-century Egypt that resulted in a certain dominant paradigm. I must emphasize this point, which I regard as very exciting. We have here potentially a new tool for understanding the forces that transformed Romano-Byzantine Egypt: Coptic usages themselves may reveal the social and cultural worlds of their authors to an extent that has not previously been envisaged.

iii). P. Harr. 107

Finally, I will now illustrate how the Ismant material can be utilized to reclassify previously known texts, to advance research as regards other archives, and even to solve long established problems.

In 1999, Alanna Nobbs and Malcolm Choat, both of whom are working on the 'Corpus of Christian Papyri' project at Macquarie University, and knowing of my work on the identification of Manichaean documents, such as personal letters, from late antiquity, brought this text to my attention. P. Harr. 107 is a personal letter written in Greek that was originally published in 1936, in the Rendel Harris volume of papyri of unknown provenance edited by J. Enoch Powell.[4] It reads:

> To my most honoured mother Maria, from Besas, many greetings in God.
> Before all things: I pray to the Father, the God of Truth, and to the Paraclete Spirit, that they may preserve you in soul, body and spirit; for the body health, for the spirit joy, and for the soul life eternal. Whoever you find coming my way, do not hesitate to write to me about your health, so that I might hear and rejoice. Do not fail to send me the cloak for the pascha festival; and send my brother to me.
> I greet my father and my brothers. I pray for your health for many years.

Powell had dated the document, on palaeographic grounds, to the third century, with a query. Subsequently, H. I. Bell (1944, 197) dated the text to the same.[5] The papyrus has always attracted some degree of interest, not least because it has been considered possibly the earliest Christian letter; though the absence of any reference to the Son, alongside the prayer to the Father and Spirit, did call for some explanation. Origenist thinking, gnostic speculation and a Jewish background were all considered.[6] The Manichaean possibility could not be seriously explored, though believers identified Mani himself, in his spiritual persona, as the 'Paraclete' whose coming was foretold by Jesus, because of the considered opinion that the papyrus was best placed in the first half of third century; and because of the lack of comparative material.

Of course, Manichaean authorship would be inconceivable before the latter third century, with the first Manichaean mission perhaps reaching Alexandria about 260 CE. However, Malcolm Choat had already begun to cast doubts on the traditional early date given to the piece, and this opened the possibility of a Manichaean author; this together, of course, with the fact that the Ismant material now allows us to know what a Manichaean letter might look like! Consequently, I compared P. Harr. 107 with Coptic letters that I had identified as Manichaean, and which were not yet published at that stage, and immediately one can discern a characteristic formula whereby the author opens his letter with a prayer to the Father, 'the God of Truth'; this is known Manichaean

nomenclature, but can not be supposed unique to that religion. Here are four of the most obvious examples, three now published in P.Kell. V:

P.Kell. V Copt. 25, 12–22 (Matthaios to his mother Maria): 'This is my prayer to the Father, the God of Truth, and his beloved Son the Christ, and his Holy Spirit, and his light angels: That he will watch over you together, you being healthy in your body, joyful in heart and rejoicing in soul and spirit, all the time we will pass in the body, free from any evil and any temptation by Satan and any sickness of the body'.

P.Kell. V Copt. 29, 7–13 (Piene to his mother Maria, the same as above): 'This is my prayer every hour to the Father, the God of Truth: That he may preserve you healthy in your body, joyful in your soul and firm [in] your spirit; for all the time that you [will] spend in this place. Also, after this place, you may find life in the kingdom for eternity'.

P.Kell. V Copt. 32, 19–24 (unnamed male author to the catechumen Eirene): 'I am praying that you may continue in health of the body, and gladness of the spirit, and joy of the soul, until we see you again'.

P81C, II. 4–9 (Pamour to his sister Partheni): 'Before everything I pray to the Father, the God of Truth: That you will live for me a long time and a great period; being healthy in body, flourishing in soul, and rejoicing in spirit, safe from all the temptations of Satan ...'.

For further discussion of this text and the formula I refer to the published article by Gardner, Nobbs and Choat (2000); but the conclusion to this research, of course, is that possibly the earliest known Christian letter can now be reclassified as probably the earliest known Manichaean document of any kind!

Author's Address:
Department of Studies in Religion
Woolley Building (A20)
University of Sydney,
N. S. W. 2006,
Australia

---

[4] See now M. Naldini, Il Cristianesimo in Egitto. Lettere private nei papiri dei secoli ii–iv, Le Monnier, Firenze, 1998[2], number 5, 76–8 and 427.

[5] This date, and the judgment that the papyrus was Christian, was endorsed by C. H. Roberts, *Manuscript, Society and Belief in Early Christian Egypt*, Oxford University Press for the British Academy, London (1979), 1, note 2.

[6] A. Nobbs has previously discussed (with a bibliography) the reasons for considering a Christian attribution, see Emmett, 1985 A. M. Emmett, The concept of spirit in papyrus letters of the third and fourth century: problems posed by P. Harr. 107, *Prudentia*, supplement (1985), 73–9.

REFERENCES

Bagnall, R. S., ed., 1997 *The Kellis Agricultural Account Book*, Oxbow Books, Oxford.

Bell, H. I., 1944 Evidences of Christianity in Egypt during the Roman Period, *Harvard Theological Review* 37, 185–208.

Gardner, I., ed., 1996 *Kellis Literary Texts Volume 1*, Oxbow Books, Oxford.

Gardner, I., 1999 An Old Coptic Ostracon from Ismant el-Kharab?, *Zeitschrift für Papyrologie und Epigraphik* 125, 195–200.

Gardner, I., A. Alcock and W–P. Funk, eds, 1999 *Coptic Documentary Texts from Kellis Volume 1*, Oxbow Books, Oxford.

Gardner, I. and M. Choat, in press, Towards a Palaeography of Fourth Century Documentary Coptic, in J. van der Vliet and M. Immerzeel, eds, *Acts of the VIIth International Coptic Congress, Leiden, 2000*, Peeters, Louvain.

Gardner, I., A. Nobbs and M. Choat, 2000 P. Harr. 107: Is this another Greek Manichaean letter?, *Zeitschrift für Papyrologie und Epigraphik* 131, 118–24.

Worp, K. A., ed., 1995 *Greek Papyri from Kellis: I*, Oxbow Books, Oxford.

Worp, K. A. and A. Rijksbaron, eds, 1997 *The Kellis Isocrates Codex*, Oxbow Books, Oxford.

The Excavations at Ismant el-Kharab from 2000 to 2002

Colin A. Hope

with contributions by Olaf E. Kaper and Helen Whitehouse, and an appendix by Olaf E. Kaper

At The Third International Dakhleh Oasis Project Conference I presented a discussion of the results of the excavations at Ismant el-Kharab, ancient Kellis of the Mothite Nome, during the 2000 season. Subsequently, two further excavation seasons have been conducted and I take the opportunity here to incorporate the results of those two seasons into this report, thus completing the preliminary reporting on the excavations at the site.[1] Preliminary reports on all three seasons have been published elsewhere (Hope 2000, 2001a; Hope et al. 2002), and the current report represents an amalgam of and an elaboration upon those discussions, with a more extensive range of illustrative material.

The three seasons of excavations described here were conducted between 9 January and 17 February 2000; 21 January and 10 February 2001; and 19 January and 28 January 2002. In each season work was undertaken in different parts of the site, however, the discussion that follows will present the data according to excavation area, sub-grouped according to season; all of these excavation areas are indicated on Figure 1. An exception to this is the reporting of the work in the Small East Church, which is described elsewhere by Gillian Bowen (Bowen this volume a). In addition to the excavation, significant progress was made in recording the backlog of ceramics, glass, textiles and other artefacts, throughout these seasons; this aspect of the work is not discussed here. Whilst much of the work formed a continuation of that which had been commenced in earlier seasons, such as within the Temple of Tutu and its associated structures, the residential complex immediately to its north-west, the East Church Complex and Area C, new work was commenced in the cemeteries located adjacent to the site.

Excavations within the Settlement

I Within the Temenos of the Temple of Tutu

Excavations within the Inner Temenos of the temple (Figure 2) were conducted in its north-western corner where a complex of magazines associated with a well are located, within the three rooms of Shrine I, two rooms of Shrine IV and in the south-eastern corner of the temple forecourt. Some clearance of surface sand from the eastern end of the forecourt also took place, though floor deposits were not reached.

I.1 North-Western Corner of the Inner Temenos: Area D/1

Previous excavation conducted within the north-western corner of the Inner Temenos, Area D/1 Zones XVIII–XX (Hope and Bowen 1997, 54–6; Hope 2002, 182–6), revealed the existence of three possible architectural phases of development:

1. an original barrel-vaulted, mud-brick room that appeared to have occupied most of the excavated area,
2. this room was then cut into for the building of a rectangular stone structure that may have been a well; its revealed dimensions were 5.65 x 3.50 m east-west by north-south and it abutted the walls of the earlier room, and finally,
3. the construction of storage chambers over the stone structure, surrounding an oval mud-brick well, which abutted the western and northern sections of the temenos wall. These chambers are below the floor of the rear court of the temple and access was provided by two stairways; some flimsy brick structures were erected at floor level. Red clay dredged out from the earlier well was found below the floors of the lower chambers.

---

[1] The contributions to this report by Kaper and Whitehouse comprise the description of the excavations in Room 2 of Shrine I in 2002, for which see also Hope et al. 2002, while the descriptions of the decorative scheme of Room 1 of that shrine are based upon information provided by Kaper.

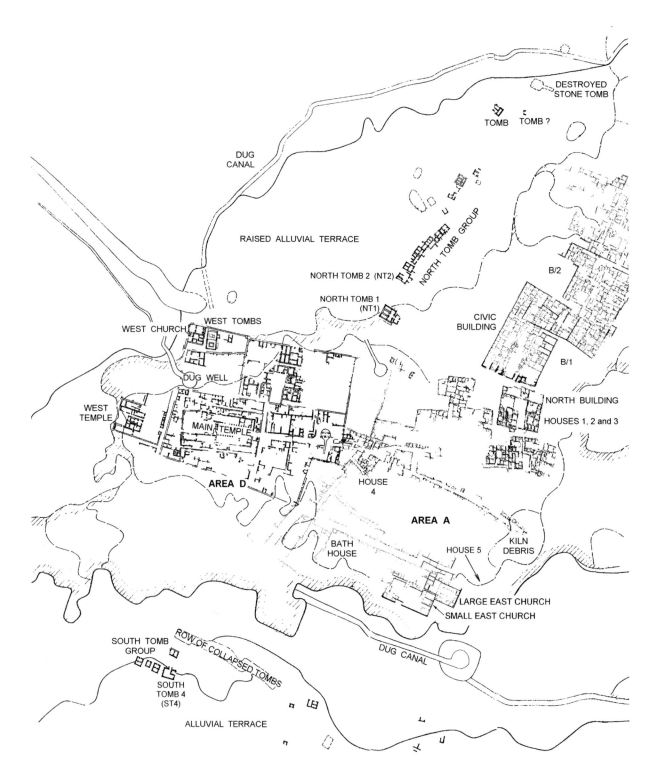

Figure 1 Plan of Ismant el-Kharab showing main excavation areas (original drawing by J. E. Knudstad

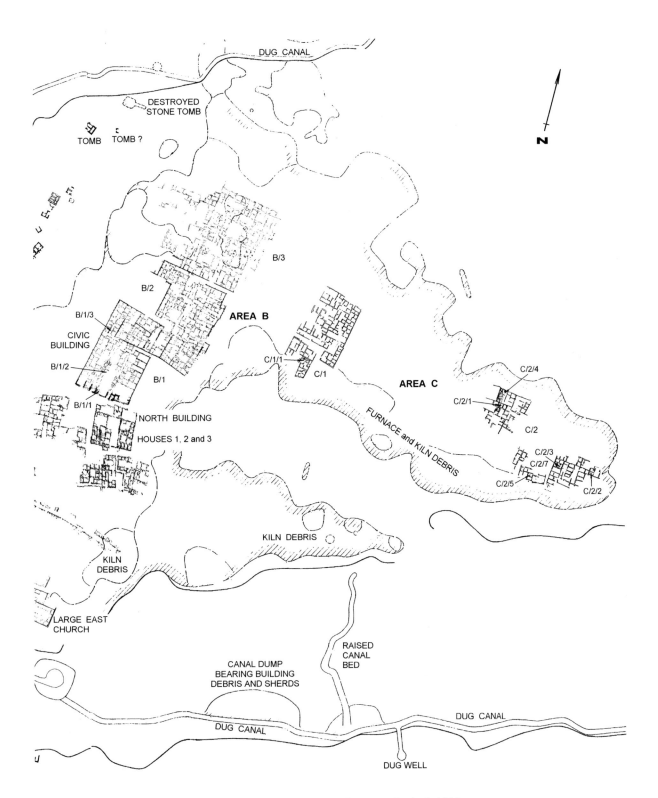

supplemented by J. Dobrowolski and B. Rowney and compiled by B. Parr). Scale 1:4000.

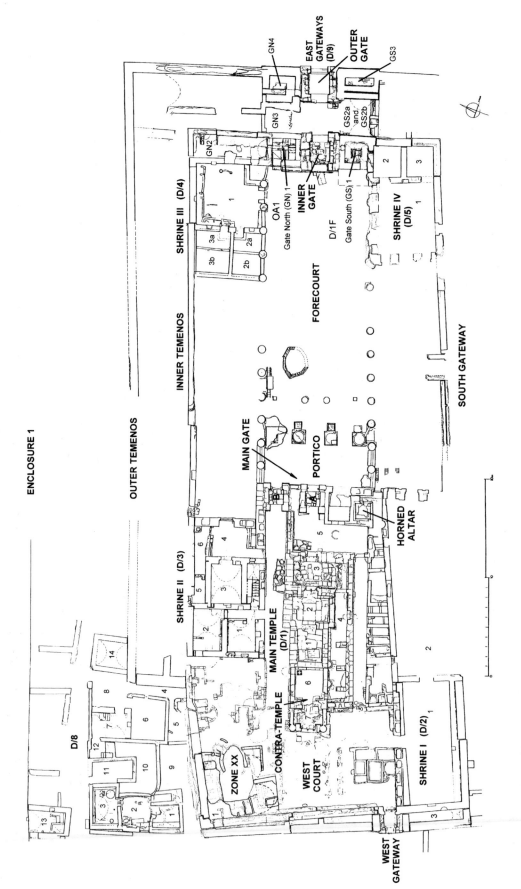

Figure 2 Plan of the Main Temple Complex and associated structures (original drawing by J. E. Knudstad supplemented by J. Dobrowolski and B. Rowney).

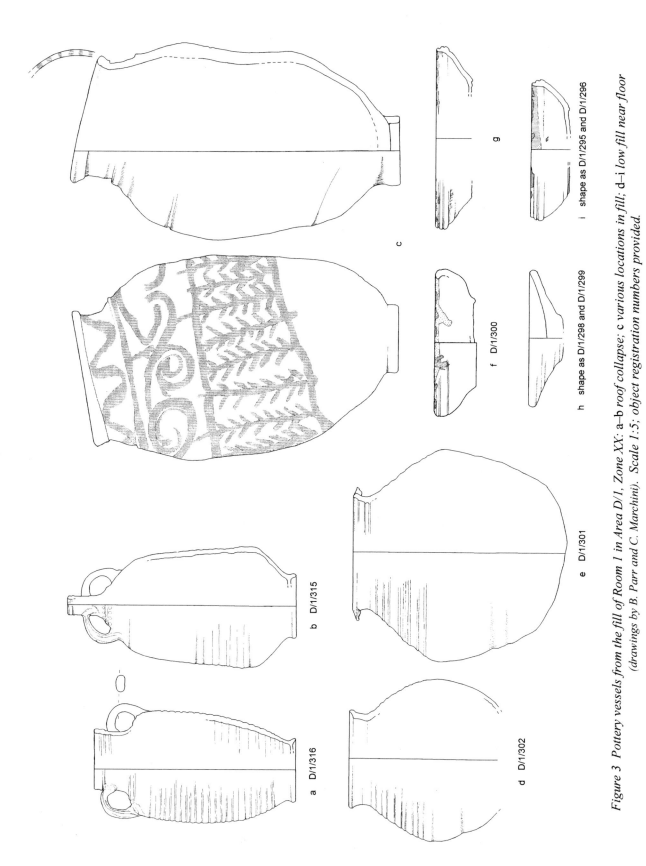

Figure 3 Pottery vessels from the fill of Room 1 in Area D/1, Zone XX: a–b roof collapse; c various locations in fill; d–i low fill near floor (drawings by B. Parr and C. Marchini). Scale 1:5; object registration numbers provided.

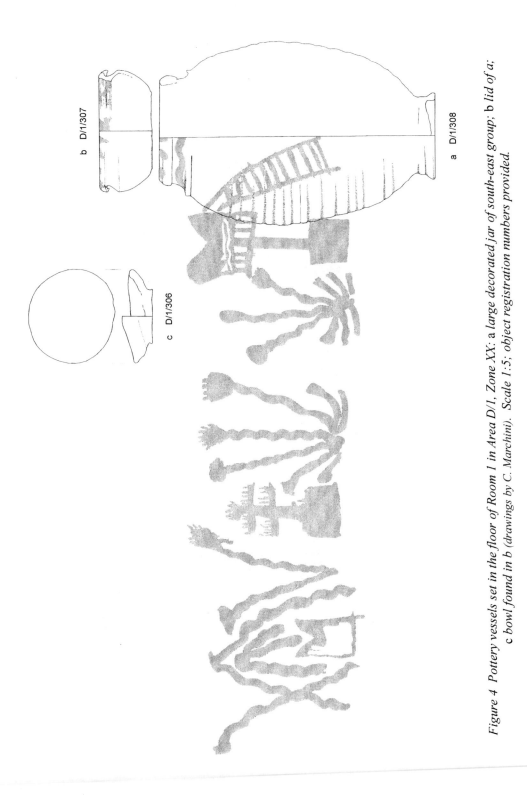

Figure 4 Pottery vessels set in the floor of Room 1 in Area D/1, Zone XX: a large decorated jar of south-east group; b lid of a; c bowl found in b (drawings by C. Marchini). Scale 1:5; object registration numbers provided.

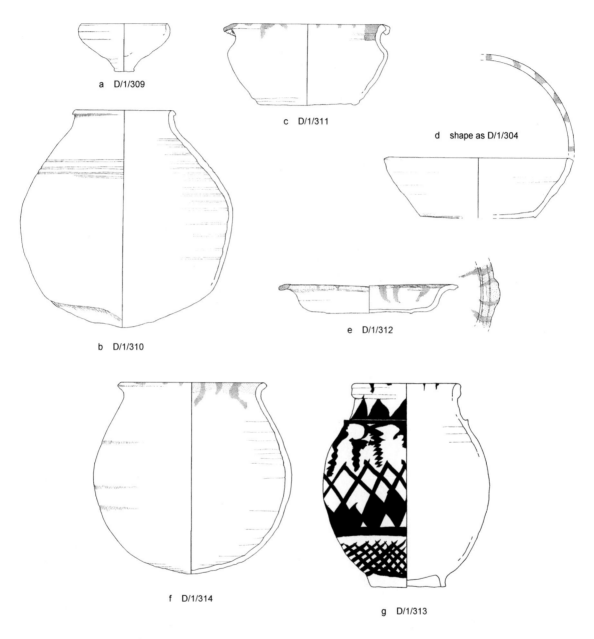

a   D/1/309

c   D/1/311

d   shape as D/1/304

b   D/1/310

e   D/1/312

f   D/1/314

g   D/1/313

*Figure 5 Pottery vessels set into floor of Room 1, Area D/1, Zone XX: a–b jar and lid, north-eastern group;
c lid from north-western group; d shape of lid from south-western group; e lid of group west of the bench;
f–j jars found below Tutu Stela, east of pottery vessels (drawings by B. Parr).
Scale 1:4; object registration numbers provided.*

*Plate 1 North-west corner of Inner Temenos showing pottery vessels in the floor of Room 1 of Area D/1,
Zone XX; looking north.*

*Plate 2 Remains of mud-brick wall built atop stone wall revealed beneath floor of Room 1 of Area D/1, Zone XX,
and rectangular bin in which pottery vessels were set; looking south.*

Mud seals with impressions of Nemesis (Hope 2002, 187, plate 9), found at the entrance to one of the lower rooms, showed that these rooms were contemporary with the use of the temple in the celebration of the cult of Tutu, currently believed to have lasted until the second quarter of the fourth century CE,[2] whilst pottery from the rooms could be ascribed to the late third or early fourth century (Dunsmore 2002, 129–31). As the depth of the oval well had not been determined and parts of the lower chambers awaited examination, and the sequence outlined above needed further confirmation, it was decided to excavate in this area. In the 2000 season it was not possible to determine the depth of the well and work focused upon the excavation of the remaining lower chamber. It may be noted that the mud-brick oval structure was identified as a well rather than some other feature, such as a grain silo, because of its depth and the apparent inaccessibility of the lower part, and the emplacement for a cross beam in its upper wall.[3] Further, the reason for locating a silo within the Inner Temenos of the Main Temple might be questioned, whereas a facility for the provision of water for ablutions and offerings in such a location is understandable. That water was accessible in this part of the site is shown by the discovery of the edge of a probable well in Area D/8 immediately to the north (Hope 2002, 202, plate 22). If the identification of the oval mud-brick structure as a well is correct then it is assumed that its lowest courses will be of stone.

The lower chamber that was explored, numbered 1, is located within the north-western corner of the area; it measures 2.18 m east-west by 1.05 m north-south. Its roof had fallen into the chamber and pottery vessels that were once on the roof had been tipped into the chamber; others were found on the floor level (Figure 3). All of these appear to be of fourth-century date. In addition, there was a quantity of sherds from formed, but unfired, vessels and also a piece of a glass ingot.[4] The floor of the room, like those to its east, was of compacted earth, and it had a low mud bench 1.28 m long against the southern wall, in which there were four depressions and part of a fifth at the eastern end (Plate 1). A large decorated jar was set into the floor of the room adjacent to the western end of the bench and against the western temenos wall; its

mouth had originally been closed with a bowl (Plate 1, Figure 5e). Four other large jars were also set into the floor of the western end of the room, and again their mouths had been closed with bowls (Plate 1, Figure 5a–e).[5] Two of these jars are of the same decorated type as that found at the western end of the bench, and the most elaborate one is illustrated here (Figure 4a); another example was found in the fill of the room (Figure 3c). The other two are undecorated and of similar shape (Figure 5b). The lower parts of these jars were located within a pit, the walls of which were formed by the northern and western temenos walls, a narrow wall on the south, 46 cm long formed from bricks laid on their edges, and an eastern wall 61 cm from the western temenos wall (Plate 2). This pit had a plastered floor at 71 cm below the floor of the room; together with its pots and the vessel at the western end of the bench, it was put in place before the bench.

This installation may be ascribed to the late third to fourth century on the basis of the morphology and decoration of the ceramic vessels, the use of the area in general while the temple functioned for the veneration of Tutu[6] and the architecture of the installation itself (see below). The large decorated jars are especially diagnostic. They are made in a low-fired fabric containing numerous limestone inclusions that is very porous; the decoration is on a cream surface and executed in red paint before firing. Such vessels are a regular feature of the ceramic assemblage across the site, and on present evidence, principally context and association with coins and dated texts, appear to be restricted to the late third to fourth century. Whilst the format of the decoration on such jars is similar, no two have the same decorative scheme (Dunsmore 2002, 137–9).

Unfortunately, there is no evidence for the function of the installation. All of the buried jars were empty on discovery; the fabric of the jars, as noted above, is porous and thus, presumably, they were not used for the storage of liquids for any length of time. There are no deposits on the interiors that might indicate original contents. It does seem, however, that we are dealing with some storage and distribution facility that is contemporary with the final phase of use of this part of the temple. It is of interest to note that large decorated jars of the type found buried in

---

[2] This estimate is based upon the occurrence of the name of a priest of Tutu, one Stonios, in a contract dated 335 (K. A. Worp, *Greek Papyri from Kellis*, Oxbow Books, Oxford,1995, number 13); for other texts from the temple relating to this person see K. A. Worp, Short Texts from the Temple of Tutu, in C. A. Hope and G. E. Bowen, eds, *Dakhleh Oasis Project: Preliminary Reports from the 1995–6 to 1998–9 Field Seasons*, Oxbow Books, Oxford, 2002.

[3] The dissimilarity to the grain storage facilities at contemporary Karanis may be noted (Boak and Peterson 1931, 18–23 and for the semi-public ones Husselman 1979, 56–62).

[4] Other fragmentary glass ingots have been found within a domestic context in a small room within the West Court of the temple, due east of the West Gateway (Figure 2; Hope 2002, 182); such material probably relates to the use of the temple enclosure for secular activity during the mid and late fourth century (Hope 2001b, 50–1).

[5] Similar large decorated jars were found buried in the floor of the D/8 domestic complex due north of this part of the Main Temple (Hope 2002, 202, Plate 20); the same practice was encountered at Karanis (Boak and Peterson 1931, 27, Figure 40; Husselman 1979, 23, Plate 7).

[6] Based upon the occurrence of the mud seals with the impression of Nemesis referred to above.

Plate 3 Room 1 of Area D/1, Zone XX, after removal of floor, showing mud-brick wall atop stone wall (foreground), and south wall of Room 1 (left) with part of roofing of the area to its south still in place; looking west.

Plate 4 Two parts of the Tutu stela set into the floor at the eastern end of Room 1, Area D/1, Zone XX; looking south.

Plate 5   Tutu Stela (D/1/294) from Room 1, Area D/1, Zone XX.

the floor of Room 1 have been found elsewhere on the site also set into floors, and it is apparent that the decoration does not relate to this function and, therefore, that we are encountering a secondary usage of these vessels. Whilst this is not the place to undertake a detailed analysis of the decorative motifs on such vessels, it is worth noting that in addition to linear and abstract motifs, what may be identified as palm fronds (Figure 3c; Dunsmore 2002, Figures 7b, 7d)[7] and items of cult paraphernalia (Figure 4a) do feature. This may imply that certain vessels were produced originally for ritual use.[8]

The floor of Room 1 and those to its east were removed. Under the compacted earth of the floor of Room 1 and the gypsum on compacted earth of the floors of the others, earlier features were immediately encountered. These show that the suggested phase 1 vaulted structure mentioned above was contemporary with the stone structure defined as phase 2, which served as a foundation or support for it (Plate 3). Thus the stone structure may not, as originally postulated, have been a well. Further, it would seem that the walls of this vaulted room probably abut both the western and northern temenos walls. The east wall of the pit with the pottery jars is a part of this early structure. When the storage chambers were constructed the early vaulted room was cut through so that some of their walls could be set on the underlying stone structure. It was then

necessary to refill the areas between the vault and the temenos walls to form a secure base for the floors of the new rooms. This was done with clay dredged from the sinking of the oval well. When this was done not only were the pit and bench constructed, but two other jars (Figures 5f–g) were completely buried in the north-eastern corner of Room 1, and their mouths sealed with the two halves of a small limestone stela depicting Tutu (Plate 4). Over the stela was placed a mud brick and then the floor was laid. Like all of the vessels from within the floor of Room 1, these two contained no indication of their original contents.

The stela (Plate 5; Registration Number 31/420-D6-1/ D/1/294), despite being broken, is in very good condition; it measures 31.0 x 22.0 x 3.7 cm. Tutu is shown in the form of a sphinx facing right with a lion's head attached at the rear of its human head. He wears a *nemes*-headcloth and a crown was once attached separately by a dowel into the upper edge of the piece. A crocodile's head emerges from his chest, his tail ends with a rearing cobra wearing the white crown and he is accompanied by a serpent. The lappets of the *nemes* are painted and there are two cross-bands painted on the body; the eyes of the cobra, serpent, crocodile, lion and Tutu were all originally inlaid, as was the body of the cobra. The inlays that survive are of blue, red and white glass. Tentatively, the piece is ascribed to

---

[7] The same motif occurs on other contemporary ceramic forms (Dunsmore 2002, Figures 1a–b, 6k).

[8] On the ritual usage of the palm rib in various religious ceremonies and as a symbol of fertility see Kaper 1997, 167–80, and Venit 2002, 155–6, Figures 132–3, 135. In addition to this, the occurrence of depictions of palm fronds within a funerary context in Dakhleh on coffins (for example Figure 24) and tomb walls should be noted. It occurs also on a variety of ceramic vessels and objects from the Old Kingdom and Second Intermediate Period.

Plate 6 North-eastern corner of Room 1 of the mammisi, *Area D/2; looking east.*

the first or second century CE; it is uncertain whether it had outlived its original function and was being used simply as a lid, or whether it may have been buried as a votive object despite, or because of, its broken state. It was certainly buried while the cult of Tutu still functioned within the temple.[9]

I.2 Shrine 1, Area D/2: the *Mammisi*

I.2.1 Room 1

In 2000 the excavation and study of Shrine I concentrated upon the lifting of the remaining roofing blocks from the central part of the eastern half of the Room 1 and the clearance to floor level of the north-eastern quarter.[10] Only the lifting of the lower blocks in the south-eastern quarter remains to complete the clearance of the inner room of this important structure. The most significant additions to our knowledge of the decoration of the room will be reviewed.

Centrally located within the northern wall of the shrine is a door communicating with the West Court of the Main Temple (Figure 2). Most of the decoration of its jambs has now been recovered, though the lower parts are blackened from the pouring of oil during ritual practice and from exposure to burning. They were decorated with

scenes of divinities who receive offerings: on one side are three goddesses including Tapshay, and on the other are three gods including Amon-Ra and Amon-nakht. The lintel carried a large depiction of a bird (unidentified) with outstretched wings and the reveals were inscribed with hymns to Tutu and Neith. Upon the cornice was a painting of a scarab with four wings and the cartouches of Tutu and Neith on the right and Tutu and Tapshay on the left.

Amongst the procession of the gods of Lower Egyptian nomes that adorned the northern upper register upon the vault in this part of the room, Sobek-Ra and Horus have been identified receiving offerings from Amon and Hathor. In the register below, which contains a long row of gods worshipping Tutu, the following have been recognized: Horus of the East, Amon of Balamun and the desert god Ha. Little of the original decoration of the eastern wall survives. There was a *sm3-t3wy* scene above the doorway flanked by 12 deities probably representing the hours of the day. Seth and Nephthys of Dakhleh were depicted in the upper register.

The excavations also revealed the classical decoration upon the eastern part of the northern wall and the northern part of the eastern wall, and sections of the decorated vault from the eastern part of the room (Plate 6). Above the dado representing masonry blocks, the walls are painted with panels with central squares, topped by birds, that

---

[9] The piece is discussed by Kaper elsewhere in this volume.

[10] The previous work in this section of the shrine is described in Hope and Bowen 1997, 56–8; Kaper 2002 presents an overview and interpretation of the decorative scheme prior to the work described here.

Plate 7 South-eastern corner of Room 1 of the mammisi, *Area D/2, showing money boxes as found; looking east.*

Plate 8 Detail of money boxes (D/2/43 and 42), see Plate 7; looking south-east.

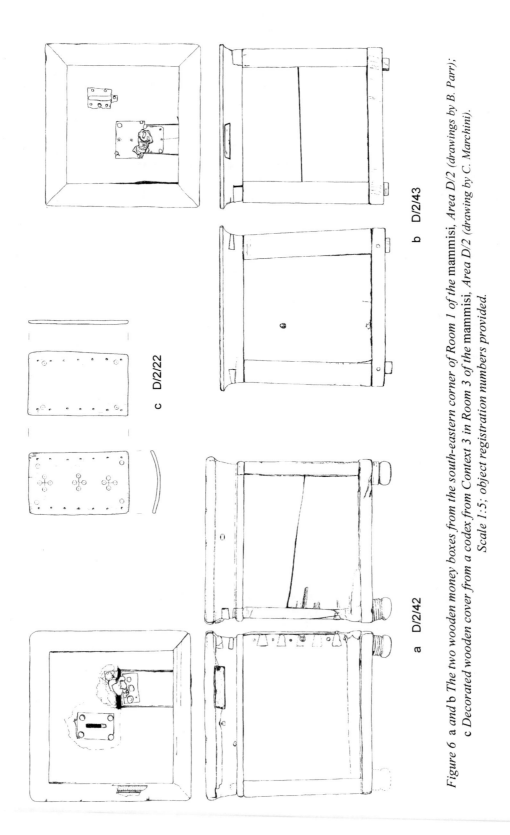

Figure 6 a and b The two wooden money boxes from the south-eastern corner of Room 1 of the mammisi, Area D/2 (drawings by B. Parr); c Decorated wooden cover from a codex from Context 3 in Room 3 of the mammisi, Area D/2 (drawing by C. Marchini). Scale 1:5; object registration numbers provided.

b D/2/43

c D/2/22

a D/2/42

contain female heads and are alternately coloured red and orange, and are separated and topped by vines. The same design is encountered around the walls of the room. The execution of these squares may well have proceeded from west to east as there is only half of a square adjacent to the northern jamb of the eastern door into the room, and the next panel on the eastern wall extends onto the northern wall, all indicating a rather casual approach to the layout of the classical decorative scheme. The vault decoration recalls that of mosaics:

> ... fragments of painted vault plaster ... confirmed that the design of the eastern half of the ceiling was a complex geometric one based on squares and 8-point stars, a pattern more commonly found in mosaic floors. This fits with the rest of the vault scheme, which uses mosaic-type patterns to create a simulated coffered ceiling centred on a portrait tondo[11] within an imbricated shield supported by kneeling figures within a square frame. The scheme has parallels in the 'zodiac ceilings' of Egyptian temples and tombs of the Roman period, and also Roman temples elsewhere in the Eastern Mediterranean; of closer significance, the portrait-in-a-shield can be paralleled in Alexandrian mosaics, including new examples retrieved in the current French and Polish excavations (Whitehouse in Hope *et al.* 2002, 104).

From the deposits excavated this season it is possible to confirm the sequence of collapse and reuse of the room. The eastern half of the vault fell first, together with the cornice and jambs of the northern door. Following this the room was used as a stable for donkeys and graffiti were drawn upon the walls of the western half; animal manure overlies the fallen sections of the northern door. It is probable that the damage to the pharaonic figures in the decoration of the western half of the room was done at this stage, sometime within the mid- to late-fourth century.

During the 2001 season the final sections of collapse and fill within the south-eastern corner were removed, the decorated plaster and artefacts collected and the wall paintings recorded. This enabled us to undertake excavation below the floor of the shrine to the basal clay upon which the site is built, bringing to an end the study of this part of the monument.

Amongst the collapse within the south-eastern corner sections of decoration belonging to the southern and eastern walls were retrieved. This enabled the completion of the restoration in separate sections, but eventually in full on paper, of the eastern end of the uppermost register on the southern wall that depicts a procession of the nome-gods of Upper Egypt. Figures of Antaios (Antaiopolis), Wepwawet (Assiut), Neferhotep (Diospolis Parva), Hathor (Dendera), Amon-Re (Thebes) and Nekhbet (el-Kab) were recovered. No trace was found of the initial gods of this procession nor of the gods worshipping them. The names and crowns of the gods in the register below this procession are also lacking due to the very fragile nature of the plaster from this section of the wall.

Fragments from the decoration of the eastern wall of the room, and those sections surviving upon the wall, show that the principal scene represented Tutu as a striding sphinx upon the *sm3-t3wy* symbol with Nile gods on either side uniting the two heraldic plants that form this depiction of the unification of the two lands of Egypt. These figures are each followed by six goddesses who represent the 12 hours of the night. The inner face of the centrally-located doorway in the eastern wall appears to have been decorated entirely with pharaonic scenes, though only fragments survive. Upon the lower part of the southern jamb (Plate 7) is preserved the only figure of a king within the entire room; unfortunately, he is not named! The king extends his hand, reciting the offering formula for Tutu; above him is a short inscription containing the offering formula. Above this only the yellow legs of a god remain. The cornice is decorated on the south with the cartouches of Tutu and Neith topped by their respective crowns, while the door lintel carried figures of a variety of deities, including a winged serpent, Heh and Tutu as a striding sphinx with a crocodile's head projecting from his chest.[12]

Underlying the wall collapse, the stable deposit found across the majority of the room was encountered here also. Within this material, lying upon a broken section of the earth floor in the south-eastern corner of the room, were two, almost intact, wooden money boxes (Plates 7–8 and Figure 6a–b). They are both square, 20.2 ± 0.2 cm and 21.5 cm, in the form of shrines with cavetto cornices, standing 23.2 cm and 25.5 cm high upon four short feet. Set into their tops are metal-framed slots through which coins could be inserted into the box. Sliding wooden panels adjacent to these would have enabled the boxes to be emptied with ease, while lead seals prevented them from being opened at will. The seal upon one box was broken before discovery but that upon the other remained intact; unfortunately both boxes contained only sand. A single bronze coin of Constantine the Great was found on the floor against the southern wall. The only other find of significance in this part of the room was seven fragments of gilded plaster sculpture; similar fragments were also found at floor level against the western wall of the room many seasons ago.[13]

A cut to basal clay was then made through the earth floor adjacent to the eastern wall of the room; it was one metre wide and extended from the southern wall 2.43 m to the north, terminating at a mid-point through the eastern

---

[11] This is illustrated in Hope 2002, Plate 12.

[12] This is a regular feature of the god's iconography and occurs on the image on the western wall of the room, see O. E. Kaper, 'The God Tutu (Tithoes) and his Temple in the Dakhleh Oasis', *Bulletin of the Australian Centre for Egyptology* 2 (1991), Figure 4.

[13] For a discussion and illustration of similar plaster sculptures from elsewhere in the temple see Hope 1998, 821–5.

Plate 9 Excavation to basal clay in the south-eastern corner of Room 1 of the mammisi, *Area D/2; looking east.*

doorway. An area of the earth floor immediately west of the door, 80 x 87 cm in area, formed a slight mound with three approximately circular depressions in it, and was harder than the surrounding floor material. The mound appears to have been exposed to oil, possibly from the pouring of libations; the jambs of the eastern door also have traces of such material. Amongst the artefacts lying upon the floor in this part of the room was a fragment from the upper edge of a sandstone altar upon which such offerings may have been made. Removal of the oily material revealed the earth floor that extends across the entire section of the room up to the walls and door sill; patches of gypsum occurred intermittently, either indicating that the floor had once been coated with this material or that some spillage had occurred when the walls and vault were coated with gypsum plaster. The wall plaster terminated at the upper surface of this flooring.

Beneath the earth floor the upper surface of what resembled a mud-brick wall emerged on the north (Plate 9, upper left). It extends from the northern edge of the trench to a point 15 cm from the southern edge of the southern doorjamb; the remainder of the trench was filled with mud-brick rubble. Removal of the rubble fill showed that the wall was only three courses, 25 cm, high and sits upon hard red clay. This basal clay has been cut into to form a pit, the northern edge of which was cut vertically, with which the southern face of the brick wall was aligned.

As the brick rubble was removed, it was found to extend under the northern section of the eastern wall and also under the southern wall, which terminate one course below floor level. The southern 65 cm of the eastern wall, however, continues down (Plate 9, upper right). It extends a further five and a half courses, 47 cm, lower than the northern section and stands upon what may be the south-eastern edge of the same pit, which the three-course northern walls is set upon. A distinct crack was noted extending vertically from the northern edge of this lower section of the eastern wall, indicating that the upper section is probably part of the same construction phase. The brick fill, with some variations in compactness and composition, continued down a further 36 cm below the base of the southern section of the eastern wall, at which point the base of the pit was revealed (Plate 9). Only the northern edge of this pit, standing 58 cm high, and the south-eastern edge, 36 cm high above the floor of the pit, were revealed. Close examination of the north-eastern corner of the cut showed that some brick rubble occurs below the southern door jamb but east of the three-course brick wall, indicating that it might terminate there rather than extending under the jamb and doorway.

This excavation has shown that the southern part of the eastern wall of Room 1 is part of a structure that predates the *mammisi,* and the southern walls of the latter abut this earlier wall.[14] In places, traces of a pale-green-painted

[14] The architectural study of this room by J. Dobrowalski has shown that the walls of the *mammisi* were inserted into a pre-existing structure, see Dobrowalski 2002,125–6.

Plate 10 Doorway into Room 1 from Room 2 of the mammisi, *Area D/2; looking south-west.*

plaster are visible on the eastern face of this wall within Room 2, most of which now carries a panel decoration upon a red ground that is painted upon plaster overlying the original green-painted plaster. A similar situation pertains upon that part of the eastern wall north of the doorway: its eastern face has panel decoration upon a red ground, but within the reveal of the doorway original green-painted plaster is covered by outer plaster, in this case added to form the northern, inner jamb of the door. This would imply that the northern part of the eastern wall is contemporary with the earlier section on the south. The northern part of the eastern wall abuts the southern wall of the court west of the Main Temple, which in turn aligns with the southern edge of the inner door of the West Gateway through the two temenos walls surrounding the temple.[15] This southern wall of the court, may, therefore, also be a part of the earlier structure, as would be the western wall of the shrine as this is part of the inner, earlier, temenos wall.

Decorated plaster with a pale-green basal colour has been found at various other places within the Inner Temenos (Figure 2): on remains of the original temple façade south of the main axial doorway (1A), on the screen walls of the Portico, on the inner face of the southern wall of the Inner Temenos west of the South Gateway, on the

northern and eastern walls of Room 1 of Shrine III, upon the inner face of the northern wall of Temenos 1 concealed behind the eastern wall of Room 6 of Shrine II, upon the southern wall due west of Shrine II, upon the exterior of the northern wall of Shrine IV and in Room 2 of Shrine I. Thus, the original structure located on the site of the *mammisi* is part of a decorative/structural phase of the entire complex. It cannot be dated with precision, but is early in the overall evolution of the Inner Temenos complex, and may be ascribed to the late first to mid-second centuries CE.[16] The *mammisi* was formed by extending the southern section of the eastern wall, and building its northern and southern walls directly against the walls of an existing room. The three-course mud-brick wall found below the floor of the *mammisi* may be a part of the earlier structure but further excavation is necessary to clarify its function.

I.2.2 Room 2

In 2001 a two-metre section adjacent to the doorway into Room 1 was selected for investigation to determine whether Room 2, like its neighbour, was decorated and to locate its southern wall, which was not visible at surface level. A deposit of wind-blown sand 0.9–1.2 m deep overlay

---

[15] For a discussion of the West Court and West Gateway see Hope 2002, 178–82; further comments can be found in Dobrowolski 2002, 121–6.

[16] For a discussion of the criteria available for dating the various phases of the evolution of the Main Temple (written in 1996/7) see Hope 2001b, 44–51.

Plate 11 *Inscribed wooden boards and papyri within a stable deposit on the floor against the northern section of the west wall of Room 2 of the* mammisi, *Area D/2; looking west.*

mud-brick collapse, the majority from walls. Only one section of vaulting bricks was found, due south of the southern door jamb, and this preserved painted plaster with a motif known from the eastern and western extremities of the ceiling of Room 1 (see above). This may indicate that Room 2 originally possessed a decorated vaulted ceiling also with classical motifs. A few fragments of plaster decorated in pharaonic style were found that apparently derive from the upper part of the door jambs. Available time precluded the removal of the brick deposit, so that only the upper sections of the walls were revealed. This was sufficient to show that the western walls are decorated with a classical panel motif upon a red ground; at the centres of the panels are squares from the corners of which extend stylised floral sprays. The decoration is preserved most clearly on the south.

The southern wall of Room 2 was located at a distance of 2.0 m from the southern door jamb; the northern wall is 1.8 m from the northern door jamb. This makes the room just over a metre wider than Room 1, being 6.13 m in width. Its northern wall aligns with the original northern wall of Room 1, whilst its southern wall aligns with neither of the southern walls of Room 1. At the western end of the southern wall an original doorway 87.5 cm wide has been bricked up; its reveals preserve a green-painted plaster enabling this feature to be identified as part of the earlier decorative phase within the Inner Temenos mentioned above. A doorway of similar size, 0.88 m in width, also bricked in, is located in the northern wall 1.35 m east of

the western wall; this originally communicated with the area south of the Main Temple.

The aims of the 2002 excavations in the antechamber of the *mammisi*, Room 2, were twofold: to determine the nature of the painted plaster decoration of the outer room and the method of covering of this room, which measures more than 6 m in width. Two trenches were excavated, one at each end of the room.

The western end of Room 2 was first excavated, after the area cleared during the 2001 season had been exposed again. In the previous season, only the upper layer of wind-blown sand had been removed and the upper layer of mud-brick collapse revealed. This season, the trench was laid out against the length of the western wall with a width of two metres along its northern half and one metre along the southern half. This area was fully excavated to floor level in its northern half, as was a smaller section along the southern end of the western wall (Plate 10).

The rubble collapse consisted of standard-size mud bricks; no vaulting bricks were found or other kinds of roofing material. It was concluded from this that the room had been open to the sky in the manner of a court, contra to the implication of the discovery of vaulting bricks in this area during the previous season. The rubble collapse contained a few dressed-sandstone blocks, which must have been introduced during the dismantling of the Main Temple. Two fragments of the same block were found in different parts of this collapse. Also among the collapse in the south-western corner of the room were various fragments of a plaster bust of a goddess, similar to earlier

Plate 12 Images of four of the Seven Demons associated with Tutu within a pedestal upon which a figure of that god stands, from above the door in the west wall of Room 2 of the mammisi, *Area D/2.*

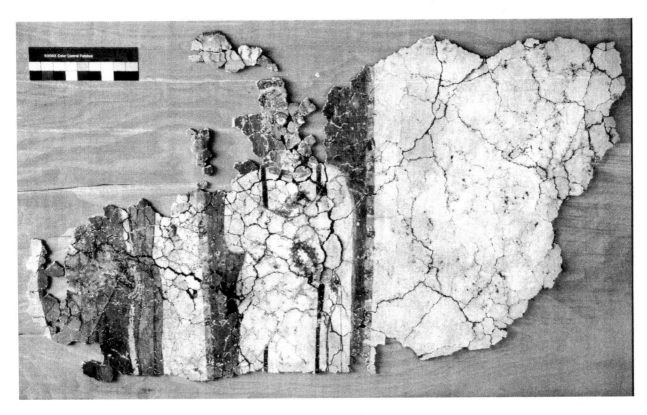

Plate 13 Figures in classical dress from the west wall of Room 2 of the mammisi, *Area D/2.*

finds around the Main Temple (see footnote 13). This sculpture had originally been gilded. In the same context another fragmentary plaster sculpture was found, preserving a pair of legs in classical style with an enveloping garment. Numerous fragments of plaster wall decoration were among the collapse. Beneath the collapse, at approximately 1.75 m depth, several layers of earth floors could be distinguished, the uppermost of which contained much stable material. Within this, a group of Greek papyrus documents was found along with two miniature wooden codices, one of four leaves and one of three leaves with their string binding *in situ*, and one single wooden board, all inscribed in Greek (Plate 11; see below). These were found together against the northern part of the western wall.

Classical decoration remains upon the walls (see below). Amongst the bricks from the collapsed walls, large segments of decoration could be retrieved, which had originally been present above the main wall zone. North of the doorway upon the western wall, the classical decoration was surmounted by a painting of a series of personages, above which was a painting of a horse, probably with a horseman, but not much of this element has survived. To the left of the doorway were figures of Egyptian gods in pharaonic style, but the excavations have not exposed all of the relevant fragments from this side of the wall.

The doorway itself, the entrance into the *mammisi*, was again decorated with the same classical panels and the decoration continued above with pharaonic imagery. Several scenes of gods in pharaonic style may be reconstructed here, covering the upper jambs and lintel. The cavetto cornice above the door was painted with a winged solar disc. Above the cornice was a painting of the principal god of the temple, Tutu, in the form of a sphinx set upon a pedestal facing right. Inside the pedestal were images of the seven demons who were associated with the god (Plate 12). To the left of this central image was a large human figure dressed in military boots, who seems to represent a deity, but not many fragments could be retrieved of this figure. To the right of Tutu was the aforementioned horseman.

A trench at the eastern end of Room 2 with a width of two metres was commenced across the entrance into the shrine. Time constraints did not allow this to be completed, but the results confirmed the conclusions drawn from the work at the western end of the room, as the depth of deposit at this end of the room is much less, *circa* 90 cm. There is again no roofing material to be found among the collapse, which consists of mud bricks from the walls only. The painted plaster here is much more weathered; the decoration upon the walls and doorways has lost nearly all of its painted detail, and only small fragments of floral decoration could be retrieved from amongst the fill. The floor level was only reached inside the northernmost part of the triple doorway, and no finds were recorded.

Initial clearance at the western end of Room 2 revealed a classical-style panel scheme on a red ground, partly

observed last season and fully recorded this year. This overlies an earlier layer of painted plaster on the eastern and southern walls and is related to structural modifications observable in the mud-brick walls. The decoration is comparable to the panel-design on the *mammisi* walls (Room 1), but this season's work showed that it was topped by an acanthus scroll which also relates it to a scroll and panel design, on a green ground, painted all round the inner surface of the Inner Temenos of the temple (Hope 2002, 192–3, 199). The similarity suggests a uniform redecoration of the temple, perhaps related to one of the major renovations of the late first to second centuries CE attested in inscriptions.

As clearance progressed downwards, substantial amounts of painted plaster from a higher part of the wall were retrieved from the fill: many of these fragments required on-site conservation before they could be lifted. Luckily, it was possible to consolidate and move large pieces of the painted decoration in this way, which will help us to understand and piece together the rest that is very fragmentary and also visually very complex. The upper part of the western wall seems to have been painted at a later date than the panel scheme below with possibly two registers of figures centring on Tutu, above a winged-disk cornice over the doorway into the *mammisi*. The flanking figures include both pharaonic-style divinities and others painted in Roman style: Isis-like goddesses, a hero-god in military dress and a horse-rider. These paintings are crude in execution, but vivid and colourful, and they are unique in content, not only within the range of motifs so far discovered in this temple, but also in the corpus of Graeco-Roman temple décor in Egypt. Most surprisingly they also include the full-length portrayal of a man and woman (Plate 13), evidently private citizens of Kellis, depicted in the manner of contemporary funerary portraiture (compare Whitehouse 1998) but apparently here associated with divinities as donors to the temple, or commemorated dead. Parallels for some of the other elements in this décor can be drawn from wall paintings excavated at Karanis and Theadelphia in the Fayum, and the rare panel-paintings of individual divinities (Whitehouse 1999), tentatively dated second–third century. But the ensemble here, and the mélange of pharaonic and Roman motifs painted by the same hand, are unparalleled.

A more limited clearance at the eastern end of Room 2 confirmed that the red-ground scheme with additional white details had been used in the decoration of the entrance system and walls here, too, and presumably extended throughout the interior of the room. In parts this decor clearly overlay an earlier green scheme; small fragments of other coloured painting retrieved at the eastern end await further examination and assessment. Concerning the cache of inscribed wooden boards found at the western end of Room 2, Klaas Worp writes:

On the basis of photographs supplied to me I have been able to make the following identifications:
Object 31/420-D6-1/D/2/44: a single wooden board inscribed with eight lines of Greek text. Each line

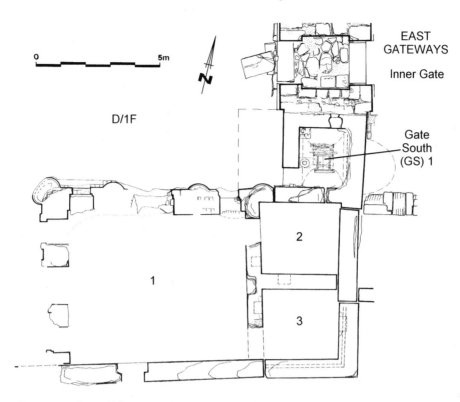

*Figure 7 Plan of Shrine IV, Area D/5, and adjacent sections of the East Gateways,
Area D/9, Room Gate South 1 and the south-eastern corner of the Forecourt,
Area D/1F (drawing by J Dobrowolski and B. Rowney). Scale 1:150.*

*Plate 14 Large Stela, registration number D/1F/5, as found against exterior wall of Gate South 1 at the eastern end of
Area D/1F; looking east.*

contains, in theory, a Greek verb in the first person singular active, but the forms in lines 3 and 7 do not correspond with any known verb.

Object 31/420-D6-1/D/2/45: three faces of the two wooden boards contain calculations made by a schoolboy supposed to calculate a series of fractions of a given number.

Object 31/420-D6-1/D/2/46: five faces of three of the wooden boards preserve 12 lines presenting part of a parody of Homer's *Iliad*. While the genre itself is not unknown (Olson and Sens 1999), the new text is apparently not found elsewhere.

I.2.3 Room 3

When the Outer Temenos was constructed around the inner one (Figure 2), and the stone section of the West Gateway was added, a narrow room, 1 m by wide, was created at the rear of Room 1, extending the full width of the latter. The excavation of this unusual feature was commenced during the 2000 season and completed in 2001, when a trench two metres reducing to one metre wide was opened to basal clay level.

In the 2000 season the room was cleared of its fill, comprising first wind-blown sand and then sand with brick rubble, straw, branches and much palm frond, to the earth floor. A maximum preserved height of 2.82 m at the south-western corner was recorded for the room; it is considerably less on the north. The room was originally roofed with a vault. Within the fill were several ceramic vessels and the outer cover from a wooden codex decorated with three cruciform motifs comprising four circles attached to short lines (Figure 6c).

The cut to basal clay enabled the building and depositional sequences to be determined. The basal clay slopes considerably from west to east, and north to south, and is lower here than under the eastern part of Room 1. Over it are deposits of earth containing charcoal and predominantly small potsherds, below a narrow lens of sand with stones, and then a deposit of compact earth fill containing some mud-brick fragments and pieces of sandstone. They occupy a depth of 68 cm on the west within the southern section of the trench to 1.16 m on the east. The western wall of Shrine I, which is part of the Inner Temenos wall, was built atop the compact earth deposit apparently without any foundation trench, and the surface of this deposit formed the contemporary ground level outside the temple complex. Over this, and against the wall, straw, sand, miscellaneous flora and some ash gradually accumulated. The exterior face of the shrine wall was mud-plastered and contained several features. The main one is a semicircular niche, 63 cm wide, 39.5 cm deep and preserved to 97 cm in height, located

approximately 2.4 m above ground level[17] and situated south of the centre of the wall. There may also have been a square niche, 50 cm wide, at a similar height above ground and 1.98m north of the larger one. Between the two, a vertical groove 36 cm wide implies the existence of another, presently unidentifiable, feature. These elements may indicate cultic activity at the rear of Room 1; when revealed they were found to have been either bricked in or plastered over.

The stone section of the West Gateway was then constructed[18] with a mud-brick wall facing to its southern exterior. This wall, which forms the northern wall of Room 3, was set into the straw and sand deposits, again without any real foundation trench. Its southern face preserves patches of mud plaster, which may indicate that at some stage it was a visible external face of the complex. The western, and probably also southern, wall was then constructed in a much sturdier manner than the earlier walls: a foundation trench was cut through the straw and sand deposit, and the compact earth to the sand and stone lens, and the wall was constructed within this trench. A deposit of earth was then laid and a new earth floor created at 92.5 cm above the original ground level. Two sets of foot-holes cut into the eastern and western walls at their northern end indicate that access to this narrow chamber was required, though if the entire room was roofed then how access was gained to these is uncertain. No evidence was forthcoming on the actual function of this room.

I.3 Shrine IV, Area D/5, adjacent Area D/1F and Gate South 1, Area D/GS1

Shrine IV (D/5) is located in the south-eastern corner of the Inner Temenos of the Temple of Tutu (Figure 2) and comprises three mud-brick rooms, two abutting the eastern temenos wall that are of equal size (Rooms 2–3) and a third, much larger room (Room 1), to the west of these (Figure 7). Work conducted within the structure during previous seasons showed that Room 1 is decorated with a classical design on its southern wall comprising octagons with bowls of fruit on an aubergine-coloured base. Further, Room 3 preserves three layers of plaster with *dipinti* of Tutu, Seth, Bes and a vulture deity upon the lowest, and an elaborate classical design with birds, flowers and octagons on the uppermost (Hope 2002, 198–9; Kaper 2002; Whitehouse 2002). Three doorways provide access into the shrine on the west and its northern wall is integral with the eastern end of the southern colonnade that frames the approach to the temple itself. To permit the depth of preservation to be ascertained and the structure of the decorative design in Room 1 to be determined, a section of the western end of the southern wall was exposed in 2000 and work was also undertaken in Room 2 and an

---

[17] Whilst this may appear extremely high above ground level, a similarly-located niche was found in the north wall of Room 1 of Shrine III (Hope 2002, 193).

[18] See Dobrowolski 2002 for further details.

Plate 15 Stela of Septimius Severus worshipping Neith and Tutu, registration number D/1F/5, from Area D/1F.

Plate 16 Room Gate South 1 and the eastern end of the entrance system into Shrine IV, Area D/5, from Forecourt, Area D/1F; looking east.

Plate 17 Door closing the crypt in Room Gate South 1; looking south.

Plate 18 The crypt in Room Gate South 1 and two ceramic jars buried in the floor.

area within the Forecourt immediately to the north of Shrine IV. Unfortunately, the decoration upon the southern wall of Room 1 is not well preserved and it is in a fragile condition so that work had to be stopped. Some removal of surface sand from around the doorways on the west revealed that yellow geometric designs upon an aubergine-coloured background adorn the entrance system and the corners of the room.

Clearance of upper collapse in Room 2 showed that there are several layers of plaster on its northern and eastern walls, but there is no evidence for the elaborate classical design found in the Room 3. The southern and western walls of the room each contain niches and only have one layer of white plaster. The original layout of this part of the Inner Temenos was quite different from that which now exists and Shrine IV once consisted of a single very large room. It was only after it had been subdivided that the elaborate decoration of Room 3 was added.

Immediately north of Room 1 an area of the Forecourt of the temple was excavated; it is designated D/1F. Wind-blown sand overlay considerable collapse from the shrine's northern wall. Three doorways were found to provide access into Room 1 of Shrine IV through this wall. All of these were once fitted with pivoted wooden doors that opened into the shrine, and from which there is a single step down into the Forecourt of the temple. The doorways are set between short sections of screen walls and were topped by cavetto cornices supported upon wooden lintels. Half columns, fashioned in mud brick, are attached to the walls on either side of the central doorway and on the east of the eastern doorway, while to the west of the western doorway the walls are attached to a full column. The shafts of the columns and the screen walls are now white-plastered but were once plastered and painted green; the capitals were papyriform and painted in typical pharaonic fashion to represent the open umbel and calyx of this plant. The details of the latter are painted alternately red and yellow on the capitals of outer columns, but red and pale green on the capitals of the inner columns. Large sections of shaft and pieces from the capitals were found fallen to the north. Here were also numerous fragments from plaster sculptures, all apparently representing the goddesses Isis, which appear to have been attached to the screen walls (compare Hope 1998, 821–5). A fragment of a limestone sandalled-foot from a statue possibly of this goddess was found here also, similar to others found within the East Gateways and at the western end of the Forecourt (Hope 1998, 814–5). Thus the architecture and decoration of the exterior of the northern wall of Shrine IV is traditionally pharaonic in contrast to the decoration within. Amongst the collapse in this area the shaft and attached papyriform capital from a small column were found made from mud plaster around a palm-rib frame, the pieces of which are tied together with rope. Details of the capital are painted to resemble the open calyx of the papyrus. Fragments of

such small columns have been found during previous seasons as have small, elaborately-modelled plaster capitals, raising the possibility that there was once a second colonnade atop the larger one.

Between Room 2 of Shrine IV and the innermost of the East Gateways through the Inner Temenos (Figure 7) there is a single small room, termed Gate South 1 (D/GS1). This was also excavated in 2000. Within the brick collapse abutting the exterior of its western wall an intact sandstone stela was found (registration number 31/420-D6-1/D/1F/5, Plates 14 and 15; Kaper this volume a). It measures 80.0 x 59.0 x 8.6 cm and carries representations of a king making offering to seated figures of Neith and Tutu below the sign for heaven, while in the lunette there is a winged sun's disc with two dependent uraei. The figures are carved in relief and painted; at some stage areas of the background have been carelessly painted red. The figure of Neith has been altered in antiquity and is covered with a stain that has resulted from the pouring of oil libations. Two short columns of hieroglyphic text are written in front of the gods and a double cartouche in front of the king enables him to be identified Septimius Severus (193–211). To the south of this stela an inverted pedestal was found which might once have supported a statue. The original location of both of these items is uncertain, but it may be suggested that they were positioned along the processional route through the Forecourt.

Gate South 1 (Plate 16) was filled with collapse from its roof and the walls of a probable second level room. Approximately in the centre of the room, a well-preserved wooden trap door was found abutting four wooden beams on its north (Plate 17). The door and beams covered a rectangular pit 82–88 x 88–91 cm in size, which is contained by brick walls extending to the edges of the room. At a depth of 65.5–67.5 cm the pit becomes circular with a diameter of 91 cm; at a total depth of 1.3–1.5 m there is a smoothed mud floor 98 cm in diameter (Plate 18). This structure may have functioned as a crypt for the storage of temple possessions; when excavated it contained the remains of several late-third to fourth-century ceramic vessels, including pieces from a large decorated jar of the type buried at the rear of the temple in the area of the well (see above). From the sand fill came three fourth-century bronze coins and a further two were found on the floor, one of which dates to the reign of Constantine I. Numerous pieces of green crystalline stone were found in its fill and on its floor, which have been identified as beryl (low-grade emerald).[19] This is not native to Dakhleh and may have come from the mines in the Eastern Desert between Myos Hormos and Berenice (Shaw *et al.* 1999). Set into the floor of the room against its western wall were two large ceramic vessels, originally covered with ceramic lids (Plate 18); each was found to be filled only with earth.

To determine whether the construction of Gate South 1 and the south colonnade/northern wall of Shrine IV were

---

[19] I am grateful to Maxine Kleindienst for this identification.

Plate 19 South-eastern corner of the Main Temple Forecourt, Area D/1F, with entrances into Room Gate South 1 and Room 1 of Shrine IV, Area D/5; looking south-east.

Plate 20 Excavation to basal clay in the south-eastern corner of the Main Temple Forecourt, Area D/1F, showing foundation wall for the south colonnade and its intersection with the wall of Gate South 1; looking south.

Plate 21 Sub-floor walls in Room 3 of the Large East Church, Area A/7; looking west.

Plate 22 Earlier wall used as the foundation for the northern wall of the southern rooms of the Large East Church, Area A/7; looking south-east.

contemporary, a trench 2.0 m wide was excavated adjacent to the exterior of the western wall of Gate South 1. This extended on the north to the edge of the southern jamb of the Inner Gate of the East Gateways and on the south to the colonnade (Plate 19). This showed that the step into the eastern door of Shrine IV was actually the upper part of a foundation wall to support the colonnade; this extends to the west under all of the columns. Underlying a series of floor deposits and construction surfaces was hard red clay of the Mut Formation. This had been dug into for a foundation trench into which the stone gate was set and filled with yellow sand; other similar trenches may have been cut for the walls of Gate South 1 and the colonnade but they could not be detected. That Gate South 1 and the colonnade were constructed at the same time is shown by the bonding of the lowest two courses of the former's western wall with the fifth and sixth courses of the support wall for the colonnade (Plate 20). Above this the wall of Gate South 1 abuts that of the colonnade, which continues to the east to form the wall common to Gate South 1 and Room 2 of Shrine IV (Plate 19). This test shows that the original stage of Shrine IV as a single room is contemporary with the construction of the colonnade, Gate South 1 and the Inner Gate of the Eastern Gateways. The alterations to the internal arrangement of Shrine IV caused considerable damage to the dividing wall between its eastern end and Gate South 1, which necessitated repairs to the wall that can now be seen as an original mud-plastered surface has fallen away (Plate 19).

II Domestic Structure north of the rear of Main Temple, Area D/8

Immediately to the north of the north-western corner of the Inner Temenos, between its wall and that of Enclosure 1 containing the entire Temple of Tutu and its administrative/storage facilities, lies a domestic structure of 13 spaces, Area D/8 (Figure 2). This occupies the area where the northern part of the second or Outer Temenos wall around the temple, set some five metres away from the first one, would have extended to join its western wall. Between the two temenos walls and Enclosure 1 elsewhere there are various well-defined chambers; D/8 interrupts the general pattern of their layout. Work in the area during previous seasons (Hope 2002,199–204) has indicated a fourth-century date for this complex, has shown that its Room 1 is built over a well and that a northern extension of the western wall of the Inner Temenos was cut down to its lowest courses when D/8 was built. The area also yielded quantities of papyrus inscribed in Greek and the latest dated document from Ismant el-Kharab: a horoscope drawn up in Greek for the year 392 CE (de Jong and Worp 2001, 203–6).

During the 2000 season clearance of two chambers in the eastern part of D/8 was commenced. These are a north/south corridor, Room 4, which provides access to a small kitchen, Room 5, at its southern end abutting the exterior of the Inner Temenos (Figure 2). The eastern wall of Room

4 is much thicker than all others in the structure and comprises the western wall of a structure or series of rooms between the Inner and Outer Temenos walls due north of Shrine II. More small fragments of papyrus inscribed in Greek were found amongst the collapse of the roof of the corridor, along with quantities of domestic garbage above the earth floor. Removal of this floor showed that the lower sections of both of the walls of the corridor are wider than the upper parts, that of the western wall considerably so. In addition, study of the western extant end of the Outer Temenos wall shows that it has been cut back to form the eastern jamb of the door into Room 4. These features confirm that the original layout of this area was quite different from what existed in the fourth century.

III Area A

III.1 The East Church Complex, Area A/7

During the seasons covered by this report the major focus of excavation within the East Church Complex (Figure 1) was the clearance of the Small East Church; this is discussed elsewhere in this volume by G. E. Bowen. Two test trenches were, however, opened in the previously-excavated Large East Church (Bowen 2002, 67–75) in order to determine whether there were earlier structures beneath the floors. The areas selected for examination were in the south aisle, immediately outside the doorway to Room 3, one of a sequence of four rooms that opens off that aisle on the south, and all of Room 3 (Bowen this volume, Figure 1).

In 2000 excavation was carried out beneath the floor of Room 3; it revealed a substructure within that room and also a substantial wall upon which the northern wall of the room were built. The substructure, within the western half of the room only, comprises part of an east-west wall abutting a section of north-south wall at its eastern end (Plate 21). The northern end of the north-south wall is built over a hardened earth feature that runs for the entire width of Room 3 at a slight angle to the lower section of wall beneath its northern wall; this feature has a concave surface. The northern edge of this feature and the end of the north-south wall appear to have been cut away when the northern wall of Room 3 wall built. The western wall of Room 3 was built over the extant top of the western end of the east-west wall and over the hardened earth feature; the eastern wall of Room 3 is also built over the latter. All of the lower features are built upon a layer of compact earth.

During the 2001 season the trench in the south aisle was excavated from the centre of the doorway (Plate 22) and continued in an easterly direction for 2.5 m; it spanned the width of the south aisle (1.8 m). The section of wall revealed beneath the northern wall of Room 3 in 2000 could be studied further as a result of this. It is preserved 40 cm in height and extends a further 56 cm into the south aisle than does the wall built on top of it. Other sections of the same wall have been revealed both to the east and

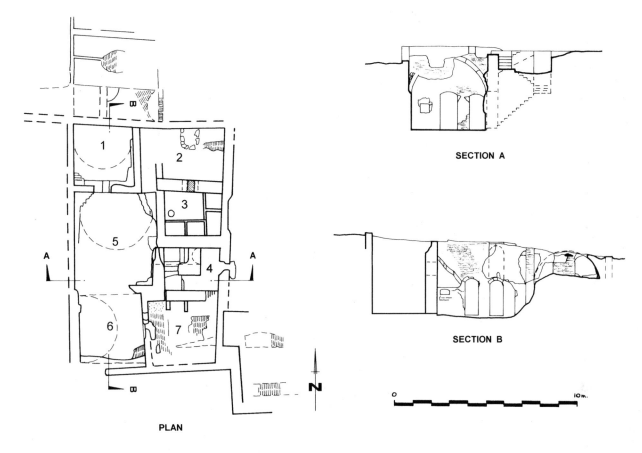

Figure 8 Plan and section of House 5, Area A/9 (drawings by B. Rowney).

Plate 23 Northern end of Room 5 of House 5, Area A/9, with Room 1; looking north.

Plate 24 The eastern wall of Room 5 of House 5, Area A/9, with doors into Rooms 3 and 4; looking east.

Plate 25 Drawing of head in ink upon a potsherd, registration number A/10/22, from Context 11 in the Rubbish Dumps, Area A/10.

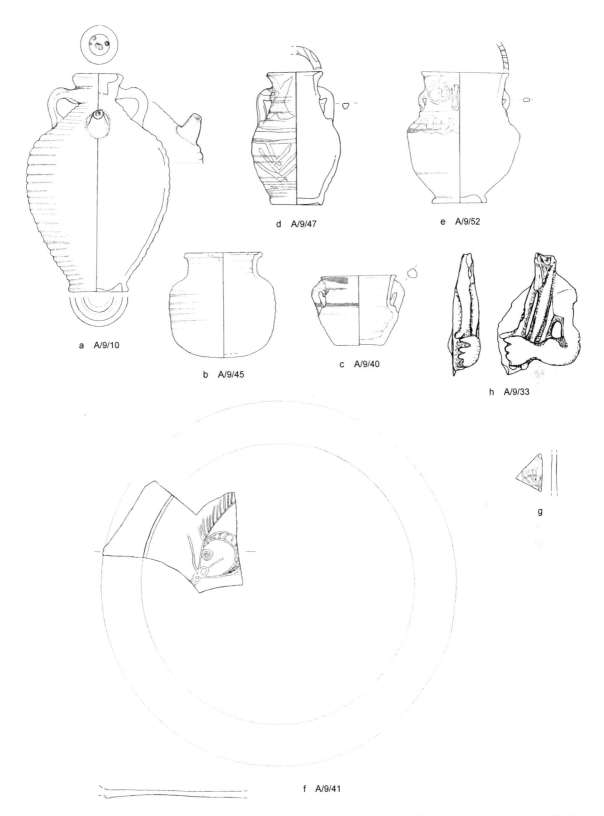

Figure 9 Objects from House 5, Area A/9: a *Imported spouted jug from fill of vault against west wall of Room 5;* b *Imported Nile silt jar from the fill of Room 1;* c–e *Oasis Red Ware vessels from the floor in Room 5;* f–g *Fragments of an imported Fish Plate from the floor of Room 5;* h *Arm and shoulder from a human figure in slate from fill in Room 5 (drawings by C. Marchini, A. Dunsmore and B. Parr). Scale* a–g *1:4,* h *1:2; object registration numbers provided.*

west (Bowen 2002, Figure 1), and it is clear that it represents an earlier wall that has been used as foundation for the northern wall of all of the southern rooms. It extends beyond the church to the east; it was laid directly onto a compact earth layer that may well be contiguous with that found below the early features in Room 3. The hardened earth layer is 70 cm below the floor of the aisle. A purposely-built foundation wall for the southern colonnade of the nave was revealed, and it also was built upon the earth layer. The fill between this layer and the floor of the aisle comprised mud-brick rubble, ash, bones and potsherds. The ceramic assemblage was identified as fourth-century. The earth layer was sterile and no features were detected below it; it clearly extends under the entire building as it has been found at various other locations (Bowen 2002, 73).

III.2 House 5, Area A/9

House 5 is located immediately north-east of the East Church Complex (Figure 1). Excavation of the building was commenced in 1997 (Hope 2002, 170) and completed in 2000. Only two rooms (1 and 5) could be cleared to floor level because of the instability of the walls of the house resulting from removal of wooden fittings. The structure is preserved on two levels. The upper level with storage bins is extant on the east and because of this and the weakness of the structure, the exact layout has not been determined (Figure 8). The core comprises three rooms (1, 5 and 6) on a north-south axis on the west and four rooms similarly arranged on the east (2, 3, 4 and 7). All rooms except the stairway (Room 4) were roofed with barrel vaults. Other rooms abut to the east and north, but whether access to these can be gained from the core rooms of House 5 is unknown, as is the point of entry into the house.

Room 5, the middle room on the west, appears to have been central to the arrangement of rooms as revealed; from it access is gained to all others (Plates 23 and 24) as clearance to floor at ground level revealed in 2000. This room preserves open niches in its northern, eastern and western walls; the southern wall has almost completely collapsed. These niches are surrounded by areas of white plaster, and there is a square of white plaster in the centre of the northern wall of Room 1 to the north. There is a clerestory window in the northern wall of the main room (Plate 23).

Unlike the other houses excavated in Area A, this one yielded very few texts, only a few documentary ostraka in Greek of the fourth century (Worp forthcoming, O. Kell. 59, 86, 142). Of these O. Kell. 59 is dated after 322 and was found in the fill of the vault of Room 5, and O. Kell. 86 from the floor of that room is dated 324/5 or later. Four bronze coins were found in fill of the vault of Room 5 and upper fill of the room, and nine others at floor level;

they are all but one fourth century issues dating from the reigns of Constantius II to Valens or Valentinian II. The exception is a third century tetradrachm found at floor level.

Ceramics throughout all of the deposits proved it to be fourth century. Figure 9a is extremely well-made in a light-fired fabric and the only complete example of the form from the site; it was found in the vault fill of Room 5 and is an import. Figure 9b illustrates a vessel from the fill of Room 1, manufactured in the Nile Valley in Nile silt fabric B2. Fragments of two bowls found at floor level in Room 5 (Figure 9f–g) were also imported from the Nile Valley, one is a piece from a 'Fish Plate' (Figure 9f). The three red-painted handled vessels (Figure 9c–e) are in Oasis Red Ware, a hallmark of fourth- and fifth-century pottery manufactured in Dakhleh and Kharga (Hope 1999, 235–6);[20] they were found at floor level in Room 5. A fragment from a figurine and a lamp in the same ware were also found in the same location. Other figurines from the house have been published elsewhere (Stevens 2002, numbers 5, 8, 24 and 31). An extremely interesting discovery was the left arm and shoulder from a human figure in light-grey slate (Figure 9h).

III.3 Rubbish Dumps, Area A/10

Areas to the north-east of the East Church Complex and House 5 (Figure 1) have been shown to be possible locations for pottery kilns from the amount of vitrified clay on the surface and as a result of an archaeo-magnetometer survey. Testing during the 2000 season in several areas revealed the existence of numerous rubbish dumps but little in the way of structures. The dumped material includes domestic material within ash, though some pieces of metal slag were found. In one test some 40 ostraka inscribed in Greek with documentary texts were found, amongst which were numerous receipts for payment of the poll tax dating to the first half of the third century, from 212 to *circa* 250 (Worp forthcoming, O. Kell. 27, 35–51). The large quantities of potsherds included material of the first-fourth centuries CE, and an interesting figured ostrakon (Plate 25).

IV Area C

Upon the most easterly of the two mounds that comprise Area C (C/2; Figure 1) a magnetometer survey conducted in 1998 (Smekalova 2002, 35–9) revealed the presence of various anomalies that could be circular in shape and possibly pottery kilns. Two such anomalies were particularly intense but they had been buried by dumps from our earlier work on the mound in units C/2/2 and C/2/5. As a part of the study of technology practiced at the site we are attempting to locate any activity that might be related to pottery, glass and faience manufacture, and the

---

[20] This term is preferable to that previously used, namely Oasis Red Slip, as the surface is polished or burnished rather than slipped; the much older term Kharga Red Slip is inaccurate.

Plate 26 Room 1 of Area C/2/7; looking north-west.

Plate 27 Room 3 in Area C/2/7, looking south, showing the area of floor through which excavations were conducted against the eatern wall.

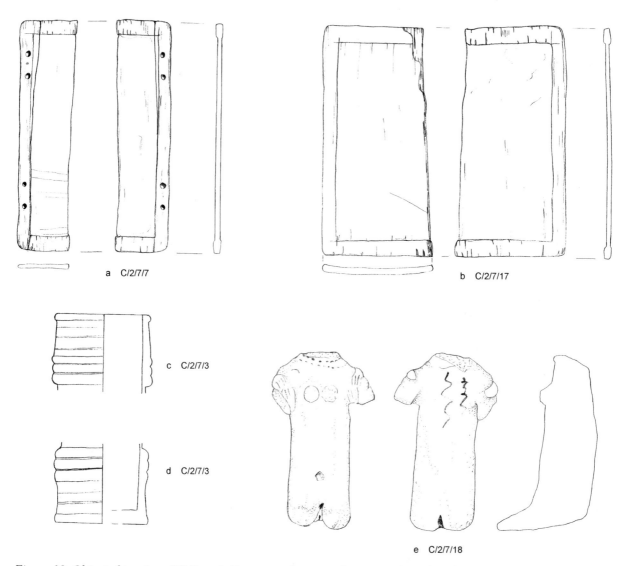

Figure 10 Objects from Area C/2/7: a–b *Fragments from wooden writing boards,* a *from Room 1 and* b *from Room 2;* c–d *Fragments from painted wooden boxes from Room 1;* e *Terracotta figurine from Room 3 (drawings by C. Marchini). Scale 1:2; object registration numbers provided.*

working of metals. Mound C/2 has already yielded pottery- and metalworking kilns; its surface is littered with iron slag (Hope 2002, 176–8; Eccleston 2002). The excavation of the two intense anomalies was undertaken in 2000.

Earlier dump material was cleared and three contiguous rooms in the corner of a mud-brick domestic structure were revealed (C/2/7), but no material to account for the strength of the magnetometer reading. The rooms are arranged within an L-shape: in the corner is Room 1 with Room 2 to its south and Room 3 to its west. Room 1 connects with the others through doorways in its south and west walls. To the west of Room 2 and south of Room 3 is another area accessed from Room 2; from Room 3 another space is accessed to the west. The full distribution of rooms was not determined. It is assumed that the structure had a flat roof and a stairway in the south-west corner of Room 3 may have led to roof level; the floors are of trampled earth throughout and the walls are unplastered.

Room 1 is 4.40–4.75 m east-west and 3.10–3.62 north-south; it has a depression in the floor against the western

end of the south wall and what may be the remains of a hearth against the centre of the same wall (Plate 26). Other than the stairway in Room 3 (Plate 27), there is a free-standing buttress against the south wall; the room is 3.65–4.11 m north-south by 3.83–4.00 m east-west. Room 2 is the largest of the three, being 3.50–3.55 m north-south by 5.85–6.30 m east-west. Flimsy mud-brick structures in the western end of the room showed that it had been used for the stabling of animals, at which time the door from Room 2 to the space on the west was blocked. The maximum preserved height of the structure is 0.84 m.

In case the magnetic anomalies were produced by earlier features it was decided to excavate through the floor against the eastern wall of Room 3 where an intense anomaly appeared during the geophysical survey. Several superimposed earth floors were found, some of which contained concentrations of iron filings and small pieces of corroded iron that may have resulted from smithing. No structures were revealed and it can be assumed that the concentration of filings accounts for the high magnetic

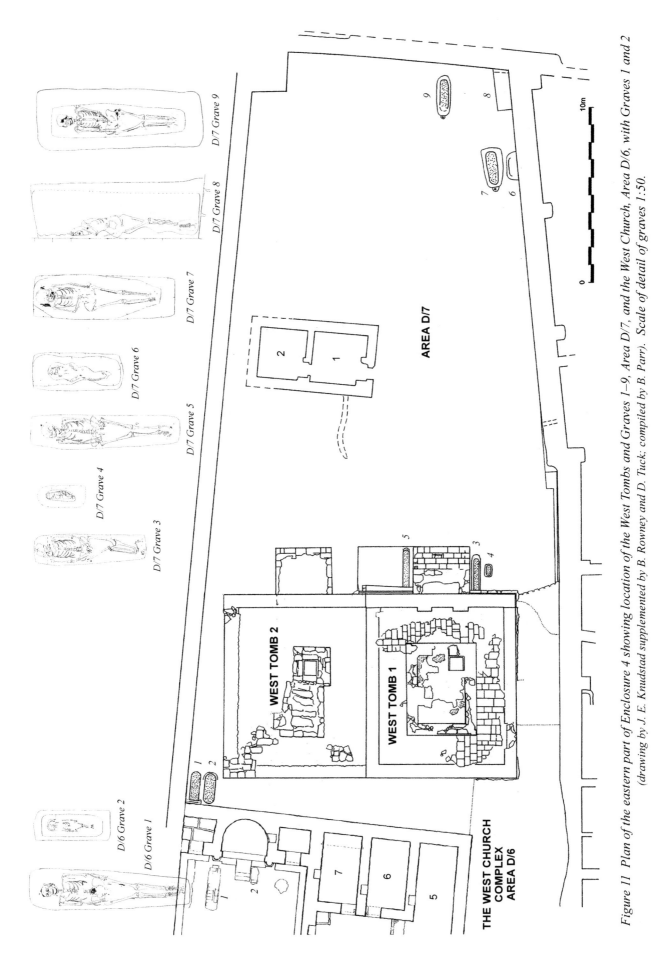

Figure 11 Plan of the eastern part of Enclosure 4 showing location of the West Tombs and Graves 1–9, Area D/7, and the West Church, Area D/6, with Graves 1 and 2 (drawing by J. E. Knudstad supplemented by B. Rowney and D. Tuck; compiled by B. Parr). Scale of detail of graves 1:50.

Plate 28 Grave 5 adjacent to the northern side of the steps of West Tomb 1, Area D/7; looking west.

*Plate 29 Burials in the south-eastern corner of Enclosure 4, Area D/7, Graves 6–9 with North Tomb 1 in the upper
left; looking east.*

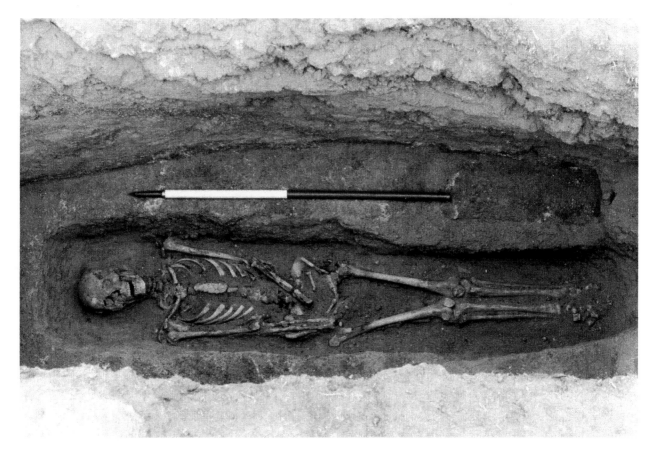

Plate 30 Grave 9 at the eastern end of Enclosure 4, Area D/7; looking north.

Plate 31 Grave 6 against the southern wall at the eastern end of Enclosure 4, Area D/7; looking north.

reading, the circular shape on the magnetic map indicating the area of their distribution rather than the shape of a specific built feature. It is clear that within the area in general future excavation will reveal substantial evidence of metalworking activity.

As with other structures on C/2 those found in C/2/7 would appear to date to the first and second centuries CE, as indicated by the discovery of fragments of papyrus inscribed in Demotic, ostraka in Greek and ceramics. Two of the ostraka are poll-tax receipts, one datable to between 116–7 and 179–80, and the other to either 168–9 or 200–1 CE (Worp forthcoming, O. Kell. 29 and 31). The latter was drawn up for Exones, son of Tithoes. A wide variety of domestic objects were found amongst the wall and roof collapse that filled each roof to floor level. Of note are four fragments from wooden writing boards of the type intended to be inscribed upon a wax base (Figure 10a–b), unfortunately no text was preserved. Those illustrated are 12.4 cm and 12.2 cm respectively in height but the widths are uncertain;[21] the type is distinct from those frequently encountered in Area A and less commonly in Areas B and D (Hope 1997, 9–11). There are fragments from two small, turned wooden receptacles (Figure 10c–d) painted with bands of colour, both from Room 1; the colours comprise yellowish-orange, turquoise, red, black and brown. The body from a terracotta female figurine (Figure 10e) is of a type rare at the site. Other objects include wooden spindle whorls, mud loom weights, wooden toggles, fibre shoes and mud jar sealings.

The excavations indicated that this structure had been used as a blacksmith's workshop and, because of the rarity of such, it was decided to conduct further work here in 2001. This concentrated on the floor deposits in Room 1. A three by two metre grid was set up in the south-western corner of the room and this was subdivided into 50 x 50 cm units. The deposits were excavated separately within each sub-unit and the entire matrix was kept; the magnetic component of each was isolated and the weight of magnetic and non-magnetic fractions determined. This showed that the upper deposits may derive from use of the room by animals, while the main phase of activity definitely relates to the smithing of iron, with large quantities of micro slag being present. In some units the matrix comprised between 15–30% micro and macro slag. This is supported by the discovery of fragments from smithing-hearth bottoms, vitrified linings and fuel as slag, some found *in situ*.

Pottery associated with the deposits from which the slag derived can be assigned to the first to second centuries CE, and appears to attest a domestic assemblage, suggesting that we have a household workshop.[22]

Cemeteries Adjacent to or in the Settlement

I Cemetery within Enclosure 4, Areas D/6 and D/7

Enclosure 4 is the last of a series of additions on the north of Enclosure 1, which contains the Main Temple (Knudstad and Frey 1999, 193–202); it forms the extreme north-west of the site (Figure 1). Before the enclosure was constructed there were two classical-style monumental tombs in the area, termed West Tombs 1 and 2, probably constructed during the first centuries of Roman rule (Hope and McKenzie 1999). Interments found within one indicate that it was reused for the burials of eleven adults and sub-adults probably at the end of the third century CE, and that they may have derived from a wealthy sector of the community. In the mid-fourth century a two-roomed church, termed the West Church, with a seven-roomed domestic annex was built west of these tombs (Bowen 2002, 75–81, 83); its western and northern walls form part of the walls of Enclosure 4. Two single-interment graves with mud-brick superstructures, oriented east/west, were found built against the northern end of the exterior of the eastern wall of the church (Hope 1995, 57–8; Bowen, 2002, 78; Molto *et al.* this volume); these are numbered D/7 graves 1 and 2. In 1999 another grave was discovered against the steps leading to the southernmost of the two monumental tombs, West Tomb 1. It was decided, therefore, that the interior of Enclosure 4 should be investigated systematically for further graves; this was undertaken in the 2000 season.

A further seven single-interment pit graves were located within the area east of the monumental tombs (Figure 11): three beside West Tomb 1, numbered D/7 Graves 3–5 (Plate 28), and four in the south-eastern corner of the enclosure, numbered D/7 Graves 6–9 (Plate 29). They are all oriented east/west and contained skeletonized, human remains with the heads placed on the west (Plate 30; Molto *et al.* this volume). Traces of linen or impressions from such indicate that the bodies were wrapped in some way; however, the only substantive remains of wrapping were found upon a sub-adult (Plate 31). No grave goods were found. At the head end of Grave 9, however, a small bowl was set into the ground and within it was another bowl, while the emplacement for a bowl was found at the head end of Grave 7. The bowls are of fourth century types. All of the graves were sealed with mud bricks.

Two similar burials were found within the nave of the West Church, Area D/6. Their location had been noted some years ago when the church was excavated, but their

---

[21] For recently-published comparisons see H. Willems and W. Clarysse, eds, *Les Empereurs du Nil*, Peeters, Leuven, 2000, 308–9.

[22] This work forms part of the study of high temperature industries at Kellis being undertaken for a PhD thesis at Monash University by Mark Eccleston.

Plate 32 Grave 1 in the West Church, Area D/6; looking east.

Plate 33 Grave 2 in the West Church, Area D/6; looking north-east.

Plate 34 Burial of a child in Grave 2 in the West Church, Area D/6; looking south.

Plate 35 Two-roomed, mud-brick structure (?chapel) in the centre of Area D/7; looking north.

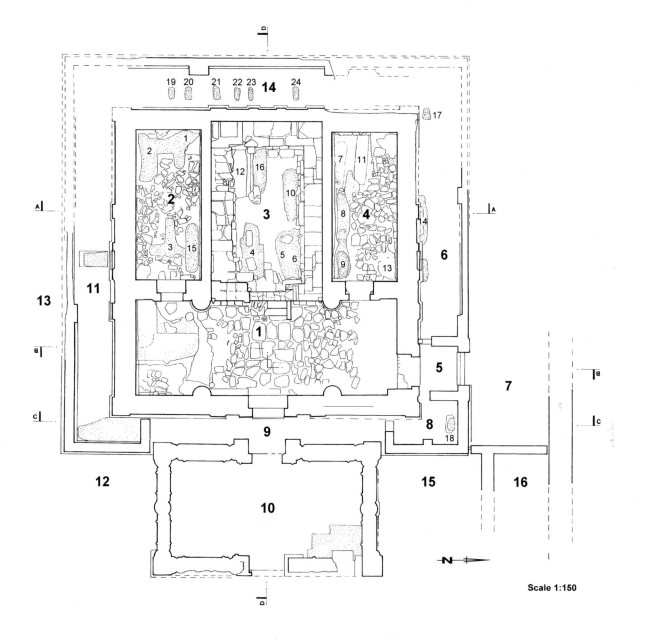

Figure 12 Plan of North Tomb 1 showing location of rooms (and spaces) and Christian graves (drawing by B. Rowney, adapted by B. Parr).

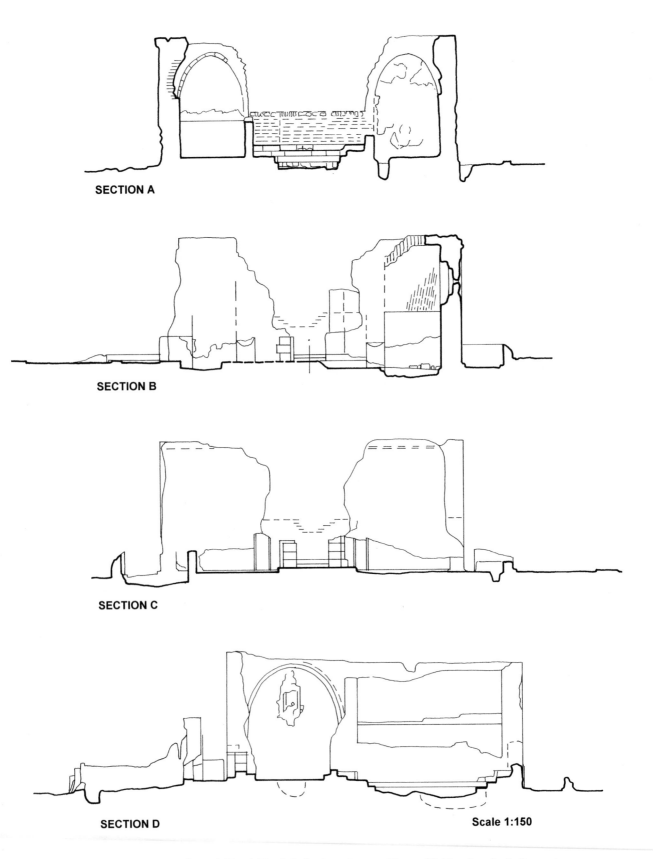

SECTION A

SECTION B

SECTION C

SECTION D   Scale 1:150

Figure 13 Sections through North Tomb 1, for location see Figure 12 (drawings by B. Rowney).

Plate 36 Portico, east and north walls of North Tomb 1 photographed by Winlock in 1908 (reproduced courtesy of the Department of Egyptian Art, The Metropolitan Museum of Art, New York); looking south-west.

Plate 37 West and south walls of North Tomb 1 photographed by Winlock in 1908 (reproduced courtesy of the Department of Egyptian Art, The Metropolitan Museum of Art, New York); looking north-east.

Plate 38 The west wall of North Tomb 1 photographed by Winlock in 1908 (reproduced courtesy of the Department of Egyptian Art, The Metropolitan Museum of Art, New York); looking east.

Plate 39 The southern end of Room 1 of North Tomb 1 with the eastern wall of Room 3 photographed by Winlock in 1908 (reproduced courtesy of the Department of Egyptian Art, The Metropolitan Museum of Art, New York); looking south.

Plate 40 The northern wall of Room 3 of North Tomb 1 photographed by Winlock in 1908 (reproduced courtesy of the Department of Egyptian Art, The Metropolitan Museum of Art, New York); looking north-west.

Plate 41 Portico and north-eastern corner of North Tomb 1 after excavation; looking south-west.

exact identity had not been determined. One, D/6 Grave 1, is located due north of the *bema* to the west of the attached column on the northern side of the apse (Plate 32), and the other, D/6 Grave 2, is immediately to the south of the *bema* (Plate 33). The former was covered with mud bricks and contained the burial of an adult, while the latter contained the burial of a child and was not covered with bricks (Plate 34). They both appear to have been positioned specifically in relation to the apse and therefore to post-date the construction of the church (*contra* Hope 2000, 58), ascribed to the second half of the fourth century on numismatic evidence (Bowen 2002, 83). Thus, D/7 Graves 1 and 2 can also be given a similar date, and it is assumed that the others in this area are contemporary, and that all are the burials of Christians (Bowen this volume b).

A two-roomed mud-brick building on a north-south alignment is situated within Enclosure 4 east of the monumental tombs, almost abutting its northern wall (Plate 35). The outer room (1) contained a hearth in the south-eastern corner and ash deposits on the floor; against its western wall were traces of a low bench. The contents of the structure, mostly ceramics, were domestic in nature and certainly fourth century in date. Four coins were found in contexts immediately above the floor: three were struck by sons of Constantine I, two while Caesar (318–24) and one while Augustus (336–40), and one by Constantine I between 324–30.[23] The area to its south appears to have been delineated with narrow walls and a channel enters this area from the north-west. A brick-lined channel enters from the south through the wall of the enclosure. These features again present a domestic aspect. Whilst the purpose of the structure has not been determined, a connection with the burials of D/7 is difficult to avoid (see Bowen this volume b). The building was constructed after the superstructure of the West Tombs had begun to erode, as a deposit of sand and small pieces of sandstone undoubtedly from those tombs underlies both rooms.

During the removal of salt-compacted brick collapse and sand against the northern wall of the enclosure, due east of the two-roomed structure, two deposits of glass vessels were found. These were, unfortunately, in a fragmentary state and await conservation and cleaning; they comprise five and two vessels respectively, and were found 20–30 cm below the surface. It is uncertain whether any of these vessels are to be associated with the brick structure or whether they were simply dropped here. Two of the items are of particular note. One is a mould-blown vessel in the form of a child's head and the other a unique jug painted with scenes of combatant gladiators. All of these vessels may be dated to the fourth century; they are discussed elsewhere in this volume with a focus upon the gladiator vase (Hope *et al.* this volume).

II The North Tomb Group

A series of mud-brick mausolea located on the north-western edge of the site have been termed the North Tomb Group and another group on the south is termed the South Tomb Group (Figure 1; Knudstad and Frey 1999, 208–13).[24] The examination of the two largest structures in the northern group was commenced in 2000 and completed in 2001, whilst work on one of the South Tombs was undertaken in 2001. During the 2002 field season examination of the surface of the site to the south-west and north-west of the North Tomb Group revealed the remains of further mud-brick tombs, preserved only to the lower courses of their walls. Another structure, probably a tomb, was discovered approximately 15 m north of the West Tombs that preserves the vault of a subterranean chamber. Thus, it is conceivable that rather than being isolated structures, the West Tombs form the southern limit of a second row of mausolea that lined the north-western side of the site, paralleling the distribution of the South Tomb Group.

II.1 North Tomb 1

This structure is the largest of any occurring in either of the two groups (Figures 12 and 13) and is located at the southern end of the eastern row of the northern group, isolated from the remainder. Before excavation commenced in 2000 it was known that the central chamber was sandstone-lined and decorated with mortuary scenes of pharaonic type painted upon gypsum plaster. These scenes were photographed by H. E. Winlock when he visited Dakhleh in 1908 and a single view was included in the publication of that trip along with other general views of the monument (Winlock 1936, 20–1, plates XI–XIII). The room had been cleared by B. Moritz during a brief trip to Dakhleh in 1900 but only a preliminary account of the work was ever published (Moritz 1900, 466–71).

Since Winlock's recording of the monument considerable deterioration has occurred, the majority of the stone from the central chamber having either been removed or destroyed. For this reason it seemed advantageous to reproduce here all of Winlock's photographs of the tomb to enable a better appreciation of the significance of this structure (Plates 36–40).[25] A discussion of the pharaonic-style painted decoration in the central chamber is presented elsewhere in this volume by Olaf Kaper, who assigns a date in the early second century CE to the paintings.

North Tomb 1 consists of a free-standing entrance porch (Room 10; Plate 41) on the east that leads into a transverse

---

[23] I am grateful to Gillian Bowen for providing identifications of all coins referred to in this article.

[24] The discussion of the architecture of these tombs in that study is based on surface reconnaissance and therefore differs from that presented here.

[25] I am most grateful to Dr Dorothea Arnold of the Egyptian Department of The Metropolitan Museum of Art, New York, for providing copies of these photographs and permission to reproduce them in this report.

Plate 42 South wall of North Tomb 1; looking north.

Plate 43 West wall of North Tomb 1; looking east.

Plate 44 Entrance into Room 1 of North Tomb 1 from the Portico; looking west.

Plate 45 Part of the Greek inscription from Room 1 of North Tomb 1.

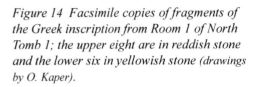

Figure 14 Facsimile copies of fragments of the Greek inscription from Room 1 of North Tomb 1; the upper eight are in reddish stone and the lower six in yellowish stone (drawings by O. Kaper).

Plate 46 Southern section of the floor of Room 1 of North Tomb 1; looking south-west.

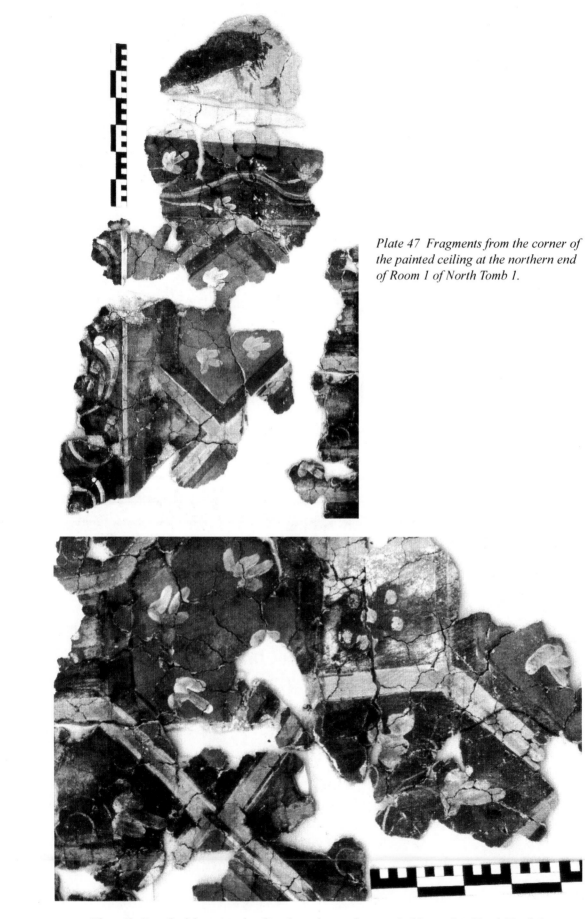

Plate 47 Fragments from the corner of the painted ceiling at the northern end of Room 1 of North Tomb 1.

Plate 48 Detail of the painted ceiling from the northern end of Room 1 in North Tomb 1.

hall (Room 1) off which open three similarly-sized chambers to the west (Rooms 2–4); the core of the tomb is about 12 m square and stood about five metres in height (Plate 42).[26] Around the tomb is an inner corridor comprising three spaces (Rooms 6, 11 and 14) that could originally be accessed only from a small room (5) at the east end of northern corridor (6). This room also provides a point of entry to the tomb through a door in the northern wall of Room 1, while another small room (8) at the north-eastern exterior corner of the tomb is reached via Room 5 also. None of these side rooms communicates with the corridor (9) separating the porch from the tomb. The whole complex appears to be set within a wall some five metres from the tomb (Figure 12; Plate 41, bottom right). This wall can be traced on the north and extends for a considerable distance to the east of the actual tomb, approximately 37 m, at which point it appears to turn through 90 degrees to the south, but its full length on the east could not be determined and there is no clear trace of it on the south or west of the tomb. There is a semblance of a *dromos* leading to the porch that again awaits definition. The area between the porch and exterior enclosure wall is subdivided into at least two spaces (15–16) that block access to the northern entrance system into the tomb, via space 7, from this direction.

In the exterior faces of the northern, southern and western walls there are pilasters with papyriform capitals framing central false doors with cavetto cornices supporting small niches; at each corner there is another pilaster (Plates 37, 41–3). The rear, western, wall is badly damaged at the centre (Plate 38) but the lower parts of the pilasters and the false door remain (Plate 43). The façade of the building had pilasters flanking the central door and corner pilasters. Around the top of all walls there is a plain architrave and cavetto cornice. All of these features and the walls were once coated with gypsum plaster; the walls are battered.

The porch is entered from the east via a door on the same axial alignment as those from the porch into the tomb and then into the tomb's central stone chamber. It has screen walls set between 10 columns, with attached vertical torus mouldings that may once have supported cavetto cornices; the walls are painted alternately in monochrome red or yellow both inside and out. The corner columns are double-engaged and have piers at the exterior to form the corners; those columns flanking the doors have attached piers to form the doorjambs. The porch is separated from the mausoleum proper by a sandstone-paved corridor (Room 9), closed by short walls from the corridor surrounding the exterior on the north, south and west (Rooms 6, 11 and 14). There is a sandstone door-sill from the porch into this corridor (Plate 44).

Entry into the transverse hall was through a doorway with sandstone jambs (Plate 44), originally closed by double doors. Twenty-four fragments of sandstone inscribed in Greek were discovered in Room 1; the stone of eight is reddish in colour while that of the remainder, which partly join, is yellowish (Figure 14; Plate 45). It is uncertain whether the colour variation should be used to identify two original inscriptions given the range found within single blocks employed elsewhere on the site. Two further pieces were found by Moritz (1900, 467) during his clearance of the central stone room. He identified them as from a lintel from a door into that room. It is possible, however, that these pieces and those found in 2000 are from a lintel over the outer door into the tomb. It has not proved possible to translate the inscription because of its fragmentary nature, but it appears to have commemorated the construction of the tomb and those for whom it was built.[27] Fragments of painted sandstone, one with a uraeus, were found in the fill of the transverse hall, indicating that either the outer or inner stone door may have supported a cornice decorated with a winged disc flanked by uraei. A short flight of stone steps descends into the hall, which has the remains of a floor of irregularly-shaped sandstone blocks (Plate 46); on either side of the door half columns are attached to the wall. These are aligned with others that are located at the junction of the walls of the central chamber and those flanking it. There is the remains of a niche centrally-located in the southern wall. It is possible that the central section of this hall in front of the Room 3 was not roofed, while those parts to the north and south in front of the other chambers were certainly barrel-vaulted (Plate 39).

The northern vaulted section was originally decorated with a classical coffer motif. This comprises a foliate scroll border (Plate 47) around interconnecting, horizontal and vertical hexagons, some of which contain birds within foliage and others a stylized floral design (Plate 48). The background is salmon pink. The horizontal hexagons are outlined in light green and red, and coloured orange; they contain white flowers or birds. The vertical hexagons are similar but lack the red outline; the intervening squares are coloured blue-black with what are probably grapes in maroon. The walls in the northern section are yellow. The southern section of vault may have had a similar design but only small sections were recovered decorated with a maroon vine motif on a white ground, with purple grapes. The walls there are originally red with yellow squares on the lower part, but this was over-painted in purple with an unidentified yellow design. The attached columns on either side of the door into the central stone room are also

---

[26] The numbering of the rooms reflects the sequence of their identification and excavation, and whilst not entirely logical, will be retained here as the find spots of a considerable number of burials and artefacts were recorded at the time of excavation in relation to contexts within the rooms so numbered.

[27] I am grateful to Klaas Worp for information on this inscription, the contents of which he identifies on the basis of the occurrence twice of a verb characteristically found in such building inscriptions and for which he refers the reader to M. C. Hellmann, *Les signatures d'architectes en langue grecque, Zeitschrift für Papyrologie und Epigraphik* 104 (1994), 151–78.

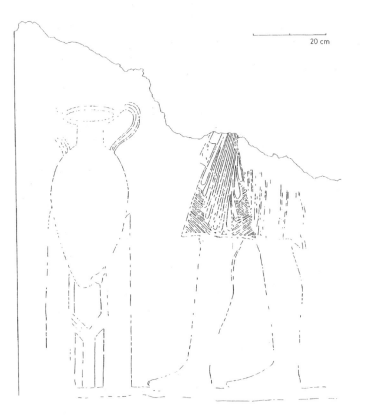

*Figure 15 Facsimile copy of painting on the wall south of the
entrance into Room 1 of North Tomb 1 (drawing by O. Kaper).*

Plate 49 Painting on the wall south of the entrance into Room 1 of North Tomb 1; looking east.

Plate 50 Room 3 of North Tomb 1; looking west.

Plate 51 Room 1 of North Tomb 1; looking west.

Plate 52 Room 4 of North Tomb 1; looking west.

Plate 53 Graves 4–6 in Room 3 of North Tomb 1; looking west.

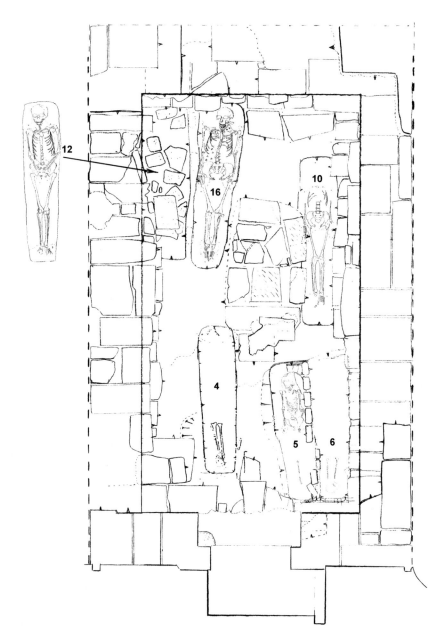

Figure 16 Plan of Room 3 of North Tomb 1
(drawing by B. Rowney and D. Tuck and C. McGregor, compiled by B. Parr).   Scale 1:50.

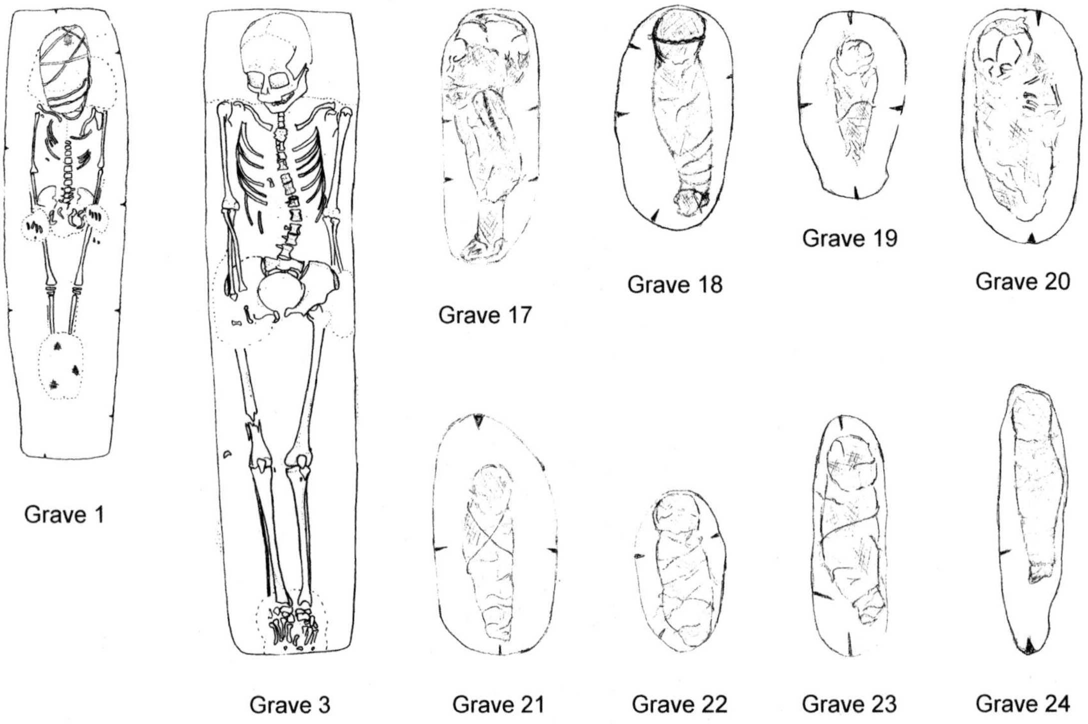

Grave 1

Grave 3   Grave 21   Grave 22   Grave 23   Grave 24

Grave 17

Grave 18

Grave 19

Grave 20

Figure 17 Burials from North Tomb 1: Graves 1 and 3 from Room 2; Grave 17 from Space 6, Grave 18 from Room 8;
Graves 19–24 from Space 14 (drawings by W. Dolling and D. Tuck). Scale 1:20.

decorated. The northern one is yellow with purple vertical stripes, rounded at the bases, above a horizontal purple band; the decoration imitates fluting. The southern one has traces of a similar decoration, but an earlier design on a red base is visible.

Decorating the interior of the wall on either side of the entrance into the transverse hall are the remains of figures Only that on the south wall is clear and only its lower part survives. A male figure faces towards the door, wearing a kilt and standing beside a large amphora in a tripod support all upon a baseline (Figure 15; Plate 49). The skin colour is red, as is the amphora and support, while the kilt was originally white with a pale green, decorative frontal section, flanked by stripes and a green tassel suspended from its belt. The features of the kilt enable the figure to be identified as divine, and it is suggested by Olaf Kaper (personal communication, 2003) that along with the northern counterpart, he may be represent either Horus or Thoth, possibly pouring a libation. Details of execution distinguish the painting from those in the central chamber described elsewhere in this volume by Kaper.

The central chamber on the west, Room 1, now preserves only the lower parts of its stone walls and part of its stone floor (Plate 50); only a few traces of the original pharaonic decoration were recovered amongst the stone and brick rubble filling the room. A flight of two or three stone steps with a low balustrade provides access into this room.

What appears to be a central niche in its western wall (Winlock 1936, plate XIII) is the result of missing wall blocks. From Winlock's photographs (Plates 38–40) and the information provided by Moritz (Kaper this volume), the height of the stone walls in this chamber at the time of discovery can be determined as 2.70 m.[28] The room was probably stone vaulted. The chambers flanking it, Rooms 2 and 4, are paved with irregularly-shaped blocks of sandstone, but the walls and roofs are of mud-brick, the latter being barrel-vaulted (Plates 51 and 52). The northern room is painted red and the southern room yellow to heights of 1.41 and 1.38 m respectively. It is probable that all doors throughout the tomb were of wood, the timbers being secured to a frame with large iron nails, numerous examples of which were found.

In addition to the evidence of alterations yielded by the painting of the southern part of the transverse hall, features of other rooms indicate at least two architectural phases. The steps leading into Room 3 are built against and obscure the original jambs of the door into the room, while the stone floor of Room 1 is at a higher level than the bases of the attached brick columns against its western wall. Another lower floor in Room 1 is revealed by cuts through the upper floor. Three fragments from a well-carved sandstone offering table were found built into the jamb of the door through the northern wall of Room 1 into Room 5 (Figure 18a–b). Two distinct floors were noted in Rooms

---

[28] The dimensions provided by Moritz for the chamber, 5.40 by 2.94 m, are incorrect, and represent that part of the room where the floor is missing. The chamber is actually 6.45 by 4.50 m.

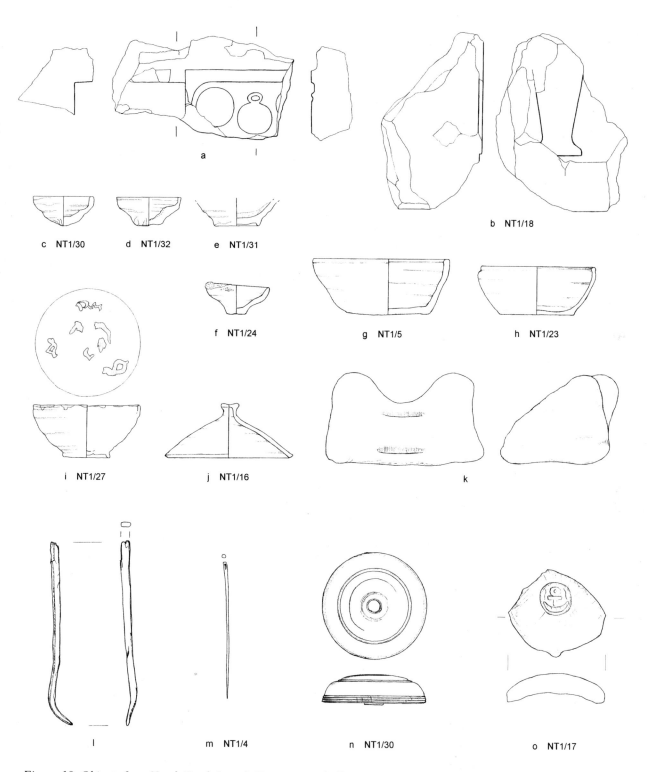

Figure 18 Objects from North Tomb 1: a–b *Fragments of offering tables from Room 1;* c–j *Ceramics from various locations;* k *Ceramic headrest (?) from Room 8;* l–m *Copper-alloy pins from Space 12;* n *Wooden spindle whorl from Space 12;* o *Gypsum sealing with crux ansata from Grave 3 (drawings by B. Parr, C. Marchini and A. Dunsmore). Scale* a–j *1:4 and* l–o *1:2; object registration numbers provided.*

2 and 4; the doors into Room 5 from space 7 and into Room 6 from 5 were blocked with mud bricks.

Little evidence survives to indicate the location of the original burials. The floors of the three western rooms are pitted and later burials, mostly all disturbed, were found in graves cut through the stone floors in Rooms 2 and 3 (Figures 12, 16 and 17, Graves 1–6; Dupras and Tocheri this volume a). In Room 2 Graves 1 and 3 contained remains (Figure 17), while 2 was empty; in Room 3 (Figure 16) Grave 4 contained remains from two individuals, while bones from the individual interred in Grave 6 were found mixed with those in Grave 5. All were oriented east-west with heads on the west and little in the way of grave goods that could be associated directly with the burials was found; they may well be the burials of Christians. Grave 3 in Room 2 yielded part of a gypsum sealing in the upper fill bearing the impression from a seal carved with a *crux ansata* (Figure 18o), which lends support to this interpretation. Skeletal material was found in highly disturbed circumstances in all rooms of the tomb. Ceramic from the tomb is mostly fourth century in date (Figure 18c–j); the two copper-alloy pins (Figures 18l–m) could also be of this date or earlier. Items that predate the suggested Christian usage are the fragments from the finely-worked offering table and what resembles a ceramic headrest (Figure 18k).

During the 2001 season the focus of the excavation within this monument was the locating and recording of all intrusive burials and, hopefully, evidence for the location of the original burials. Eighteen further graves, numbered 7–24, were investigated that contained burials in various states of preservation (Dupras and Tocheri this volume a). Of these complete or near-complete bodies were preserved in Graves 10, 12 and 16 in Room 3 (Figure 16, Plate 53), Grave 13 in Room 4, Grave 17 in Room 6, Grave 18 in Room 8 and Graves 19–24 in Room 14 (Figures 12 and 17). All other cuts contained disarticulated and disturbed human remains with the exception of one, Grave 15 in Room 2, which was completely empty. Graves 14 and 17–24 are located within the corridor and rooms surrounding the main part of the tomb, and all contained the remains of small children. None of the burials was accompanied by artefacts.

Work within Rooms 1–4, which form the core of the tomb, concentrated on floor level and sub-floor activity, and it could be demonstrated clearly that the original gypsum-plastered floor in Rooms 1, 2 and 4 had been replaced by stone floors comprising randomly-cut sandstone blocks. The floor in Room 3 was originally of stone, but this had been removed almost completely, either before or at the time the burials in that room (4–6, 10, 12 and 16) were made.

The majority of the graves post-date the original use of the tomb. Those cuts within the tomb that were obviously graves were all dug through the stone floors or made when the latter had been partially removed. Again, they are oriented east-west; where the body remained its head was always positioned on the west. Those who cut the graves and those who were buried in them may, therefore, be identified as Christians, and a date in the second half of the fourth century suggested. Most of the bodies of adults had been disturbed to some degree. In some cases it appeared as though the body had been dug up, the wrappings carelessly pulled away and the body then thrown back into the grave. Where this had not happened (Graves 7 and 10) it seems as though the western end of the grave was dug into, as though the head was targeted specifically. This feature has also been observed in the contemporary cemetery immediately to the east of the settlement (31/405-C5-2, Kellis 2).

A careful search was made for the location of original burials, including under the stone paving in the transverse hall (Room 1) and below floors in rooms within and outside of the tomb. No subterranean chambers were located. Room 1 did contain two pits in its south-western corner (Figure 12): an earlier north-south pit extending from the centre of the southern wall is cut by another that is east-west against the southern wall. Unfortunately it could not be determined whether either predate the laying of the floor of the room, and neither contained remains of interments of any type, though their fill, context 45, did contain human skeletal material. If the earlier pit was dug for a burial then, because of its orientation, it is distinct from the majority of those found in the tomb; furthermore, whilst the pit against the southern wall is east-west, such a location for a non-Christian burial is paralleled by the finds in North Tomb 2, there within pottery coffins. It must be concluded that the original burials were probably placed within the three rear rooms of the tomb, either in coffins or upon funerary beds, though no trace of these was found. The total minimum number of burials represented by the skeletal material is estimated at 35, 20 adults and 15 juveniles (Dupras and Tocheri this volume a), a number that exceeds that of the graves. Unless there were more multiple burials than the two noted (4 and 24), then if all of the material originates from burials made within the tomb we must conclude that these interments were not always within graves, and some may represent the people for whom the tomb was erected or those buried within it before its substantial reuse by Christians.

During the course of this study substantial evidence was accumulated on the building techniques of the tomb, and the main phases of construction. The tomb is built onto the basal clay of the site with foundations set into trenches; the floors of the portico and external rooms rest upon a foundation of red clay and crushed sandstone. Only the central stone-lined room has substantial foundation courses of stone blocks.

II.2 North Tomb 2

The examination of this tomb commenced in 2000; it is situated 25 m to the north of Tomb 1 (Figure 1). It was

Plate 54 The western end of North Tomb 2 photographed by Winlock in 1908 (reproduced courtesy of the Department of Egyptian Art, The Metropolitan Museum of Art, New York); looking south-east.

Plate 55 The entrance into North Tomb 2 and remains of its portico; looking north-west.

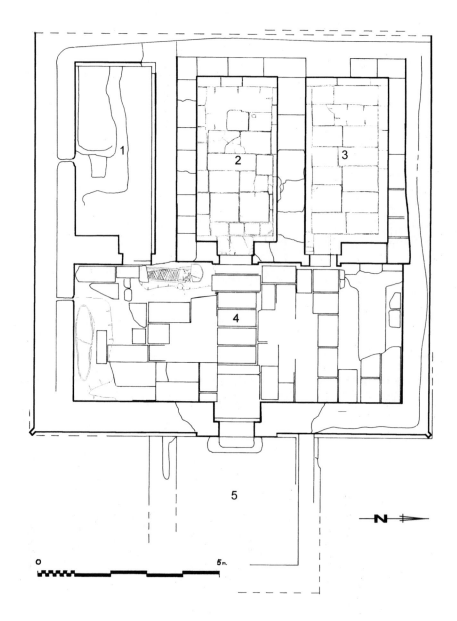

Figure 19 Plan of North Tomb 2
(drawing by B. Rowney, supplemented by D. Tuck, compiled by B. Parr). Scale 1:100.

Plate 56 Eastern end of North Tomb 2 showing Room 4 and with Rooms 2–3 on the right; looking south-east.

Plate 57 Rooms 2 and 3 of North Tomb 2; looking east.

*Plate 58 Room 4 of North Tomb 2;
looking south.*

Plate 59 Burials in the floor of Room 2 in North Tomb 2; looking south.

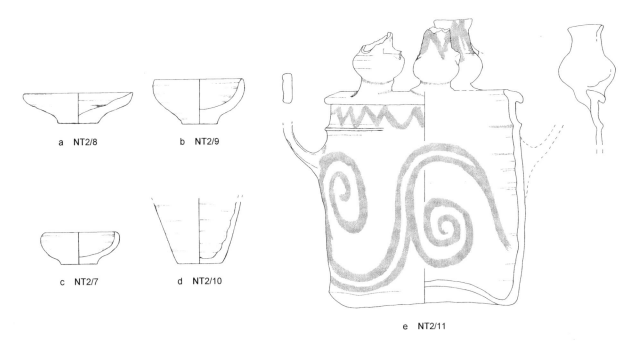

Figure 20 Ceramics from North Tomb 2: a–d *from Room 2;* e *from Rooms 2 and 3 (drawings by A. Dunsmore and B. Parr). Scale 1:4; object registration numbers provided.*

Plate 60 Sandstone offering table, object registration number NT2/5, found on the floor of Room 2 in North Tomb 2.

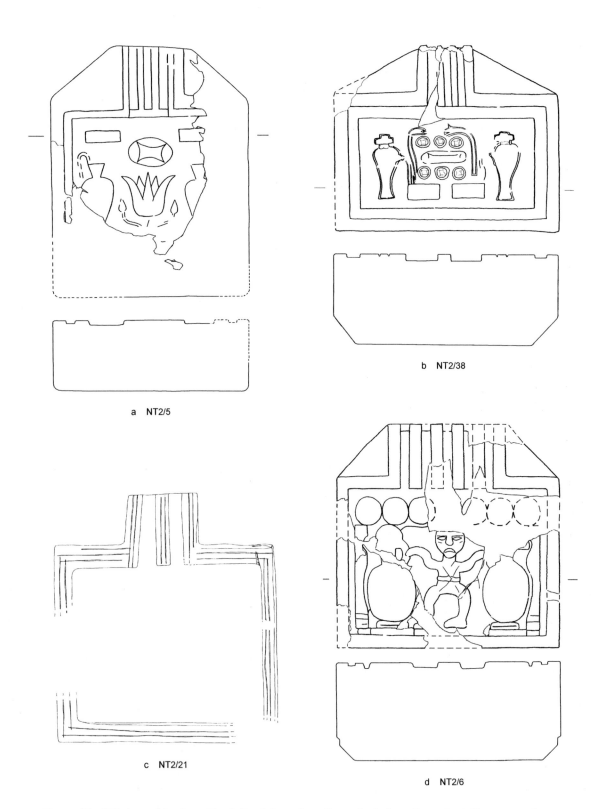

a   NT2/5

b   NT2/38

c   NT2/21

d   NT2/6

*Figure 21 Offering tables from North Tomb 2: a from Room 2; b from Room 3; c Fragments from
Rooms 2–4; d Fragments from Rooms 1 and 4 (drawings by B. Parr and O. Kaper).
Scale 1:5; object registration numbers provided.*

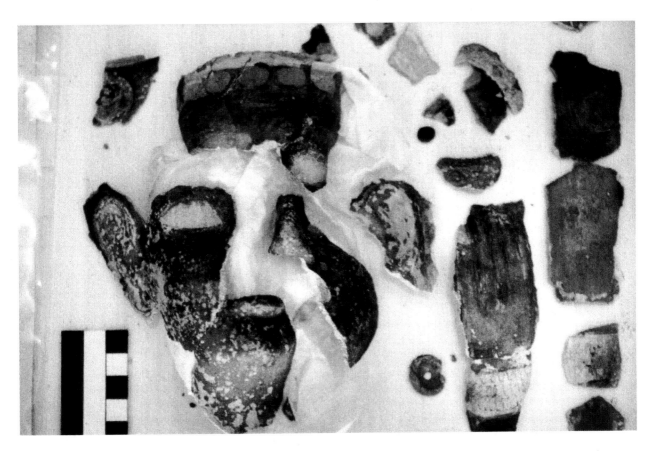

Plate 61 Fragments from a painted cartonnage coffin or coffins from North Tomb 2; face from Room 2 found near Body 2 and the hand from Room 3.

Plate 62 Fragmentary green glass heart scarab and one polychrome glass wing from Room 3 in North Tomb 2.

also photographed by Winlock during his visit to the site (Plate 54). The architecture (Figure 19) basically represents a simplified version of that of North Tomb 1.[29] It has three chambers on the west, Rooms 1–3, which all open off a transverse hall, Room 4, entered through the centre of its eastern wall; a small poorly-preserved porch, Room 5, fronts this entrance (Plate 55). As in North Tomb 1, the doors into North Tomb 2 were probably of wood and numerous iron nails from their construction were found. Surviving door pivots indicate that double-doors opened into Room 2, and all others were single. The core of the tomb is about 10 m square, it stands to just less than five metres in height and is set upon a platform. Its exterior walls are battered and adorned only with a cavetto cornice above a torus moulding on all but the eastern wall, and corner mouldings. The exterior walls were originally white-plastered. The lower parts of pilasters survive framing the entrance into the tomb in the centre of the eastern wall, and it is likely that this door supported a cavetto cornice (Knudstad and Frey 1999, Figure 13.37). Unlike North Tomb 1, the central and northern chambers, Rooms 2 and 3, are both of sandstone, with stone-paved floors and possibly once stone vaults; only the lower parts of the walls survive (Plates 56 and 57). Fragments from a sandstone cavetto cornice were found in Room 4, as were five fragments of painted sandstone, several of which join to preserve part of an image of a solar disc flanked by uraei. These undoubtedly derive from over the doors into Rooms 2 and 3. Pieces of plaster decorated in red and black were also found in Room 4. The southern chamber, Room 1, is of mud brick and its barrel-vaulted roof is well preserved (Plate 54). The transverse hall, Room 4, is also of mud brick, with a barrel-vault, but it has a sandstone-paved floor (Plates 56 and 58); as with all of the stone floors in the tomb, this one was coated with a layer of plaster. All external walls are mud brick. There was a parapet wall approximately one metre in height above the roof of the tomb (Knudstad and Frey 1999, 211, Figure 13.37).

Removal of collapse in Room 1 revealed east-west pitting in the floor that may represent cuts for graves through the floor, most of which had been removed. Just above floor level in the Room 2 the remains of the burials of a least four adults, skeletonized, and one wrapped infant were found (Dupras and Tocheri this volume a). The skeletal remains were oriented east-west with the heads on the east (Plate 59), but it is uncertain if this represents their original placement as none of the them was complete and there is evidence for extensive disturbance throughout the tomb. Furthermore, the matrix in which they were found comprises crushed sandstone, charcoal, ash and sand that appears to derive from an episode of looting and destruction. They were accompanied by a small selection of objects including pottery and a sandstone offering table;

some fragments of decorated cartonnage were also recovered. The intrusive burial of an infant wrapped completely in linen and oriented north-south, with the head to the south, was found in a pit cut through one of the other burials and into the stone floor of the room.

The pottery (Figure 20a–e) included bowls that may be ascribed to the second to third century CE and an unusual vessel painted with an interlocking-spiral motif and with small jars attached at the rim. Fragments from the latter were found elsewhere in the tomb. The sandstone offering table (Plate 60; Figure 21a) is decorated with two one-handled vessels flanking an open lotus flower with buds, above which is a loaf of bread, all in incised relief, within an incised groove that connects to channels for the draining of libations. The cartonnage, from Body 2, is extremely fragmentary. Some pieces are red-coloured and amongst them are parts of a face with a wreath at the forehead; similarly-coloured fragments preserving arms and a hand with a bracelet at the wrist were found in Room 3 to the north (Plate 61). Amongst the same matrix in which the bodies were found there was a quantity of burnt and gilded wood that clearly derived from either a coffin, a shrine or box.

The northern chamber, Room 3, had witnessed a fire of considerable temperature at some stage that reduced much of the burial furniture to charcoal and turned parts of the human skeletal material into a substance resembling glass. It is evident from the preliminary study of the fragments that the chamber contained what may have been either a decorated funerary bed upon which the body was laid, a coffin or a box, as shown by fragments with friezes of uraei and small columns supporting papyrus capitals, and other carved elements, all with traces of gilding. The majority of this material was burnt, some to the point of being unrecognisable; it appeared to concentrate in two rows parallel to the north and south walls of the room. The matrix in which these pieces were found was identical to that in which the bodies of Room 2 were situated, and the two undoubtedly result from the same event. Other items of significance include more decorated cartonnage, a plaster eye socket with glass inlay, and a moulded, dark-green glass, heart scarab with wings of red glass and details in yellow and white (Plate 62). More fragments of cartonnage were found adjacent to the exterior wall of Room 3. Amongst the cartonnage is one piece, coloured blue and red, that preserves a representation of a crouching jackal and a dependant uraeus; another preserves part of a hieroglyphic text in black on a blue ground. Room 3 also yielded pieces from three offering tables, one of which could be restored (Figure 21b, Plate 63); fragments from one of the others (Figure 21c) were also found in Rooms 2 and 4.

The fire seems to have been restricted to Rooms 2 and 3, although the floor of the transverse hall was covered with a blackened oily material that may have been burnt

---

[29] The room numbering reflects the sequence in which they were identified during the excavations. Again, the description of this monument and the drawings published in Knudstad and Frey 1999, 211 and Figure 13.37, need revising in the light of the excavations.

Plate 63 Sandstone offering table, object registration number NT2/38, from Room 3 in North Tomb 2.

Plate 64 Fragments from one of the short ends of a funerary bed, object registration number NT2/35, from Room 4 of North Tomb 2.

*Figure 22   Fragments from one of the short ends of a funerary bed, object registration number NT2/35,
from Room 4 of North Tomb 2 (drawings by B. Parr and O. Kaper).   Scale 1:4.*

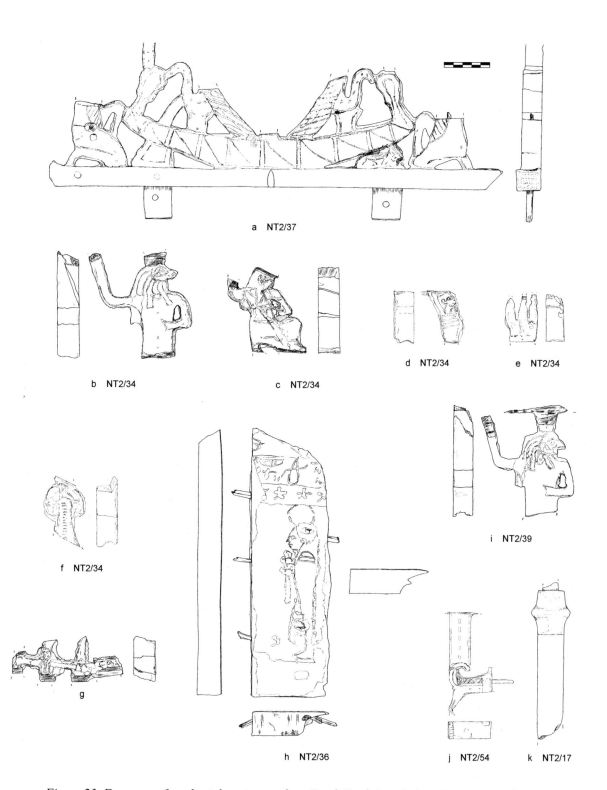

Figure 23 Fragments from burial equipment from North Tomb 2: a–h *from Room 4 near floor;*
i *from fill of grave in the northern end of Room 4;* j *from fill of grave in the southern end of Room 4;*
k *from Room 2 (drawings by B. Parr and O. Kaper). Scale: 1:4; object registration numbers provided.*

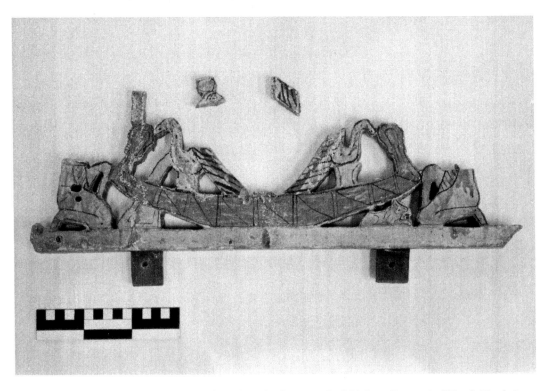

Plate 65 Open-work barque from the sides of a funerary bed(?) from Room 4 of North Tomb 2.

Plate 66 Remains of a burial in a pit through the floor of Room 1 in North Tomb 2; looking west.

(Plate 59). Amongst the low fill in this room were found fragments from at least one polychrome-decorated, inscribed wooden funerary bed and a box. The fragments from the bed include parts from one of the short ends with lower panels carrying representations of a falcon-headed and a jackal-headed deity, Horus and Anubis, pouring libations, and an upper panel with another jackal-headed deity, Duamutef, presenting offerings of linen and oil/ointment (Figure 22, Plate 64). The figures of Anubis and Duamutef are on the right and Horus on the left. Above the figures are rows of stars and a cavetto cornice with a scale or feather pattern. Dowels in the top of the upper panel indicate that another element was affixed here. The figures are drawn in black outlines and have internal details in black also, in which colour the offerings and libations are shown. They are set upon a background that is divided vertically into two colours, with green behind the figure and red in front. The stars are on a black ground above Horus and a turquoise ground above Anubis and Duamutef; the feather (or scale) pattern on the cornices are green and red. The vertical corner post preserves sections of text in hieroglyphic writing coloured pale green. This has been studied by Olaf Kaper, whose comments are reproduced in Appendix 1.

Other polychrome wooden fragments from various places within the same room include part of a funerary boat with winged uraei, flanked by kneeling figures who probably represent the Souls of Pe and Nekhen (Figure 23a, Plate 65). The boat is coloured red on a green base; the figures and uraei are yellow with black details. Various other fragments may come from a similar composition and the same object, possibly a funerary bed (Figure 23b–g). The fragment from a box (Figure 23h) was also found; it is also polychrome-painted and carries a figure of Imsety in yellow, standing upon an area coloured red, with pale green in front of him and pale red behind. A row of white stars on a black ground is above the figure and above this is part of a hieroglyphic text in black on a yellow ground and then a red area. Dowels on the left and right edges of the piece indicate that it was attached to further panels. Whether the burnt and carbonised fragments of funerary furniture found in Rooms 2 and 3 come from the same items as the fragments from Room 4 cannot be determined. It is also uncertain how many items are represented by this assemblage. The fragments from the end of the funerary bed have interior faces coated with gesso and painted red as do the fragments from the boat, while some of the figures have the same treatment inside and others are plain. This latter may be the result of erosion.

Human remains from several other bodies (Dupras and Tocheri this volume a) were found in Room 4, some preserving tissue and elaborate bandaging. The upper part of a well-preserved mummified male, discovered at floor level in the south central part of the room, may originally have been interred in one of the damaged ceramic coffins buried below the floor of the room (see below). Distributed throughout the tomb were pieces from several carved, sandstone offering tables, one of which was of extremely high-quality workmanship (Figure 21d). Provisional study

of the objects would indicate dates for the burials within the first or second centuries CE.

Following the 2000 season the excavation of the floor deposits in the transverse hall, Room 4, and portico, Room 5, remained to be completed, as did the examination of any sub-floor deposits. This work was completed in 2001.

It appears that the construction of the tomb was undertaken in a single phase; unlike in Tomb 1, there is no evidence of changes to floor level. The stone chambers of tomb sit upon foundations with a specially-dug pit while the other rooms are built directly upon the basal clay. No subterranean chambers were located, though, unlike in Tomb 1, the stone flooring was not lifted as it was extremely-well preserved except in the southern rear room. Here a deep pit was found in the south-western corner that appears to have been executed by robbers in an effort to locate subterranean burials; it is 2.7 m deep and irregularly shaped. Several sandstone paving slabs were found in it at a depth of 1.65 m and 1.8 m; below the former were the remains of the burial of a child placed in a crouched position within sand (Plate 66). Only the torso and lower limbs survived; associated with it was a large quantity of linen. Several fragments from an elaborately-carved, sandstone offering table were found at a similar depth but they do not appear to have been associated with this burial, which seems to be late in date. Other fragments from the same table were found in sand deposits elsewhere within the same room (Figure 21d).

In the transverse outer room three graves were located: one each against the northern and southern walls, and one against the western wall between the doors into the central and southern rear rooms. None of these was original in that they were cut into the foundation trenches for the neighbouring walls and they disturbed the original distribution of paving slabs (Plate 67). Each grave originally contained a single burial within a ceramic coffin. The paving stones of the floor had been removed completely for the northern and southern graves, while they had been replaced, somewhat randomly, over the western one (Plate 67, right). The burial in the northern grave was represented only by fragments of bone and linen, and the coffin had been completely broken. From the fill, which consisted of sand containing some pieces of mud brick, sandstone and charcoal, came further painted wooden fragments representing divine figures, including the ancestral spirits (Figure 23i). The southern burial was again poorly preserved though the coffin was almost intact. The fill of the grave comprised material similar to that within the northern grave, with large quantities of human bone and linen, and a small number of fragmentary objects including pieces of painted wood, one showing a figure on a funerary bed (Figure 23j). The coffin contained the same material as the pit but with little bone. It is possible that the torso of a mummified male found on the floor of Room 4 was originally interred in this coffin.

The third burial, on the west, was in a better state of preservation. The well-wrapped remains of a female were found within a ceramic coffin, the lid of which had been broken through in antiquity and then repaired with gypsum plaster. The fill above the burial comprised sand with

*Plate 67 Floor at the southern end
of Room 4 in North Tomb 2 showing
relaid paving stones over the burial
of Senpsais; looking south-east.*

Plate 68 The mummy of Senpsais in her ceramic coffin in Room 4 of North Tomb 2; looking west.

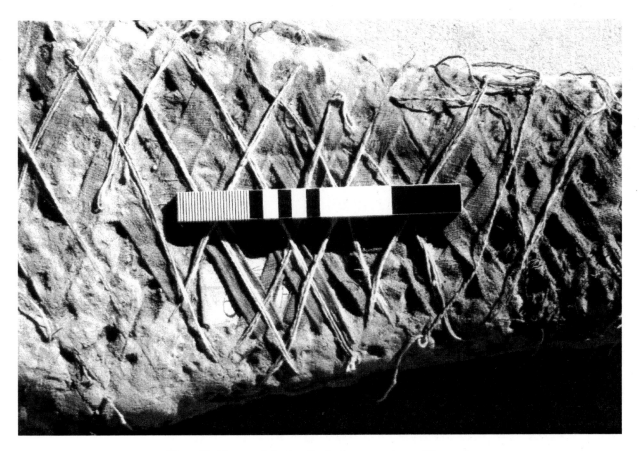

Plate 69 Mummy label in situ *in the wrappings of Senpsais.*

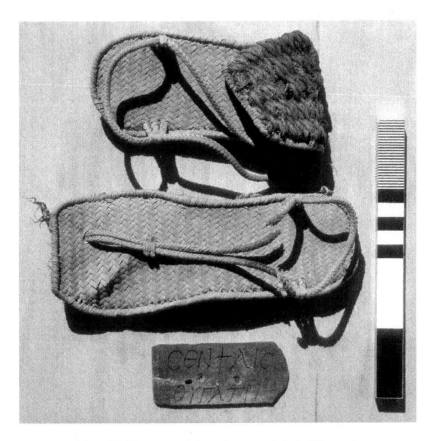

Plate 70 Woven sandals and mummy label of Senpsais.

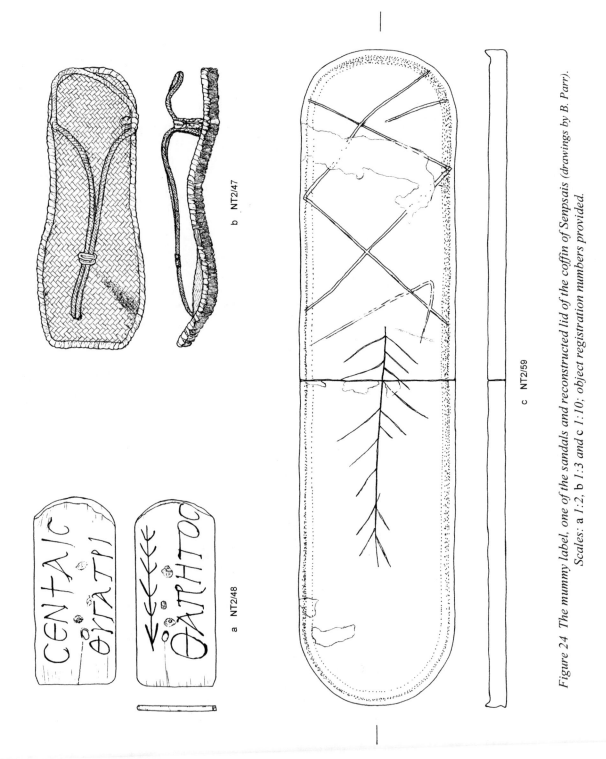

Figure 24 The mummy label, one of the sandals and reconstructed lid of the coffin of Senpsais (drawings by B. Parr). Scales: a 1:2, b 1:3 and c 1:10; object registration numbers provided.

Plate 71 The northern wall, entrance and remains of the portico of South Tomb 4 with niche in the southern wall of Room 3; looking south.

Plate 72 South Tomb 4 showing poorly-preserved eastern wall; looking south-west.

some sandstone rubble; in it were a loop-shaped handle from a metal vessel, two fragments from a burnt sandstone offering table and a small piece of gilded plaster. The head was found disarticulated and partly unwrapped (Plate 68). The remainder of the body was intact; it was wrapped first with wide bandages and then narrow bandages in a lozenge design over this, and then string also in a lozenge pattern (Plates 68 and 9). Well-preserved basketry sandals were attached to the exterior at the foot end, and a wooden 'mummy label' was secured to the body by the outer bandages (Plates 69 and 70; Figure 24). The label provides the identity of the deceased, reading on the one side ΘΑΤΡΗΤΟC and on the other CΕΝΨΑΙC ΘΥΓΑΤΡΙ: 'Senpsais, daughter of Thatres'.[30] This is the first discovery of such a label at the site. It is interesting to note that the side upon which the father's name is written was placed uppermost within the wrappings, thus identifying the person to whom the mummy was to be delivered. Furthermore, as no destination for delivery is indicated, it is possible that the mummification took place at Kellis, on which see most recently Aufderheide *et al.* (this volume). The lack of the element Aurelios in the father's name may indicate a date for the burial prior to the early third century. The style of all of these burials is similar and implies a degree of contemporaneity; the only preserved body was oriented north-south with the head on the north. The other two graves are oriented east-west. It would, therefore, appear that orientation was not a major concern for those making the interments, which are in all probability not those of Christians.

Again, it would seem that the original burials, which may be represented by finds from the previous season, were placed in the rear chambers and at least one was laid upon a funerary bed, and they were accompanied by ceramics and offering tables. At least one of these burials was within a painted cartonnage coffin, from which the winged heart scarab may also originate. The burials in the ceramic coffins represent a second phase of burial within North Tomb 2; the single burial in Room 1 is undated and may be comparatively recent. Whether there were burials of the fourth century as in North Tomb 1 is uncertain; if there were, none was placed within a grave cut through the floor of the tomb. The estimate for the minimum number of individuals attested by the skeletal remains is 32, 22 adults and 10 juveniles (Dupras and Tocheri this volume a). The original placement of all of the interments cannot be determined.

It is possible to present a tentative reconstruction of the main phases in the desecration and destruction of the tomb. Following the secondary phase of use of the tomb for the burials in the ceramic coffins by an unknown length of time, the destruction and burning of the original interments occurred. From the distribution of burnt bone and wooden

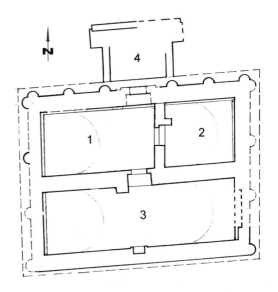

Figure 25 Plan of South Tomb 4 (drawing by J. E. Knudstad, modified by B. Parr). Scale 1:200.

objects, it would seem that this took place simultaneously in Rooms 2 and 3, but during this process some skeletal material was thrown into Room 4 along with fragments of broken wooden furniture before the burning. At this time the secondary burials in the northern and southern ends of the floor of Room 4 were broken into and despoiled, during which process some fragments from the painted wooden objects were deposited in the graves after they had been robbed. There followed an episode of sand accumulation during which further disturbance of the skeletal material and broken objects occurred. Another phase of vandalism then followed; pits were dug through the sand at certain points to floor level, paving stones in the western ends of Rooms 2 and 3 were removed and pits dug into basal clay below, presumably in the search for subterranean burials. The paving stones and clay material were deposited on top of the sand accumulation in Room 4. There was then another phase of sand fill before the brick structure of the tomb began to collapse. When the bulk of the stonework from Rooms 2 and 3 was removed is uncertain, but at that time further distribution of skeletal and other material will have resulted.

III South Tomb 4

The South Tombs are located immediately to the south-west of the settlement, beyond the remains of an ancient canal that provided irrigation for the field network around this part of the site (Figure 1; Knudstad and Frey 1999, 211–3). The exact number of mausolea within this group is uncertain as many are poorly preserved; on the west is a group of five comparatively well-preserved examples. The

---

[30] Despite grammatical inaccuracies, this seems to be the preferred reading; I am grateful to Klaas Worp for his comments upon this piece. For a recent discussions of these objects see J. Quaegebeur, Mummy Labels: An Orientation, in E. Boswinkel and P. W. Pestman, *Textes Grecs, Démotiques et Bilingues (P. L. Bat. 19)*, E. J. Brill, Leiden, 1978, 232–59; W. Scheidel, The meaning of dates on mummy labels: seasonal mortality and mortuary practice in Roman Egypt, *Journal of Roman Archaeology* 11 (1998), 285–92.

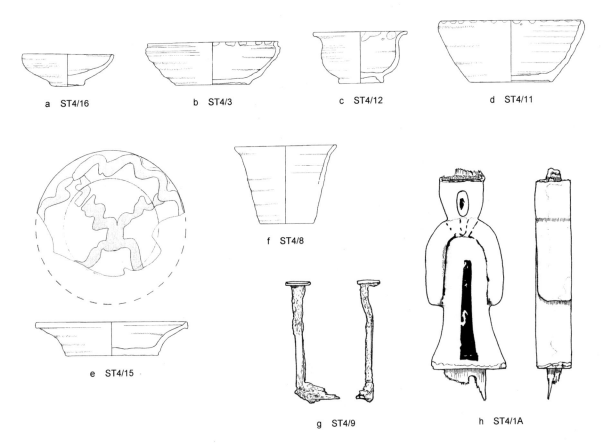

a ST4/16   b ST4/3   c ST4/12   d ST4/11

f ST4/8

e ST4/15

g ST4/9   h ST4/1A

Figure 26 Objects from South Tomb 4 (drawings by C. Marchini and B. Parr). Scales: a–f 1:4, g–h 1:2;
object registration numbers provided.

most elaborate of these, number 4, was selected for excavation (Figure 25; Plates 71 and 72).[31]

A T-shaped entrance porch (Room 4), poorly preserved and measuring approximately 3.00 x 3.65 m, fronts the structure on the north. Only its side walls and the western end of the northern wall can be traced, and then only at the level of the foundation or lower course. It is assumed that there was a centrally-located doorway in the northern wall. This porch leads into what was originally a single transverse chamber, measuring 10.5 x 3.5 m, now Rooms 1 and 2, via a poorly-preserved doorway in the centre of the common wall. Another room, Room 3, of approximately equal size is accessed through a central door in the southern wall. This doorway may have had a stone frame; the door itself was single-leafed and opened to the west into Room 3. A partition wall, erected immediately east of the door into the outer room, subdivides this room into areas of unequal size, now termed Room 1 on the west, which is the larger space, and Room 2 on the east; it is a secondary alteration to the layout and clearly abuts the original wall plaster. The floors of Rooms 1 and 2 are of compact earth; that in Room 2 is at a slightly higher level and there is a step up into the room. The floor of this room was relaid when the room was created. The door into Room 2 was single-leafed and opened to the north into the room.

In the rear (southern) wall of Room 3, which is 10.16 x 3.43 m, there is a central niche, 58 cm above the floor level, measuring 61 cm wide, 28 cm deep and preserved to a height of 70 cm. There appears to have been another niche in the eastern wall that had a stone base and an arched top, possibly with some sort of frame at the sides, but it is now poorly preserved. The floor of the inner room is of mud bricks laid obliquely from north-west to south-east, covered by a layer of mud plaster. In the centre of this floor is a deposit of what appears to be oil-rich mud.

Externally, the tomb is provided with two half-columns on the eastern and western sides, and two half-columns on either side of the entrance. At the north-eastern and north-western corners there were double half-columns, while at south edge of the eastern and western sides there was a further half column. The columns support papyriform capitals; whether there was a cavetto cornice above cannot be determined. The roofs throughout were barrel-vaulted and walls mud-plastered; there is no evidence for the use of white plaster on the walls.

Within the tomb brick collapse overlay sand fill to almost floor level. On and near the floors throughout there

---

[31] As in the case of the North Tombs 1 and 2, excavation of South Tomb 4 necessitates a revision of the plan and description of this monument provided in Knudstad and Frey 1999.

were the very disturbed remains of the interments, some, though not all, burnt (Dupras and Tocheri this volume b). In Room 1 some human remains, linen and broken objects were piled up and burnt; in Room 3 the walls and floor had been exposed to severe burning while the human remains and linen were not. The burials have clearly been exposed to wanton destruction. Associated with the human remains was a variety of incomplete artefacts. These included fragments from a gilded sandstone statue probably of Isis, fragments from a terracotta figurine of a female, pieces of plastered and painted wood that may come from funerary furniture (Figure 26h), pieces from glass and ceramic vessels (Figure 26a–f); the latter are of types that may be ascribed to the second to third centuries CE. Iron nails (Figure 26g) indicate that doors of similar construction to those in the North Tomb 1 and 2 were fitted in this tomb also. A study of the skeletal material (Dupras and Tocheri this volume b) indicates that six adults, two juveniles and one infant were buried in the tomb; whether these were all relatively contemporary cannot be determined because of the extent of disturbance.

During the 2002 field season a study of the floors of the tomb was undertaken to determine whether there were any burial chambers below. This took the form of examination of damaged sections of the floor especially in the Room 3, none of which provided evidence that can be regarded as conclusive but which does not seem to indicate their presence. In one such damaged area, south of the door into the room, fragments from a gilded limestone statue of a male with a moustache were found.

Concluding Remarks

The excavations described above continue to show that there is much still to be learned about the ancient village of Kellis. We have now excavated *in situ* material in Area C and possibly in the North Tombs of the early Roman Period that can be related to the material of similar date discovered in the cemetery on the north-west of the site (31/420-C5-1, Kellis 1; Birrell 1999), and small amounts of which have been found elsewhere in Areas A, B and D (Patten 1999, 87–8). This will enable us to gain a far clearer picture of life at Kellis during its formative period, though yet earlier material can be expected as there is growing evidence that the site was first settled in the Ptolemaic Period.[32]

The excavations have seen the completion of both long-term and short-term projects. We are now able to proceed with the preparation of final conservation and recording

of the decoration of the pharaonic-style decoration from Room 1 of the *mammisi* of the Temple of Tutu and to define its constructional phases with greater certainty. This, together with the two stelae found in 2000, will elucidate many aspects of the cult of Tutu.[33] The work in the East Churches themselves is complete, though a clear understanding of the functioning and evolution of the complex within which they stand requires further study. As they are amongst the oldest surviving in Egypt, their significance for the study of church architecture and liturgy cannot be underestimated. Further, the discovery of another cemetery of the fourth century in Areas D/6–7 containing single burials that are oriented east/west and that lack grave goods, and which may be proposed as Christian, emphasises the significant contribution the site and its associated cemeteries are making to our understanding of early Christian traditions.

The examination of both North Tombs 1 and 2 has been completed and their use from the late first or second centuries into the fourth century can be documented. That no burial crypts were discovered, raising the probability that the primary interments were located within the rear chambers at ground level, is problematic for the seeming lack of security that such arrangements provide the burials. A similar situation may be observed in South Tomb 4, though no excavation below floor level was conducted there.

Other Roman Period mud-brick mausolea within Dakhleh confirm this practice, for example those at Beyout el-Qureysh (Mills 1982, 98) to the south of Ismant el-Kharab, whilst yet others attest the use of crypts, for example some of those near Mut el-Kharab at Bir Shugalah.[34] Subterranean burials were found in some of the tombs at el-Bagawat in Kharga Oasis (Hauser 1932), and other features of their architecture resemble, in general terms, those of the Ismant el-Kharab tombs. The stone-built mausolea of similar date to the latter at Ezbet el-Bashendi (Moursi and Osing 1982; Yemani 2001) show that sarcophagi containing the deceased could be placed below the stone floors, while at Ismant el-Kharab itself, the stone and brick structures designated West Tombs 1 and 2 were both provided with subterranean vaulted burial apartments. Nothing is yet known of the burial style within the mud-brick tombs at Amheida (ancient Trimithis; Mills 1980, 269–71), but they will undoubtedly yield valuable comparable data as the superstructures have numerous features in common with the tombs at Ismant el-Kharab. From within the Nile Valley parallels to several of the features of the Ismant el-Kharab tombs can be found in

[32] This is based upon assessments of the date of some of the painted cartonnage from the cemetery to the north-west of the settlement (Schweitzer 2002), some of the Demotic texts and isolated finds of ceramics.

[33] For a study of this god that incorporates much of the Kellis material see O. E. Kaper, *The Egyptian God Tutu. A Study of the Sphinx-God and Master of Demons with a Corpus of Monuments*, Peeters, Leuven, in press.

[34] A preliminary examination of this group of tombs, first examined during the course of the survey, was undertaken in conjunction with our work at Mut el-Kharab in 2001. The site has subsequently been selected for excavation by the inspectors of the Dakhleh and Farafra Inspectorate, which has shown the tombs to be more elaborate that any others of similar date in Dakhleh.

the stone tombs at Tuna el-Gebel, though of course many of the latter are more elaborate, as are the tombs at el-Bagawat, which the Ismant el-Kharab tombs predate.

Aspects of the architecture of the Tuna el-Gebel tombs have recently been suggested to derive from the tomb chapels of the XXVth Dynasty (Arnold 1999, 49). In examining features of the Ismant el-Kharab tombs, especially those within the North Tomb Group, connections with temple architecture become apparent. The three burial chambers fronted by a longitudinal chamber, as seen in North Tomb 1 and 2,[35] occur from at least the XVIIIth Dynasty, for example at the Temple of Ptah at Karnak and Nekhbet at el-Kab (Arnold 1999, Plans VIII and XII), and consistently thereafter throughout Egypt into the Roman Period (Arnold 1999, Plans XII and XV, Figures 45, 91, 115, 119, 123, 124, 161 and 225). These include the Late Period temple at Qasr Ghweita in Kharga Oasis and the Roman temple at Deir el-Hagar in Dakhleh itself, and possibly the Ptolemaic temple at 'Ain Birbiyeh (Mills 1999, Figure 1). There is a striking similarity at the so-called chapel dedicated to Alexander the Great at Kom Madi (Bresciani 1980), which rather interestingly contains what the excavator identified as a *kline*. The façades of many of the tombs, with their cavetto cornices and torus mouldings, resemble those of what Arnold (1999, 356–7) has termed the temple house (Arnold 1999, Figures 96, 97, 160 and 220). Furthermore, the entrances to many of the tombs at Ismant el-Kharab are fronted by either an attached portico or porch, or, in the case of North Tomb 1, by a free-standing porch with columns and screen walls. These resemble the porches or kiosks erected in temples from the XXVth Dynasty onwards (Arnold 1999, 44–5, 282–5). The connection between temple and tomb is also reflected in the decorative schemes, though not in North Tomb 1 (see comments by Kaper this volume b). The architecture of these tombs and others at Ismant el-Kharab, namely the West Tombs (Hope and Mckenzie 1999), indicates the degree of elaboration that occurred in the oases during the early Roman Period.

The discovery of fragments from what were probably funerary beds in North Tomb 2 is of significance in light of the small corpus of examples that survives.[36] These objects appear within the repertoire of funerary furniture during the Roman Period; they also display distinctive elements derived from temple architecture. Whether their appearance is at all associated with the inclusion of *kline* in the Ptolemaic tombs at Alexandria is possibly worth exploring. While this is not the place to undertake a detailed typological or iconographic study of such items, a few comments are necessary to confirm the identification of the North Tomb 2 fragments. The shape of the larger pieces from the short end of the bed, representing a portal with broken lintel, and the decoration of the panels, are paralleled by several other examples. From Tomb 66 at el-Bagawat in Kharga Oasis (Metropolitan Museum of Art 31.8.1: Hauser 1932, 48, Figures 7 and 19; Parlasca 1995, 203, note 27, Plate XXIV.1)[37] comes a bed upon which the sides of the imitation portal are painted with crowned serpents that wind around a vertical sceptre. Panels flanking this element are decorated with images of gods making offerings, here Horus and Thoth, below rows of stars; it was originally supported on short legs, those at the same end as the portal originally being decorated with lions' heads. The sides are open-work and preserve panels with a checker-board motif that alternate with papiriform columns. Also from Kharga, Dush Tomb 20 (Dunand *et al.* 1992, 55, Figure 4, Plate 61.1–3), comes a fragmentary example with the portal decorated in a similar manner to that from Bagawat Tomb 66, the lion legs preserved, and with painted representations of the barque of Sokar carrying a mummified human figure. If the open-work figures and the boat found in North Tomb 2 at Ismant el-Kharab do derive from such an item, then this bed provides a parallel for the use of a boat motif. Another example preserved in Berlin (West Berlin 1683: Kurth 1990, 17, Plates 8.2 and 9.1–3; Parlasca 1991, Figures 10–11) has a pseudo-portal with panels decorated with images of Osiris, Qebesenuef and Anubis, flanked by representations of crowned serpents. This example does not have lion-headed decoration on the legs.

This feature seems to be one of the most important in the iconography of the funerary beds. In addition to those just mentioned, it occurs upon the late Ptolemaic or early Roman period example from Akhmim belonging to Nedjemib in the Egyptian Museum Cairo (CG 3263: Grimm 1975a, number 40, Plates 76–7),[38] another from Akhmim in Berlin (East Berlin 12708: Grimm 1974, 117, Plate 137.1; Kanawati 1987, 55),[39] the possible Theban example in the Royal Ontario Museum (910.27: Needler 1963), another from Thebes in Berlin (East Berlin 12442:

---

[35] A variation on this layout can be seen in the tomb of Kytinos at Ezbet Bashendi (Osing *et al.* 1982, 57).

[36] I wish to acknowledge the kind assistance of Olaf Kaper in assembling references to these items and providing me with copies of studies not available in Australia, also to Roberta Shaw for providing me with photographs of the bed in the Royal Ontario Museum and a copy of Needler 1963.

[37] I am grateful to Dr Dorothea Arnold for providing me with photographs of this and other items found at Bagawat by the Metropolitan Museum of Art Egyptian Expedition.

[38] This example is particularly important in documenting the full appearance of the beds: an open-work canopy set upon a separate base with lion-headed legs; it enables other so-called canopies or shrines to be identified as the upper section from such objects.

[39] This item has been described as an offering chest; Needler (1963, 7, footnote 42) assigns this to the Ptolemaic–Roman Period, whilst Olaf Kaper and Harco Willems (personal communication 2003) and Kanawati (1987, 55) accept a date within the First Intermediate Period or early Middle Kingdom.

Grimm 1974, 117–8, Plate 137.2; Kurth 1990, 20–2, Figure 5), and a second example from Bagawat Grave 66 (Cairo JE 56229: Hauser 1932, 45, Figures 7, 14–16, 18; Parlasca 1995, 203, footnote 26, Plates XXIV.3–4; Dunand and Lichtenberg 1998, 106), whilst wooden feet ornamented with lions heads found in several other tombs at Dush have been identified as also from such beds (Dunand *et al.* 1992, 225).[40] Another feature is the occurrence of open-work sides or panels that can be raised, thus enabling the body within to be seen: the Nedjemib bed, the example in Berlin formerly part of the West Berlin collection (1683) and one of the examples formerly in the East Berlin collection (12708), both beds from Bagawat Grave 66, all mentioned above, and also one from Dush Tomb 6 (Dunand *et al.* 1992, 27–8, Plate 60.1–3). It is possible that the canopy found by Rhind (1862, frontispiece) in the Theban tomb of Montuemsaf formed part of such a bed, as also the 'shrine' of Inaros in Hamburg (Behrmann *et al.* 1987), thus similar to the upper section of the Nedjemib bed. Amongst the charred and burnt wooden fragments found in North Tomb 2 were curved sections and panels, friezes of uraei and papyriform columns, all of which are features found on such funerary beds.

Fragments from what may also have been painted wooden funerary beds have been found in the cemetery to the north-west of the site (31/420-C5-1, Tomb 1), but of a quality far inferior to those from North Tomb 2. They possibly parallel the shape of one of the beds found at Dush in Tomb 6 (Dunand *et al.* 1992, 27–8, Plate 60.1–3), an example with straight legs.

Examples of funerary beds have been found placed within tombs and bearing human remains, such as the examples from Bagawat Grave 66 and Dush Tomb 6.[41] It has been suggested that they were not, in fact, manufactured for this purpose, but rather to display the mummified or otherwise prepared body in the home and possibly to transport it to the tomb (Needler 1963, 4–7; Castel and Dunand 1981, 107; Behrmann *et al.* 1987, 175–9). Their close resemblance to the lion-headed biers upon which the mummy is laid while the final rites are performed over it, has also been pointed out by both Needler (1963, 4–7) and Dunand (Castel and Dunand 1981, 107), while Dunand also connects them with the more classical beds (*kline*) that are both depicted and included in the Alexandrian tombs. The latter are discussed most recently by Venit (2002, 13–4 and 186–8).

The North and South Tombs at Ismant el-Kharab present features that indicate potential associations with classical traditions. Whilst the locations of built tombs on the perimeter of settlements occurs elsewhere in Egypt, and

they may be on an axial alignment, as some at Alexandria such as those in the earlier Moustapha Pasha and Anfushy cemeteries (Venit 2002, 44–5, 73–7, 189–90, Figures 28, 56) and at el-Bagawat (Fakhry 1951, Plate II), this is not always the case (for example, Tuna el-Gebel: Grimm 1975b, 227). Streets of tombs as found at Ismant el-Kharab are a regular feature of Roman cemeteries in Italy (Toynbee 1971, 73–4, 79–91, 120–1) and elsewhere. In addition, in the use of pilasters and even false doors, further parallels can be found amongst classical tomb architecture (Toynbee 1971, chapter 5, especially 132–42; Venit 2002, 166). The use of torus mouldings and cavetto cornices is, of course, quintessentially Egyptian, but the final ensemble presents a mixed appearance, and highlights the process of assimilation of various cultural traditions attested throughout the site of Ismant el-Kharab, typical of Egypt under Roman rule.

Acknowledgements

The excavations at Ismant el-Kharab are carried as part of the fieldwork of the Dakhleh Oasis Project through a concession granted to Anthony J. Mills by the Supreme Council of Antiquities. I wish to thank Ashraf el-Tarboushi and Amad ed-Din, the inspectors seconded to the Project by that organization, for all of their assistance during the excavations, and also Maher Bashendi and Sayed Yamani, the officers of the Dakhleh Inspectorate of Antiquities, for their support.

The major funding source in 2000 and 2001 was Monash University, Australia, through grants awarded to the writer and Gillian Bowen. Additional support in 2000 was received from Nederlandse Organisatie voor Wetenschappelijk Onderzoek, through Olaf Kaper, then Leuven University, and Klaas Worp, University of Amsterdam, and The Seven Pillars of Wisdom Trust, through Iain Gardner, University of Sydney. In 2000 and 2002 the Griffith Institute, Oxford, funded part of the work through Helen Whitehouse, Ashmolean Museum. In each season Rosemary Cromby provided a studentship that enabled one Monash University student to participate in the excavations, and during the 2001 season various participants, mostly Monash University postgraduate students, covered their own expenses. To all I extend my sincere appreciation. I am grateful to Professor Naguib Kanawati, Macquarie University, Sydney, for permission to use the texts of the previously-published discussions, which appeared in the *Bulletin of the Australian Centre for Egyptology* 11–13, as the basis for this present contribution.

---

[40] Dunand has estimated that fragments from 16 tombs at Dush, excluding the examples from Tombs 6 and 20, derive from funerary beds (Dunand *et al.* 1992, 225), and there may have been other examples at Bagawat as Hauser (1932, 48) mentions an unspecified number of fragmentary biers with legs. These could, of course, attest actual beds such as have been found in tombs at Dush, again in Tomb 6 for example, and also at Ismant el-Kharab (Hope and McKenzie 1999, Plate 3).

[41] I think that it is advisable to distinguish specially-made funerary beds from the undecorated domestic examples that may also be used as supports for the body in tombs.

The following participated in the field work during the seasons reported here, to all of whom I extend my thanks: Beatrice Amadei, Michelle Berry, Laurence Blondaux, Gillian Bowen, Wendy Dolling, Amanda Dunsmore, Mark Eccleston, Janelle Jakawenko, Andrew Jamieson, Olaf Kaper, Carla Marchini, Caroline McGregor, Bruce Parr, Barry Rowney, Martin Rowney, Annie Schweitzer, Dan Tuck and Helen Whitehouse. Without the able assistance of the Egyptian site supervisors our work would have been more difficult, therefore I wish to thank Juma'a Mutawalli, Anwar Amr Senussi and Anwar Omar es-Sayed.

Appendix: Note on the Inscriptions upon a Funerary Bed from North Tomb 2

The two inscriptions on the end of a funerary bed from North Tomb 2 are situated on the same corner post, one on the head end (1) and one on its right lateral face (2). The inscriptions are rendered here in lines of standardized hieroglyphs, not all of them certain, with the direction of some signs reversed for greater clarity.

The two inscriptions do not yield a running translation, and no transliteration can therefore be presented. There is a frequent confusion in the direction and order of the signs, for instance in the group 𓊨𓁹 ('Osiris'), which indicates that the author of these columns was not trained in writing hieroglyphs. Even so, most of the signs can be identified easily and the two columns have several groups of signs in common, suggesting a deliberate arrangement. It is significant that several of the same signs are again to be found upon the inscribed cartonnage masks from the cemetery 31/420-C5-1 (Kellis 1), as yet unpublished. The origin of these signs can be traced by the occurrence of the phrase *sšm skr-wsir*, 'leading Sokar-Osiris' in the form 𓌞𓊨𓁹 and 𓌞𓊨𓁹 respectively, which occurs several times in the inscriptions of the tomb of Kitinos at Bashendi and in the tomb of Petosiris at el-Muzawwaqa (Osing *et al.* 1982). The phrase refers to a ritual during the Osiris festivities in the month of Khoiak, in which the deceased hopes to participate. These particular funerary inscriptions are unique to the Dakhleh Oasis, and their inclusion upon the funerary furniture, as on some cartonnage masks, is a further indication of their importance in the oasis.

Principal Author's Address:
Centre for Archaeology and Ancient History
School of Historical Studies
Building 11, Clayton Campus,
Monash University,
Victoria 3800,
Australia

REFERENCES

Arnold, D., 1999 *Temples of the Last Pharaohs*, Oxford University Press, Oxford.

Aufderheide, A. C., L. Cartmell and M. Zlonis, this volume Bio-anthropological Features of Human Mummies from the Kellis 1 Cemetery: The Database for Mummification Methods, 137–51.

Behrmann, A., H. Felber and D. Kurth, 1987 Der Schrein des Inaros, Sohn des Peteisis, *Mitteilungen aus den Musem für Völkerkunde Hamburg*, Neue Folge 17, 159–200.

Birrell, M., 1999 Excavations in the Cemeteries of Ismant el-Kharab, in C. A. Hope and A. J. Mills, eds, *Dakhleh Oasis Project: Preliminary Reports on the 1992–1993 and 1993–1994 Field Seasons*, Oxbow Books, Oxford, 29–41.

Boak, A. E. R. and E. E. Peterson, 1931 *Karanis. Topographical and Architectural report of Excavations during the Seasons 1924–28*, University of Michigan Press, Ann Arbor.

Bowen, G. E., 2002 The Fourth-Century Churches at Ismant el-Kharab, in C. A. Hope and G. E. Bowen, *Dakhleh Oasis Project: Preliminary Reports on the 1994–5 to 1998–9 Field Seasons*, Oxbow Books, Oxford, 64–85.

Bowen, G. E., this volume a The Small East Church at Ismant el-Kharab, 153–65.

Bowen, G. E., this volume b Some Observations on Christian Burial Practices at Kellis, 167–82.

Bresciani, E., 1980 *Kom Madi 1997 e 1978. Le pitture murali del cenotafio di Alessandro Magno*, Pisa.

Castel, G. and F. Dunand, 1981 Deux lits funeraire d'epoque romaine de la necropole de Douch, *Bulletin de l'Institut Francais d'Archeologie Oreintale* 81, 79–110.

De Jong, T. and K. A. Worp, 2001 More Greek Horoscopes from Kellis (Dakhleh Oasis), *Zeitschrift für Papyrologie und Epigraphik* 137, 203–19.

Dobrowolski, J., 2002 Remarks on the Construction Stages of the Main Temple and Shrines I–II, in C. A. Hope and G. E. Bowen, eds, *Dakhleh Oasis Project: Preliminary Reports on the 1994–5 to 1998–9 Field Seasons*, Oxbow Books, Oxford, 120–8.

Dunand, F. and R. Lichtenberg, 1998 *Les Momies et la Mort en Égypte*, Editions Errance, Paris.

Dunand, F., J-L. Heim, N. Henein and R. Lichtenberg, 1992 *La Necropole de Douch*, L'Institut Français d'Archéologie Orientale, Cairo.

Dunsmore, A., 2002 Ceramics from Ismant el-Kharab, in C. A. Hope and G. E. Bowen, eds, *Dakhleh Oasis Project: Preliminary Reports on the 1994–5 to 1998–9 Field Seasons*, Oxbow Books, Oxford, 129–42.

Dupras, T. L. and M. W. Tocheri, this volume a A Preliminary Analysis of the Human Skeletal Remains from North Tombs 1 and 2, 183–96.

Dupras, T. L. and M. W. Tocheri, this volume b Preliminary Analysis of Human Skeletal Remains from South Tomb 4, 197–9.

Eccleston, M. A. J., 2002 Metalworking at Kellis: A Preliminary Report, in C. A. Hope and G. E. Bowen, eds, *Dakhleh Oasis*

Project: *Preliminary Reports on the 1994–5 to 1998–9 Field Seasons*, Oxbow Books, Oxford, 143–9.

Fakhry, A., 1951 *The Necropolis of el-Bagawat in Kharga Oasis*, Government Pres, Cairo.

Grimm, G., 1974 *Die Römischen Mumienmasken ays Ägypten*, Franz Steiner Verlag GMBH, Wiesbaden.

Grimm, G., 1975a *Kunst der Ptolemäer- und Römerzeit in Ägyptischen Museums Kairo*, Philipp von Zabern, Mainz.

Grimm, G., 1975b Tuna el-Gebel 1913–1973, *Mitteilungen des Deutschen Archäologischen Instituts Abteilung Kairo* 31, 221–36.

Hauser, W., 1932 The Christian Necropolis in Khargeh Oasis, *Bulletin of the Metropolitan Museum of Art* 27, 38–50.

Hope, C. A., 1995 The Excavations at Ismant el-Kharab in 1995: A Brief Report, *Bulletin of the Australian Centre for Egyptology* 6, 51–8.

Hope, C. A., 1997 The Find Context of the Kellis Agricultural Account Book, in R. S. Bagnall, ed., *The Kellis Agricultural Account Book*, Oxbow Books, Oxford, 5–16.

Hope, C. A., 1999 Pottery Manufacture in the Dakhleh Oasis, in C. S. Churcher and A. J. Mills, eds, *Reports from the Survey of Dakhleh Oasis 1977–1987*, Oxbow Books, Oxford, 215–43.

Hope, C. A., 2000 The Excavations at Ismant el-Kharab in 2000: A Brief Report, *Bulletin of the Australian Centre for Egyptology* 11, 49–66.

Hope, C. A., 2001a The Excavations at Ismant el-Kharab and Mut el-Kharab in 2001, *Bulletin of the Australian Centre for Egyptology* 12, 35–63.

Hope, C. A., 2001b Observations on the dating of the occupation at Ismant el-Kharab, in C. A. Marlow and A. J. Mills, eds, *The Oasis Papers 1: The Proceedings of the First Conference of the Dakhleh Oasis Project*, Oxbow Books, Oxford, 43–59.

Hope, C. A., 2002 Excavations in the Settlement of Ismant el-Kharab in 1995–1999, in C. A. Hope and G. E. Bowen, eds, *Dakhleh Oasis Project: Preliminary Reports on the 1994–5 to 1998–9 Field Seasons*, Oxbow Book, Oxford, 167–208.

Hope, C. A. and G. E. Bowen, 1997 The Excavations at Ismant el-Kharab 1995/6 and 1996/7: A Brief Report, *Bulletin of the Australian Centre for Egyptology* 8, 49–64.

Hope, C. A. and J. McKenzie, 1999 Interim Report on the West Tombs, in C. A. Hope and A. J. Mills, eds, *Dakhleh Oasis Project: Preliminary Reports on the 1992–1993 and 1993–1994 Field Seasons*, Oxbow Books, Oxford, 53–68.

Hope, C. A., O. E. Kaper, H. Whitehouse and K. A. Worp, 2002 Excavations at Mut el-Kharab and Ismant el-Kharab in 2001–2, *Bulletin of the Australian Centre for Egyptology* 13, 85–107.

Husselman, E. M., 1979 *Karanis Excavations of the University of Michigan in Egypt 1928–1935 Topography and Architecture*, University of Michigan Press, Ann Arbor.

Kanawati, N., 1987 *The Rock Tombs of el-Hawawish* VII, The Ancient History Documentary Research Centre, Macquarie University, Sydney.

Kaper, O. E., 1997 *Temples and Gods in Roman Dakhleh: Studies in the indigenous cults of an Egyptian Oasis*, privately published Ph.D. dissertation, Rijksuniversiteit Groningen.

Kaper, O. E., 2002 A Group of *Dipinti* in Shrine IV at Ismant el-Kharab, in C. A. Hope and G. E. Bowen, eds, Dakhleh Oasis Project: *Preliminary Reports on the 1994–1995 to 1998–1999 Field Seasons*, 209–16.

Kaper, O. E., this volume a The God Tutu at Kellis: On two Stelae found at Ismant el-Kharab in 2000, 311–21.

Kaper, O. E., this volume b The Lost Decoration of North Tomb 1, 323–30.

Knudstad, J. E. and R. A. Frey, 1999 Kellis: The Architectural Survey of the Romano-Byzantine Town at Ismant el-Kharab, in C. S. Churcher and A. J. Mills, eds, *Reports from the Survey of Dakhleh Oasis 1977–1987*, Oxbow Books, Oxford, 189–214.

Kurth, D., 1990 *Der Sarg der Teüris*, Philipp von Zabern.

Mills, A. J., 1980 Dakhleh Oasis Project – Report on the Second Season of Survey, September–December, 1979, *Journal of the Society for the Study of Egyptian Antiquities* X, 251–82.

Mills, A. J., 1982 Dakhleh Oasis Project: Report on the Fourth Season of Survey. October 1981 – January 1982, *Journal of the Society for the Study of Egyptian Antiquities* XII, 93–101.

Mills, A. J., 1999 ʻEin Birbiyeh, in C. A. Hope and A. J. Mills, eds, *Dakhleh Oasis Project: Preliminary Reports on the 1992–1993 and 1993–1994 Field Seasons*, Oxbow Books, Oxford, 23–4.

Molto, J. E., P. Sheldrick, A. Cerroni and S. Haddow, this volume Late Roman Period Human Skeletal Remains from Areas D/6 and D/7 and North Tomb 1 at Kellis, 345–63.

Moritz, B., 1900 Excursion aux Oasis de Désert Libyque, *Bulletin de la Societé Khédiviale de Géographie*, Ve Série No. 8, 429–75.

Moursi, M. and J. Osing, 1982 ʻEzbet Baschendi, in J. Osing *et al.*, *Denkmäler der Oase Dachla aus dem Nachlass von Ahmed Fakhry*, Philip von Zabern, Mainz am Rhein, 57–69.

Needler, W., 1963 *An Egyptian Funerary Bed of the Roman period in The Royal Ontario Museum*, The University of Chicago Press, Chicago.

Olson, S. D. and A. Sens 1999 *Matro of Pitane and the Tradition of Epic Parody in the Fourth Century BCE. Text, Translation and Commentary*, Scholars Press, Atlanta.

Osing, J., M. Moursi, Do. Arnold, O. Neugebauer, R. A. Parker, D. Pingree and M. A. Nur-el-Din, 1982 *Denkmäler der Oase Dachla*, Philipp von Zabern, Mainz am Rhein.

Parlasca, K., 1991 Hellenistische und Kaiserzeitliche Holzsarkophage aus Ägypten, in S. Stucchi and M. B. Aravantinos, eds, *Giornate di Studio in Onore di Achille Adriani*, "L'Erma" di Bretschneider, Rome, 115–27.

Parlasca, K., 1995 Neue Beobachtungen ze den paganen Grabbauten in el-Bagawat (Kharga Oase) und ihren Funden, in *Alessandria e il Mondo Ellenistico-Romano. I Centenario del Museo Greco-Romano*, "L'Erma" di Bretschneider, Rome, 202–4.

Patten, S. F., 1999 Report on the Study of the Ceramics: 1993–1994 Seasons, in C. A. Hope and A. J. Mills, eds, *Dakhleh Oasis Project: Preliminary Reports on the 1992–1993 and 1993–1994 Field Seasons*, Oxbow Books, Oxford, 83–8.

Rhind, A. H., 1862 *Thebes: Its Tombs and their Tenants*, London.

Shaw, I., J. Bunbury and R. Jameson, 1999 Emerald mining in Roman and Byzantine Egypt, *Journal of Roman Archaeology* 12, 203–15.

Smekalova, T., 2002 Magnetic Testing using Overhauser Gradiometer GSM-19WG and Cesium Magnetometer MM-60, in C. A. Hope and G. E Bowen, eds, *Dakhleh Oasis Project: Preliminary Reports on the 1994–5 to 1998–9 Field Seasons*, Oxbow Books, Oxford, 31–41.

Stevens, A., 2002 Terracottas from Ismant el-Kharab, in C. A. Hope and G. E. Bowen, eds, *Dakhleh Oasis Project: Preliminary Reports on the 1994–1995 to 1998–1999 Field Seasons*, Oxbow Books, Oxford, 277–95.

Toynbee, J. M. C., 1971 *Death and Burial in the Roman World*, The John Hopkins University Press, Baltimore and London.

Venit, M. S., 2002 *Monumental Tombs of Ancient Alexandria*, Cambridge University Press, Cambridge.

Whitehouse, H., 1999 A Painted Panel of Isis, in C. A. Hope and A. J. Mills, eds, *Dakhleh Oasis Project: Preliminary Reports on the 1992–1993 and 1993–1994 Field Seasons*, Oxbow Books, Oxford, 95–100.

Whitehouse, H., 2002 Wall Paintings in Shrine IV of the Temple of Tutu, in C. A. Hope and G. E. Bowen, eds, *Dakhleh Oasis Project: Preliminary Reports on the 1994–1995 to 1998–1999 Field Seasons*, Oxbow Books, Oxford, 311–21.

Whitehouse, H., 1998 Roman in Life, Egyptian in Death: The painted tomb of Petosiris in Dakhleh Oasis, in O. E. Kaper, ed., *Life on the Fringe, Living in the Southern Egyptian Deserts during the Roman and early-Byzantine Periods*, Research School, Centre for non-Western Studies, Leiden university, Leiden, 53–70.

Winlock, H. E., 1936 *Ed Dakhleh Oasis, Journal of a Camel trip made in 1908*, Metropolitan Museum of Art, New York.

Worp, K. A., forthcoming, Greek Ostraka from Kellis, Oxbow Books, Oxford.

Yamani, S., 2001 Roman Monumental Tombs in Ezbet Bashendi, *Bulletin de L'Institut Francais d'Archeologie Orientale* 101, 393–414.

The Gladiator Jug from Ismant el-Kharab

Colin A. Hope and Helen V. Whitehouse

The excavations at Ismant el-Kharab, ancient Kellis, since 1986 have produced a considerable quantity of glass of a wide variety of types,[1] including plain and decorated wares.[2] On 2 February 2000, however, a quite exceptional discovery of two adjacent deposits of glass was made within Enclosure 4 of Area D, amongst one of which were fragments from a jug painted with well-preserved scenes of combatant gladiators (Hope 2000, 58–9). This vessel forms the focus of the present contribution, which aims to place the piece within its broader context and to explore the question of its place of manufacture.[3] The vessels that comprise the two groups were all found in fragments, not all of which from each vessel were recovered. Surface deposits on the pieces, of sand and salt crusts,[4] some over the broken edges, indicate that the vessels were dropped where they were found and broke upon impact with the ground; that a considerable number of joinable pieces from each vessel was retrieved indicates that there was little subsequent disturbance following abandonment. This study is intended as an exploration of issues raised by the discovery of the painted jug and further refinement of many of these will undoubtedly be undertaken by authorities on ancient glass.

Find Context

Enclosure 4 lies at the north-eastern corner of the site, and is the last of a series of enclosures added on the northern side of Enclosure 1, which contains the Main Temple of Tutu and its associated structures (Hope this volume, Figure 1). The enclosure contains the West Church and its adjacent complex dated to the mid-fourth century (Bowen 2002, 75–81, 83), to the east of which are the two West Tombs (Hope and McKenzie 1999); slightly to the east of these there is a two-roomed mud-brick structure (Hope this volume, Figure 11). At various locations within the enclosure are east-west-oriented, single human burials presumed to be those of Christians (Bowen this volume; Hope this volume). The West Tombs predate the construction of the wall of Enclosure 4, which, in its north-western corner, is identical with the wall of the West Church. This indicates that the enclosure is contemporary with the West Church.

The two deposits of glass were found near to the inner face of the northern wall of the enclosure, Group 1 (Figure 1) 8.4 m west of the north-eastern corner and Group 2 (Figure 2) 0.6 m farther to the west, thus both to the immediate east of the two-roomed structure. They were found 20 cm and 30 cm respectively below the surface of the site within a deposit of sand and mud brick eroded from the northern enclosure wall. The area in which they were discovered was not excavated below the point of their discovery, but, from the excavations within the two-roomed building, it can be ascertained that they lay 1.3 and 1.2 m above the compact clay surface upon which this structure was constructed.

It would appear that the glass vessels were deposited in their find spot after there had been considerable accumulation of material against the northern wall of the enclosure subsequent to the construction of the two-roomed

---

[1] This has been studied by Carla Marchini who, through illness, has unfortunately been prevented from contributing to the present study. This has resulted in a lack of the necessary technical data being included.

[2] It is not possible to elaborate upon the range of material here, but it can be noted that examples of gold-sandwich glass, mosaic glass, both bichrome and polychrome, facet-cut glass, incised glass and painted glass have all been found; glass beads containing silver have also been recovered. A substantial part of a large colourless bowl in a shape resembling North African Red Slip ware bowls of the third-fourth centuries has also been recovered.

[3] Helen Whitehouse has contributed the description of the vessel.

[4] I wish to acknowledge the care and skill of Laurence Blondaux in cleaning the gladiator jug, and Michelle Berry in reconstructing the assemblage.

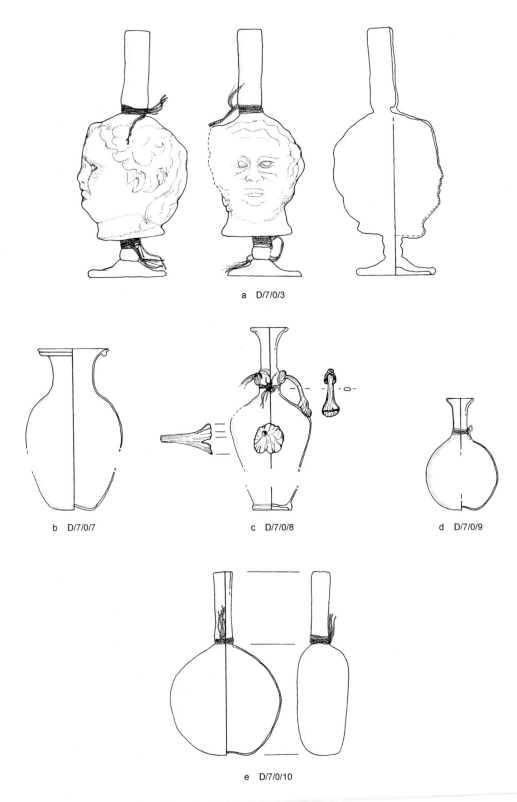

a　D/7/0/3

b　D/7/0/7　　　　　　　　c　D/7/0/8　　　　　　　d　D/7/0/9

e　D/7/0/10

Figure 1　Area D/7 glass vessels in Group 1 (drawings by C. Marchini and B. Parr).
Scale 1:3; object registration numbers provided.

structure. Whilst the exact date at which this building was erected cannot be determined, this must have been during the second half of the fourth century. The glass vessels cannot be related with any certainty to the use of this structure. There is currently no evidence for occupation at Kellis after the early 390s (Hope 1999; 2002, 204-6). It is therefore probable that the glass vessels were dropped during the course of the abandonment of the site at the end of the fourth century or possibly very early in the fifth century, although why in the spot where they were found, given that it is not an obvious point of exiting the village, cannot be determined. The find context does not, therefore, assist in the dating of the manufacture of the vessels, but does indicate generally the period until which they continued in use.

Description of the Vessels

In the descriptions the dimensions are given in centimetres and the following abbreviations are employed: H height, D diameter, W width, Th thickness.

Group 1: Figure 1

Figure **1a:** 31/420-D6-1/D/7/0/3[5]

Form: single head-shaped bottle with tall cylindrical neck, unaccentuated rim, applied bead stem and foot with fire-rounded edge; the face is of the chubby child-like type with blurred details.[6]

Colour: pale green.

Technique: head mould-blown; neck, foot and stem free-blown.[7]

Dimensions: Ht 19.8; D of head 9; H of head 10.2; D of head at base 5.7; H of neck 6.9; D of rim 2.1; H of foot/stem 3; D of foot 6.6; Th of wall at head and neck 0.2–0.3.

Contents: residue of pine, cedar or fir resin (Ross and Stern, this volume).

Stopper: String wound around top of stem of the foot and at the base of the neck; the two sections may once have joined thus forming a means of raising the vessel, or they could have been attached to a stopper used to close the vessel, on which see Stern 1995, 31 footnote 64.

Date:[8] Provisionally the piece may be assigned to the late third or early fourth century; this date is confirmed by the use of pale green glass (Price and Cottam 1998, 16), which is the colour of all of the pieces in both deposits.[9]

Stern (1995, 204–15) has outlined the evolution of mould-blown head-shaped vessels during the first to fourth centuries CE based upon dated examples from excavations. Those with chubby child-like faces she identifies as representing Dionysos or Eros and notes that they were most common in the eastern Mediterranean. The largest number of head-shaped vessels was manufactured in that region during the second and third centuries, and production ceased during the mid-fourth century. Vessels with single heads were made predominantly in the first–second and fourth centuries. Of those detailed in her survey an early fourth century vessel from Worms in Germany has a foot similar in external shape to Figure 1a, though the stem is not beaded, and also a tall neck with an unaccentuated rim; however, the neck is funnel-shaped and the vessel has two faces (see also Harden *et al.* 1987, number 95). The shape of the eyes resembles those of Figure 1a. No other piece in both Stern's survey and catalogue has a similar foot; a single-head vessel of the first half of the third century (Stern 1995, number 148) possesses a similar neck and rim type, but has the usual flat base.

Jennifer Price (personal communication, 2003) has pointed out that parallels to the bead stem and foot of this piece occur in the late second and third century in the west (for example Isings' 1957 forms 91b–c), which might indicate a slightly earlier date for this vessel than is indicated by reference to Stern's study. These features occur on two flutes from Sedeinga assigned a date in the third century CE (see below; pointed out by J. Price personal communication, 2003).

Plates 1 and 3.

Figure **1b:** 31/420-D6-1/D/7/0/7

Form: flask with a diagonal rim, fire-rounded edge, funnel mouth with applied trail, wide neck, convex body and a concave base.

Colour: pale green.

Technique: blown.

Dimensions: H estimated 12.9; D of rim 5.85; D of body 8.1; H of neck 3.6; Th of wall 0.2–0.3.

Date: fourth century.

The rim type occurs frequently at Kellis on flasks of various sizes and shapes, and jugs: see Marchini 1999, Figures 1c, 3h. A fragment preserving the rim to upper body from a similar flask was found at Alexandria in Gabbari Tomb B3 and ascribed to the fourth to fifth centuries (Nenna 2001a, 508 number 6).

---

[5] This is the object registration catalogue number.

[6] In the descriptions I have provided details following suggestions made by Jennifer Price.

[7] I follow the terminology and data on manufacture and morphology provided in Price and Cottam 1998, 22–9.

[8] In discussing the date of the vessels in both deposits I will only refer to parallels from well-dated contexts that serve as a guide to the date of the Kellis pieces; I will not discuss the distribution pattern of each type. As the dating of the glass from Karanis is acknowledged to need revision (D. Whitehouse, The Date of the Glass from Karanis, *Journal of Glass Studies* 41, 168–70), I have used the publication of this material sparingly.

[9] Jennifer Price (personal communication 2003) has pointed out that pale green glass appears from the second century in some contexts in Egypt.

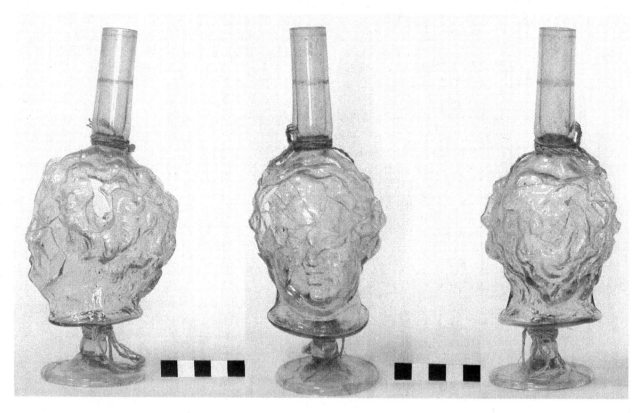

Plate 1   Group 1: head-shaped vessel, object registration number 31/420-D6-1/D/7/0/3.

Plate 2   Group 1: flask, object registration number
31/420-D6-1/D/7/0/9.

Plate 3   Group 1: flask, object registration number
31/420-D6-1/D/7/0/10.

Figure 1c: 31/420-D6-1/D/7/0/8

Form: two-handled, spouted jug with a tall neck, flaring unaccentuated rim, conical body and low trailed ring base.
Colour: pale green body and neck, darker green handles and spout.
Technique: blown; ribbon handles applied to upper body and attached to base of neck and faceted spout drawn.
Dimensions: H estimated 13.5; D of body 6.6; D of rim 3; D of base 3.3; H of neck 5.1; Th of wall 0.1–0.3.
Stopper: string tied around the base of the neck between the handles indicates that the vessel was once closed with a stopper.
Date: fourth century.

The shape represents a combination of the features of single-handled, spouted jugs with globular bodies, and two-handled jugs with taller, narrower bodies, as found in forms 123b and 124 of Goethert-Polaschek 1977, both ascribed to the early fourth century on the basis of finds excavated in Germany.

The shape is attested by several examples from Kellis: for one with a single handle see Marchini 1999, Figure 3f.

Figure 1d: 31/420-D6-1/D/7/0/9

Form: flask with tall neck and flaring unaccentuated rim, globular body and concave base.
Colour: pale green.
Technique: blown.
Dimensions: H 9; D of body 6; D of rim 2.2; H of neck 3; Th of wall 0.2–0.3.
Contents: unidentified brown residue.
Stopper: string wound around the base of the neck indicates the original existence of a stopper.
Date: fourth century; compare forms 79c–d and 80 of Goethart-Polaschek (1977).
Plate 2.

Figure 1e: 31/420-D6-1/D/7/0/10

Form: flask with a vertical rim, tall neck constricted at base, flattened convex (lentoid) body and convex base.
Colour: pale green.
Technique: blown.
Dimensions: H 14.7; D of body 9.3 and 4.2; D of rim 1.5; H of neck 5.7; Th of wall 0.15–0.3.
Contents: unidentified brown residue.
Stopper: the presence of string wound around the base of the neck indicates the existence originally of a stopper.
Date: late third to fourth centuries.

Harden *et al.* (1987, numbers 116 and 151) have published two comparable flasks but with spherical bodies and decoration, the former being one of a group of nine similar flasks with abraded decoration representing Baiae and Puteoli, the second being enamelled and gilded with a mythological scene; they (1987, 125) note the rarity of bottles with flattened bodies. Undecorated examples, some without the restriction at the base of the neck, comprise Goethert-Polaschek's (1977, 150–2) form 93; both undecorated and painted are Isings' (1957, 121–2) form 103.
Plate 3.

Group 2: Figure 2

Figure 2a: 31/420-D6-1/D/7/0/6

Form: two-handled jug a tall neck, slightly-accentuated rim, inverted piriform body and flattened ribbed ring base; the broad ribbon handles, applied to shoulder and attached to the neck, have a central groove and three rounded trails; the neck narrows above the flange at the junction of the handles on the neck, where there is a horizontal scroll.
Colour: pale green body and neck; handles and ring base darker green.
Technique: either blown into a ribbed one- or more piece mould, or fluting on body produced by optic-blowing (Price and Cottam 1998, 12–3; Flemming 1999, 107–9); neck free-blown; handles drawn.
Dimensions: H 27.6; D of body 14.1; D of rim 3.3; D of base 6; H of neck 12; Th of wall 0.15–0.3.
Stopper: string wound around the base of the neck between the handles for attachment of a stopper.
Date: fourth century; compare Isings 1957 form 129; Harden 1969, 64–5, Plate XIIc; Goethert-Polaschek 1977 forms 143 and 144; Harden *et al.* 1987, number 47.
Plates 4 and 5.

Figure 2b: 31/420-D6-1/D/7/0/4

Form: one-handled jug with diagonal rim and fire-rounded edge, funnel mouth, cylindrical neck not off-set and with low ridge, narrow ovoid body, and low ring base; double-rod handle attached to a low thumb-piece at rim.
Colour: pale green with darker green handle and ring base.
Technique: blown; handle drawn and applied after enamelled/cold-painted decoration executed.
Dimensions: H 26.1; D of body 9; D of rim 6.3; D of base 6; Th of wall 0.2.
Decoration: see following section.
Date: For late third to fourth century parallels to the shape of the jug see Isings 1957 form 120b; Goethert-Polaschek 1977 form 124; Harden *et al.* 1987, numbers 70–2; Nenna 2003a, 366, Figure 19; none of these is painted. A close parallel exists in the Daphne Ewer from Kerch in the Crimea; this opaque white glass jug has cold-painted and gilded decoration. It is ascribed to the late second to early third century (Harden *et al.* 1987, number 150; Whitehouse 2001, 266-70 no. 864), as are fragments from another vessel of similar shape preserving the head of the goddess Thetis found at Dura Europos (Clairmont 1963, 34–5). Another jug of similar shape, but with a curved handle that rises above the rim, and with gilded decoration of a Dionysiac scene, was found at Begram (Kurz 1954, 106 number 154; Menninger 1996, 23–5); Whitehouse (1989a, 97–8; 1989b, 1553) has suggested a date within the late first or early second centuries for this vessel, another in the Corning Museum of Glass and an undecorated example of similar shape from Begram.

Examples of glass painted with scenes of gladiatorial combat occur from the late first to third centuries CE, and parallels to such scenes in mosaics occur from the second to early fourth centuries CE (see below). In theory at least,

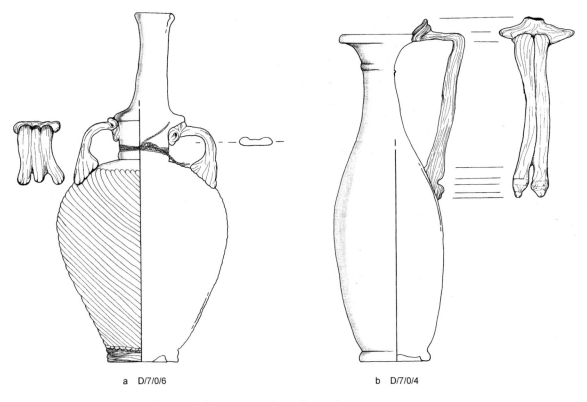

a   D/7/0/6   b   D/7/0/4

Figure 2 Area D/7 glass vessels in Group 2 (drawings by C. Marchini).
Scale 1:3; object registration numbers provided.

the use of such designs could occur until the demise of these combats in the fourth century.

A date for this vessel within the third or first half of the fourth centuries seems reasonable.

Plates 5–7 and frontispiece.

Decoration of the Gladiator Jug

Frontispiece and Plates 5–7.

The other surviving examples of painted gladiator scenes are on the comparatively simple forms of cups or conical beakers, with one or two registers of combat scenes demarcated by plain lines or surrounded with a floral frame: for example, the Begram beakers in the Musée Guimet (Coarelli 1963, Plates xi.2 and xii; Menninger 1996, Plate 19.3-4) and the Lübsow beakers (Coarelli 1963, Plates vii.1–x; Menninger 1996, Plate 20.2). As befits the more complicated shape of the flask, the decorative scheme is more ornate: the body of the jug is decorated with a single principal register occupied by two pairs of combatants, each with a referee. The entire decorative scheme (total height about 201 mm) is defined top and bottom by a band of black wave-ornament on a yellow ground demarcated above and below with reddish-brown lines; a third such band forms the ground-line to the principal figure scene. Below the top band of wave ornament, which is wider (16 mm) than the others, and shades from pale reddish-brown into yellow, the neck of the flask is decorated with a lotus frieze, the petals of each bloom

drawn in dark outline, and coloured alternately yellow and blue tipped in reddish-brown, with the occasional green bloom; a pair of yellow lanceolate leaves flanks each bloom. Below is a band of black herringbone on a pale reddish-brown/yellow background like that of the top wave-band, and similarly demarcated with reddish-brown lines. Below this is a yellow scroll dotted with blue and red blobs, demarcated below by a yellow then a reddish-brown line. Between the wave-band which closes the gladiatorial scenes and the lowest wave-band, is a similar but larger scroll, with the addition of green dots of foliage as well as the red and blue.

Within the principal figure zone (minimum height 77 mm), the two scenes of combat occupy the whole area: to the left of the handle, a gladiator with bare head and abundant curly dark hair faces right, with a slight smile on his features. A metal-scale protector *(manica)* worn slantwise across his upper chest covers his left shoulder and entire left arm, ending above a deep belt of yellow bounded top and bottom by reddish-brown strips with yellow studs. The right side of his chest and his right arm are bare, save for a green armband on the upper arm and a yellow wristband. In his right hand he grasps a metal dagger or short sword. He wears a loincloth *(subligaculum)*, white with black decoration, yellow ties above and below either knee, and green and yellow anklets. His feet are bare, and behind his left foot lies a trident with blue metal prongs and a yellow handle. His mailed left fist makes contact with the boss of the rectangular

Plate 4 Group 2: two-handled jug, object registration number 31/420-D6-1/D/7/0/06.

Plate 5   Two-handled jug, head-shaped vessel and one-handled jug,
object registration numbers 31/420-D6-1/D/7/0/ 6, 3 and 4.

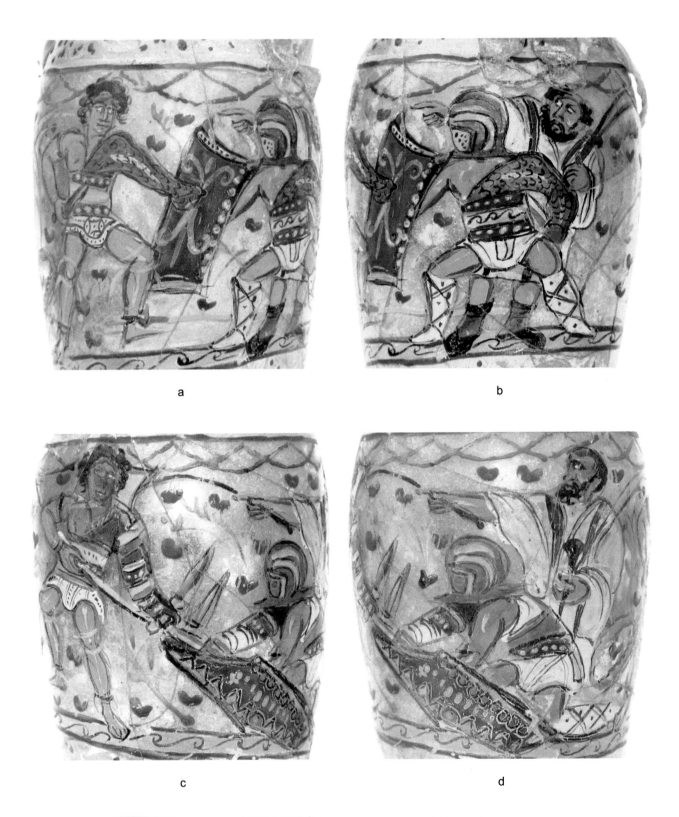

a

b

c

d

Plate 6 Details of the decoration on the one-handled jug, object registration number 31/420-D6-1/D/7/0/4.
Colour enhanced for clarity.

Plate 7 One-handled jug showing handle attachment.

reddish-brown shield held in the left hand of his opponent, who is seen in a rather clumsily-depicted rear view. The shield is edged with blue studs on a yellow strip, and ornamented in yellow with a central rib and a scrolling X-device terminating in blue studs. This second gladiator also wears a continuous metal *manica*, protecting his right shoulder and arm, above a similar wide belt, this time decorated with a band of wave-pattern in black, again with bands of yellow-studded brown above and below; a flap of yellow cloth hangs below, over a white loincloth. Below the knees, the gladiator's lower legs and feet are protected with white wrappings *(fasciae)*, cross-banded and studded in black and reddish-brown. His head is turned left to face his opponent and is entirely covered with a globular metal helmet, blue and yellow, with a fin-like crest, a yellow grating over the face and a horizontal rim protecting the neck. In his mailed right hand is a metal blade with a handle – a dagger or a short sword. Although still on his feet, he seems to be losing the fight: behind him stands a black-haired, bearded referee, wearing a knee-length baggy white tunic with reddish-brown stripes *(clavi)*; with the forefinger of his raised right hand the referee points to the other gladiator, at whom his gaze is directed. In his left hand he holds a couple of slightly curving rods. Below the loincloth of the losing gladiator can be seen the hemline of the referee's tunic, but now painted yellow with dark-brown stripes, and his bare legs and feet, shod in short dark-brown boots, planted firmly on the wave-patterned 'ground-line'.

The other group, to the right of the handle, likewise consists of a pair of combatants and a referee. Another bare-headed, curly-haired gladiator seems to be delivering the winning blow at his opponent: his facial features are less clear than those of the other winning gladiator, but he seems to be smiling, and leaping with the triumphant force of the blow – his left leg is planted firmly on the wave-band 'ground-line', his right leg, bent at the knee, is raised in the air. Both legs are bare, save for yellow ties above and below the knees, and yellow and green anklets. He wears a dark-patterned white loincloth and a deep belt striped blue, yellow with black dots, reddish-brown with yellow studs, and green. At his left shoulder rises a yellow metal shoulder-guard *(galerus, spongia)* held by a hatched yellow strip slantwise across his chest. His left arm is protected with an arm guard, striped yellow, blue, reddish-brown and white, with yellow studs on the central reddish-brown band, and he grasps a short sword with blue metal blade and yellow handle in his left hand. His right arm is bare save for a green and yellow armband and blue wristband, and with his right hand he holds the yellow handle of a trident whose blue metal prongs threaten his opponent over the top of the latter's shield. The shield is a reddish-brown rectangle seen sideways-on, with yellow border, blue studs, yellow dots and a yellow/blue central boss (?) with yellow sawtooth ornament above and below. Behind it crouches the other gladiator, holding the shield with his bare left arm and attempting to stave off the attack with a short sword or dagger in his right hand. The right arm is covered with a guard of white strips below a yellow-studded band of reddish-brown, then blue. His head is completely covered in a globular helmet of blue and yellow metal with a fin-like crest and a wide rim over his shoulders, but instead of a grating over his face, there is a solid metal piece with perhaps a slit for the eyes. He wears a short white tunic with a wide blue belt above a narrower reddish-brown strip with yellow studs; a flap of yellow cloth hangs below at the back. His left leg, kneeling on the ground, is protected from the knee down with white *fasciae*, cross-banded and studded in reddish-brown and black; only part of his bare upper right leg is visible. Behind him a standing referee dressed like the other and similarly bearded, faces full left and points with his raised right hand, which holds a curving rod, at the other gladiator. In his left hand he holds two further rods and a trumpet(?) coloured black.

The background to these scenes of combat is surprisingly floral, and more elaborate than that on the other surviving examples: around the top runs a chain formed by two green festoons. Below this the whole background is scattered with heart-shaped red blooms with a yellow calix, seen in isolation or attached to tall, leafy green stems. A green wreath, similar to those seen in more spriggy form on other gladiator glasses, lies just above the left leg of the kneeling gladiator, and a sprigged green stem between his shield and the left leg of his opponent may be a palm branch.

The painting is detailed and vivid, with sharp white highlights on the bronzed skin of the gladiators and the metal of the mailed arm-guards, the plates of which are indicated with little black strokes. The folds of the referees' white tunics are shaded with pale blue. The figures and their equipment are delineated with a thin brownish-black outline and seem to have been created as line-drawings which were then filled in with colour. The basic skin-colour is a thin reddish-brown with body contours outlined in stronger reddish-brown. Within the range of colours used, blue and yellow are apparently chosen to represent two different metallic surfaces (bronze and tinned bronze?), yellow perhaps also signifies wood and dense reddish-brown may be leather. The handle of the flask lies over the painted decoration and was clearly applied afterwards (Plate 7).

In each pair of combatants, the helmeted fighter may be identified as a *secutor*, from his distinctive helmet and other fighting equipment. His bare-headed opponent fighting with a trident should be a *retiarius*, but the net proper to this category of gladiator is nowhere apparent. This may be compared with the similarly netless figure in the Kos gladiator mosaic of the third century (Robert 1948, 98–9); for a unique example of the net shown in use see Junkelmann 2000a, 137. The referee (*summa rudis*) holds his typical pliant rod (Robert 1948, 84–6). The continuous scale-armour *manica* worn by both fighters of the pair to left of the handle is an item seen from the second–third century on in two-dimensional depictions and also bronze figures of gladiators (Junkelmann 2000a, 82; see also the early fourth-century 'Borghese' gladiators mosaic from Torrenova on the via Casalina, Rome: Junkelmann 2000a,

144 Figures 228–30). Despite their general similarity to the other painted gladiator representations on glass, the details and poses of the figures on the flask are more closely paralleled by representations on mosaic pavements; gladiatorial combats were a particularly popular subject in the Eastern Mediterranean in the second–third centuries (for the examples from Kos, Patras and Kourion see Dunbabin 1999, 216, 229). The gladiator seen in rear view may be compared with a variety of such figures in the 'amphitheatre mosaic' from Zliten now in Tripoli Museum (Ville 1965, Figures 17, 18, with a suggested dating late Flavian–early Antonine, though later dates have also been suggested, Ville 1965, 147, 152). This parallel was also noted by Coarelli (1963, 64) with reference to the better-preserved of the two gladiator glasses found at Lübsow in Pomerania, citing in addition the Gallo-Belgian relief illustrated by Robert (1949, Plate XXI).

Place of Origin of the Gladiator Jug

One of the most interesting questions raised by the discovery of this remarkable vessel at Ismant el-Kharab is its place of manufacture. In exploring this various avenues of investigation can be pursued: the distribution of painted glass in general, and specifically within Egypt, and suggestions for centres of its manufacture; in light of the possibility that Alexandria was the place of origin, what evidence exists for both glass manufacture there and the performance of gladiatorial games that could have inspired the production of such decorated vessels or created a market for them. The form of the jug does not provide unequivocal evidence for its place of manufacture, as variations on the type are found throughout Europe, around the Mediterranean and into the East.

I. Distribution of Painted Glass

Painter (1987, 259–62), Rutti (1991; 2003) and Nenna (in press) have outlined the development of painted glass from its appearance in Italy in the first century CE, where it was introduced from Syria or possibly Egypt. The material of the first century CE, *circa* 20–70 (Rutti 2003, 349), comprises hemispherical bowls and amphorisks in coloured glass, the latter only from Cyprus and Kerch on the northern shore of the Black Sea, the former from throughout Europe to Egypt, but mostly from the west. Rutti (2003, 357) lists 12 out of 76 examples as having been found in Egypt. It is suggested that many of the bowls were made in one factory, but that there was likely one factory in the east (? Egypt) and another in northern Italy. The motifs employed comprise predominantly birds and vegetation; recent finds, included in Rutti's count, at Berenike on the Red Sea coast conform to this pattern (Wendrich 1996, 137; Nicholson 1999, 233–4; Nicholson 2000, 206). Amongst exceptions to the standard decorative format of the early bowls is one from Nîmes decorated with pygmies and cranes (Rutti 1991, 130, Plate XXXVc; 2003, Figure 1).

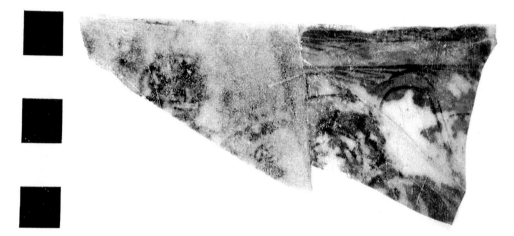

Plate 8 Large East Church (Area A/7): painted glass preserving the upper parts of three human figures.

Plate 9 Large East Church (Area A/7): painted glass preserving parts of two human figures.

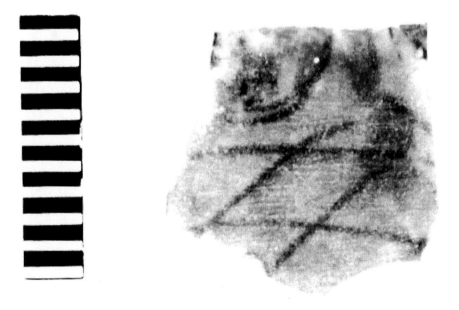

*Plate 10 Large East Church (Area A/7): painted glass preserving part of a wrapped
human figure, possibly Lazarus.*

From Berenike, however, also come fragments from an exceptional, clear-glass bowl painted in polychrome with marine life, shells and vegetation, dated to the third quarter of the first century (Nicholson and Price 2003). Its fabric, form and decoration distinguish it from other first-century bowls and, along with pieces in the Corning Museum of Glass (Whitehouse 2001, 849–50), it may derive from an eastern source (Rutti 2003, 354-5) and may attest a distinct tradition. From the point of view of the present study, an even more interesting bowl derives from Algiers, which is decorated with figures of gladiators and foliage (Kurz 1954, 105, Figure 377; Coarelli 1963, 69, Plate XV).[10] Painter (1987, 259) mentions this bowl as an example of the early manufactures, though it is morphologically distinct from them and also has a colourless base fabric; it may post-date them (J. Price personal communication, 2003).

Another group of painted glass, which includes a different range of shapes to those of the early group, has been thought to occur in the east from the late second century and in the west from the beginning of the third century (Painter 1987, 260–1; Rutti 2003, 354 with references). Others examples not from these sources are referred to by Hill and Nenna (2003, 89). Painter's dating of this group needs to be modified in light of suggestions that some of the material from the east (especially Begram) should be dated to the late first to early second centuries (see below). In the western examples the base material is colourless and the form, cylindrical cups, is very common and only found in the north-western provinces of the Roman empire; approximately 50 examples, some complete but most represented by fragments, are enamelled. They have been found around the North Sea in northern Germany, Denmark, Britain, western France and the Rhineland (Rutti 2003, Figure 9), and presumably were manufactured within the area. Seven or eight only show parts of gladiatorial scenes.[11]

Amongst the painted glass from the east, of a variety of forms, Egypt has produced fragments, the Sudan has produced fragments and several more-or-less complete vessels, there are pieces from Syria, or ascribed to Syria, and an important collection has been found at Begram in Afghanistan. Those found in Syria or thought to have been made there comprise the Daphne Ewer and pieces from a similar form found at Dura Europos, mentioned above, and the Paris Plate with mythological scenes (Harden *et al.* 1987, number 149).

The pieces from Egypt originate from 'Ain et-Turba and Dush in Kharga Oasis, Oxyrhynchos, Karanis, Quseir el-Khadim, Berenike and Krokodilô, plus a few without specific provenance. To these can be added not only the jug decorated with gladiatorial scenes from Ismant el-Kharab but also fragments found in the Large East Church at the same site (Marchini in Bowen 2002, 84). The latter may all derive from one or two flat panels, one of which was originally provided with a frame of turquoise glass rods and may have been set within a wooden frame into the altar of the church. The fragments are decorated in polychrome and preserve figurative, floral and geometric motifs. Amongst the former can be seen: a group of three figures with, on the left, a standing male figure with head turned to the right, a central figure looking straight ahead, and a figure on the right, bent and with head raised to look at the figure on the right (Plate 8); parts of two figures with that on the left with raised right hand (Plate 9); a small figure completely wrapped, possibly to be identified as Lazarus (Plate 10);[12] and a group with adults and a child at lower right (Plate 11). The identity of the scenes is uncertain, but given the find context it is tempting to suggest that they are biblical.

The 'Ain et-Turba fragments (Hill and Nenna 2003, 88–9) comprise those from a tall blue goblet decorated in red and with gold, and three fragments of thin colourless glass one decorated with a large feline (panther?) attacking a gazelle from a wild animal fight (*venationes*?), and two from the same object with the head of Eros or Victory and two figures, one making a libation. From Dush come fragments from a large plate decorated with the 36 decans (Nenna in press). Three pieces from Oxyrhynchos (Harden 1936, 100, Figure 2b; Coarelli 1963, 68, Plate XIV.4) derive from a bowl and are decorated with what may have been a circus scene: one fragment has the leg of a man wearing a tunic and boots before a bull, another a palm frond between two figures, and a third what resembles a naked child.[13] Karanis (Harden 1936, 122, Plate XIV)

---

[10] It is of interest to note that in the mid-first century CE mould-blown cylindrical cups and ovoid beakers with scenes of the arena were produced in the West, probably Roman Gaul: G. Ville, Les coupes de Trimalcion figurant des gladiateurs et une série de verres 'sigillés' gaulois, in M. Renard and R. Schilling, *Hommages à Jean Bayet*, Collection Latomus LXX, Bruxelles-Berchem, 1964, 721–33; Harden *et al.* 1987, numbers 88–90; J. Price, Decorated Mould-Blown Glass Tablewares in the First Century A.D., in M. Newby and K. Painter, eds, *Roman Glass: Two Centuries of Art and Invention*, The Society of Antiquaries of London, London, 1991, 56–75; Nenna 2001b, 176–7, and numbers 286–99 with additional information in D. Foy and M-D. Nenna, Productions et importations de verre antique dans la vallée du Rhône et le Midi méditerranéen de la France (Ier–IIIe siècles), in D. Foy and M-D. Nenna, eds, *Échanges et Commerce du verre dans le monde antique*, Éditions Monique Mergoil, Montagnac, 2003, 227–96.

[11] This information has been provided courtesy of Jennifer Price; for another recently-discovered piece see G. Sennequier and S. Le Mahéo, À propos d'un verre à décor peint trouvé à Rouen, *Annales du 13e congrès de l'Association Internationale pour l'Histoire du Verre*, l'Association Internationale pour l'Histoire du Verre, Lochem 1996, 175–84 and V. Arveiller-Dulong, G. Sennequier and N. Vanpeene, Verreries du Nord-Ouest de la Gaule: productions et importations, in D. Foy and M-D. Nenna, eds, *Échanges et Commerce du verre dans le monde antique*, Éditions Monique Mergoil, Montagnac 2003, 150.

[12] This identification has been proposed variously by Gillian Bowen, Carla Marchini and Helen Whitehouse.

[13] A fourth fragment mentioned by Harden (1936, 138) as possibly from a goblet with a pad-base and floral polychrome decoration is actually a piece of *millefiori* glass (M-D. Nenna personal communication, 2003).

Plate 11 Large East Church (Area A/7): painted glass preserving parts of a group of three human figures.

yielded three pieces from a bowl with floral decoration. Amongst the Quseir el-Qadim fragments, eight in number (Roth 1979, 149; Meyer 1992, 38–9), floral and geometric designs occur, although one preserves the forepart of an animal identified as a dog (Meyer 1992, 38 number 342). From Berenike three fragments are reported, two from a flaring beaker and one with decoration of an animal (Nicholson 1998, 386–7).[14] A single sherd from the Eastern Desert fort at Krokodilô (al-Muwayh) is decorated with what may be a bird (Brun 2003, 383). Of possible Egyptian provenance are: a cylindrical vase in the Metropolitan Museum of Art decorated with Nilotic scenes (Hill and Nenna 2003, 89), two fragments in the same collection from a tall goblet decorated with scenes of gladiatorial combat and animals possibly from the Fayum (Kurz 1954, 104, Figures 374 and 376; Coarelli 1954, 68, Plate VII.2–3), and two fragments in the Corning Museum of Glass, one decorated with a *putto* riding a hippopotamus and the other with a figure in boots (Whitehouse 2001, 259 numbers 854–5).

Painted glass found in the Sudan comes from Sedeinga and Meroe. Three vessels are known from the Meroitic cemetery at Sedeinga. Two are tall narrow, dark blue flutes with beaded stems and feet similar to the head vase from Ismant el-Kharab, and carry painted and gilded decoration showing pharaonic-style offering scenes; they were found in pyramid WT8 (Leclant 1973) and have recently been dated to the second half of the third century and assigned a local manufacture (Wildung 1997, 364–7), though this has been questioned (M-D. Nenna personal communication, 2003). The third is a tall goblet from grave T56 in sector II of the cemetery, dated also to the third century, decorated with a Dionysiac theme and also thought to be a local manufacture (Berger-el Naggar and Drieux 1997; Berger el-Naggar 1999). Fragments of another blue glass goblet(?) were found in Tomb 5 of the northern cemetery at Meroe, with gilded decoration of a man with a shield and the legs and head of a lion (Dunham 1957, 127, 21-12-47c, 52, 70f). This tomb also yielded other painted fragments (Dunham 1957, 127, 21-12-50, 56). Tomb 13 there yielded other fragments from a green glass vessel thought to have originated in Tomb 5, including one with a royal or sphinx's head and a wreath, one with Nefertum on a lotus and another with a priest before a god

---

[14] A further two fragments from Berenike are reported, but no detail or date provided; see J. W. Hayes, Summary of the Pottery and Glass Finds, in S. E. Sidebotham and W. Z. Wendrich, eds, *Berenike 1994. Preliminary Report of the 1994 Excavations at Berenike (Egyptian Red Sea Coast) and the Survey of the Eastern Desert*, Research School Centre for Non-Western Studies, Leiden University, Leiden, 1995, 38.

(Dunham 1957, 76, 22-1-47).[15] They are assigned to the third century (Hill and Nenna 2003, 89).

One of the most significant discoveries of cold-painted/ enamelled glass vessels was made at Begram between 1937 and 1939 in Rooms 10 and 13 of the so-called 'palace'. This material has been published with discussions by Hamelin (1953; 1953; 1954), Kurz (1954) and recently by Menninger (1996). Amongst the 179 glass vessels in the hoards were at least 18 cold-painted vessels, including cups, tall goblets and jugs, with the goblets being particularly common. They are decorated with mythological scenes: Zeus and Ganymede, Europa and the bull; the combat of Hector and Achilles, Orpheus; an Isiac ritual; several battle scenes; fishing and hunting scenes, including a panther attacking a gazelle; and at least two goblets had scenes of gladiatorial combat (numbers 199 and 201: Robert 1946, 128–36; Kurz 1954, 102–3; Menninger 1996, 56–7). Kurz (1954, 104) dated the goblets to the first century; Menninger (1996, 63) has assigned a date to the enamelled glass of late second to third century, while Whitehouse has on several occasions argued for a late first to early second century date (1989a, 153; 1989b, 97; 1998, 640–1), which has been accepted by Nenna (1999, 155). Amongst this find was one vessel decorated with what is regularly identified as the Pharos lighthouse. The place of manufacture of the painted glass from Begram has regularly been surmised to be Egypt,[16] though Raschke (1978, 633 and note 510) has pointed out that this provenance is largely an assumption. The finds of painted glass from a wide variety of locations within Egypt and the Sudan, however, do render the possibility worthy of serious consideration, especially in light of the recent finds at Berenike,[17] as does the similarity of the fabric of one of the painted goblets from Begram to second-century glass fabrics at Karanis (Whitehouse 1989a, 98–9; 1989b, 154). If these painted vessels were made in Egypt, then other goblets of similar type found at Lübsow in Pomerania and Sedeinga could also have an Egyptian place of manufacture (Coarelli 1963, 65). Other western types, namely two bowls from Denmark, are connected to some of the Begram finds by the use of the motif of a blue leopard with black spots (Kurz 1954, 105; Coarelli 1963,

Plate XIII.3–4), which is also found upon one of the pieces possibly from the Fayum (Coarelli 1963, 68, Plate VII.2). The similarity in the choice of the repertoire of motifs, the range of colours employed and the details of style, between pieces found in Egypt, Pomerania and at Begram has been observed (Kurz 1954, 104–5; Coarelli 1963, 65–6).

II: Glass Manufacture in Egypt

Nenna (1998, 152; Nenna *et al.* 2000, 107) has proposed that Alexandria played a significant role in the development of polychrome glass in the Ptolemaic Period, and that city's continued importance as a centre of glass manufacture is generally assumed (Harden 1936, 38–46; 1969, *passim*). Discoveries of kiln sites of Roman Period date confirm production and working at several sites in the Delta: Alexandria, Taposiris Magna, Marea and three in the Wadi Natrun (Nenna *et al.* 2000; Thirion-Merle *et al.* 2002–3); Thmuis (Bagnall 2001, 233)[18] and Athribis (cited in Meyer 1992, 45). References amongst classical authors to Egyptian glass, glass manufacture and export, documentary evidence, and evidence for the working of glass at various sites (reviewed in Nenna *et al.* 2000, 107–12) all indicate activity from the Delta as far south as Edfu. At Ismant el-Kharab, while no kilns used for the working of glass have been found, several glass ingots have been recovered (Hope 2002, 182; this volume).

Various categories of glass have been identified as manufactured in Egypt. These types include, in addition to painted glass: a wide variety of engraved, facet-cut and high-relief-work glass from the first to fourth centuries, often inscribed and some with mythological scenes;[19] mosaic glass from the Ptolemaic to late Roman Periods (Nenna 2002, 2003a–b); various types of mould-blown glass (Nenna 2003b) and inlays (Nenna 1995; 1998). Recent analyses have identified specific fabrics as Egyptian manufactures (Foy *et al.* 2003; Picon and Vichy 2003).

III. Gladiatorial Games in Egypt

The performance of gladiatorial games was linked to the imperial cult, the Roman army and Roman attitudes to

---

[15] I am grateful to Joyce Haynes of the Museum of Fine Arts Boston for providing further information on these pieces, which are now in that collection and numbered 21.11757 and 21.11758.

[16] Seyrig 1941, 261–3; Kurz 1954, 108–9; Coarelli 1963, 65; Harden 1969, 59; Price 1983, 215; Painter 1987, 260; Harden *et al.* 1987, 273; Whitehouse 1989a, 97; Whitehouse 1989b, 153; Menninger 1996, 71; Nenna 1998, 155. Whitehouse (1989a, 98–9; 1989b, 155) has suggested that some of the Begram pieces, especially the fish-shaped vessels and the goblets with openwork trailing, were made from cullet exported from Egypt to Mousa on the south-western tip of the Arabian peninsula and to Barbarike on the north-western coast of India, where it was made into vessels that later reached Begram. This suggestion is based upon analysis of samples from Begram and the similarity of their fabric to the group of early fabrics at Karanis.

[17] This helps to confirm suggestions that glass was transported by ship down the Red Sea to India and then overland to sites such as Begram.

[18] The source cited by Bagnall for this information (*Orientalia* 68, 313–420) was not available to me at the time of writing this article.

[19] Kurz 1954, 100; Coarelli 1963, 73–8; Harden 1969, 54; Harden *et al.* 1987, 182, 190; Delacour 1993, 66; Nicholson 1999, 236–7; Hill and Nenna 2003; Nenna 2003a.

death and manhood (Wiedemann 1992, 44–7). Wiedemann (1992, 46–7) has proposed that amphitheatres situated on the margins of the Roman Empire assured soldiers that they were Roman, defined what belonged to Rome and symbolized, from a Roman perspective, confrontation with and triumph over barbarism. Attendance at the games marked acceptance of Roman ideology and cultural superiority. Thus, the celebration of the games following Roman conquest might be regarded as axiomatic in a city such as Alexandria, despite reservations that have been expressed in relation to their limited popularity in the Hellenized East (Robert 1940, 23–4). Their performance is certainly attested in Antioch, Beirut, Athens and Corinth and other sites in Greece, Rhodes and throughout Asia Minor (Robert 1940; 1946; 1948; 1949; 1950; Papapostolou 1989; Weidemann 1992, 43–4, 129). Whilst the following discussion does not lay claim to representing an exhaustive study of the data, it does aim to draw attention to the variety of material that can be used to indicate the probability of the games having been performed in Alexandria.[20]

A small but significant body of textual evidence attests the existence of gladiatorial training schools (*ludi*) in Egypt. An inscription from Naples from the reign of Domitian mentions this school and its procurator, and implies that it was created under imperial patronage (Robert 1940, 124–5; Lindsay 1965, 177; Ville 1981, 284), while other evidence indicates that it was in existence at least from the time of Nero (Ville 1981, 284–5, note 136) and even Augustus (Wiedemann 1992, 170). Juvenal (*Satire* VI, 82–3) refers to a Roman gladiator fleeing to Alexandria where, presumably, he would continue to fight.

From a military archive of the camp at Babylon (in modern Cairo) come documents relating to a *familia gladiatoria* attached to the camp (Robert 1946, 142–3) that mention gladiators, including a *retiarius*, wild animal fights and fights between men and animals. One fragment refers to a *ludos* at Nico ..., which Robert restores to read Nicopolis where the Roman army was stationed east of Alexandria. He believes that the school was attached to the army and was not for public performances. Whether the find spot of the documents indicates that there was a training school also at Babylon is uncertain.

From 260 comes a document recording the requisitioning of clothes on behalf of a *ludus* (P. Lips I 57: Robert 1940, 125; Lindsay 1965, 177), but which one is not specified, though it is assumed to be that at Alexandria. A second-century song, written upon one side of a papyrus the other side of which contains a tax-account from the Arsinoite nome, contains the complaint by a woman that her lover, a gladiator (*mirmillo*) has abandoned her (P. Rylands I, 15: Robert 1940, 125; Lindsay 1965, 176–7). Finally, gladiators are mentioned in Greek magical papyri

from Egypt (Robert 1940, 242 and note 3; Betz 1986: *PGM* IV. 1390, 1394, 2163; *PGM* VII.175; *PGM* XXXV.18). Of these one (*PGM* VII.175) is worth quoting here; it occurs in a collection headed 'table gimmicks': "*To make the gladiators painted [on the cups] 'fight':* Smoke some 'hare's-head' underneath them"; the accompanying editorial note reads "It seems likely that the reference is to translucent, painted glass which, when lit, produces the effect" (Betz 1986, 120 note 6). This conveniently not only alludes to gladiators but glass painted with scenes of combatant gladiators being used in Egypt.

Gladiators of Alexandrian origin are attested throughout the empire especially in the West, from the first to third centuries, some specifically stated as from the Alexandrian *ludus*, though whether they all received their training in Alexandria is not known (Ville 1981, 264–7; Lindsay 1965, 177). A text of 113 implies the presence of gladiators in Alexandria (Lindsay 1965, 178). Whilst Dio Chrysostom (*Discourse* XXXII) at the end of the first century does not mention gladiatorial spectacles specifically amongst the pleasures of the Alexandrians, he does berate them upon their love of the games; Clement of Alexandria (*Paedagogus* 3, 11.77), late second to early third, warns against the moral dangers of attending the spectacles of the arena (Robert 1940, 243; Wiedemann 1992, 147).

The venue *par excellence* in which gladiatorial games were conducted was the amphitheatre. While no remains of such a structure in Alexandria have been discovered, there is textual evidence for one in Nicopolis. Strabo (*Geography* 17.1.10) refers to an amphitheatre and stadium there being new constructions; Josephus (*Jewish War* II. 490–91) records that in the reign of Nero the presence of large numbers of Jews at a public meeting in the amphitheatre prompted a riot. Other scenes of entertainment that included combat sports were the stadium and theatres, but these would only be used in the absence of an amphitheatre (Robert 1940, 34–66). Such buildings are also known in Alexandria, and at Antinoë and Oxyrhynchos (Bailey 1990, 122–3); Bailey (1990, 123) disputes the existence of amphitheatres outside of Alexandria. One theatre recently identified to the east of Pelusium has been claimed to have been used for gladiatorial games (Bagnall 2001, 232 and note 29, citing P. Grossmann), but no evidence to support this suggestion has been published.

One final category of data that may be reviewed here is representations of gladiators upon small finds.[21] Reservations concerning the use of such material in a discussion of the location of gladiatorial games have been expressed, quite correctly, by Robert (1940, 37; 1946, 127–8). Such items as glass, lamps, terracotta and bronze figures, and ceramic vessels, decorated with gladiators were easily transportable, and their discovery at a site does not

---

[20] I would like to thank Klaas A. Worp for checking references to gladiators in documents from Egypt on my behalf.

[21] My intention here is to indicate the range of objects that carry representations of gladiators not to present an exhaustive list of all examples.

indicate in all cases that games were conducted there. Robert (1946, 127) cites in this regard the glass vessels from Begram and Denmark, and a single lamp from Byblos, all sites or regions where there is no other evidence for the games. Whilst his reservations are acknowledged here, in the case of Egypt where inscriptional evidence proves the existence of at least one gladiatorial school and where suitable venues for the games existed, a brief review of such objects seems warranted. The manufacture of a variety of small items commemorating the games reflects their popularity, especially amongst the army. It has been noted that the frequency of such items is greater in areas with a strong military presence, and less in other regions (Hellmann 1987, 83–4). From the outset it should be noted that the number of such items is not large; for the glassware from Egypt see the discussion above.

Of terracotta figurines depicting gladiators there is one in the Graeco-Roman Museum at Alexandria[22] (Breccia 1922, 263), one from Abukir and another from Middle Egypt[23] (Perdrizet 1921, 156–7 numbers 443–4), and one in Hamburg (Hamburg 1991, 80 number 86). Several others represent charioteers: two were found in the Fayum, one actually in a kiln (Perdrizet 1921, 156 numbers 440–1), several derive from Antinoë (Dunand 1990, numbers 609–11), one from Hawara now in the Ashmolean Museum (1888.776) (H. Whitehouse personal communication, 2003) and another lacks specific provenance (Dunand 1990, number 608). The identification of two figures from the Sieglin and Schreiber collections (Fischer 1994, 389 numbers 1002–3) as gladiators has been suggested; they appear to be equestrian. Finally, a figure in the Louvre of a monkey assuming the role of a gladiator may be noted (Dunand 1990 number 909; Willems and Clarysse 2000, 243 number 163). From the brief descriptions provided of the fabrics in which these pieces are made they appear to be Egyptian.

Another category of object made in local clay may be described, for want of a better term, as plaques. In the Graeco-Roman Museum at Alexandria there is a rectangular curved plaque (GR 22342; Bernand 1995, 43), made in a Nile silt fabric, decorated with two similarly-attired combatant gladiators (Breccia 1934, 50 number 320).[24] It was purchased from Nahman in 1930. Another plaque in brown clay from the Fayum (Perdrizet 1921, 115–6, number 439) bears a depiction of four *quadrigae* in a circus race.[25] Ceramic vessels were also decorated with gladiatorial themes. A fragment from Kom Firin, from a closed form in red clay, is decorated on the exterior in high relief with a combat between a *secutor* and what

may be a *retiarius* (Perdrizet 1921, 156, number 442). From Alexandria comes most of a bowl, in red-coated yellow clay, that has relief decoration on the interior of armour identified as that of gladiators (Perdrizet 1921, 157, number 446), but which could be that of soldiers.

Lamps and bronze figures form the final categories to be reviewed. Of 17 lamps or fragments from lamps, four derive from the recent excavations in the Gabbari cemetery.[26] Three of these are identified as imports on the basis of their fabrics; two depict single gladiators and the third gladiatorial armour (Georges 2001, 444 number 42). The fourth is made from a local fine clay and bears an indistinct representation of a gladiator shown from the rear. It appears to have been made from either an old mould or one made from a lamp that might have been imported (C. Georges, personal communication 2002). Kom Firin has yielded the handle from a lamp that is decorated with a figure of Nike crowing a triumphant gladiator while his opponent allows his sword to fall to the ground; it is made in yellow clay (Perdrizet 1921, 157 number 445). The remainder were discovered in Egypt, but lack further indication of provenance. Four are in the Alexandria Museum (registration numbers 28070, 28302, 28497, 25147; Breccia 1914, 237 Figure 91, 265 Figure 126; Michalowski n.d., Plate 83), three in the British Museum (Bailey 1988, numbers Q1909-10, Q1957) ascribed to the first and second centuries, and the others were part of a private collection (cited in Hellmann 1987, 85 note 8). The sole bronze figure of a gladiator published is from Xois and formed the handle of a knife (Perdrizet 1911, 75–6 number 112).

Conclusions

From the evidence that has been presented above it is possible to draw some tentative conclusions in relation to the place of manufacture of the jug decorated with gladiatorial combat found at Ismant el-Kharab. Egypt, and more specifically Alexandria, emerges as a possible candidate. The manufacture of a wide variety of glass in Egypt throughout the Roman Period is now accepted, amongst which enamel-painted glass, some with scenes of gladiatorial contests and other games, is one probable category.[27] Most of these examples of painted glass are ascribed to the late first century and the second century, but some are third to fourth centuries. If the flutes found at Lübsow and Begram were indeed made in Egypt, then there was a tradition for producing painted vessels in sets. The Alexandrian glassmakers, and other craftsmen, could

---

[22] For information on items in this collection I am most grateful to Mervat Seif-el-Din.

[23] In the publication this is described as a lamp; however, while it possesses a handle and a hole at the front at the figure's genitals, there is also a hole in the rear at the shoulders, which renders its use as a lamp improbable.

[24] They wear crested helmets, a right arm guard, greaves and boots or leggings, and carry square shields and short swords.

[25] A third plaque possibly from Memphis in a silt clay carries a representation of Harpocrates as a Roman general (Willems and Clarysse 2000, 269 number 198).

[26] I am most grateful to Marie-Dominique Nenna for enabling me to see these items, and Camélia Georges for information.

[27] Examples from Ismant el-Kharab, 'Ain et-Turba, Oxyrhynchos, Meroe and possibly the Fayum; see the discussion above.

have witnessed gladiatorial games held at Nicopolis, if the performances there by members of the imperial school were not restricted to spectators from the military. In view of the suggested date of the jug from Ismant el-Kharab, it should be noted that gladiatorial games continued to be celebrated in various parts of the Roman world throughout the fourth century despite a series of rescripts by the emperors, and gladiators were still depicted upon consuls' medallions into the first half of the fifth century (Weidemann 1992, 156–9). How long games were celebrated in Alexandria is not known. They appear to have ceased in the west after the third century (Weidemann 1992, 159) but examples of engraved glass with representations of gladiators and the circus continued to be manufactured into the first half of the fourth century as examples found in Germany and Italy illustrate (Goethert-Polaschek 1977, 38 number 104, 48–9 number 150; Harden *et al.* 1987, 210–12).

The manufacture of small items decorated with gladiatorial or related themes does not need to have resulted from first-hand observation but could have drawn upon a repertoire of widely-available, accepted standard compositions. Indeed, the detail that is often included in such representations would have required either extremely good knowledge by the artisans of the differences in the armament of the various gladiators or access to descriptions/illustrations upon which to draw. The scenes depicted upon these items tend to be similar despite the type of object being produced. They focus upon the highlights, especially the end of the combat (Hellmann 1987, 84; Weidemann 1992, 92–3; Junkelmann 2000a, *passim*; 2000b, 31–74). As noted by Helen Whitehouse above, the iconography of the glasses with gladiatorial scenes resembles that found on mosaics, of which there are several in the eastern Mediterranean and North Africa (Dunbabin 1978; Wiedemann 1992, 25) as well as Europe. This is particularly obvious from the posture of the figures, the inclusion of the referee and the victor's prizes (palm-frond and crown). The similarity of one of the pairs of figures on a glass goblet found at Begram and figures in mosaics from Zliten in North Africa, Kreuznach in Germany and Reims in France, has been commented upon by Robert (1946, 129–36).

The decoration on the painted jug from Ismant el-Kharab conforms to the formats found upon the other glass with similar scenes despite it post-dating them by at least a century. This can be seen in the composition and colour scheme employed. Other close parallels can be found on a variety of clay medallions from Europe (Junkelmann 2000a, illustrations 213, 218 and 220). Weidemann (1992, 25) states that in mosaics from the late third century onwards representations of gladiatorial combat became rare and were replaced by those of the hunting and capture of wild animals, though some are known of the early fourth century (for example Junkelmann 2000a, illustrations 215–6 and 228–30).

Whether the Kellis jug was decorated by an artist who had personally observed gladiatorial games or was drawing upon the standard repertoires may not have been important to the person/s who acquired it. We cannot know what significance the decoration held for the purchaser/s: was it a memento of a visit to the games or simply an item with interesting decoration? It certainly was a luxury piece; but was it brought to Kellis because of its decorative or ideological value, or for its contents, likely some precious oil or resin such as that once within the head-vase found nearby? Was it bought in Alexandria when new by its owner at Kellis or traded via middle-men, and when viewed at Kellis what significance could the decoration have held for those who had not seen the games, for which there is no evidence in the Egyptian countryside? It certainly must have acquired greater value because of the rarity of such items in the provinces, probably being a veritable antique when it was dropped, broke and abandoned. Its discovery offers the possibility of extending the time frame during which painted glass with gladiatorial scenes was produced, apart from being, without doubt, the best preserved of all such vessels. Items in the two deposits also indicate that some of the residents of ancient Kellis had access to luxury products of the highest quality.

Acknowledgements

Colin Hope would like to thank a number of colleagues for their assistance. Marie-Dominique Nenna most generously made available copies of various of her studies of glass prior to publication and also of published material that could not be obtained in Australia; she provided a wide variety of information on glass from Egypt. Helen Whitehouse and Olaf Kaper have also aided me in matters bibliographic. Marie-Dominique Nenna and Jennifer Price have both kindly commented upon a first draft of the full article, made suggestions for its improvement, provided information for inclusion and saved me from a variety of assumptions and errors; however, any that remain are entirely my responsibility.

Postscript

Following the completion of this study the final text of Nenna (in press) was made available and F. Kayser's study, *La Gladiature en Egypte* (*Revue d'Etudes Anciennes* 102 [2000], 459–78) came to my attention. It has not been possible, therefore, to incorporate the results of these works into this article.

Authors' Addresses:

Colin A. Hope
Centre for Archaeology and Ancient History
Building 11, Clayton Campus
Monash University
Clayton, Victoria 3800,
Australia

Helen V. Whitehouse
Department of Antiquities
The Ashmolean Museum
Beaumont Street,
Oxford OX1 2PH,
United Kingdom

REFERENCES

Ancient Sources

Dio Chrysostom: III Discourses XXXI–XXXVI, translated by J. W. Cohoon and H. Lamar Crosby, William Heinemann Ltd, London and Harvard University Press, Cambridge, 1940.

Juvenal, *The Sixteen Satires*, translated by P. Green, Penguin Books, Harmondsworth, 1974.

Josephus, *The Jewish War, Books I–III*, translated by H. St. J. Thackeray, William Heinemann Ltd, London and Harvard University Press, Cambridge, 1947.

Strabo, *Geography*, translated by H. L. Jones, W. Heinemann Ltd, London and Harvard University Press, Cambridge, Volume VIII, 1947.

Modern Sources

Bagnall, R. S., 2001 Archaeological Work on Hellenistic and Roman Egypt, 1995–2000, *American Journal of Archaeology* 105, 227–43.

Bailey, D. M., 1988 *Catalogue of the Lamps in the British Museum. III: Roman Provincial Lamps*, British Museum Publications, London.

Bailey, D. M., 1990 Classical Architecture in Roman Egypt, in M. Henig, ed., *Architecture and Architectural Sculpture in the Roman Empire*, Oxford University Press, Oxford, 121–37.

Berger el-Naggar, C., 1999 Un enrichissement notable des collections d'archéologie nubienne au musée du Louvre: Les Fouilles de Sedeinga, *Revue du Louvre Études* 2, 31–4.

Berger el-Naggar, C. and M. Drieux, 1997 Une nouvelle verrerie découverte en Nubie soudanese, *Techne* 6, 19–20.

Bernand, A., 1995 *Alexandrie des Ptolémées*, Editions du Centre National de la Recherche Scientifique, Paris.

Betz, H. D., ed., 1986 *The Greek Magical Papyri in Translation*, The University of Chicago Press, Chicago.

Bowen, G. E., 2002 The Fourth-Century Churches, in C. A. Hope and G. E. Bowen, eds, *Dakhleh Oasis Project: Preliminary Reports on the 1994–1995 and 1998–1999 Field Seasons*, Oxbow Books, Oxford, 65–85.

Bowen, G. E., this volume Some Observations on Christian Burial Practices at Kellis, 167–81.

Breccia, E., 1914 *Alexandrea ad Aegyptum: Guide de la ville ancienne et moderne et du musée gréco-romain*, Instituto italiano d'arti grafiche, Bergamo.

Breccia, E., 1922 *Alexandrea ad Aegyptum*, Instituto italiano d'arti grafiche, Bergamo.

Breccia, E., 1934 *Terracotte figurante greche e greco-egiziane dell Museo di Alessandria*, Instituto italiano d'arti grafiche, Bergamo.

Brun, J.-P., 2003 Le verre dans le désert orientale d'Égypte: contextes datés du Haut Empire romain, in D. Foy and M-D. Nenna, eds, *Échanges et commerce du verre dans le monde antique*, Éditions Monique Mergoil, Montagnac, 377–87.

Clairmont, C. W., 1963 *The Excavations at Dura-Europos Final Report IV, Part V: The Glass Vessels*, Dura-Europos Publications, New Haven.

Coarelli, F., 1963 Su alcuni vetri dipinti scoperti nella Germania indipendente e sul commercio alessandrino in occidente nei primi due secoli dell'impero, *Archeologia Classica* 15, 61–83.

Delacour, C., 1993 Redécouvrir les verres du trésor de Begram, *Arts Asiatiques* XLVIII, 53–71.

Dunand, F., 1990 *Catalogue des terres cuites gréco-romaines d'Egypte*, Musée du Louvre, Paris.

Dunbabin, K. M. D., 1978 *The Mosaics of Roman North Africa*, Clarendon Press, Oxford.

Dunbabin, K. M. D., 1999 *Mosaics of the Greek and Roman World*, Cambridge University Press, Cambridge.

Dunham, D., 1957 *The Royal Cemeteries of Kush Volume IV: Royal Tombs at Meroë and Barkal*, Museum of Fine Arts, Boston.

Empereur, J-Y., 1998 *Alexandria Rediscovered*, British Museum Press, London.

Fischer, J., 1994 *Griechisch-Römische Terrakotten aus Ägypten*, Ernst Wasmuth, Tübingen.

Flemming, S. J., 1999 *Roman Glass. Reflections on Cultural Change*, University of Pennsylvania Museum, Philadelphia.

Foy, D. and M-D. Nenna, eds, 2001 *Tout feu, tout sable: Mille ans de verre antique dans le Midi de La France*, Musées de Marseille/Editions Edisud, Aix-en-Provence.

Foy, D., M. Picon, M. Vichy and V. Thirion-Merle, 2003 Caractérisation des verres de l'Antiquité tardive en Méditerranée occidentale: l'émergence de nouveaux courants commerciaux, in D. Foy and M-D. Nenna, eds, *Échanges et commerce du verre dans le monde antique*, Éditions Monique Mergoil, Montagnac, 41–85.

Georges, C., 2001 Les lampes, in J-Y. Empereur and M-D. Nenna, eds, *Nécropolis 1*, Institut Français d'Archéologie Orientale, Cairo, 423–504.

Goethert-Polaschek, K., 1977 *Katalog der Römischen Gläser des Rheinischen Landesmuseums Trier*, Philipp von Zabern, Mainz am Rhein.

Hamburg, 1991 *Götter, Graber und Grotesken*, Museums für Kunst und Gewerbe, Hamburg.

Hamelin, P., 1952 Sur quelques verreries de Begram, *Cahiers de Byrsa* 2, 11–25.

Hamelin, P., 1953 Matériaux pour servir à l'étude des verreries de Begram, *Cahiers de Byrsa* 3, 121–8.

Hamelin, P., 1954 Matériaux pour servir à l'étude des verreries de Begram (suite), *Cahiers de Byrsa* 4, 153–83.

Harden, D. B., 1936 *Roman Glass from Karanis*, University of Michigan Press, Ann Arbor.

Harden D. B., 1969 Ancient Glass, II: Roman, *Archaeological Journal* 126, 44–77.

Harden, D. B., H. Hellenkemper, K. Painter and D. Whitehouse, 1987 *Glass of the Caesars*, Olivetti, Milan.

Hellmann, M-C., 1987 Les représentations de gladiateurs sur les lampes romaines, in C. Landes and D. Cazes, eds, *Les Gladiateurs*, Musée archéologiques de Lattes, Lattes, 83–5.

Hill, M. and M-D. Nenna, 2003 Glass from Ain et-Turba and Bagawat Necropolis in the Kharga Oasis, Egypt, *Annales du 15ᵉ Congrès de l'Association Internationale pour l'Histoire du Verre, New York 2001*, Association Internationale pour l'Histoire du Verre, Nottingham, 88–92.

Hope, C. A., 1999 Observations upon the dating of the occupation at Ismant el-Kharab, in C. A. Marlow and A. J. Mills, eds, *The Oasis Papers 1: The Proceedings of the First Conference of the Dakhleh Oasis Project*, Oxbow Books, Oxford, 43–59.

Hope, C. A., 2000 The Excavations at Ismant el-Kharab in 2000: A Brief Report, *Bulletin of the Australian centre for Egyptology* 11, 49–66.

Hope, C. A., 2002 The Excavations at Ismant el-Kharab in 1994–5 to 1998–9, in C. A. Hope and G. E. Bowen, eds, *Dakhleh Oasis Project: Preliminary Reports on the 1994–1995 and 1998–1999 Field Seasons*, Oxbow Books, Oxford, 167–208.

Hope, C. A., this volume The Excavations at Ismant el-Kharab from 2000 to 2002, 207–89.

Hope, C. A. and J. McKenzie, 1999 Interim Report on the West Tombs, in C. A. Hope and A. J. Mills, eds, *Dakhleh Oasis Project: Preliminary Reports on the 1992–1993 and 1993–1994 Field Seasons*, Oxbow Books, Oxford, 53–68.

Isings, C., 1957 *Roman Glass from Dated Finds*, J. B. Wolters, Groningen and Djakarta.

Junkelmann, M., 2000a *Das Spiel mit dem Tod. So kämpften Roms Gladiatoren*, Philipp von Zabern, Mainz am Rhein.

Junkelmann, M., 2000b *Familia gladiatoria*: The Heroes of the Amphitheatre, in E. Köhne, C. Ewigleben and R. Jackson, eds, *Gladiators and Caesars. The Power of Spectacle in Ancient Rome*, British Museum Press, London, 31–74.

Kurz, O., 1954 Begram et L'Occident Gréco-Romain, in J. Hackin, J-R. Hackin, O. Kurz and P. Hamelin, *Nouvelles recherches archéologiques à Begram (ancient Kâpicî) (1939–1940)*, Imprimerie Nationale – Presses Universitaires, Paris, 91–293.

Leclant, J., 1973 Glass from the Meroitic Necropolis of Sedeinga (Sudanese Nubia), *Journal of Glass Studies* 15, 52–68.

Lindsay, J., 1965 *Leisure and Pleasure in Roman Egypt*, Frederick Muller Limited, London.

Marchini, C., 1999 Glass from the 1993 Excavations at Ismant el-Kharab, in C. A. Hope and A. J. Mills, eds, *Dakhleh Oasis Project: Preliminary Reports on the 1992–1993 and 1993–1994 Field Seasons*, Oxbow Books, Oxford, 75–82.

Menninger, M., 1996 *Untersuchungen zu den Gläsern und Gipsabgüssen aus dem Fund von Begram (Afghanistan)*, Ergon Verlag, Würzburg.

Meyer, C., 1992 *Glass from Quseir el-Qadim and the Indian Ocean Trade*, The Oriental Institute, Chicago.

Michalowski, K., n.d. *Alexandria*, Anton Schroll & Co., Wien-München.

Nenna, M-D., 1995 Les éléments d'incrustation: une industrie égyptienne du verre, in *Alessandria e il Mondo ellenistico-romano. I Centenario del Museo Greco-Romano*, "L'Erma" di Bretschneider, Rome, 377–84.

Nenna, M-D., 1998 Le rôle d'Alexandrie et de l'Égypte dans les arts verriers à l'époque hellénistique, in *La Gloire d'Alexandrie* (exhibition catalogue), Paris-Musées et l'Association Française d'Action Artistique, Paris, 152–5.

Nenna, M-D., 2001a Le mobilier en verre, in J-Y. Empereur and M-D. Nenna, eds, *Nécropolis 1*, Institut Français d'Archéologie Orientale, Cairo, 505–12.

Nenna, M-D., 2001b Les gobelets soufflés dans un moule, in D. Foy and M-D. Nenna, eds, *Tout Feu, Tout Sable*, Musées de Marseille/Editions Edisud, Marseille, 176–81.

Nenna, M-D., 2002 New Research on Mosaic Glass: Preliminary Results, in G. Kordas, ed., *Actes du congrès Hyalos, vitrum, glass (Rhodes 2001)*, Athens,153–8.

Nenna, M-D., 2003a Verres gravés d'Égypte du Iᵉʳ au Vᵉ siècle ap. J.-C., in D. Foy and M-D. Nenna, eds, *Échanges et commerce du verre dans la monde antique*, Éditions Monique Mergoil, Montagnac, 359–75.

Nenna, M-D., 2003b Verreries de luxe de l'antiquité tardive découvertes à Douch, Oasis de Kharga, Egypte, *Annales du 15e Congrès de l'Association Internationale pour l'Histoire du Verre*, Association Internationale pour l'Histoire du Verre, Nottingham, 93–7.

Nenna, M-D., in press De Douch (oasis de Kharga) à Grand (Vosges): un disque en verre peint à représentations astrologiques, *Bulletin de l'Institut Français de Archéologie Orientale* 103.

Nenna, M-D., M. Picon and M. Vichy, 2000 Ateliers primaires et secondaires en Egypte à l'époque gréco-romaine, in M-D. Nenna, ed., *La Route de Verre: ateliers primaires et secondaires de second millénaire av. J.-C. au Moyen Age*, Maison de l'Orient Méditerranéen-Jean Poilloux, Lyon, 97–112.

Nicholson, P. T., 1998 The Glass, in S. E. Sidebotham and W. Z. Wendrich, eds, *Berenike 1996. Preliminary Report of the 1996 Excavations at Berenike (Egyptian Red Sea Coast) and the Survey of the Eastern Desert*, Research School Centre for Non-Western Studies, Leiden University, Leiden, 279–88.

Nicholson, P. T., 1999 The Glass, in S. E. Sidebotham and W. Z. Wendrich, eds, *Berenike 1997. Preliminary Report of the 1997 Excavations at Berenike (Egyptian Red Sea Coast) and the Survey of the Egyptian Eastern Desert, including Excavations at Shensef*, Research School Centre for Non-Western Studies, Leiden University, Leiden, 231–41.

Nicholson, P. T., 2000 The Glass, in S. E. Sidebotham and W. Z. Wendrich, eds, *Berenike 1998. Report of the 1998 Excavations at Berenike and the Survey of the Egyptian Eastern Desert, including Excavations in Wadi Kalalat*, Research School Centre for Non-Western Studies, Leiden University, Leiden, 203–9.

Nicholson, P. T. and J. Price, 2003 Glass from the Port of Berenike, Red Sea Coast, Egypt, in D. Foy and M-D. Nenna, eds, *Écahnges et commerce du verre dans le monde antique*, Éditions Monique Mergoil, Montagnac, 389–93.

Painter, K., 1987 Groups J and K: Introduction, in D. B. Harden, H. Hellenkemper, K. Painter and D. Whitehouse, *Glass of the Caesars*, Olivetti, Milan, 259–86.

Papapostolou, I. A., 1989 Monuments des combats de gladiateurs à Patras, *Bulletin de Correspondance Hellénique* CXIII, 351–401.

Perdrizet, P., 1911 *Bronzes grecs d'Egypte de la Collection Fouquet*, La Bibliotheque d'art et d'archéologie, Paris.

Perdrizet, P., 1921 *Les terres cuites grecques d'Égypte de la Collection Fouquet*, Berger-Levraulet, Nancy-Paris-Strasbourg.

Picon, M. and M. Vichy, 2003 D'Orient en Occident: l'origine de verre à l'époque romaine et durant le haut Moyen Âge, in D. Foy and M-D. Nenna, eds, *Échanges et commerce du verre dans le monde antique*, Éditions Monique Mergoil, Montagnac, 17–31.

Price, J., 1983 Glass, in M. Henig, ed., *A Handbook of Roman Art*, Phaidon Press Ltd, Oxford, 205–19.

Price, J. and S. Cottam, 1998 *Romano-British Glass Vessels: A Handbook*, Council for British Archaeology, York.

Raschke, M. G., 1978 New Studies in Roman Commerce with the East, in H. Temporini, ed., *Aufstieg und Niedergang der Römischen Welt*, II: Principat, Part 9.2, Walter de Gruyter, Berlin and New York, 605–1163.

Robert, L., 1940 *Les Gladiateurs dans l'Orient Grec*, Paris; reprinted Adolf M. Hakkert, Amsterdam, 1971.

Robert, L., 1946 Monuments de Gladiateurs dans l'Orient Grec, *Hellenica* 3, 112–50.

Robert, L., 1948 Monuments de Gladiateurs dans l'Orient Grec, *Hellenica* 5, 77–99.

Robert, L., 1949 Monuments de Gladiateurs dans l'Orient Grec, *Hellenica* 7, 126–151.

Robert, L., 1950 Monuments de Gladiateurs dans l'Orient Grec, *Hellenica* 8, 39–72.

Ross, A. and B. Stern, this volume A Preliminary Report on the Analysis of Organic Materials from Ismant el-Kharab, 365–71.

Roth, A. M., 1978 Glass, in D. S. Whitcomb and J. H. Johnson, eds, *Quseir el-Qadim 1978 Preliminary Report*, American Research Center in Egypt, Cairo, 144–81.

Rütti, B., 1991 Early Enamelled Glass, in M. Newby and K. Painter, eds, *Roman Glass: Two Centuries of Art and Invention*, The Society of Antiquaries of London, London, 122–36.

Rutti, B., 2003 Les verres peints du Hait Empire: centres de production et de diffusion, in D. Foy and M-D. Nenna, eds, *Échanges et commerce du verre dans le monde antique*, Éditions Monique Mergoil, Montagnac, 349–57.

Seyrig, H., 1941 Antiquités syriennes 38. Inscriptions grecques de l'Agora de Palmyre, *Syria* 22, 223–70.

Stern, E. M., 1991 Early Roman Export Glass in India, in V. Begley and R. D. De Puma, eds, *Rome and India: The Ancient Sea Trade*, The University of Wisconsin Press, Madison, 113–24.

Stern, E. M., 1995 *Roman Mold-Blown Glass: The First through Sixth Centuries*, "L'Erma" di Bretschneider in association with the Toledo Museum of Art, Rome.

Thirion-Merle, V., M-D. Nenna, M. Picon and M. Vichy, 2002-3 Un nouvel atelier primaire dans le Wadi Natrun (Égypte) et les compositions des verres produits dans cette région, *Bulletin de l'Association Française pour l'Archéologie du Verre*, 21–4.

Ville, G., 1965 Essai de datation de la mosaïque des gladiateurs de Zliten, in *La mosaïque gréco-romaine*, Editions du Centre National de la Recherche Scientifique, Paris, 147–55.

Ville, G., 1981 *La Gladiature en Occident des Origines à la mort de Domitien*, Ecole Française de Rome, Rome.

Wendrich, W. Z., 1996 The Finds, Introduction, in S. E. Sidebotham and W. Z. Wendrich, eds, *Berenike 1995. Preliminary Report of the 1995 Excavations at Berenike (Egyptian Red Sea Coast) and the Survey of the Eastern Desert*, Research School Centre for Non-Western Studies, Leiden University, Leiden, 127–45.

Whitehouse, D., 1989a Begram, the *Periplus* and Gandharan Art, *Journal of Roman Archaeology* 2, 93–9.

Whitehouse, D., 1989b Begram Reconsidered, *Kölner Jahrbuch für Vor- und Frühgeschichte* 22, 151–7.

Whitehouse, D., 2001 *Roman Glass in the Corning Museum of Glass* II, Corning Museum of Glass, New York.

Wiedemann, T., 1992 *Emperors and Gladiators*, Routledge, London and New York.

Willems, H. and W. Clarysse, eds, 2000 *Les Empereurs du Nil*, Peeters, Leuven.

Wildung, D., ed., 1997 *Soudan, Royaumes sur le Nil*, Paris and Munich.

The God Tutu at Kellis:
On Two Stelae Found at Ismant el-Kharab in 2000

Olaf E. Kaper

Introduction

The temple of Ismant el-Kharab, ancient Kellis, has been under excavation by the Dakhleh Oasis Project since 1991 (most recently see Hope 2002 and this volume). This is the only known temple in Egypt to be dedicated to the god Tutu, who was known in Greek as Totoes or Tithoes. The numerous representations of this god that have come to light during these excavations have provided the impetus for a monograph entitled *The Egyptian God Tutu* (Kaper 2003), for which a total of 186 attestations of the god were collected from all parts of Egypt, including 32 from the temple at Ismant el-Kharab.

In 2000, the excavations yielded two stelae depicting the god from within the Inner Enclosure of the Main Temple (Hope this volume). Their find context is important, because of the 67 stelae known for the god, only one other (Kaper 2003, S-1) has a known provenance, from the temple of Koptos. The new finds thus help to confirm the cultic setting for this type of stela. The Third Dakhleh Oasis Project Conference provided the opportunity to present a more detailed discussion of the pieces concerned, and to discuss some other representations of the god Tutu at Ismant el-Kharab. This paper aims not to repeat arguments already made elsewhere, and for the material regarding the god Tutu not treated *in extenso* here, the reader is referred to the said monograph (Kaper 2003).

The God Tutu

As a background, a basic outline of the current state of knowledge regarding the god Tutu is presented first. The god did not originate in the oases, but probably in the Nile Delta town of Sais. Tutu rose to prominence during the Late Period and in the Ptolemaic and Roman Periods; he was venerated throughout the country. The principal information concerning the god was first collected by Sauneron (1960), and Quaegebeur (1986) summarized some important additional insights.

The name of Tutu is first attested in the town of Sais during the 26th Dynasty and the popularity of the god spread rapidly throughout Egypt during the early Ptolemaic Period. He is often encountered in private names at this time, as Tutu in Egyptian or Totoes in Greek, which shows the god's origins in the private realm. It was only during the second half of the Ptolemaic Period that Tutu was included in temple decoration in various locations. Tutu was the son of Neith and he provided his worshippers with protection against the actions of demons. He was the master of demons, controlling the seven fearsome beings that were sent out by his mother Neith or by other goddesses such as Bastet. They could be referred to as the Arrow Demons, because they were identified with the arrows from the bow of Neith. These demons were responsible for bringing illness and misfortune into the world and their influence could be averted by enlisting the help of Tutu.

In stelae, statues and sometimes in temple reliefs the god may appear as a striding sphinx. He was usually depicted wearing the *tni* crown 𓊽 composed of horns and two ostrich feathers or, more rarely, with other crowns or with a solar disk. The solar disk indicates that Tutu could be considered as a manifestation of the sun god, which is further shown by his close association with the god Amon-Re. Tutu was venerated in temples all over Egypt, especially during the Roman Period, from Kalabsha in the south to Alexandria in the north. The widespread use of the name attests his veneration in considerably more locations.

A Stela from the Reign of Septimius Severus

As stated above, two stelae depicting Tutu were found at Ismant el-Kharab during the 2000 field season. In the following, I provide a description of these two pieces and situate them within the context of the epigraphic material from the site. Together, these stelae show the different aspects of the appearance of Tutu in this particular temple,

0   20 cm

Figure 1 Facsimile (by the author) of the stela of Septimius Severus.

some elements of which are not found in other locations in Egypt.

The first stela was found against the inner face of the eastern end of the Inner Temenos, to the left of the entrance gate (Hope this volume). No obvious architectural setting for this large stela has come to light, so its exact original location remains unknown. The piece is intact, it is made of sandstone and measures 80.5 cm in height, 60 cm in width and 11 cm in thickness.

The stela is carved in raised relief with a scene of two seated divinities receiving an offering from a pharaoh (Figure 1; Hope this volume, Plate 15). The first recipient is a goddess wearing a short wig and with traces of a Red Crown visible on her head; the second is a male deity wearing the Double Crown. They are identified as Neith and Tutu, two of the principal gods of Kellis, on the basis of their iconography and the hieroglyphic legends (see below). The stela was once covered in gypsum and painted and there are traces of extensive gilding on the upper bodies and crowns of the three figures, as well as remains of red paint that may once have covered the entire scene. The lower section of the stela has been left free for the addition of inscriptions, perhaps in paint, but no trace of these remains, and it has to be doubted whether a text was ever added here.

The stela is of a type erected by private persons as a means of communication with the gods of the temple. The donor, or group of donors, would erect such a votive stela as a request for aid, specifically for healing, or in gratitude for such aid having been delivered, or it may have been the intention to propitiate the deity with a gift. The name of the donor or donors responsible for the erection of the stela is expected at the base of the relief, as in the case of similar votive stelae found elsewhere (for example Vleeming 2001 for earlier Demotic stelae and Bernand 1989, no. 6 for a Greek stela). Nevertheless, there are many other examples that show that the name of the donor was regularly omitted, and its addition was apparently not essential for the intended purpose of the piece. The second Tutu stela, described below, is another case in point.

The rectangular shape of the stela has been modified in the upper section by carving a rounded top with three rectangular projections in relief. The central projection has been made to fit within the outlines of the stela by sinking it into the curve of the vault. The resulting shape resembles that of the *pr nw*, or *itrt šmᶜw*, the traditional Lower Egyptian temple. This shape may have been chosen because Neith and Tutu, the principal deities represented, were both of Lower Egyptian origin, but it is more likely to be a more general reference to divine architecture.

The rounded upper section of the stela, with its winged sun disc, symbolises the heavenly vault (Westendorf 1966, 75). This disc has two depending cobras wearing the crowns of Upper Egypt (left) and Lower Egypt (right), and two *ḥwi* sceptres are extended to either side. Both the cobras and the sceptres are symbols of protection, like the winged disc itself, and the same decoration was common on funerary stelae. Below it, the stela contains the

hieroglyph for sky, which rests on two supports at either end. This element serves to emphasize further the divine nature of the scene.

The stela depicts a king offering a tray of bread to Neith and Tutu. There are hieroglyphic legends with all three figures:

With the king: ⟦⟧, *nb tȝ⟨wy⟩ swyrys*, 'Lord of the Two Lands, Severus', and ⟦⟧, *sȝ rᶜ ḳsrs*, 'the son of Re, Caesar'.

With Neith: ⟦⟧, ⟨*nt*⟩ *wrt ms*, '(Neith) the great, who gave birth (to Re)'.

With Tutu: ⟦⟧, *ḏd mdw in twtw ᶜȝ pḥty ḥry ššrw sȝ rᶜ*, 'Words spoken by Tutu great of strength, Master of the Arrow Demons, the son of Re'.

The king is identified in the cartouche as the emperor Septimius Severus, which provides a date range for the manufacture of the stela between 193 and 211 CE. He is depicted in full Egyptian costume, with a composite crown set atop a short wig. The crown consists of horizontal ram's horns, an *atef* crown flanked by two feathers, two spirals and two small cobras. Solar disks are set on top of the crown, the feathers and the spirals. The king is dressed in a kilt with a triangular apron and a bull's tail is appended from its belt. The remains of a collar can be made out, but no other jewellery is present, nor is there a beard. The offering by the king consists of a tray with four different shapes of bread. In front of him is an offering stand shaped as a papyrus plant on which a bouquet is placed composed of a large lotus flower and two buds on bound stems.

The goddess Neith is seated on a block throne decorated in the traditional manner with falcon feathers. Originally she was depicted wearing the Red Crown, but this was at some stage and for unknown reasons altered into a smaller head with a short round wig. The wig is otherwise not attested for Neith at Kellis. In her left hand the goddess holds an *ankh* sign and her right hand grasps a papyrus staff (*wadj*) on which a rearing cobra is set. Together with this, Neith holds her emblematic bow and arrows. There are traces of a collar and remains of an armlet on her upper left arm. It is likely that other elements of jewellery were once present, but these are no longer visible owing to the damaged surface of the relief.

Tutu is depicted seated behind Neith upon a block throne that remained undecorated. The god is depicted wearing the Double Crown set upon a long striated tripartite wig. There are cobras added both upon his brow and upon the front of the crown. The god's clothes consist of a kilt and a corselet complemented by pairs of armlets and bracelets and the divine beard. He holds an *ankh* sign in his left hand and a *was* staff in his right hand, the latter combined with a small knife.

The unbalanced nature of the composition is noticeable. The two deities have not been accorded the same amount of space, so that Tutu has a visibly wider pedestal and throne, and the figure of Neith appears somewhat compressed between the other two figures. Moreover, Neith's left arm with its hand holding the *ankh* has been drawn too long, so that the *ankh* overlaps with the bow

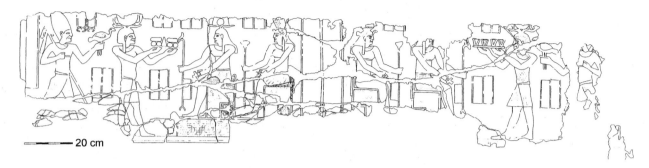

20 cm

Figure 2 Reconstructed lintel from Doorway 1B of the Main Temple at Kellis (drawing by O. Kaper).

held in her other hand. Her figure is also shorter than that of Tutu, and it was shorter even before the original Red Crown was removed. The reasons for this difference between the two figures are unclear. When the Red Crown of Neith was removed, the inscription panel belonging to the goddess was also modified, as is suggested by the remains of a vertical groove in the stone where a second inscription column is expected, as with Tutu. This column was later removed, probably together with the crown of the goddess. I suggest the following scenario to explain the changes to the design.

The stela was once gilded, traces of which remain on the head and crown of Tutu and on the crown of the king. At some stage the upper half of the central scene was overpainted in red, perhaps after most of the gilding had been removed. It is, however, not certain in which order the gilding and the red paint were applied. The red paint was coarsely applied in a manner which suggests a later reuse of the stela, perhaps at the moment when the figure of Neith was recut. The gilding of the stela may have been restricted to the area of the faces and crowns. When the gilding was removed with a chisel or a similar tool, it left the surface of the stela badly damaged. This was subsequently repaired by recutting the figure of Neith and perhaps by overpainting the recut surface in red. The red paint may have been intended as a grounding for a renewed gilding, which was never applied. During the last stage of its use, the stela was covered by libation fluids, probably with the same ritual oil that was applied inside the temple (Ross 2002). The libations were aimed at the figure of Neith in particular.

Tutu in Human Form at Ismant el-Kharab

The stela of Severus demonstrates that Tutu could be depicted in human form at Kellis, wearing the Double Crown. This is confirmed by several other depictions of the god in the temple. For instance, the decorated lintels from three doorways of the Main Temple contained two symmetrical depictions of the god in human form, wearing the *tni* crown on the left (southern) side and the Double Crown on the right (northern) side. Tutu is accompanied by his mother Neith on the left side of each lintel and the goddess Tapsais on the right side. These lintels have been discussed briefly elsewhere (Kaper 1997b, 31) and the reconstructed lintel from Doorway 1B is depicted here in Figure 2, being the most complete of the three decorated lintels. This lintel can be dated provisionally to the end of the second century CE on stylistic grounds, because it resembles a relief found in the Contra-Temple dated to the reign of Pertinax (Kaper and Worp 1995, 112–13).

Several scenes in the *mammisi* of Tutu, which probably dates from the early part of the second century (Kaper 2002a), depict the god in human form. The decoration of the vaulted ceiling was painted on

Figure 3 Facsimile of Tutu seated upon the Nine Bows from the south-western corner of the mammisi *(drawing by O. Kaper).*

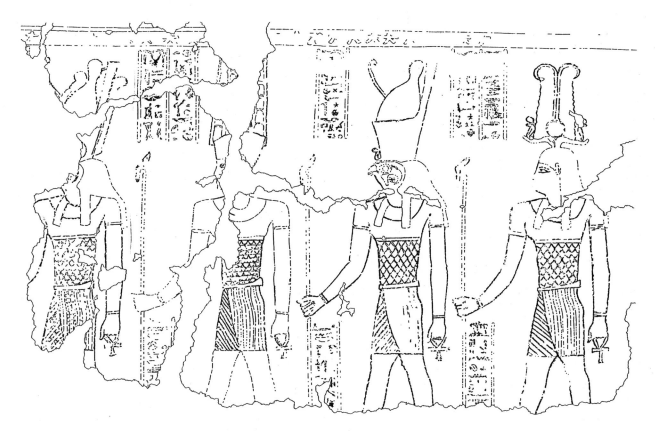

Figure 4 Facsimile of the four principal gods of the Dakhleh Oasis upon the southern half of the vaulted ceiling of Room 1 of the mammisi *(drawing by O. Kaper).*

plaster that is still being reconstructed. Upon the southern side of this ceiling, the penultimate figure on the western end of the upper register depicted Tutu seated upon a block throne (Figure 3). The throne is decorated with falcon feathers and a wheel appears in its lower right corner, which represents the wheel of fortune, the attribute of the Greek goddess Nemesis. Tutu exerted influence over the fate of men and for this reason the Greek concept of divine retribution (*nemesis*) became linked to the god. The pedestal underneath the throne was originally filled with nine images of bows, as a symbol for the traditional enemies of Egypt. Their place underneath the feet of the god indicates that they are in his power. Tutu has a blue skin colour in this scene and a yellow tripartite wig, as is common for the principal male gods in this shrine. His crown is the *ṯni* crown.

Another scene from the same register of the *mammisi* depicts the four principal gods of Dakhleh Oasis (Figure 4). A long procession of the nome gods of Upper Egypt is followed without interruption by depictions of the gods Seth of Mut el-Kharab, Amon-Re of Deir el-Hagar and Amon-nakht of ʿAin Birbiyeh. The final god in this series is Tutu of Kellis, who is depicted in human form wearing the *ṯni* crown. A human form for the god is that most commonly encountered in the *mammisi*, and the same iconography is known from other sites, such as Philae (for example Junker and Winter 1965, 70–1).

The goddesses associated with Tutu in Kellis were Neith and Tapsais. Neith was the god's mother, as is well known also from other parts of Egypt. She was depicted wearing the Red Crown, sometimes with two rearing cobras on top that wear the crowns of Upper and Lower Egypt. Tapsais, on the other hand, was strictly a local goddess. In Egyptian her name was Tap(a)shay and in Greek Tapsais. She was depicted wearing the feather crown of Hathor, or the Red Crown, or a combination of both. An exceptional bronze was found in the Contra-Temple that depicts the goddess (Kaper and Worp 1995) and it is likely that she may have been a private person who was divinised after her death. There is no historical information available about her, but the phenomenon of divinised persons is well-known in Egypt and the oases. In Kharga, a local saint called Piyris was venerated at ʿAin el-Labakha (Hussein 2000, 107–8).

A Stela depicting Tutu as a Sphinx

The second stela discovered in the 2000 field season depicts Tutu of Kellis as a sphinx (Plate 1). The stela was found in the subterranean magazines in the north-western corner of the Inner Temenos (Hope this volume). This stela is made of limestone that had once been covered with gypsum and paint. Only traces of the gypsum now remain. It measures 30.5 cm in width, 22.3 cm in height and 3.6 cm in thickness. The stela was found in two pieces, each of which was used as a lid for a pottery vessel while

Plate 1 Stela of Tutu as a sphinx.

the temple was still in operation, as described by Hope in this volume.

The stela is carved in a high raised relief with the addition of inlaid pieces of coloured glass, which would originally have numbered eleven, but two are no longer extant. In the edge of the stela at the top of the head of the sphinx is a square dowel hole for the insertion of a crown of a different material. Traces of gypsum around the hole confirm that a crown had once been present.

Tutu is depicted as a striding sphinx facing right, with a lion's head of equal size against the back of the human head. A crocodile's head is added to the chest, and the tail of the sphinx ends in a large cobra wearing the White Crown. Behind the paws of the sphinx lies a serpent, as is common in this type of image of the god.

The human head of Tutu is exceptionally rendered in a three-dimensional view. The ear stands out towards the viewer and the right end of the eyebrow curves in towards the back. The head has no beard and no uraeus. The inlaid eye of the head seems to have been painted to resemble a human eye and it has a cosmetic line added in blue. The wig is of the long striated type, falling over the back and the chest in two equal parts. The lion's head is stylized and has a noticeably large ear.

The lion's body has been emphatically modelled with much emphasis on the musculature of the legs. No sex has been indicated. Traces of gypsum upon the body indicate the former presence of two painted intersecting chains that had a small circle at their meeting point. The tail is shaped as a cobra and once had six inlaid pieces of glass in its chest. The two lower pieces are blue, in the middle they are red, and there were again two blue pieces above, of which the right one is now missing. The eye of the cobra is inlaid with blue glass.

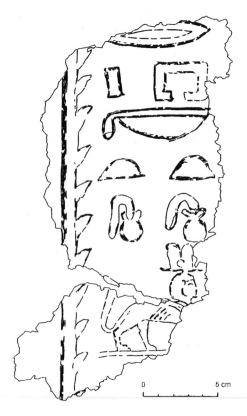

Figure 5 Facsimile the inscription on the western reveal of the lateral door of the mammisi *containing the name of Tutu (drawing by O. Kaper).*

Figure 6   Facsimile of the Dipinto *of Tutu on the east wall of Room 3 of Shrine IV (drawing by O. Kaper).*

The crocodile's head at the chest is foreshortened owing to a lack of space. Its rounded shapes and oversized features make it look like a caricature. The teeth have been stylized as a zigzag line. The large eye has been emphasised with blue glass paste, and there are remains of green or blue paint on its skin.

The mane of the sphinx has been stylized in the conventional way but it was decorated with a grid of incised lines to which the painted layer once added colours. The traces of gypsum indicate that the painted version of this grid did not exactly coincide with the incised grid. This pattern is exceptional on the mane of the Tutu sphinx and does not occur outside Kellis. It is noteworthy that there are two further images of Tutu from Ismant el-Kharab that show the same chequered pattern upon the mane. One of these is located on the rear wall of the *mammisi* and the other was painted above the entrance into the inner room of that shrine, on the interior face. This feature may have been a specific local trait of the god in the Dakhleh Oasis, and it increases the likelihood that the stela was a local product of the artisans of Kellis. It is conceivable that the cult statue of Tutu at Kellis possessed such a chequered pattern upon the mane, but there is no further information about its appearance.

Tutu as a Sphinx or Lion-God elsewhere in Ismant el-Kharab

The popular veneration of Tutu elsewhere in the Dakhleh Oasis is shown by the depiction of the god in the temple of Deir el-Hagar and in the two painted tombs at el-Muzawwaqa, where he appears as a sphinx wearing the Double Crown or the *tni* crown as at Kellis. The sphinx was the most commonly-encountered manifestation of the god Tutu at Kellis. This iconography once serves as a determinative with the name of Tutu upon the reveal of the lateral entrance to the *mammisi* (Figure 5). This sphinx is shown striding, wearing the *tni* crown and with a curving tail that may originally have been shaped as a cobra.

The excavation of Shrine IV at Ismant el-Kharab, opposite the entrance to the *mammisi*, revealed a series of four drawings of local gods upon the eastern and southern walls of its Room 3 (Kaper 2002b). One of these depicts Tutu as a striding sphinx (Figure 6) wearing the *atef* crown and with a ceremonial beard. His tail ends in a cobra crowned with a large Double Crown. The head of a crocodile emerges from the god's chest, as a symbol for the group of seven demons whom he controls, and two knives, two scorpions and a dressed cobra are other symbols of the god's might added at the paws. A larger cobra with an undulating body extends underneath the figure, crowned with a solar disk. This *dipinto*, even though it has little aesthetic merit, is significant because it depicts Tutu with a large number of attributes comparable to the sphinx upon the stela.

The god was depicted in the form of a sphinx in several scenes in the *mammisi*. In a badly damaged scene upon the rear wall, Tutu appeared as a striding sphinx upon a pedestal (Figure 7 and Kaper 1991, 65, Plate 13). The

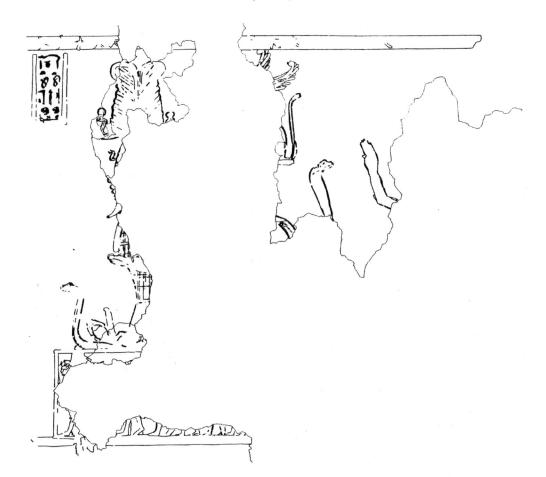

Figure 7 Facsimile of the sphinx of Tutu on the western wall of Room 1 of the mammisi *(drawing by O. Kaper).*

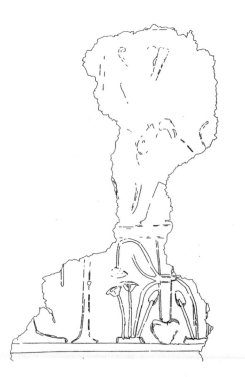

Figure 8 Facsimile of the sphinx of Tutu from the eastern wall of Room 1 of the mammisi, upon the symbol for the unification of the Two Lands (drawing by O. Kaper).

Figure 9 Reconstruction of the face of Tutu in a scene on the northern half of the vault of Room 1 of the mammisi *(drawing by O. Kaper).*

surviving traces show that the image had a beard and the long wig with an uraeus upon its head. It is not clear whether a head band was originally present. His crown was the *ṯni* crown. Upon the chest, the mane showed the chequered pattern, mentioned above, and the head of a crocodile can be detected also. The tail ended in a cobra and another cobra reared its head in front, with its body trapped underneath the first paw of the sphinx. The remaining three paws are lost. A knife and a scorpion have been added at the first paw and similar elements may have appeared at the other paws. Over the back of the sphinx are the remains of a seated leonine figure with wings, set upon its own baseline. There is no doubt that this was originally a representation of the griffin of Nemesis holding the wheel of fate in its paw. The pedestal underneath Tutu has been almost completely destroyed, but traces indicate that a row of nine bound captives was represented inside. Only the feet of these figures remain, but the similar image in Figure 3 may be cited as a parallel, the pedestal of which contains the Nine Bows.

One further depiction of Tutu as a sphinx is located over the axial doorway of the inner room (Room 1) of the *mammisi*, on the exterior face, and three more were located on the interior face of the same wall. Upon the exterior face, the central image above the doorway into Room 1 depicted Tutu as a sphinx upon a pedestal in which was a representation of the seven demons whom the god controlled (partly in Hope this volume, Plate 12). The parallel scene upon the interior face of the same wall, located above the doorway into the shrine, depicted the sphinx of Tutu upon the symbol for the unification of the Two Lands (), which again stresses the royal aspect of the god. The scene in Figure 8 is located lower on the same wall and even though this painting is almost completely weathered away, it still preserves the faint traces of a seated sphinx wearing the Double Crown upon the symbol of the unification of the Two Lands.

Thus, Tutu could be depicted either in human form or as a sphinx in Kellis, but the temple shows an exceptional third type that is a mixture of the two. Fragments from the vaulted ceiling of the *mammisi*, from the northern side, preserve two human representations of Tutu with multiple heads. The usual human face of the god on the first of these has been juxtaposed with a lion's head that has the opposite orientation, like a Janus head. The crown upon the head is the usual *ṯni* crown. The second image combines the same Janus head with a crocodile's head, as is shown in the reconstruction drawing in Figure 9. In this case the crown is lost. The latter image especially can be considered as a connection between the human representations of Tutu and the sphinx. The crocodile was the third part of the composite Tutu sphinxes that was often added to the chest of the sphinx but which has here been incorporated into the head of the god in human form.

The Nature of Tutu of Kellis

The inscriptions and images from the temple at Ismant el-Kharab provide much specific information about Tutu. The god's name is always followed by the title 'great-of-strength' (*ꜥꜣ pḥty*), which indicates the god's protective powers. The title is commonly associated with powerful deities such as Seth, Horus of Edfu, or Amon-nakht of 'Ain Birbiyeh. In addition, the title refers to a demon called 'Great of Strength', who was the first of the group of seven demons over whom Tutu held sway and whose principal manifestation was the crocodile. This was often combined with the image of Tutu (as in Figures 6, 7 and 9) as an expression of the close relationship between the god and the demon 'Great-of-Strength'. Tutu's control over these demons is of great importance at Kellis, as appears from the god's title 'Master of Demons' (*ḥry šmꜣyw* or *ḥry šsrw*), found in inscriptions from the Main Temple and upon the stela of Severus discussed here. In addition, Tutu was depicted together with the Seven Demons upon the façade of Room 1 of the *mammisi*, as mentioned above.

Other scenes in the *mammisi* show Tutu as the god who controls human destiny. He once carries the title *ꜥḥꜥ nfr m-ḫnw n niwt=f*, 'Agathos Daimon in his town', which indicates that he was held responsible for the good fortune of the inhabitants of his town, namely Kellis. Elsewhere, the griffin of the Greek goddess Nemesis could be added to the image of Tutu (Figure 7), or the wheel of fate (Figure 3). This aspect of the god as controller of fate was considered important, as is confirmed by sources from other locations in Egypt.

There are several specifically local traits of Tutu to be seen upon the rear wall of the *mammisi* of Kellis. One scene shows Tutu in human form with what seems to be a lion's head, according to a rare iconography of the god known from the temple at Kalabsha. He was accompanied by another god, who can be identified by the surviving fragments of his crown as Shesmu, the god of perfume and the wine press. Not much is known about the role of Shesmu in Roman times and he has not been encountered before in Dakhleh, but it may be significant that immediately below this god is another image of Tutu (Figure 7), who is being presented with the local produce of Dakhleh, including grapes. When considering the profusion of vines in the classical decoration, upon the Inner Temenos and inside the *mammisi*, then it seems warranted to assume a relation between Tutu of Kellis and the local wine production as personified in Shesmu. Unfortunately, there are as yet no inscriptions that confirm this supposition.

The second aspect of the god that seems of special importance in Kellis is Tutu's role as king. Even though there is no historical king represented in the *mammisi*, it is striking to find many references to kingship in the titles and iconography of Tutu. The god's name is sometimes written in a cartouche, he can wear the Double Crown, and he is depicted subjugating the enemies of Egypt who are trapped inside the pedestal beneath his feet. As for his titles, two scenes designate the god as '*nsw*-king of Upper Egypt and *bity*-king of Lower Egypt' and several times he is 'king of the gods'. Whereas *mammisis* always emphasise the royal aspects in their decoration, the Kellis *mammisi* can be said to have a more than usual emphasis on the royal status of its god. This was stressed even at the cost of other aspects of the temple decoration, such as the depiction of the historical king or the birth of the god. One unparalleled scene in the *mammisi* shows Tutu and Neith receiving an offering of incense from the god Horus-Iunmutef. This is originally a specifically royal ancestor ritual carried out in front of the king or his ancestors (as in Junker and Winter 1965, 227) and it is unparalleled for a god.

Apart from its royal significance, the title 'king of the gods' may also be taken as a reference to the god Amon-Re, who was normally designated with this epithet. In some temples, Tutu was effectively considered as a manifestation of Amon-Re and a double cult of the two gods is known in the southern part of Koptos and at Behbeit el-Hagar (Kaper 1998). In Kellis, this close relationship with Amon-Re was present prominently also. The portable barque shrine in which the image of Tutu was transported in and out of his temple displayed images of Amon on its exterior rather than of Tutu himself (Hope 1998, 841). Conversely, the great god Amon-Re of Hibis, the principal god of the Great Oasis (Kharga and Dakhleh), was absent from the *mammisi* decoration. This omission of Amon-Re is all the more remarkable, because every other god of Dakhleh Oasis seems to have been represented on the walls of the *mammisi* (Kaper 1997a; 1997b, Chapter 2), and the temple reliefs at Deir el-Hagar and 'Ain Birbiyeh in the same oasis contain images of Amon-Re of Hibis in various prominent positions. Perhaps the role of Amon in the temple decoration at Kellis was taken over by Tutu, because the two gods were thought to be closely linked. Upon the barque shrine the reverse situation seems to have applied for the same reason. Amon-Re could be represented by Tutu in Kellis or *vice versa*, as an indication that the two gods were interchangeable to a high degree.

The two stelae found in the temple enclosure of Ismant el-Kharab depict the god Tutu in his two most common manifestations: in human form and as a striding sphinx. The Severus stela demonstrates a local trait of Tutu in the use of the Double Crown, which is particularly common at Kellis, and the sphinx stela attests the chequered pattern on the mane, which is another local peculiarity of the god's iconography. The god's relationship with the group of seven demons is demonstrated by his title 'Master of Demons' on the Severus stela and by the addition of the head of the first demon, a crocodile, to the chest of the sphinx on the second stela.

The two stelae are votive pieces of a well-known type, and thanks to their find context in the temple enclosure, there can be no doubt that they were intended as gifts to the temple itself. The same may apply to the numerous other Tutu stelae kept in museum collections, for which a lack of archaeological context had necessitated that this matter remain largely undecided. Even though the exact purpose for their erection has not been recorded, the two stelae from Kellis attest the practice of propitiating Tutu with votive gifts. Obtaining the good favour of the sphinx-god was a major preoccupation that will have resulted in the embellishment of his cult centres throughout Egypt.

Acknowledgements

My work on the god Tutu and his temple in Ismant el-Kharab was sponsored by the Alexander von Humboldt Foundation, Bonn, in 1999–2000 and the Netherlands Foundation for Scientific Research (NWO) financed the 2000 season of excavations in the *mammisi*, when part of the material described was excavated. I am grateful to Colin Hope for providing me with full access to the material from Ismant el-Kharab, and to him and Gillian Bowen for valuable editorial comments.

Author's Addresses:

Honorary Reseach Associate
Centre for Archaeology and Ancient History
School of Historical Studies
Building 11, Clayton Campus,
Monash University,
Victoria 3800,
Australia

and

Netherlands-Flemish Institute in Cairo
1 Dr Mahmoud Azmi Street,
Post Office Box 50,
11211 Zamalek,
Cairo,
Egypt

REFERENCES

Bernand, A., 1989 *De Thèbes à Syène*, Centre National de la Recherche Scientifique, Paris.

Hope, C. A., 1998 Objects from the Temple of Tutu, in W. Clarysse, A. Schoors and H. O. Willems, eds, *Egyptian Religion, the Last 1000 Years: Studies Dedicated to the Memory of Jan Quaegebeur*, Volume 2, Peeters Publishers, Louvain, 803–58.

Hope, C. A., 2002 Excavations in the Settlement of Ismant el-Kharab in 1995–1999, in C. A. Hope and G. E. Bowen, eds, *Dakhleh Oasis Project: Preliminary Reports on the 1994–1995 to 1998–1999 Field Seasons*, Oxbow Books, Oxford, 167–208.

Hussein, A., 2000 *Le sanctuaire rupestre de Piyris à Ayn al-Labakha*, Institut Français d'Archéologie Orientale, Cairo.

Junker, H. and E. Winter, 1965 *Das Geburtshaus des Tempels der Isis in Philae*, Akademie der Wissenschaften, Vienna.

Kaper, O. E., 1991 The God Tutu (Tithoes) and his Temple in the Dakhleh Oasis, *The Bulletin of the Australian Centre for Egyptology* 2, 59–67.

Kaper, O. E., 1997a A Painting of the Gods of Dakhla in the Temple of Ismant el Kharab, in S. Quirke, ed., *The Temple in Ancient Egypt: New Discoveries and Recent Research*, British Museum Press, London, 204–15.

Kaper, O. E., 1997b *Temples and Gods in Roman Dakhleh: Studies in the Indigenous Cults of an Egyptian Oasis*, privately published Ph.D. dissertation, Groningen University.

Kaper, O. E., 1998 The God Tutu in Behbeit el Haggar and in Shenhur, in W. Clarysse, A. Schoors and H.O. Willems, eds, *Egyptian Religion, the Last 1000 Years: Studies dedicated to the memory of Jan Quaegebeur*, Peeters Publishers, Louvain, 139–57.

Kaper, O. E., 2002a Pharaonic-Style Decoration in the *Mammisi* at Ismant el-Kharab: New Insights after the 1996–1997 Field Season, in C. A. Hope and G. E. Bowen, eds, *Dakhleh Oasis Project: Preliminary Reports on the 1994–1995 to 1998–1999 Field Seasons*, Oxbow Books, Oxford, 217–23.

Kaper, O. E., 2002b A Group of Priestly *Dipinti* in Shrine IV at Ismant el-Kharab, in C. A. Hope and G. E. Bowen, eds, *Dakhleh Oasis Project: Preliminary Reports on the 1994–1995 to 1998–1999 Field Seasons*, Oxbow Books, Oxford, 209–16.

Kaper, O. E., 2003 *The Egyptian God Tutu: A Study of the Sphinx-God and Master of Demons with a Corpus of Monuments*, Peeters Publishers, Louvain.

Kaper, O. E. and K. A. Worp, 1995 A Bronze Representing Tapsais of Kellis, *Revue d'Égyptologie* 46, 107–18.

Quaegebeur, J., 1986 Tithoes, in W. Helck and W. Westendorf, eds, *Lexikon der Ägyptologie*, Volume VI, Otto Harrassowitz, Wiesbaden, 602–6.

Ross, A., 2002 Identifying the Oil used in the Rituals in the Temple of Tutu, in C. A. Hope and G. E. Bowen, eds, *Dakhleh Oasis Project: Preliminary Reports on the 1994–1995 to 1998–1999 Field Seasons*, Oxbow Books, Oxford, 263–7.

Sauneron, S., 1960 Le nouveau sphinx composite du Brooklyn Museum et le rôle du dieu Toutou-Tithoès, *Journal of Near Eastern Studies* 19, 269–87.

Vleeming, S. P., 2001 *Some Coins of Artaxerxes and Other Short Texts in the Demotic Script Found on Various Objects and Gathered from Many Publications*, Peeters Publishers, Louvain.

Westendorf, W., 1966 *Altägyptische Darstellungen des Sonnenlaufes auf der abschüssigen Himmelsbahn*, Verlag Bruno Hessling, Berlin.

The Decoration of North Tomb 1

Olaf E. Kaper

Introduction

North Tomb 1 at Ismant el-Kharab possessed a cult chamber decorated with paintings in pharaonic style. A description of the architecture is provided by Colin Hope in this volume, from which it is clear that there was only one room built of stone in this mausoleum; this central chamber was singled out with figurative paintings. The remaining rooms of the tomb were built of mud brick and decorated with painted plaster in classical style. The tomb had always been a conspicuous free-standing structure at Ismant el-Kharab, and several modern travellers have referred to it in their descriptions, usually referring to it as a 'temple'. Gerhard Rohlfs, who visited the site in 1874 (Kaper 2001, 246–7) describes a stone structure, which was called *birbeh* ('temple'), which he considered to be "ein aus römischer Periode stammendes Kastell". It possessed "drei Hauptgemächern und zwei Nebenkammern, deren Decke, wie deutlich zu erkennen war, ursprünglich gewölbt war" (Rohlfs 1875, 301).

The central chamber of the mausoleum was excavated by Bernard Moritz (Kaper 1997, 4–5) in February 1900, and again a hundred years later by the Dakhleh Oasis Project. The latter work is described by Colin Hope in this volume, but it is interesting to quote Moritz's description of the central room as he found it, because it was so thoroughly robbed afterwards:

"Bâti en blocs de grès taillés, il a une longueur intérieure de 5m,40 sur 2m,94. On y pénètre en descendant un escalier de 3 marches. L'architrave qui portait une inscription grecque a disparu et nous n'en avons pu retrouver que deux petits fragments. Le sol est pavé de briques crues. Le toit sans doute voûté, a cédé probablement sous la pression des sables, lorsque les dunes firent irruption. L'intérieur a actuellement une hauteur de 2m,70, mais était apparemment plus haut. La paroi occidentale a été aussi détruite, on ne sait par quel agent.

Après avoir déblayé l'intérieur, nous trouvâmes sur le plancher des débris d'un tronc de palmier brûlé, puis des bouquets d'oliviers et de saules, une quantité de coins en bois de Sant, qui servaient probablement pour la consolidation de la voûte. Devant la paroi occidentale gisaient les restes de quelques momies brûlées et en partie calcinées" (Moritz 1900, 467).

The central cult chamber may have had a vaulted roof, as Moritz believed, in either mud brick or stone, of which he will have found the remains. Painted decoration was noted upon all four walls of the room, most of which had, however, disappeared before 1900. The remaining walls were last mentioned in 1917 by Girgis Elias (1917), who describes the tomb as "un temple en pierre, sans plafond, ayant environ 3 mètres de longueur, 2 mètres de largeur et 2 mètres et demi de hauteur. L'entrée et la muraille ouest sont démolies; sur les murs nord et sud il y a des peintures, mais tellement endommagées qu'il n'est plus possible de reconnaître les personnages. Aucune inscription n'est visible sur ces murs". The walls were robbed subsequently and during the recent excavations in 2000 by the Dakhleh Oasis Project only a few traces of the painted blocks were found (Hope, this volume). Nevertheless, there remain four sources of information about the original appearance of these walls, which are the following:

1. An article published by Bernhard Moritz (1900), which describes his excavation of the mausoleum and the discovery of the decoration. It includes a description of the paintings on the basis of remarks by Friedrich W. von Bissing, who commented on photographs shown to him by Moritz in Cairo. This implies that a complete photographic record had been made by Moritz, which is now lost.[1]

2. One of the detailed photographs taken by Moritz was published, however, and this shows a part of the walls not known from later photographs (Plate 1). It was included in a popular introduction to ancient Egypt written by Gaston Maspero under the title *Égypte*, and which was published

---

[1] A search for these photographs and the *Nachlass* of Bernard Moritz in Berlin was fruitless; Kaper 1997, 5, Footnote 34.

FIG. 53o. — PEINTURE D'UN HYPOGÉE DANS L'OASIS
BAHARIÉH.
(Cliché Moritz Bey.)

Plate 1 Part of the southern wall in a photograph by Moritz, incorrectly attributed to Bahariya.

Plate 2 Detail of the northern wall in a photograph by Winlock.

Plate 3 The right half of the southern wall in a photograph by Winlock.

in two editions in 1912 and 1919 (Beinlich-Seeber 1998, no. 13096). Figure 530 in that book is entitled 'Peinture d'un hypogée dans l'oasis Bahariéh. *(Cliché Moritz Bey.)*'. Apart from the fact that the painting in the photograph is not known from Bahariya, Moritz did not travel there.[2] The correct attribution is confirmed by Moritz and von Bissing's description of the iconography of the eastern end of the southern wall in the cult chamber of North Tomb 1 (below).

3. Herbert Winlock visited the tomb in 1908 and took several photographs. He published a description of the tomb in 1936, together with a plan (Winlock 1936, Plate 13, bottom left). His remark "This sanctuary has been dug out recently" shows that he was not aware of the journey undertaken by Moritz eight years previously. The condition of the paintings was already much worse than when first uncovered, and the paintings were partly obscured by mud streaks brought on by rainwater.[3] One photograph of part of the decoration was published in Winlock's travelogue (1936) as Plate 12 (upper), here Plate 2.

4. Two unpublished photographs of the room taken by Winlock are kept in the Metropolitan Museum of Art, New York, and these are reproduced here in Plate 3 and in Hope, this volume, Plate 40. The first shows the western half of the southern wall and the other a view of the northern wall of the chamber.

Moritz remarked that the walls of the chamber still stood to a height of 2.70 m, which probably indicates the height of the northern wall, which shows 10 courses of stone on one of Winlock's unpublished photographs (Hope, this volume, Plate 40). The original decoration can be described in some detail thanks to the extensive descriptions given by Moritz. In the following overview, his words will be quoted *verbatim*, and this information will be used to interpret the surviving photographs. On the basis of the combined data, the accompanying two diagrams have been produced (Figures 1 and 2), which though incomplete, may serve as the basis for a renewed appreciation of the iconography of this tomb.

The Decoration on the Northern Wall

"En entrant par la porte, on aperçoit au milieu de la paroi, à droite, la momie d'Osiris debout entre Isis et Nephthys, qui la protègent de leurs ailes. Devant les déesses pousent deux fleurs de *nymphea cœrulea* avec deux boutons chacune, derrière elles on voit deux

---

[2] Moritz travelled from Assiut to Kharga and Dakhleh and back again to Assiut (Moritz 1900, 472), from 17 January to 9 February 1900. The photo is found re-attributed incorrectly to the tombs at el-Muzawwaqa in Porter and Moss 1952, 298: 'called Bahrîya, but perhaps from here'.

[3] Beadnell 1901, 84 records heavy rains in the oasis in February 1901.

Figure 1 Reconstruction of the northern wall decoration.

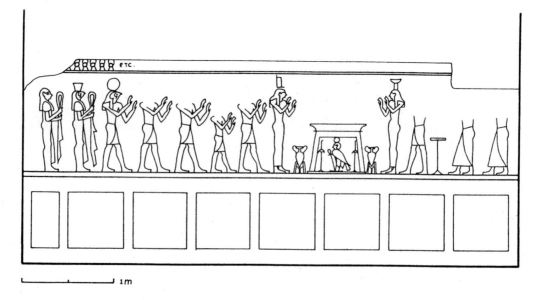

Figure 2 Reconstruction of the southern wall decoration.

tiges de papyrus (?) ou de "lis" accompagnées aussi de deux boutons. A droite, des porteurs d'offrandes arrivent avec une oie, des pains, etc. Le dernier paraît avoir une coiffure étrange que je ne distingue pas très bien. Y a-t-il deux uræus au-dessus du front et serait-ce un prince de l'oasis? On pourrait y reconnaître le dédicateur du temple. Son costume diffère aussi de celui des deux autres qui portent sur la robe des prêtres la peau de panthère, insigne de certains prètres des morts. Cette peau semble manquer au troisième qui ne porte qu'une robe longue, laissant à nu la partie supérieure du corps. Entre lui et le second prètre on remarque des offrandes et des fleurs. Mais qu'y a-t-il au-dessus? On dirait deux oiseaux en face l'un de l'autre, peut-être une forme spéciale du disque ailé? A gauche de l'Osiris momie, nous voyons Osiris (?) assis sur un siège à pieds de lion qui est posé sur un escabeau. Devant lui se trouve un insigne assez fréquent aux basses époques: un bâton finissant en uræus coiffée de la double couronne" (Moritz 1900, 468).

In Winlock's time, the condition of the paintings was already much diminished. Winlock could not make out the same amount of detail as Moritz, and on his plan he gave the location of only two images on the north wall, as *a* on the right and *b* on the left: 'At *a* offering bearers advance towards a now destroyed seated figure, *b*, in front of which stands a figure facing *a*'.

The mummiform figure of Osiris can not be made out on Winlock's photograph (Hope, this volume, Plate 40). In the diagram, the iconography of the god has been adapted from depictions of the god in the *mammisi* at Ismant el-Kharab (compare Kaper 2002). The relative position of Isis and Nephthys is also not certain, but their order upon the southern wall could be copied here. The wings of Isis extend over her upper body, quite unconventionally (Plate 2). Normally, the torso and one breast would be visible between the arms. The two goddesses probably held ostrich feathers in their hands, but other elements also sometimes occur, such as a flagellum, so that this has not been reconstructed.

There are two priests bringing food offerings to the deceased (Plate 2). They are identified as mortuary priests by the animal skin, which covers their bodies, and by their shaven heads. The first priest holds a goose with both hands in a manner not known from elsewhere. The second priest holds a duck in his right hand and his other hand appears to point at the pile of bread on a small table. The heads of the two priests were probably covered with a cone-like insignia indicative of the priestly rank, which is also worn by the priests Kytinos and Petubastis in Dakhleh, whose tombs are described further below. Traces of such an item are certainly visible on the head of the priest on the right. The headgear of the man in the corner was apparently of a special kind, and it could not be reconstructed. The element in front of him is also intriguing. On Winlock's published photograph (Plate 2), the rear part of a flying bird can be seen, so Moritz's

suggestion of two birds has been followed in the reconstruction.

The seated figure on the left, whose location on the wall is indicated on Winlock's plan, is of uncertain nature. The type of chair seems to preclude an identification as Osiris, also because Osiris is already present elsewhere in the same scene. The 'insigne assez fréquent' which was said to be in front of this figure is not clear to me.

The scene was probably topped by a *kheker* frieze, as on the opposite wall, but Moritz does not note its presence. The decoration of the dado with a regular row of small square panels has been adopted from Winlock's photograph of the southern wall (Plate 3). This element remains uncertain, because Moritz (1900, 470) speaks of a single red panel on each wall, whereas Winlock's photograph appears to show a series of rectangular panels. The latter would be more in accordance with classical taste and has parallels in contemporaneous tombs in Tuna el-Gebel and Akhmim, on which more will be said below. It remains a problematic part of the reconstruction of the decoration, but it is clear that no pharaonic elements were present here.

The Decoration on the Southern Wall

"La paroi gauche est bordée en haut par une frise de *cheker*, ornement des plus communs dans l'art égyptien. En commençant par le coin, à côté de la porte, on voit une procession de personnages qui se dirige vers un but malheureusement détruit; ce sont d'abord deux des "enfants d'Horus", chacun avec le nœud qu'on nomme "sang d'Isis", puis Horus lui-même levant les mains en adoration. Devant Horus se trouvent trois hommes dont la partie supérieure est détruite. Si je ne me trompe, le troisième, de taille moindre, serait le fils du personnage placé derrière lui. Comme les autres, il fait le geste de la prière.

L'objet de leur adoration est posé sur une sorte de table dont le rebord et les pieds sont ornés d'un feston. Une amphore sur un pied se trouve à gauche et à droite de la table sous laquelle se voit une âme imberbe en forme d'oiseau, avec le disque solaire sur la tête. Devant l'âme se trouve le signe de la vie et des tiges de papyrus d'où sortent des flammes (?) sont placés des deux côtés de l'âme. Je me rapelle avoir vu dans le commerce, des candélabres en faïence, d'époque gréco-romaine, qui imitaient la forme du papyrus. S'il s'agissait ici de pareille chose, il faudrait naturellement penser que les candélabres étaient placés devant la table et non au-dessous.

L'objet qui est sur la table me paraît avoir la forme d'un naos; on distingue encore un des symboles ailés de l'Égypte sans pouvoir en dire rien de plus. Des deux côtés se tiennent debout Isis et Nephthys (son hiéroglyphe se voit sur la tête de la déesse à droite); il s'agirait donc de la caisse sacrée qui renferme les restes d'Osiris.

Plus à droite, encore une autre procession arrive avec des offrandes; le premier personnage semble correspondre par le costume à la première personne arrivant de gauche, les autres portent de longues robes et sont peut-être des prêtres et prêtresses. On remarquera la table d'offrande placée au milieu de la procession" (Moritz 1900, 468–70).

For this scene there is additional information in Winlock's photograph of the right half (Plate 3), and in Moritz's published photograph for the left end (Plate 1). There is a problem, however, in matching the description of this scene with the photographs. According to Moritz, the scene starts with the two sons of Horus on the left, followed by a Horus-type figure and three adoring males in front of the small shrine. The third is said to be smaller than the preceding two. Yet, the photograph of Winlock shows a full-sized divine figure following Isis and on Moritz's photograph there is another full-sized figure preceding Horus. The small figure must, therefore, have been positioned in between the others, and the number of persons described by Moritz has to be increased.

It is unusual that only two of the four sons of Horus should appear in the tomb. Yet, there was certainly no room for the remaining two on the opposite wall.

Perhaps there was a falcon perched on the shrine, as is suggested by the dark shape still visible in Winlock's photograph (Plate 3), and by a parallel depiction in el-Muzawwaqa, in the first chamber of the tomb of Petosiris (Osing *et al.* 1982, Plate 25a). Moritz suggests that a winged disk could have been present above this element. The figurative painting in the vestibule of North Tomb 1, mentioned by Colin Hope (this volume), has provided the details for the two amphorae stands on either side of the shrine in the diagram.

There does not seem to be room on the wall for more than two (male) priests and one offering table in the corner on the right. Moritz seems to suggest a larger number, also including females, but this has not been followed here.

The Decoration on the Eastern Wall

"Quant aux deux personnes qui se voient sur le mur aux deux côtés de la porte, je supposerais que, à gauche et à droite d'Osiris, Horus et Anoubis se tiennent debout et lui tendent probablement le signe de la vie ou quelque autre symbole divin" (Moritz 1900, 470).

Apparently, there was one scene on either side of the doorway, both showing Osiris who was depicted once together with Horus and once with Anubis. It is unclear exactly which god appeared on which side of the doorway, and no photographs survive of these scenes, so they could, therefore, not be reconstructed.

The Decoration on the Western Wall

"Le mur du fond est malheureusement presque entièrement détruit. On y voit, peints en jaune, deux pieds d'un meuble qui descendent jusqu'au sol, c'est-à-dire plus bas que les fresques des côtés latéraux. Un bouquet de nymphées de teinte verdâtre naît près de chaque pied. Entre ces pieds il y a le même rectangle rouge foncé qui se trouve aussi à la base des autres parois.

Le meuble que ces pieds supportaient a disparu. Peut-être était-ce un lit funéraire sur lequel était posée la momie d'Osiris. Des traces, à droite, à gauche et sur le plan même du lit, pourraient appartenir à la partie inférieure de deux déesses qui seraient Isis et Nephthys. Mais tout celà est bien indédis" (Moritz 1900, 470).

This information by Moritz is important, because it contradicts Winlock's observation of a broad niche 'above floor level' in the rear wall (Winlock 1936, 21, plate 13). Apparently, this feature had not been there originally, and it may have been created though robbery or collapse of a part of the west wall subsequent to Moritz's departure. The notes of Wilkinson in 1825 contain a plan of North Tomb 1, which also shows the rear wall unbroken.[4] The decoration of the west wall could well have contained a funerary bier with a depiction of the deceased, especially as this was an almost obligatory element in the decorative scheme that is lacking upon the side walls. Moritz notes its low position upon the wall, which may have been intended to suggest that the bed rested on the floor of the chamber, possibly corresponding with an actual wooden funerary bed placed in the room. The tomb of Kytinos in Dakhleh depicts two mummies on biers upon its rear wall (Osing *et al.* 1982, 61, Plate 15).

General Remarks on the Decoration

The paintings were applied on a gesso layer upon the sandstone walls of the sanctuary. About the original colour scheme not much can be said. Moritz does not record the colours of the scenes he describes, except for the west wall, where he notes yellow legs of what may have been a funerary bed, and the greenish lotus flowers on either side. The red panelling upon the dado of the entire room is briefly mentioned as well. From the photographs it is clear that many of the male figures were depicted with a dark skin, probably red, whereas the female figures had a lighter, probably yellow, skin, in accordance with the traditional colour conventions. This rule is not consistently applied, however, because on the south wall, the male deity to the right of the small shrine has a light skin as does the *ba* bird inside the shrine, whereas it had undoubtedly a male head. Moritz describes it as having a beard.

---

[4] Unpublished manuscript in the Bodleian Library, Oxford, with the title 'Cairo to Siouah + Fayoum + Oases to Thebes, 1824–5'.

There are a few other decorated tombs in Dakhleh, notably two rock-cut tombs at el-Muzawwaqa, but these do not much resemble either each other or the decoration of North Tomb 1. The tomb of Kytinos (*Ktyns*; Κύτινος; compare Wagner 1987, 245, Footnote 3) in Bashendi (Osing *et al.* 1982, 58–69, Plates 64–69), however, contains a number of similarities in its decoration and it is comparable with North Tomb 1 in several respects. First, both tombs consist of several chambers with an axial cult chamber oriented east-west. Second, the axial chapel was decorated with pharaonic-style reliefs containing images of gods and priests as offering bearers.

The cult chamber of North Tomb 1 differed significantly from Kytinos' tomb in execution, because the latter was slightly smaller and decorated with sculpted reliefs. There were also significant differences in iconography; as Dieter Kurth (1990, 59) has pointed out, the tomb of Kytinos is a notable example of the use of temple decoration in a private tomb, but this is entirely absent from North Tomb 1. Kurth referred to the souls of Pe and Nekhen over the doorway of Kytinos' cult chamber, its *soubassement* with Upper and Lower Egyptian symbols and *rekhyt* birds, the bandeau inscriptions and the two registers with ritual scenes, and finally the *kheker* frieze that tops its walls. It is certainly not a coincidence that this decorative scheme resembles that of the sanctuaries at 'Ain Birbiyeh and Deir el-Hagar in the same oasis.[5] The use of ritual scenes in private tombs was not restricted to Dakhleh, as may be observed, for instance, in Chapel 21 in Tuna el-Gebel (Gabra and Drioton 1954, Plates 25 and 28). In Dakhleh, the tomb of Petosiris in el-Muzawwaqa yields a further example with its depiction of fecundity figures on the walls, which is also derived from temple decoration (Kurth 1990, 63). No such elements were present in the cult chamber of North Tomb 1.

In the tomb of Kytinos, the decoration focuses on the aspect of the deceased as Osiris. The god Shu is depicted giving him the breath of life and a libation, as an indication of his divine status after death (Osing *et al.* 1982, 61–2, plate 17a–b; Kurth 1990, 63). Next to the doorway are depictions of the four sons of Horus, two of whom recur in the same location in North Tomb 1, possibly with the role of a guardian (compare Kákosy 1969, 66–8). The most notable difference between North Tomb 1 and other contemporary tomb chapels, such as that of Kytinos, lies in the absence of mortuary scenes, such as the mummy of the deceased on a bier and scenes derived from the Book of the Dead. As Moritz suggested, it is likely that the bier had been represented on the rear wall of the chapel, but there is no place for the scene of the weighing of the heart, which is almost universally present in other tombs. As an example I cite the rock-cut tombs in as-Salamuni (Akhmim), for instance, which were mostly decorated with a combination of images of deities, the tomb owner, and different mortuary scenes (Kuhlmann 1983, Plates 33–8; Kanawati 1990, Plates 40–2).

The decoration in North Tomb 1, as far as we know, centred upon the veneration of the deceased in two of his manifestations. In the central image upon the northern wall he was depicted in the guise of Osiris flanked by the goddesses Isis and Nephthys. That this image depicts the deceased himself, as opposed to the god Osiris, is clear from the row of priests carrying food offerings to him. This scene is comparable to the scene in the tomb of Kytinos, which depicts the tomb owner as a mummy. On the southern wall, however, the central image is different and shows the *ba* bird, symbolising the soul of the deceased who resides in heaven. The bird is enclosed inside a small shine as a divine icon, and it is flanked by Isis and Nephthys. The divine status of this image is confirmed by the row of deities that face it in adoration.

The *ba* represents the second form in which the deceased continued its existence after death. It is, in fact, one of the central themes in the mortuary beliefs of Roman Egypt. Osiris had been the focus of these beliefs since time immemorial, and this prominence persisted until the demise of the old religion. The role of the *ba* soul in these beliefs had increased over time and became highly important in many parts of the country in Roman times (Kurth 1990, 63–4; Beinlich 2000; Willems and Clarysse 2000, 124 and 126). In Dakhleh and Kharga this is clear from the addition of small wooden statues of the *ba* placed upon the mummy in this period, which is attested at 'Ain el-Labakha and Dush in Kharga (Dunand 1998, 131), and Ismant el-Kharab in Dakhleh (Birrell 1999, 38). Dieter Kurth (1990, 64) has summarized the situation as follows: "Die für die Auferstehung wesentlichen Gestalten sind also die des Osiris und die des Ba-Vogels". This is what is depicted in the chapel of North Tomb 1. It shows the deceased resurrected in heaven as a *ba*, and in the netherworld as an Osiris.

The Date of the Paintings

Moritz dated the paintings to the Roman Period on the basis of their artistic style and the Greek inscription over the doorway, of which he had found two fragments (Moritz 1900, 467; Hope this volume). The iconography led him (Moritz 1900, 470) to conclude correctly that it was a tomb chapel: "Il est certain que de pareilles scènes ne pouvaient se trouver que dans un temple Osirien où dans un temple funéraire", and he compared it to the mortuary temples in Thebes: "Ce temple pouvait bien être ou en rapport direct avec le tombeau, ou bien isolé comme les grands temples de la nécropole de Thèbes". It is now clear that there were burials in this type of tomb, and it may therefore be compared to other tombs of the same period.

Many tombs from Roman Egypt, both rock-cut tombs and built chapels, show a combination of two different artistic styles, such as a classical-style dado combined with religious scenes in pharaonic style (Castiglione 1961). The

---

[5] The decorative scheme of the sanctuary of Deir el-Hagar is partly published in Winlock 1936, Plate 22. The publication of the sanctuary at 'Ain Birbiyeh by the Dakhleh Oasis Project awaits the completion of its excavation and conservation.

decoration of North Tomb 1 belongs to this tradition. Unfortunately, as long as the tomb decoration of the Roman Period remains largely unpublished, as it is today, this aspect can not yet assist in the dating of the tomb. We are confronted with the problem that tomb decoration in Roman Egypt varied considerably, even within a small region such as the Dakhleh Oasis.

One major difference between the Kytinos tomb and North Tomb 1 is the occurrence of hieroglyphic legends and bandeau inscriptions in the former. The pharaonic-style decoration in North Tomb 1 seems to have been devoid of such, and it is possible that the Greek inscription found in front of the room was the only text present. This suggests a similar date for the tomb as that of Petosiris in el-Muzawwaqa, which remained largely without inscriptions, and which has been dated to the early second century CE (Whitehouse 1998, 262).

Acknowledgement

I am grateful to the Alexander von Humboldt Foundation for supporting my research.

Author's Addresses:

Honorary Reseach Associate
Centre for Archaeology and Ancient History
School of Historical Studies
Building 11, Clayton Campus,
Monash University, Victoria 3800,
Australia

and

Netherlands-Flemish Institute in Cairo
1 Dr Mahmoud Azmi Street,
Post Office Box 50,
11211 Zamalek, Cairo,
Egypt

REFERENCES

Beadnell, H. J. Ll., 1901 *Dakhla Oasis: Its Topography and Geology*, Survey Department, Cairo.

Beinlich, H., 2000 *Das Buch vom Ba*, Harrassowitz, Wiesbaden.

Beinlich-Seeber, Ch., 1998 *Bibliographie Altägypten 1822–1946*, Harrassowitz, Wiesbaden.

Birrell, M., 1999 Excavations in the Cemeteries of Ismant el-Kharab, in C. A. Hope and A. J. Mills, eds, *Dakhleh Oasis Project: Preliminary Reports on the 1992–1993 and 1993–1994 Field Seasons*, Oxbow Books, Oxford, 29–41.

Castiglione, L., 1961 Dualité du style dans l'art sépulchral égyptien à l'époque romaine, *Acta antiqua Academiae scientiarum hungaricae* 9, 209–30.

Dunand, F., 1998 Pratiques et croyances funéraires, in O. E. Kaper, ed., *Life on the Fringe*, Research School Centre for Non-Western Studies, Leiden University, Leiden, 128–38.

Elias, G., 1917 Inspection de l'oasis de Dakhleh, *Annales du Service des Antiquités de l'Égypte*, 17, 141–3.

Gabra, S. and É. Drioton, 1954 *Peintures à fresques et scènes peintes à Hermoupolis-ouest (Touna el-Gebel)*, Egyptian Antiquities Organization, Cairo.

Hope, C. A., this volume The Excavations at Ismant el-Kharab from 2000 to 2002, 207–89.

Kákosy, L., 1969 Probleme der ägyptische Jenseitsvorstellungen in der Ptolemäer- und Kaiserzeit, in *Religions en Égypte Hellénistique et Romaine: Colloque de Strasbourg 16–18 mai 1967*, Paris, 59–68.

Kanawati, N., 1990 *Sohag in Upper Egypt, A Glorious History*, Prism Archaeological Series 4, Giza.

Kaper, O. E., 1997 *Temples and Gods in Roman Dakhleh; Studies in the Indigenous Cults of an Egyptian Oasis*, privately published Ph.D. Dissertation, Groningen.

Kaper, O. E., 2001 Archäologische Forschungen der Rohlfs'schen Expedition in der Oase Dachla (1874), in C.-B. Arnst, I. Hafemann and A. Lohwasser, eds, *Begegnungen: Antike Kulturen im Niltal. Festgabe für Erika Endesfelder, Karl-Heinz Priese, Walter Friedrich Reineke, Steffen Wenig von Schülern und Mitarbeitern*, Verlag H. Wodtke und K. Stegbauer, Leipzig, 233–51.

Kaper, O. E., 2002 Pharaonic-Style Decoration in the Mammisi at Ismant el-Kharab: New Insights after the 1996–1997 Field Season, in C. A. Hope and G. E. Bowen, eds, *Dakhleh Oasis Project: Preliminary Reports on the 1994–1995 to 1998–1999 Field Seasons*, Oxbow Books, Oxford.

Kuhlmann, K.-P., 1983 *Materialien zur Archäologie und Geschichte des Raumes von Achmim*, Philipp von Zabern, Mainz am Rhein.

Kurth, D., 1990 *Der Sarg der Teüris: Eine Studie zum Totenglauben im Römerzeitlichen Ägypten*, Philipp von Zabern, Mainz am Rhein.

Maspero, G., 1912 *Égypte*, second edition 1919, Histoire générale de l'art 4, Paris.

Moritz, B., 1900 Excursion aux oasis du désert libyque, *Bulletin de la Société khédiviale de Géographie*, Series V, no. 8, 429–75.

Osing, J., M. Moursi, Do. Arnold, O. Neugebauer, R. A. Parker, D. Pingree and M. A. Nur-el-Din, 1982 *Denkmäler der Oase Dachla. Aus dem Nachlass von Ahmed Fakhry*, Philipp von Zabern, Mainz am Rhein.

Porter, B. and R. L. B. Moss, 1952 *Topographical Bibliography of Ancient Egyptian Hieroglyphic Texts, Reliefs and Paintings*, Volume VII, *Nubia the Deserts, and Outside Egypt*, Griffith Institute, Oxford

Rohlfs, G., 1875 *Drei Monate in der Libyschen Wüste*, Fischer, Kassel.

Wagner, G., 1987 *Les oasis d'Égypte à l'époque grecque, romaine et byzantine d'après les documents grecs*, Institut français d'archéologie orientale, Cairo.

Whitehouse, H., 1998 Roman in Life, Egyptian in Death: The painted tomb of Petosiris in the Dakhleh Oasis, in O. Kaper, ed., *Life on the Fringe*, Research School Centre for Non-Western Studies, Leiden University, Leiden, 253–70.

Willems, H. and W. Clarysse, eds, 2000 *Les Empereurs du Nil*, Lourain, Peeters.

Winlock, H. E., 1936 *Ed Dakhleh Oasis, Journal of a Camel Trip Made in 1908*, Metropolitan Museum of Art, New York.

Ancient Antibiotics: Evidence of Tetracycline in Human and Animal Bone from Kellis

Corey Maggiano, Tosha L. Dupras and John Biggerstaff

Abstract

Two decades ago archaeologists in northern Africa discovered evidence that an antibiotic was in some way included in the diet of ancient peoples, possibly affecting the health of the population. It has been proposed that the causative organisms were *Streptomyces aureofaciens*: ubiquitous, mould-like, tetracycline-producing bacteria that could have contaminated grain products. Upon consumption, tetracyclines are incorporated into developing or remodelling bone, remaining observable under ultraviolet light for thousands of years. The current pilot project focuses on an analysis of Egyptian human and non-human animal bone (N=30) from Kellis in the Dakhleh Oasis in south-western Egypt *circa* 100 BCE to 400 CE. Confocal Laser Scanning Microscopy is used to determine whether or not the population had been exposed to antibiotics, taking advantage of tetracycline's natural fluorescent properties. Results suggest that, though nearly every sample shows tetracycline fluorescence described in previous literature, bone from the Kellis 1 and Kellis 2 cemeteries display distinct differences in florescent patterning. Confocal Laser Scanning Microscopy allows three-dimensional viewing and high-resolution imaging, lending new perspective and increased accuracy to the analysis. Previously-published theories regarding the means of exposure and resulting health affects are reconsidered.

Introduction

Twenty-two years ago researchers in Africa made a discovery that surprised not only themselves but the medical community as well. Quite by accident, they had discovered tetracycline, a type of antibiotic, embedded in human bone over 1400 years old from a site in ancient Nubia, present day Sudan (Bassett *et al.* 1980). They attributed its presence to common antibiotic-producing, gram-positive bacteria called *Streptomyces aureofaciens*.

Shortly thereafter, researchers working in Egypt made similar findings (Cook *et al.* 1989). Now, the topic of ancient antibiotics is revisited, focusing on bone collected from the ancient village of Kellis and its two associated cemeteries located in the Dakhleh Oasis, Egypt, *circa* 100 BCE to 400 CE.

Bassett and fellow researchers (1980) were the first to document the existence of antibiotics in archaeological material from a site in Sudanese Nubia, *circa* 350 to 550 CE. Due to the extremely dry environment, levels of bone preservation are very high and natural mummification is common, resulting in preserved remains perfect for histological analysis. During microscopic examination of the Nubian skeletal material, researchers discovered something unexpected. Under a 490 angstrom UV lamp, all of the 42 individuals tested displayed fluorescence in their bone. Upon closer examination Bassett *et al.* (1980) and Keith and Armelagos (1988) ruled out post-mortem fungal invasion as the origin of fluorochrome (fluorescent material) in the sample. The occurrence of labelled areas of bone overlapped by, or even adjacent to, non-fluorescent areas demonstrates that the fluorescence follows all rules of bone formation and maintenance. Fungal osteoclasia, on the other hand, results in diffuse fluorescence and is accompanied by obvious bone damage referred to as tunnelling; neither were observed in the Nubian remains. Bassett and colleagues (1980) conclude that the patterning of the label, its hue and absorption wavelength were all congruent with antibiotic labelling *in vivo*, specifically by oxytetracycline, a member of the tetracycline group of antibiotics.

Arguing that the antibiotics were not intentionally used for medicinal purposes, Bassett *et al.* (1980) proffered a strong hypothesis regarding exposure. Mould-like bacteria that naturally produce tetracyclines (*Streptomyces aureofaciens*) could have infested wheat or various other grains stored for safekeeping. Upon consumption of these spoiled foodstuffs, tetracyclines would be locked into forming or remodelling bone. The authors suggest that the presence of this compound in the bones of the Nubian population could have had many effects on health, including: prevention of infectious disease, disruption of infant bone formation, and the disturbance of spermatogenic and phagocytic activity.

Using the same fluorescent microscopy technique as Bassett *et al.* (1980), Cook, Molto and Anderson (1989) discovered similar staining in human bone and teeth from 'Ain Tirghi, *circa* 800 BCE,[1] a cemetery to the west of Kellis. This material also displayed the fluorescent qualities, differential labelling, and patterning indicative of pre-mortem tetracycline incorporation. Every individual (n=40) tested positive for tetracycline fluorescence when compared to 25 known modern examples obtained from hospital biopsies. Cook *et al.* (1989) observed that labels within an osteon were often separated by non-fluoresced bone. They surmised that gaps between exposures could be explained by seasonal food scarcities, perhaps forcing consumption of typically discarded, contaminated grain. This, they argue, would not result in therapeutic doses of antibiotics, but may have prevented bone infection.

More recently, Armelagos (2000) adopts a new perspective on tetracycline incorporation, discarding the theory of contaminated grain for one of contaminated ale. In this article Armelagos (2000) alludes to tests that show 'significant' amounts of tetracycline being produced during the ale-making process. Although these findings are non-quantitative, they do testify to the importance of considering *S. aureofaciens'* environment when discussing tetracycline production. Unlike Cook *et al.* (1989), however, Armelagos (as stated in Keith and Armelagos 1988), maintains that therapeutic levels of tetracycline were produced and consumed in the ancient world.

Since the discovery of ancient antibiotics in 1980, a few researchers have worked diligently to define further the topic and its implications. The current research at Kellis is designed to expand this effort by testing for the presence of tetracycline in human and non-human bones to expand the geographic and temporal spread of the phenomenon. To facilitate discussion regarding ancient antibiotics and their effects on health, however, issues of bacterial ecology and tetracycline incorporation must first be addressed.

Life History and Ecology of *Streptomyces aureofaciens*

Members of the Actinomycetes' order, *Streptomyces aureofaciens* included, share unique morphological and life history traits such as branching hyphae, extensions or projections of the cell's body, and reproduction through aerial spores (Buchanan and Gibbons 1974; Goodfellow *et al.* 1984). A bacterium of this type will spend most of its lifetime in a non-active, protected state called a spore (Waksman 1967; Tate 1995). Only in this state are the

bacteria resistant to hostile conditions such as xeric environments. When conditions are more favourable to growth, bacteria respond by entering a vegetative phase of growth. This is when the colony forms, expanding its boarders in search of more nutrients. The predominant macrostructure of the colony is made up of a network of undifferentiated cells forming a homologous collection of bacteria termed the substrate mycelium (Waksman 1967). Once the colony has achieved the proper size and has enough nutrients at its disposal, cells begin to differentiate, growing away from the substrate and forming aerial hyphae. Polyps at the terminal apex of these structures are the locations for sporulation (Waksman 1967; Goodfellow *et al.* 1988). Although, bits of mycelium will replicate by standard cellular division, reproduction through aerial spores is primary for settlement of near viable colonies (Buchanan and Gibbons 1974). Thus, the process begins all over again.

The growth pattern of *Streptomyces aureofaciens* is extremely sporadic, consisting of periods of colony development followed by dormancy; this in contrast to slow steady growth seen in other bacteria (Williams 1985). Goodfellow *et al.* (1984) and Williams (1985) agree that the average doubling rate, a measure of growth, for soil-dwelling members of *Streptomyces* is 1.7 days, fairly slow considering that some bacteria will double in number every hour. Armelagos (2000) also asserts that the growth rate for *S. aureofaciens*, in particular, is rather slow in comparison with other bacteria, about one week to 10 days for colony maturation.

Aside from sharing reproductive techniques and basic morphology, most Actinomycetes share similar tolerance levels for their environment, though outliers, such as thermophylic species, are not uncommon (Starr *et al.* 1981). Most are neutrophils, preferring pH levels between 5 and 9 (Buchanan and Gibbons 1974; Goodfellow *et al.* 1984) and are generally halophilic, that is, 'salt loving' (Buchannan and Gibbons 1974). *Streptomyces aureofaciens,* are highly aerobic and tolerant of extremely xeric environments, when in an inactive state, as discussed previously, relative to other bacteria (Starr *et al.* 1981; Goodfellow *et al.* 1988). Like many of its relatives, *S. aureofaciens* is a popular saprophyte in the later stages of plant and animal decomposition (Buchanan and Gibbons 1974; Starr *et al.* 1981; Goodfellow *et al.* 1984; Williams 1985). They are by far not the only micro-organisms occupying this niche, and have therefore developed an interesting, and useful, mechanism of competition.

Tetracycline (TC) synthesis involves a complex secondary metabolic pathway that is activated under certain stimuli and circumstance (Waksman 1967). Colonies of *S. aureofaciens* only produce tetracycline after their vegetative phase is secure (Goodfellow *et al.* 1988; Tate 1995). Before primary growth is complete, colonies are

---

[1] Date based on C14 testing of Body 42 from this tomb provided in Molto 2001, 86.

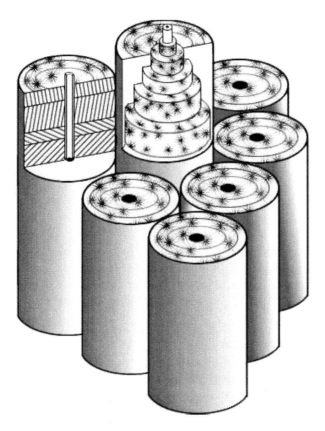

Figure 1 Illustration of osteon formation within a bone.
Each circular structure is an osteon.
Image courtesy of L. Williams.

unable to shunt metabolic energy into antibiotic production (Waksman 1967; Goodfellow *et al.* 1988) without losing their tenuous hold on the territory. Not only is the process of antibiotic synthesis 'expensive' metabolically and genetically (Hopwood and Merrik 1977), it is also dangerous (Hopwood and Merrik 1977; Goodfellow *et al.* 1988). *S. aureofaciens* are not above being destroyed by their own weapon; special defences have to be maintained against even their own antibiotic products, (J. F. Charba personal communication, 2001). The reality of the situation is that under favourable conditions a colony may reach and far out-grow the vegetative stage, never producing peak amounts of tetracycline (J. F. Charba personal communication, 2001). Though antibiotic production is 'expensive' for the organism, it lends *S. aureofaciens* an advantage when maintaining its presence in an area. At the level of the micro-site, other bacteria are presumably held at bay by tetracycline long enough that the new generation of Streptomycetes can gain purchase on the territory. In summary, synthesis of antibiotics in species like *S. aureofaciens* is a response to competition or otherwise sub-optimal conditions. In a natural environment such as soil, very little tetracycline is produced anyway; without a competitive or challenging environment tetracycline is produced in *even smaller* amounts (J. F. Charba personal communication, 2001).

Bacterial contamination of stored food, however, could easily result in enough tetracycline to label human bone. Once consumed, the compound permeates the whole body, including the skeletal system. Determining the effect that bone-incorporated tetracycline will have on the body requires familiarity with bone growth and maintenance.

Bone Structure and Tetracycline Incorporation

On a microscopic level, bone may be classified into two different types: woven and lamellar. The former is characterized by its disorganized collagen structure and is found in newly formed foetal bone and in areas of intense repair, after damage or breakage for example, (Eriksen *et al.* 1994). The latter is more solid, has a more organized collagen orientation, and is more mature, the result of remodelling (Eriksen *et al.* 1994).

Lamellar bone is laid down in concentric layers at the periosteum during bone growth and, after extensive remodelling, forms discrete units called osteons (Figure 1). Each osteon forms around a Haversian canal that encases a longitudinal blood vessel supplying that area with nutrients. Likewise, Volkmann's canals run perpendicular to the length of the bone for the same purpose. In its advanced form lamellar bone ossifies in lamelae, rings surrounding the Haversian canal, that are riddled with bone cells housed in lacunae: small cavities in the bone (White 2000). These cells, called osteocytes, maintain the bone and are supplied with nutrients via fluid filled passages, or cannaliculi (White 2000). In fully mature bone, the result is a system of osteons that in cross-section appear as tightly packed circular structures.

Though it may seem that bone tissue is stable and standardized, in reality, it is extremely dynamic, not just during development, growth, and healing, but also at all times between. The remodelling of bone is a constant process. After an area of old bone is resorped it takes only a month and a half for an average osteon to form completely (Skinner and Nalbandian 1975). In the healthy individual complete renewal, or turnover, of all bone in the body occurs approximately every 10 years (Manolagas 2000, 116).

Upon ingestion, tetracycline pervades all intra- and extra-cellular space, including hard tissues. About 10% of the tetracycline introduced to the body finds its way to bone tissue (Urist 1963). Frost (1965) discusses the two main ways tetracyclines interact with hard tissue: adsorption and incorporation. Adsorption, the temporary 'stickiness' occurring between hydroxyapatite crystals on the surface of a bone and deposited tetracycline molecules (Frost 1965), is created by a system of hydrogen bonds (Misra 1991). This type of bonding is strong but is of temporary duration, all traces having been wiped from the bone within about three days (Frost 1965). The chemical nature of tetracycline is completely unchanged by this process; in fact, the orientation of the tetracycline molecule

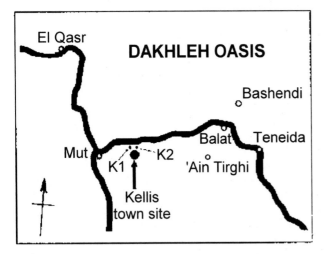

*Figure 2 Location of Kellis 1 (K1) and Kellis 2 (K2)
cemeteries in the Dakhleh Oasis.*

on the hydroxyapatite surface is such that the antibiotically active portion sticks up (Misra 1991).

The second type of interaction between hard tissues and tetracycline is full incorporation or permanent labelling. Currently forming or remodelling bones, or developing teeth, lay down new bone material in layers, between lamellae, that subsequently mineralize, much like layers of sediment on the bottom of a lake. Whereas adsorption temporarily rests tetracycline molecules on the surface of one of these layers, to be swept away in non-actively altering bone, permanent labelling in active bone occurs when tetracycline molecules are sandwiched between mineralizing layers, locking them in whatever structures were forming at the time (Frost 1965). Any area of bone fluorescing due to the presence of a fluorochrome is generally called a 'label'. Frost (1965, 460) ironically notes, "[…] there is every reason to believe that many of them [tetracycline labels] will still be present after 30 years or more". Little did he know, 15 years later someone would show that tetracycline labels can last for thousands of years.

At the microscopic level, different bone structures accept labels in unique ways, giving rise to several distinct patterns of fluorescence. It is important to describe and discuss each type of fluorescence observed in the sample in order to determine if tetracycline is actually present in bone from Kellis 1, Kellis 2 and faunal remains from the village of Kellis. It is toward this goal that the research at Kellis is focused.

Materials and Methods

A total of 30 skeletal samples, 22 human and eight non-humans, were selected from Kellis and its two adjacent cemeteries (Figure 2). Nine individuals from Tomb 13 in the Kellis 1 cemetery (31/420-C5-1) were selected for analysis. This cemetery lies north-west of the village, and its complete boundaries are unknown (Birrell 1999, 29).

Presently the excavation of 21 tombs has been completed. The period of use of this cemetery is under debate, but based on burial style and artefacts it is thought that the cemetery was in use during the late Ptolemaic and early Roman periods (Birrell 1999, 38; Schweitzer, 2002, 269–76). Usually consisting of one chamber, the tombs contained multiple burials (Birrell 1999, 33–5). Although many tombs in the Kellis 1 cemetery contained artificially mummified remains, Tomb 13 contained only fully skeletonized individuals (Cook 1994). Due to the disturbed nature of all the interments in Tomb 13, reconstruction of age at death, beyond assessing maturity, and sex was impossible (see Table 1 for sample numbers).

Thirteen samples were selected from the Kellis 2 cemetery (31/420-C5-2). Of those, three are adult females, two are adult males, five are infant/juveniles and three represent foetal remains (refer to Table 2 for sample demographics). The structure of the Kellis 2 cemetery is very different from that of Kellis 1. All individuals in the Kellis 2 cemetery are buried in a Christian fashion, with each individual in a single interment grave, with the head oriented to the west (Bowen this volume). Although the preservation of soft tissue is evident, there is no evidence of artificial mummification. The exact date of use of the cemetery is under consideration, however, C14 dates indicate that the cemetery was in use from approximately 100 to 450 CE (Molto 2001). Onomastic evidence from the village of Kellis, however, reveals the earliest evidence of Christianity possibly occurring *circa* 250 CE (Bowen this volume) and the village site being abandoned by *circa* 400 CE (Hope 2001). At present 450 individuals have been excavated, but the site limitations indicate perhaps as many as 4000 individuals in the cemetery.

Archaeological faunal material (n=8) from the village of Kellis was also sampled for analysis, including chicken (2), cow (2), donkey, goat, pig and gazelle (see Table 3 for sample description). These species include many of those used as food resources by the inhabitants of the Dakhleh Oasis; several even display prominent cut marks as possible evidence of consumption (Churcher 2002). Though several of these samples may be of questionable antiquity, they provide reasonable justification for faunal examination. All samples in this study were examined using the fluorescence detection abilities of Confocal Laser Scanning Microscopy.

Using a Foredom® rotary handsaw, the bone tissue was first sectioned into approximately 4 cm segments in order to fit into Peel-A-Way® embedding moulds, unless the original fragment was already of appropriate size. These sections were made perpendicular to length of the bone to emphasis recognizable histological features. Once reduced in size the samples were placed into moulds with corresponding identification numbers and were embedded in Epo-fix® Embedding Fluid (bisphenol-a-diglycidylether) and Epo-fix® Hardening Solution (triethylenetetramine). Once embedded and removed from their moulds, bone sections were cut 70 to 85 microns thick on a Buehler Isomet® Low Speed Saw. Loctite® Extra Time Epoxy (an

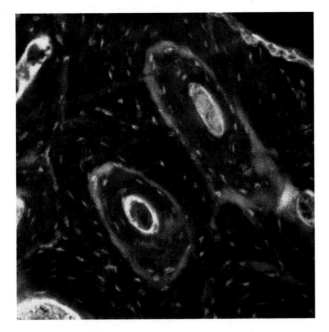

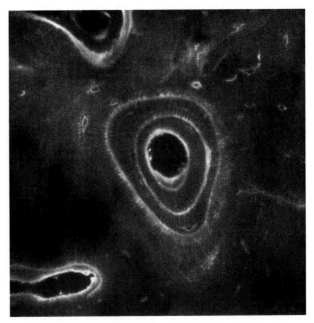

Plate 1 Cloudy ring fluorescence from Kellis 1, Tomb 13, Burial 4.

Plate 2 Distinct multiple ring fluorescence from Kellis 2 cemetery Burial 42.

Epoxy and Amine resin) was used to adhere bone thin-sections to slides. Carborundum sandpaper of 400 and 600 grit was used to reduce sample thickness to approximately 30–40 microns.

To view, test, and photograph these samples, a LSM 510 Confocal Laser Scanning Microscope (CLSM) was considered ideal. The excitation wavelength used for the purposes of this experiment was delivered via argon laser at 458 nm, as close to the optimum range as equipment would allow. The advantage of using a laser, however, is that, at this wavelength, its sheer intensity adequately excites the target, despite the fact that it is narrowly clipping the trailing end of tetracycline's fluorescent spectrum.

The microscope was otherwise optimized for tetracycline detection by setting the argon laser at 48% power, the detector gain (how sensitive the detector is) at ~470–570, and the amp gain (amplification of detected light) at ~1.2–1.4. Filters within the microscope were engaged to allow through only light of a wavelength between 505–550 nm (the emitting wavelength of tetracycline). Several of these settings, especially the detector gain and pinhole size were constantly adjusted from slide to slide due to variation caused by the angle of the sample on the microscope slide and variation in thickness.

Each bone section was observed for florescent structures similar to those reported in previous studies (Bassett *et al.* 1980; Cook *et al.* 1989). Preliminary searching was accomplished more easily with a 10x objective, relying on the digital magnification capabilities of the operating software. At least one image was taken of an area of the bone section deemed 'representative' of the whole; others captured diagnostic structures and fluorescent patterns. Later, specific samples were revisited for high-resolution/ 40x objective or three-dimensional imaging. All images were saved into a database, accessible through specialized viewing software for proper image quality and manipulation during analysis. The total number of samples exhibiting fluorescence was tallied, as well as the number of fluorescence patterns displayed in each sample. When possible, the frequency of specific patterns of fluorescence was estimated.

Results

The primary interest in this pilot project was to observe different types of fluorescence to determination tetracycline presence and variation in the fluorescent patterning, rather than gather quantitative information such as growth rates, osteon counts, and other histological observations. Unfortunately, small sample size, time constraints, and limited financial resources restricted the method of analysis such that the number of fluorescent structures per area of bone and total fluorescent area could not be counted or measured. In addition, control groups of bone were inaccessible at the time of experimentation. For this reason, analysis of results was performed through comparison with images and information published in previous literature by Bassett *et al.* (1980) and Keith and Armelagos (1988) for the Sudanese-Nubian bone, 350–550 CE and Cook *et al.* (1989) for the Dakhleh Oasis, 'Ain Tirghi, ~800 BCE.

Nearly all samples from the Dakhleh Oasis showed some form of fluorescence. In fact, Confocal Laser Scanning Microscopy examination of the Kellis material reveals six distinct patterns of fluorescence, based on the structure labelled and its shape. For purposes of analysis these patterns are referred to as 'ring fluorescence', 'complete

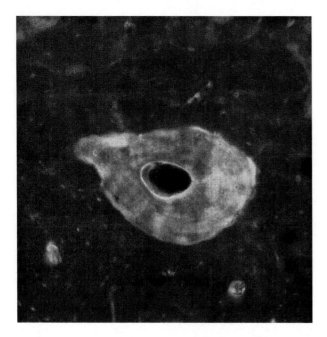

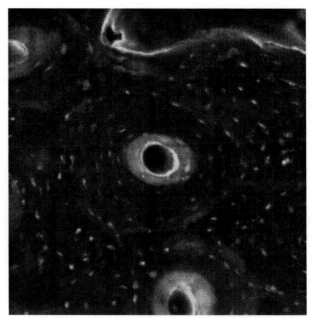

Plate 3 A completely fluoresced osteon from the Kellis 1, Tomb 13, Burial 5.

Plate 4 Partially fluoresced osteon from the Kellis 1, Tomb 13, Burial 18.

fluorescence', 'partial fluorescence', 'cement line fluorescence', 'lamellar fluorescence' and 'general fluorescence'. All of these forms have been documented in Sudanese-Nubian bone (Bassett *et al.* 1980; Keith and Armelagos 1988) or at 'Ain Tirghi, Egypt (Cook *et al.* 1989), but apparently there has been no synthesis of their reports: Bassett *et al.* observed ring, complete, and cement fluorescence; Cook *et al.* reported ring, and lamellar fluorescence. In order to determine whether tetracycline is the fluorochrome observed in this the material from Kellis and its associated cemeteries, each form of fluorescence found is compared to similar forms of fluorescence attributed to tetracycline in the literature.

Ring fluorescence is characterized by one or more ring-shaped labels within a single osteon. It is one of the most commonly used fluorescent markers in modern analyses of bone histology. This type of fluorescence is extremely important in the context of ancient antibiotics. Unlike other patterns of fluorescence, labels that take the form of rings within an osteon relate directly to a single, short exposure event. Therefore if an osteon has three rings of fluorescence, the individual consumed fluorochrome-laden material exactly three times during that osteon's formation. Rings of fluorescence are formed when tetracycline is adsorbed to the surface of currently forming lamellae. The osteon continues to grow toward the Haversian canal at its centre, in a fashion comparable to, but the reverse of, growing tree rings. New lamellae cover the tetracycline label, sandwiching it in between non-fluorescent lamellae, giving the fluoresced osteon a 'bull's eye' appearance.

Results of Confocal Laser Scanning Microscopy testing on Kellis bone samples show fluorescent ring structures in all sample groups, especially in the Kellis 2 cemetery. Osteons with one fluoresced ring are much more common

than those with two or three rings. In general, this type of fluorescence is also more rare than others within a specific individual. Ring fluorescence in bone from Kellis is indistinguishable from those reported by Bassett *et al.* (1980) and Cook *et al.* (1989). Kellis bone displays two separate types of ring fluorescence based on the continuity and clarity of the label. These fluorescence sub-types have been given the designations 'cloudy' (Plate 1) or 'distinct' (Plate 2).

This type of fluorescence is not to be confused with bright rings present at the edge of Haversian canals, which are not due to fluorescence. These rings appear in almost every osteon, and often at the outer and inner boarders of the bone section itself, and are most likely the result of refracted light passing horizontally through the thickness of the sample.

Complete fluorescence is defined by the external border of an osteon and continues, through all lamellae, to the Haversian canal, resulting in an osteon that is wholly fluoresced (Plate 3). Across the Kellis sample, this type of fluorescence is the most common. Comparison with images from the Nubian population (Bassett *et al.* 1980) shows identical fluorescent structure. Interestingly though, Cook *et al.* (1989) do not describe this type of fluorescence in the context of their archaeological sample from 'Ain Tirghi, but in the context of a modern medical biopsy used as a positive control, originating from a patient treated with continual doses of tetracycline.

The last of the three forms of intra-osteon labelling, partial fluorescence, can be described as a mean between ring and complete fluorescence. These labels originate at some level within the osteon and continue to the Haversian canal (Plate 4). They are differentiated from ring fluorescence by the fact that they have never been observed

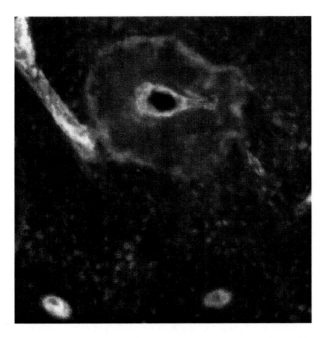

Plate 5 Cement Line fluorescence in an osteon from the Kellis 1, Tomb 13, Burial 13.

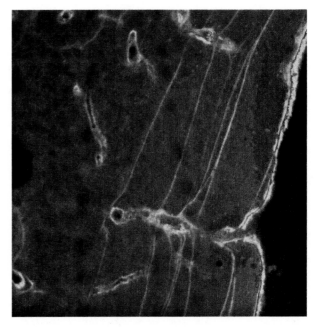

Plate 6 Lamellar fluorescence from the Kellis 2 cemetery, Burial 22.

anywhere but adjacent to the Haversian canal and are usually quite thick in comparison. Partial fluorescence is also not confused with complete fluorescence because outer lamellae are not labelled whatsoever. Representation of partial fluorescence is second in frequency only to complete fluorescence within the Kellis groups.

The fluorescence of cement lines, observed in this context by Bassett *et al.* (1980), is a bit more subjective. Perhaps for that reason Cook *et al.* (1989) make no mention of it. In this form, only the external rim of an osteon is lit, albeit in a faint, cloudy fashion (Plate 5). Cement line incorporation of fluorochrome occurs during the first steps involved in the formation of an osteon after an area is resorbed. For this reason, this type is most noticeable when the osteon's perimeter is made obvious by a backdrop of lamellar bone, in younger bone, or, in older bone, when it abuts or overlaps adjacent osteon structures.

In general, but most notably in the Kellis 1 cemetery, cement line fluorescence is prolific, matching closely those viewed by Keith and Armelagos (1988). It is important to consider that the cement line fluorescence is quite similar to cloudy ring fluorescence in appearance and seems to be somehow related, as they are seen in the same sample predominantly from Kellis 1.

The last type of fluorescence attributed to tetracycline labelling in the literature is lamellar fluorescence (Plate 6). Fluorescence within the lamellar bone that does not contain osteons is observed as rings along the diameter of the bone in Cook *et al.* (1989), observed in these samples as a small portion of the ring: a nearly straight line. This form of fluorescence would result from fluorochrome incorporation during the formation of lamellar bone. Bassett *et al.* (1980), however, did not observe this form

of fluorescence in their sample. This type of labelling is represented in Kellis 2 material.

Though no fungal osteoclasia is present in the Kellis bones, it seems that several of the samples from extremely young individuals displayed some general fluorescence. These, however, seem to fall into two categories: diffuse fluorescence resulting from fungal activity (Plate 7) and general brightness. The first is the result of fungal invasion post mortem, the second, thickness of the sample or some other artefact of the analysis process.

As is the case with most human and non-human remains from African desert environs, bone used in this experiment was in remarkably good physical condition; there were few if any indications of deterioration, microscopic or otherwise. Histological structure was nearly perfectly preserved; no evidence for micro-organism occupation or damage, that is, foci, or tunnels, could be found. High alkaline, extremely xeric, sandy soils are responsible for this degree of preservation. Very few fungal decomposers survive in these conditions, and even fewer perform with any efficacy on bone.

Kellis 1 Cemetery Sample

When exposed to the appropriate excitation wavelength, every sample from the Kellis 1 cemetery (n=9) showed patterns of fluorescence that previous researchers have attributed to tetracycline incorporation (Table 1). The most common form of fluorescence was complete fluorescence, observed in every individual. Partial, cement line, and ring fluorescence appeared in the same number of samples but had varying frequencies within an individual. For example, while partial and cement line fluorescence was nearly as frequent as complete within an individual, ring

Table 1 Types of fluorescent patterns documented in the Kellis 1, Tomb 13, individuals.

Sample ID	Sex	Age	TC	Ring	Complete	Partial	Cement	Lamellar	General
K1-B1	?	?	Yes		X		X		
K1-B2	?	?	Yes	X	X	X	X		
K1-B3	?	?	Yes		X		X		
K1-B4	?	?	Yes	X	X		X		
K1-B5	?	?	Yes		X		X		
K1-B6	?	?	Yes	X	X	X			
K1-B14	?	?	Yes		X	X			
K1-B17	?	?	Yes	X	X	X			
K1-B18	?	?	Yes	X	X	X			

Table 2 Demographic information and types of fluorescent patterns documented in the Kellis 2 cemetery.

Sample ID	Sex	Age	TC	Ring	Complete	Partial	Cement	Lamellar	General
K2-B13	?	4	Yes	X				X	
K2-B15	?	9m	?						X
K2-B22	F	45	Yes	X	X		X	X	
K2-B30	F	40	Yes	X	X	X		X	
K2-B39	?	11	?						X
K2-B42	M	45	Yes	X		X	X	X	
K2-B69	M	29	Yes		X	X	X	X	
K2-B70	?	18m	Yes	X					
K2-B71	?	3	Yes	X					
K2-B73	F	38	Yes	X	X				
K2-B390	?	< 0	Yes			X	X		X
K2-B406	?	< 0	?						
K2-B446	?	< 0	Yes?		X				X

Table 3 Types of fluorescent patterns documented from each animal sample from the village of Kellis.

Sample ID	Animal	TC	Ring	Complete	Partial	Cement	Lamellar	General
D/8 Room 12 (3)	chicken	Yes?	X					
A/7 E. Nave, S. (2)	chicken	Yes	X	X				
D/10 Locus 1 (2)	gazelle	Yes?		X				
D/9 Gtwy Ctrl (2)	cow	Yes	X	X	X	X		
C/1/1 Room 4 (2B)	cow	Yes		X		X		
C/1/1 Room 5 (3B)	pig	Yes?					X	
C/1/1 Room 4 (2B)	goat	Yes?					X	
C/1/1 Room 4 (1A)	donkey	Yes	X	X	X			

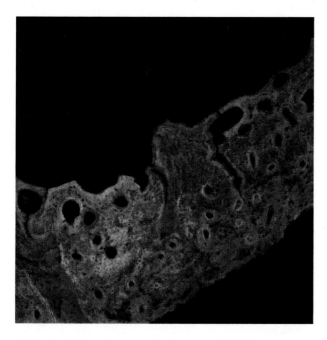

Plate 7 Diffuse fluorescence from the Kellis 2 cemetery, Burial 17.

fluorescence was actually quite rare in comparison. It is also important to note that it was never observed in the distinct bands reported by Cook *et al.* (1989). Instead it appeared as a single cloudy halo within the osteon, much like Bassett *et al.* (1980) and Keith and Armelagos (1988) documented. Lamellar fluorescence was not recorded in any images during testing; however, it is possible that it did occur in at least some of these samples. General fluorescence was not present in any of the samples from Kellis 1.

Kellis 2 Cemetery Sample

Of the total number of samples collected from Kellis 2 (n=13), 10 display definitive evidence of tetracycline incorporation (Table 2). Much more common within the cemetery and within individuals, ring fluorescence is distinct and, in several cases, consists of two or three rings per osteon (Plate 2). Quite the reverse of Kellis 1, complete, partial, and cement fluorescence are observed in decreased frequency, both in the site overall, and within samples. Lamellar fluorescence, by sheer chance, is represented in this set of samples. Its occurrence is as underestimated as it is in Kellis 1, hinting that it may be much more frequent in Kellis 2. Also different from Kellis 1, diffuse fluorescence was noted. More often it could be described as general brightness, but in at least one sample fluorescence is obvious and has an appearance not unlike that resulting from post-mortem fungal invasion, though no actual damage to the bone is evident.

Faunal Remains from the Village of Kellis

Though, histologically, bone structure varies considerably with the species examined, tetracycline labelling was easily

identified in four out of the total number of animal samples (n=8). The other four display some of the characteristics of certain fluorescent patterns, but are not convincing enough report as positive for tetracycline-like fluorescence either because of the extremely limited appearance of noted fluorescent structures (Room 12 chicken), or because the structures viewed are otherwise unknown or ambiguous (Table 3). It is safe to say, however, that the type of fluorescence most represented in these samples is complete fluorescence. Ring structures are rare and when present are feint, diffuse, or incomplete: interrupted or disturbed by other structures.

Discussion

Comprehensive review of the literature and results of Confocal Laser Scanning Microscopy fluorescence testing can be combined to draw several important conclusions regarding the presence of tetracycline in human and animal bones from the Dakhleh Oasis. Implications of this study could have far ranging effects on the study of ancient antibiotics in general and on today's perspective on antibiotics, their history and modern application. In specific, the current study has shed much light on the nature of the antibiotic presence at the Dakhleh Oasis, illuminating several aspects of the phenomenon previously not addressed. The various forms of fluorescence observed, and their differential representation, suggest that tetracycline labels could be used as a tool through which various social and health factors could be addressed. The ecological, behavioural, and reproductive habits of *Streptomyces* spp. have offered clues that may aid in the determination of the source of ancient antibiotics. In addition, the possibility of tetracycline affecting the health of historic populations can be reconsidered from a more holistic perspective.

Analysis of the Kellis material could be made through comparison with data published by Bassett *et al.* (1980), Keith and Armelagos (1988) and Cook *et al.* (1989). All of the six types of fluorescence observed at Kellis were identical to what these researchers have concluded is tetracycline fluorescence, resulting from *in vivo* antibiotic incorporation in forming bone. In addition, the Kellis bone itself, suggests that the phenomena occurred during the lifetime of the individuals. Fluorescence in Kellis remains, except in individuals displaying general fluorescence, follows all natural laws of bone formation and is strictly limited to structural boundaries created by the different types of bone in the body. Many samples showed one fluoresced osteon immediately adjacent to several unfluoresced osteons or even overlapped by more recently formed non-fluorescent tissue. A combination of all these bits of evidence supports the conclusion that tetracycline was indeed incorporated into the bones of the Dakhleh Oasis' inhabitants, their infants and even their domestic animals while they lived.

Both Bassett *et al.* (1980) and Cook *et al.* (1989) note that tetracycline was present in every individual tested.

While this is not the finding of the current study (22 of 30 samples showed evidence of tetracycline labelling and most of the remainder showed some evidence), this could be explained by several factors unique to the current project. The fact that archaeological foetal and animal bones have never been tested for tetracycline and the fact that it is possible for one to simply miss tetracycline labels due to the random chance involved in sectioning and surveying bone could account for the few cases where tetracycline was not definitively observed. The pervasive nature of tetracycline fluorescence in populations tested suggests that causative behaviour is shared among different individuals despite differences in age, sex, and social status. This is not to say that there are no differences between the types or frequency of fluorescence observed between different groups of individuals.

One of the most important findings of this project has been differential representation of fluorescent forms in the two cemeteries. Kellis 1, for example, shows a much more obvious occurrence of complete fluorescence and partial fluorescence than Kellis 2. Kellis 2, however, is the source for every observed case of distinct ring fluorescence and lamellar fluorescence. Implications of the various types of tetracycline fluorescence have not been addressed by previous anthropological research. It becomes obvious, however, that fluorescent structure is directly related to certain aspects of growth and development. This simple observation can result in some very informative conclusions.

In general, labels in Kellis 1 bone are cloudier and less distinct than in Kellis 2. This fact is most easily noticed when observing ring fluorescence. The phenomena accounting for variation in fluorescent ring structure are unknown. Bassett *et al.* (1980) suggests that interruption of formation during exposure, or vice versa, is a possible explanation. Though this hypothesis makes logical sense, data from the Kellis cemeteries does not support it. Cloudy rings were only recorded in the Kellis 1 sample and distinct only in Kellis 2. If cloudy structures were caused by interruption of growth or incorporation of tetracycline they should be observable in all affected bone equally as this would be an occurrence in every sample set. This is not the case, however, suggesting instead that some basic difference in the type of exposure is responsible, perhaps resulting from a different type of tetracycline or even different concentrations. Though it is impossible to measure the concentration of tetracycline in an individual from fluorescent intensity, this does not mean it is impossible to determine concentration of one set of individuals versus another. In any case, the fact that there is such a correlation between Kellis 1 and Bassett *et alii*'s Sudanese-Nubian material is significant. Similar results imply similar mechanisms.

Shape is not the only important consideration to be made when discussing the importance of ring fluorescence. The number of rings is also noteworthy. Multiple rings are very rare in the Kellis material and only appear in individuals from Kellis 2. Three, or more commonly, two

rings, represent only a few exposure events during the approximate month and a half it takes for an osteon to form in the metabolically normal individual (Skinner and Nalbandian 1975). If consumption of tetracycline were regular, many bands would be visible in a single osteon but again this is not the case in Kellis 2. Cook *et al.* (1989) suggest that ring structures may be indicative of seasonal consumption of tetracycline. Though the same type of multiple ring structure is seen in Kellis 2 individuals, it is hard to agree with this reasoning. Certainly, multiple rings do indicate infrequency of consumption, but seasonality would not be evidenced by tetracycline incorporation every 10 days. Rather, it would be suggested by sustained or even infrequent tetracycline consumption for periods of one or a couple months out of a year.

Complete fluorescence seems also to have extremely significant implications. Cook *et al.* (1989) published an image taken from one of their modern medical controls, an individual who had been 'constantly' given tetracycline to treat acne. This type of fluorescence is exactly the same type reported by Bassett *et al.* (1980) and the same as documented in the material from Kellis 1, though Kellis 2 also displayed complete fluorescence, it was much less common than in Kellis 1; again this finding seems to correlate to that of previous research, this time with work in 1989 by Cook *et al.* Not discussed by Bassett *et al.* (1980), however, is the fact that complete fluorescence seems to be the direct result of many consecutive doses of tetracycline over the period of osteon development. Because many osteons do not display this type of fluorescence, it would seem that occasionally, and in some cases quite frequently, tetracycline was consumed steadily for periods in excess of one or more months. Similar in its frequency, partial fluorescence can be interpreted in much the same fashion but with a decreased duration, resulting in half a fluoresced osteon.

Determination of cement line fluorescence, observed by Bassett *et al.* in 1980, was extremely subjective in this experiment, perhaps due to the decreased emission of tetracycline. Even when fluorescence was not obvious, the cement line, in many cases, was. This results from the fact that this feature marks a very real border between individual osteons or between an osteon and surrounding lamellar bone.

Lamellar fluorescence, though under-represented, was very distinct and histologically unmistakable. Running in long, bright, streaks through otherwise homogenous bone, lamellar fluorescence results from tetracycline incorporated into the tissue during lamellar bone formation, before osteon proliferation marks the truly mature state of the bone.

General fluorescence or brightness in a sample was rare and probably resulted from some sort of refractive scattering of light. There was however, at least one case where the appearance of the lit structures matched true fluorescence caused by post-mortem fungal invasion via the pre-existing channels throughout the Haversian system. This was not an occurrence in any of the other samples in the study.

In the event that the age or sex of an individual was known, as in Kellis 2, even more information can be gained regarding the nature of tetracycline incorporation. The total number of aged and sexed samples in this study was not high enough to make reliable conclusions. It is important to at least note that the ages of individuals with the 'most' fluorescence was not what was expected. Because younger individuals have more actively mineralizing bone, they should show more evidence of tetracycline labelling than older individuals. In the Kellis 2 sample, however, the older individuals, that is those above 29, showed not only more fluorescence, in general, but normally displayed more types of fluorescence as well. If this pattern is reliable, it could be surmised that tetracycline-laden food was more often consumed by older individuals, though a larger sample size would be necessary to test hypotheses of this type.

Source and Method of Consumption

Determining that tetracycline is present in the bones of the Dakhleh Oasis people is quite a bit easier than uncovering its source. Review of the literature has provided some insight into this very important question, supporting the original hypothesis put forth by Bassett *et al.* (1980) and accepted by Cook *et al.* (1989) with only slight modification: seasonality of exposure. The assertion that perhaps ale could be a primary source of tetracycline for the population, as proffered by Armelagos (2000), seems to be debatable.

The first key to this puzzle is the amazingly high frequency of tetracycline labelling in the population. For so many people to have been exposed to tetracycline sometime in the last ten years of their life, the source of the fluorochrome would have to be extremely common. The extreme similarity between the results of Cook *et al.* and those of this study suggest that the method of incorporation has remained fairly constant or at least is similar between 'Ain Tirghi and Kellis 2. As noted before the differences in dates between Kellis 1 and Kellis 2 are significant. What all this means is that whatever the source of tetracycline, it has persisted for at least 1200 years. Thus, the quest is simplified. All new Roman imports can be ignored; foods that varied in accessibility or popularity can also be disregarded.

The next clue that can be used to address possible agents of tetracycline consumption is the nature of the organism responsible for tetracycline production, *Streptomyces aureofaciens*. These bacteria are involved in the late stages of decomposition processes, infesting nearly all organic materials, plant or animal. Bacteria in general, including *S. aureofaciens*, have extremely demanding water requirements; the moisture content of their environment has to be very high. Last of all, when nutrient content in the surrounding medium is low, spores survive but the bacteria are not active, therefore, nutrient availability must also be high in order for the bacteria to shunt metabolic energy into the production of tetracycline before sporulation.

All these considerations made, relatively few food products remain as possibilities. In fact, it becomes arguable that only one type of food satisfies all these criteria: grain. Long storage time, a stable substrate environment, high nutrient content, and antagonistic interactions with other micro-organisms are all ecological necessities for tetracycline production that are found in stored grain. Given that *S. aureofaciens* is a late stage decomposer, even dried grain can fulfil moisture requirements for colony formation (Priest and Campbell 1987). Fungi and insect activity at the centre of the grain's mass releases carbon dioxide and heat by-products; thus allowing condensation of moisture in cooler areas (Priest and Campbell 1987). Colonies of *S. aureofaciens* would remain physically undisturbed for long enough to accumulate tetracycline in the spoiling grain. From there it could be incorporated into many different food products including, bread, cakes, gruel and ale. It can be speculated that infested grain would have been thrown out, or perhaps used as domestic animal fodder, except in times of food scarcity or famine. Thus, the 'seasonality' hypothesis is supported, not by ring fluorescence, but by the fact that many non-fluorescent osteons exist in individuals, especially Kellis 2, representing months where no tetracycline was consumed.

Though grain seems to be the most likely candidate for tetracycline content, Armelagos (2000) has reasoned that perhaps ale would be a more suitable environment for tetracycline production. Indeed a liquid medium is capable of hosting large populations of *S. aureofaciens*. In fact, this is the method used during modern synthesis of tetracycline: huge vats of aerated medium. The problem that plagues this theory, however, is that *S. aureofaciens* in a liquid medium, like many antibiotic producing *Actinomycetes*, grow in a disturbed manner, decreasing the potential for formation of secondary metabolites (Waksman 1967, 117; Goodfellow *et al.*1988, 191) unless the concentration is maintained and monitored perfectly. This problem is avoided in today's liquid batch cultures by the use of aerators and impellers, as well as a barrage of systems designed to monitor the 'concentration' of the medium, its viscosity, heat, and requisite chemical composition (Goodfellow *et al.*1988, 196). Left to their own devices, large populations of *S. aureofaciens* growing in ale would only result in a foul-tasting beverage. It is perhaps important to note, however, that Armelagos (2001) comments that two undergraduate students produced 'tetracycline in quantity' by adding *Streptomyces* to a mixture of malted grain and bread. This has not been addressed by peer review, however, and is not able to be verified. It is not impossible that more experimentation could prove that, by sheer coincidence, the traditional ale-making process simulates the exact medium concentration and chemical constituents required to create enough tetracycline to label hard tissues in the human body; though, from a review of the literature surrounding tetracycline production it does seem improbable.

Tetracycline and its Effects on Health in Ancient Populations

It cannot be denied that tetracycline has been shown to benefit human health in many ways, curing disease through destruction of harmful bacteria, effectively treating various bone degenerative disorders, and limiting the growth of cancerous tumours. Negative side effects are rare, although under certain conditions tetracycline can inhibit normal formation and development of hard tissues in the body. The question asked by those studying antibiotics in an archaeological context, however, is which, if any of these effects, could have had an impact on the health of ancient peoples.

In order for tetracycline to function as an antibiotic in the human body, about two grams per day must be ingested, ideally spread out over several doses over the course of four days to a week or more (Walsh 2000, 1528). Inhibition of matrix metalloprotienases in adults and inhibition of bone mineralization in the foetus also both require significant doses (Frost 1965). In neither case is one dose sufficient; exposure must continue for days. In contrast, only one exposure of 0.2 ìg/ml tetracycline is required for the formation of detectable fluorescent labels in bone (Fukutani *et al.* 1985).

Bassett *et al.* (1980) argue that the amount of fluorescence in their sample is indicative of clinical concentrations of tetracycline. Keith and Armelagos (1988, 599) announce, without any explanation or corroboration, that "Many Nubians did, in fact, ingest therapeutic doses of tetracycline during their lifetime". Cook *et al.* (1989, 143) hypothesize that the amount of ingested tetracycline was "... considerably less than modern prescribed dosages". They suggest that perhaps small amounts could inhibit certain types of bone infection, lamenting the fact that "... it is impossible to determine the amounts of tetracycline ingested at a given time ...". Obviously opinions abound. This is not surprising considering the number of variables that complicate the issue. The body is variably sensitive to tetracycline based not just on concentration but also on the duration of exposure, weight of the individual, and the disease involved. Basic bioavailability of the compound is inhibited by simultaneous ingestion of food, not to mention being produced on or in a food product.

Problems in concentration estimation abound even at the level of antibiosis due to the fact that tetracycline synthesis by *S. aureofaciens* is intermittent at best. Production of tetracycline is limited by the life cycle of *S. aureofaciens*, its immediate physical environment, pH levels, oxygen availability, nitrogen presence, and phosphorous content. Interactions between *S. aureofaciens* and other micro-organisms and fungi also become important. Even the production of tetracycline itself can limit the growth of *S. aureofaciens* colonies and act as a regulator of antibiotic production.

Further complicating matters are the various difficulties researchers must overcome to measure *S. aureofaciens'* production capacity under natural conditions. Because tetracycline acts at the level of the micro-site, only small concentrations are produced in non-regulated environments. In a more suitable environment for growth, such as a nutrient-rich media like grain, measurable concentrations of tetracycline will be produced, but no verifiable evidence exists to support concentrations reaching anything close to therapeutic levels without massive application of modern technology. Modern science must employ drastic measures in order to produce useable concentrations of tetracycline. Bacteria used for tetracycline synthesis are modified significantly through directed mutation (hybridization), manipulation of regulatory genes, deletion of restricting genes, increasing production genes, recombination (including protoplast fusion), developed bioreactor technology, various bioreactor properties, media optimization, and even direct chemical alteration of the metabolites produced (Goodfellow *et al.* 1988). In this fashion, large amounts of tetracycline are made for use in modern therapy.

Examining the types of fluorescence seen in the bone offers some information, mainly regarding age at exposure and exposure duration or frequency within the time frame of a single osteon's development. In the case of complete, partial, and multi-ring fluorescence, dosage duration is satisfactory, but evidence is lacking to suggest maintenance of high blood plasma levels of tetracycline in the body during this time. This cannot be determined in an individual with unknown medical history because it is impossible to separate exposure events that could have taken place up to ten years apart. Even a sustained sub-therapeutic concentration would have had little effect on disease, because the concentration would not be high enough to actively guard the body against invasion. The resulting confusion can be simplified. Due to the various limitations on *S. aureofaciens'* synthesis of tetracycline and tetracycline bioavailability, attaining therapeutic tetracycline levels in the human body through unintentional means would be extremely unlikely. As a result, tetracycline in the ancient world was not likely to have systematic antibiotic or hard tissue effects.

In the case of penetrative bone infections, however, some medical benefit may have been gained due to ingestion of tetracycline, not because it reached therapeutic levels in the body, but because it did not have to. As infectious micro-organisms penetrate tetracycline labelled bone, they would encounter functional tetracycline molecules freed by deterioration of the bone. This could account for the uncommonly low incidence of bone infection in the Dakhleh Oasis population (Cook *et al.* 1989) and perhaps even contribute positively to the level of bone preservation post mortem.

Conclusion

Confocal Laser Scanning Microscopy proves itself a versatile, efficient, and accurate technique for observing fluorescent tetracycline labels in human and animal bone. The use of this technology results in high-resolution, three-dimensional images of tetracycline labels offering as yet unprecedented detail to observable features. Results of Confocal Laser Scanning Microscopy testing, compared with those of previous researchers on the topic, show that tetracycline was incorporated *in vivo* into the bones of at least 22 of the 30 humans and animals examined from the Dakhleh Oasis, Kellis area (*circa* 100 BCE to 400 CE) establishing a continuance of the phenomenon in the Dakhleh Oasis for over 1200 years.

Six different patterns of fluorescence were observed, based on the structure that incorporated tetracycline during its formation: ring fluorescence (cloudy and distinct/single ring and multiple ring), complete osteon fluorescence, partial osteon fluorescence, cement line fluorescence, lamellar fluorescence, and general fluorescence. Each type of fluorescence offers information regarding the exposure's length and age during labelling. Differential frequencies of these forms between the Kellis 1 and Kellis 2 cemeteries offers evidence that there may be some basic difference in the mode of incorporation between these two time periods. Young children and even infants show some tetracycline fluorescence but the most prolific labelling occurs in older individuals, contrary to what is to be expected due to the rapid mineralization rate in the young. Domestic animals even display evidence of tetracycline exposure. This suggests perhaps that kept animals were consuming some contaminated food source as well. What food products could be responsible in the faunal case has not been evaluated. The gazelle, however, as an example of non-domestic fauna, merely showed diffuse or general fluorescence from some post-mortem bacterial invasion or artefact of the testing procedure.

For the human population, stored grain seems to offer the most likely situation for tetracycline accumulation and consumption due to the environmental instability of ale production, the second most popular hypothesis.

Contrary to the unfounded assumptions of previous research, comprehensive review of the literature behind the habits of *Streptomyces aureofaciens* and tetracycline production, both natural and artificial, reveals no evidence to suggest that therapeutic concentrations could have been maintained in the human body. In the specific case of bone infection, however, there may have been some benefit gained due to direct contact with concentrated tetracycline locked in the bone.

Acknowledgements

The authors would like to thank the Egyptian Supreme Council of Antiquities and members of the Dakhleh Oasis Project for their support. In particular we thank A. J. Mills, J. E. Molto, P. Sheldrick, M. Tocheri, C. A. Hope, G. E. Bowen, U. Thanheiser and C. Churcher. In addition we thank G. Bertetta and S. Charba at the University of Central Florida for their guidance and thoughts on our project. This research was supported by grants from The Wenner-Gren Foundation for Anthropological Research, an In-House Grant from the University of Central Florida, and the Honors College at the University of Central Florida, and through the generosity of the Molecular and Microbiology Department at the University of Central Florida.

Authors' Addresses:

Corey Maggiano
Department of Biology
University of Central Florida
Orlando,
Florida 32816,
U. S. A.

gnosLs@hotmail.com

Tosha L. Dupras
Department of Sociology and Anthropology
University of Central Florida
Orlando,
Florida 32816,
U. S. A.

tdupras@pegasus.cc.ucf.edu

John Biggerstaff
Department of Microbiology and Molecular Biology
University of Central Florida
Orlando,
Florida 32816,
U. S. A.

jbiggers@mail.ucf.edu

REFERENCES

Armelagos, G. J., 2000 Take two beers and call me in 1,600 years, *Natural History* 109, 50–4.

Bassett E, M. Keith, G. J. Armelagos, D. Martin and A. Villanueva, 1980 Tetracycline-labeled human bone from ancient sudanese nubia (A.D. 350), *Science* 209, 1532–4.

Birrell, M., 1999 Excavations in the Cemeteries of Ismant el-Kharab, in C. A. Hope and A. J. Mills, eds, *Dakhleh Oasis Project: Preliminary Reports on the 1992–1993 and 1993–1994 Field Seasons*, Oxbow Books, Oxford, 29–41.

Bowen, G. E., this volume Some Observations on Christian Burial Practices at Kellis, 167–81.

Buchanan, R. E. and N. E. Gibbons, eds, 1974 *Bergey's Manual of Determinative Bacteriology*, Eighth Edition, The Williams and Wilkins Company, Baltimore.

Churcher, C. S., 2002 Faunal Remains from Kellis, in C. A. Hope and G. E. Bowen, eds, *Dakhleh Oasis Project: Preliminary Reports on the 1994–1995 to 1998–1999 Field Seasons*, Oxbow Books, Oxford, 105–13.

Cook, M. A., 1994 The mummies of Dakhleh, in A. Herring and L. Chan, eds, *Strength in Diversity: a reader in physical anthropology*, Canadian Scholar's Press Inc., Toronto.

Cook, M., E. Molto and C. Anderson, 1989 Fluorochrome labelling in Roman period skeletons from Dakhleh Oasis, Egypt, *American Journal of Physical Anthropology* 80, 137–43.

Dupras, T. L., 1999 Dining in the Dakhleh Oasis: Determination of Diet from Documents and Stable Isotope Analysis, unpublished Ph.D. dissertation, McMaster University, Canada.

Dupras, T. L., H. P. Schwarcz and S. I. Fairgrieve, 2001 Infant feeding and weaning practices in Roman Egypt, *American Journal of Physical Anthropology* 115, 204–12.

Eriksen, E. F., D. W. Axelrod and F. Melsen, 1994 *Bone Histomorphometry*, Raven Press, New York.

Frost, H. M., 1965 Tetracyclines and fetal bones, *Henry Ford Hospital Medical Journal* 13, 403–10.

Fukutani, S, Y. Tsukamoto and M. Mori, 1985 Determination of fluorescent oxytetracycline complexes in dental and skeletal hard tissues by rapid and accurate quantitative method, *Progress in Clinical & Biological Research* 187, 215–24.

Goodfellow, M., M. Mordarski and S. T. Williams, 1984 *Biology of the Actinomycetes*, Academic Press Inc., New York.

Goodfellow, M., S. T. Williams and M. Mordarski, 1988 *Actinomycetes in biotechnology*, Academic Press Inc., New York.

Hope, C. A., 2001 Observations on the dating of the occupation at Ismant el-Kharab, in C. A. Marlow and A. J. Mills, eds, *The Oasis Papers 1: The Proceedings of the First Conference of the Dakhleh Oasis Project*, Oxbow Books, Oxford, 43–59.

Hopwood, D. A. and M. J. Merrik, 1977 Genetics of antibiotic production, *Bacteriological Reviews* 41, 595–635.

Keith, M. and G. J. Armelagos, 1983 Naturally Occurring Antibiotics and Human Health, in L. Romanucci, D. Moerman and L. Tancredi, eds, *The Anthropology of Medicine*, Bergin and Garvey Publishers, New York.

Keith, M. S. and G. J. Armelagos, 1988 An example of in vivo tetracycline labeling: Reply to Piepenbrink, *Journal of Archaeological Science* 15, 595–601.

Manolagas, S., 2000 Birth and death of bone cells: Basic regulatory mechanism and implications for the pathogenesis and treatment of osteoporosis, *Endocrine Review* 21, 115–37.

Misra, D. N., 1991 Adsorption and orientation of tetracycline on hydroxyapatite, *Calcified Tissue International* 48, 362–7.

Molto, J. E., 2001 The comparative skeletal biology and palaeoepidemiology of the people from Ein Tirghi and Kellis, Dakhleh Oasis, Egypt, in C. A. Marlow and A. J. Mills, eds, *The Oasis Papers 1: The Proceedings of the First Conference of the Dakhleh Oasis Project*, Oxbow Books, Oxford, 81–100.

Piepenbrink, H., B. Herrmann and P. Hoffman, 1983 Tetracylintypische fluoreszenzen and bodengelagerten skeletteilen, *Zeitschrift für Rechtsmedizin* 91, 71–4.

Priest, F. G. and I. Campbell, 1987 *Brewing Microbiology*, Elsivier Applied Science, New York.

Skinner, H. C. and J. Nalbandian, 1975 Tetracyclines and mineralized tissues: review and perspectives, *Yale Journal of Biology & Medicine* 48, 377–97.

Starr, M. P., H. Stolp, H. G. Truper, A. Balows and H. G. Schlegel, eds, 1981 *The Prokaryotes: a handbook on habitats, isolation, and identification of bacteria*, Springer-Verlag, New York.

Schweitzer, A., 2002 Les parures de cartonnage des momies d'une nécropole d'Ismant el-Kharab, in C. A. Hope and G. E. Bowen, eds, *Dakhleh Oasis Project: Preliminary Reports on the 1994–1995 to 1998–1999 Field Seasons*, Oxbow Books, Oxford, 269–76.

Tate, R. L., 1995 *Soil Microbiology*, John Wiley and Sons Inc., New York.

Urist, M. R. and K. H. Ibsen, 1963 Chemical reactivity of mineralized tissue with oxytetracycline, *Archives of Pathology* 76, 484–96.

Van Der Bijl, P. and G. Pitigoi-Aron, 1995 Tetracyclines and Calcified Tissues, *Annals of Dentistry* 54 (1–2), 69–72.

Walsh, P., 2000 *Physicians' Desk Reference*, Medical Economics Company Inc., Montvale.

Waksman, S. A., 1967 *The Actinomycetes: a summary of current knowledge*, Ronald, New York.

White, T. D., 2000 *Human Osteology*, 2nd edition, Academic Press, New York.

Williams, S. T., 1985 Oligotrophy in soil: fact or fiction?, in M. Fletcher and G. D. Floodgate, eds, *Bacteria in their Natural Environments*, Academic Press, New York.

Late Roman Period Human Skeletal Remains
from Areas D/6 and D/7 and North Tomb 1 at Kellis

J. Eldon Molto, Peter Sheldrick, Antonietta Cerroni and Scott Haddow

Introduction

This paper describes the skeletal biology and palaeopathology of two small skeletal samples associated with the village of Kellis, (Hope this volume Figure 1). Designated herein as the Town Site Burials (TSBs), they were recovered from areas D/6, D/7 and North Tomb 1, the latter located adjacent to Kellis, the former being on the perimeter of the town site. These burials, analyzed during the 2001 and 2002 field seasons of the Dakhleh Oasis Project, were chosen for their relative completeness and likely represent the later Roman period occupants of Kellis typified by the Christian burial position. During the late Roman Period (*circa* 280–400 CE) the people of Kellis primarily interred their dead in the Kellis 2 cemetery located immediately north-east of the town site. Why and exactly when the people of Kellis used areas D/6, D/7 and North Tomb 1 are unknown. Our current understanding is that at least one of these town site tombs was reused during the late phase of the Kellis occupation, and thus likely date to the period when Kellis was abandoned in the late fourth century CE (Hope 2001, 56–7; 2002, 205–6). In addition, is the question of representation? Are the TSBs random accretions or do they represent groups with possible close kinship ties? The biological relationships among the bodies within these tombs and their genetic relationships to Kellis 2 constitute the primary research questions addressed herein.

Material and Methods

The archaeology of North Tomb 1 and the Area D/6 and D/7 burials is described elsewhere (Hope this volume) as is the demography of the total commingled samples in North Tombs 1 and 2 (Dupras and Tocheri this volume). Their criteria for ageing the burials is more limited than the present study which relies on a multiplicity of methods to provide a consensus age estimate when a disconcordance between the different methods occurs. Nineteen burials were analyzed and they are summarized in Table 1. The basic skeletal research methods, for example stature and age estimates, involved in their analysis are outlined elsewhere (Molto 2001). The morphogenetic statistical comparisons are restricted to non-metric data. The Mean Measure of Divergence statistic (Sjovold 1973; 1977) is used for the intersample comparisons, whereas intragroup comparisons are based on a model proposed independently by Molto (1979) and Sjovold (1976/77) using the binomial distribution.

The Burials: A Brief Description

Area D/6 and D/7

These two designations represent two adjacent zones in Area D; the distribution of the eleven burials is shown (Hope this volume Figure 11). The two burials in D/6 are inside a church and may represent statused individuals (Colin Hope personal communication December, 2002).

Burial D/7-1, is the complete skeleton of a female estimated to be 55 ± 5 years of age. Age was estimated from the stage of rib morphogenesis (V - 43–58), heavy dental attrition and ante-mortem tooth loss (N = 9), widespread osteoporosis and extensive degenerative change in the cervical spine and the knee. Concerning the latter, the articular surfaces of both patellae show wear striations with extensive eburnation being present on the left patella. Consistent with her older age estimate is ossification of the costal cartilage of the first rib. Her symphysis pubis score provided a younger age estimate that was not concordant with the rest of the ageing data. There is evidence that this individual experienced anaemia in childhood as bilateral (healed) cribra orbitalia is present. Despite the osteopenia and osteoporosis there is no ante-mortem trauma. The only noteworthy non-metric trait present is bilateral incomplete bridges of the hypoglossal canal. Her stature is estimated at 157.12 ± 3.28 cm.

Burial D/7-2, is the complete skeleton of a female with dental and skeletal age estimates of 20 ± 2 years. There is virtually no dental attrition, the spheno-occipital synchondrosis is fused, all the long bone epiphyses except the medial clavicles are fused and or in the final stages of fusing, and the rib morphology is a stage 2. Also, the iliac crests remain unfused. Both symphysis pubes, especially the left, have superior border erosions and destruction of the billowing of the face, which would suggest an older age if they were the sole ageing criteria. There is no trauma and the only evidence of infection is a large periapical abscess with sequel loss of the mandibular left M1. Non-metric traits present include; bilateral infra-orbital sutures, left hypoglossal canal spurring and accessory ossicles in both sides of the lambdoidal suture. The manubrium and 1st sternal body are completely fused which is an anomalous for such a young individual. Her stature is estimated at 160.65 ± 3.28 cm.

Burial D/7-3 is the complete skeleton of a female with an estimated age of 60 ± 5 years. Age was estimated on the basis of respective rib (VI) and symphysis pubis (VI) morphogenesis values of 59–71 and 60 ± 12.4 years. That this individual may be in the upper range of these estimates is supported by widespread osteoporosis with fractures, extensive osteoarthritis, particularly evident in the dens articulation with the atlas (eburnation) and the knee (femoral patellar articulation), extensive spondylosis deformans (osteophytosis) in the cervical (neck) and the lumbar regions, fused costal cartilage of the right 1st rib, plus advanced dental attrition and ante-mortem tooth loss (at least nine teeth). Moreover, a large piece of atherosclerotic plaque, likely from the aorta, was recovered from the associated grave fill. This person likely died from complications sequel to a major intertrochanteric (femur) fracture, which showed no resorptive changes associated with osseous healing. In addition, there was a healed fracture of a left true rib (likely 4,5/6), and the left second proximal phalanx of the foot. The latter fractures are well healed and suggest that the trauma occurred long before her death. The only evidence of infection in this skeleton is the presence of slight periosteal newbone on the posterior surface of the right radius. Key non-metric traits present include a complete metopic suture, a right divided hypoglossal canal, a small but distinct precondylar tubercle, partial division of the left jugular canal, a sagittal wormian bone and divided superior articular facets of the atlas. In addition, an anomalous canal patent with the latero-superior suprascapular fossa and the gleno-acromial notch, which exits at the base of the coracoid process, is present. It likely transmits an emissary branch of the suprascapular vessels. Her stature is estimated at 155.4 ± 3.28 cm.

Burial D/7-4 is the complete skeleton of a late foetus or perinate. The remains were wrapped in a cloth. There is no evidence of pathology or key non-metric traits.

Burial D/7-5 is the complete skeleton of a female with an estimated age of 48 ± 5 years. Age was estimated using rib (43–58), symphysis pubis (48.1 ± 14.6), dental pathology, 10 teeth lost ante-mortem, and degenerative joint changes, namely slight osteophytosis in the lumbar region and advanced osteoarthritis of the patellae. In addition, the bones were well mineralized, not osteopenic, including the ribs. Although the dental attrition was less than expected for an individual in this age group, the extensive ante-mortem tooth loss, 10 teeth, likely contributed to the low attritional score. Key non-metric traits present include large precondylar tubercles, an ossified right pterygospinous ligament, bilateral spurring of the pterygo-alar ligament, a trochlear spur in right orbit, a left divided hypoglossal canal, and a foramen in the left lateral pterygoid plate. Finding so many hyperostotic traits in a female skeleton is unusual. Her stature is estimated at 165.43 ± 3.28 cm.

Burial D/7-6 is the fairly complete but poorly preserved skeleton of an infant with an estimated age of 18 ± 3 months. Many of the bones and skeletal elements were broken and were covered in a crystalline matrix likely composed of calcium salts. The deciduous incisors and molars were fully erupted, the canine were in the emergence stage of eruption, while the deciduous M2s were beginning to erupt and may have begun to emerge. The laminal plates of the individual vertebrae had fused though none of the neural arches were fused to the centra. Only two long bones were measurable. There was no osseous or dental pathology. The only non-metric trait of note was ossification into the pterygo-spinous and pterygo-alar ligaments.

Burial D/7-7 is the complete and well-preserved skeleton of a female with estimated age of 40 ± 5 years: rib estimate = 43–58; symphysis pubis 38.2 ± 10.9; 7 teeth lost ante-mortem with extensive attrition. The bones were well mineralized and there was no evidence of osteophytosis, although osteoarthritis was advanced in both patellae. The skeleton was otherwise healthy. Key non-metric traits present include, bilateral Os Japonicum and infra-orbital sutures, a left divided hypoglossal canal, ossification (large spur) of the right pterygo-alar ligament and a right mylohyoid bridge. Her stature is estimated at 153.62 ± 3.28 cm.

Burial D/7-8 is the complete skeleton of a male estimated to be 45 ± 5 years of age: rib score 33–42; symphysis pubis 45.6 ± 10.4; 13 teeth lost ante-mortem; osteophytosis in lumbar and lower thoracic vertebrae. The bones are well mineralized. Considerable trauma was present including a healed circular lesion of his right parietal that measured 24 mm across, a major impact fracture of his left proximal humerus and a fracture of his 1st left rib. Spina bifida occulta was present in his 1st sacral vertebrae. Ossification into the medial collateral ligament is an anomalous condition present. The dental health of this individual was poor. In addition to the extensive ante-mortem tooth loss, noted above, the crowns of three teeth, maxillary canines and the right 1st mandibular premolar, were destroyed by dental caries with one of these, the premolar, supporting a large periapical abscess. Periodontal disease was extensive. There were no noteworthy morphogenetic traits present in this skeleton. His stature is estimated at 170.63 ± 3.53 cm.

Burial D/7-9 is the complete skeleton of a male with an estimated age of 27 ± 3 years: rib score 26–32; symphysis pubis score 28.7 ± 6.5; medial clavicle fusing; no ante-mortem tooth loss, slight to moderate attrition. This individual showed a mosaic of skeletal ageing characteristics. The S1-S2 bodies were fused, which normally indicates an individual in the late 20s or early 30s, yet the medial clavicular epiphysis is not completely fused suggesting a person in the mid 20s. The latter agrees with the degree of dental attrition in this skeleton, whereas the sacral data closely approximate the rib and symphysis pubis scores. Also of note is the fusion of his coccyx and sacrum. Spina bifida occulta, measuring 10 mm, is present in S1. There is no dental pathology. Key morphogenetic traits present are, ossification, spurring, of the right pterygo-spinous and pterygo-alar ligaments, the presence of an anomalous pathway for the right temporal artery, bilateral intermediate condylar canals, an accessory ossicle at lambda and a cervical rib. His stature is estimated at 163.2 ± 3.53 cm.

Burial D/6-1 is the complete burial of a robust male with an estimated skeletal-dental age of 27 ± 3 years. Age was assessed from the following: symphysis pubis 23.4 ± 3.6; rib 24-28; medial clavicle just fusing ~ 25 years; S1-S2 fused = 28-32; dental attrition moderate 27 years; no ante-mortem tooth loss). The age was assigned to the upper limits of the symphysis pubis and rib score because of the amount of dental attrition, which is most consistent with Kellis 2 dentitions in late 20s. The bones are well mineralized. Healed fractures occur in left ribs 2 and 3 and the lower margins of the nasal bones. In addition, there is a slight compression fracture of L1 with small schmorl nodes on its inferior posterior surface and the inferior posterior surface of T12 and the superior surface of L2. Possibly related to the above traumas is the isolated occurrence of erosive osteoarthritis, exposing the cancellous bone and showing a grainy appearance, on the head and rib facet of 11th rib. The only additional evidence of degenerative joint changes is slight erosion in the left acetabulum and sclerosing of the femoral articular surfaces of both patellae. Spina bifida occulta occurs in L5 and S1. Four teeth have carious lesions only one of which, maxillary left M2, was likely to have caused pain. The extreme calculus build-up, limited to the left mandibular

teeth, particularly the molars, may be a concomitant of the latter, with masticatory preference given to the use of the right side of the dentition. Key morphological variants present in this skeleton include; ossification into the pterygo-spinous (+) and pterygo-basal ligaments (++), a large precondylar tubercle and the formation of divided articular surfaces of both occipital condyles and both superior articular facets of the atlas. His stature is estimated at 176.8 ± 3.53 cm.

Burial D/6-2 is the complete and well-preserved skeleton of an infant with dental age estimate of 6 ± 3 months. No teeth have begun to emerge and the roots of many of the deciduous teeth vary from partially formed to at most 1/2 the length. Interestingly, the *symphysis menti* is fully fused, except for a small remnant in the superior alveolus between the central incisors. There is no evidence of bone pathology with both orbits being healthy: no porotic hyperostosis. The presence of bilateral lambdoidal accessory ossicles is the only non-metric variant present.

North Tomb 1 Burials

A total of seven burials and one skull from a disturbed burial were analyzed from several rooms in the North Tomb 1; their locations are shown in Hope this volume Figures 12, 16 and 17.[1]

North Tomb 1, Room 1, Context 8 is the skull of a female with an estimated age of 20 ± 2 years of age. The spheno-occipital synchondrosis is fully fused, the maxillary 3rd molars have fully erupted, and there is slight enamel polishing on the M1 and M2s. While there is no ante-mortem tooth loss a large periapical abscess is present in the alveolus of the maxillary left lateral incisor. The tooth was lost post mortem but it most likely possessed a carious lesion with dentin exposure. The right maxillary and mandibular molars and premolars have extensive calculus build-up completely covering the buccal, cheek, surfaces of these teeth. A small pit and fissure carious lesion occurs on the left mandibular M2. Key morphological variants present include; bilateral Os Japonicum, a possible staphne defect on the right mandible, bilateral divided hypoglossal canals, a left intermediate condylar canal, and a left accessory ossicle at Pterion.

North Tomb 1, Room 2, Burial 3 is the complete and well preserved skeleton of an adolescent of unknown sex, with an estimated age of 15 ± 2 years. All three elements of the hip bone are fully fused except a small portion of right os pubis, which is just fusing to the ilium, while the only long bone epiphyses fused are in the elbow: distal humerus and proximal ulna. The second permanent molars have fully erupted and on the right side they show enamel

---

[1] It should be noted that the burials were numbered continuously throughout the tomb in the order of their excavation and not by rooms.

polishing with no dentine exposure. The third molar crowns are formed, the roots are not developed and the process of eruption has not started. There is no evidence of skeletal infection, trauma, or dental pathology. Key variations present include spina bifida occulta of S1, bilateral Os Japonicum, bilateral divided hypoglossal canas, ossification into the left pterygo-alar ligament (+), a divided right jugular canal, and bilateral mylohyoid bridges.

North Tomb 1, Room 3, Burials 5a and 5b

Two burials were commingled in the field number NT1/5. Their ages were similar, but could be sorted by size differences. 5b was originally interred in grave 6 where both fibulae and feet were found.

Burial 5a is the incomplete skeleton, only hips and left fibula in lower appendicular skeleton, hands and right radius missing in upper appendicular skeleton, of a female with an estimated age of 22 ± 2 years. Age was based on the following: symphysis pubis 25.0 ± 4.9; rib morphogenesis 20–24; limited fusing medial clavicle epiphyses 20–25, only tiny dentine exposure of the mesial-buccal cusps of the right M1s; dental attrition 18–22 years; lack of dental pathology; fusion of the spheno-occipital synchondrosis 17–22 and full eruption of the maxillary 3rd molars >18 years. The bones are well mineralized and there is no evidence of infection, trauma or degenerative joint disease. Of interest is the complete fusion of the sternomanubrial joint and the extreme development of shovelling of the right lateral maxillary incisor which approximates a barrel shaped expression. Other morphological traits of note are: left Os Japonicum, slight ossification (+) of the right pterygo-spinous ligament, bilateral presence of a divided hypoglossal canal, complete on right, ++ on left, a right mylohyoid bridge, possible trace of the occipital suture, an accessory ossicle at lambda, bilateral presence of the intermediate condylar canal, a left incomplete foramen transversarium of the atlas, ossification of the apical ligament of the axis, and a right septal aperture. Her stature is estimated at 165.18 ± 3.857 cm.

Burial 5b is the incomplete skeleton of a male with an estimated skeletal age of 23 ± 4 years of age. Missing the skull, most of the hands and feet, the right hip, several vertebrae, and most of the upper appendicular, the scapulae, humeri, left clavicle and left radius, lower appendicular: all bones except the left patella and the tali. Age is based on rib, 20–23, and symphysis pubis, 20–26, morphogenesis, plus the fusing nature of medial clavicular epiphysis and epiphyseal rings of the vertebrae 20–25 years. There is no degenerative changes in the bones present including the three lumbar vertebrae present (L3-L5). There is no osteopathology or key morphological variants present. As expected of an individual of this age bone mineralization is excellent.

North Tomb 1, Room 3, Burial 10 is the incomplete (no skull and many vertebrae are missing) burial of an adult male likely in his 40s or 50s;. Age is difficult to estimate as there are no sternal rib ends or teeth and the pubic symphysis have variant morphological profiles with the right suggesting a person 45 ± 10 and the left a least a stage older (stage 5; 55 ± 10 years). The later age estimate is supported by the presence of considerable osteoarthritic changes in the knees and spine and osteoporosis in his tibia. This person suffered considerable pathology in both feet which may have produced some disuse atrophy in his legs after earlier development of osteoarthritis. In both his feet ankylosing of the tarsal bones occurs and there is considerable build-up of bone of the major articular areas. As well the bones are slightly osteopenic. These changes are similar to those found in NT1/12. There are no noteworthy osteological variants present. His stature is estimated at 173.74 ± 3.53 cm.

North Tomb 1, Room 3, Burial 12 is the complete skeleton of a male with an estimated age of 27 ± 3 years. Age was estimated from: associated changes in the ribs (28–32 years); symphysis pubis (35 ± 9.2 years); dental attrition (25–30 years) and lack of dental pathology, no ante-mortem tooth loss; the fused medial clavicular epiphyses and the fusion of S1-S2. The slight degree of attrition is atypical of individuals older than 30 in the Kellis samples and this was the deciding factor assigning of the age range. This individual suffered from a number of pathological conditions. First, his skull is considerably asymmetrical in shape, which suggests that he suffered from chronic torticollis. The asymmetry is reflected in all views of the skull. In the basi-occiput region the dens facet is considerably lipped and eroded with cancellous bone showing and the right transverse tubercle is considerable smaller than the left. From the posterior view the skull has a decided left orientation including the nuchal crest, which also shows more left side rugosity. These changes suggest a congenital condition, although wry-neck can also be acquired. Of interest is the fact that this individual has considerable degenerative joint changes in the upper limb, thoracic and lumber spines. In the bones of elbows, particularly the ulnae, the degree of arthritis is advanced to a point of showing bilateral lipping, erosion, and eburnation only found in very elderly individuals (60+) in the Kellis 2 population. Included in the upper limb changes were the bilateral fusion of the lunate and scaphoid bones, which on the right side were ankylosed to the distal radius. The reason for this degree of advanced arthritic change is the bilateral and long standing infections in his feet, with concomitant but slight osteoblastic changes, considerable osteolytic destruction, ankylosing of many bones in each foot, and widespread osteoporosis. The osteoporosis was also found in the leg bones, particularly the tibia. This advanced bilateral osteoporosis is interpreted as a function of disuse atrophy. Whether the latter was from neurological disorder leading to infection or whether it was from a long standing infection that led to lack of use of the legs is difficult to determine. That this individual was severely compromised in terms of locomotion and may have come to rely entirely on his

Table 1 Summary of Burials from D6/–D/7 and North Tomb 1 at Kellis.

Burial	Age Estimate	Sex	Inventory	Comments
D/7-1	55 ± 5	F	complete	very osteoporotic without fractures, advanced osteoarthritis, bilateral spurs of hypoglossal canal
D/7-2	20 ± 2	F	complete	no osteopathology, large periapical abscess of mandibular left first molar, fusion of manubrium and sternum
D/7-3	60 ± 5	F	complete	osteoporotic, unfused intertrochanteric fracture, metopism, nine teeth lost ante-mortem, suprscapular canal, precon tub
D/7-4	perinate	?	complete	could be last trimester fetus, no hyperostotic traits present
D/7-5	48 ± 5	F	complete	slight osteoporosis of ribs, 10 teeth lost ante-mortem, advanced patellar arthritis, pterygospinous bridge, precondylar tubercle, trochlear spur, no fractures or infection
D/7-6	18m ± 3m	?	~ complete	no osteo or dental pathology, pterygoid (basal) bridge
D/7-7	40 ± 5	F	complete	no osteoporosis, advanced patellar OA, fusion of costal cartilage (1st rib), seven teeth lost ante-mortem R. Os Japonicum, left divided hypoglossal canal, chondromalacia patella, no infection
D/7-8	45 ± 5	M	complete	healed fractures of right parietal, left proximal humerus and left rib, 'Pelligrini syndrome' left tibia, spondylitis deformans of the lower thoracic and lumbar vertebrae, no osteoporosis, slight osteoarthritis of patellae, spina bifida occulta S1,13 teeth lost ante-mortem
D/7-9	27 ± 3	M	complete	S1-S2 already fused, no ante-mortem tooth loss, no infection or trauma, spina bifida occulta of S1, anomalous temporal artery, cervical ribs, fused coccyx to sacrum
D/6-1	27 ± 3	M	complete	Spina bifida occulta L5 and S1, infection in posterior T12, centrum, compression fracture of L1, smorl nodes L2 and 3 no ante-mortem tooth loss, healed fractures of left ribs 2 and 3, healed fracture of lower nasal bone
D/6-2	6m ± 3m	?	complete	symphysis menti already fused, no patholoogy, lambdic ossicle
NT1	20 ± 2	F	skull only	slight attrition, no ante-mortem tooth loss, considerable calculus build-up, healed depression fractures R. frontal
NT1/2-3	15 ± 2	?	complete	no osteo or dental pathology, Os japonicum, right divided jugular canal, rodent knawing of r. frontal
NT1/3-5a	22 ± 3	F	incomplete	no dental or osteo pathology, manub-stern fused, L. Os Japonicum, trace of r. occipital suture
NT1/3-5b	23.4 ± 3.6	M	no skull	no osteo pathology, no key anomalies
NT1/3-10	45 ± 5	M	no skull	advanced osteoarthritis of major joints, osteoporosis of tibia, ankylosing of small tarsus bones and MT II and III in feet
NT1/3-12	27 ± 3	M	~ complete	torticollis with skull assymetry, extensive osteoarthritis in elbow and shoulder, fusion of lunate and scaphoids on each side, these bones ankylosed with right radius, osteoporosis of leg bones particularly tibia, infection, osteoporosis and fusion of foot bones, resportive changes in hands
NT1/3-16	30 ± 5	M	complete	no pathology, no ante-mortem tooth loss, bilateral post. arch foramina, r. septal aperture, bilateral spurs of pterygo basal. ligament, left carotico-clinoid bridge, bilateral intermediate condylar canals, healed fracture of metacarpal 5
NT1/4-8	23 ± 3	M?	incomplete	no osteo or dental pathology, bilateral posterior arch foramina of atlas

upper limbs for movement can be advanced judging from the advanced degenerative disease in the upper appendicular skeleton of this young person. Moreover, there was considerable osteoarthritis in the apophysial joints throughout his spine, particularly in the lumbar region. This may suggest locomotory accommodation from a sitting position rather than benefiting from the use of crutches. The general lack of osteophytosis in the lower spine, slight lateral osteophytes on superior bodies of L5 and S1, may also support this hypothesis. In terms of differential diagnosis two possibilities can be postulated at this time: a Madura foot infection, of fungal or bacterial origin, or paralysis from a disease such as poliomyelitis. Though some of the foot changes resemble leprosy, for example concentric resorption of one of the metatarsals, the total lack of skull changes, that is, rhinomaxillary syndrome, pathognomonic of the lepromatous form of this disease, precludes it as a serious candidate (Steinbock 1976, 201; Aufderheide and Rodriguez-Martin 1998, 144). Determining the precise cause of the pathological changes noted in this skeleton will take time and will involve the use of radiology and DNA. The only evidence of dental pathology is a carious lesion of the maxillary right central incisor with a sequel periapical abscess. The carious lesion likely developed in lacunae made from a dental fracture to the mesial surface of the tooth. Key morphogenetic traits present in this skeleton are; bilateral ossification into the pterygo-alar ligament (++), bilateral ossification of the clino-clinoid ligament, complete right; +++ left, bilateral presence of the divided hypoglossal canal, a left divided jugular canal, bilateral intermediate condylar canals, and complete ossification of the left suprascapular ligament. An anomalous pathway for a emissary branch of the suprascapular vessels noted for D/7-3 is also present in this burial. Partial ossification into the suprascapular ligament is also present, the complete bridging of which will normally house the suprascapular nerve and vessels. His stature is estimated at 177.42 ± 3.53 cm.

North Tomb 1, Room 3, Burial 16 is the complete skeleton of a male with an estimated age of 30 ± 5 years. Age was estimated from rib, 28–34, and symphysis pubis, 35.2 ± 9.2, morphogenesis, dental attrition 25–32 and pathology, no ante-mortem tooth loss, the fusion of all epiphyses and the S1-S2 centra 28–32. Calcification of thyroid cartilage is also present: estimate 30–40 years. The bones of this skeleton are well mineralized. A well healed fracture of the left metacarpal 5 is the only evidence of osteopathology. There is no dental pathology. Key morphological variants present are; ossification into the right (+) and left (++) pterygo-alar ligaments, complete ossification of the left carotico-clinoid ligament, a right divided jugular canal, bilateral mylohyoid bridges, bilateral intermediate condylar canals, bilateral posterior arch foramina of the atlas, and a left septal aperture. His stature is estimated at 175.35 ± 3.53 cm.

North Tomb 1, Room 4, Burial 8 is the incomplete skeleton of a 20–26 year old of unknown sex (no pelvis, mandible only from the skull, only shaft of left femur from the infracranial skeleton). Age was estimated on the basis of rib morphogenesis, 19–24 using male and female standards, the incomplete fusion of the medial clavicular epiphysis < 25 years, the eruption of the 3rd mandibular molars and the slight degree of attrition on the molar teeth. The vertebral column was complete and healthy and all bones present were well mineralized and healthy. The only non-metric variants present were bilateral posterior arch foramina, divided foramen transversaria of the C4 to C7 and slight ossification into the right suprascapular ligament (+).

Various aspects of the above burials are shown in Plates 1–10. These were selected in terms of their usefulness for illustrating the results that follow.

Results

The results are categorized under the following: demography, skeletal characteristics, palaeopathology, and non-metric morphology. The latter is used to address the issue of bio-genetic relationships in the discussion section.

Demography

The information for the 19 burials in Table 1 has been summarized demographically as follows:

	Qty	%
Perinates	2	10.5
Infants (6 months to 2.99 years)	2	10.5
Children (3 to 12.99 years)	0	0
Adolescents (13 to 19.9 years)	1	5.3
Young Adults (20 to 35 years)	9	47.4
Middle Adults (36 to 50 years)	3	15.8
Older Adults (50+ years)	2	10.5
Sex Ratio (% Male/Female)	7/7	50

Although information on such a small sample is biased, such as, the low subadult (5/19 = 26.3 %) and the perinatal/infant mortality (4/19 = 21.0%), the absence of children, and the low middle adult mortality, the fact that all major age groups are present is significant in terms of representation, as is the balanced sex ratio. Moreover, of the middle and older adults, females predominate, which is similar to the pattern identified at Kellis 2 (Molto 2002). Collectively, these burials do not seem to represent random interments but sampling from a population, a hypothesis best supported by the morphogenetic data shown below.

Skeletal Characteristics

In terms of general skeletal appearance the TSBs are not overly robust and are of short stature. Males on average

Table 2 Summary craniometric statistics of the Kellis Town Site Burials versus Kellis 2.

| | Males | | | | | | | | Females | | | | | | |
| | Kellis 2 | | | | Town Site | | | | Kellis 2 | | | | Town Site | | |
	N	Mean	S.D.	Range	N	Mean	S.D.	Range	N	Mean	S.D.	Range	N	Mean	S.D.	Range
GOL	45	179.6	5.1	169–190	5	184.8	4	180–190	60	171.1	6	160–186	6	176.2	4.4	170–182
XCB	45	137.2	4.7	127–149	5	136.8	4.3	128–139	61	133.5	4.7	122–145	6	137.5	4.5	132–143
BBH	44	131.5	4.7	123–140	5	132.2	5	128–139	57	126	4.4	115–137	5	127.6	3	124–131
BPL	36	91.6	4	85–100	5	98.4	3.5	95–104	57	89.3	4.4	82–98	5	92.8	3.6	91–98
BNL	43	99.9	3.8	92–109	5	103.2	4.8	96–109	57	94.3	4	85–106	5	96.2	3.2	90–103
FOL	46	36	2.1	31–40	5	35.2	2.8	31–38	58	34.2	2.4	28–39	5	35.8	0.4	35–36
FOB	26	30.6	1.9	27–34	5	29.6	1.3	28–31	38	28.1	2.2	24–31	5	31.4	1.1	30–33
OVB	42	43.8	2.8	39–49	5	47.6	2.5	44–50	59	42.6	3.1	37–52	6	45.8	3.7	42–51
SMB	44	82.1	3.7	77–90	5	84.8	2.4	82–88	59	78	4	72–89	6	83	4.4	77–89
ASB	37	107.6	4.6	99–120	4	105.5	4.8	100–110	55	102.7	4.1	94–113	6	105.6	2.3	103–108
MAB	37	61.1	2.9	55–67	5	62.8	1.3	61–64	45	58.5	4.1	50–72	5	63.2	3.7	59–68
ZYB	42	127.6	4	120–136	5	129.6	3.2	125–133	54	119.6	3.9	110–126	6	126.8	2.6	122–129
FRC	44	95	3.9	87–102	5	96.4	3.6	92–100	60	92.4	3.3	85–100	6	97.6	1	96–99
OBB	42	38.3	1.6	36–42	5	40.4	2.3	38–44	58	37.6	1.8	33–42	6	39.3	1.2	37–40
OBH	42	33.2	1.5	31–36	5	34.8	1.6	34–37	58	33.8	1.9	29–37	6	33.5	3.2	30–38
EKB	41	94.6	3.9	85–104	5	96.4	2	94–99	54	92.4	3.4	87–98	6	98	1.4	96–100
NPH	37	70	4.8	60–85	5	75	2.8	71–79	57	66.6	4.3	56–72	6	65.8	3.9	62–71
NAH	42	51.5	2.3	46–57	5	53.6	1.8	52–56	58	49.5	2.6	45–56	6	50.6	3.8	46–56
NAB	42	24.2	1.7	21–28	5	24.6	1.1	23–26	58	23.3	3.8	19–27	6	25.3	2.9	23–30
WNB	43	10.7	1.7	8 to 14	5	9.8	1.6	7to11	57	10.2	1.8	7 to14	6	11	2.4	8 to15
MFB	46	94	4.1	88–103	5	96.4	4.4	89–101	61	92	3.8	85–100	6	97.5	3.4	93–102
NBC	46	109.4	5	99–121	5	113	6.8	103–121	61	106.8	4.3	97–117	6	108.5	3.7	103–111
BLC	42	111.1	5.2	98–120	5	112.6	3	110–117	58	107.8	5.4	95–115	6	110.3	6.5	98–116
LOC	41	95.6	4.5	88–114	5	100.2	2.4	97–103	55	92	4.3	84–108	6	96.7	3.6	93–103

Table 3 Summary of cranial indices.

| | | | | | | | | | | | | | Male | | Female | |
Measure	D/7-1	D/7-2	D/7-3	D/7-5	D7-7	D/7-8	D/7-9	D/6-1	NT1/1-8	NT1/2-3	NT1/3-12	NT1/3-16	Mean	S.D.	Mean	S.D.
Cranial index	77.6	79.4	79.1	80.5	79.3	74.6	72.2	75.3	72.5	73.2	74.7	73.3	74	1.3	78.1	2.9
Orbital Index	75	90	81.1	95	84.6	89.5	87.2	92.5	85	85	81.8	80.5	86.3	5.1	85.1	6.9
Nasal Index	53.1	42.6	53.6	52.9	50	43.6	44.2	46.4	44.2	44	44.2	48.1	45.3	1.9	49.4	4.8
Upper fac hgt Index	48.8	56.3	50.4	54.3	53.3	56.8	60	56.4	48.4	53.7	61.7	54.6	57.9	2.9	51.9	3.2
Fronto-parietal index	70.5	67.1	72.9	72.1	69.6	70.3	68.5	68.5	73.5	71.2	69	73.7	70	2.2	71	2.4
Cranial Module	142.3	150.7	148.7	148.3	145.3	151	146	149	x	155.3	157	153.3	151.3	4.2	147.1	3.3

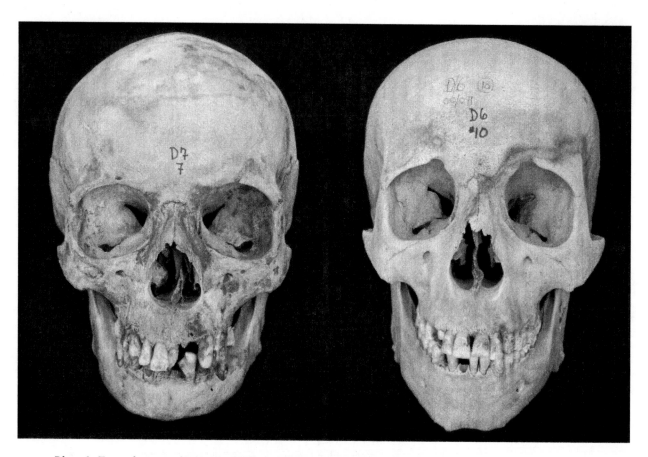

Plate 1 Frontal views of D/7-7 and D/6-1 showing typical shape characteristics of Kellis skulls; for most characteristics these skulls have average values (see text).

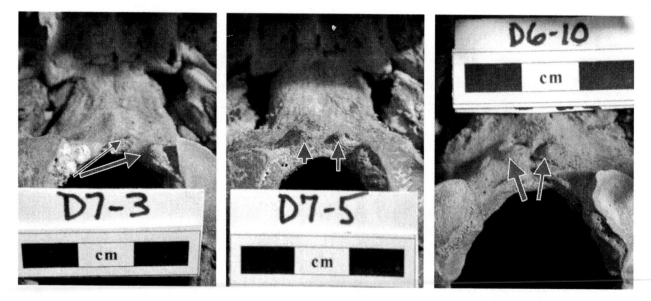

Plate 2 Precondylar tubercles (arrows) in burials D/7-3, D/7-5, and D/6-1; this rare, highly genetic trait, suggests these individuals are related.

Table 4 Select non-metric traits in Kellis Town Site Burials and Kellis 2; those with percentages
for Mean Measure of Divergence.

Trait	M	F	D/6-D/7	NT1	Group	%	Kellis 2	%
Metopic suture*	0(5)	1(6)	1(8)	0(5)	1(13)	7.7	6(105)	5.7
Os Japonicum*	0(5)	2(6)	1(9)	2(4)	3(13)	23.1	7(101)	6.9
Open Spinosum*	1(5)	1(6)	2(7)	1(5)	3(13)	23.1	51(105)	48.6
Infraorbtial suture*	2(5)	4(7)	3(8)	2(5)	5(13)	38.5	50(105)	47.6
Tympanic dehiscence*	0(5)	2(7)	2(8)	0(5)	3(13)	23.1	26(106)	24.5
Mendosal suture - trace	0(5)	4(7)	3(8)	2(5)	5(13)	38.5		
Marginal foramen*	0(5)	0(7)	0(8)	0(5)	0(12)	0	10(105)	9.6
Pterygospinous spur/bridge	1(5)	1(6)	3(10)	0(5)	3(15)	20	19(104)	18.2
Pterygobasal ossification	4(5)	2(7)	4(10)	3(5)	7(15)	46.7	42(103)	40.7
Clino-clinoid bridge	1(5)	1(7)	0(10)	2(5)	2(15)	13.3		
Carotico-clinoid ossification	0(5)	0(7)	0(10)	0(5)	2(15)	13.3	20(98)	20.4
Squamoparietal synostosis	0(5)	0(7)	0(8)	0(5)	0(13)	0		
Trochlear spur	0(5)	1(7)	1(8)	0(7)	1(15)	6.7	12(104)	11.5
Divided hypoglossal canal	3(5)	6(6)	7(10)	3(4)	10(14)	71.4	60(104)	57.7
Precondylar tubercle	1(5)	2(7)	3(10)	0(5)	3(15)	20	2(95)	2
Divided jugular	1(5)	0(6)	0(8)	2(4)	2(12)	16.7	37(101)	36.7
Mylohoid bridge*	1(5)	1(7)	1(8)	2(5)	3(13)	23.1	26(104)	25
Lat. Pterygo-plate foramen	0(5)	1(7)	1(8)	0(5)	1(13)	7.7	6(100)	6
Absent zygo-fac. For.	0(5)	3(7)	2(10)	1(5)	3(15)	20	14(101)	13.9
Absent poster. condylar canal	2(5)	1(6)	1(8)	4(4)	5(15)	33.3	10(102)	9.8
Frontal grooves	2(5)	3(7)	5(8)	1(5)	6(13)	46.2	40(100)	40
Supraorbital foramen	3(5)	3(7)	3(8)	3(5)	6(13)	46.2		
Anomalous temporal artery*	1(5)	0(7)	1(8)	0(5)	1(13)	7.7	4(100)	4
Accessory optic canal	0(5)	1(7)	1(10)	0(4)	1(14)	7.1	5(101)	5
Frontal temporal articulation	0(5)	0(7)	0(8)	0(5)	0(13)	0		
Occipital suture	0(5)	1(6)	0(8)	1(5)	1(13)	7.7		
Notochord remnant	0(5)	0(7)	0(9)	0(5)	0(14)	0		
Intermediate condylar canal	2(5)	1(7)	1(8)	2(4)	3(12)	25		
Ossicle at pterion	0(5)	2(7)	1(8)	1(4)	2(12)	16.7	20(99)	20.2
Ossicle at lambda	1(5)	0(7)	1(8)	0(5)	1(13)	7.7		
Skulls without sutural bones	1(5)	4(7)	4(8)	1(5)	5(13)	38.5		
3rd molar agenesis - mx*	2(5)	2(5)	3(6)	0(5)	3(11)	27.3	17(91)	18.7
Divided occipital condyle	1(5)	0(5)	1(8)	0(4)	1(12)	8.3		
Atlas - divided superior facet	1(5)	0(5)	1(8)	0(3)	1(11)	9.1		
Atlas - lateral bridge/spur	1(5)	0(7)	1(11)	0(3)	1(14)	7.1		
Atlas - posterior bridge/spur	1(5)	1(7)	2(11)	0(3)	2(14)	14.2		
Atlas - posterior arch foramen	2(5)	1(5)	2(11)	1(3)	3(14)	21.4		
Atlas - incomplete trans. for.	0(5)	1(6)	1(8)	0(3)	1(11)	9.1		
Axis - incomplete trans. For.	0(5)	2(6)	1(8)	2(4)	3(12)	25		
Septal aperture	4(5)	1(5)	3(8)	2(2)	5(10)	50		
Supratrochlear spur	0(5)	0(7)	0(10)	0(3)	0(13)	0		
Suprascapular bridge/spur	4(5)	3(5)	5(8)	2(3)	7(11)	63.6		
Unfused acromial epiphysis	0(5)	0(5)	0(8)	0(2)	0(10)	0		
Bifid rib	0(5)	0(5)	0(8)	0(2)	0(10)	0		
Acetabular defect	1(4)	3(5)	2(8)	2(3)	4(11)	36.4		
Divided anter. calcaneal facet	1(5)	0(6)	1(8)	0(3)	1(11)	9.1		

M = male; F = female; NT1 = North Tomb 1; p(n); * adult-adolescent data only for Mean Measure of Divergence

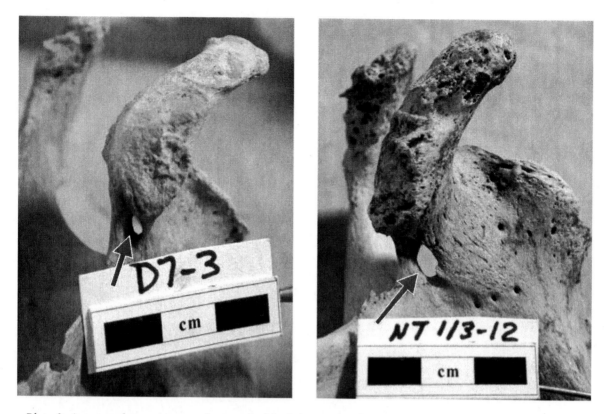

Plate 3 An anomalous neurovascular canal of the left scapula of burials D/7-3 and NT1/12. This rare canal likely has a genetic basis; if so, these two individuals may be related.

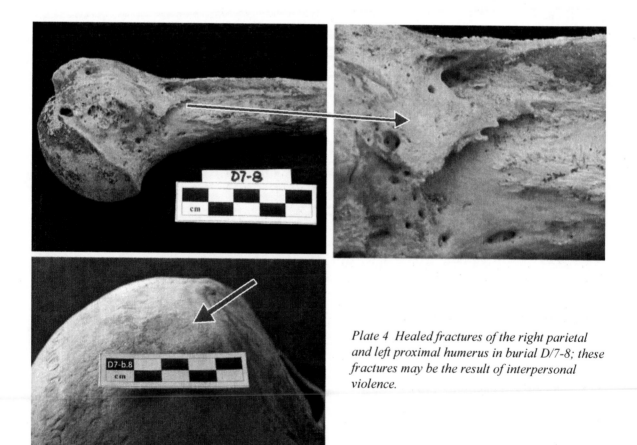

Plate 4 Healed fractures of the right parietal and left proximal humerus in burial D/7-8; these fractures may be the result of interpersonal violence.

were 172.8 ± 5.3 cm, whereas females averaged 159.3 ± 4.6 cm. Both values are slightly higher than those reported for Kellis 2 (Molto 2001, 90–1), although the degree of sexual dimorphism, average female to male stature, in height is identical at 92%. This consistency may suggest that measurement error is not a factor in the statural differences noted between Kellis 2 and the TSBs. Tables 2 and 3 summarize the craniometric data for the TSBs skulls relative to the Kellis 2 sample. For all general characteristics of size and shape these burials fit within the range of the Kellis 2 sample, although they are somewhat skewed to the higher values for many of the traits (see for example GOL, XCB and BBH in Table 2). Like the Kellis 2 skulls, these crania are not characterized by any extremes and this is reflected in the mean and modal values shown in Table 3. For most of the measures, except the cranial module (males = 151.3 and females = 147.1), which is an indicator of overall size of the skull, male-female differences are negligible and are pooled. These crania, as indicated by the cranial module, are also slightly larger than the Kellis mean values (unpublished data). In terms of shape characteristics, they have medium cranial shape as seen from above (76.0 = mesocranic or average length and breadth characteristics), with medium height, medium orbits (85.6 = mesochny) with borderline narrow to medium noses, upper end of leptorrhiny, and somewhat broad appearing vaults, lower border of broad using the *fronto-parietal* index. Some of these relationships are shown in Plate 1.

Non-Metric Morphology

Table 4 summarizes key non-metric cranial and infracranial traits in the TSBs. The table also includes select traits from Kellis 2 for use in the distance analysis (see below). D/6, D/7 and North Tomb 1 show a number of succinct differences, which may represent different lineages within a population. Most noteworthy in this regard is the high relative frequency of the precondylar tubercle, a rare genetic trait, which occurs in 3 of 10 individuals in D/6 and D/7 but is absent in North Tomb 1 (Plate 2). In addition, two burials, one each from D/7 (number 3) and North Tomb 1 (Burial 12), have an anomalous suprascapular canal (Plate 3). To my knowledge, this variant has never been described before in the skeletal literature and these are the only examples in all the burials the senior author has examined in Egypt (n > 1000). Many of the traits that are common in Kellis 2 are also observed frequently in the TSBs, such as, pterygobasal spurring, mylohyoid bridging, the infra-orbital suture, frontal grooves, partial ossification of suprascapular ligament and the hypoglossal canal bridging. Information on the key non-metric traits observed is found with the burial descriptions and in Table 1.

Palaeopathology

The above descriptions indicate considerable pathology in these skeletons that include trauma, dental pathology,

degenerative change, infection, haematological, metabolic and congenital disorders. General analysis of pathological lesions are described in Steinbock (1976), Ortner and Putschar (1985) and Aufderheide and Rodriguez-Martin (1998). As many pathologies are age and sex related some summary comments on the palaeopathology of this sample follow the categorical descriptions.

Trauma

Five adults in the TSBs experienced skeletal trauma. Four most likely represent malintent cases, namely; a healed fracture of the left metacarpal 5 in burial NT1/16, a healed fracture of the right nasal bone in individual D/6-1, a healed depression fracture of the right parietal in burial D/7-8 (Plate 4) and a healed fracture of the right frontal in burial NT1/8. The first two fractures are likely from fisticuffs, whereas the latter are impact wounds from instruments. The lesion on the right parietal of D/7-8, which is approximately 24 mm circular, was made by a different type of weapon than that which caused the frontal trauma in NT1/8. These malintent fractures represent cases of interpersonal violence. The overall prevalence of malintent trauma in this sample is relatively high at 33% (3/15). In the Kellis 2 sample ~7% of individuals experienced trauma from interpersonal violence and all cases were males (Molto 2001, 97–8). The presence of malintent fracture in a female (NT1/8) burial is anomalous for this population.

Individual D/7-8, a middle-aged male with the right parietal lesion, also had long healed fractures of the left proximal humerus and a left true rib. Normally such fractures would be considered accidental, but given the malintent wound to his right parietal the latter fractures may also be a concomitant of the same malintent event that caused the parietal lesion. Similarly, burial D/6-1 had healed fractures of left ribs 2 and 3 and a slight compression fracture of the L1 with associated schmorl's nodes in the adjacent vertebrae. These latter acute fractures could have been from a fall.

Individual D/7-3, an elderly female likely 60–70 years of age, suffered a severe intertrochanteric fracture with minimal evidence of healing. Based on the latter it is likely that the trauma, probably a fall, and no doubt figured prominently in her death. Severe and widespread osteoporosis was unequivocally the contributing risk factor for this trauma.

Dental Pathology

Dental pathology is common in all well represented archaeological samples. The TSBs provide evidence of dental caries, ante-mortem tooth trauma, periodontitis, calculus, ante-mortem tooth loss and periapical abscesses (Plate 5). These data are reported herein by age cohort since all dental disease is positively correlated with chronological age. The small sample size and representation, necessitates using broader age categories, namely:12–18; 19–35; 36–50 and 50+. In total there were 12 TSB dentitions suitable for analysis. Methodologically,

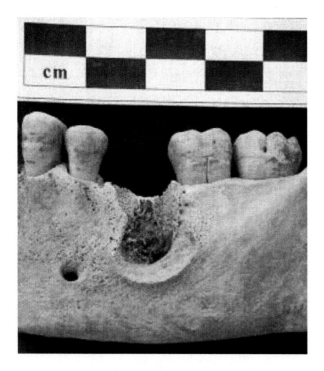

Plate 5 Periapical abscess in the alveolus of left mandibular M1 in individual D/7-2. The young age of this individual suggests that the ultimate cause of the abscess was a large carious lesion; if the infectious bacteria in this abscess spread through the blood it could have caused the death of this individual.

Table 5 Summary of Dental Pathology by Individual.

Age	Burial	Mean Age	Sex	Qty Anal	Lost PM	Lost AM	Fract	Caries	Absc	Calc	Peridon	Other
12 to 18	NT1/2-3	15	?	24	0 of 28	0/28	0/24	0/24	0/28	0	0	3 unerupted
19 to 35	D/7-2	20	F	29	0 of 31	1 of 31	0/29	4 of 29	1 of 31	slight	0	cal. On man inci, ATM and ab MnLm1
	NT1/3-5a	22	F	16	0/16	0/16	0/16	0/16	0/16	0	0	no dental pathology, maxilla only
	NT1/1-8	20	F	12	16/30	0/30	0/12	2 of 12	1 of 30	slight	0	mn3ms con mis, mx AN MN M1s caries
	NT1/4-8	23	M									
	D/7-9	27	M	26	0/30	0/30	7 of 28	2 of 28	0 of 29	slight	0	cal mn incisors + can
	D/6-1	27	M	30	1 of 31	0/31	1 of 29	4 of 30	0 of 31	slight	0	mn r can missing con.
	NT1/3-12	28	M	32	0/32	0/32	2 of 32	2 of 32	1 of 32	slight	0	Mx R I with abscess sequel to trauma
	NT1/3-16	30	M	32	0/32	0/32	0/30	0/30	0/32	slight	0	
36 to 50	D/7-5	48	F	17	2 of 32	10 of 32	0 of 17	5 of 18	2 of 24	advanced	slight	r mx m2 covered by calculus
	D/7-7	40	F	22	2 of 29	7 of 29	2 of 21	2 of 21	1 of 27	moderate	advanced	
	D/7-8	45	M	13	4 of 30	13 of 30	1 of 14	4 of 14	1 of 16	slight	moderate	
50+	D/7-1	55	F	14	6 of 28	9 of 28	0 of 14	0 of 14	2 of 21	slight	slight	
	D/7-3	60	F	17	1 of 29	9 of 29	3 of 17	1 of 17	6 of 20	slight	advanced	

the determination of the prevalence of dental disease is complicated, as the types of the pathologies are interdependent. For example, ante-mortem tooth loss can be a sequel to periodontitis and dental caries. Dental caries, however, can result from pulpal exposure from extreme wear and/or a highly cariogenic diet, that is, high carbohydrate content. Moreover, when a tooth is lost ante-mortem the underlying cause is no longer analyzable except by inference, to other dentitions in the sample, and so important data are unavailable. For example, in the TSBs, D/7-8, a middle aged adult male (~45 years), lost 13 teeth ante-mortem and many of these likely had dental caries. Of the teeth in his alveolus at death only four had caries for a prevalence of 28.6%. The true rate of carious teeth in this individual, however, was likely closer to 50% if we assume that most, or all, of the 13 teeth lost had dental caries. Also, there is considerable variation in the prevalence of dental disease for individuals of similar age for a variety of reasons. These are cautionary concerns for generalizing about the state of dental health in the TSBs. The dental pathology is summarized by age cohort in Table 5 and the general patterns are described below.

Adolescent Dental Health

Only one dentition, NT1/2-3, is available for analysis and there is no dental pathology present. As expected, dental attrition in this individual is very slight and no teeth showed evidence of dental trauma.

Young Adults (19 to 35). A total of 177 teeth were analyzable in the six young adult dentitions. Of these 14 (7.9%) had dental caries and 5.6 % (N=10) were fractured. The distribution of the carious are: molars (10) premolars (2) and incisors (2). Of the two carious lesions on the incisor teeth both were sequel to ante-mortem fractures. Of the fractured teeth 60% occurred on the molars, 30% on the incisors plus one premolar. Noteworthy is the fact that 70% of the fractured teeth occurred in one individual (D/7-9) and four individuals had no ante-mortem fractures. In each of the six dentitions there was slight dental calculus build-up and no evidence of periodontal disease. One tooth of the 202 analyzable tooth sites was lost ante-mortem (~0.5%) in the young adults. It should be noted that all of the these young adults were likely in their 20s with at least 40% in the early stage of this cohort.

Middle Adult (36 to 50). There were 53 teeth analyzable in the three dentitions represented in this age category. Each individual dentition had dental caries with an overall prevalence of 20.7%. As well, only 5.7% (3/53) of the teeth have dental fractures which may reflect that a lot of the teeth with fractures may have been lost ante-mortem as the 33% (30/91) prevalence of ante-mortem tooth loss reflects. Similarly there is a low rate of periapical abscesses (4/57 = 3.5%), which again may be a function of the ante-mortem tooth loss prevalence. There is considerable variation in alveolar health with periodontitis being

advanced in one individual (D/7-7), moderate in another and slight in the 3rd dentition. Similarly the three dentitions were characterized as having slight, moderate and advanced dental calculus, although the individual with the most dental calculus has the least periodontal resorption. It is important to note than none of the individuals in this category may have been less than 40 years of age. Plate 5 demonstrates a case of ante-mortem tooth loss in a young adult (D/7-2) that is likely a concomitant of a carious lesion with sequel infection: an abscess.

Older Adults (50+). Only two dentitions are represented in this age cohort; one aged 55 (D/7-1), the other with an estimated age of 60 (D/7-3). As expected there is considerable ante-mortem tooth loss (32.6 % - 18/57), and for reasons discussed above both the rate of dental caries and ante-mortem trauma are respectively low at 3.2% (1/31) and 10% (3/31). In both cases dental calculus build-up is slight and the older individual has advanced periodontitis.

Degenerative Joint Disease

Degenerative skeletal changes have multiple causes, although the most common are categorized as osteoarthritis in the joints and spondylitis (osteophytosis) in the vertebral bodies (Steinbock 1976). These changes, categorically called Degenerative Joint Disease, like dental pathology, are highly correlated with age as they are thought to reflect cumulative wear and tear with time. Personal idiosyncrasies and life style differences are often reflected in the intra-individual patterns of Degenerative Joint Disease. The specific changes in the TSBs are detailed in the descriptions above, whereas this discussion addresses general trends.

As expected, degenerative joint disease is absent in the adolescent, NT1/3, and it is more common in the middle and old adults relative to the young adults. In the latter category, of the burials sufficiently well preserved and represented, only two show evidence of degenerative joint disease, namely D/6-1 and NT1/12. The former shows slight degenerative erosion in the left acetabulum, the head and facet of the 11th right rib and sclerotic build-up on the femoral articular surfaces of both patellae. The rib erosion may be a sequel to trauma, while the patellar changes may represent the initial changes seen in chondromalacia patellae. The extensive degenerative changes described above in burial NT1/12 are anomalous for this age group and relate to the fact that he suffered a debilitating disease that required the use of the arms for support and locomotion. Noteworthy is that his spine is free of vertebral osteophytosis, although the interarticular facets of most of the vertebrae have slight osteoarthritis. This pattern may be a concomitant of his compromised posture and locomotion. The three middle adults (D/7-5, D/7-7 and D/7-8) collectively experienced slight vertebral osteophytosis in the lumbar and thoracic regions with the most severe changes being noted in D/7-7 where the

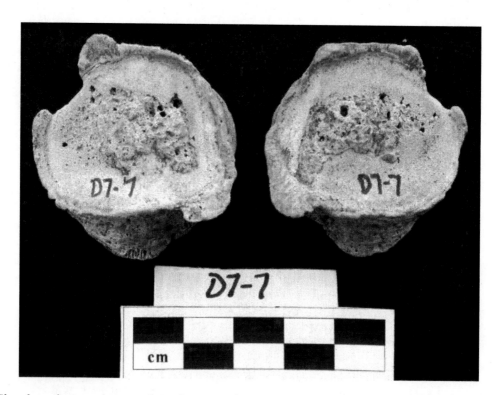

Plate 6 Chondromalacia and osteoarthritic lipping in both patellae of burial D/7-7 an older adult female. Note the combination of erosion and sclerotic build-up; the patella is one of the first bones to show degenerative changes in this population.

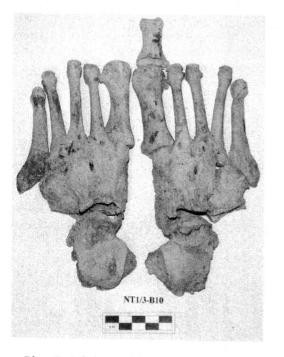

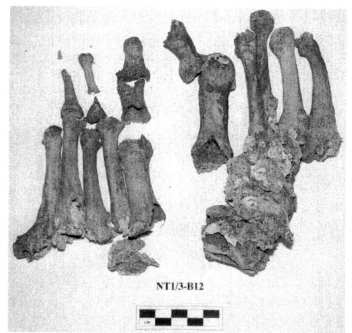

Plate 7 Ankylosis of the foot bones in burial NT1/10; that this may represent a response to a debilitating condition is evidenced by extremely osteoporotic tibia which suggests that the legs were immobilized.

Plate 8 Ankylosis and extensive osteosclerotic bone changes in the feet of NT1/12; these changes represent a response to chronic infectious condition that may have involved the nerves.

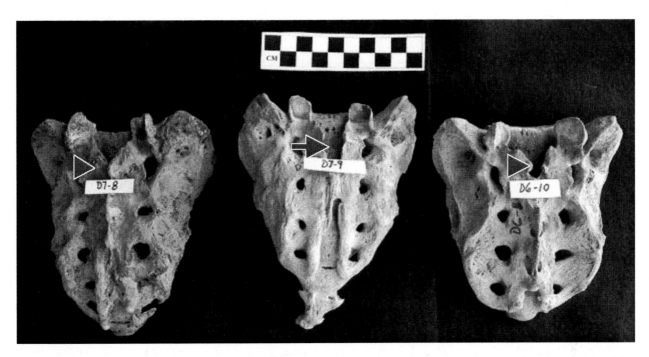

Plate 9 Spina bifida occulta in the sacra of burials D/7-8, D/7-9 and D/6-1. This is common in these, as well as Kellis 2, skeletons, but the relative frequency is elevated in the D/6–D/7 sample suggesting these individuals may be related.

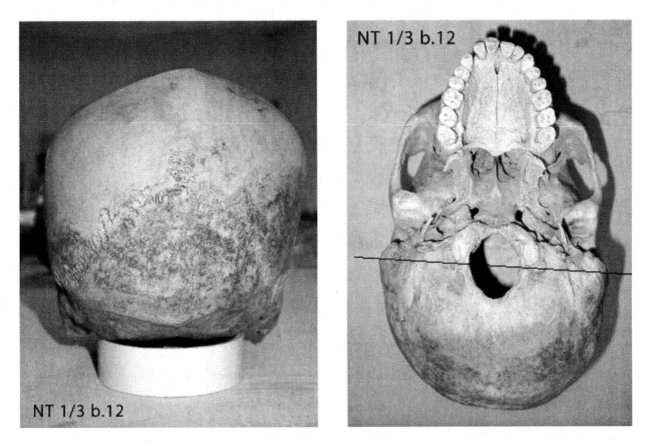

Plate 10 Posterior (left) and inferior (right) views of skull NT1/12 showing asymmetry (line) from long standing (congenital) torticollis (wry neck).

osteophytotic lipping is more advanced (in C7, L4 and L5). For the most part osteoarthritis in these individuals is slight in the spine and the major synovial joints, although in D/7-7 vertebral osteoarthritis is advanced in the L5/S1 articulation exhibiting lipping, pitting, joint enlargement and eburnation occurring. In the two older adults, both females (D/7-1 and D/7-3) in their late fifties or early sixties, osteoarthritis and vertebral osteophytosis are advanced, for example, both have eburnation in the spine and advanced chondromalacia patella (Plate 6). Degenerative Joint Disease in the TSBs follows expectations, although there is considerable variation between and within age groups.

Infection The skeleton responds to infectious agents by producing excess bone, that is, periosteal new-bone formation, destroying bone, lytic lesions, or a combination of both processes. These reactions are, in part, a response to an inflammatory process. Moreover, it is possible to differentiate active versus inactive disease states. In most cases specific diagnosis of the causative agent is not possible, although recent DNA research is improving diagnostics. In the D/6–D/7 sample the only evidence of infection is some slight periosteal new-bone formation on the posterior surface of the right radius. In the North Tomb 1 sample, two individuals (10 and 12), both from Room 3, show extensive infectious changes in their feet and lower legs. As noted above, this is characterized by excess bone formation and ankylosis of the tarsal bones (Plates 7 and 8). Both these skeletons also have severe osteoporosis of the tibia which is an indication of disuse atrophy. Whether the disuse was a concomitant of being disabled from foot infections or experiencing a debilitating neurological disease cannot at this time be determined. DNA analysis may, in future, assist in diagnosing these pathologies. Given their close proximity in Room 3 of North Tomb 1, the hypothesis of a congenital, genetic determined pathology emerges. Unfortunately, Burial 10 was missing many infracranial bones and the skull, so a morphological comparison of the two burials is not possible. Comparison of the DNA profiles for these burials is a future research venue which may help determine their specific genetic relationship.

Haematological Disorders

Porotic hyperostosis of the orbit and vault, which is characterized by sieve-like porosity in normal smooth bone, is argued to be a concomitant of iron deficiency anaemia (Steinbock 1976, 246–7). Though the causes of anaemia are many (Fairgrieve and Molto 2000) the condition is most common in children and thus skeletal lesions are usually more prevalent in this cohort. Porotic hyperostosis is absent in the two children (D/7-6 and D/6-2) and one adolescent (NT1/2-3) analyzable in the TSB sample. In the adults only two individuals (D/7-1, and D/7-9) had evidence of orbital porotic hyperostosis (2/8 – 25.0 %), although the condition was inactive at the time of death.

Clearly, the TSBs have a low prevalence of porotic hyperostosis relative to the Kellis 2 data, in which approximately 80% of the subadults and 50% of the adults had evidence of porotic hyperostosis (Fairgrieve and Molto 2000).

Metabolic Disorders

Loss of bone density is a well-known concomitant of hormonal decline with age, especially in women. Osteopenia and osteoporosis can, however, have other causes including disuse atrophy due to trauma or other forms of pathology. In the TSBs, osteoporosis occurs in both older adult females; in one case (D/7-3) leading to a hip fracture and eventual loss of life. Although the other older female had widespread and significant bone loss there were no osteoporosis-related fractures. In the two females, D/7-5 and D/7-7, respectively judged to be in their early and late 40s, only the latter has evidence of moderate osteoporosis, which is limited to the ribs and vertebrae. D/7-8, a male in his mid to late 40s, has similar but less osteoporosis than D/7-7. In the younger adults, only NT1/10 and 12, have evidence of bone loss for reasons presented earlier.

Congenital Conditions

Spina bifida is a neural tube defect characterized by the failure of the laminal plates of the vertebrae to ossify. Spina bifida occulta (= hidden), is the least severe of the various forms and is often listed as subclinical, since the cleft is too narrow to allow the protrusion of the spinal nerve and its meninges. Spina bifida occulta can occur in any vertebrae, but is most common in the sacrum (especially S1), L5 and C1. Spina bifida occulta occurs in the sacra of three males (Plate 9) in D/6–D/7 for a group prevalence of 42.8% (3/7). Only in one case (D/7) are two segments (S1 and S2) involved. These individuals may be closely related genetically. In the North Tomb sample, one individual (NT1/3) also has spina bifida occulta of S1 for a group prevalence of 25%. The overall prevalence of spina bifida occulta in the TSBs is 36.4%. In no case is spina bifida occulta associated with ankylosed vertebrae.

'Wry neck' or torticollis, a rare condition characterized by "involuntary turning of the head secondary to dystonic muscle contraction" (Aufderheide and Rodriguez-Martin 1998, 259) can be either acquired or congenital. A long standing 'likely congenital' case of torticollis is present in burial NT1/12 (Plate 10). The condition has resulted in considerable asymmetry favouring the left side of the skull. Of interest, is the presence of left side congenital ankylosis of C7-T1 in the spine, which could be associated with torticollis.

Palaeogenetic Interpretation

As noted in the introduction, the key research problem addressed herein is the determination and interpretation of the genetic relationships within the two groups of town site burials, and their relationship to Kellis 2. This aspect of the research relies on non-metric morphology as it has many advantages over craniometrics for dealing with small samples (Molto 1983). Previous research using the Mean Measure of Divergence statistic incorporating the Freeman-Tukey angular transformation has shown that all the Dakhleh samples studied to date ('Ain Tirghi, Kellis 1 and Kellis 2) represent an evolving deme (Molto 2001, 90). For the present analysis Kellis 2 obviously provides the most relevant comparative data for the TSBs. For the Mean Measure of Divergence comparison the data for D/6–D/7 and North Tomb 1 are pooled. This is justifiable on four counts: *1)* it increases sample size, *2)* they both likely represent contemporaneous occupants of Kellis in the late Roman period, *3)* the Kellis 2 data to which the TSBs are being compared also represent pooled data from many lineages (Molto 2002) and *4)* the TSBs have in common many morphological traits. Key among the latter is a particularly interesting variant, the anomalous vascular suprascapular canal, shared by two individuals, one each from the two areas. As noted, this rare trait has only been observed in these two burials in all the Dakhleh skeletons studied to date and has never been described in the osteological literature. Twenty-two non-metric cranial traits are used to compare Kellis 2 and the TSBs (see Table 4). These traits were selected for their known variability in the Dakhleh samples (Molto 2001) and because many of them have variant relative frequencies between the TSBs and Kellis 2. This selection for variability mitigates against creating a Type II error where the null hypothesis (H_o) is actually incorrect but is accepted. Using too many low variable traits in a trait battery is biased towards accepting the null hypothesis, that is that TSBs and Kellis 2 represent individuals who share a common gene pool. Using a large number of highly variable traits provides a fairer testing of the H_o. The alternative hypothesis in this study may be advanced by the separation of the TSBs from the Kellis 2 sample. For the comparisons the adult individual, for the majority of the traits and all the data from Kellis 2, is the unit of observation: versus the side count.

The resulting Mean Measure of Divergence of 0.0069 has a standard deviation of 0.0247. In terms of interpretation, a Mean Measure of Divergence that is equal to or greater than twice its standard deviation is statistically significant at $p \leq 0.05$ (Sjovold 1977). In this case the Mean Measure of Divergence is not significant suggesting that the TSBs and Kellis 2 represent sampling from the same breeding population.

In the TSBs at least one highly genetic trait, the precondylar tubercle, has an elevated relative frequency, that can be used with the Kellis 2 data to examine within-group relationships. In fact, the precondylar tubercle is limited to the D/6–D/7 sample and was present in three of 10 analyzable crania for a relative frequency of 30%. In the Kellis 2 population the precondylar tubercle occurs in adults and subadults in equal relative frequencies (respectively 2/95 and 2/90), which justifies their pooling

for a sampling model. That is, this trait in the hypothetical Kellis population occurs in 2% of individuals. What then is the probability of obtaining the distribution of the precondylar tubercle in the D/6–D/7 sample? To address this the binomial distribution following Sjovold (1976/77) and Molto (1978) is used. The probability (p) of obtaining the relative frequency of the precondylar facet (x) in a sample of 10 individuals can be calculated using the following formula:

$$Pr\,(x) = \frac{n!}{x!\,(n-x)!}\,(0.02)^3\,(0.98)^7$$

where n = the sample size and 0.02 and 0.98 represent the relative frequencies of absence and presence of the precondylar facet in the sampling population (Kellis 2) and the superscripts represent the number of individuals with trait presence (3) and absence (7). ! represents factorial and is used to calculate the number of orders these proportions can occur in a sample of 10 (= 120). Thus the probability of obtaining this result by chance is 8 in 10,000 ($120 \times [(0.02)^3 \times (0.98)^7]$) or slightly less than 1 in 1000. In rejecting the null hypothesis the most parsimonious interpretation is that the individuals with the trait are genetically related rather than this being a stochastic result; chance would produce this finding 1 in 1000 times. The precise relationships among those individuals with the trait cannot at this time be determined. These data, however, suggest that the burial areas in and adjacent to Kellis, most likely represent family or lineage mortuary complexes rather than random accretions.

Discussion

This paper describes the better preserved skeletal remains from D/6–D/7 (n =11) and North Tomb 1 (n = 8) from the Kellis town site. From a demographic standpoint the composite sample is considered representative in that most age groups and both sexes are represented, although as expected of small samples, many demographic categories are under-represented, for example, perinates. The small sample size precludes making comparative/interpretive statements from some of the findings. For example, relative to Kellis 2 these bodies have respectively low and high rates of porotic hyperostosis and malintent trauma, which could suggest fewer anaemias and more violence if the sample size was large. Herein these results are considered stochastic.

Despite the sample size limitations the TSBs provide a number of interesting results, particularly with regard to palaeopathology and palaeogenetics. Concerning the former, the people represented by the TSBs had very good skeletal and dental health at least until the mid-third decade of life. Following this they suffered considerable decline in their dental and skeletal health. Ante-mortem tooth loss was considerable by the early 40s and by the mid-40s osteoporosis was present in both the female and male skeletons. An older adult female likely died of complications of an osteoporotic related hip fracture. The most noteworthy palaeopathology was an unusual disease that afflicted two adult males buried in the same room (Room 3) in the North Tomb 1. This disease, characterized by infection in the feet with sequel ankylosis of many foot bones, plus osteoporosis of the lower limb, left both individuals debilitated particularly the younger male (NT1/ 12). This individual suffered considerable early onset osteoarthritis in his upper limb probably because he could not walk and used his arms for propulsion while in the sitting position. The advanced state of the arthritis suggests that he had suffered for considerable time and this may provide strong evidence of long term care. He also suffered from congenital torticollis (wry neck) which is the first case of this disorder in the Dakhleh skeletons.

In terms of palaeogenetics the TSBs clearly share a common breeding population with Kellis 2. This is not unexpected given the location and the similarity in burial position, extended burials oriented east-west with head to the latter direction, which are used to place the TSBs in the later Roman period. Of note is the fact that the TSBs provide new genetic evidence supporting the hypothesis that the people of Kellis buried their dead in specific areas according to kinship rather than randomly accretioning burials when people died. Finding the precondylar tubercle, a rare and highly genetic trait, in three of 10 bodies in D/6–D/7 provides the strongest support yet for the kinship hypothesis. Also, three males (D/7-8, D/7-9 and D/6-1) in this area had spina bifida occulta. Though spina bifida occulta has a complex etiology, genetics plays a role in its development and this clustering is additional support for the kinship hypothesis. The 'familial' hypothesis has been developed for Kellis 2 based on the clustering of rare morphogenetic traits in that cemetery (Molto 2002), although the burials at Kellis 2 are so closely packed that succinct spatial clusterings are difficult to delineate (Molto 2002). This and the longer temporal dimension of Kellis 2, minimally 100 years, have made testing of this hypothesis difficult. Noteworthy in terms of the hypothesized familial clusterings in Kellis 2, is the fact that the four individuals with precondylar tubercles in Kellis 2 are found in two areas rather than being randomly distributed throughout the cemetery: adults 211 and 227 in the southern part of Kellis 2 and subadults 71 and 239 in the northern part of Kellis 2. The exact genetic relationships, father, mother etc., between the bodies with precondylar tubercles, and spina bifida occulta, within and between these cemeteries requires DNA testing. This research is under way using both mitochondrial and STR analyses. The latter includes y-chromosome STRs which will allow a comparison of the paternal and maternal, from the mitochondrial DNA, lineages. The clustering of these skeletal variations in the D/6–D/7 burials may also suggest a limited period of time for their interment, possibly towards the final occupancy of Kellis. Finally, finding a rare, unique morphological trait, the suprascapular neurovascular canal, in two bodies, one each from D/7 and North Tomb 1, provides some possible evidence linking these two mortuary areas genetically and temporally. Clearly, the precise temporal position for the TSBs requires radiocarbon dating.

Current thinking suggests that the town of Kellis was abandoned in the late 4th century CE (Hope 2001, 56–7). It is likely during this period that burials were interred in D/6–D/7 and the North Tomb 1 complex was reused. Why Kellis 2 was not used exclusively in the late Roman period is a matter of speculation. One possibility is that the D/6–D/7 complex and by inference North Tomb 1, may represent higher statused families and hence their segregated mortuary treatment (personal communication Colin Hope, December 2002). The morphological evidence however, shows that TSBs were not foreigners who occupied Kellis after it was abandoned.

Acknowledgements

The authors thank Colin A. Hope for the opportunity to study these burials and Anthony J. Mills for his logistical support. This research was funded by a major grant from the Social Science and Humanity Research Council of Canada (Grant 50-1603-0500) awarded to the senior author.

Authors' Addresses:

J. Eldon Molto
Department of Anthropology
Lakehead University
955 Oliver Road,
Thunder Bay,
Ontario P7B 5E1,
Canada

Peter Sheldrick
209 Victoria Avenue,
Chatham,
Ontario N7L 3A7,
Canada

Antonietta Cerroni
Department of Anthropology
University of Toronto
100 St. George Street,
Toronto,
Ontario,
Canada

Scott Haddow
Institute of Archaeology
University College London
Gower Street,
London WC1E 6BT,
United Kingdom

REFERENCES

Aufderheide, A. and C. Rodriguez-Martin, 1998 *The Cambridge Encyclopedia of Human Paleopathology*, Cambridge University Press, London.

Bowen, G., 1998 The Spread of Christianity in Egypt in light of recent discoveries from ancient Kellis, unpublished Ph.D. Thesis, Monash University, Melbourne.

Dupras, T. D. and M. W. Tocheri, this volume *Preliminary Analysis of the Human Skeletal Remains from North Tombs 1 and 2*, 183–96.

Fairgrieve, S. and E. Molto, 2000 Cribra orbitalia in two temporally disjunct population samples from the Dakhleh Oasis, Egypt, *American Journal of Physical Anthropology*, 111, 319–31.

Hope, C. A., 2001 Observations on the Dating of the Occupation at Ismant el-Kharab, in C. A. Marlow and A. J. Mills, eds, *The Oasis Papers 1: Proceedings from the First International Symposium of the Dakhleh Oasis Project*, Oxbow Books, Oxford, 43–59.

Hope, C. A., 2002 Excavations in the Settlement of Ismant el-Kharab in 1995–1999, in C. A. Hope and G. E. Bowen, eds, *Dakhleh Oasis Project: Preliminary Reports on the 1994–1995 to 1998–1999 Field Seasons*, Oxbow Books, Oxford, 167–208.

Hope, C. A., this volume The Excavations at Ismant el-Kharab from 2000 to 2002, 207–89.

Molto, J. E., 1979 *Genes in Prehistory: A model for determining familial status among excavated burial samples*, Paper presented at the Annual Canadian Archaeological Association Meetings, Vancouver.

Molto, J. E., 1983 *Biological Relationships of Southern Ontario Woodland Peoples: The Evidence of Discontinuous Cranial Morphology*, National Museum of Man, Mercury Series, Paper No. 117, Ottawa.

Molto, J. E., 2001 The skeletal biology and paleoepidemiology of the people from Ein Tirghi and Kellis, Dakhleh, Egypt, in C. A. Marlow and A. J. Mills, eds, *The Oasis Papers 1: Proceedings from the First International Symposium of the Dakhleh Oasis Project*, Oxbow Books, Oxford, 81–99.

Molto, J. E., 2002 Bio-archaeological Research of Kellis 2: An Overview, in C. A. Hope and G. E. Bowen, eds, *Dakhleh Oasis Project: Preliminary Reports on the 1994–1995 to 1998–1999 Field Seasons*, Oxbow Books, Oxford, 239–55.

Ortner, D. and W. Putschar, 1985 *Identification of Paleopathological Conditions in Human Skeletal Remains*, Smithsonian Institution Press, Washington, DC.

Steinbock, R. T., 1976 *Paleopathological Diagnosis and Interpretation*, C. C. Thomas, Springfield.

Sjovold, T., 1973 The occurrence of minor nonmetric variants in the skeleton and their quantitative treatment for population comparisons, *Homo* 24, 204–33.

Sjovold T., 1976/77 A Method for familial studies based on minor non-metric traits, *Ossa*, Volume 3/4, 97–107.

Sjovold, T., 1977 Non-metrical divergence between skeletal populations: The theoretical foundation and biological importance of C.A.B. Smith's mean measure of divergence, *Ossa* 4 (supplement 1), 1–133.

A Preliminary Report on the Analysis of Organic Materials from Ismant el-Kharab

Andrew Ross and Benjamin Stern

Introduction

Excavations at Ismant el-Kharab, ancient Kellis, have produced substances that appear to be oils or similar materials and residues found in containers. In this paper we report the preliminary results of analysis of samples of materials from various locations at the site: two from a temple, three from a church, two from a tomb, two from domestic contexts and one sample of residue from a glass vessel. As it was not possible to analyse all of the available samples, these were selected to represent a range of find contexts. The samples were received as small fragments in sealed plastic bags, which were a possible source of contamination by plasticisers.[1]

The samples were analysed by gas chromatography and gas chromatography-mass spectrometry. Only samples containing compounds other than fatty acids were selected for gas chromatography-mass spectrometry as it is generally not possible to identify the origin of mixtures or degraded fatty acids with any degree of certainty. It is likely, however, that the material used in offerings was olive oil; this was discussed in previous work (Ross, 2000a; 2002b).

Experimental Procedure

Approximately 1 ml of dichloromethane:methanol (50:50 v/v) was added to a small portion (~ 0.1 g) of each sample. The solvent extract was then transferred to another clean vial and the excess solvent removed under a stream of nitrogen. Extracts were methylated with diazomethane. Diazomethane in diethyl ether was prepared by the addition of sodium hydroxide to 1-Methyl-3-nitro-1-nitrosoguanidine (Sigma) in a diazomethane generator (Pierce) after the method of Fales *et al.* (1973).

Gas chromatography was performed on a Hewlett Packard 6890 Gas Chromatograph fitted with a fused silica column. It was equipped with a flame ionization detector and split/splitless injector. A split ratio of 5:1 was used for the first two minutes and the carrier gas was helium. The injector and flame ionization detector were maintained at 300°C and 350°C respectively. The oven temperature was programmed from 50°C (2 minutes) to 340°C (12 minutes) at 10°C/min. Combined gas chromatography-mass spectrometry was carried out using a Hewlett Packard 5980 Series 2 Gas Chromatograph connected to a 5972 series Mass Selective Detector. The gas chromatograph was equipped with a split/splitless injector operating in splitless mode. The carrier gas was helium, delivered with a constant head pressure. The injector and interface were maintained at 340°C and the oven temperature was programmed as before. The column was inserted directly into the ion source. Electron impact spectra were obtained at 70 eV with full scan from m/z 50 to 700.

Phthalate plasticisers were found in the samples and were not present in the blanks. This is indicative of sample contamination, possibly from the plastic bags in which they had been placed after collection.

Results of Analysis

Sample 1 (D/7 S2000.56) is part of the contents of a glass vessel found in the 2000 field season in Area D/7 (Hope this volume). It is in the form of a child's head with a tall cylindrical neck section (registration number 31/420-D6-1-D/7/0/3; Hope and Whitehouse this volume, Figure 1a and Plate 1a). It is of late third or early fourth century CE date. Analysis by gas chromatography and gas chromatography-mass spectrometry showed that it contained retene and the methyl ester of dehydroabietic acid, the methyl ester of 7-oxodehydroabietic acid, and possibly two other methylation products of 7-oxodehydroabietic acid. Traces of $C_{16:0}$ and $C_{18:0}$ fatty acid methyl esters were also found. This is consistent

---

[1] This work was undertaken as part of the research for a M.A. thesis at Monash University (Ross 2002c).

with the presence of aged resin from a species of *Pinacea*, either pine, cedar or fir, together with a small amount of oil or fat of unknown origin. The presence of the aromatic compound retene may indicate that the material is pine or cedar tar that was produced by heating under reducing conditions. The presence of 7-oxodehydroabietic acid, however, may indicate otherwise (Mills and White 1977, 24). Heron and Pollard (1988, 440), contend that the absence or presence of this material depends on the burial environment; it will be produced in oxygenated systems, whereas reducing conditions will produce aromatic diterpenes.

Sample 2 (A/5 S91.26) is from Area A, House 3 (A/5), Room 6 (Hope 1997, Figure 2.). Gas chromatography and gas chromatography-mass spectrometry showed this to be virtually identical to Sample 1 and so is almost certainly aged *Pinacea* resin.

Sample 3 (D/8 S2000.20) is from Room 8 in Area D/8, north of the north-west corner of the Temple of Tutu (Hope this volume, Figure 2) and is identified as a domestic structure (Hope 2000, 57). Analysis of this sample showed that it consisted of a complex mixture of components: C_6, C_8 and C_9 dicarboxylic fatty acids; $C_{16:0}$, $C_{17:0}$, $C_{18:0}$ and $C_{20:0}$ fatty acids; and C40, C41, C42, C43, C44, C45, C46, C47, C48 and C50 wax esters. Although this sample contains a wax it would be difficult to identify it as beeswax in particular. The composition of beeswax is quite distinctive (dominant C_{30} alcohol, with C40 to C48 wax esters, (Regert *et al.* 2001). There are other potential sources such as plant waxes (Bonfield 1997). In addition, fresh beeswax does not contain dicarboxylic acids or free fatty acids of chain length under 24 (Charters *et al.* 1995, 122–3). The presence of the $C_{16:0}$ acid, palmitic acid could be explained by the hydrolysis of the wax esters that would produce this acid together with C24 to C36 alcohols. These alcohols, however, were not detected in Sample 3, whilst analyses of other aged samples of beeswax have detected these alcohols and palmitic acid. For example, Charters *et al.* (1995, 122–3) noted long-chain alcohols in five samples of Late Saxon and Medieval pottery from the United Kingdom; Evershed *et al.* (1997, 980–1) found them in residues from lamps of the Late Minoan I Period from Mochlos. In both of these cases little or no palmitic acid was present in the samples. Evershed *et al.* (1997, 982) attributed this to the formation of soluble salts in alkaline soil conditions that were then lost by solution in ground water. This would certainly explain why palmitic acid remains in samples from the dry environment of Ismant el-Kharab.

As mentioned above, the absence of long-chain alcohols from Sample 3 suggests the possibility that an oil or fat was mixed with a wax and this is further reinforced by the presence of short-chain dicarboxylic acids in the sample. Mills and White (1994, 34–5) have shown that when oils and fats are degraded by the action of soil bacteria the resulting product has a composition high in saturated fatty acids, particularly $C_{16:0}$ and $C_{18:0}$ and that the amounts of

unsaturated fatty acids such as the $C_{18:1}$ acid oleic acid tend to be much reduced, some of it being converted to palmitic acid. Mills and White (1994, 39–40) also showed that oxidation can break $C_{18:1}$ fatty acid chains near their centre, forming $C_{8:0}$, $C_{9:0}$ and $C_{10:0}$ dicarboxylic acids and smaller amounts of $C_{9:0}$ and other monocarboxylic acids. This sample can therefore be identified confidently as degraded wax that probably also originally contained a fat or vegetable oil.

Sample 4 (A/7 S97.23) is from the bema of the Large East Church (A/7), where it was presumed to be the spill of oil from lamps (Bowen 2002, 70; Hope this volume, Figure 1). Chemical analysis by Gas Chromatography showed the presence of $C_{16:0}$ and $C_{18:0}$ fatty acids, suggesting that the material could have been a vegetable oil but it was not possible to identify the source.

Sample 5 (A/7 S97.23) is from paving stones east of a feature adjacent to the central column at the west end of the nave of the Large East Church (Bowen 2002, 73). The function of this feature is uncertain, but Bowen (2002, 73) considered that the oil deposit was the result of some aspect of church ritual. Chemical analysis of this by Gas Chromatography provided similar results to the previous sample.

Sample 6 (A/7 S97.132) is from the top of a large feature, comprising two pedestals once joined by a screen, situated directly in front of the sanctuary of the Large East Church (Bowen 2002, 70). The quantity of organic residue that remains on this feature, together with its prominent location, again indicates an association with church ritual (G. Bowen personal communication, 2003). Once again, chemical analysis of this by Gas Chromatography was inconclusive, other than showing the presence of $C_{16:0}$ and $C_{18:0}$ fatty acids of uncertain origin.

Sample 7 (NT2 S2001.38) is from Room 5 of North Tomb 2 (Hope this volume). Chemical analysis of this by gas chromatography was again inconclusive, showing the presence of a mixture of $C_{16:0}$ and $C_{18:0}$ fatty acids of unknown origin.

Sample 8 (NT2 S2001.38a) is from a paving stone in the same room as Sample 7. Chemical analysis of this by gas chromatography showed, once more, the presence of a mixture of $C_{16:0}$ and $C_{18:0}$ fatty acids of unknown origin.

Sample 9 (D/1 S94.760) is from a pedestal from Room 6 of the Temple of Tutu, one of several found in the temple (Hope 1998, 837–9; Hope this volume, Figure 2). Chemical analysis by gas chromatography and gas chromatography-mass spectrometry showed the presence of a range of fatty acids of chain lengths $C_{14:0}$, $C_{15:0}$, $C_{16:0}$, $C_{17:0}$, $C_{18:0}$ $C_{18:1}$, $C_{20:0}$, $C_{22:0}$, $C_{24:0}$, $C_{26:0}$ and $C_{28:0}$, three long chain alkanes, methyl moronate, methyl oleanolate and wax esters of chain length C40, C42, C44, C46 and C48. As discussed under Sample 3 above, the presence of long-chain fatty acids of chain length 24 and above, together with the presence of wax esters, indicates the presence of a wax. This is supported by the detection of long chain alkanes, which are also found in beeswax (Charters *et al.* 1995, 122; Evershed *et al.* 1997, 980–1), although these may be due to sample contamination.

The $C_{14:0}$ to $C_{20:0}$ fatty acids are either the decomposition products of longer chain compounds or from another source such as a vegetable oil or animal fat. The presence of the $C_{18:1}$ fatty acid also suggests that another material was present, for beeswax, as analysed by Charters *et al.* (1995, 122), does not contain this or any other unsaturated acid. The absence of short chain dicarboxylic acids suggests that the material is better preserved than Sample 3. Finally, the detection of methyl moronate and methyl oleanolate are of considerable significance as these triterpenoids are biomarkers for *Pistacia* resin (Serpico 2000, 447; Stern *et al.* in press). The absence of oleanonic, isomasticadienonic and masticadienonic acids, however, usually found in *Pistacia* resin is unusual. This sample appears to have been originally a mixture of wax, *Pistacia* resin and probably an oil or fat.

Sample 10 (D/1 S93.320) is from another pedestal in the same temple. This fragmentary pedestal was found in the north corridor of the temple and was decorated with a cavetto cornice and a winged sun's disc (Hope 1998, 837–8, Plate 12). Chemical analysis of Sample 10 by gas chromatography showed the presence of a number of fatty acids of unknown origin, including the $C_{16:0}$, $C_{18:0}$ and $C_{18:1}$ acids. The presence of oleic acid ($C_{18:1}$), which is abundant in plant oils shows that this sample is slightly better preserved than Samples 4 to 8 but does not help to narrow the identification to anything other than a fat or oil of unknown origin.

Discussion of Sources on Ancient Oils

A number of textual sources give information on materials used in Egyptian ritual and these could indicate those used in the temple at Kellis. The texts from the 'Laboratory' in the Temple of Horus at Edfu (Chassinat 1987, 189–230) contain formulae for the manufacture of substances used in religious ritual in the temple. There are also Egyptian texts that provide useful information on the materials used in mummification in the Ritual of Embalming (Goyon 1972, 18–84) and the Opening of the Mouth Ritual (Goyon 1972, 85–182).

Rooms identified as 'laboratories' have also been identified in other temples of the Ptolemaic and Roman Periods (Paszthory 1988, 1–5), but as the texts at Edfu are very well preserved and a recent translation (Wilson 2002) exists, the other texts are not included in this discussion. The most important recipes contained in the Edfu texts as far as this paper is concerned, are those for *Kyphi*, the

nine unguents for the Opening of the Mouth Ritual, God's Stone, *mḏt*-ointment and God's Sweat.

The recipe for *Kyphi* (Chassinat 1987, II, 203, 7-204, 8 and Wilson 2002, 10–12) contains instructions for making 100 *deben* of *Kyphi* from a total of sixteen ingredients. Plutarch (*De Iside et Osiride:* 80) claimed that the components of *Kyphi* were: honey, wine, raisins, cyperus, resin, myrrh, camel's thorn, hartwort, mastic, asphalt, rush, monk's rhubarb, two types of juniper, cardamon and sweet flag. In discussing Plutarch's sources for *De Iside et Osiride*, Griffiths (1970, 80) suggested that the main source for information on Egyptian religion was Manetho's now-lost *The Sacred Book* that may have contained information on the preparation of *Kyphi*. If this is the case, it might be expected that Plutarch's description of *Kyphi* was accurate. Manniche (1999, 51) interpreted the ingredients of the Edfu recipe as being raisins, wine, honey, frankincense, myrrh, mastic, pine resin, sweet flag, aspalathos, camel grass, mint, cyperus, juniper, pine kernels, peker and cinnamon. This is a similar number of ingredients to the recipe given by Plutarch and in the majority of cases the ingredients are the same.[2] This implies that Plutarch's information probably came from the same source, but has been abbreviated. Another detailed recipe for *Kyphi* was given by Dioscorides (*De Materia Medica* I, 24), who noted that it was used in antidotes and as a treatment for asthma. This recipe contained only ten ingredients, but the major components were the same, being raisins, resin, honey, and wine, with lesser amounts of myrrh, cyperus, juniper berries, aspalathos, sweet flag and camel grass.

The recipe for the nine unguents used in the Opening of the Mouth ritual (Chassinat 1987, II, 210, 1–8 and Wilson 2002, 13) consists of lists of ingredients but not their proportions. Seven of these unguents contain *mnn*. The identity of this material is by no means certain. Serpico (2000, 460–8) considered this may have referred to bitumen and noted (2000, 460 and 466–8) that bitumen has been identified by chemical analysis in a number of funerary contexts, whereas Manniche (1999, 45, note 24) is of the opinion that it was more likely to be wood tar, pitch or a coniferous oil or resin.[3] Perhaps the best evidence for the identity of *mnn* is provided by the Ritual of Embalming, in which Goyon (1972, 48–9) identified the material as originating from *ḏȝhy*, *kbny*, Coptos and *dprw*, and also from Punt (Goyon 1972, 64). He (Goyon 1972, 49, 336–7) identified *ḏȝhy*, *kbny* and *dprw* as Phoenicia, Byblos and the biblical Tophel, a bitumen producing region south of the Dead Sea. In Antiquity, bitumen was available in large quantities in the Levant and smaller amounts were found in Egypt (Serpico 2000, 454–5).

Six of the oils in the Edfu list contain *ḥḏw* which Chassinat (1931, 30) identified as 'aromatics', that is, a number of aromatic plant materials were added and

---

[2] All of the ingredients may be the same as it is difficult to identify many of these accurately by their Egyptian and Greek names.

[3] See both of these for sources concerning the difficulty in identifying *mnn*.

intended to be listed in full later in the text. The word *ḥdw* may be derived from the Old Kingdom *ꜥdw stjw*, perfumed fats (Altenmuller 1976, 7). The word may also mean milk or milk fat. Mesnil du Buisson (1935, 43) noted that milk was sometimes referred to as *ḥd* or *ḥdt* and that the name for a vase used to carry milk was *ḥdw*. The alternative identification of *ḥdw* as onions (Manniche 1989, 69) does not seem appropriate here. Three of the oils contained *ꜥnḫ-imy*, which, according to Manniche (1989, 114), may refer to henna (*Lawsonia inermis*).

The standard Old Kingdom offering list, Barta's Type A (Barta 1963, 47–9) contained seven items identified as oils by oil-jar determinatives. These were, *sti-ḥꜣb*, *ḥknw*, *sft*, *nḥnm*, *tw3wt*, *ḥꜣt-ꜥš* and *ḥꜣt-tḥnw*. The Edfu list retains these in the same order, although some of the names are slightly different, with the addition of *mdt*-oil at the start and *ḳb* at the end. The inclusion of *mdt*-oil is not surprising, considering the importance given to it in the Edfu texts as shown below. The word *ḳb* is a variant of *b3k* that was considered by Faulkner (1962, 78) to signify moringa oil. Here, however, it must refer to a mixture of several ingredients. A list of ten unguents and oils is contained in the Opening of the Mouth Ritual and here the ritual function of some of the materials is mentioned:

mdt-unguent: Osiris N, Take the Eye of Horus, *mdt*-unguent.
sti-ḥꜥb: Osiris N, Take the Eye of Horus, festival perfume.
ḥknw-unguent: Osiris N, Take the Eye of Horus. Your two eyes will be made whole by the unguent, and it will not run down your face.
šft-unguent: Osiris N, Take the Eye of Horus, for, by wearing it, Seth is dispirited.
nḥnm-unguent: Osiris N, Take the Eye of Horus, apply the unguent.
tw3wt-unguent: Osiris N, Take the Eye of Horus which one brings him and by favour of whom the gods support him.
Best quality *ꜥš*-unguent: Osiris N, Take the Eye of Horus, take possession of it for your face.
Best quality *tḥnw*-oil: Osiris N, Take the Eye of Horus, take it for your forehead.
ibr-unguent: Osiris N, Take the Eye of Horus, by whose power Seth will have been kept away, but which will not withdraw from you.
b3k-oil: Osiris N, Take the Eye of Horus which is allowed to you and which brightens your face (translated from Goyon 1972, 148–9).

The Edfu recipe for God's Stone (Chassinat 1987, II 214,7–II 215,1 and Wilson 2002, 16), used for anointing the statue of Min-Amun, shows that its major ingredient was *mnn*, to which were added incense, resin, other plant materials and small amounts of precious metals and gemstones. The same material is mentioned in the Ritual of Embalming, where it is associated with Osiris and Min (Goyon 1972, 63). Here, *mnn* is the exudation from the body of Osiris. Later in the same ritual another material is used for anointing the soles of the feet and lower legs

(Goyon 1972, 78). This is the 'oil of the mineral that blackens' which Goyon (1972, 78, note 3) suggests is probably an oil containing 'God's Stone'.

The recipe for *mdt*-ointment (Chassinat 1987, II, 227, 3–16 and Wilson 2002, 24–5) shows that this preparation was fat from a young bull that had been purified, coloured red with a plant-derived dye, and perfumed with a number of different substances. It is possible that *mdt*-ointment was in use as early as the Third Dynasty; *mḥ ib dt* or *mḥ dt* is mentioned in a list of materials from the tomb of Hesire at Saqqara (Altenmuller 1976, 14, Abb.3, 21). The ritual function of *mdt*-ointment, according to the Edfu texts, was to anoint the gods' statues and the material was also used for candles used in the temple.

The recipe for 'God's Sweat' (Chassinat 1987, II, 229, 1-230, 6 and Wilson 2002, 25–6) is for a material to be used for anointing the statue of Hathor in order to make it smell like her sweat. This recipe does not contain *mnn*.

As some of the samples analysed derived from the Large East Church it is worthwhile to consider what is known of oils used in church ritual. It should be noted that a number of texts from the site, indicate a Manichaean presence in the village (Gardner *et al.* 1999, 72–82). There is no evidence, however, to suggest that the Large East Church was used by the Manichaean community (G. Bowen, personal communication 2003). Clearly, the oil deposits in the church may have been the result of religious practice. A formula for anointing oil was given in the Septuagint (Exodus 30, 23–5):

Take also the aromatics: the best flower of myrrh, five hundred shekels; of sweet-smelling cinnamon, half as much, two hundred and fifty; of iris, five hundred shekels of the sanctuary, and of olive oil, one hin; and you shall make it a holy anointing oil, a fragrance of the perfumery according to the art of the perfumer.

This oil was to be used in anointing the sacred objects in order to sanctify them. The recipe reflects practice at the time the Septuagint was translated, that is, in Alexandria by the end of the third century BCE (Fraser 1972, 690), and may provide an indication of the materials used in Egyptian ritual at the time. The Jewish tradition reflected in the Septuagint may explain the use of oils in Christian ritual where they are used in baptism, consecration and blessing.

Some of the Coptic texts from Ismant el-Kharab (Gardner *et al.* 1999, 70) refer to oil in connection with the *Agape*, a communal meal celebrated by Christians and Manicheans. P.Kell. Copt. 17 (Gardner *et al.* 1999, 150) contains a clear reference to the use of oil in this ceremony:

It is I, Horion, I greet you warmly; in the Lord, greetings. After I had finished writing(?), the agon of oil ... I wrote this ... Lautine, that he could send it by way of the outsiders (?); but our son Timotheos ... Look, I have left a portion with them like you said. Also, the other agon of oil that I received from Sabes [with the] holokittinos, I left it (with them). For we take in much oil for the agape, in that we are many, and they consume much oil.

The finds in House 3, where this document was discovered, were dated by Hope (1999, 109–16) to the fourth century

CE. Oil is mentioned in a number of the recently-translated Greek ostraka from Ismant el-Kharab (Worp, forthcoming) and one particular text may have a religious significance. O. Kell. 138 reads:

> Hieronymos to the komarch of Ei. Immediately after the receipt of this letter collect from Pisechtis son of Para 3000 silver talents and send these to me today for the (purchase of) public oil. I pray for your health (Worp forthcoming).

This text was found in House 4, Room 4 and dates from the second half of the fourth century CE (Worp forthcoming). It describes the purchase of 'public' oil for an unknown purpose but it may, as suggested by Worp (forthcoming), have been for use in the church at Kellis as other texts from the house indicate a Christian presence (G. Bowen personal communication, 2003).

Conclusions

While many of the results of chemical analyses of materials from Ismant el-Kharab are inconclusive, some provide definite identifications; even the results which are difficult to assign to a certain source show that in many cases the material used was an oil or fat without further addition. The results from Samples 1 and 2 show that resin from the *Pinacea* family was used at Kellis, but as the species of *Pinacea* could not be identified, then it is not possible to suggest where it originated. Dioscorides (*De Materia Medica* I. 92–5) gave a number of medicinal uses for coniferous resins and related substances, including relieving asthma, chest infections and a variety of skin conditions, and so the glass vessel could have contained a medicinal preparation. The discovery context of the glass vessel (Hope this volume) reveals little indication of the function of the container, although the presence nearby of a number of Christian burials (Hope this volume) may suggest a funerary or mortuary association. The building near where the glass vessel was found contained domestic ceramics, but these could have been used in a mortuary or funerary context (C. Hope personal communication, 2002).

Sample 2 was almost identical to Sample 1 and so has the same possible origins. It was found in House 3 (A/5) Room 6. Magical texts and Manichean material were found in the house and so there is a possibility that the resin was connected with magical or religious practice. None of the surviving magical texts (P.Kell. I Gr. 82–8, Worp 1995, 205–21) refers to resin, but a fragmentary medical prescription (P.Kell I Gr. 89, Worp 1995, 223) includes myrrh, and so may also have included other resinous materials. Two of the Manichean letters from the house (P.Kell. Copt. 22. 23, P.Kell. Copt. 24. 43, Gardner *et al.* 1999, 174–8 and 182–4) mention a material called ⲕⲙⲙⲉ, which, according to Gardner, Alcock and Funk (1999, 286), referred to 'gum'. The word may, however, have a wider meaning, as the Middle Egyptian qmyt was considered by Faulkner (1962, 279) to refer to gum or resin. There is, therefore, a possibility that ⲕⲙⲙⲉ is resin and refers to the material detected by analysis. The use of this material is uncertain.

Sample 3 is identified as a wax, possibly mixed with an oil or fat. This is a simple material with many possible uses and so the original use of Sample 3 cannot be established with any confidence. Furthermore, the domestic context of its discovery (Hope 2000, 57) makes a ritual use less likely. The fact that no resin was found associated with the sample means, however, that it cannot be the residue from the material *Kyphi*, discussed above, as the ancient recipes for this material all contain resin. The wax may be of local origin, as honey is mentioned once in the Kellis Agricultural Account Book (Bagnall 1997, 174–5, line 1670).

Sample 9 contains wax and probably an oil or fat; there is also evidence for the presence of *Pistacia* resin, a material with a long history of use in Egypt that was probably imported from the Levant (Serpico *et al.* in press). This sample was found associated with a sandstone pedestal (Hope 1998, 839, Plate 14) in the sanctuary of the Contra Temple of the Temple of Tutu (Hope 1998, Figure 3). The discovery of this sample in a religious context suggests that it is the residue of a ritual material, perhaps a type of *Kyphi*. The discovery near this pedestal of a small bronze votive figure (Hope 1998, 819, Figure 5.6; Kaper and Worp 1995) of Tapshay, the consort of Tutu, could suggest that the pedestal was connected with her cult. There was a thick coating of organic residue around the pedestal and the figurine had been preserved in it. None of the recipes for *Kyphi*, other materials from the Edfu texts or other sources discussed above specifically mention beeswax and so a possible identity for Sample 9 cannot be suggested. The combination of *Pistacia* resin and fatty acids is found on linen wicks found in the Workmen's Village at Amarna (Serpico 1997, 183–5), where it was considered that oil or fat had been added to the resin either to help it burn more easily or perhaps because the mixture had a religious significance. The sample from Ismant el-Kharab is unlikely, however, to have been the residue from a lamp or candle used in temple ritual as it is from a very substantial deposit.

The material found on this pedestal contrasts with the less complex residue found on another pedestal (Sample 10). The function of these pedestals is uncertain: Hope (1998, 838–9) suggested that they were used to support offering bowls, shrines or statues, but as the remains of the cult objects in the temple are in most cases extremely fragmentary and widely scattered throughout the building (Hope 1998, 814), it is not clear which objects are associated with the pedestals. The remains of some of the cult objects, such as a statue of Tutu (Hope 1998, 817), a squatting sandstone figure (Hope 1998, 819), and a number of shrines (Hope 1998, 831–6), were also covered with residues of oil or resinous material.

The remaining samples reveal little about their original composition but they do show that in the Temple of Tutu, the Large East Church and at other locations on the site there was extensive use of one or more oils or fats of unidentified origin.

The texts from the 'Laboratory' in the Temple of Horus at Edfu show that a considerable number of materials were used to make ritual preparations. Most of the materials mentioned in the texts are complex mixtures of ingredients that include animal fat, vegetable oil, different kinds of resins, possibly bitumen and a number of plant-derived materials that were used as colourings, aromatics and perhaps thickeners. This is in sharp contrast to the materials found in the temple, churches and other locations at Ismant el-Kharab, which are at most mixtures of two or three ingredients and the majority of which consist of some kind of oil or fat. No traces of resins from species of *Commiphora* or *Boswellia* were found in the samples, whereas these appear to be frequently mentioned in the Edfu texts. This may suggest that these materials were particularly expensive or that their supply was restricted to the major temples in the Nile Valley. Clearly, however, expensive imported materials such as pine resin or tar and *Pistacia* resin were available and used at Kellis. In the Edfu Laboratory texts, *mnn* is an ingredient of incense, most of the nine 'sacred oils' and in materials for anointing statues in the temple. If, therefore, similar materials were used in the Temple of Tutu, then residues of these materials should include *mnn*.

There is clearly scope for further analytical work on samples from Ismant el-Kharab. Analysis of further deposits from pedestals and other cult objects may reveal useful information on cult practice in the Temple of Tutu, and analysis of more samples from the site could provide further evidence on the wider use of resins and other materials.

Authors' Addresses:

Andrew Ross
Centre for Archaeology and Ancient History
School of Historical Studies
Building 11, Clayton Campus,
Monash University,
Victoria 3800,
Australia

Benjamin Stern
Department of Archaeological Sciences
University of Bradford
Bradford BD7 1DP,
United Kingdom

REFERENCES

Ancient Sources:

Dioscorides *De Materia Medica,* translated by John Goodyer and edited by Robert T. Gunther, Hafner, London 1934.

Plutarch *De Iside et Osiride,* translated by J. G. Griffiths, University of Wales Press, 1970.

The Septuagint, Volume 2, Exodus, translated by A. Le Boullueq and P. Sandevoir, Éditions du Cerf, Paris, 1989.

Modern Sources:

Altenmuller, H., 1976 Das Ömagasin im Grab des Hesire in Saqqara (QS2405), *Studien zur Altägyptischen Kultur* 4, 1–29.

Bagnall, R. S., 1997 *The Kellis Agricultural Account Book (P.Kell. IV Gr 96),* Oxbow Books, Oxford.

Barta, W., 1963 *Die altägyptische Opferliste von der Frühzeit bis zu griechische-römischen Epoche,* Bruno Hessling, Berlin.

Bonfield, K. M., 1997 The analysis and interpretation of lipid residues associated with prehistoric pottery: pitfalls and potential, unpublished Ph.D. thesis, University of Bradford.

Bowen, G. E., 2002 The Fourth Century Churches at Ismant el-Kharab, in C. A. Hope and G. E. Bowen, eds, *Dakhleh Oasis Project: Preliminary Reports on the 1994–1995 to 1998–1999 Field Seasons,* Oxbow Books, Oxford, 65–85.

Charters, S., R. P. Evershed, P. W. Blinkhorn and V. Denham, 1995 Evidence for the Mixing of Fats and Waxes in Archaeological Ceramics, *Archaeometry* 37, 113–27.

Chassinat, E., 1931 Quelques parfums et onguents en usage dans les temples de l'Égypte ancienne, *Revue de l'Égypte ancienne* 3, 117–67.

Chassinat, E., 1987 *Le Temple d'Edfou,* S. Cauville and D Devauchelle, eds, Institut Français d'Archaeologie Orientale, Cairo.

Evershed, R. P., S. J. Vaughan, S. N. Dudd and J. Soles, 1997 Fuel for Thought? Beeswax and Lamps and Conical cups from Late Minoan Crete, *Antiquity* 71, 979–86.

Fales, H. M., T. M. Jauni, and J. F. Babashak, 1973 Simple Device for Preparing Ethereal Diazomethane Without Resorting to Codistillation, *Analytical Chemistry* 45, 2302–3.

Faulkner, R. O., 1962 *A Concise Dictionary of Middle Egyptian,* Griffith Institute, Oxford.

Fraser, P. M., 1972 *Ptolemaic Alexandria,* Clarendon Press, Oxford.

Gardner, I., A. Alcock and W-P. Funk, eds, 1999 *Coptic Documentary Texts from Kellis Volume 1,* Oxbow Books, Oxford.

Goyon, J-C., 1972 *Rituels Funéraires de L'Ancienne Égypte,* Éditions du Cerf, Paris.

Griffiths, J. G., 1970 *Plutarch's De Iside et Osiride,* University of Wales Press.

Heron, C., and A. M. Pollard, 1988 The Analysis of Natural Resinous Materials from Roman Amphoras, in E. Slater and J. Tate, eds, *Science and Archaeology,* BAR, Oxford, 429–47.

Hope, C. A., 1997 The Find Context of the Kellis Agricultural Account Book, in R. S. Bagnall, ed., *The Kellis Agricultural Account Book (P.Kell. IV Gr 96)*, Oxbow Books, Oxford, 5–16.

Hope, C. A., 1998 Objects From The Temple Of Tutu, in W. Clarysse, A. Schoors and H.Willems, eds, *Egyptian Religion The Last Thousand Years Part II*, Peeters, Leuven, 803–58.

Hope, C. A., 1999 The Archaeological Context, in I. Gardner, A. Alcock and W-P. Funk, eds, *Coptic Documentary Texts from Kellis Volume 1*, Oxbow Books, Oxford, 96–122.

Hope, C. A., 2000 Excavations at Ismant el-Kharab in 2000: A Brief Report, *Bulletin of the Australian Centre for Egyptology* 11, 49–66.

Hope, C. A., 2001 Excavations at Ismant el-Kharab and Mut el-Kharab in 2001, *Bulletin of the Australian Centre for Egyptology* 12, 35–64.

Hope, C. A., this volume The Excavations at Ismant el-Kharab from 2000 to 2002, 207–89.

Hope. C. A. and H. V. Whitehouse, this volume The Gladiator Jug from Ismant el-Kharab, 291–310.

Kaper, O. and K. Worp, 1995 A Bronze Representing Tapsais of Kellis, *Revue d'Égyptologie* 46, 107–18.

Manniche, L., 1989 *An Ancient Egyptian Herbal*, University of Texas Press, Austin.

Manniche, L., 1999 *Sacred Luxuries: Fragrance, Aromatherapy and Cosmetics in Ancient Egypt*, Cornell University Press, New York.

Mesnil du Buisson (Comte du), 1935 *Les Noms Et Signes Égyptiens Designant Des Vases Ou Objets Similaires*, Librairie Orientaliste Paul Geuthner, Paris.

Mills, J. S. and R. White, 1977 Natural Resins of Art and Archaeology: Their Sources, Chemistry and Identification, *Studies in Conservation* 22, 12–31.

Mills, J. S. and R. White, 1994 *Organic Chemistry of Museum Objects*, Butterworth-Heinemann, Oxford.

Paszthory, E., 1988 Laboratorien in ptolemaischen Tempelanlagen, *Antike Welt* 21, 3–20.

Regert M., S. Colinart, L. Degrand and O. Decavallas 2001 Chemical alteration and use of beeswax through time: accelerated ageing tests and analysis of archaeological samples from various environmental contexts, *Archaeometry* 43, 549–69.

Ross, A. C., 2000a An Investigation into the Use of Oils and Fats in Ancient Egyptian Ceremonial and Religious Practice, unpublished B.Litt (Honours) dissertation, Monash University.

Ross, A. C., 2002b The Oil Used in the Rituals in the Temple of Tutu at Kellis, in C. A. Hope and G. E. Bowen, eds, *Dakhleh Oasis Project: Preliminary Reports on the 1994–1995 to 1998–1999 Field Seasons*, Oxford, 263–7.

Ross, A. C., 2002c Ritual and Private Use of Oils and Related Materials in Roman Egypt, unpublished Masters dissertation, Monash University.

Serpico, M., 1997 Mediterranean Resins in New Kingdom Egypt a Multi-Disciplinary Approach to Trade and Usage, unpublished Ph.D. dissertation, University College London.

Serpico, M., 2000 Resins, Amber and Bitumen, in P. Nicholson and 1. Shaw, eds, *Ancient Egyptian Materials and Technology*, Cambridge University Press, Cambridge, 430–74.

Serpico M., J. Bourriau, L. Smith, Y. Goren, B. Stern and C. Heron in press Commodities and Containers: A Project to Study Canaanite Amphorae Imported into Egypt during the New Kingdom, in M. Bietak, ed., *The Synchronisation of Civilisations in the Eastern Mediterranean in the Second Millennium* BC (II). Proceedings of the SCIEM 2000 EuroConference, Haindorf, May 2001.

Stern B., C. Heron, L. Corr, M. Serpico and J. Bourriau, in press Compositional variations in aged and heated *Pistacia* resin found in Late Bronze Age Canaanite amphorae and bowls from Amarna, Egypt, *Archaeometry*.

Wilson P., 2002 Temple Laboratory Texts from Edfu, unpublished translation by P. Wilson after H. W. Fairman.

Worp, K. A., ed., 1995 *Greek Papyri From Kellis: 1*, Oxbow Books, Oxford.

Worp, K. A., forthcoming *Greek Ostraca from Kellis*.

The Chronology of Kellis 2: The Interpretative Significance of Radiocarbon Dating of Human Remains

Joe D. Stewart, J. Eldon Molto and Paula J. Reimer

Introduction

The village of Kellis was important in the political, religious and economic spheres of the Dakhleh Oasis during the Ptolemaic and Roman times. The exact temporal span of the village is unknown, although archaeological data mainly from coins and texts recovered in the village suggest that it was abandoned by the end of the fourth century CE (Hope 2001, 57). The exact date of origin is more obscure, although there is some ceramic and other evidence in the village and the Kellis 1 cemetery that indicates that this was in the Late Ptolemaic Period (Hope 2002, 205; Schweitzer 2002,). In terms of mortuary customs the citizenry of Kellis interred their dead adjacent to the town site and in two cemeteries north-west (Kellis 1: 31/420-C5-1) and north-east (Kellis 2: 31/420-C5-2) of the village proper. Conversion to Christianity at Kellis resulted in a shift in burial customs from that found in the pagan tombs of Kellis 1 to the traditional Christian burials found in Kellis 2. The latter were characterized by single interments with the head oriented to the west, while the former were multiple burials located in rock-cut tombs (Birrell 1999). The tombs of Kellis 1 investigated to date have all been disturbed, although the abundant archaeological material recovered indicates both Ptolemaic and Roman Period presence. At least one of these tombs, K1-13, has yielded ceramic, cartonnage and radiocarbon dates of Ptolemaic age. The time when the Roman-Period inhabitants changed their inhumation program from large crypts to mostly single burials in the Christian burial mode is debated (Bowen this volume; Molto 2002a, 241). Establishing the temporal range for Kellis 2 is important for the interpretation not only of the origins of the Christian attitude toward interment, but also for the genetic and epidemiological data that are accruing from analysis of the Kellis 2 skeletons. It is the purpose of this paper to present and interpret the radiocarbon dating results obtained thus far from human skeletons recovered from the Kellis 2 cemetery.

The Kellis 2 Cemetery

Kellis 2 likely housed between 3,000 and 4,000 burials (Molto 2002a, 241), of which 450 have been excavated and analyzed (Figure 1). Unfortunately, very few grave goods are associated with Kellis 2 burials making archaeological dating difficult (Bowen 1998, 307; Sheldrick forthcoming). There is, however, considerable variation in tomb construction, which may eventually yield some information on chronology (Sheldrick forthcoming). The burial position and absence of grave goods are the primary factors in identifying the interments as those of Christians while the study of onomastics indicates the presence of Christians at the site by the mid-third century (Bowen this volume). An osteo-chemical biography of each of these burials is being generated, which includes DNA, both nuclear and mitochondrial, stable isotopes and morphology. A main objective of the research is to identify genetic relationships among each of the burials. Establishing the relative chronological position of the burials is critical for interpreting intra-site biological relationships. For example, two burials that share rare morphogenetic traits and DNA genotypes may be grandmother-grand-daughter, mother-son etc., although the interpretation of this necessarily depends on their relative chronological positions. Moreover, there are burials with key pathologies, namely tuberculosis and leprosy, that need to be evaluated in terms of their possible contemporaneity in order to assess the relationship between the diseases and their influence on the population over time. In fact, as shown in Figure 2, most of the radiocarbon dates (n=8 of 11) available for Kellis 2 have been performed on individuals because they represent individuals with these mycobacterial diseases (tuberculosis and leprosy).

In sum, defining the overall temporal span Kellis 2, as well as any internal spatial-temporal patterning that might correlate with factors such as mortuary practices, genetic and/or kin relationships, or health and disease is the ultimate goal of this aspect of the bioarchaeological

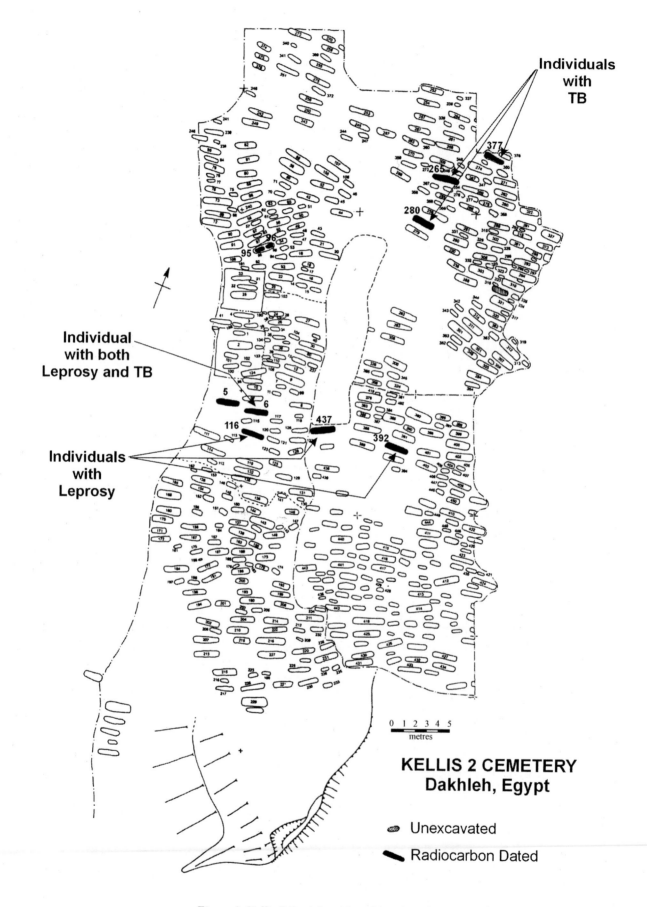

Figure 1 Kellis 2 Burials with radiocarbon dates.

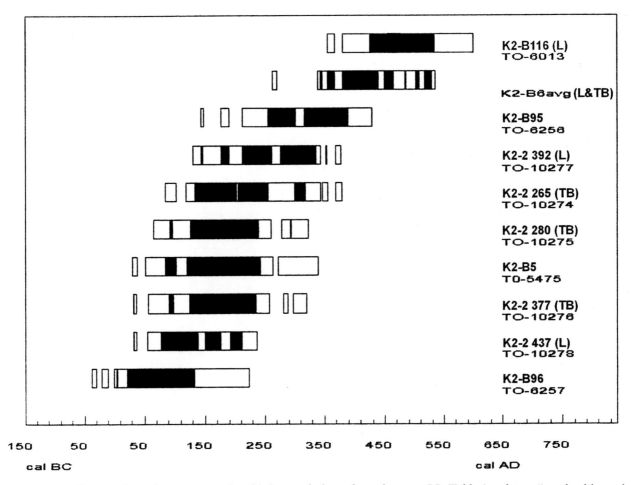

Figure 2 Kellis 2 Radiocarbon Dates, ordered left-to-right by radiocarbon age BP (Table 1, column 4) and calibrated to cal BC (BCE)/cal AD(CE). Solid bars display 1-sigma cal age ranges (Table 1, column 6); open bars display 2-sigma cal age ranges (Table 1, column 7).

research. Whether stratigraphic ordering of the individual tombs is possible in future is an additional research problem that may correlate with the chronometric results.

Materials and Methods

Radiocarbon dates on nine burials and two on a tenth burial from Kellis 2 cemetery (Table 1) are reported here. This represents the beginning of a program to radiocarbon date approximately 40–60 burials from Kellis 2. All eleven accelerated mass spectrometry determinations are 'conventional radiocarbon ages' (Stuiver and Polach 1977, 356) on human bone collagen extracted and dated at IsoTrace Laboratory. High precision measurements, using four rather than two graphite targets, were made on the five most-recently assayed samples (TO-10274 through TO-10278). Statistical analysis of the radiocarbon ages with standard deviations was performed following Ward and Wilson (1978) by testing the statistic T' (T for multiple determinations on the same object) against Chi-square (at the 95.5% c.i.), as programmed in Calib 4.3 (Stuiver *et al.* 2000). The same program was used to calibrate the radiocarbon ages via the INTCAL 98 decadal atmospheric

calibration curve (Stuiver *et al.* 1998). No laboratory multiplier error was provided nor was any added variance input. Most of the individuals were aged 30+years at death. However, no sample age spans to smooth the calibration curve were input, due to the relatively short turnover time (15–30 years) of collagen in living bone (Wild *et al.* 1998).

Results

TO-5476 and TO-6104 are dates on two samples (K2-B6a and K2-B6b) from the same individual. Testing found them to be statistically the same (T $0.89 < \chi^2$ 3.84), permitting pooled averaging (K2-B6avg). This average then was calibrated, along with all the individual radiocarbon ages. Although TO-5476 and TO-6104 were each calibrated, the calibrated average was used in further statistical analysis and in plotting the 1- and 2-sigma calibrated age ranges (Figure 2). A problem is presented by TO-6256 and TO-6257. They represent two infant individuals (Burials 95 and 96) from the same crypt, Grave 92, yet they are statistically different from each other (T' $7.29 < \chi^2$ 3.84). If, as appears from the archaeological context, they were contemporaneous (Bowen 1998, 307),

Table 1 Kellis 2 radiocarbon database.

Sample Identification			14C Age bp	s.d. of 14C age	1-sigma Cal Age Range(s)*	2-sigma Cal Age Range(s)*
Lab Code	Sample Code	Sample Information				
T0-5475	K2-B5	Rib	1840	60	85–103 [0.094] 120–243 [0.906]	30–39 [0.008] 53–263 [0.875] 273–339 [0.117]
TO-5476	K2-B6a	Rib. Same individual as K2-B6b (TO-6104); see K2-B6avg.	1670	50	261–278 [0.115] 324–331 [0.034] 336–428 [0.851]	252–443 [0.896] 447–469 [0.034] 481–530 [0.070]
TO-6104	K2-B6b	Rib. Same individual as K2-B6a (TO-5476); see K2-B6avg.	1600	50	418–474 [0.499] 476–532 [0.501]	342–372 [0.042] 378–565 [0.932] 567–581 [0.014] 587–597 [0.012]
K2-B6avg	K2-B6avg	K2-B6 average. T' 0.89 < X2 (.05) 3.84 Skeletal and DNA evidence for leprosy DNA evidence for tuberculosis	1635	37	345–348 [0.016] 356–368 [0.081] 381–440 [0.703] 450–466 [0.092] 484–486 [0.011] 502–508 [0.027] 518–529 [0.070]	264–271 [0.012] 340–535 [0.988]
TO-6256	K2-B95	Rib; double infant burial with K2-96	1720	50	256–303 [0.399] 317–390 [0.601]	144–149 [0.003] 177–191 [0.011] 213–429 [0.986]
TO-6257	K2-B96	Rib; double infant burial, with K2-95	1920	50	5–6 [0.005] 22–132 [0.995]	-38 – -30[0.011] -21 – -11[0.017] -1–224 [0.972]
TO-6013	K2-B116	Rib. Skeletal and DNA evidence for leprosy	1590	50	426–533 [1.000]	356–368 [0.013] 381–599 [0.987]
TO-10274	K2-2 265	Rib. Skeletal and DNA evidence for tuberculosis. High precision date	1800	50	134–164 [0.215] 166–202 [0.258] 206–257 [0.404] 302–318 [0.123]	84–103 [0.025] 120–345 [0.955] 347–356 [0.008] 369–380 [0.012]
TO-10275	K2-2 280	Rib. Skeletal evidence for tuberculosis High precision date	1840	50	93–97 [0.025] 127–239 [0.975]	66–260 [0.924] 279–294 [0.020] 296–324 [0.056]
TO-10276	K2-2 377	Rib. Skeletal and DNA evidence for tuberculosis. High precision date	1850	50	90–99 [0.058] 126–236 [0.942]	33–36 [0.003] 56–258 [0.950] 282–289 [0.008] 299–321 [0.039]
TO-10277	K2-2 392	Rib. Skeletal and DNA evidence for leprosy. High precision date	1780	40	144–147 [0.016] 178–191 [0.074] 213–262 [0.435] 277–337 [0.475]	131–345 [0.979] 353–355 [0.004] 370–379 [0.017]
TO-10278	K2-2 437	Rib. Skeletal and DNA evidence for leprosy. High precision date	1880	40	77–138 [0.640] 151–176 [0.200]	33–37 [0.009] 55–237 [0.991]

* Positive age ranges are cal CE; negative age ranges are cal BCE.

then one of the dates must be erroneous. It is tempting to suspect that TO-6257 is too early, but the only solution for this dilemma will be to date the specimens again. For the present, both dates are left in the analysis. If TO-6257 is valid, the 2-sigma calibrated age ranges extend from about the calibrated BCE/CE boundary to calibrated 600 CE. It is quite unlikely, however, that the actual time span covered is this broad. Taking the late end of the earliest date and early end of the latest date as the minimal termini, the 2-sigma calibrated age ranges span approximately calibrated 220 to calibrated 380 CE, again, unlikely. The true age range must lie somewhere between these extreme possibilities given the greater statistical likelihood.

Testing of the set of 10 uncalibrated radiocarbon ages reveals two statistical groups, whose compositions differ slightly, depending on whether one starts searching for outliers from the early end or the late end of the array. This can be visualized in Figure 2, where the dates are ordered by radiocarbon age. Starting at the early (left) end, TO-6257 through TO-6256 comprise an early group (T' $10.77 < \chi^2$ 14.10), which is followed by a late group comprised of the B6 average and TO-6013. Starting at the late (right) end, however, TO-6256 is relegated to a group of the latest three dates (T' $3.21 < \chi^2$ 5.99). This statistical exercise is very provisional, given plans for much more extensive dating of Kellis 2. The groupings may not persist when more samples have been dated. This is supported by the fact that all adjacent pairs of calibrated age ranges (both 1- and 2-sigma) overlap, if all intercepts for each date are considered.

More enlightening at this stage than the statistical analysis is the temporal distribution of pathologies (Table 1). Tuberculosis, as diagnosed by both skeletal and DNA evidence (Molto and Matheson 2001, 3), afflicted four individuals covering almost the entire chronology (TO-10278, TO-10277, the B6 averaged date, and TO-6013), and individuals with leprosy span an even larger time. The two cases of tuberculosis fall into the early to middle portion of the time span. The three cases of skeletal tuberculosis, Burials 265, 280 and 377, which clustered in the northern part of the excavated area of the cemetery (Molto and Matheson 2001), fall in the early to middle portion of the chronology. Their closely overlapping radiocarbon ages indicate that they were contemporaneous, which is evident even without statistical testing. Radiocarbon dating is not sufficiently precise to establish the relative dating of the three individuals. Burial 6, an individual with both skeletal and DNA evidence of lepromatous leprosy (Molto 2002b), and which tested positive for *M. tuberculosis* DNA, overlaps statistically with Tuberculosis at 95.5% c.i.

Discussion

The radiocarbon dates summarized for Kellis 2, though difficult to interpret at this stage, *vis à vis* determining the temporal span represented by the cemetery, hint at a longer use than the historical evidence from the 'Christian' burial

position (Bowen 1998, this volume). Complicating the interpretation of the radiocarbon dates is the large temporal range from the two child burials, 95 and 96, interred in the same grave (grave 92). To quote Bowen (1998, 307): "The grave was assumed to be that of an adult and it was not until the mud pavement was removed that two bodies were revealed. The infants must have been buried together and presumably died within a short time of one another, yet the radiocarbon dates may separate them by as much as 260 years, although it must be admitted that they fall within the standard deviation at 95.5% c.i. The radiocarbon dates do not permit an accurate dating of the cemetery". In light of the new dates obtained, this conclusion needs to be modified.

The radiocarbon dates available do, however, facilitate the interpretation of mycobacterial disease at Kellis. First, it is clear that both tuberculosis and leprosy were contemporaneous in this Roman Period population. This fact is more clearly evidenced by the isolation of the DNA of both diseases in Burial 6 who showed pathognomonic evidence of leprosy, but had no skeletal lesions associated with tuberculosis (Molto 2002b). The association of these diseases in different parts of the cemetery probably reflects familial or extended lineage clusters rather than claustering or segregation because of their diseases (Molto 2002b). The fact that the four burials with leprosy traverse the whole temporal dimension so far determined for Kellis 2 is important as it establishes the endemic nature of this disease at Kellis, rather than Kellis being an early Egyptian 'leprosaria' (Molto 2002b). In this regard it is important to note that earliest evidence of leprosy in the paleoepidemiological record comes from Ptolemaic Dakhleh and these four early cases were interpreted as representing high ranking foreigners (Europeans) who were banished to Dakhleh because of their affliction (Dzierykray-Rogalski 1980). This interpretation has now been challenged (Molto 2002b, 186), although it is clear that leprosy was an endemic disease in Dakhleh by the Roman Period. Although four cases may seem too few to hypothesize an endemic disease, it is important to note that leprosy is not highly infectious and in a given population only about 1% of those exposed to the bacillus will develop the disease and of these only a small percentage, ~5% of hospitalized victims, will show bone lesions (Aufderheide and Rodriguez-Martin 1998, 145).

In summary, the additional radiocarbon dates (n=40–50) planned as part of the Kellis 2 bioarchaeology project, including redating child burials in grave 92, should provide a more rigorous statistical basis for interpreting the temporal period represented at Kellis 2. Establishing the exact temporal span of Kellis 2 is important for interpreting all skeletal data sets including paleodemography, paleopathology and paleogenetics (Molto 2002b). A possible future strategy is to compute several radiocarbon dates in select skeletons as opposed to conducting high precision testing. Clearly, radiocarbon dating is essential for understanding the bioarchaeology of the Kellis population in the Roman Period.

Acknowlegements

This research was funded by major grants from the Social Science and Humanity Research Council of Canada (Grant 50-1603-0500) and The Lawrence Livermore National Laboratory.

Authors' Addresses:

Joe D. Stewart
Department of Anthropology
Lakehead University
955 Oliver Road,
Thunder Bay,
Ontario P7B,
Canada

J. Eldon Molto
Department of Anthropology
Lakehead University
955 Oliver Road,
Thunder Bay,
Ontario P7B,
Canada

Paula J. Reimer
Centre for Accelerator Mass Spectrometry L-397
Lawrence Livermore National Laboratory
Post Office Box 808,
Livermore,
California 94550,
U. S. A.

REFERENCES

Aufderheide, A. and C. Rodriguez-Martin, 1998 *Human Paleopathology*, Cambridge University Press, New York.

Birrell, M. 1999 Excavations in the Cemeteries of Ismant el-Kharab, in C. A. Hope and A. J. Mills, eds, *Dakhleh Oasis Project: Preliminary Reports on the 1992–1993 and 1993–1994 Field Seasons*, Oxbow Books, Oxford, 29–41.

Bowen, G. E., 1998 The Spread of Christianity in Light of Recent Discoveries from Ancient Kellis, unpublished Ph.D. dissertation, Monash University, Australia.

Bowen, G. E., this volume Some Observations on Christian Burial Practices at Kellis, 168–82.

Dzierykray-Rogalski, T., 1980 Paleopathology of the Ptolemaic Inhabitants of the Dakhleh Oasis, Egypt, *Journal of Human Evolution* 9, 71–4.

Hope, C. A., 2001 Observations on the dating of occupation at Ismant el-Kharab, in C. A. Marlow and A. J. Mills, eds, *The Oasis Papers 1: The Proceedings of the First Conference of the Dakhleh Oasis Project*, Oxbow Books, Oxford, 43–59.

Hope, C. A., 2002 Excavations in the Settlement of Ismant el-Kharab in 1995–1999, in C. A. Hope and G. E. Bowen, eds, *Dakhleh Oasis Project: Preliminary Reports on the 1994–1995 to 1998–1999 Field Seasons*, Oxbow Books, Oxford, 167–208.

Molto, J. E., 2002a Bio-archaeological Research of Kellis 2: An Overview, in C. A. Hope and G. E. Bowen, eds, *Dakhleh Oasis Project: Preliminary Reports on the 1994–1995 to 1998–1999 Field Seasons*, Oxbow Books, Oxford, 239–55.

Molto, J. E., 2002b Leprosy in Roman Period Burials from Kellis 2, Dakhleh, Egypt, in C. Roberts and K. Manchester, eds, *Past and Present of Leprosy: Archaeological, Historical, Paleopathological and Clinical Approaches*, BAR, London, 186–96.

Molto, J. E. and C. Matheson, 2001 *Vertebral Pathologies at Kellis 2: A Study in Differential Diagnosis*, unpublished paper presented at the 29th Annual Canadian Association for Physical Anthropology Meetings, Winnipeg, Manitoba.

Schweitzer, A., 2002 Les parures de cartonnage des momies d'une nécropole d'Ismant el-Kharab, in C. A. Hope and G. E. Bowen, eds, *Dakhleh Oasis Project: Preliminary Reports on the 1994–1995 to 1998–1999 Field Seasons*, Oxbow Books, Oxford, 269–76.

Sheldrick, P., forthcoming The Archaeology of Kellis 2, in M. Wiseman, ed., *The Oasis Papers II: Proceedings of the Second International Conference of the Dakhleh Oasis Project*, Oxbow Books, Oxford.

Stuiver, M. and H. A. Polach, 1977 Discussion: Reporting of Radiocarbon Data, *Radiocarbon* 19, 355–63.

Stuiver, M., P. J. Reimer, E. Bard, J. Warren Beck, G. S. Burr, K. A. Hugen, B. Kromer, G. McCormac, J. van der Plicht and M. Spurk, 1998 INTCAL 98 Radiocarbon Age Calibration, 24,000–0 cal bp, *Radiocarbon* (40) 3, 1041–83.

Stuiver, M., P. J. Reimer and R. W. Reimer, 2000 CALIB Version 4.3 (computer software), URL http://www.calib.org/

Ward, G. K. and S. R. Wilson, 1978 Procedures for Comparing and Combing Radiocarbon Age Determinations: A Critique, *Archaeometry* 20, 19–31.

Wild, E., R. Golser, P. Hille, W. Kutschera, A. Priller, S. Puchegger, Werner Rom, P. Steier and W. Vycudilik, 1998 First ^{14}C Results from Archaeological and Forensic Studies at the Vienna Environmental Research Accelerator, *Radiocarbon* 40 (1–2), 273–82.

A Mythological Ostrakon from Kellis

Klaas A. Worp

The ostrakon presented below was found in January 1996 in Zone XXVI, which is located due west of Shrine II (Area D/3; Hope this volume Figure 2) of the central village temple. It was found in a chaff deposit beneath a fragment of a sandstone pedestal that had been used as a doorstep into a door through the northern wall of the Inner Temenos, immediately due east of Shrine II (Hope 2002, 192–3).[1] It bears the Kellis object registration D/3/90 (SCA 2564) and its dimensions are 6.8 (high) x 7.3 (wide) cm. The sherd's ware is P1b; both sides of it are inscribed. A palaeographical date is not easy to establish but a dating of the cursive handwriting to the later 3rd or first half of the 4th century seems reasonable when taking into account the other datable documents from area D/3.

The text on the sherd starts on the convex side and appears to continue on the concave side. It provides a version of the myth of Kyknos son of Poseidon, who first married Prokleia daughter of Laomedon and fathered two children, a son Ten(n)es and a daughter Hemithea. After his wife Prokleia died, Kyknos remarried a certain Philonome daughter of Tragasos. She, however, fell madly in love with her stepson Ten(n)es and when he did not respond to her advances, she slandered him with his father Kyknos. The latter then exposed his own children by putting them into a basket and dropping this into the sea. Due to the fact that the verso of the text is mostly illegible, the rest of the myth is not relevant for our story. For the complete myth see *Der Kleine Pauly* V 586 under 'Tennes

1'; P. Grimal, *Dictionnaire de la Mythologie grecque et romaine* (Presses Universitaires de France, Paris 1963[3]) 109, under 'Cycnos 2' and 443–4 under 'Ténès'. Grimal mentions as ancient classical sources for this story of Kyknos especially Strabo XIII.1.19, 589; Pausanias X.14.1 following; Apollodorus Mythographus, *Epitome* III 23 following; Diodorus Siculus V 83, and Conon, *Narrationes*, 28. None of these authors, however, presents a text offering a verbatim model for the text on the ostrakon.[2] The rendering of the story given by Photius, *Bibliotheca*, cod. 186, 135b Bekker, lines 19 following, comes relatively close to the version found here, but it is the work of a much later, 9th century, author. Perhaps Photius presents a version adapted from that of the original author of our own text?

Whatever the answer to this question, the text on the ostrakon does not appear to provide new details for the ancient myth. In itself, however, it is interesting to see that knowledge of the myth spread as far from Greece as to the Dakhleh Oasis in Egypt.[3] It seems quite possible that the story was taught in an ancient school in Kellis, and that we are dealing with a schoolboy's homework on an ostrakon.[4] There are other signs of educational activity at Kellis, see especially the Kellis Isocrates Codex from House 3 (Area A/5; Worp and Rijksbaron 1997) and the Homer fragment from the temple, Shrine III (Area D/4; Hope and Worp 1998, 206–10).[5] There is insufficient ground for thinking that at some point in time Shrine II

---

[1] I am most grateful to the director of the Australian excavations at Ismant el-Kharab, Dr C. A. Hope (Monash University, Melbourne), for his kind permission to publish this object. Likewise, I should like to express my gratitude to the Dakhleh Oasis Project and its director, A. J. Mills, for extending hospitality to me during my stay in the Dakhleh Oasis.

[2] Consultation, moreover, of the Leuven Database on Ancient books (accessible via: http://ldab.arts.kuleuven.ac.be) reveals that to date there is apparently no literary papyrus which presents the story of Kyknos in recognizable form. For another relevant database available on the Internet see also below, footnote 3.

[3] For a catalogue of ancient mythographical papyri see now the website developed by M. Huys and Th. Schmidt: 'http://cmp.arts.kuleuven.ac.be/searchform.html'.

[4] For such ostraca texts in general see R. Cribiore, *Writing, Teachers and Students in Graeco-Roman Egypt*, Scholars Press, Atlanta 1996, 63–4; 'mythological' ostraka are to be found in her catalogue of texts under numbers 108, 141, 146, 183, 273, 274, 346, 351, 392 and 406; there is, however, no parallel for the story of Kyknos in her catalogue of school texts.

[5] Also in this publication a detailed description of the finds in this shrine is provided.

Mythological Ostrakon from Zone XXVI, object registration number 31/420-D6-1/D/3/90.

housed a local school, however, it is of interest to note that several other ostraka were found in the same context as this one, some of which also reflect schoolboy activity (Hope 2002, 193; Worp forthcoming, O.Kell. 153 and 161, also 157).

This introduction must end with a note of caution. Following its discovery I studied the original sherd in the excavation house on the site and made there a first transcript of a text on the potsherd, which is not easy to read. Subsequently, photographs of the sherd were made available to me for further study, but even though they are of good quality, it turned out to be impossible to arrive at reliable readings of two words in lines 4 and 9, while there is also a problem in establishing the text in lines 12ff.[6]

Convex side:

1	Κύκνος ὁ Ποσιδῶνος	"Kyknos the son of Poseidon
2	βασιλεύων τῆς Τρῷ-	who reigned over Cape Troy
3	ας ἀκτῆς ἔσχεν δύο παῖδας,	begot two children,
4	† αιλεγον† καὶ Ἡμιθέαν.	(Tennes?) and Hemithea.
5	Ἀποθανούσης δὲ τῆς τού-	And after their mother died,
6	των μητρὸς ἀπηγάγετο	he married a
7	μητρυιάν· ἡ δὲ ἐπιμανεῖσα	stepmother. But she went
8	τῷ ἥρωι λόγῳ προήνεγκεν	madly after her young hero and with
9	† λιμισεως†· μὴ δυναμένη	words displayed her ... but when she
10	δὲ αὐτὸν πεῖσαι διέβαλεν τῷ πα-	could not persuade him, she slandered him with
11	τρὶ ὡς ἐπιμιγήσοντα αὐτῇ·	his father as if he would have wanted sex with her;
12	καὶ αὐτὸς ἀποβιάσασθαι τὴν δ[ια-]	and he, ... to remove the slander with force (?)
13	βολὴν ὡς αὐτὴν vacat.	

1 Ποσειδῶνος   3–4 At the left-hand side there is a big blot over the written text, making it extremely difficult to read the text underneath the blot   6 Or read ἐπηγάγετο?   8 Or, less likely, read προηνέγκετο?

The concave side features 13 more lines; after three mostly illegible and incomprehensible lines (14–16) the text continues with:

17	τὴν ἀδελφὴν αὐτοῦ κλέου-	his sister, weeping (?),
18	σαν ἐπὶ τοῦτο ἀμφοτέρους	both into it ..."

Due to the bad preservation of the other lines on the verso, which features extremely tiny 'sawtooth' writing, the remainder of the text on this side of the ostrakon, lines 19–26, is illegible.

While the general character of the text is clear, there remain a few textual problems, viz.:

Line 4. One expects at the start the name Τέ(ν)νην (acc.), therefore, the transcript in the text above, αιλεγον, probably contains a mistake. One could, of course, separate the letters -αι from the following λεγον and take these as part of the copula καὶ, with a very unrecognizable kappa at the start. Furthermore, in Greek cursive writing it is sometimes easy enough to confuse λ and τ.[7] Despite the similarity between these letters it is, however, in the present case difficult to convince oneself from the photo that the letters at the end of the word allow of reading here καὶ Τένην.

Lines 7–8. The Greek verb ἐπιμαίνομαι indeed governs the dative τῷ ἥρωι. The use of the latter word, our 'hero', for a young boy is surprising.

Lines 8–9. While the verb ʼπροήνεγκεν or, less likely, προηνέγκετο, may be rendered as "she displayed, she put forward", in the context the verb's subject is the stepmother, of course, it is far less clear what λιμισεως should mean. Going with the verb one would expect an object, in the accusative, and a genitive in -εως makes no sense. Probably the reading is mistaken, but I have no convincing alternative to offer; an interpretation to the effect that μισεως should be separated from the preceding l. ἡμίσεως and be interpreted as "in a half (hearted) way" does seem not really attractive, the more so as it offers no solution for the preceding part of the line.

Line 11. The form ἐπιμιγήσοντα (Part. fut. act.) is problematic; if it is connected, as seems obvious enough, with the verb ἐπιμίσγω, one expects a medial form ἐπιμιγησόμενον, see Liddell, Scott and Jones 1940 under ἐπιμίσγω; for future forms in -μιγήσομαι etc. < -μείγνυμι, see the electronic Thesaurus Linguae Graecae at http://stephanus.tlg.uci.edu/inst/textsearch. Maybe the error can

[6] I am grateful to Professor M. Huys (Leuven) for discussing this text with me and offering a number of interesting and helpful comments; I do hope that this new version of my transcript will provide him with inspiration for removing problems remaining in this text.

[7] An illuminating case is that of the Hermopolitan village name Πρήκτεως where it was once proposed to change this name into an aberrant name Πρήκλεως (cf. the indices to *Berichtigungsliste der griechischen Papyrusurkunden aus Aegypten* V, 184 and 198).

be attributed to a school boy? To be sure, changing ἐπιμιγήσοντα (part. fut. act.) into ἐπιμιγήσαντα (part. aor. act.) does not help.

Lines 12ff. Reference is made here, of course, to the development in the myth that Kyknos threw his two children (line 18, ἀμφοτέρους) into a box and let that be dropped into the sea, but the precise grammatical construction is unclear and one cannot be certain as to how the text runs. I would expect the infinitive ἀποβιάσασθαι to depend from a finite verb or a participle (θέλων ἀποβιάσασθαι τὴν δια-Ιβολὴν = 'as he wanted to put the slander away with force'), but no applicable form offers itself. Besides, there is the question that the readings in lines 12–13 are not all absolutely secure and that the rendering of ἀποβιάζομαι, translated by Liddell, Scott and Jones 1940 as 'to force back, to treat with violence, to use force', as suggested above is not normal. In itself one could think that it is more natural to think of the stepmother as the subject of the infinitive ἀποβιάσασθαι, but then we must jettison the reading of δια-Ιβολήν.

Lines 17–18. Within the context of the development of the story it seems far more natural to take the participle κλέου-Ισαν as a spelling error for κλαίου- | σαν ('weeping') while connecting it with the young baby daughter that was to be put into the box, rather than connecting it with the verb κλέω = 'to make famous'.

Author's Addresses:
Department of Papyrology
Archeologisch Historisch Instituut der
Universiteit van Amsterdam,
Oude Turfmarkt 129,
NL-1012GC Amsterdam,
The Netherlands

and

Leids Papyrologisch Instituut
Witte Singel 27,
NL-2311BG Leiden,
The Netherlands

REFERENCES

Hope, C. A., 2002 Excavations in the Settlement of Ismant el-Kharab in 1995–1999, in C. A. Hope and G. E. Bowen, eds, *Dakhleh Oasis Project: Preliminary Reports on the 1994–1995 to 1998–1999 Field Seasons*, Oxbow Books, Oxford, 167–208.

Hope, C. A, this volume The Excavations at Ismant el-Kharab from 2000 to 2002, 207–289.

Hope, C. A. and K. A. Worp, 1998 A New Fragment of Homer, *Mnemosyne* 51, 206–10.

Liddell, H. G., R. Scott and H. S. Jones, 1925–1940 *A Greek-English Lexicon*, The Clarendon Press, Oxford.

Worp, K. A. and A. Rijksbaron, eds, 1997 *The Kellis Isocrates Codex*, Oxbow Books, Oxford.